ALDERWOOD

DISCARD

SOUTH AMERICA
1978

Note: The *Bolivia* chapter in this edition has not been revised in our usual manner due to the loss of manuscripts in the mail from that country on two occasions. We apologize to our readers for any inconvenience this omission may cause.

A definitive handbook of
the 13 nations of the New World's southern continent;
610 pages of text; map of the continent;
city plans; archeological site plans;
photographs and illustrations.

FODOR'S MODERN GUIDES
FOUNDED BY EUGENE FODOR

Editorial Staff
ROBERT C. FISHER
editor

RICHARD MOORE
executive editor, London

LESLIE BROWN
managing editor

DOROTHY FOSTER
research director

Production Staff
C. R. BLOODGOOD
director

EILEEN ROLPH
managing director, London

Advertising Staff
E. W. NEWSOM
director

SANDRA LANG
assistant director

South America 78:

Area Editors: RICHARD BRILL, H. BUENCRISTIANO, ANDRE FODOR, DONALD
GRIFFIS, WILLIAM HORSEY, PENNY LERNOUX, ALLEN LOWRIE, MARY LOWRIE,
JOHN NELSON, EDUARDO PROANO, HUGO SCHOFFER, WILLIAM P.
WILLIAMSON

Editorial Contributors: JERRY KVARDA, RICHARD P. LEAVITT,
MARCEL NIEDERGANG

Drawings: LASZLO ROTH

Photographs: J. ALLEN CASH, E. FODOR, MAGNUM PHOTOS INC., PAN
AMERICAN WORLD AIRWAYS, GEORGE PENDLE, RAPHO GUILLUMETTE
PICTURES

Maps and City Plans: C. W. BACON M.S.I.A., JOHN HUTCHINSON, DYNO
LOWENSTEIN, LESLIE S. HAYWOOD

Cover: ROLAND DUBOIS

FODOR'S

SOUTH AMERICA 1978

CREATED BY EUGENE FODOR

ROBERT C. FISHER
LESLIE BROWN
editors

DAVID McKAY COMPANY INC. - NEW YORK

The following Fodor Travel Books are current in 1978:

AREA GUIDES:

AUSTRALIA, NEW ZEALAND AND SOUTH PACIFIC
CANADA
CARIBBEAN, BAHAMAS AND BERMUDA
EUROPE
EUROPE ON A BUDGET
INDIA
JAPAN AND KOREA
MEXICO
SCANDINAVIA
SOUTH AMERICA
SOUTHEAST ASIA
SOVIET UNION

U.S.A. (1 vol.)

COUNTRY GUIDES:

AUSTRIA
BELGIUM AND LUXEMBOURG
CZECHOSLOVAKIA
EGYPT
FRANCE
GERMANY
GREAT BRITAIN
GREECE
HOLLAND
HUNGARY*
IRAN
IRELAND
ISRAEL
ITALY
MOROCCO
PORTUGAL
SPAIN
SWITZERLAND
TUNISIA*
TURKEY
YUGOSLAVIA

USA GUIDES:

FAR WEST*
HAWAII
MID-ATLANTIC*
MID-WEST*
NEW ENGLAND*
NEW YORK AND NEW JERSEY*
ROCKIES AND PLAINS*
SOUTH*
SOUTHWEST*

CITY GUIDES:

LONDON
VENICE*
PARIS
VIENNA
PEKING

LANGUAGE GUIDE:

EUROPE TALKING*

SPECIAL INTEREST GUIDES:

CRUISES EVERYWHERE*
INDIAN AMERICA
OLD WEST*
OLD SOUTH*
ONLY-IN-AMERICA VACATIONS*
OUTDOORS AMERICA*
RAILWAYS OF THE WORLD
SEASIDE AMERICA*

LATEST ADDITIONS TO THE SERIES:

JORDAN AND THE HOLY LAND
BRAZIL

*Not available in Hodder and Stoughton editions

MANUFACTURED IN THE UNITED STATES OF AMERICA

TABLE OF CONTENTS

THE FACE OF SOUTH AMERICA

EDITORS' FOREWORD

Why South America?

South America is a bright newcomer to international tourism. There are no special flights today to Caracas for the "peak" season—no rush to Rio for the glorious summer months on Copacabana—no great pilgrimage to the mysterious lost cities of Peru.

To the knowing international traveler, South America is a true land of discovery—a land of new sights, sounds, sports, people, history, ideas, and traditions. To the visitor who has already traveled there, South America is a treasured memory of uncrowded beaches and hotels, the Amazon and the Pampas, restaurants with the kind of old-time service hotel managers dream about—in short, an entirely new continent that's now ready and waiting to welcome a future wave of tourism.

The travel boom to South America is just beginning. The first pioneer tourists are now being welcomed with all the attention, courtesy and friendliness that exists in countries before the tourist rush begins. Taxi drivers are helpful, bell boys do not solicit tips—the welcome is genuine.

The fact that you are now holding this book in your hands makes you a pioneer in this discovery. It takes people like yourself to read about (and travel to) South America, and to tell your friends about it to make the area popular. In this book, and later in South America, you'll discover a dynamic new world where millions of people are building better lives and nations.

In South America you can't help catching the spirit of Brasilia—the capital city that a dynamic country has just moved a thousand miles into the wilderness. You'll feel the history of ancient cities that date to the beginning of recorded time—join in the excitement of booming cities where every hour a new building is started. South America is growing and you'll grow along with it. You'll dance along with Latin rhythms, ski in the middle of July, and enjoy a steak dinner for a dollar you wouldn't have believed unless you ate it yourself.

These are a few reasons to visit South America and why this book has been published. South America is all dressed up and ready to welcome visitors with magnificent hotels, excellent jet and steamship service, reasonable prices, and probably the best service in the world.

Consider this book an invitation to travel soon to South America. Everywhere its editors went, the South Americans put out their hands in friendship and said, "Welcome—our home is yours."

And, they mean it.

What's Where?

As everybody knows, South America is one of the two continents of the western hemisphere and forms a giant triangle. A close look at a map of the continent will familiarize one with the general location of coasts and countries.

Beginning with Colombia, which, with Panama, separates the Caribbean from the Pacific, South America extends as a broad continent in the north to a narrow point in the south. Colombia's capital, Bogota, lies on a plateau in the Andes, a great mountain chain that forms the backbone of the continent and lies closer to the Pacific than to the Atlantic.

An hour and 10 minutes by jet south of Bogota is Quito, Ecuador, best preserved of all Spain's great Colonial cities. Tiny Ecuador borders Peru—a country with a treasury of rich history and fascinating contrast. From Lima the Pacific coast continues southward to Chile—a spectacular country extending 2,600 miles south from the deserts of Atacama to the subantarctic tip of the Americas at Tierra del Fuego.

From the bleak, frozen wastelands of Chile the continent follows the Atlantic northward through moderate climates to the Amazon country and eventually to the torrid tropical zones of interior Venezuela and the Guianas.

Argentina borders Chile and the Atlantic, and the great Republic stretches 2,300 miles from south to north. Coastal Uruguay and landlocked Paraguay and Bolivia all border Argentina, in addition to the giant of South America—Brazil.

Brazil—largest country in South America—sprawls over half of the continent and embraces the world's mightiest river—the Amazon. From the giant bulge of Brazil, the continent curves northwestward through the Guianas to Venezuela, and returns again to the shores of the Caribbean.

Travellers leaving New York City and flying on the standard Round South America tours usually cover more than 12,000 miles in their journey around the great continent.

Distances and contrasts are great in South America and at first many of the names are new and curious—but a few moments spent studying a map will greatly aid trip planning.

CHOOSING YOUR VACATION SPOT

A brief alphabetical rundown of South America—country-by-country—will give an idea of the vastness and the variety the continent has to offer the visitor.

Argentina. Cosmopolitan Buenos Aires and Mar del Plata beach resorts; Bariloche Alpine Lake District in the Andes; the colorful vineyards of Mendoza; gourmet food everywhere (huge steaks $2.50 to $4.00). You may see the highest mountain in the New World, Mount Aconcagua (22,834 ft.), the world's largest glacier (the Upsala, 50 miles long), jungles (with big game), deserts and vast wildernesses, a continental ice-cap second only to that of Greenland, millenary larch forests, numberless lakes and the huge Iguazu Fall.

Bolivia. An unforgettable Shangri-La where Inca culture and its centuries-old civilization are perfectly preserved. Tours from La Paz to Lake Titicaca and the monolithic wonders of Tiahuanaco.

Brazil. Land of contrasts from ultra-sophisticated Rio, dynamic São Paulo, futuristic Brasilia, colorful Bahia to the vast, mysterious Amazon. Tropical beaches, exciting night life, friendly people.

Chile. Championship skiing at Portillo (U.S. summer); record-breaking fish in lakes amidst the Andes and in the ocean. In Santiago, world-famous wines, continental cuisine, fine shops. In nearby Viña del Mar, excellent beaches and a cosmopolitan casino.

Colombia. Historic, colonial Cartagena, bustling Barranquilla and the fjörd-like bays of Santa Marta on the Tropical Spanish Main; the exhilarating mountain cities of Bogota and Medellin. Pre-Colombian artifacts and hand-woven textiles. Good buys for shoppers are emeralds, jewelry and antiques.

Ecuador. Eternal Spring on the Equator, breathtaking scenery; awe-inspiring cathedrals and museums of the Hispanic period. Gateway to the Galápagos. A source of the Amazon.

French Guiana. Virtually unexplored, just now beginning to welcome international visitors. Adventurous river trips and launch service to the infamous penal colony of Devil's Island. Wild, primitive land of lush jungle and greatly varied wildlife.

Guyana. Almost unknown to tourists; breathtaking Kaieteur Falls, five times higher than Niagara, just an hour's flight from the capital Georgetown; a blending of six peoples and cultures; Africans, Amerindians, East Indians, Portuguese, Chinese and European, wild virgin jungle land.

Paraguay. Shop for exquisite lace in Asunción, important historic city of Spanish period. Interesting trips on river steamers. Visit Iguassu Falls; unexcelled hunting and fishing along wide rivers for the fighting *dorado*.

Peru. Land of the Inca and the most important archaeological discoveries in the West. Luxurious hotels in Lima and fine beach resorts. Exciting shopping; unsurpassed cuisine.

Surinam. Modern hotels with casinos minutes from the jungle. River trips past Indian villages by steamer or dugout canoe. Dutch, Javanese, Hindu and Bush Negro cultures.

Uruguay. Also know as the "Gaucho Land", with its main *estancias*, where the hospitality of its people is added to authentic native traditions. Cosmopolitan Montevideo, the capital, one of the most beautiful cities in the Western Hemisphere, welcomes the foreigner. Vacation in Punta del Este with its world-famed beaches.

Venezuela. Excellent tours from modern Caracas, with its skyscrapers and luxurious hotels, to rural Valencia, historic Merida, Ciudad Bolivar, Margarita Island for pearl fishing, the awesome canyons of the Great Savannah and Angel Falls, Macuto for deep-sea fishing.

ACKNOWLEDGEMENTS

Our guide is a result of several extended trips through the Continent. We were greatly helped by a large number of people in the travel field, in public life, and by those who extended advice as personal friends. No conventional list of "acknowledgements" could truly express our gratitude to the many who helped us in our task.

The following were extremely helpful:

U.S.A.: Louis J. Garcia, Vice President and Director of Public Relations, Braniff International Airways, New York; Francisco J. Hernandez, Chief of Travel Division, Pan American Union, Washington, D.C.; Robert Booth, Braniff International Airways; William J. Bird, Vice President, Braniff; James C. Seix, New York; Luis Zalamea, Luis Zalamea Associates, Miami; Peter Grace, President of W. R. Grace & Co.; Carlos V. Pellerano, former Executive Director S.A.T.O.

Colombia: René Garcia Vélez, former Director Nacional de Turismo; Juan Ucros, Vice President, Braniff, Colombia; Allen and Mary Lowrie, travel agents.

Ecuador: Graciela Levi Castillo, former Director General, Ecuadorian Government Tourist Bureau, Quito; former Ambassador Dr. Jose R. Chiriboga; William MacIntosh, Ecuadorian Tours.

Peru: Gordon K. McCoun, District Director, Braniff, Washington, D.C.; Drew W. Kohler, formerly of Lima; H.E. Ambassador Cesar de la Fuente, Peruvian Ambassador to Netherlands; former Ambassador to U.S., Dr. Fernando Berkemeyer; Eduardo Dibos, former President of Peruvian Automobile Club; Frank A. Mau, Commercial Attaché, U.S. Embassy; J. W. Thoman, Information Officer, U.S. Embassy; Peter J. De La Mare; George Althaus, Lima Tours, Lima.

Bolivia: Former Ambassador Don Victor Andrade.

Chile: Don Luis Valdes Pereira, Ex-director de Turismo, Santiago de Chile; Guillermo Vivado, ex-Press and Public Relations Officer.

Argentina: Alberto Sauter, former President Argentina National Tourist Organization, Buenos Aires; Hector V. Sabato, Direccion Nacional de Turismo; Sergio A. Betancourt, Public Relations, Pan Am, Buenos Aires.

Brazil: André Fodor, our South American Representative, Rio de Janeiro; C. D. Hellyer, formerly of Rio de Janeiro; John Blashill, Former Chief of Bureau, Time-Life International; Lucy Mendes Bloch, Former Director of Tourism, Brazil; Dr. Victor

Boueas, Former Director Department Turismo, Guanabara (Rio province); Oberon Bastos, Press Officer, Pan Am, as well as Pan Am's Joe Sims; Paulo Einhorn; and Count Gyula Dessewffy, Curitiba.

Surinam: F. L. de Rooy, Director Surinam Tourist Development Board.

Venezuela: Luis J. Perez Barreto, former Director Tourism; Peter Wenzel, formerly District Manager, Pan Am, Caracas; Messrs. Hamilton Wright Sr. and Jr.

For the current revision, we are particularly indebted to: Darius Morgan, Crillon Tours Ltda., La Paz (Bolivia); Richard G. Brill, President, Amazon Explorers; Parlin, N. J. (Amazon chapter, Brazil); Allen and Mary Lowrie and Earl M. Hanks, Allen & Mary Lowrie Travel Service, Bogota (Colombia); Eduardo Proano, Metropolitan Touring, Quito (Ecuador); Hugo Schoffer, Braniff International, Asuncion (Paraguay); John H. Nelson, Surinam Tourist Bureau, New York (Surinam); Herbert Buencristiano, Bueme's Travel Service, Montevideo (Uruguay); Luis Zalamea; Jerry Kvarda, Tariffs-Marketing, Pan Am; and to Esther G. Johnston, of Fodor's editorial offices, Litchfield, Conn.

A Final Note

All comments in this guide, whether favorable or adverse, are based on the editors' personal experience. We feel that the first responsibility of a guide is to inform and protect the reader, rather than to praise indiscriminately. All comments are made in the spirit of constructive criticism and in the hope of stimulating improvements where they are needed.

Although we make a last-minute check just before going to press, much of the information herein is perishable. We cannot, therefore, be responsible for the sudden closing of a restaurant, bankruptcy of a hotel, or bad mood of an otherwise excellent chef, any (or all) of which can make one of our comments out-of-date. We welcome letters from readers whose opinions are at variance with ours (or who agree!), and are always ready to revise our opinions when the situation warrants. In the meantime, the editors asume responsibility for all the judgments in the book.

Send your letters to the editors at one of these addresses: **In the USA,** Fodor's Modern Guides, 750 Third Avenue, New York, N.Y. 10017; **in Europe,** Fodor's Modern Guides, 27b, Old Gloucester St., London WCIN 3 AF, England.

FACTS AT YOUR FINGERTIPS

FACTS AT YOUR FINGERTIPS

PLANNING YOUR TRIP

> **DEVALUATION, REVALUATION, INFLATION.** With constant changes in rates for currency, not to mention the value of the dollar and sterling, the prices throughout this book, and ratios, are bound to change. So keep this in mind, please . . .

$P£ **WHAT WILL IT COST?** See individual country chapters for some attempts to answer this disturbing question. Some idea about getting there, however, follows: Most visitors to South America arrive by air. While some excursion fares are available the majority of air tickets sold are the standard all-year jet fares.

To give an idea of jet transportation from several key world cities, the chart below presents a sampling of all year, round-trip regular economy class:

To:	From: New York	Los Angeles	London
Lima	$782	$846	£797
Buenos Aires	$1,048	$1,178	£819
Rio de Janeiro	$1,014	$1,160	£768

Air fares to South America are constantly changing, and seem to be going up at the moment. You would be wise to look into the special excursion fares, some for 17 days, others for 30 days, which are considerably less than the standard round-trip fares listed above. For instance, new low excursion fares are being introduced between New York and the Caribbean Coast of South America (Colombia, Venezuela).

Don't neglect to look into the number of permissible stopovers you can have with your ticket. See the *Airlines* section, below, for further details.

Luxury steamship service to South America is more expensive than flying by jet.

These are top prices and less luxurious steamers and passenger carrying cargo vessels can cut the above fares in half, from North America and Europe.

From Europe a small selection of ocean transport is available. Sample one-way fare: the Ybarra Line service from Barcelona to La Guaira (Port for Caracas) starts at $515-590 cabin class, and from $440-520 up, tourist class.

 COST OF A TYPICAL DAY. Peru is a popular South American country with international travelers. A day and night in Lima is not typical, of course, for all South America, but the prices there are very near standard for most capital cities.

A breakdown of the average tourist's expenses in *Lima* for a day and night (exchange rates *approx.*):

1st Class Hotel

(one person sharing Double)	$15.00	£8.35
Three Meals (including service)	$15.00	8.35
Four Taxi Rides	$4.00	2.25
Two Drinks (Pisco Sours)	$2.00	1.10
Theater Ticket (Reserved Seat)	$1.50	.85
Movie	.60	.35
City Sightseeing Tour	$8.50	4.75
Laundry (Shirt)	.50	.27
Dry Clean Suit	$2.00 (Dress $1.00)	1.10
Pack of American Cigarettes	$1.00	.55
Total Cost	$50.10	£27.92

The approximate cost per day in other countries, including first-class hotel, meals, transfers, tips and incidentals (no shopping, of course) would be:

	APPROX. COST PER DAY	
Argentina	US$35-40	£22.25*
Bolivia	30-35	19.45
Brazil	40-50	27.80
Chile	25-40	22.25
Colombia	40-50	27.80
Ecuador	25-35	19.45
Paraguay	35-40	22.25
Peru	40-50	27.80
Surinam	30-35	19.45
Uruguay	25-35	19.45
Venezuela	40-50	27.80

    * at $1.80 to £ sterling

Recent devaluations in several countries have increased there the purchasing power of the dollar, but tourists still must know how to shop around for "buys" in accommodation and services.

MONEY MATTERS. South American money seems complicated at first glance. Many currencies are classified as "soft" meaning that they change value often very suddenly.

Best advice is to change only what you anticipate spending in each country. Check with a reputable bank and see if it is to your advantage to change a permitted amount of your money before entering some countries.

Travelers checks and single U.S. one-dollar bills are accepted almost everywhere in South America's larger cities. Hotels will generally change travelers checks at rates slightly lower than banks or currency exchange houses.

Here's a list of South American countries, their local currencies and exchange rates (at presstime) to U.S. dollar:

Argentina	peso	265.00	Guyana	dollar	2.54
Bolivia	peso	20.00	Paraguay	guarani	124.33
Brazil	cruzeiro	12.23	Peru	sol	69.14
Chile	peso	17.35	Surinam	guilder	1.78
Colombia	peso	36.25	Uruguay	peso	3.96
Ecuador	sucre	24.58	Venezuela	bolivar	4.28
French Guiana	franc	4.05			

These figures represent exchange rates valid at publication time. However, check with your bank or travel agent for the latest rates.

Credit Travel and Credit Cards. A number of organizations in the United States, Canada and Britain make credit cards available which enable you to sign for hotel and restaurant bills, car rentals, purchases, and so forth, and pay the resulting total at one time on a monthly bill, either pay-as-you-go or in installments after you return home. This is particularly advantageous for businessmen traveling on an expense account or on business trips whose cost is deductible for income tax, since the bill provides a voucher for your expenditures. In these days of currency exchange rate fluctuations, cards save you the trouble of converting, as you'll be billed in dollars back home at current exchange rate on date of purchase. Such organizations are the *Diners Club, American Express Card, Carte Blanche, Eurocard, Access* and *Barclaycard.*

Travelers checks are the best way to safeguard travel funds. They are sold by various banks and companies in terms of American and Canadian dollars and pounds sterling. Most universally accepted are those of *American Express*, while those issued by *Bank of America* are also widely used.

Best known and easily exchanged British travelers checks are those issued by *Thos. Cook & Son* and the "Big Four" banks: *Barclays, Lloyds, Midland,* and *National Westminster.*

Changing travelers' checks or cash is easiest at your hotel, but will cost you more (and it will be worse in shops and restaurants!). So change at banks, if you can afford the extra time, and try to avoid doing so at weekends, when rates are less advantageous. Also try to have on hand enough local currency for arrival at the next port of call, to get you through the unnerving procedures at airports with porters, taxi drivers, bellhops at the hotel, etc. You can buy small packets for this purpose at many banks and at *Perera, Deak* and similar agencies.

HOW TO GO. The traveler to South America may choose a variety of ways to travel—in a group, on tour, alone on a pre-arranged itinerary, or free lance "plan as you go".

A serious talk with a travel agent will usually answer the question of which is best for you, and a few lines here may help make the decision.

Group Travel. Group travel often saves money. Several attractive group fares from the United States to South America are now in effect and substantially reduce the transportation costs of the traveler.

Restrictions on these fares include the following: group must consist of at least 10 persons traveling together; all group members must travel together on the full itinerary.

Sample fares to South America in U.S. dollars for economy jet service are shown later in this *Planning* section.

 ON TOUR. Inclusive tours allow one to pre-pay the land arrangements and leave the worries of booking hotel rooms and other facilities to the tour organizer. Typically the tour price includes hotel accommodations, two or three meals a day, tips and taxes, transfers to and from the hotel and sightseeing trips. Air fares may be quoted separately.

The following are sample prices of individual tours to South America intended to provide a rough idea of the cost involved. *All prices are exclusive of air transportation.*

Avianca (the Colombian international airline) offers several inclusive tour packages, example: 14 night *"Colombian Contrasts"* covers Cartagena, the resort area of Santa Marta, Bogotá and Medellín. The costs, including air fare and hotels starts at $601 from Miami and $726 from New York.

Pan Am's World has a 23-day *Round South America* tour starting at $661 or a 22-day *Grand Tour* from $709. Less expensive tours of shorter duration are also available.

Maupintour in conjunction with *Avianca* and *Varig* features a 22-day grand tour of South America with twice a week departures from Miami. The land package is from $1,398.

SOME TOUR OPERATORS SPECIALIZING IN SOUTH AMERICA

In the U.S.:

AMAZON EXPLORERS
Professional Bldg., Rte. 9
Parlin, N.J. 08859

AMERICAN EXPRESS
1110 Brickell Avenue
Miami, Florida 33131

ASENSIO TOURS & TRAVEL
501 Fifth Ave.
New York, N. Y. 10017

BENNETT TOURS
270 Madison Ave.
New York, N.Y. 10016

LADATCO TOURS
c/o Americana Tours
245 S.E. First Street
Miami, Florida 33131

CARIBBEAN HOLIDAYS
711 Third Avenue
New York, N.Y. 10017

THOS. COOK & SON
587 Fifth Ave.
New York, N.Y. 10017

EXPRINTER INTERNATIONAL
500 Fifth Ave.
New York, N.Y. 10036

FOUR WINDS TRAVEL
175 Fifth Avenue
New York, N.Y. 10010

HEMPHILL/HARRIS TRAVEL
10100 Santa Monica Blvd.
Los Angeles, California 90067

LINDBLAD TRAVEL
133 East 55 St.
New York, N.Y. 10022

LISLIND INTERNATIONAL
5 World Trade Center
New York, N.Y. 10048

MARTIN EMPIRE TOURS
711 Third Avenue
New York, N.Y. 10017

MAUPINTOUR ASSOCIATES
900 Massachusetts St.
Lawrence, Kansas 66044

NATRAC TOURS
150 State St.
Boston, Mass. 02109

SITA WORLD TRAVEL
275 Post St., Rm. 503
San Francisco, Calif. 94108
and 2960 Wilshire Blvd.
Los Angeles, Calif. 90010
and 10 Columbus Circle
New York, N.Y. 10019

TRAVELWORLD INC.
6922 Hollywood Blvd. Suite 302
Los Angeles, California 90028

VACATIONLAND TRAVEL SERVICE
300 Madison Ave.
New York, N.Y. 10017

WRIGHT WAY TOURS
Box 6038
Glendale, Calif. 91204

In the U.K.:

ALTA HOLIDAYS
57 Victoria St.
London SW1
England

HOULDERS WORLD HOLIDAYS
Deepdene House
Dorking, Surrey
England

Special Interest Tours. In the past few years several special interest tours have been organized to visit South America. Your travel agent will have information on camera tours, horticultural tours, agricultural tours and many others. Amazon River cruises and hunting safaris, special package tours to Carnival in Rio are all available.

Amazon Explorers, Parlin, N.J. 08859, specializes in safaris to the Amazon Basin.

Adventures Anywhere, (57½ Wyckoff St. Brooklyn, N.Y. 11201) features a *Realm of the Inca* trip geared to archeology and anthropology. The 18 day package to Quito, Lima, Cuzco and Machu Picchu costs $1,795, including air fare from Miami.

Lindblad Travel Inc., 133 East 55, New York, N.Y. 10022, specializes in tours "off-the-beaten path" to such places as Easter Island, the Galápagos, Antarctica, the Amazon, etc.

You can book a 2-week tour of the Galapagos Islands through *Houlders World Holidays*, Deepdene House, Dorking, Surrey, England. Regular cruises around the Galápagos are now available on a yacht providing berths for 60 passengers. Contact: Metropolitan Touring, P.O. Box 2542, Quito, Ecuador.

Thru the Lens Tours, Inc., 5301 Laurel Canyon Blvd., North Hollywood, California 91607 runs 24-day photography tours of Peru and Ecuador for about $1900 plus air fare.

La Rana, Calle 27B No. 6–73, Bogotá, Colombia, specializes in exotic tours throughout Colombia (Amazon, Leyva, La Goajira, San Agustin).

From Great Britain, Louis Duforest Travel Service Ltd. offers "Decorum Holidays" covering one or several countries.

Pennworld Ltd., (122 Knightsbridge, London SW1) offers a 5 week Trans-Andes coach trek for the adventurous which roams from Rio de Janeiro on the Atlantic coast to Lima on the Pacific coast. £970 includes air fare from London, allow £48 for excursions and £9 a day for accommodations and meals.

Pre-arranged Itinerary. The traveler visiting South America independently and expecting to visit certain areas in peak or popular seasons should plan an itinerary with a professional travel advisor. First, the total cost of the trip can be accurately estimated and, secondly, advance reservations can be secured for transportations and hotels. For example, hotel reservations are necessary in *Punta del Este* at the height of the season, few rooms exist in *Rio* at Carnival, and a large convention in any South American capital will put the unprepared visitor almost out in the street.

Plan-As-You-Go Travel. Wandering in South America on a plan-as-you-go basis can be the most rewarding way of all, or it can be a disaster, depending on the individual. To do it successfully you need a knowledge of Spanish, some experience in foreign travel already, an open schedule and a good deal of willingness to take things, and people, as they are.

South America is still a virgin land for tourism and there are not the traveler's information booths, translators, and guides everywhere as there now are in Europe and other popular travel destinations.

There is no friendlier continent than South America to the stranger. Nevertheless the novice international traveler is advised to make some definite plans and reservations before he leaves.

In-Between. A formula that provides experienced planning and guidance but that avoids the sterility of standardized international hotels and airports and gets you much closer to the real life of the countries you visit is touring by motorcoach and either staying in small hotels or camping out. Two agencies specialize in this style of travel: *World Trek*, 801 Second Ave. Suite 501, New York, N.Y. 10017; and *Pennworld*, 44 Brattle St., Cambridge, Massachusetts 02138. This kind of travel is not only more colorful, it is obviously less expensive, too. Typically: 36 days for $885, 45 days for $1298. Both plus air fare.

Official Tourist Information Offices. Because tourism is a relative newcomer to South America, few official or government travel information offices have been established abroad.

To meet the increasing demand for information, the *South American Travel Organization* was formed in 1963 by the various tourism interests in South America. SATO, as the new organization is popularly called, now maintains offices in Lima, Peru, and will supply both the travel trade and interested persons with up-to-date information on all South American countries.

For information on any aspect of travel to South America, write or visit: South American Travel Organization, El Rosario 240, 1er piso, Miraflores, Lima, Peru.

Individual countries with travel information centers in the United States:

Bolivia
Bolivian Consulate General
10 Rockefeller Plaza
New York, N.Y. 10020

Brazil
Brazilian Consulate General
630 Fifth Avenue
New York, N.Y. 10020

Colombia
Colombian Govt. Tourist Office
140 E. 57 St.
New York, N.Y. 10022

Ecuador
Ecuador Tourist Agents
% Ecuadorian Airline
500 Fifth Avenue, Room 310
New York, N.Y. 10020

French Guiana
French Government Tourist
  Office
610 Fifth Avenue
New York, N.Y. 10020
Tel: 757-1125

Guyana
Guyana Tourist Information
  Office
Consulate of Guyana
622 Third Ave.
New York, N.Y. 10017
Tel: 953-0920

Peru
Peruvian Consulate
10 Rockefeller Plaza
New York, N.Y. 10020

Surinam
Surinam Tourist Bureau
1 Rockefeller Plaza
New York, N.Y. 10020
Tel: LT 1-3063

Uruguay
Uruguay Consulate
301 E. 47 St., Suite 19A
New York, N.Y. 10017

Venezuela
Venezuelan Govt. Tourist Bureau
450 Park Avenue
New York, N.Y. 10022
Tel: 355-1101

 STUDENT AND EDUCATIONAL TRAVEL OPPOR-TUNITIES. An increasing number of foreign students are being admitted to Colleges and Universities in South America—both as full-time students and at summer sessions. Registration procedures vary for each school and prospective students should contact the university directly or write the *Institute of International Education*, 809 UN Plaza, New York, N.Y. 10017.

 YEAR 'ROUND TRAVEL. South America may be pleasantly visited *anytime*. Because of the reversed seasons below the equator and the great variations in geography, altitude and climate on the continent, the traveler heading South can always find delightful weather.

Nature has been kind to South America. Her people residing on the equator do not live in sweltering cities but, due to their elevation, they enjoy spring-like climates the year 'round. Bogota, Quito, La Paz and Cuzco are always pleasant. South America's Caribbean coast and sunny ski lands are good examples of how attractive the continent really is.

New Year's Eve in Punta del Este is a wonderful summer night, and the height of the swimming season on Rio's famed Copacabana Beach is Christmas Day. Summer weather is absolutely guaranteed from December through March.

Tropical rains are always intermittent and allow time for outdoor

FACTS AT YOUR FINGERTIPS

AVERAGE TEMPERATURE CHART IN ° FAHRENHEIT

		Jan.	Feb.	Mar.	Apr.	May	Jun.	Jul.	Aug.	Sept.	Oct.	Nov.	Dec.
Buenos Aires (Argentina)	Max.	85°	83°	79°	72°	64°	57°	57°	60°	64°	69°	76°	82°
	Min.	63	63	60	53	47	41	42	43	46	50	56	61
La Paz (Bolivia)	Max.	64	64	64	66	66	60	61	62	62	65	67	64
	Min.	43	43	43	40	35	36	34	35	38	40	42	43
Rio de Janeiro (Brazil)	Max.	84	85	83	80	77	76	75	76	75	77	79	82
	Min.	73	73	72	69	66	64	63	64	65	66	68	71
Bogotá (Colombia)	Max.	67	68	67	67	66	65	64	65	66	66	66	66
	Min.	48	49	50	51	51	51	50	50	49	50	50	49
Quito (Ecuador)	Max.	69	69	69	69	69	70	71	71	72	70	70	70
	Min.	46	47	47	47	47	46	44	44	45	46	46	46
Lima (Peru)	Max.	82	83	83	80	74	68	67	66	68	71	74	78
	Min.	66	67	66	63	60	58	57	56	57	58	60	62
Montevideo (Uruguay)	Max.	83	82	78	71	64	59	58	59	63	68	74	79
	Min.	62	61	59	53	48	43	43	43	46	49	54	59
Caracas (Venezuela)	Max.	79	77	79	81	80	78	78	79	80	79	77	78
	Min.	56	56	58	60	62	62	61	61	61	61	60	58

activities. In most towns the rain comes at a certain time during the day and thus seldom interrupts activities because they are planned around it.

There are festivals, special events, and sporting attractions year round.

As a general guide, the chart (preceding) outlines South American climates:

Seasons below the Equator are the reverse of the north—Summer, December 21 to March 20; Winter from June 21 to September 20. Temperatures vary with altitudes—warm along the coast, colder in the highlands.

 FESTIVALS AND SPECIAL EVENTS. South America is a land of fairs and festivals. Listed below are a great many of the special events regularly scheduled each year. Because most of the continent is Roman Catholic, a great many events are religious holidays and the dates change from year to year. Holy Days and special celebrations are colorful and numerous.

For more facts on festivals and special events, see country chapters.

HOLIDAYS. The following legal holidays are observed in South America. Also see listing of Fairs and Festivals in the country chapters.

ARGENTINA. January 1; January 6; Maundy Thursday; Good Friday; May 1, May 25; Corpus Christi; June 20; July 9; August 15; August 17; October 12; November 1; December 8 and 25. Not all are obligatory holidays.

BOLIVIA. January 1; (Carnival normally in February); April 9; May 1; Corpus Christi; August 5, 6 and 7 (National Festival); October 12; November 1; November 2; December 8; December 25.

BRAZIL. January 1; January 20 (Rio); January 25 (São Paulo); Carnival Monday, Tuesday and Wednesday morning; Good Friday; April 21; May 1; Corpus Christi; September 7; November 1; November 15; December 25.

CHILE. January 1; Holy Week; May 1; May 21; August 15; September 18 and 19; October 12; November 1; December 8; December 25.

COLOMBIA. January 1 and 6; March 19; Holy Week; Easter; May 1; May 8; May 29; June 6; July 20; August 7 and 15; October 12; November 1 and 11; December 8 and 25.

ECUADOR. January 1; January 6; Carnival on the Monday and Tuesday before Lent; Maundy Thursday; Good Friday; May 1 and 24; July 24; August 10; October 9 and 12; November 1 and 3; December 6 and 25.

FRENCH GUIANA. Pre-Lenten celebrations from January 6 to Ash Wednesday; July 14; October 15 to 25 (Feast of Cayenne); November 11.

GUYANA. January 1; March 27, 28 and 30; May 18 and 24; August 3; October 12; November 9; December 25 and 26.

PARAGUAY. January 1; February 3; March 1; March 26 and 27; May 1, 14, 15 and 28; June 12; August 15; September 29; October 12; November 1; December 8 and 25.

PERU. January 1; Holy Week; May 1; June 29; July 28, 29; August 30; October 9 (Dignity's Day); November 1; December 8 and 25.

SURINAM. January 1; March 27, 30; April 30; May 7, 18; July 1; December 15, 25.

URUGUAY. January 1 and 6; March 1-2; April 15, 16, 17; April 19; May 1; June 19; July 18; August 25; October 12; November 2; December 25.

VENEZUELA. June 24; July 5 and 24; October 12; December 25.

CARNIVAL WEEK. Brazil and most South American countries start Carnival on the weekend preceding Ash Wednesday in early February. A word of caution about "carnival-time" visits. Many returning tourists have complained about minimal hotel services where their rooms went uncleaned and the beds unmade for days. Many instances of late or no breakfasts. Gas pumps and garage services often closed down. Be prepared for the otherwise orderly system to break down during such holiday time.

CLOSING HOURS. Opening and closing hours naturally vary from city to city and country to country. Best rule to follow is to remember many shops close for the customary two or three hour Latin luncheon. Plan your shopping between ten a.m. and noon and three p.m. and six p.m. and you'll find stores open in every country.

In the larger cities many of the big department stores are now staying open during the lunch hours. In Buenos Aires, for example, the larger stores now open at nine a.m. and don't close until seven p.m.

Chile has the latest regular hours with stores normally open from 9:30 a.m. to 1:00 p.m. and then reopening at 3:30 p.m. until 8 p.m. Some are converting to the "jornada unica", staying open during lunch time, and opening at 9 a.m., and closing at 5 or 5:30 p.m. Rio stores open 8 a.m.-6:30 p.m. Sat. 8:30 a.m.-1 p.m.

PASSPORTS AND VISAS. Although U.S. laws do not require a passport for travel to or in any part of the Western Hemisphere, a passport is required by the laws and regulations of some of the countries concerned. Thus it is a good idea for travelers to South America to have a valid passport, and most countries there will require an onward or return ticket. Except for Venezuela, which readily issues visas for 45 days, South American countries do not require visas of U.S. citizens for visits of up to three months. Some countries require Tourist Cards; see individual country chapters for full details on this subject.

The U.S. Government issues both individual and family passports. Individual passports are more expensive ($13 each) but they offer more flexibility, as you may need to separate—for business, illness, or special interests. Plan for maximum freedom of movement. It is a good idea to have children wear I.D. bracelets listing their names and passport numbers.

U.S. citizens should apply several months in advance of their expected departure date. U.S. residents must apply in person to the U.S. Passport Agency in New York, Boston, Philadelphia, Washington, D.C., Miami, Chicago, New Orleans, Seattle, San Francisco, Los Angeles, or Honolulu, or to their local County Courthouse. In some areas selected post offices are also equipped to take passport applications. If you still have your latest passport, issued within the past eight years, you may use this to apply by mail. Otherwise, take with you: 1) a birth certificate or certified copy thereof, or other proof of citizenship; 2) two identical photographs 2½ inches square, full face, black and white or color and taken within the past six months; 3) $13 ($10 if you apply by mail); 4) proof of identity, such as a driver's license, previous passport, any governmental I.D. card. Social Security and credit cards are NOT acceptable. U.S. passports are valid for five years.

If a non-citizen, you need a Treasury Sailing Permit, Form 1040 C, certifying that Federal taxes have been paid; apply to your District Director of Internal Revenue for this. You will have to present various documents: 1) blue or green alien registration card; 2) passport; 3) travel tickets; 4) most recently filed Form 1040; 5) W-2 forms for the most recent full year; 6) most recent current payroll stubs or letter; 7) check to be sure this is all! To return to the U.S. you need a re-entry permit if you plan to stay abroad more than 1 year. Apply for it in person at least six weeks before departure at the nearest office of the Immigration and Naturalization Service, or by mail to the Service, Washington, D.C.

HEALTH CERTIFICATES. Travelers to South America will need a valid smallpox vaccination certificate (less than three years old) in their possession for entry into all South American countries as well.

The vaccination certificate must bear the stamp of the local or state health department where the inoculation was given.

In addition to the required smallpox vaccination, the U.S. Public Health Service advises the following inoculations for travelers to South America: Yellow fever for travelers to the northern third of South America; typhus for the Andean region; and typhoid for an extensive trip around South America. A tetanus shot is also recommended by the Service for all international travel.

CUSTOMS REGULATIONS. Travel to and within South America has become relatively uncomplicated in the past few years. Customs regulations vary from country to country. See the country chapters for specific information.

WHAT SHALL I WEAR IN SOUTH AMERICA? This depends entirely on who you are, where you go, and what you do. A corporation executive on a business trip, staying in sleek hotels and attending formal conferences will hardly pack the same clothes as a college student on vacation, staying in pensions and riding in local buses. Most people who read this will fall somewhere in between.

If you expect to attend formal or business functions, to be invited out or to go to concerts or the theater you will need, as in the United States or Europe, a dark suit and tie for men, and at least one long dress plus a cocktail dress for women. In season, that dark suit can be a summer or a Palm Beach light-weight suit (with an unobtrusive sweater, or extra underwear, if it is unexpectedly chilly). Black ties and dinner jackets are rare in South America today, and in most capitals and major cities you can hire formal dress, and have it fitted, on 24 hours notice, if need be. Men should bring at least one pair of black shoes, and women at least one dress pair, for special occasions. Otherwise, wear what is comfortable, and strong if you plan to climb about ruins or be out in villages, countryside or forest. Sandals may or may not be practical in muddy or dirty streets.

On a more average level, although most local middle-class and business people still dress conservatively, men tourists will not have difficulty wearing good sports shirts without ties in most places. Take a couple of ties along anyway, but don't worry about them. The easiest thing to remember, when packing, is that in South America as almost everywhere in the world today you can get what you need locally. Buenos Aires, after all, is not the Gobi Desert. In fact, with the assistance of numerous French and Italian designers, and Argentina's excellent wool and leather, it has become a leading center for fashion. You can buy smart, latest-model dresses there for much less than in the U.S. and know that they are made from high-quality natural materials. Argentina also has a large ready-to-wear clothing industry that caters to all tastes and budgets. U.S. brands, such as Arrow, Manhattan and Van Heusen shirts, are made there under licence, and are drip-dry.

More informally still, if you belong to that large group of tourists who have no formal engagements, you can dress largely to suit yourself. Open-necked sports shirts for men, and pants-suits or short skirts for women are acceptable. Buenos Aires's top hotel, the 800-room Sheraton, does not seem to mind informal dress in its public rooms, nor does the Plaza place any restrictions, even though it is a favorite with upper-class residents. In Rio de Janeiro, at Copacabana, you can wear your bathing suit into most hotels, as they provide separate entrances and elevators for direct access to and from the beach. Women may wear backless, halter-type dresses on hot days, and men may go without jackets. Few people wear hats for style anymore; wear them for protection as you see fit.

Most young people can get by with T-shirts, pull-overs and jeans. Jeans put out by the Argentine subsidiaries of Levi's and Lee's are very popular with all classes hit by hard times, and come in many models. Shorts may be worn in public if they are neither too brief nor too tight; and in Buenos Aires pairs of Tourist Police women patrol shopping streets both to assist visitors and to discourage the Latin custom of fanny-pinching.

A few cautions: 1) Cities like Quito, Bogotá, La Paz and Arequipa can be cold at night because of their altitude. Bring along at least one sweater, extra underwear, and a light scarf. 2) Electricity—most hotels are fitted for 220-volt A.C., though some of the newer ones carry points for 110 volts that will operate U.S. electric razors and other gadgets. 3) Bring your own shoe shine equipment; except in the barber shops of large hotels stands are hard to find. 4) Local druggists have preparations for local problems, but you might carry some anti-diarrhoea capsules. Most stomach upsets come from over-indulgence—strong seasonings, shell-fish, heavy wines, etc. Try to eat lightly your first day or two in a new place. 5) When you buy drip-dry clothing, be sure to get dacron-cotton blends in preference to nylon, which can be very hot and damp in the tropics. 6) A brief summary of climate conditions is given for each country of South America in the *Practical Information* section of that country's chapter; see also the temperature chart in this present chapter, above. 7) Finally, your airline allowance is 30 kilos (66 pounds) for First Class and 20 kilos (44 pounds) for Economy. And it makes sense in any case to—travel light!

A few additional reminders for your packing checklist would include: *Ball-Point Pen* for plane travel on the continent. *Detergent* for do-it-yourself laundry. *Laundry Gadgets* to hang up those articles you wish to rinse out. *Tooth Paste* or powder if you are addicted to a special brand. *Camera Gadgets*, lightmeter, filters, if you use them and plenty of film. *Sun Glasses*, a must for sunny South America. *Extra Eyeglasses* if you're dependent upon them. *Prescribed Medicines* you take regularly. *Vitamins*.

Plastic Bags for lingerie, shoes, bottles that might break, costume jewelry, damp laundry and swim suits. *Binoculars. Travel Clock. Spot-Remover Powder*—easier and less dangerous to carry than liquids. *Manicure Set. Sewing Kit* supplied with pins and with thread in colors you'll be wearing. *Cigarette Lighter*, if you're a smoker. Windproof style more practical, for use at sea. *Notebook* for recording what you see and buy and spend on shore, and for addresses of friends you'll make en route. *Sunburn Preventative*.

Imported liquors are expensive in South America, so you might want to stock up on your favorite brands at duty-free shops in international airports such as London, New York, Miami or Los Angeles. (See individual country sections for their respective liquor customs allowances).

 PHOTOGRAPHER'S HINTS. Best advice is to carry sufficient color film. Several of the smaller countries still do not stock fresh color film in all sizes, and to avoid disappointment, carry more color film than you plan to use (you'll end up using it all in highly photogenic South America). Film is very expensive, especially in Brazil. Black and white film (usually fresh) is usually available in the capital cities. A good filter for bright sunlight is a must on your photo checklist, as well as mailing containers for sending color film home, if you plan to be gone more than three months. Airmail your film home—don't use surface mail—it's painfully slow between South and North America.

X-rays. When you fly, remember that in spite of official claims to the contrary, airport security x-ray machines do in fact damage your photographic films in about 17% of the cases. Have them inspected separately, or pack them in specially-lined protective bags available in photo supply stores.

A final hint—a small tip to those whom you use as models, before you shoot, insures a smooth relationship.

 USEFUL ADDRESSES. The *Organization of American States*, Washington, D.C., issues several inexpensive booklets on all South American countries. The *U.S. Government Printing Office*, Washington, D.C., sells maps of South American countries. The *Chamber of Commerce of Latin America in the U.S.A.*, 1 World Trade Center, Rm. 3549, New York, N.Y. 10048, has business information.

Also the *London Chamber of Commerce, Latin American Section*, 69 Cannon St., E.C.4.

The Hispanic Council, Canning House, 2, Belgrave Square, London, S.W.1. issues *British Bulletin of Publications on Latin America*.

A list of addresses of the local SATO Chapters in South America may be obtained from the *South American Travel Organization*, Avenida Arequipa 340, Oficina 603, Lima, Peru, and in New York at 708 Third Ave., New York 10017.

HOW TO GET THERE?

AIRLINES FROM THE U.S. AND CANADA. A study released recently showed that 97.07 per cent of all departures from North to South America were by air. There are many factors responsible for this startlingly high figure of air travelers—but the best reason is probably that air travel to South America is a real bargain.

In fact, South America offers the world's greatest international air travel bargain. A traveler purchasing a 'round South America ticket buys over 12,724 miles of transportation, has up to a full year to travel (or 30 days if he buys an excursion ticket), and by making a circle tour around the continent can take in as stopovers almost every major city, important sightseeing spot and glamorous resort in South America.

A good example is the Miami-Buenos Aires round trip ($944 tourist class) or the New York-Buenos Aires routing ($1048 tourist class). Both tickets allow stopovers in many South American and Central American countries plus several Caribbean islands and cities in the U.S.A. Comparable fares to European and Pacific destinations are more expensive per mile. Probably the best way to dramatically illustrate the 'round South America air bargain is to list all possible cities for stopovers on a New York-Buenos Aires round trip ticket. However, a surcharge of $131 on the outward portion would be assessed if you made *all* the stops listed.

> New York—San Juan (or Jamaica, Haiti, Dominican Republic)—Caracas, Venezuela—Port of Spain, Trinidad—Georgetown, Guyana—Paramaribo, Surinam—Cayenne, French Guiana—Belem, Brazil—Brasilia, Brazil—Rio de Janeiro, Brazil—São Paulo, Brazil—Asuncion, Paraguay (Iguassu Falls)—Montevideo, Uruguay—Buenos Aires, Argentina.

The return from Buenos Aires may be taken up South America's Pacific Coast and allows the stopovers listed below. However, if *all* are taken, the surcharge again would be $105 more than the regular fare, less if some points are omitted.

> Santiago, Chile—Antofagasta, Chile—La Paz, Bolivia—Lima, Peru—Guayaquil, Ecuador—Quito, Ecuador—Cali, Colombia—Panama City, Panama—San José, Costa Rica—Managua, Nicaragua—Tegucigalpa, Honduras—San Salvador, El Salvador—Guatemala City, Guatemala—New York.

The last few years, however, have seen a dramatic growth in various types of charter flight/package tours. These give you a fixed itinerary, with hotels and most meals included, and no stopovers, of course, but at considerable savings. An example would be *Lan-Chile-Pan Am's* 16 day tour of four countries for $394 plus GIT air fare of $573 from Miami, $620 from New York, or $778 from Los Angeles. Another such package offers one-week tours of Lima for $128; Lima, Cuzco and Machu Picchu for $314; Lima, Machu Picchu and the Amazon for $325; plus air fares varying from $372 to $655.

Checking Your Car. A convenient way to get to the airport and have your car waiting on return is offered by *Autobaby Sitters*, 827 Sterling Place, Brooklyn, N.Y., who will take care of your car from the moment you leave it at the airport, and have it there on your return.

INDIVIDUAL EXCURSIONS AND GROUP INCLUSIVE TOUR FARES

(Prices quoted are round trips)

Courtesy Pan American World Airways

	NEW YORK		MIAMI		LOS ANGELES	
	Excursion	Group	Excursion	Group	Excursion	Group
ANTOFAGASTA	$835 (1)	—	$670 (1)	—	—	—
ASUNCION	884 (1)	$712 (8)	835 (1)	$676 (8)	$989 (1)	$853 (8)
	782 (7)	635 (9)	734 (7)	589 (9)	916 (7)	771 (9)
BARRANQUILLA	408 (2)	311 (10)	231 (2)	197 (10)	582 (4)	451 (10)
	428 (3)	—	253 (3)	—	—	—
BELEM	696 (1)	574 (8)	597 (1)	499 (8)	895 (4)	727 (8)
	649 (7)	519 (9)	563 (7)	455 (9)	824 (7)	662 (9)
BOGOTA	435 (2)	365 (10)	273 (2)	235 (10)	621 (5)	474 (10)
	455 (3)	—	294 (3)	—	—	—
BRASILIA	846 (1)	687 (8)	797 (1)	608 (8)	1017 (1)	792 (8)
	782 (7)	635 (9)	734 (7)	589 (9)	916 (7)	771 (9)
BUENOS AIRES	886 (1)	744 (8)	837 (1)	678 (8)	991 (1)	856 (8)
	782 (7)	635 (9)	734 (7)	589 (9)	886 (7)	771 (9)
CALI	457 (2)	380 (10)	297 (2)	253 (11)	650 (5)	507 (10)
	477 (3)	—	318 (3)	—	—	—
GUAYAQUIL	620 (5)	500 (11)	421 (5)	343 (11)	686 (5)	594 (11)
LA PAZ	855 (6)	635 (11)	730 (1)	569 (11)	929 (1)	766 (11)

	NEW YORK Excursion	NEW YORK Group	MIAMI Excursion	MIAMI Group	LOS ANGELES Excursion	LOS ANGELES Group
LIMA	719 (5)	595 (11)	558 (5)	478 (11)	766 (5)	662 (11)
MEDELLIN	424 (2)	337 (10)	259 (2)	215 (10)	604 (4)	469 (10)
	444 (3)	—	280 (3)	—	—	—
MONTEVIDEO	886 (1)	744 (8)	837 (1)	678 (8)	991 (1)	856 (8)
	782 (7)	635 (9)	734 (7)	589 (9)	916 (7)	771 (9)
QUITO	597 (5)	479 (11)	390 (5)	314 (11)	669 (5)	577 (11)
RIO DE JANEIRO	848 (1)	697 (8)	800 (1)	616 (8)	1019 (1)	799 (8)
	782 (7)	635 (9)	734 (7)	589 (9)	916 (7)	771 (9)
SANTIAGO	872 (1)	725 (8)	747 (1)	644 (8)	935 (1)	822 (8)
	782 (7)	635 (9)	734 (7)	589 (9)	916 (7)	771 (9)

Notes: (1) Ticket limit 14 to 28 days.

(2) Ticket limit 10 to 30 days; applicable September thru May only.

(3) Ticket limit 10 to 30 days; applicable June, July, August only.

(4) Ticket limit 30 days.

(5) Ticket limit 10 to 30 days.

(6) Ticket limit 10 to 28 days.

(7) Ticket limit 29 to 45 days; applicable Sept. 15 thru March 31 only.

(8) Minimum group—10 passengers. Ticket limit 14 to 21 days*

(9) Minimum group—10 passengers. Ticket limit 7 to 21 days. Applicable Sept. 16 thru November 30 and January 15 thru May 31*

(10) Minimum group—10 passengers. Ticket limit 7 to 14 days*

(11) Minimum group—5 passengers. Ticket limit 7 to 14 days*

* Prices indicate air fare only. Additional ground tour must be purchased in conjunction with these fares.

Planning a trip to South America?

British Caledonian is the British airline serving the whole of that vibrant, exciting and colourful continent.

From London Gatwick British Caledonian fly to the major cities of Argentina, Brazil, Chile, Colombia, Peru and Venezuela.

You will experience on our DC-10 and 707 flights a standard of service that has made us the experienced traveller's favourite airline.

If your South American journey is a holiday British Caledonian will be delighted to make any special booking arrangements.

Contact your travel agent for full details of British Caledonian South America scheduled services and reservations.

CARACAS

BOGOTÁ

RECIFE

LIMA

RIO DE JANEIRO

SÃO PAULO

BUENOS AIRES

SANTIAGO

BRITISH CALEDONIAN

LANGUAGE/30
For the Business or Vacationing International Traveler

Now in 20 languages! A basic language course on cassette tapes (up to 2 hours) complete with a pocket phrase dictionary and social guide...Only $14.95 EA. (plus shipping)

BONUS STOPOVERS

From North America

If you are going to Buenos Aires and other South American cities, why not stopover at Lima or the Caribbean's Leeward Islands, Caracas or Cayenne? These and many other South American and Caribbean points may be usually visited without extra charge when you purchase a ticket from New York to Buenos Aires. In some cases a slight supplement applies.

You'll be pleasantly surprised at the way an ordinary roundtrip can be broadened in scope into a very comprehensive circle trip. When you buy a ticket to Buenos Aires you are entitled to 6,362 miles transportation in each direction.

Stopovers are, of course, entirely optional. You can fly nonstop from New York to the Argentine capital. However, if you wish to add a number of countries en route these privileges are certainly useful.

Let's examine some of the available routings from New York to Buenos Aires. You can fly from New York to Miami and after a stopover at the Florida gateway continue down the island chain to Montego Bay and Kingston, Jamaica. Then comes a short hop to Curacao, Netherlands West Indies. First landfall on the South American continent using this itinerary would be Caracas, Venezuela, a city with modern hotels and interesting sightseeing possibilities.

Next comes Bogota, Colombia, another city which is attracting more and more visitors during their Round South America trips or RSAs as they are known in the travel industry.

After a stopover in Bogota your ticket entitles you to visit Cali, Colombia; Quito, Ecuador; Guayaquil, Ecuador; and Lima, Peru. Lima is another city which is a prime tourist draw. It is also a jumping off point for trips to Cuzco, 11,400 feet above sea level and gateway to the Inca country. The side trip from Lima to Cuzco is charged separately from the New York/Buenos Aires ticket.

Heading towards Buenos Aires from Lima, the passenger has a choice of two routings. You can travel down the Coast of Chile to Arica, the country's most northerly seaport, Antofagasta, another major port steeped in history and finally Santiago, the capital.

With about 2,500,000 inhabitants, Santiago sits at the foot of the Andes and is a good center for sightseeing in the nearby countryside. After a visit to Chile, you board a flight for the short crossing of the Andes to your turning point, Buenos Aires.

The other route from Lima to Buenos Aires takes you to La Paz, Bolivia, a city 12,500 feet high. Here visitors can embark on fishing trips to the nearby Lake Titicaca area, shop for native handicrafts or just enjoy the rugged scenery.

What about other routings from New York and Buenos Aires? Leaving New York you can fly first to San Juan and then to Port of Spain, Trinidad. Many businessmen combine a South American visit with a Caribbean vacation because the fare is often the same and a variety of stopovers are possible.

Heading down South America's East Coast from Port of Spain, you may visit Georgetown, Guyana; Paramaribo, Surinam; and Cayenne, French Guiana. Of the three territories, Surinam has perhaps made the biggest attempt to win tourist traffic. River trips are an added attraction

From Europe

Between Europe and South America, one of the most popular itineraries involves a circle trip. You fly first to New York, then continue via Miami, the Caribbean and other South American points to your final destination. Returning, you cross the South Atlantic to Dakar, West Africa, and fly on to Europe.

Depending on your destination, the fare via New York in one direction can be the same as going via the South Atlantic. Where you originate in Europe also is a determining point. But ask your travel agent to explore your particular situation; you may be pleasantly surprised.

AIRLINES SERVING SOUTH AMERICA FROM U.S.A. AND CANADA

A great number of carriers now operate between North and South America. Over 30 lines now fly south from New York, Miami, New Orleans, Houston and Los Angeles—the major gateway to South America.

Leading carriers and a brief summary of their services from the U.S.A. are listed below (*note*: subject to change!):

Aerocondor Airlines—Boeing 720 service from Miami to Barranquilla, Medellin, Bogotá and Cali. Also two weekly flights from Miami to San Andres Island.

Aerolineas Argentinas (Argentine Airlines)—Direct New York-Buenos Aires; also from New York via Rio de Janeiro and São Paulo. Non-stop New York-Rio de Janeiro. From Miami to: Lima, Santiago, La Paz, Buenos Aires. From Los Angeles to Bogotá, Lima, Buenos Aires.

Aeroperu—DC-8 jet service from Miami to Panama, Lima, Santiago and Buenos Aires. Also three weekly flights from Los Angeles with a stop enroute at Mexico City.

Air Panama—Boeing 727 service from New York, Los Angeles and Miami to Panama, Guayaquil and Lima, and from Panama to Bogotá.

Avianca (The Colombia International Airline)—Excellent non-stop jet service from New York and Miami to Bogotá, Barranquilla, Cali, Cartagena, Santa Marta and Medellin, Colombia; and from Los Angeles to Bogotá via Mexico plus a non-stop Thurs. and Sat. from Los Angeles to Bogotá. Flights continue to Quito, Lima, Santiago, Buenos Aires, São Paulo and Rio. Also has extensive domestic network serving over 150 cities within Colombia and regular jet service to Caracas, San Juan, and Europe. Ask about special $110 "Visit Colombia" ticket.

Braniff International Airways—Offers a wide choice of flights from the United States and serves more cities in South America than any other carrier. Provides excellent regular jet flights from Miami, New York, Washington, Chicago, Dallas, Houston, New Orleans, Los Angeles, San Francisco, Minneapolis, Omaha, Oklahoma City, Wichita. Serves Panama City, Cali, Bogotá, Guayaquil, Quito, Lima, La Paz, Asunción, São Paulo, Rio, Santiago and Buenos Aires.

CP Air (Canadian Pacific)—Excellent jet service from Vancouver, Toronto and Montreal to South America via Mexico City. Cities served are Lima, Santiago and Buenos Aires.

STANDARD JET FARES

(Courtesy of Pan American World Airways)

All prices quoted are one way. Round trips are twice these figures.

The airline prices shown are merely a guide. As with all other airline prices nowadays, they are erratic and subject to sudden changes. Therefore, be sure to consult your airline or travel agent for current rates before booking.

	From New York		From Miami		From Houston		From Los Angeles	
	FIRST	ECON.	FIRST	ECON.	FIRST	ECON.	FIRST	ECON.
ANTOFAGASTA	$724	$455	$611	$374	$706	$441	$783	$491
ASUNCION	795	513	711	459	825	532	878	587
BARRANQUILLA	358	255	222	161	349	248	471	329
BELEM	636	410	550	355	679	438	812	524
BOGOTA	395	282	258	189	385	275	508	356
BRASILIA	772	498	687	443	801	517	867	573
BUENOS AIRES	812	524	732	472	835	539	880	589
CALI	431	296	294	204	421	289	544	370
GUAYAQUIL	498	231	358	231	487	314	598	383
LA PAZ	698	450	572	369	676	436	748	491
LIMA	606	391	467	291	569	367	652	423
MEDELLIN	385	273	249	180	375	266	499	347
MONTEVIDEO	812	524	732	472	835	539	880	589
QUITO	471	304	322	214	460	297	584	374
RIO DE JANEIRO	786	507	701	452	818	528	867	580
SANTIAGO	778	502	659	425	763	492	798	543

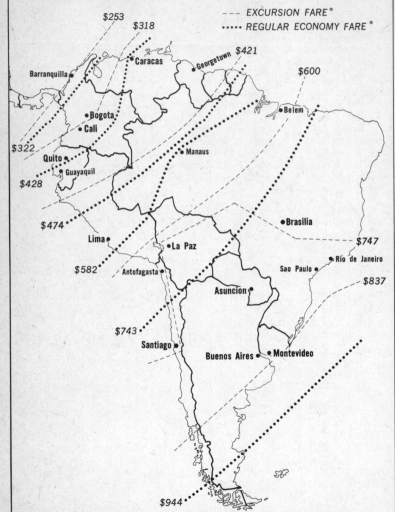

Air Fares by Dollars and Distance (Approximate)

ROUND TRIP FARES, WINTER, FROM MIAMI TO SELECTED SOUTH AMERICAN DESTINATIONS

--- EXCURSION FARE*
•••• REGULAR ECONOMY FARE*

$253
$318
$421
$600
Caracas
Georgetown
Barranquilla
Belem
$322
Bogota
Cali
Quito
Manaus
Guayaquil
$428
Brasilia
$474
Lima
La Paz
$747
Antofagasta
Sao Paulo
Rio de Janeiro
$582
$837
Asuncion
$743
Santiago
Buenos Aires
Montevideo
$944

*See fare tables and text for details, and for other fares, higher and lower.
Figures here based on IATA fares at presstime, subject to change

Delta—Regular jet service from Las Vegas, Dallas, and New Orleans direct to Caracas via Maracaibo, with good connections in New Orleans from Detroit, Indianapolis, Los Angeles, San Francisco, and Memphis.

KLM (Royal Dutch Airlines)—Serves Maracaibo, Barranquilla, Medellin, Georgetown, Port of Spain, Paramaribo, Guayaquil, Lima and Quito from New York via Curacao and/or Aruba.

LAN-Chile Airlines—Serves South America and the South Pacific from New York and Miami with B707 and B727 jets. Stops include Panama, Cali, Guayaquil, Lima, Santiago, Buenos Aires, Rio, Montevideo and Asuncion as well as extensive service within Chile. South Pacific route stops at Easter Island en route to Tahiti.

PanAm—This American flag carrier operates by far the most extensive and frequent jet service to and within South America. Daily jet service to almost all South America from Los Angeles, San Francisco, Houston, New Orleans, Washington, Philadelphia, Baltimore, Boston, Chicago, Tampa, Miami, and New York. Nearly 40 years ago, Pan American began building a network in South America and today's Latin service features flights like the New York-Buenos Aires non-stop jet (10½ hours), and daily service almost all countries. Round trip economy-class jet excursion fare to Argentina from New York is only $886, and is available all year round.

Varig (Brazilian Airlines)—Daily jet service from New York to Rio de Janeiro, São Paulo, Buenos Aires, and Asunción, 4 times a week to Montevideo and 3 times a week to Santiago; from Miami to Caracas, Manaus, Belem, Brasilia, Rio de Janeiro, São Paulo, Buenos Aires, Montevideo, Asunción, Santiago; DC-10 service also from N.Y. and Miami. Daily jet service from Los Angeles to Lima, Rio de Janeiro, São Paulo, Buenos Aires, Montevideo, Asunción and Santiago; from Mexico to Bogotá, Manaus, Brasilia, Rio de Janeiro, São Paulo. Also operates an extensive domestic service within Brazil.

Viasa (Venezuelan International Airways)—Regular jet service to Caracas from New York, Miami, Washington, D.C., San Juan and Santo Domingo.

AIRLINES SERVING SOUTH AMERICA FROM EUROPE

Several airlines now link Europe directly with South America. The most direct routes are by way of Africa and most flights stop at Dakar, the capital of Senegal, which is Africa's closest point to the South American continent.

Many experienced travelers plan a triangle trip to South America from Europe or vice versa. It is possible to include a visit to the United States on a Europe-South American flight at little extra cost. For example, a London-Dakar-Rio round trip costs £717.00, while London-Dakar-Rio-New York-London increases the ticket to only £806, while the London-Lima fare allows a stopover in New York at no extra cost. All fares jet economy. Also London, Capetown, Buenos Aires, New York.

Listed below are the major transatlantic airlines offering European-South America service:

Aerolineas Argentinas—Regular jet service from Zurich, Frankfurt, London, Rome, Paris, and Madrid to Rio de Janeiro, São Paulo and Buenos Aires.

Air France—Daily jet departures from Paris non-stop or via Madrid to Rio; via Madrid, Nice or Dakar to Buenos Aires and Santiago; via Madrid to São Paulo and Montevideo; non-stop or via Lisbon to Caracas; from Paris and Lisbon via Fort de France or Pointe-à-Pitre to Cayenne, Paramaribo, Bogotá, Quito, Lima and Santiago. Also twice a week SST Concorde service Paris-Rio via Dakar.

Avianca (The Colombia International Airline)—Four trans-Atlantic jet flights a week offer a choice of service from Frankfurt, Paris, Zurich and Madrid to San Juan, Caracas, Barranquilla, Bogotá, Quito, Lima, Santiago, Buenos Aires, São Paulo and Rio.

British Airways (BOAC)—Several weekly jet flights to South America with a choice of mid-Atlantic routes. Regular direct service from London to Georgetown, Trinidad and Panama. Connections at London for British Airways flights to and from many European cities.

British Caledonian Airways. From London to Recife, Rio de Janeiro, São Paulo, Buenos Aires and Santiago.

Iberia (Spanish Air Lines)—Several routes offer jet service between Madrid and South America. Bi-weekly jet flights from Madrid either nonstop to Rio or via Las Palmas and continuing to Montevideo, Buenos Aires and Santiago or continuing to São Paulo, Asuncion and Buenos Aires. Other trans-Atlantic service includes regular flights from Madrid direct or via San Juan to Caracas, Maracaibo, Bogotá, Quito, Guayaquil, Lima, La Paz and Santiago. There is a Madrid-Santo Domingo-Panama flight. Iberia now uses the DC-10's and 208-passenger Stretch DC-8-63 jets on its trans-Atlantic flights.

KLM (Royal Dutch Airlines)—A variety of trans-Atlantic jet services are offered. Best service is from Amsterdam to Caracas and Curacao via Madrid, Frankfurt, Zürich and Lisbon. KLM also operate continuing service for several of its trans-Atlantic flights to Guayaquil, Buenos Aires, Panama, Santiago, Rio de Janeiro, São Paulo, Montevideo, Lima, Quito, Port of Spain, and Paramaribo.

LAN-Chile—flies to Santiago and Panama from Frankfurt, Paris and Madrid.

Lufthansa—The German flag carrier serves South America from Frankfurt, other European cities or Dakar to Rio, São Paulo, Montevideo, Buenos Aires, Santiago, Guayaquil, Lima, La Paz, Caracas, Bogotá, Quito, and Asuncion.

PanAm—Because of Pan Am's extensive Latin American services, the fastest way to South America from Europe is often a combination of a trans-Atlantic flight to New York and from there a connection with one of Pan Am's long-range, non-stop jet flights to Rio or Buenos Aires. Pan Am also operates a direct Africa-Rio service from Johannesburg and Capetown and a mid-Atlantic service from Madrid and Lisbon to Miami, where connections may be made for all South America.

SAS—The Scandinavian carrier operates a Europe-South America jet service. Twice weekly service to South America from Copenhagen. One flight leaves Scandinavia for Zürich, Lisbon, Rio, São Paulo, Montevideo, Buenos Aires and Santiago; the other via Zürich, Monrovia, Rio, Montevideo to Santiago.

Swissair—The Airline of Switzerland operates via Dakar a DC-10 jumbo jet service from Zürich and Geneva to Rio, São Paulo, Buenos Aires and Santiago.

TAP (Intercontinental Airline of Portugal)—Direct jet service from Lisbon to Recife, and Buenos Aires twice weekly; to Rio de Janeiro five times weekly.

Varig—17 flights weekly from Copenhagen, Frankfurt, London, Zürich, Geneva, Rome, Paris, Madrid, Lisbon and Oporto to Recife, Rio de Janeiro, São Paulo, Buenos Aires, Montevideo, Asuncion, Santiago. Also twice weekly service via New York and Rio to Johannesburg.

Viasa—The Venezuelan carrier offers seven Europe-South American routes to Caracas. Regular flights link Amsterdam, Paris, Madrid, Lisbon, Rome, and Milan. The trans-Atlantic flights continue in South America to serve several cities, including Curaçao, Bogotá, Cali and Lima.

AIRLINES SERVING SOUTH AMERICA FROM THE PACIFIC AREA AND AFRICA

Direct or through plane service from the Orient, Far East, Australia or Hawaii to South America is offered by *CP Air*, which has frequent services from Hong Kong and Tokyo to Lima, Santiago and Buenos Aires through Vancouver and Mexico City. *Qantas*, operating since 1965, flies from Australia to London through Tahiti, Acapulco and Mexico City, where direct flights to South America can be had. *LAN-Chile* now has regular jet service between Santiago, Easter Island, Tahiti and Fiji.

The Pacific traveler heading for South America can utilize *Pan Am's* B-747 SP service offering non-stop flights Tokyo-New York and Sydney or Auckland to San Francisco which make excellent connection points for onward service to South American destinations; from Los Angeles or San Francisco take *Braniff* direct jet flights all the way to Lima, La Paz, Rio, São Paulo, Santiago, and Buenos Aires or *Pan Am* to Panama, Venezuela, Brazil and Argentina. *CP Air* also offers fine service from Vancouver, Montreal and Toronto to South America via Mexico City. *Varig* offers a service from Los Angeles to Lima and Rio de Janeiro. Another route by *Varig* links Tokyo with Lima, Rio de Janeiro and São Paulo. Braniff also links Honolulu and Hilo with Dallas, Houston, New Orleans and Miami from where it connects to flights serving Central and South America.

South African Airways flies from Australia, Mauritius, Johannesburg to Rio; also; Australia, Mauritius, Johannesburg, Capetown to Buenos Aires. *Varig* also flies from Johannesburg. *Aerolineas Argentinas* flies between Buenos Aires to Capetown.

BY SEA. A great many steamship companies offer various kinds of service between world ports and the South American continent, although passenger service has been steadily diminishing throughout the world with the expansion of containerization. Alcoa Steamship Co., for example, formerly an important carrier of tourists to the southern continent, now has no passenger service whatever. However, more cruises call at South American ports than before.

From North America:

Costa Line, 245 Park Ave., New York 10017 *and* One Biscayne Tower, Miami Fla., 33131. Sailings from Florida and Puerto Rico to Venezuela and from Florida to Colombia. Ten cruises are offered from December to May with fares starting at $695.

Prudential Lines, Inc., 1 California St., San Francisco, Calif. 94106 and 1, World Trade Center, New York, N.Y. 10048 operates four modern liners to and around South America from West Coast ports. 100-passenger, air-conditioned, stabilized vessels, all first class. Sailings twice a month to: Manzanillo, Mexico, Balboa, Panama Canal, Cartagena, Curaçao, La Guaira, Puerto Cabello, Venezuela, Rio, Santos, Paranagua, Buenos Aires, Straits of Magellan, Valparaiso, Callao, Buenaventura. Cruise may begin or end in any port. Rates: per person double occupancy, from Los Angeles, about $4,205–$7,800.

A variety of Prudential cargo freighters also sail from East Coast to South American ports.

Royal Netherlands SS Co., c/o Lislind International, 5 World Trade Center, 6383, New York 10048. From New York and New Orleans to Guyana, Surinam, and Venezuela.

Norwegian Caribbean Lines, One Biscayne Tower, Miami, Florida 33131; *Costa Line,* 245 Park Ave., New York 10017, and One Biscayne Tower, Miami, Fla. 33131 has sailings from Florida and Puerto Rico to Venezuela and from Florida to Colombia. Fares are about $400 to $900. *Swedish American Line,* 636 Fifth Ave., New York 10020, has yearly cruises scheduled to call at South American ports either on cruises *Around South America* or on West Indies-South America cruises, either from New York or Port Everglades.

More and more cruise lines stop regularly at La Guaira, Venezuela, Cartagena and San Andres Island, Colombia. Others are featuring long trips around South America. Among the cruise lines are:

Carras, 75 Rockefeller Plaza, Suite 505, New York, N.Y. 10019. The *Daphne* sails from New Orleans to Central America, Caribbean and South American ports of San Andres, Cartagena, Colombia.

Costa Line, 245 Park Ave., New York, N.Y. 10017, and One Biscayne Tower, Miami, Fla. 33131 has sailings from Florida and Puerto Rico to Venezuela and from Florida to Colombia.

Chandris, Inc., 666 Fifth Avenue, New York, N.Y. 10019, has sailings in winter and spring from San Juan which call at La Guaira, Venezuela.

Cunard, Ltd., 555 Fifth Avenue, New York, N.Y. 10017 has the *Cunard Countess* sailing year-round from San Juan with a stop at La Guaira, Venezuela, on weekly cruises.

Flagship Cruises, 522 Fifth Avenue, New York, N.Y. 10036, schedules the *Kungsholm* for at least one cruise a year that covers South America extensively. This is usually in the fall or winter season, calling at such ports as Buenos Aires, Santos, Rio, and Bahia.

Holland America Cruises, Two Pennsylvania Plaza, New York, N.Y. 10001, usually schedules its *Statendam* to call at La Guaira, Venezuela during its winter cruises out of Miami, Fla.

Home Lines Agency, Inc., One World Trade Center, Suite 3969, New York, N.Y. 10048, includes La Guaira, Venezuela and Cartagena, Colombia, for the *Oceanic* sailing out of New York and for its *Doric* out of Port Everglades, Fla. during the winter cruise season.

Lauro Line Cruises, Inc., One Biscayne Tower, Miami, Fla. 33131, schedules the *Angelina Lauro* out of Port Everglades during winter and spring to include, on different trips, such South American ports as La Guaira, Venezuela, Cartagena and San Andres, Colombia.

Lindblad Travel, Inc., 133 East 55 Street, New York, N.Y. 10002, puts its *Lindblad Explorer* into Amazon River cruises in spring and other very off-beat trips to that part of the world.

Monarch Cruise Lines, Inc., 1428 Brickell Avenue, Miami, Fla. 33131, has La Guaira, Venezuela, and Cartagena, Colombia, as regular ports of call for the winter and spring season for its *Monarch Star* (formerly the *Veendam*) out of Miami. Monarch Cruise Lines, Inc., is a division of Holland America Line, Inc.

Paquet French Cruises, 1370 Avenue of the Americas, New York, N.Y. 10019 is scheduling its *Renaissance* into 44-day "Around South America" cruise program which is expected to be repeated annually every fall. Ports include Callao or Lima, Peru, Valparaiso, Chile, Puerto Montt, Punta Arenas, Buenos Aires, Santos, Salvador in Brazil, French Guiana. Departure is from Port Everglades, Fla. The line's *Mermoz* sails out of San Juan in winter and spring and includes La Guaira, Venezuela in its itinerary.

Princess Cruises, 2020 Avenue of the Stars, Los Angeles, Ca. 90067, has two ships alternate out of San Juan which include calls at both La Guaira, Venezuela and Cartagena, Colombia. The *Island Princess* and the *Sun Princess* visit the South American ports during winter and spring from Los Angeles.

Royal Caribbean Line, Inc., 903 South America Way, Miami, Fla. 33132, puts La Guaira, Venezuela as a regular port of call for both its *Sun Viking* and *Nordic Prince* which sail on alternate Saturdays from Miami year-round.

Royal Viking Line, One Embarcadero Center, San Francisco, Ca. 94111 is thinking more South America with a chance that its October and December 1977 South America trips will become annual events. The *Royal Viking Sea* and the *Royal Viking Star* sail from both San Francisco and Los Angeles to Callao, Peru, Arica, Valparaiso, Puerto Montt and Punta Arenas, Chile; Bueno Aires, Argentina, Montevideo, Uruguay; Santos, Rio and Salvador, Brazil and La Guaira, Venezuela. The line also features trans-Canal cruises from West to East Coast and reverse, stopping at both Cartagena, Colombia and La Guaira, Venezuela, usually in spring and fall. In mid-November and through December, the same line sails from both Port Everglades, Fla. and New Orleans on a series of Gulf of Mexico/Caribbean trips which include stops at Cartagena, and San Andres Island, Colombia and La Guaira, Venezuela.

Sitmar Cruises, 10100 Santa Monica Boulevard, Los Angeles, Ca. 90067 featured a cruise from both New York and Port Everglades, Fla.

on its *Fairwind* to Lima, Peru with a stop at Cartagena, Colombia in May 1977 with a repeat (not out of New York) in the fall. It looks like it might be repeated in 1978. Ordinarily the *Fairwind* sails out of Port Everglades with a call at La Guaira, Venezuela on its Caribbean runs, most of the year with some exceptions. The line's other ship, the *Fairsea* sails from Los Angeles to Mexico and the Caribbean in the winter and spring with a stop also at La Guaira, Venezuela.

Strand Cruises, 60 East 42 Street, New York, N.Y., Suite 2025, has chartered the *Veracruz* from the Bahama Cruise Line. In winter and spring the ship sails from San Juan and includes La Guaira, Venezuela and Cartagena, Colombia as ports of call.

Sun Line Cruises, One Rockefeller Plaza, Suite 315, New York, N.Y. 10020, features cruises in winter from Port Everglades and other ports such as Tampa, Fla. and Houston and Galveston, Texas. South American ports include Cartagena, San Andres Island, Colombia and La Guaira, Venezuela. The line's *Stella Solaris* and *Stella Maris* usually make the trips. In addition, the *Stella Maris* has also for the past few years (and looks like it will in the future) cruises in January, February and early March to Ciudad Guayana and travels on the Orinoco River, in the heart of Venezuela.

A great number of banana boats, tramp steamers, and tankers also cross the Caribbean from Tampa, New Orleans, and Texas ports bound for South America. Their schedules and prices often depend on where their cargo takes them, and a good travel agent can track down the right ship for you. Freighter travel is adventurous, relaxing, and often very inexpensive—it's well worth investigating. There are well over 100 travel agencies in the U.S. that specialize in freighter travel. A complete listing is given in *Ford's Freighter Travel Guide*, P.O. Box 505, 22030 Ventura Blvd., Woodland Hills, Calif. 91365 ($4.50); however, two leading ones are: Air/Ship Travel Service, 630 Fifth Avenue, New York, N.Y. 10020, and Freighter Travel Service, 201 East 77th Street, New York, N.Y. 10021. Plan to at least book several months in advance.

A final note: the "air-sea" cruises that are so popular in other parts of the world are beginning to catch on for South America too. These are package tours that take you to South America by ship and you return by plane—or vice versa, and they are easily arranged. Under present agreements, the price works out to half the round-trip air fare plus the one-way steamship fare less 10 per cent. For example, *Travelguide* offers a 23-day and a 31-day package by air (Pan Am, Lan Chile) to the West Coast of South America (Ecuador, Peru, Chile) and return (by Santaliner) to Ecuador, Colombia and the U.S. (West Coast). Optional side trips to Easter Island, Cuzco/Machu Picchu, and the Amazon River.

In addition to the American lines listed above, many Scandinavian and several other foreign lines offer service from the U.S.A. and Canada to South America. These lines usually begin the voyage in their own country, stop at a U.S. port, and continue to South America.

The following lines offer frequent U.S.A.-South America service: Torm Lines (Denmark)—C.A. Venezolana de Navegacion (Venezuela)—Chilean Line (Chile)—Barber SS Lines, Inc.— Nopal Line—Argentine Lines (ELMA).

From Europe:

Ships of many nations connect European and South American ports with a great variety of service. Major British-South American services are detailed below, and in addition the names of several other European lines are listed.

Italian Line, World Cruises, Inc., One Whitehall St., New York 10004. Monthly sailings from Mediterranean ports to Brazil, Argentina, Panama, Venezuela, Colombia, Ecuador, Peru and Chile.

Lamport and Holt Line, Ltd., Royal Liver Building, Liverpool 3. Regular service from a United Kingdom port via Las Palmas to Rio de Janeiro, Santos, Montevideo and Buenos Aires.

Royal Netherlands SS Co., Lislind International, 5 World Trade Center, New York, 10048, has regular roundtrip sailings by modern 12-passenger freighters from Amsterdam to Paramaribo, via Curaçao and Aruba; from Rotterdam and Le Havre to Cristobal, Buenaventura, Guayaquil, Callao, Matarani, Arica, Antofagasta, Valparaiso; and monthly roundtrip service from Amsterdam, Le Havre or Bilbao to La Guaira, Puerto Cabello, Maracaibo, Cartagena, Barranquilla, Santa Marta.

Because of rising maintenance costs and low rentability, most passenger shiplines are stopping or reducing their regular services to South America, preferring to rent or use their ships for long cruises. Some passenger and cargo ships which serve this area are:

Compagnie Maritime Belge S.A. (Belgian)—*Hanseatic Line* (German)—*Houlder Bros. & Co. Ltd.* (British)—*Rotterdam-South America Line* (Dutch)—*Laeisz Line* (German)—*Compagnie Fabre S.G.T.M.* (French)—*Linea "C"* (Italian)—*Hamburg-South American Line* (German).

 SHIPBOARD TIPPING. A hard question to answer is "How much to tip?" Tipping is a personal matter. The amount depends upon service received, length of trip and type of accommodations. Those who serve are: Bedroom Steward and Waitress who have the most to do for you and should be tipped accordingly; Stewards who may be called upon for breakfast in bed, or for special service; Deck Steward; and Night Steward if he serves you; Wine Steward if you order wines with meals; Tips to Bar Steward as you are served, or percentage of total bar bill at end of cruise. Bellhop: tips for errands. Passengers usually tip on shipboard as they would in a first-class resort hotel under the American Plan (room and all meals).

 TRAVELING BY CAR TO SOUTH AMERICA. Road-building in Central and South America has progressed to the point that one can drive all the way from the United States to Chile, Argentina or

Brazil with just one short sea voyage. There is no road yet from Panama to Colombia, but several shipping lines transport cars and passengers from Panama to Buenaventura or Cartagena in Colombia, or La Guaira in Venezuela. *Latin American Travel and Pan American Highway Guide*, published by Compsco Publishing Co., 663 Fifth Ave., New York 10022, $7.95. About 85 per cent of the principal highways and main roads are good to excellent and hard surfaced. The rest with few exceptions are adequate dirt roads, open year round, but there are still too many rough and hazardous areas to make driving pleasurable. Good hotels exist along the entire route; with careful planning, a room with bath or shower can be had every night.

A reliable, fairly new car is a must, preferably of a well-known make, for which spare parts are available in South America. Good repair facilities are available; gasoline and oil can be obtained everywhere, but high-test premium gasoline is hard to come by except in the capitals. Use tires with tubes, and take extra tubes along. Consult your automobile dealer about what spare parts to carry, and be sure to take a towing cable, hand pump, pressure gauge, tube repair kit.

For border crossings, beside car registration and license, you'll need about 25 passport size photos, and a *Carnet de Passages en Douane*. The AAA, 8111 Gatchouse Rd., Falls Church, Va. 22042, will issue one for $185, refunding $150 when you surrender the Carnet. No carnet needed for a tourist vehicle to enter Brazil for up to 60 days. Formalities completed at the border. Also required are Inter-American driving permits and Inter-American registration papers plus a country identification plaque on the automobile. You cannot sell your car in South America; plan to drive or ship it.

Buy insurance in the U.S. beforehand. If you have an accident, pay the judgments against you and collect the amount afterwards. Never leave your car unguarded or unlocked—there are organized gangs in every major city, expert at breaking into and stealing cars.

Shipping cars. There are ample facilities for shipping automobiles from the U.S., but unless the owner is planning to reside in South America for some time, it is advisable to rent a car.

Best suggestion for travelers wanting to see South America by car is to rent automobiles in the various cities.

For those determined to drive around the continent, several good maps of South American roads, mountain passes, etc., may be obtained free from automobile clubs and some oil company touring services.

ARRIVING IN SOUTH AMERICA

CUSTOMS. See Customs Regulations outline in previous section, *Planning Your Trip,* and other additional requirements in country chapters.

MONEY. There is a great fluctuation of many South American currencies due to recent devaluation. Best advice is to change only what you anticipate spending in each country, thus saving money, since exchange bureaus and banks generally charge a commission when you buy and again when you exchange any unspent balance back to U.S. dollars or other currency.

Travelers checks are usually changed at hotels but banks and currency exchange houses give a better rate.

 LANGUAGES. Spanish and Portuguese are the two major languages of South America. Spanish is the official language of Argentina, Bolivia, Chile, Colombia, Ecuador, Paraguay, Peru, Uruguay and Venezuela. Portuguese is the official language of Brazil.

Dutch is the official language in Surinam, French in French Guiana and English in Guyana.

South America also abounds with Indian languages and native dialects. Most interesting example is Surinam where Dutch is the official language and the inhabitants speak either Dutch, English, Javanese, Hindi or a Pidgin English called "talkie talkie". *Guarani* is the second official language of Paraguay.

English is widely understood in the larger cities of South America and English speaking visitors will have little language difficulty in leading hotels, restaurants, travel agencies, airports and shops.

TIME ZONES. There are four time zones in South America. The table below shows the corresponding time changes for major cities:

When it is *noon* in New York City: It is also noon in: Bogota—Quito—Lima—Santiago. It is one p.m. in: Caracas—Georgetown—Paramaribo—Cayenne—La Paz—Asuncion—Buenos Aires—Montevideo. It is two p.m. in: Brasilia—Rio—São Paulo. It is three p.m. in: Recife, Brazil. It is four p.m. in: Lisbon. It is five p.m. in: London.

 TIPPING. Tipping and service charges in South America are usually included in hotel, restaurant and bar bills. In several countries recent formal legislation has set service charges at various percentages of the bill. The legal charges run as high as 24 per cent in Argentine and Uruguayan hotels, although most are fixed at 10 per cent. In Chile, 10 per cent is the legal charge.

Best advice is to always check your bill for service (*servicio* in Spanish and Portuguese) and if a charge is included, you are not obligated to tip. However, if the service has been special (and it usually will be in most of South America), it is perfectly correct to tip an additional five per cent.

Small tips for taxi drivers and other services are *usually* accepted in most cities. However, in several places where tipping is not the custom, foreign visitors are often astonished to see their tip politely refused.

Tipping practices are covered more specifically in country chapters.

STAYING IN SOUTH AMERICA

HOTELS. South America offers several of the world's most splendid hotels. From the dramatic *Tamanaco* sitting impressively upon a mountainside above Caracas, to the *Copacabana Palace* beside the Atlantic on Rio's world-famed beach, to the glittering resort hotels of Punta del Este and Mar del Plata—South American hotels will surely satisfy even the most fastidious visitor.

For the budget-minded and student traveler, a great number of inexpensive inns, pensions and lodges are available in almost every town of importance.

Country chapters later in the book contain more details on hotels.

FOOD AND DRINK. Dining in South America is an experience. One has never really tasted charcoal-broiled steak until dining with the gauchos of Uruguay. Their *parrillada* is a giant-sized serving of half-a-dozen grilled meats that would tempt even the strictest vegetarian. Argentina's *asado* or roasted meat on an open fire is equally as memorable.

The seafood of South America is just as succulent—whether one enjoys Venezuela's tiny oysters and clams (with a dash of sweet lemon) on the beach at Macuto, or sits beside the brilliant sea with the smart set in Viña del Mar sampling delicate steamed shrimp and perfect white wine.

In Chile the *langostinos* are also long remembered (baby crawfish). Peru offers *seviche*—raw fish marinated in a spicy pepper, onion, and lemon sauce that makes the perfect snack after a day riding the surf at Lima's Waikiki Beach.

Brazilians enjoy *feipoada completa*—a masterly blending of rice, black beans, and a variety of smoked pork. Also in Brazil—don't fail to sample *vatapa*—a heavy fish and shrimp combination spiced with peppers and paprika. Brazilian seafood is tops on the continent and not expensive. The most varied and tasty cuisine in Brazil is found in Bahia.

For the adventurous, there's Bolivia's really hot *aji* pepper, the sharp Indian curry dishes of Guyana, or the traditional 20-course, spicy Dutch *rijsttafel* in Surinam. On the not-to-miss list also put Panama's *sancocho*, a savory chicken soup with local vegetables, and Colombia's *Ajiaco*, thick potato soup.

Prices vary from very reasonable to about the same as in most U.S. or English restaurants. In the smaller cities three good meals in the best restaurants normally run from five to six dollars. In the larger cities and capitals, three good meals in the best places will normally run from ten to fifteen dollars daily—and that's really eating in style.

In the more out-of-the-way places, food can be a real bargain. A filet mignon—not just a slice of it—but the entire strip—charcoaled on an outdoor grill and served in a garden under the bright evening sky of Asuncion—can be enjoyed for as little as $2 (U.S.), and for less than four dollars in a modest middle class restaurant in Buenos Aires. Conversely, a mediocre dinner in one of the better restaurants in La Paz can run close to ten U.S. dollars.

It's hard to set an average—but with 20 U.S. dollars a day you'll normally dine royally in South America. Lima, Caracas, Buenos Aires, Santiago, Bogotá and Rio have the best restaurants and finest food, and also higher prices than the smaller cities.

Drinking is also an adventure. Chilean wine is rapidly gaining world renown—and rightly so. The wines from Chile's central region are second to none anywhere in the world. Peru's *Pisco*, a brandy made in the Ica valley, is also rapidly gaining fame. Colombia's excellent *Medellin Añejo* rum (which sells at the Bogota airport tax free shop for about $1 (U.S.) a bottle) is outstanding. Uruguay's barley beer is one of many excellent, very inexpensive beers in South America. The large German immigration to South America brought some master brewers to the continent and you'll appreciate their labors after a long walk in the sun along Punta del Este's perfect, endless beach.

And when you celebrate in South America, you'll do it with Chile's or Argentina's excellent, inexpensive champagne.

DRINKING WATER AND MILK. Best general rule is to drink bottled water in South America. Many of the public water systems date almost to Colonial times and are not 100 per cent safe. Notable exceptions are the splendid public systems in the larger towns of Argentina, Colombia, Surinam and Uruguay—everywhere else be sure and ask for bottled water (it is usually in your hotel room when you arrive). There are several excellent mineral waters bottled in South America that make drinking bottled water a pleasure rather than a hardship.

Pasteurized milk is available in almost every major city in South America. The one rule to remember is to have the bottle opened at your table.

ROUGHING IT. There are no hostels operated in South America by the International Youth Hostel Organization, nor are there many camping areas, as in most European countries. However, the adventurous traveler may often find adequate lodging in South America for the small fee usually charged at most American or European camping grounds. Despite no formal organization or marked zones, camping is possible and pleasant, and becoming more popular.

SPORTS. South America is a sportsman's paradise —whether participant or spectator. Hunting, fishing, swimming, hiking, horseback riding, tennis, boxing, golf, and baseball are the standard favorites of South America.

In addition, the continent offers visitors thrilling sports seldom seen elsewhere in the world. The world-wide game of *soccer* takes on a new meaning in South America. Anyone fortunate enough to witness a soccer match in Rio de Janeiro's Maracanã Stadium will never forget the sheer spectacle of the day. Rio's Maracaná stadium is the world's largest, seating 200,000 and regularly hosts soccer's most brilliant stars. South American enthusiasm for the game often runs to near madness.

Bull fighting and *Jai Alai* are also South American favorites. The world's top bull fighters annually visit the South American rings. *Jai Alai*, the world's fastest game, has traveled from Spain's Basque country to South America, with some variation, and the handball game is becoming a betting favorite of Latins.

For more details on Sports, see country chapters.

 **SHOPPING.** Shopping is one of South America's prime attractions. From the antique Colonial silver in the quaint shops of Quito and Lima to Paraguay's dainty lace, to the curious native handicrafts of Surinam, the South American visitor will find an endless array of irresistible shopping bargains.

See country chapters for more information.

 MEDICAL TREATMENT. In most South American countries there is no shortage of competent, trained, English-speaking doctors. The International Association for Medical Assistance for Travelers (IAMAT), Suite 5620, Empire State Bldg., 350 5th Ave., N.Y. City, 10001, has participating doctors in every South American country. All speak English. The rates are standardized at: $15 office call, $20 house or hotel call, and $25 for night or holiday calls. They will send, on request, a booklet listing these physicians, which you can carry on your trip.

Pharmaceuticals pose no problem for the visitor. All major cities have excellent drugstores and many offer "round the clock" service.

 READING MATTER AND NEWS. English-language newspapers and magazines are for sale in all leading South American cities. With the fine jet schedules to South America, there is little delay in receiving airmail editions of New York and Miami newspapers. International editions of news magazines are on sale in all of South America's leading hotels.

Daily English-language newspapers are published in Buenos Aires, Bogota, Rio, Georgetown, Panama and Caracas.

 DRY CLEANING AND LAUNDRY. Good service available in the better hotels. Usually the best dry cleaning and laundry service in South America is done in the private plants of such leading hotels as those in the Intercontinental chain (*Tamanaco, Caracas; Tequendama, Bogota*), the *Guarani-Asuncion*, or *San Cristobal Sheraton*.

Prices run from expensive to outrageous for dry cleaning, but in all fairness, it's extremely expensive to maintain these pioneer cleaning plants.

 COSMETICS. No problem here. In fact, the ultra *chic* women of Santiago, Lima, Rio, São Paulo and Buenos Aires usually introduce visitors to many of the latest beauty aids and cosmetics. In the world of fashion, the leading South American capitals are as smart as Paris, Rome, or New York.

TOBACCO. Available in great variety everywhere. Every country produces its own cigarettes and cigars—some excellent—some very poor. Quality tobacco products are always available everywhere—but often at inflated prices. A pack of American cigarettes will usually cost approx. $1 (U.S.) in most of South America.

Best bet is to buy the tax-free cigarettes on your air flights. Most international flights offer American or English cigarettes for sale at considerable savings.

 MAIL AND TELEGRAPHIC SERVICES. Major hotels will hold mail for arriving guests. Another possibility is to have the mail forwarded to the local *American Express* office or agency. General Delivery in most of South America is not recommended for visitors. Telegraphic service is available everywhere, as well as wireless service to the Falkland Islands. Many hotels have cable facilities.

 ELECTRICAL CURRENT. It varies from country to country in South America. Most of the top hotels have transformers for current and adapters for plugs for guests with foreign electric razors, slide projectors, etc.

Argentina. 220 volts, 50 cycle, AC, need European-type plugs.

Bolivia. 110 volts in La Paz; rest of towns 220 volts; American and European-type plugs used.

Brazil. Usually 110 or 120 volts, 60 cycle in Rio and São Paulo.

Chile. 220 volts, 50 cycle, AC.

Colombia. Voltage varies from 150 in Bogota to 110 and 120 elsewhere. U.S. type plugs.

Ecuador. 110 volts, 60 cycle, AC, U.S. type plugs.

Paraguay. 220 and 380 volts, 50 cycles.

Peru. 220 volts, 60 cycle, AC, transformers usually available.

Surinam. 127 volts, 50 cycle, AC, in Paramaribo. 115 volts, 60 cycle, AC elsewhere.

Uruguay. 220 volts, 50 cycle, AC.

Venezuela. 110 volts, AC, in Caracas and elsewhere 60 cycle.

 GUIDE SERVICES. Excellent guide service is available in all South American countries from several tour operators. Best advice is to check if the tour agent or office is a member of the *South American Travel Organization* (SATO). All SATO members are the local leaders in tourism and offer competent, honest service.

GETTING AROUND IN SOUTH AMERICA

AIR SERVICE WITHIN SOUTH AMERICA. In the past decade the airplane has opened vast areas of South America to development. In many countries regular air service links many cities that are not joined by any surface transportation.

Small international lines and a great many domestic carriers serve practically every city of consequence on the South American continent.

A good example of domestic fares is provided by the chart below giving sample fares (in U.S. dollars) within Argentina on *Aerolineas Argentinas* from Buenos Aires:

To:	One Way	To:	One Way
Bahia Blanca	$ 57.40	Resistencia	$ 68.60
Bariloche	115.90	Rio Gallegos	111.80
Com. Rivadavia	86.60	Rosario	34.60
Cordoba	64.20	Salta	98.20
Corrientes	68.60	San Juan	86.80
Iguazu	79.00	Santa Fe	40.60
Mar del Plata	43.20	Tucuman	92.80
Mendoza	86.80		

TRAIN SERVICE IN SOUTH AMERICA. As a general rule travel by train in South America is not recommended. Most countries have limited passenger services, equipment is apt to be old, trips are often arduous. There is a notable exception, however, in the 30,000 mile network in Argentina, Bolivia, Brazil, Chile, Paraguay and Uruguay.

Amerailpass allows unlimited travel during a limited time period in and between these countries. Rates vary: *approx.* $50 each for one month; $75 for two months; $90 for three months. Children from 3 to 12 are charged half-fare; children under 3 years can travel free of charge. A first-class ticket entitles the traveler the right to buy sleeping accommodations for $3 per night. For detailed information, write Asociacion Latino-Americana de Ferrocarriles, ALAF, Florida 783, Buenos Aires, Argentina. *Note:* rates subject to change!

BUS SERVICE WITHIN SOUTH AMERICA. TISA (principal office: Bernardo de Irigoyen 1370, Buenos Aires) has international service to Peru, Colombia, Uruguay, Brazil, Venezuela, Paraguay, Bolivia, Chile and Ecuador, in modern, air-conditioned buses, and is now offering a pass valid for first-class bus travel throughout South America called *Amerbuspass*, valid for 180 days. Tickets are available in all capital cities.

Otherwise, while service is good on major highways and prices low, no schedule or tariff books are published and distributed outside of the local areas. Schedules and fares change constantly, and there is little or no cooperation between lines.

Best advice for budget travelers planning extensive overland trips in South America is to write the *South American Travel Organization*, El Rosario 240, 1er piso, Miraflores, Lima, Peru, and request specific bus information be forwarded from the organization's representative in the respective area. Bus service is always available in South America over practically every road shown on a map. The local interior services are often crowded trucks with plank seats and few comforts. On the other hand, excellent buses run regularly between major capitals and oceanside resorts.

 RENTAL CARS IN SOUTH AMERICA. Most major South American cities have local or international Rent-A-Car Services. Avis has extensive operations throughout the continent and there are several good local car-rental services in various cities. Hertz is also well represented.

CAR RENTAL

Argentina: Rates for Fiat 600: $8.25 a day and 8 cents per km. $50 weekly. Fiat 128: $12 a day, 12 cents per km. $72 weekly. Add 1% tax.

Bolivia: Rates begin at $12 a day and 10 cents per km. Weekly rates $66 plus mileage. No tax.

Brazil: Rates for Volkswagen 1300: $27 a day with unlimited mileage, $165 weekly. Add 5% tax. $72 a day for most luxurious Ford.

Chile: Rates for Peugeot 404 or Fiat 125 begin at $16.50 a day plus 16 cents per km. Weekly $98.80 plus mileage. Add 20% tax.

Colombia: Rates begin at $13.60 plus 14 cents per km. Weekly $81.60. No tax.

Ecuador: Rates begin at $12 a day and 12 cents per km. Weekly $72 plus mileage. Add 4% tax.

Paraguay: Rates begin at $23.65 a day and 24 cents per km. Weekly $141.50 plus mileage. No tax.

Peru: Rates begin at $12.90 a day and 11 cents per km. Weekly $77.35 plus mileage. Add 2% tax.

Venezuela: Rates for a Ford Maverick: $12.85 a day plus 13 cents per km. Weekly $76.95. No tax.

Rates do not include gas! Prices: courtesy of *Avis*.

Miles into Kilometers

Miles	Kms.	Miles	Kms.	Miles	Kms.
1	1.6093	10	16.09	100	161.
2	3.22	20	32.19	200	322.
3	4.83	30	48.28	300	483.
4	6.44	40	64.37	400	644.
5	8.05	50	80.5	500	805.
6	9.66	60	96.6	600	966.
7	11.27	70	112.7	700	1127.
8	12.87	80	128.7	800	1287.
9	14.48	90	144.8	900	1448.
				1000	1609.3

FOR TIRE PRESSURE

Kilograms into Pounds				Pounds into Kilograms			
Kgs.	Pounds	Kgs.	Pounds	Pounds	Kgs.	Pounds	Kgs.
1	2.2046	40	88.18	1	0.45359	40	18.14
2	4.4	50	110.23	2	0.907	50	22.68
3	6.6	60	132.28	3	1.36	60	27.22
4	8.8	70	154.32	4	1.81	70	31.75
5	11.0	80	176.37	5	2.27	80	36.29
6	13.2	90	198.42	6	2.72	90	40.82
7	15.43	100	220.46	7	3.18	100	45.36
8	17.64	200	440.92	8	3.63	200	90.72
9	19.84	300	661.39	9	4.08	300	136.08
10	22.05	400	881.85	10	4.54	400	181.44
20	44.09	500	1102.31	20	9.07	500	226.8
30	66.14	1000	2204.62	30	13.61	1000	453.59

CONVERSION TABLES FOR MOTOR FUELS AND OILS
Liters into Quarts and Gallons

1 U.S. gallon equals 0.8327 Imperial (British) gallon or 3.78 liters.
To arrive at British gallons equivalent for liters,
multiply U.S. figures by 0.83.

Liters	Qts. (U.S.)	Liters	Gals. (U.S.)	Liters	Gals. (U.S.)
1	1.0567	1	0.2641	40	10.57
2	2.11	2	0.53	50	13.21
3	3.17	3	0.79	60	15.85
4	4.23	4	1.06	70	18.49
5	5.28	5	1.32	80	21.13
6	6.34	6	1.59	90	23.78
7	7.40	7	1.85	100	26.42
8	8.45	8	2.11	200	52.84
9	9.51	9	2.38	300	79.25
10	10.57	10	2.64 *	400	105.67
		20	5.28	500	132.09
		30	7.93	1000	264.18

CUSTOMS—RETURNING HOME

At this writing, **American residents** who are out of the USA at least 48 hours and have claimed no exemption during the previous 30 days are entitled to bring in duty-free up to $100 worth of bona fide gifts or items for their own personal use.

The $100 duty free allowance (years ago, it was $500!) is based on the full fair *retail* value of the goods (previously, the customs' estimation was on the wholesale value). You must now list the items

Quarts and Gallons into Liters

1 Imperial (British) gallon equals 1.2 U.S. gallons or 4.5 liters.
Add 20% to liters in table to arrive at equivalents in British gallons.

Qts. (U.S.)	Liters	Gals. (U.S.)	Liters	Gals. (U.S.)	Liters
1	0.9463	1	3.7853	40	151.41
2	1.89	2	7.57	50	189.27
3	2.84	3	11.36	60	227.12
4	3.79	4	15.14	70	265.
5	4.73	5	18.93	80	302.8
6	5.68	6	22.71	90	340.7
7	6.62	7	26.50	100	378.5
8	7.57	8	30.28	200	757.1
9	8.52	9	34.07	300	1135.6
10	9.5	10	37.85	400	1514.1
		20	75.71	500	1892.7
		30	113.56	1000	3785.3

purchased and *they must accompany you when you return*. So keep all receipts handy with the detailed list, and it is obviously wise to pack the goods together in one case. The $10 mailed gift scheme (see below) is also based on the retail value. Every member of a family is entitled to this same exemption, regardless of age, and their exemption can be pooled.

One quart of alcoholic beverages may be included in the exemption if you are 21 years of age or older. Alcoholic beverages in excess of one quart are subject to customs duty and internal revenue tax. Approximate rates are (1/5 gallon); brandy or liquor, $2-$3; champagne, 90¢; wine, 15¢. The importation must not be in violation of the laws of the state of arrival.

British residents, except those under the age of 17 years, may import duty-free from *any* country the following: 200 cigarettes or 100 cigarillos or 50 cigars or 250 grams of tobacco; 1 litre of spirits or 2 litres of wine in excess of 38.8% proof, and 2 litres of still table wine. Also 50 grams of perfume, ¼ litre of toilet water and £10 worth of other normally dutiable goods.

Canadian residents: In addition to personal effects, the following articles may be brought in duty free: a maximum of 50 cigars, 200 cigarettes, 2 pounds of tobacco and 40 ounces of liquor, provided these are declared to customs on arrival. The total exemption is $150, and unsolicited gift mailings may be up to $15 in value. Canadian customs regulations are strictly enforced; you are recommended to check what your allowances are and to make sure you have kept receipts for whatever you have bought abroad. For complete details ask for the Canadian Customs brochure "I Declare."

BY WAY OF BACKGROUND

INITIATION TO SOUTH AMERICA

The Continent of Beauty and Grandeur

BY

MARCEL NIEDERGANG

(Marcel Niedergang, Latin American correspondent of Le Monde, *is the author of the outstanding two-volume book* The Twenty Latin Americas, *covering 21 Latin American countries.)*

Twelve months of the year, heat waves shimmer over Maiquetia airport at Caracas. From the air, the rolling foothills of arid mountain look like a herd of wild animals slumbering by the banks of the calm, flat, aquamarine Caribbean.

Sea, heat and hills: this is the first impression that South America offers in Venezuela, the country that crowns the continent. Arriving via Venezuela is one introduction to this world, but there are a dozen others. One might land at Barranquilla or Cartagena in Colombia. Or, coming from Panama on the classical route for North American travelers, you spiral blindly through an eternal gray mantle, down and down until, suddenly, there is Lima, the most languid and wondrous of Spanish cities in this hemisphere. Or there is that scenic skydrive right down Sugarloaf and into the tangle of bays, capes, rocks, beaches, verdant crags and ultramodern skyscrapers, the glory that goes by the name of Rio de Janeiro. Or, by ship, you can make your landfall in front of the gash in a cliff where Salvador (Bahia), city of all saints and sins, stews in the sun of the Brazilian Northeast.

Just about everywhere, there is this same moist, tropical, humming heat. Just about everywhere, there is this same color of the sea. And, from the Atlantic coast of Colombia to Tierra del Fuego

37

and Patagonia, there is this same powerful surge of brutal and primitive mountains, bristling with glaciers, domes and peaks more jagged than in any other mountain range in the world. This sky, this dampness, this sea and this power locked in nature certainly give South America immediate and perceptible unity, a flavor of its own that sets it apart from Europe or Africa.

Ignorance, distances, lack of curiosity and stubborn legends are the reasons why South America has remained one of the most discredited and most slandered—in short, the most unknown—of all continents. For this apparent unity must be corrected right away. The truth is that no other region of the world contains so much diversity and so many startling contradictions in such a relatively small space. "Land of contrasts" is a cliché so overworked that one hesitates to use it again. Yet if any continent is filled with contrasts, it is certainly South America. Tropical Africa also offers this apparent unity composed of immense distances, heat, laterite tracks stretching out to the horizon, and burnt-out forests. Yet when you travel through this part of Africa, you meet up with few true frontiers and no real differences from Dakar to Salisbury. This is not the case here. Everything changes, everything is modified, nothing is the same . . . and often within a single country. To sense this, you need enough will to forsake the speed of air travel and stick to this changing, disrupted and tortured soil, cracked by the sun and dying of thirst as in Venezuela's Barquisimeto or soaked by incessant tropical rains as in the Magdalena valley of Colombia.

Brazil alone, the biggest of all South American countries, is nothing less than a continent within a continent. With its 3,300,000 square miles, it is bigger than the United States without Alaska. It has the longest river, the biggest cataracts, and the densest and most extensive virgin forest in the world along with what is doubtlessly the deadliest desert and a head-spinning variety of insects and animals, from the dreaded ants of Amazonia to the anacondas slithering beneath giant water lilies. There is more of a difference between the great plains of Rio Grande do Sul, land of the horseman, and the immense beaches of the Northeast coastline planted with coconut palms tousled by the wind, than between the sierras of Spain and the plains of Germany. Recife and São Paulo are two authentically Brazilian cities and yet they are more foreign to each other and more remote in appearance and outlook than, for example, Milan and Hamburg.

But what is true of Brazil, a giant among giants, is also true of nearly every other South American nation.

Even tiny Uruguay, that Switzerland on the Rio de la Plata, offers remarkable diversity between its sandy coast, a natural choice for winter vacations and big inter American conferences, and its great grassy plains inland that butt up against the immensity of Brazil.

According to a wry saying that you often hear in Rio de Janeiro or Santiago de Chile, Argentina is supposed to enjoy every form of natural wealth. It so happens that this saying corresponds to reality. Argentina has everything: great rivers, immense plains, deserts still unexplored, more coastline than it knows what to do with, mountains, glaciers, lakes, lands gripped by Antarctic frost and others where tropical cactus grows.

In Paraguay, one can live for years in Asunción, a capital perfumed by orange blossoms, without ever having the opportunity or the possibility to enter the tempting and mysterious Chaco revealed to the world because of a war with Bolivia over some vague boundary lines.

Chile is a tongue of land sticking out nearly 2,600 miles from the Peruvian border down to Patagonia and the local geographers have found that the only way of fitting this almost endless belt into a school textbook is to cut it into three parts. So young Chileans learn their country in easy stages from the Norte Grande down to the frozen fjords of the deep south via the Norte Chico, only slightly less arid than the Norte Grande, and the island of Chiloe serving much the same purpose in Chile as the island of Djerba in Tunisia: a tourist attraction and a source of civil servants.

The Country with its Back to the Wall

Just like Mexico, Bolivia is a country of many floors and this leads once again to unusual variety that has remained unknown. While movies and documentary films have put the Bolivian *altiplano* on the map to some extent in recent years, not many people have had an opportunity to go down through those hot tropical valleys known as *yungas* into the depths of the Amazon basin. Bolivia is the most ignored of South American countries, standing tragically as it does with its back to the wall of the inhuman Andes and cut off from any outlet to the sea since the fortunes of war turned against it at the end of the 19th century. Yet this little-known Bolivia, for which a queen of England once hunted in vain in all the atlases at her disposal, also contains everything that nature can offer from sea level to 20,000 feet—that is, dizzying peaks framing steppe-like high plateaus and damp, impenetrable and treacherous jungles perhaps even less explored than certain Amazonian regions in Brazil.

The Peruvian *altiplano* is apparently nothing more than an extension of the Bolivian *altiplano* but the long, endless road that drops from the high plateaus surrounding legendary Lake Titicaca through gorges, *cordilleras* and hidden valleys to the Pacific leads to an unexpected Promised Land. This is the land of oases on the Peruvian coast cooled by the chill Humboldt Current. In a few miles, you move from a dry, yellow, sandy waste reminiscent of the Sahara to exuberant greenery, babbling canals and vegetable gardens like those surrounding Damascus.

Nor is there anything in common between the damp, low-lying

Equatorial coast devoured by mosquitoes and the cool sierra around Quito where a light breeze sways the leaves of magnificent eucalyptus forests admiring their reflections in lakes that could have come out of a Japanese print. It's hardly believable. But at a relatively short distance from this coast resembling the shores of tropical Africa in its colors, scents and people, a traveler is startled to discover rest homes for lung sufferers between Riobamba and Otavalo.

Yes, that tonic air of Switzerland's mountain pastures is only an hour away by plane from the oppressing suffocation of the Equator. Bogota, Colombia's capital 8,500 feet high, is cold, gray and melancholy under a sky that tends to be far more morose than gay. But Cali, whose very name is a caress, stretches out languorously in the warm valley of the Cauca. Hard-working industrial Medellin runs its textile factories on the flanks of coffee-growing hills 4,500 feet high in the zestful light of an eternal Mediterranean spring. Cartagena on the Caribbean coast dries its corsair sails all year long under a white sun reflected by the stagnant waters of its *cienagas*. A little bit to the east, and only a little bit, Baranquilla's big harbor smells of tar, fuel oil, fish markets, precious woods and tropical fruit. In eastern Colombia, the perfect symbol of these kaleidoscopic South America landscapes, you can travel hundreds of miles on the dry *llanos* without ever meeting a living soul, but to the west and separated by three ranges of the *cordillera* rising to about 12,000 feet, there are valleys regularly drowned by tropical rains. Only a few miles from Bogota after the famed Tequendama Falls amidst pines and cedars, you come off an acrobatic road into Girardot and its African rhythms.

Now let's go back east toward the great plains covered with rustling grass and then over the snowy and tormented peaks of Venezuela's state of San Cristobal into the scorched depths of the Orinoco. Then cross the Falcon mountains and run along the history-laden shore of the Caribbean, still echoing to the boom of galleons' cannon and gunfire from Spanish ships fighting the troops of Bolivar and Miranda. Venezuela, that "oxhide drying in the tropical sun" as it has been so aptly named by Marian Picon Salas, the national poet, also displays extremely varied natural resources over its 352,000 square miles.

To the west of Venezuela, beyond Colombia, lies the popular gateway of South America, the Republic of Panama, not itself on the continent, but very much a part of its history and culture. Traditionally first port of call for a majority of visitors to South America, this land of sunshine and jungle was once part of Colombia, having achieved its independence only in 1903. Closely linked to the United States in a kind of love-hate relationship ranging from economic and cultural interdependence to riots in the Canal Zone, Panama is a nation of proud and ambitious people. Its tourist attractions, except for the Canal Zone and the major cities are largely undeveloped, but the variety of its scenery, the opportunity for sports and shopping sprees and the general air of intrigue make it an excellent spot for a relaxed vacation.

And so we are back at our starting point. We could easily spend more time on the way to glean more images from mountain and plain, each more startling than the others. But the object of this quick bird's eye view is to supply a glimpse of the South American continent's great variety.

Dividing up the Continent

To help make things clearer, three large and characteristic regions can be staked out on this continent. André Siegfried, the great French historian, was able to distinguish them and there is not much to add to what he saw. First of all, on the Atlantic, there is an ancient backbone once linked to Africa, that geologically old Brazilian plateau from which black or purplish granite rises in the bay of Rio. Then there is the long Andean cordillera bordering the Pacific like a wall. Right at the start after the isthmus of Panama and near the Venezuelan coast, it takes on dimensions, colors and vegetation defying all comparisons. This America of the *Cordillera* and the high plateaus is certainly a second South America with a population and problems of its own. Even more than the first one, it has fascinated and it continues to fascinate generations of travelers, scientists, ethnologists and explorers. While many have already questioned its ravines, peaks, ruined temples and mysterious fortresses like that of Machu Picchu, it is quite likely that not all the answers have been supplied as yet, neither concerning the men that once lived here nor the men that still do. The third South America is to be found on its great plains: the alluvial plain of Amazonia in the north whose false dryness is riddled with gigantic ponds such as Pantanal in the Mato Grosso, and the great Argentine and Uruguayan pampas in the south where hundreds of horses roam under a dramatic sky and no one knows whether they are still wild or already tamed, because they can be one or another depending upon the season.

Still, a choice must be made. The average traveler's tastes vary according to the time of the year and the purpose of his trip. But there is no doubt that, from the viewpoint of the picturesque and the unusual, there are at least six regions in South America that deserve a longer look: the Equatorial high plateau, the Peruvian and Bolivian altiplano, the Atacama desert, the Brazilian Northeast, the Mato Grosso, and islands such as Santa Margarita off the Caribbean coast.

Avenues of Volcanoes

At the foot of ice-covered Mount Cayambe 19,440 feet high, a crude globe left by a French geodetic mission indicates that the

Northern Hemisphere has suddenly toppled over into the Southern Hemisphere. The air is so light that it is unearthly. Milky patches of hanging glaciers are reflected in the still, pure, cold mirrors of tiny lakes. Indian women with their long black hair hanging free, and their shoulders draped in turquoise shawls, beat scarlet ponchos with laundry paddles. Brown children run silently along mountain streams, for they have already learned to spare their words and to appreciate the value of silence among these men of the high plateaus. The cool breeze coming down from the mountains and the slumbering volcanoes murmurs as it crosses dark forests of pine and eucalyptus. From Riobamba lolling at the foot of Chimborazo, one of the best-known and most-celebrated of South American volcanoes, all the way to Otavalo near the Colombian border, the road crosses one of the world's most astounding spring landscapes. Canyons over 3,000 feet deep succeed necklaces of icy, translucent lakes. There are Indians everywhere of slow gestures and apparently absent stares, in the fields of immense haciendas or in villages where uniformly-whitewashed houses huddle for protection against chilly gusts. Humboldt, the German geographer, found a name for this region unique in its beauty, its charm and its deceptive South American calm: the avenue of volcanoes. There are nearly fifty of them from north to south, some covered with eternal snow like Cotopaxi or Chimborazo. It is not easy for the mountaineer of the *sierra* to tear his eyes from this assembly of icy immutable gods that strike terror when they roar. This South American Olympus is often shaken by mortal shuddering. And the Indians of the *sierra* still mingle the Virgin and ancient divinities in their incantations to those extra-terrestrial forces responsible for protecting them from the evil spells cast by lightning, thunder and the rumbling earth and mountains.

At the very end of this grand boulevard of volcanoes lies an Indian town where one is tempted to think that beautiful, peaceful and harmonious types of humanity preserved in total purity have come to the local market-place solely to provide a feast for a foreigner's eyes. For there are not very many authentically Indian villages, whether in Mexico, Central America or all along this Andean range, that can rival Otavalo in the impression it creates of a lost paradise. Market day sees endless processions of garnet, crimson and midnight-blue ponchos along dirt paths converging from all sides. In the hard golden light of the high plateau, caravans of horses and mules bearing silver-studded saddles are driven by broad-chested men and women carrying *muchachos* in a corner of a shawl. Silent and extremely clean, dignified and unobsequious, businesslike but not presumptuous, sure of themselves, childish, and terribly serious, pagans and fervent Catholics kneeling when the bishop from far-off Quito passes by, the Indians of Otavalo remain like this from dawn to nightfall to compose an eternal fresco that no painter has yet duplicated.

Center of the Inca Universe

The *altiplano*—that is, the high plateau more than 600 miles long and 60 miles wide between the two ranges of the Andes—lies at an average altitude of 13,500 feet. Most of the *altiplano* is in Bolivia, but it continues into Peru, dropping down to the Cuzco valley, the center of the universe in the days of the Incas, and further down toward the grim wild gorges of the Urubamba and the Ucayali that prefigure the enormous Amazon.

To find an equivalent of the Bolivian and Peruvian *altiplano* anywhere else in the world, one would certainly have to go all the way to the Pamir in central Asia, also walled in by snowy peaks from a universal mythology. The Indians who live, or rather subsist, on the *altiplano* strangely resemble the Mongols of the Pamir: the same broad powerful chests, the same faces hammered purple by winds racing down from the peaks and by the glacial cold of mountain nights, and the same proud and resigned silence. Except for a few scanty clumps of eucalyptus, no trees grow on the *altiplano*. Just resinous shrubs and glum grass covering the earth in patches. This is the *puna* with its cruel blue sky and harsh continental climate. During long winter nights, the mercury often drops to four below. Fifteen thousand feet high on the absolute bare slopes of the cordillera, the desolation of the *puna* becomes total, rigorous and inhuman. There, it is called the *puna brava,* an almost untranslatable expression that represents to the Indian the wildest and most fearsome land on earth. Herds of llamas occasionally leap and more frequently plod with nonchalant and suffering grace through this desert where big rust-colored slabs oozing water reveal the presence of mineral outcrops on the surface. Turquoise lakes reflect hanging glaciers, that shine strangely in these very bright nights, and the shacks of miners who dig tin and antimony. Along the rugged paths leading from the southern shores of Lake Titicaca to that tormented ravine on whose floor the Spaniards planted the foundations of La Paz, you meet men trotting one after another at night like marathon runners. They are small men, their torsoes hidden under bright but crude ponchos, the long tips of their headbands fluttering in the bitter wind from the plateau. These are the proud descendants of the Aymara people hurrying toward invisible villages, homes, families, children, emotions or tasks that no one can even imagine—for, to a Westerner, this setting is the very image of a void. But dazzling, eye-searing daylight picks out windowless, dust-colored huts of stone and mud that can hardly be distinguished from this long plain destined to be swept by the moaning wind until eternity. The harsh climate, the bare earth and the *soroche,* that mountain sickness that puts an iron clamp around your head and your heart into your mouth, all explain why this flawless but relentless landscape with its pure beauty has engendered despairing poets and unknown singers of the unjust misery of this Indian people, a people so sad that even their dance and carnival music seems to resemble laments punctuated by the monotonous rhythm of three-toned flutes.

Yet it is on this altiplano, the roof of South America, that a traveler can feel and understand more intensely than anywhere else the profound origins of the Andean Indian and the way that, over the centuries and occasionally unwittingly, he has left his mark on all the peoples living along this *cordillera* from the isthmus of Panama to the northern limits of Chile.

Fertility from an Absolute Desert

A third particularly unusual South American region is the Atacama desert in northern Chile. American engineers working for their companies in nitrate mines draw a very comfortable hardship allowance when they spend a few months in what is certainly one of our planet's most absolute deserts. The Atacama bakes under an immutable sun from the chilly and uninviting shores of the Pacific all the way to the snow-tipped peaks of the *cordillera* on the horizon. The coast is nothing but a monotonous and oppressive series of white or ochre cliffs. Some very rare coves and a few harbors like Arica, Iquique and Antofagasta break this austere line, but even these relative havens had to be considerably transformed before men could work there. Not many travelers brave this region which is also the realm of rocks, salt and iodine. True, jetliners now leap over the nitrate deserts on their direct runs from Santiago to Lima. Chilean rain gauges indicate that less than an eighth of an inch of rain comes down an average year at Iquique, just about in the center of Norte Grande on the sea. Inland in the two provinces of Tarapaca and Antofagasta, the green patches of strange stamp-sized oases exist because of light morning dew and condensed fog rather than any generosity from the sky. It was in this region that, somewhat by accident, the discovery was made of those nitrate deposits that made Chile's fortune in a bygone era. As the story goes, a group of Indians crossing the Atacama desert stopped one night to pitch their camp in a site near the present-day Maria Elena Mine. They gathered some gray stones to build a fire. Then, the earth suddenly began to crack and tongues of flame spurted into the night. Convinced that this was the devil's work, the Indians broke camp and marched into the nearest town where they told a Spanish priest what had happened to them. The priest decided to collect the ashes from the Indians' campfire. After studying it, he threw this mysterious powder into his garden with surprising results: his corn stalks grew twice as high. For the first time, saltpeter had been used as a fertilizer. Geologists have not yet been able to come up with a full explanation of how these saltpeter deposits were formed in the deserts of northern Chile. At any rate, layers of *caliche* containing nitrates among other things are found on the surface of basins that were once under water. These layers average about a foot in thickness, occasionally less, and they are consequently very easy to work.

The Polygon of Drought

What brought the Brazilian northeast out of relative obscurity was not the discovery by film directors of the *cangaceiros,* highway robbers with a sense of honor like the famed Lampiao, but rather and somewhat paradoxically the Cuban revolution. Belatedly, it was learned that, long before Fidel Castro made a name for himself in the Sierra Maestra and took over Havana, peasant leagues had sprung up in this part of Brazil to demand agrarian reform. The Brazilian northeast has begun to appear on the country's tourist map but the tourist still occasionally resembles an explorer here. And there is no doubt that the northeast is less known and less explored even by the Brazilians than Amazonia about which tons of literature have been produced or even the Mato Grosso opened up by the patient efforts of General Rondon, the protector of the Indians. Actually, the northeast consists of two fairly distinct regions: the *sertao* inland and the coast. More legends, evil spells, prophets, mysteries and violence have come out of the *sertao* than any other region in Brazil. More people, too. For as the Brazilian sociologist, Josué de Castro, has observed elsewhere in the world, misery and overpopulation go hand-in-hand here. In fact, the *sertao* has no clearly-marked frontier. It can begin fifty or one hundred miles from the coast or even further. First of all, the *sertao* is a wild, unique and startling landscape. It is the landscape of the *caatinga,* an Indian word that means something resembling "white forest". Trees in the *sertao* are bleached skeletons. Shrubs, cactus and thorns cover hard dry earth strewn with rocks or sliced into strips by long stretches of sand. A fiery sky flames over this grandiose and mystical setting where all is jagged and painful to the eye and to the flesh. Men dressed in leather or in threadbare rags but as tough and as proud as their land parade on bony horses as they hunt a problematic water point for their livestock. Geographers have found a frightening name for this *sertao* region of the northeast that stretches along the Rio Sao Francisco and over all the territory east of a line between Bahia and Fortaleza: they call it the polygon of drought. Less than fourteen inches of rain may fall here a year. Sometimes, too, no rain at all comes for several years in a row. Then the *sertao* lives up to all the curses and all the despair it has generated for centuries.

There have been at least half a dozen major droughts in the past hundred years and each of them has led to the death of hundreds of thousands of human beings and the exodus of thousands of others into central and southern Brazil. On the dusty tracks of the *sertao,* it is no longer quite so common to see starving haggard columns of pitiful refugees hunting a little bit of grass, shade and work. Yet while the exodus has become less spectacular, it has remained steady. For example, many of the workers building Brasilia came from the *sertao.* And everything is still a symbol, an omen or a premonition. Men watch the sky, the stars, the sun, the birds, the processions of ants and even the gamboling of goats to try to guess whether or not rain will fall. Here, life and death are intimately linked to the whimsical winds and clouds that turn the *sertao* green overnight.

The second part of the northeast is apparently gayer but actually not much less miserable. True, the coast contrasts sharply with the interior. Total drought and absolute aridity change almost without transition into equally total humidity and rains that never seem to stop. The jagged, sharp, rocky and sandy *sertao* gives way to aggressive green, languor, softness and rich mud where the sugar cane grows. Here, there is never less than thirty-six inches of rain a year and some years bring seventy-five inches. This is a coast of bent and twisted coconut palms as gaunt as the pines and the olive trees in the Esterel mountains of the French Riviera. It is a coast of *restingas,* those arrows of sand separating lagoons from the open sea, and also of reefs whose Portuguese name, *recife,* has been adopted by the capital of the state of Pernambuco. It is one long beach, an endless beach soaked in history and the tales of explorers and the Portuguese seamen who landed here to seek *pao brazil,* the brazilwood upon which the country's first fortune was founded. It is also soaked in the laments of slaves who fled out to sea from this coast aboard *jangadas.* Just as the horse stands for the *sertao,* the coast of the northeast is symbolized by the *jangada,* a delicate, fragile and graceful craft made of unsinkable balsa logs. It is something like a raft and the *jangadeiros* take their complicated and traditional fishing gear aboard it. When the seas are too heavy, the *jangadeiros* have to lash themselves to the frail masts of their rafts so that they will not be washed overboard. Thousands of freedom-hungry blacks slipped like this from one state to another along this coast at the end of the slavery period, trembling and crammed aboard *jangadas* awash in the long swell rolling in from Africa.

Brazilian Wild West

The Mato Grosso certainly bears one of the world's most mystery-laden names. For a long time, it was associated with Indian tribes believed to be all the more cruel and savage because they were completely unknown. Since naked men armed with bows and huddled amidst the vaguely cylindrical huts of their inaccessible villages shot arrows and shook their fists at planes flying over-head and out of range, the world concluded that the Mato Grosso was one of the most fearsome strongholds of primitive mankind, just like the land of the Borneo headhunters. It is true that the landscape of the Mato Grosso evokes such an image. It begins with the *pantanal* near Corumba in the south. This is a savannah barely rising out of the water and, during floods, it turns to mud, bogs and marshes of reeds, shrubs and thorns. Hundreds of thousands of acres of drowned forests are scored by countless canals where no canoe ever passes. South of the Mato Grosso, this immense alluvial plain sprawls over nearly 750 miles. Rivers start to rise in February in the north but not until June in the south. Up through September, the *pantanal* is nothing but a lake with a few rare islands emerging from it. Then the rivers return to their beds and the *pantanal* is transformed once more into a smiling plain of lawns, spring pastures and fertile enriched loam. North of the *pantanal,* the true Mato Grosso goes to sleep every night by the light of forest fires. Much of this Brazilian Far West has remained terra incognita on our maps. Yet, from a plane, it looks so flat and so peaceful with broad nonchalant rivers heading even further inland toward the south instead of flowing down to the sea along what should be the shortest and most reasonable route for a river to take from its source to its mouth. But this flatness is only apparent. Like the earth seen from a cosmic rocket, the Mato is flat because it is immense. Its gentle and attractive warmth decked out in violent colors can be deceiving, too. For the Mato Grosso really has not changed very much over four centuries. Its adventurers still roam an empty land and modern Brazil's great dream of westward expansion has yet to come true. For the time being, it is a slow and cautious expansion measured in inches while the smallest unit of measurement in the Mato must be at least 100 miles.

This Mato region is the anteroom of the great Amazonian forest that stretches over 750,000,000 terrifying, exuberant and partially flooded acres covering two states and four federal territories in the north. Nowhere else on our planet can one find a setting reproducing with such fearful precision the unleashed omnipotence of primitive nature and the merciless combats of the great reptiles of the Secondary Era. Everything is on the dizzying scale of the Rio Amazons 4,000 miles long. The Indians floundering along its monstrous banks have given it the same name that the Egyptians give to the Nile: the sea. Their Rio Mar has 1,100 branches and its muddy waters are not yet completely absorbed by the ocean sixty miles out to sea off its mouth. For a long time, the Mato Grosso and Amazonia were man's feared and invincible enemies, the realm of miasmas, treacherous and all-pervading waters, carnivorous flowers, cattle-eating fish and huge anacondas. Even the names of its rivers—Tapojoz, Rio Negro, Rio Madeira, Itacoai, Rio Branco or Xingu—do not have the familiar gentle ring of the streams feeding into the River Plate but the vaguely disturbing roughness of brown naked men seeking a patch of sky in the tiny clearings of the great forest. All of the species of trees and animals in Amazonia have not yet been counted. Brazilian literature itself contrasts the *selva,* the green hell, with the Rio Mar, the great river that enables man to penetrate this primitive world where water and trees are wed as they were in the earliest ages. And the Indian mythology of the Tupis and the Arawaks still tells of the incessant struggle and terror of naked and primitive man fighting for life along the walls of this immense, greenish, liquefied cavern.

A Swordfish Lying in the Sea

All along the South American continent, there is an infinity of islands, islets and archipelagoes. Some, like Marajo, are as big as Belgium or New Hampshire. Others aren't much bigger than Manhattan. Some are truly South American after sharing the fate of the nations to which they belong, but others like Aruba are still foreign. Some are strange like the ones off the Peruvian coast where guano deposits are still being worked. On San Blas off Panama live some of the most primitive tribes imaginable. The *cayos* off Colombia look like dolphin's backs, but Chile's Chiloe is a province itself. The Falklands on the way to Argentina, like rocky Villegaignon in the bay of Rio, have played historical and controversial roles. Just before reaching Brazil on the air route from Africa, you fly over Fernando do Noronha, a political penitentiary.

As you leave Trinidad for Venezuela, you cross Santa Margarita which is fairly typical of the kind of tourists' tropical paradise that you can find by the hundreds, some well-known and others unexplored. Santa Margarita falls somewhat into the second category and this explains its charm. Seen from the air, the island looks like an immense swordfish lying in the sea. A ridge of fat cottony cloud hides its spine almost constantly. With its long empty beaches where coconut palms quiver, its coves of clear water whose color never remains the same, its pueblos with their barogue churches, and its steeples looming out of high ground besieged by close-ranked battalions of cactus, Margarita is certainly Venezuela's tropical pearl. Pearl is the right word, too. Margarita's pearl oysters are famous all over the country. In September and October, a fleet of blue canoes whose white triangular sails make them resemble slightly the *jangadas* of Brazil, heads out of port. Like figureheads, the pearl fishermen stand in their bows with their sturdy torsoes that might have been carved by Praxiteles.

A Diversity of Unexplored Climates

South America, as you might expect, offers an infinite number of climates. But, generally speaking, they contrast less violently than in North America. Even on the southern tip of Argentina or Chile, winters are never as harsh as for example, in the Canadian Far North. There are more analogies between the temperate regions of the two halves of the hemisphere. The climate of the Andes often resembles that of the Rockies. There is an astounding similarity between Chilean islands and British Columbia for both are lands of forests, fjords and glaciers. The same parallel can be found in the climates of Peruvian and Californian oases. And the high plateaus of Colombia resemble those of Utah or Arizona. Still, you can run the whole gamut of climate from Panama to Chiloe and Bahia Blanca.

Most of the time, Panama is steeped in the atmosphere of a damp, heavy steam bath. Just like Guayaquil, the Ecuadorean harbor where cocoa seeds are sun-dried on the very avenues of the city. But Lima, only a few degrees to the south on the coast, is already cool. As for Bogota, Medellin, Quito, Cuzco and even Caracas, they are cities of medium or high altitudes and, naturally, they enjoy the inherent advantages of cities lying in tropical or subtropical zones but high above the dampness of the coast. This is also the case in Brazil where you need only travel a few miles from Rio to Petropolis, for example, to move from a typically tropical atmosphere to a cooler and more temperate climate. The greatest variety of South American climates is found in the Andes where, depending upon the altitude, huge differences can be encountered from one valley to another, leading to a countless number of regions and sub-regions.

South Americans are particularly sensitive about their climate. Anything that remotely recalls the colonial era irritates them with good reason. The legend of South American countries dozing in siestas and reveling in languorous tropical sloth naturally is a sore point with dynamic young nations making up in a few years for time lost over a few centuries and whose rate of population growth is the highest in the world. And, after all, it is true that it is not hotter in Rio de Janeiro during the Carnival in February—that is, at the height of the Southern Hemisphere's summer—than in Chicago during the month of August.

This sensitiveness that any traveler to South America must recognize also comes into play, and for the same reasons, where animals are concerned. In effect, another diehard legend states that Brazil has an astronomical variety of poisonous snakes. The Brazilians reply, and rightly so, that there are only 43 different species of snakes in their country while Mexico, for example, has 72. There is one type of rattlesnake in Brazil and 37 in the United States. Besides, the Brazilians have tamed their snakes. In São Paulo, there is an institute that is unique in the world. It is called Butantan. Nestling in the middle of a garden of rosewood, bougainvillaea and coffee bushes near the Rio Pintrearos, the Butantan Institute was created in 1902 by the state of São Paulo. It manufactures snakebite serum and it has several specialized laboratories studying the venoms and the viruses of scorpions and spiders. Every year, nearly 20,000 snakes are delivered to Butantan by planters or farmers who receive vials of serum in return.

Naturally, space does not permit us to make a thorough review of South American animal life. Yet it is incomparably rich. The fauna of tropical South America alone offers such a choice—it is the strangest, the most unusual and consequently the most interesting to a visitor—that it is almost impossible to underline any particular species. Naturalists themselves have not solved all of its enigmas. For example, they still do not know whether the *guacharqacas* of Amazonia belong to the gallinaceous or pigeon species because the only known species constitutes a genus and a family all by itself. The same is true for the *jaguarondi,* an apparently ordinary feline that no one has been able to classify as yet. *Aras*—bright yellow, red, violet or purple parrots—vie in sumptuousness with toucans whose enormous beaks make them the most popular of the continent's birds.

The *cabiais* in Brazil and the *chiguire* in Venezuela are one and the same, an animal the size of a large pig that lives in the water and prefers a vegetarian diet. Cicadas, howler monkeys, iguanas, caymans, and ant-eaters must all step aside before the lord of the South American forest, the jaguar. But after all, this jaguar is rarely famished and it spends most of its time tracking packs of peccaries. Though it is considered the most dangerous of South American animals, it fits very well into the image of this continent where *gentileza* rules and a sense of proportion always prevails. In fact, it is a good deal less dangerous than the Asian tiger or the African leopard. The Andes are the home of the puma much more so than the forest or the great plains of central Brazil and Argentina where it is harder to find. Brazil's favorite mascot is the charming *once,* a sort of wild cat that is very easy to tame. But then there is a host of strange creatures like the tapir, the biggest land animal in South America, or the armadillo whose features are just as archaic as those of the tapir. Equally strange is the harmless and discreet sloth, virtually incapable of moving on the ground and spending most of its life hanging head down from the branch of a tree. It must be admitted that the density of South America's animal population is relatively low when you compare it to the swarms in Africa despite an incomparably denser human population.

On the *llanos,* those immense plains in Venezuela and Colombia, giant storks prowl marshes and try to beat other hunters to their prey of frogs. Finally, further south in the Peruvian Bolivian Andes, there is the kingdom of some equally strange and fascinating animals—the *llama* that serves as the Indians' faithful companion, the vicuña and the *guanucot.*

THE SOUTH AMERICANS

Blend of Dynamism and Inertia

South America is not heavily populated. This is one of its main handicaps in the race for economic development and in its effort to fill that role of the continent of tomorrow that so many sociologists and economists have been promising it for so long. Latin America as a whole covers 15 percent of the earth's surface but its population represents only seven percent of the world total. If we just consider South America (this means subtracting Mexico, Central America and all of the Caribbean), then this proportion becomes even smaller. Take Brazil, for example. There is no denying that this is a country settled only along the coast and in a few adjoining regions like Minas Geraes and the southern states: Parana, Santa Catarina, São Paulo and Rio Grande do Sul. Two-thirds of Brazil are practically uninhabited and the immense expanses running from a line between Curitiba in the south to Macapa in the mouth of the Amazon contain less than four percent of the Brazilian population. But this is not a Brazilian characteristic. It is shared by all of South America. While United Nations statistics show that the continent is growing in population at a rate faster than any in the world, it still has a long way to go.

When the Spanish conquistadores and the Portuguese navigators discovered this continent during the 16th century and started to colonize it, it was almost empty. In addition, the first phase of this colonization was marked by heavy if not systematic extermination of any Indian populations that were met. Later, the Portuguese *bandeirantes* pushed into the depths of immense Brazil and even all the way to Amazonia in their hunt for slaves and labor supply. But this hunt brought about a weakening of the Indian factor as a racial component of the South American population. Elsewhere and particularly in the Andean countries, misery, oppression and diseases imported by the European also helped decimate the original inhabitants of the cordillera. One result of all this—which has led to the second major characteristic of South American settlement—is that groups have been scattered over clearly distinct areas without any links to each other in most cases. Even in heavily-settled rural areas, the population density has generally remained low. Compared to the West Indies and to certain Caribbean islands like Puerto Rico and especially Haiti, South America as a whole is underpopulated. With the exception of the Antioquia basin in Colombia, certain high valleys in Peru, the shores of Lake Titicaca, the Cochabamba valley in Bolivia, central Chile, the Tucuman oasis in Argentina and the Brazilian northeast, this continent is empty from the sociologist's viewpoint.

Bonds of Race and Common Interest

This has led to differences within a single country that have proved and are still proving extremely harmful from the viewpoint of national growth and of the assimilation of the masses in many countries and particularly in Brazil, Bolivia, Peru, Colombia and Venezuela. A sense of nationhood is not very deeply implanted in South America because of this situation. It is obvious, for example, that an Aymara Indian living on the southern shore of Lake Titicaca in Bolivia feels much closer to his cousin who lives and works on the other side of the border than to the *mestizos* of La Paz, his capital, or even to the Bolivian Indian farmers in the Cochabamba valley. An Indian shopkeeper in Otavalo in Ecuador has much more in common with a fellow Indian shopkeeper in Popayan or Pasto in Colombia than with the mulatto or *zambo* Ecuadoreans of Guayaquil. Venezuelan mountaineers in San Cristobal and Colombian mountaineers in Cucuta are united by bonds of race, blood and common interests. Caracas and Bogota, their respective capitals, are remote and almost unreal cities to them. Even though Colombia is one of South America's most unified countries on a human and political level, there are enormous differences between an inhabitant of Cartagena on the Caribbean coast and an inhabitant of Sogamoso near Lake Tunja in the Eastern Cordillera. There is the same gulf in Chile between the people of the Norte Grande and those of Concepcion or Valdivia. Any number of such examples could be cited.

This human concentration in clearly-defined zones that are often remote from each other has been aggravated today by the world-wide exodus from the countryside into big cities. A third consequence is to be found in transportation systems and communications networks. Most roads lead from the interior to the nearest port. Roads or railways directly linking different zones of relatively heavy population are extremely scarce and not very developed. It is very significant that the ambitious project of a Pan American Highway from Panama (that is, from the end of the present Pan American Highway beginning at the American border and not yet completed) has resulted from pressure brought to bear by bodies grouping all South American republics. The same picture is to be found within each nation. In Brazil, the building of main roads between inland cities, like the Brasilia-Belem highway, is directly linked to the relatively artificial installation and development of the new federal capital in the heart of the steppes of the state of Goias, promoted to the rank of the country's political and economic center of gravity.

Nor has the spectacular growth of air transport in South America over the past twenty years changed this situation fundamentally. Both to the east and west of the continent, the oceans remain the main means of communication between isolated population centers. South America is still the end of the world. In theory, Africa is its closest neighbor for trade. The fact that the south of the hemisphere is linked to the north by the isthmus of Panama has turned out to be more of a handicap than an advantage. The isthmus slows movement between the Pacific and the Atlantic and it is of no use at all to the roadbuilder because of dense and dangerous jungles that still must be crossed before the Pan American Highway becomes a reality. Finally, the big ports of Brazil and Argentina are much closer to Europe than to the United States. This fact has influenced and will continue to influence more and more strongly the political evolution of these countries that are among the major powers of South America.

South America's racial makeup today is extremely varied and complex. This is another characteristic of this continent. Here, in effect, race mixture has been carried out with very few restrictions or taboos and it can be said that at least half of South America's present-day inhabitants are of mixed blood. Of course, there are three basic elements in the composition of South American populations: the white man, the black and the Indian. But each of these elements has given birth to a large variety of human groups. The most classical and the most ordinary is the *mestizo,* a mixture of white and Indian blood. He is often known south of the Rio Grande as the *ladino* to set him off from the pink, blond gringo from North America. But the *ladino* himself is not a type in the proper sense of the word because he subdivides into a large number of varieties.

The Sad and Not-so-Stoic Indian

Long before the arrival of the Spaniards and the Portuguese, South America was inhabited by people who had come from Asia. They were called Indians, of course, because Columbus thought that he had discovered India. Most of them came over the Bering Strait and it is possible, though not proven, that a small number may have crossed the Pacific directly by boat. It is highly improbable that any of them came straight from Africa. South American Indians share common characteristics even though there are enormous differences between, for example, the inhabitants of the high Andean valleys and the Amazon tribes or the Indians living in the region near the border between Argentina and Paraguay. The proudest of all of them certainly are the Araucans who put up a fierce and, for a long time, victorious fight against Valdivia's Spanish troops in central Chile on the banks of the Bio Bio. The closest to primitive mankind are the remaining clusters driven into the center of the Mato Grosso. But the most common trait of the South American Indian, particularly in the Andes, is sadness. The very music that he draws out of his reed flutes is sad. "I was conceived on a stormy night. Rain and wind were my cradle . . . No one pities my misery. A curse on my birth. A curse on the world. A curse on myself . . ." Naturally, he transmitted this fundamental sadness to the conquering Spaniard who was tough but not a very gay type to begin with, either.

As for the Indian, he is stoical. Stoicism, courage, toughness and melancholy: it is not at all astounding that these are still the dominant basic traits of the people who live along the spine of the cordillera. It is significant that the dividing line is found in Colombia and Venzuela. For these two countries, while Andean in some respect and therefore indubitably Indian, also face the Caribbean where the black, whether willingly or not, has settled since the 16th century. While Bogota still displays Indian melancholy, Baranquilla on the Atlantic coast already has the black's nonchalance and exuberant gaiety. The picture is the same in Venezuela where the stern Indians of the Tachira look down with some disdain on the more turbulent and less pure population around Lake Maracaibo. The racial situation is even more complex in Brazil but the black dominates again in the northeast and for the same reasons.

The Black and the Three Americas

Yes, the black was imported. He was first brought in to work the fields of sugar cane along the coast because local Indian labor had been very quickly decimated and turned out to be insufficient. By the hundreds of thousands, these people known at the time as "Guinea coins" were crammed miserably into slavers' holds and put ashore on the South American coast and in the Caribbean. In Brazil, blacks came mainly from the Bantu region but also from Sudan and Dahomey.

Racially speaking, South America has been classified into three main zones and this classification is still valid today: an Indian

America, a mulatto America and a white America. The first lies more or less along the Andes. But as soon as you leave the coast of Argentina, Uruguay and southern Brazil to head into the pampas, you find Indians who have remained more or less pure. While the mountains have remained the Indian's choice of home, he is not completely missing on the plains. In all the Andean countries, the only whites are the descendants of old Spanish aristocratic families. This elite is no longer in control and, in a good many cases, it has not even kept the prerogatives of wealth.

White America lies to the southeast: Argentina, Uruguay and southern Brazil. It is becoming whiter and whiter. For the past half century, a veritable tidal wave from Europe has settled this area in much the same way, though much later, that European immigrants settled North America.

Then there are the tropics, the third South America. Without actually being dominant, the black has always made a major contribution here. The black ushers in the reign of gaiety, sensuality and easy-going good nature that contrast so starkly with Indian reserve, Spanish melancholy or Portuguese *saudade*. But a good many other elements must be added to these three basic ones: European, Indian and black. Combinations are countless. No one can tell you in Guayaquil or Lima whether certain human types are Indian, Chinese, mulatto or vaguely *zambo,* that is, a mixture of red and black. South American racial stock has been further seasoned by Levantine immigration mainly from Syria and Lebanon to Brazil and several Andean countries like Bolivia, and also by Japanese and Chinese colonies on the Pacific coast.

Still, in most cases and with the exception of Brazil, the continent's human types belong to one of these three main groups. In the Andean countries, there is even a scale of racial, economic and social differences. The white man is nearly always on top of the social ladder. The common man is colored. The poorer a poor man is in South America, the more Indian or black blood he has in his veins. This does not necessarily imply discrimination but this almost-universal coincidence obviously plays a very large role in inter-racial relations.

Brazil: the New Frontier

Brazil, however, is in a class by itself. It is certainly the only country in the world that has succeeded in laying the foundations of a tropical civilization. Brazilian man exists today. This cannot be denied. A visitor is always startled when he sees crowds in Rio or Bahia the day he arrives. They contain every human type between and including all extremes. In one corner of Cinelandia, there may be a Brazilian girl as blonde as wheat with delicate porcelain eyes. On the beach at Copacabana, there may be a black girl as sculptural as the girls are only in Dakar or Abidjan.

Both are Brazilian. Well, what's the answer? To get their bearings whenever they feel the need—which is very seldom—the Brazilians have an infinite series of shadings running from black to pure white. Here are the main categories: *escuro,* a mulatto with very dark skin but European features; *cabra,* a mulatto with lighter skin; *Cape Verde,* a mulatto with straight hair; *moreno,* a Portuguese very close to the usual Mediterranean type; *chulo,* very light skin but curly hair; *creolo,* swarthy skin and wavy hair; *srana,* black skin and red hair.

Despite these subtle differences and allowing for any necessary reservations, it is very easy to spot a Brazilian at home or abroad. Sociologists say that he has the following qualities and defects: kindness (that celebrated Brazilian *gentileza*), willingness to strike a compromise, cordiality, friendship, reliability when he gives his word, sadness, a taste for easy money, nonchalance, laziness, and emotionalism. According to a popular saying, if a Brazilian is sad, it is the fault of his Indian ancestors; if he is nonchalant, it is the fault of black slaves; and if he is brutal, it is the fault of Portuguese *bandeirantes.* In any case, the absence of race prejudice in Brazil is very obvious. "The Brazilians," Roy Nash has said, "are the most color-blind people in the world. They are color-blind to the point where they can look a black man in the face and see nothing but a man."

The explanation of this lack of race prejudice in Brazil must be sought in early years of Portuguese conquest and colonization. No one has studied this problem more thoroughly than the Brazilian sociologist, Gilberto Freyre. It all began with the *casa grande,* the home of the master who was the patriarchal squire of sugar cane plantations in the northeast, and the *senzalas,* the homes of the slaves attached to the plantation and over whom the master exerted all his rights, including *jus primae noctis.* This is why there was such a difference between Portuguese and Spanish colonization. This lack of any Portuguese reservations about racial mixtures has given modern Brazil a face completely different from those of other South American nations. According to Freyre, mobility was one of the secrets of the Portuguese. Without it, their victories cannot be explained. Portugal itself was almost unpopulated. It sent out handfuls of settlers drawn from all the debris and all the epidemics, famines and wars of the Middle Ages. Yet it was able to sow very virilely the remnants of its blood and civilization among peoples so diverse and so remote from each other in Asia, Africa and the Americas. As far as miscibility is concerned, no colonizing people have ever surpassed or even equalled the Portuguese. They mingled delightedly with local women as soon as they landed and produced sons of mixed blood to such a point that hardly a few thousand men were enough to take over immense areas and compete with Europe's biggest and most populous nations in the race for colonial empires. The cross-breeding of Portuguese men and Indian women gave birth at once to the race of *mamelucos* who volunteered to march under the banners of the *bandeirantes* setting out to conquer new territory inland. This mixture also partially explains the famed *saudade* of Brazil, that vague sadness that comes from afar, appears without cause, feeds on hopes and dreams, then vanishes in a burst of laughter. Portugal also experiences *saudade*. But there is an extra element in Brazilian *saudade,* an impression that nothing is worth trying because nothing can succeed, a sort of fatalism that one might be tempted to attribute to a Moorish heritage but that can be traced here to Indian blood.

Then the Indian faded into the background. And the black made his entrance. The economic and social system upon which the sugar cane plantations were founded was bound to lead to a loosening of morals. In the voluptuous atmosphere of plantation houses swarming with youthful black girls and chambermaids, venereal diseases were transmitted freely through homegrown prostitution. Modern sociologists have emphatically contradicted the vital role attributed by Freyre to the intimate relations between white masters and black or mulatto slaves.

The fact is that this mixture of races, unparalleled elsewhere, is finally turning white. Doubtlessly not to such an extent as the Brazilians themselves would prefer or would try to make one believe. In less than 50 years, four million Brazilians have been assimilated into the white group and the proportion of non-whites in Brazilian society tends to drop steadily. From this viewpoint, that deliberate policy of racial mixture preached and encouraged by the Portuguese at the start of their colonization has been a success. On the other hand, the much more rigid compartmentation between races in the other South American nations now tends to put the white man on the defensive in these countries and in the position of the white minorities in the ex-colonies of Africa and Asia. While Brazil is becoming whiter and whiter and thereby tending to integrate into the southeastern part of the continent belonging to the first group, it is clear that Indian America, on the contrary, is becoming redder and redder. This can lead to some extremely important long-term political consequences.

THE INDIAN WORLD

The Rise and Fall of Highland Empires

There is a certain parallel between the evolution of civilizations north and south of the isthmus of Panama even though the south was inhabited much later. In particular, it is clear that there are some analogies between Mexican and Peruvian civilizations. Even today, we have a long way to go before all the stones, tombs, shrines and temples of South America's known archeological sites have been inventoried and studied. Just to take the case of Peru alone, we still do not know very much about civilizations on the coast prior to the Inca period. It is therefore wise to speak of South American civilizations only with caution and modesty. We have no guarantee that new discoveries will not upset all our present-day knowledge very shortly.

As far as we now know, the greatest of these civilizations was obviously that of the Incas. Traces of Inca power first appeared in the upper Cuzco valley. Its first theme was the adaptation of the sun worship already found in the so-called Tihuanaco civilization but applied to inflexible political centralization. Linguistic unity, a complex and highly-developed road network, and an omnipresent police regime: those were the principles of a social organization unique in South America and even in both Americas. They explain the dazzling success of the Inca Empire and they also explain why this civilization has left a deep imprint on the Indians now living in Bolivia, Peru, Ecuador, and northern Chile.

Machu Picchu, one of the Inca empire's most beautiful and most typical fortresses, was discovered almost accidentally by a young American university professor. Although archeologists have been quizzing the stones of Machu Picchu since 1911, a number of irritating questions remain unanswered. It appears likely that this fortress was a forward outpost of the Incas destined to protect them against possible raids by Indian tribes coming from the Amazon plain. But this is not certain, for it is hard to imagine the Incas at the peak of their power worrying about barbarian tribes in the tropical lowlands. What is certain is that the building of Machu Picchu was rendered possible precisely by the iron discipline that the Inca clamped upon his subjects. One is immediately and perhaps rightly reminded of the building of Egypt's great pyramids by another slave population serving their Pharaoh. The ruins of Machu Picchu are certainly fascinating. When the mists rise from the gorges of the Urubamba River fighting its way through a narrow channel eight hundred yards below the fortress, you are irresistibly reminded of Delphi and of those other magnificent and battered stones on the brink of a ravine from which steam also soars. But at Machu Picchu, no oracle has ever heard the replies of the gods. A civilization died and no one has yet been able to give the exact reasons for its death. Inca domination lasted four centuries, from the 12th to the arrival of the Spaniards at the beginning of the 16th. These legendary sons of the Sun came from Lake Titicaca. Only after subduing the Aymara tribes did they settle in the warmer and more hospitable Cuzco valley that was to become, for a brief moment, the hub of the universe. At least, of the universe as it was imagined by the forerunners of Huascar and Atahualpa. At its peak, the Inca empire probably numbered 25 million inhabitants and stretched approximately over what is now the territory of Bolivia, Peru, Ecuador, northern Chile and part of Argentina. But the historian comes up against a harsh and startling fact: the Incas had no system of writing. Their history had to be reconstructed through the colorful, contradictory and certainly biased accounts written by the early chroniclers of the Spanish conquest. The main source of information is in the works of Garcilaso de la Vega, a Spaniard whose complete objectivity is all the more dubious because he had Indian ties. Another reason for wariness is the fact that this Inca civilization, perfect though it may have been, only followed on the heels of other civilizations whose state of advancement has yet to be learned. Merely on the Ancon hill near Lima, there are still 35,000 tombs to be excavated and it is likely that a gigantic Aymara empire also covered all of the Andean highlands long before the Incas appeared.

The State of Controlled Happiness

For four centuries, the Incas patiently organized their realm. Builders and administrators, these Romans of South America were less refined than the Mayas of Yucatan but more efficient. They succeeded in setting up an economic and social system planned to such a point that it has been called a communist civilization. In any case, it was a totalitarian state where nothing was left to chance, whether daily life, toil, joy, the most humble and the most indispensable tasks, a certain conception of happiness or, naturally, death. The Inca's messengers and officials traveled throughout this vast tormented and rugged empire built on apparently impassable mountains and transmitted supreme orders by means of *quipus,* colored cords, a mnemonic device to record facts, figures and events. Under this system of controlled happiness, the Indian had to die where he was born, in the place where the Inca had decided that he would be the most useful to the community, unless a decision ordered him to join some great migration needed to carry out the policy of his ruler. The community took care of the sick, the infirm and the aged. Able-bodied men worked on the lands of the state and they had to take care of plots belonging to citizens unable to work before they could turn to their own family plots. It was the Inca who supplied wool to make ponchos. Immense herds of llamas and vicuñas belonging to no one man but to all men were watched by herdsmen who were civil servants. At the head of each group of ten families was placed a chief who was responsible for them. This strict organization led to the Inca at the very top of the social pyramid, assisted by his council and by four high dignitaries who controlled the intricate mechanisms of this astounding social machine in the four provinces of Tahuantinsuyu. Food supplies were stored outside villages and along roads. Officials took from these stocks what was needed by the court, the army and the clergy.

The ostentation of the Inca's court was depicted by chroniclers in such lyrical terms that, here too, their objectivity has been questioned. According to their testimony, the Inca moved about only on a solid gold litter encrusted with emeralds. But the most grandiose and also the grimmest ceremonies of all took place when the Inca died. Then his servants and his concubines were sacrificed at the same time and, in certain cases, these funerals worthy of a Pharaoh led to the deaths of thousands.

The roads of the Inca empire were longer than Roman roads and superior in many respects. When the Spaniards landed with Pizarro at Tumbes, they were stupefied to discover this communications network built in a Dantean setting of boulders, ice, vertiginous peaks and narrow ravines. It may seem surprising that this perfect empire fell when confronted by a few horsemen from Spain. In fact, the Incas were defeated by their arrogance, their ignorance and, most of all, by their internal clashes. By their myths and legends as well. In the fall of the Inca empire, we find amazing analogies again with the defeat of the Aztecs in Mexico. Quetzelcoatl, the Aztecs' plumed serpent, had left them by sea, heading east. It was from this direction that Cortes appeared with his conquistadores. In the same way, Viracocha, the white god of the Peruvians and the lord of thunder, had also disappeared over the black waters of Lake Titicaca while announcing that he would shortly return. Like Cortes in Mexico, Pizarro in Peru cleverly used these Indian beliefs to confuse the peoples that he wanted to subdue.

The Goldsmiths of Colombia

The perfection, prestige, brilliance and Wagnerian aspects of this Inca civilization that easily took the lead in South America should not make us overlook other societies that were quite remarkable. For example, there were the Chibchas in Colombia. For a very long time, Colombia was the turntable of South America. Tribes coming from the isthmus of Panama followed the Cauca or the Magdalena toward the Andes and then used these same routes to return. Archeology has found visible traces of these wanderings even though it has hardly begun to prospect ancient Colombia. For a long time, it was believed that the Chibchas had set up a state comparable to those of the Aztecs and the Incas. But despite their remarkable degree of evolution and their exceptional skill as potters and goldsmiths, this was not the case even though they also succeeded in establishing a highly-centralized political organization at a time when their neighbors had not risen from the tribal stage. The Chibchas' sun worship demanded human sacrifices just as in the case of the Mexican Aztecs and the Peruvian Incas. And one of the Chibcha divinities bears some resemblance to the famed plumed serpent of Teotihuacan. There is one Colombian region that intrigues archeologists and travelers alike—that of San Agustin near the sources of the Magadalena. There mounds have been discovered, left by a society that is still unknown. They cover sanctuaries made of raised slabs, underground galleries and, above all, many large statues.

The Araucans, an Indian people worthy of attention, still live in southern Chile. Infinitely rougher than the Aztecs or the Incas, they clung to their country south of the Bio Bio with fierce determination. The conquerors took only two years in Peru and in Mexico to eliminate their opposition. Seventeen years of incessant combat were needed before the Araucans could be subdued and Chile conquered. And the Spanish leader, Pedro de Valdivia, paid for this conquest with his life. In fact, Araucan resistance really ended only around the middle of the 19th century. Today, it is clear that some traces of the pride and the toughness of the Araucans have remained in the blood of the Chilean *mestizos* who form more than 60 per cent of the country's population. It is not at all surprising that the two greatest Chilean writers, Pablo Neruda and Gabriela Mistral, made liberal use of Indian sources in order to sing of what they felt to be South America's most authentic aspects. Neruda haughtily goes back to primitive times "when man was earth, slime, the eyelid of the trembling mud, clay form, a Caribbean pitcher, a Chibcha stone or Araucan silica". He climbed Machu Picchu's fascinating ruins to discover the splendor of old Indian civilizations and the present-day misery of the Indian people.

18th-Century Communal Experiments

On the other hand, there is not much to be said from the viewpoint of archeology and native civilizations in other South American regions. The archeology of Amazonia, for example, is little known but it does not seem likely to contain any great surprises. Only its pottery furnishes food for thought. Other traces such as enclosures of raised stones might lead us to assume a certain degree of religious and cultural development. Similar vestiges found on the island of Marajo at the mouth of the great river are larger and certain sepulchres here recall the style of Central American tombs. Nor is there anything very noteworthy in Venezuela, a country that does not seem to have been inhabited much more than 2,000 years ago. Vestiges have been found mainly on the coast and they resemble those in the West Indies and particularly Puerto Rico. Much more worthy of interest are the Indian ways of life in the Paraña basin where men have always tended to settle. The Guaranis are the biggest group in this region originally colonized by the Jesuits.

In the Chaco, there is a group of 50,000 Indians still living in an era that looks more like the Stone Age than the 20th century. Guyanas, Cainguas and Guayakis survive in forests further south. But the main branch of Indian stock here is still formed by the Guaranis just as in the days of the Jesuit *reducciones*. With their copper skin, high cheekbones, slit eyes and long hair, the Guaranis shared and still share the Mongolian features of the Indians of the Andean highlands. In order to protect and convert them, the Jesuits set up their "reductions" here as fortified camps with, at first, an equivocal air of segregation. But this experiment finally led to an unusual attempt at collective living. Each community was autonomous. There were more than thirty of them in the 18th century and their very strict rules organized every last detail of their proteges' existence down to the least little gestures and moves, somewhat in the manner of the Incas but in a different spirit. Products of labor were distributed according to each person's needs, not according to his work. The aged, the sick and the infirm were taken care of by the community. The church was naturally the center of each reduction and military protection had to be provided against raids by Indian tribes and, above all, against Portuguese *bandeirantes* who came from nearby Brazil in search of a ready supply of labor. The decadence and the ultimate disappearance of these Indian communities were brought about in the end when the remarkable work of the Jesuits stirred jealousy abroad and they were driven out by force of arms. Once the Jesuits had been expelled from America, the reductions were sacked and completely wiped out.

A CONTINENT'S PAST
AND PRESENT

Stagnation, Turbulence and Stability

(Updating of this chapter to reflect current developments has been undertaken by Penny Lernoux of the Copley News Service.)

Historians have always admired Cortes' bold conquest of Mexico. Until the very last moment, everything hung in the balance. The very day after the conquistadores were routed during the famous *noche triste*, the scales of fate tipped in their favor. This was not the case of the conquest of the Peruvian highlands and Andean America by that illiterate genius, Francisco Pizarro. The world was stupefied—and still is—by his athletic feat of crossing the cordillera for the first time, but the outcome was never in doubt. Montezuma's defeat was temporary. Atahualpa's defeat was fatal. The Aztecs displayed fury, determination and surliness that may have only been a reflection of their natural violence and the rites of their merciless religion whose most striking symbol was the obsidian knife. On the contrary, the Inca's subjects showed kindness, fatalism and a certain sort of naiveté that predestined them for their role in history as victims. But the perspective of history is putting things back into their proper proportion. In Peru, Ecuador and Bolivia, the names of the last great Indian rulers have been expunged from the pages of history books if not from the minds and hearts of the men who live in the sierra.

In Lima, the alleged and venerated remains of Pizarro are displayed to all eyes behind a glass case in the cathedral and a statue of the cruel conquistador stands on one of the city's most beautiful squares. In Mexico City, on the other hand, there is not a single sign of Hernan Cortes on the streets. Instead, it is

Cuathemoc, the last hero of the struggle against the Spaniards, who reigns in the heart of what was once Tenochtitlan. In other words, Spain left a very different mark in the south from the start and this mark can still be felt today. Here, one must agree with the great Spanish writer, Salvador de Madariaga. It is not easy to be Spanish in South America. Spain's burden of responsibility for the conquest and subsequent colonization has been made all the heavier by other colonial powers expressing their prejudices and their criticisms. Yet this conquest was very rapid. It involved mistakes and outrageous demands, but they were on par with the mistakes and demands made by other colonial nations throughout the world. It also succeeded in quickly spreading Spanish language and culture over a huge continent and to countries separated by enormous distances and without any regular means of communicating with each other.

The Peaceful Portuguese in Brazil

The mark of Spain on a considerable part of the South American continent is totally different from that left by the Portuguese colonizers on Brazil. In fact, the history of Brazil began only at the end of the 15th century when Pope Alexander VI decided to settle the quarrel between Spain and Portugal over the control and conquest of sea routes. Through the treaty of Tordesillas signed in 1494, the Portuguese obtained from Spain the right to exercise their sovereignty over all territories discovered up to a line 370 leagues west of Cape Verde and the Azores. This ideal line ran approximately from Belem to Santa Catarina. As a result, the approximate boundaries of Brazil were laid down even before it was discovered only in 1500. Unlike what happened in the rest of South America, the Portuguese colonization of Brazil was slow, gradual and relatively peaceful. The conquistadores recruited by Pizarro, Almagro, Luque or Valdivia and led out onto the acrobatic trails of the Andes were hunting gold and fortune, the hypothetical El Dorado that fired their imaginations and multiplied their natural courage tenfold. But the first natural resource exploited by the Portuguese was simply wood. It was a red wood used in dyes, *pau brasil*, the color a burning ember and also the color of that unknown shore hemmed by coconut trees swaying in the wind. So this far-off land was named Brazil and the men who began to trade in this wood were called *brasileiros*. The dye wood ended up by dyeing the name of the whole country. After wood came sugar and sugar became the symbol of human settlement along the coast. After sugar, there was gold and diamonds— that is, the colonization of the first land in the interior and of the region that was to become the state of Minas Geraes (meaning General Mines). Then followed coffee and the appearance of planters on the red earth of São Paulo, Parana and southeastern Brazil.

The memories and the vestiges left by the colonial era, whether Portuguese or Spanish, over all of South America obviously symbolize very dissimilar temperaments and intentions. Pizarro loved Lima. He could not establish his capital at a place as remote from the sea as Cuzco. So he chose the vast terraces along the Rimac River about ten miles from chalk cliffs facing the Pacific Ocean. It was Pizarro who laid the cornerstone of the cathedral and of the viceroy's palace that are among the city's most remarkable ornaments. And all around the conqueror's exemplary tomb, bells still ring from the towers of hundreds of churches whose construction he supervised. Lima was nothing less than the capital of all Spanish possessions in South America until they won their independence. It has the oldest university in the Americas, the University of San Marcos where generations of renowed professors have taught, and a jewel of colonial architecture, the Torre y Tagle Palace now housing the Peruvian ministry of foreign affairs. There is a nostalgic Andalusian air about Lima where murmuring fountains hardly disturb the gilded silence of patios straight out of Seville. The beautiful home of La Perichola, that equally beautiful half-breed who was the viceroy's mistress, has not enjoyed as pleasant a fate as the Torre Y. Tagle Palace. Today, it is a barracks and there is no use looking in the courtyard for traces left by the carriage of this favorite immortalized by a famous short story. But the center of Lima has not changed: it is a labyrinth of streets, alleys, narrow arches, and old houses with barred windows and balconies protected by Oriental lattice-work where *sociedad* ladies and their servants could see without being seen.

Quito, though smaller than Lima, also leads a life timed by countless bells of countless churches and convents. Every night at six, their sudden panting brings out a population of Indians who take over the center of the Ecuadorean capital in order to set up their stands and light their little *braseros*. There are no less than fifty-seven churches at Quito, all jewels of Jesuit baroque and symbols of an era that was once grandiose even though they now stand in the slightly outdated setting of a sleepy provincial city.

The Fight for Independence

Between 1808 and 1823, the colonial edifice raised by Spain and Portugal crumbled for the same reasons that explain the revolt of the thirteen English colonies in North America. The driving forces of this phenomenon were the great liberal movement of the 18th century, the desire of colonies for emancipation, the internal defects of the colonial system and the exported ideas of the French and American revolutions put into practice by a few noble figures of which Bolivar is the most perfect example.

But the main difference between North and South America was this: revolt strengthened the unity of the English colonies but split and weakened the ex-Spanish colonies. This was the fault of climate and terrain, not of men. There were too many empty spaces, too many pampas, too many llanos where uncontrolled Indian tribes often roamed, too many paramos, too many deserts and too many cordilleras in South America to enable the various human nuclei born during colonization to have a chance to unite. The setback of Bolivar's great dream of a unified South America can be traced first to these purely geographical reasons. Then there was another important factor: the revolution was carried out by creoles—that is, by whites of Spanish origin but born locally. The great mass of Indians (or of blacks in the case of Brazil, but here the story of national independence is completely different) remained passive or else took the side of the Spaniard who, as a remote master, was less hated than the creole who was an immediate master. The creoles living in Venezuela, Colombia, Peru or Chile for several generations had become Venezuelans, Colombians, Peruvians or Chileans. They owned immense estates and herds. They controlled huge numbers of slaves and the economies of their countries as well. Despite this, actual political power escaped them because it was in the hands of some 300,000 Spaniards who had come from far-off Spain as high church or government officials living off the country.

Miranda had run into French revolutionaries and Bolivar took his inspiration from Napoleon. A first attempt at liberation was made on the coast of Venezuela in 1806 by Miranda but it failed. Other attempts like the one on the Rio de la Plata were no more successful. In the end, it was Napoleon's attack on Spain that helped touch off the liberation movement in South America. A French agent named Desmolard was sent by Napoleon to Venezuela and he encouraged the revolutionary movement of April, 1810, in Caracas. While the Spanish mother country was almost completely occupied by Napoleon's Grand Army and Andalusia was collapsing, South America proclaimed its independence. Venezuela in March of 1811. Ecuador in December of that same year. Chile and Argentina became free in their turn. Only Peru remained more or less in Spanish hands. On November 6, 1813, the independence of New Spain—that is, of Mexico—was proclaimed. But Spain was net yet ready to admit defeat. The first revolutionary movements were quickly overpowered. By July of 1812, Caracas was under Spanish control once more.

Enter the Libertador

It was then that Bolivar appeared on the scene. The greatest hero of South American independents was born in Caracas on July 24, 1783. Of noble and wealthy birth, Bolivar had dark eyes, a frail and almost sickly body, swarthy skin, an ardent and voluptuous temperament, arms too thin and too long, and boundless charm. During a trip to Italy, he took a romantic oath: "I swear by the God of my fathers, I swear by my honor, I swear by my fatherland that I shall allow neither respite for my arms nor rest for my soul as long as I have not shattered the chains that oppress us through the will of Spanish rule." Bolivar, the friend of Europe's greats, was devoured by ambition and he dreamt of the name that the New World's enthusiastic mobs were actually to bestow upon him later on: the Libertador. Bolivar first waged this war of liberation all alone, beginning at Cartagena on the Caribbean coast of Colombia. What has been called his "admirable campaign" took him from the shores of Colombia to the capital of Venezuela where he made a triumphant entrance. He was immediately counterattacked by Monteverde and Boves' cavalry of *llaneros*. Inch by inch, Monteverde reconquered a Venezuela covered with ruins, blood and corpses. Bolivar was a hunted man and he left for New Granada. In Jamaica and Haiti, he mapped out the rest of his campaigns just as Cortes prepared his plans the day after the *noche triste*. He realized that he had to have the people on his side to succeed. Boves' *llaneros* deserted the Spanish camp to join forces with him and the infantry of the liberating armies was suddenly filled by peasant volunteers. The other provinces became uneasy once again. From Angostura on the banks of the Orinoco, Bolivar moved up the river's valley from east to west, recruiting on the way the excellent troops of Paez the Centaur. He crossed the Andes and liberated Colombia with the help of Santander. He proclaimed the union of Venezuela, Colombia and Ecuador. Then with Sucre, Bolivar marched on Quito and Peru. In December of 1824, Sucre won the big battle of Ayacucho and inflicted lasting defeat on the armies of Spain. This time, everything collapsed from Caracas to Buenos Aires. If he had wanted it, Bolivar could have ordered his own coronation as the emperor of an empire with seven capitals: Caracas, Bogota, Quito, Chapultepec, Rio de Janeiro, Bogota and Punta del Este. In 1828, La Paz, Lima, Santiago and Buenos Aires. He did not want it and he began to lose the faith that had enabled him to march across mountains to victory with ridiculously weak forces. Plots were hatched against him. His best generals abandoned and betrayed him, conspiring to carve out principalities of their own in this South America that Bolivar wanted to see unique, free, strong and solitary. In 1828, he convened a congress at Panama City to try to bring these different states into an association, but it was a failure. Yet, despite its unhappy outcome, this Panama conference was not completely useless. Bolivar was the first to spread the idea of Pan American collaboration. Panama was a forerunner of Bolivar miraculously escaped assassination. Santander was reigning in Bogota and Paez in Venezuela. In those days, there was a saying about Bolivar: "He is applauded because he is feared. He is worshipped at times like an idol because he is great. But, to tell the truth, no one likes him." Sucre, his most loyal lieutenant, was assassinated. Bolivar himself was never to see his native Venezuela again. He stopped at Santa Marta near Cartagena and it was there that he died on December 17, 1830, exactly eleven years after the founding of Greater Colombia at the Congress of Angostura. "I have ploughed the sea . . ." the Libertador murmured in disappointment on his deathbed.

In the meanwhile, Peru was liberated once and for all by another great captain, San Martin, who began his campaign on the plains of Chile and Argentina. He dealt the first blows to the Spanish viceroy at Lima and then left a clear field and final victory to the lieutenants of Bolivar after chivalrously agreeing to step aside.

South America's Only Monarchy

Brazilian independence was not marked by the same great deeds and epic combats that we find in Spanish-speaking South America. Napoleon's armies also conquered Portugal and the regent, Dom Joao, fled the country. In January of 1808, he arrived with his court in Bahia. There was quite a contrast between this stilted, embarrassed European court so conscious of protocol and good manners and the warm and heavy truculence of Brazil's first capital. Then the government moved to Rio and all Brazilian ports were open to European trade. A treaty with England was signed in 1810. Napoleon's defeat did not change the situation. Joao became king in 1816 and he remained in Brazil until 1820 when the Portuguese revolution, an echo of the Spanish revolution, brought him back to Europe. He appointed his youngest son, Dom Pedro, as regent. But the Cortes in Lisbon stubbornly insisted on reviving a completely outmoded colonial system and this touched off an emancipation movement. To stave off complete disaster, Dom Pedro sought support from Brazilian monarchists who wanted independence but not a republic. On September 7, 1822, independence was proclaimed and on the 12th of October that same year, Dom Pedro became the constitutional emperor of Brazil. The last Portuguese garrisons were driven out the following year and the Lisbon government finally recognized this *fait accompli* in 1825. All South America was finally free.

Latin America's Political Personality

It would be very tiresome to examine or even to mention the innumerable constitutions, revolutions, *coups d'etat* and upheavals that have shaken the majority of South American nations ever since they gained their independence. In fact, you always find the same themes in their constitutions, the same bill of rights more or less inspired by the French and American models, the same separation of powers with a bi-cameral or a uni-cameral legislature and an executive power following the American example, and universal suffrage almost everywhere.

All of this verbalism is only an appearance, for reality is found here in personal power. At the time of the conquest, South America was the land of a Cortes or a Pizarro and then of a Bolivar or a Miranda during the glorious days of its independence. By the end of the 19th century, it was that of a Gomez or a Francia and, in the very recent past, of a Peron. Today, it breeds Castros. Even in Fidel Castro's revolutionary Cuba, it is not at all paradoxical to note that men still mean more than institutions or ideologies, even those of Marxism-Leninism.

The Americas invented the president and the southern half of the New World has developed this theme to an extreme. During electoral campaigns, public interest focuses on the election of the president, not of the legislature. For a president does not preside here. He governs. Most of the time, his ministers are there simply to carry out orders. This love of all-powerful presidents naturally has led in South America to abuses of power to the extent that the checks and balances serving as a brake in the United States do not work here. This is why political power in most South American countries since independence has oscillated between the "caudillo" acting as the agent of a land-owning aristocracy and the "caudillo" who appears as a demagogue to shake the masses out of their apathy for a brief moment.

The Drive for Self-Sufficiency

Two factors profoundly influenced the political evolution of South America during the early decades of the 20th century. The first was massive European immigration. The second was the replacing of European economic influence by that of the United States, the powerful neighbor to the north.

Political independence and the transformation of former colonies into full-fledged nations have not solved all the problems of this continent with its enormous natural and strategic resources. Far from it. Without things always appearing very clearly, purely colonial rule has been replaced in a number of cases by a form of collective trusteeship by the major powers and then by direct but vigilant control by American interests.

Today, the No. 1 problem of most South American countries consists of achieving a true and total sovereignty—that is, the economic independence without which all political independence is nothing but an illusion. They are in various stages of this evolution explained by the fact that some are behind the others.

The flow of white immigration from Europe that has submerged South America began during the second half of the 19th century and then developed throughout the entire beginning of the 20th century. Since 1850, more than ten million Europeans have gone to South America, mainly to the southern regions:

Argentina, Uruguay and Chile, and the south of Brazil.

Other regions and particularly Andean America were relatively neglected even though they had been the main goal of Iberian conquerors hungry for gold and precious minerals.

During the year 1910 alone, nearly two million emigrants left Europe and almost half of them headed for Brazil and the countries along the Rio de la Plata. This flow dried up only with the human hemorrhage of World War I and the great depression of 1929 and the 1930s which hit the economies of South America so closely tied to those of Europe and North America. But it started again before World War II and immediately afterwards.

Brazil, even more than Argentina and Uruguay, has been radically transformed by this immigration, not merely in its racial structure but above all in its industrial structure and efficiency. An Indian and black country at the beginning of the 18th century, Brazil is becoming within the last few decades a white country and a great industrial power.

This immigration obviously helped make South America a complement of Europe's economy by the beginning of the 20th century.

World War II did not make a great impact on South America except to force a rearrangement in her patterns of trade. Although all the countries joined the Allied cause enthusiastically, only a few sent any troops to participate in the fighting, and Argentina did not enter the war at all until it was clear the Axis would be defeated. After the holocaust, the rest of the world ignored South America as the task of rebuilding Europe and Asia was begun. The tremendous boom in the economies of Western Europe, Japan and North America was not matched in most Latin countries.

Lethargy and political mismanagement played an important role in the unhappy course of events in South America after 1945, but the most significant factor in the unrest on the continent was the decline of world markets for many of the vital products of the Latin countries. Copper, bauxite, coffee, tin and meat had all experienced a fall in comparative prices at some point during the war. The social unrest resulting from a continuous decline in jobs available and from spiraling prices during brief periods of economic boom combined with new attitudes toward government learned by the masses through the new communications media. By 1959, the situation in many countries was ripe for revolution. In Cuba, the lid blew off the boiling kettle.

The emergence of Fidel Castro as leader of the Cuban revolution was hailed by nearly everyone in both Americas, but it was not long before he revealed himself, not as the harbinger of a better life for Latin America, but as the bearer of a rigid Marxist ideology. With the enthusiasm of a convert, Castro began to export his own brand of Western Hemisphere Communism to other

Latin countries, and it was not long before officials in the United States and in other American nations began to wonder how the crude appeal of Castroism to the discontented Latin Americans could be countered.

Alianza para El Progreso

It is obvious that one of the reasons why the United States launched President Kennedy's plan of an Alliance for Progress was to thwart Castro's attempt to take over the continent. The Cuban regime boasted that it had already received millions of rubles from the Socialist camp, but America replied by offering 20 billion dollars to be distributed over ten years among the twenty nations of Latin America—with the exception of Cuba, of course. But the Kennedy plan also corresponded to Washington's legitimate and sincere desire to take a new approach to the problems of Latin America. For too many years, the United States had been accused by its southern neighbors of practicing a "big stick" policy—that is, an almost exclusive use of force to settle international and inter-American problems. As proof of this attitude very much in evidence from the beginning of the century to the eve of World War II, Latin-Americans cite the annexation of that strip of Panamanian territory wrested from Colombia and intervention by the Marines in the Caribbean, particularly in Haiti and the Dominican Republic, and in Nicaragua. In those days, some of the greatest Latin-American writers—like Juan José Arevalo, who served as president of Guatemala—used the fable of the shark and the sardines to describe hemispheric relations (with you-know-who cast as the shark). Certainly, there were many attempts made before the Kennedy plan to aid South American nations, but the Alliance for Progress was undoubtedly the broadest and the most generous undertaking of them all. Unfortunately, the intentions of the Alliance never really came to fruition, for the social, political and economic reforms implicit in the agreement never seemed to get implemented.

In fact, the signers of the Punta del Este charter assumed certain responsibilities and accepted a certain number of precise conditions in return for Washington's promise of massive aid. All Latin American countries accepting the Kennedy plan agreed to carry out a series of political and economic reforms destined to improve the welfare of their people. Here is the essence of these reforms: strengthening of democratic institutions, speeding of economic and social development, urban and rural housing programs, agrarian reform, campaigns against illiteracy, public health programs, improvement of working conditions, tax reforms and the protection of consumer purchasing power.

This short summary immediately allows one to grasp the scope of these intended reforms and the fact that this was an ideal declaration of intentions for the development of a group of nations as large as Latin America. It was agreed that the annual economic growth rate in each Latin American country signing the Punta del Este charter would not be lower than two percent. It was also agreed that illiteracy would be completely wiped out and that every school-age child in Latin America would receive at least six years of primary schooling. It cannot be denied that the charter of the Alliance for Progress went to an extreme in its efforts to nail down every last detail of future prospects. Consequently, one is forced to admit that this program was much too broad and much too ambitious, considering the frightful backwardness of most Latin American nations. This charter contained too much hope and severe disappointments were bound to come.

The apparent "benign neglect" by the Nixon and Ford administrations resulted in the almost imperceptible demise of the alliance.

The continuing turbulence in South America is no more evident than in the manner in which the continent has reached its present state. Countries previously racked by international strife and turmoil, such as Venezuela and Brazil, have emerged as surprisingly stable and prosperous nations. (It is interesting to note that Brazil thrives under a military regime, while Venezuela has enjoyed an unbroken record of four democratically elected presidents.) Argentina, on the other hand, one of the richest nations on the continent, cannot achieve economic stability because of fluctuations in her political course. Chile has sought to solve its difficulties, first with Salvador Allende's socialist government, then with a right-wing military regime, but basic social and economic problems remain unchanged. The only left-wing military regime in South America, Peru's military junta, has forced some major social changes, particularly a sweeping agrarian reform that ended centuries of feudal injustice in the countryside. By the end of last year (1975) 25 million acres of land had been redistributed to peasant families. But such reforms have been at the cost of many liberties, including a once politically diverse press. In the remaining countries no spectacular changes have transpired. None could be described as prospering.

Towards Economic Planning

When the Alianza was first inaugurated, the picture was not pleasant: while the cost of living in the United States had risen only eight percent between 1958 and 1964, for example, the index in Argentina was up 360 percent; Uruguay, 310 percent; and Chile, 230 percent. Brazil, the most extreme case, saw a rise in the cost of living of 1,500 percent! In more recent years, this runaway inflation has been somewhat mitigated; Brazil, in particular, has made enormous economic strides. But like the rest of the world, inflation is once again on the rise in most of the South

American nations, fueled by the energy crisis and inflated imported goods. Chile, for example, suffered a staggering 370 percent increase in the cost of living in 1974.

Attempts to copy the European Common Market with an 11-nation trade union known as the Latin American Free Trade Association have met with only limited success. However, the association's offspring, the six-country Andean Group, is vigorously pushing ahead with multilateral development projects and a set of common ground rules for foreign investment, including the gradual take-over by nationals of a majority control of such important sectors as banking and insurance. These new rules, or limitations, reflect an economic nationalism barely perceived in the past. Oil concessions, for example, are now looked upon as politically antiquated and economically foolish, no matter what the coloring of the government, Bolivia's right-wing military regime or Colombia's mildly progressive democracy.

Accompanying this new nationalism is a shift in political influence to the north, where oil-rich Venezuela has joined with neighboring Colombia, the two being the only stable democracies on the continent, to counter-balance the traditional poles of power in Brazil and Argentina. Using its enormous oil wealth to promote a series of novel—for Latin America—economic schemes, the Venezuelans hope to solve one of the continent's major economic headaches, the perennial swings in price in basic commodities on which so many of the area's economies depend. To shore up the Latin Americans' faltering coffee cartel, for example, Venezuela provided an $80 million loan to enable the coffee producers to maintain a stable price; similar aid has been offered to the fledgling banana cartel. The total Venezuelan commitment to its neighbors will reach $500 million, some of which may be spent in developing Latin American multinationals.

The successful example of the Organization of Petroleum Exporting Countries (OPEC) has spawned a bevy of cartels which, in addition to coffee and bananas, include copper, bauxite, meat and sugar. While none has OPEC's clout and few have been successful in stemming the recent (1975) slide in commodity prices, they signal the South Americans' desire to experiment with new solutions to traditional economic problems. With the gap between industrialized and developing nations rapidly widening, many of the South American countries find that for every step forward that they take, they are actually moving two backwards. For example, the cost of a Jeep two decades ago was 124 sacks of coffee. Today it is 344 sacks. Every time the world price per pound of coffee drops by one cent, the coffee-producing countries lose millions of dollars.

South America has made enormous strides forward, to be sure. One has only to compare a 10-year-old photograph of the cities of Bogotá, Caracas or Quito with the startling changes evident today in skyscrapers, freeways and urban suburbs to see the scope of that progress. But while thousands of new classrooms and hundreds of thousands of new houses have been built in recent years, these are not sufficient to keep up with the statistical race. With the world's highest birth rate, South America is unable to expand services fast enough to stay abreast of the exploding population. South American sociologists calculate that even if the birth rate were zero, it would take the continent's governments 15 years to build all the necessary schools, hospitals, houses and factories for the current population.

While there are several underpopulated areas that could absorb part of the explosion, such as Patagonia in southern Argentina and the plains, or "llanos," stretching across southern Venezuela and Colombia, the investment in infrastructure necessary to encourage settlement of these lands would be astronomical and certainly beyond the means of governments already in debt building services in populated areas. Brazil's Amazon Jungle often is cited as the world's last undeveloped farm land, a potential breadbasket of the continent, but agronomists and ecologists have made it clear that even if the capital necessary were available, it would be economically unfeasible. Once the delicate ecological balance of the forest is destroyed, the Amazon basin would turn into a largely barren desert.

In any case, few South Americans want to stay down on the farm. Usually one of the poorest segment of the population, the peasant dreams of going to the cities where, hard as life may be in an urban slum, at least it offers the possibility of education for his children, medical services and some small chance of a better future. Thus, there has been a massive population shift away from rural areas. While South American cities accounted for only 40 percent of the continent's population in 1950, the proportion is nearly 60 percent today. At the current rate of growth, these cities will double in size by 1990.

Traditionally an agricultural exporter, South America eventually will have to import many of its food items just to maintain the margin of malnutrition that is the lot of one-third of the population. While an extreme example, oil-rich Venezuela suggests a frightening pattern. Once an exporter of cattle and sugar, the country now imports 50 percent of the food it consumes. The United Nations' Food & Agricultural Organization (FAO) calculates that food production must increase by 3.6 percent annually in order to keep up with the population explosion and still allow for agricultural exports, but South America is unable to sustain this growth rate. And so the food exports that contribute to world supplies may decline, disrupting the world market and prices across the whole spectrum of food production and consumption, from farmer to housewives, around the globe.

No matter how poor or undernourished the South American, he possesses that one symbol of mass consumerism, the transistor radio. Consequently, even the most isolated peasant on the Peruvian altiplano has some inkling of what is going on in the world and a measure by which to compare his poverty-stricken lot. If he lives in a city slum, the South American becomes acutely aware of what he is missing. The display windows, the advertisements, his transistor radio, all awaken a desire for consumer goods he cannot afford. Out of his frustration grow the political tensions and the brief violence that periodically shake Latin American cities. But it is not violence of the stuff of revolutions. The decline and fall of so many South American guerrilla groups have demonstrated the inability of would-be revolutionaries to organize and inspire the largely apathetic masses. As Chile's former President Salvador Allende noted, "The Andes are not the Sierra Maestra (in Cuba)."

If Cuba was the political event of the sixties for South Americans, Allende's rise and fall is the most significant happening in the seventies. Although left-wing Castroite groups still are active in several countries, notably Argentina, much of Cuba's earlier romantic attraction for the disaffected young has faded with a normalization in diplomatic and commercial relations with other Latin American countries and the gradual detente with the United States. The Chilean experience is more recent and closer to home, and what it suggests is that in a continent of strong traditions and powerful political interests, it is impossible to change too much too soon. At the same time, there is a growing awareness of the need to develop South American definitions instead of borrowing unworkable political models from the United States and Europe.

It is a time of awakening, of searching for South American solutions and a growing sense of the unique character of South America in the developing world. Out of this awakening is emerging a more mature solidarity than anything the Liberator Simon Bolivar could have hoped for, a togetherness evidenced in the budding commodity cartels, in the Venezuelan aid program and in the unison of voices with which these countries now speak out on international affairs.

South America also is a young continent, with three-quarters of the population under 30, and it is these young people who offer the area's best hope of progress. Better educated than their parents, impatient with old political models, they are at the same time more skeptical of alignment with super powers, the Soviet Union or the United States. Whether they work within the "status quo" or attack it, they are highly nationalistic, desiring South American solutions to South American problems.

The outlook for the immediate future, however, is clouded, with Argentina locked in a death struggle between extreme right and extreme left, and Chile in a state of economic and political prostration. After a brief experiment in free elections, Brazil once again has slammed the lid shut on political freedom while Uruguay and Paraguay continue to be governed by military regimes. Peru still follows its peculiar course towards tentative reform. Ecuador, awash in new oil dollars, is learning to manage an economy not entirely dependent on bananas. And to the north, Colombia and Venezuela are trying to cope with the population explosion and rural migration while maintaining democratic institutions at the edge of a sea of dictatorships.

Whatever the political hue of the government however, each accepts the principle of political pluralism, because dictator and democrat realize the need for unity for economic reasons, particularly in trade relations with the United States. There also is an increasing give-and-take in the area of South American experiments in solutions to South American problems. Thus, Colombia has gone to Chile to learn how a developing country should build plants for frozen foods. The Chileans, in turn, have come to Colombia to study the Colombians' successful experiment in diversifying exports to reduce dependence on coffee and to create more labor-intensive, competitive exports such as clothes, cut flowers and pop-up books, in all three of which Colombia is one of the world's largest exporters to the United States. With Snoopy and the Three Bears earning millions of dollars for Colombia in pop-up books, it is obvious that little things can mean a lot for the developing economies of South America, once they move out of the groove of dependence on a single commodity export.

One of the brightest elements in the picture of South America today is the new cooperative spirit evident in the field of tourism. There is an increasing effort to promote South America collectively, as a total continental travel package, instead of 13 individual countries. This new attitude is showing its first results at a time when travel to other continents by North Americans is declining. South America, which had the opportunity to grab the lion's share of the North American travel market immediately after World War II (when Europe lay in ruins), is generating growing interest in the USA and Canada today. As a testing ground for closer cooperation between Latin American nations, tourism may yet show the way to the governments concerned, proving that a continental sense of cooperation may be one of the answers to the region's innumerable problems.

Not all of the South Americans' economic experiments are successful, of course, but increasingly they are based on the pragmatic view that what is good for the industrialized world may not necessarily fit the economic and social peculiarities of South America. After 150 years of independence, South America at last is beginning to search for its own economic and political identity. The outline is only now beginning to emerge, but however the picture looks when finished, it will be entirely South American.

The people of South America are as varied as their cuisine.

Photo: Pan American World Airways Inc.

Rio's Sugar Loaf has come to symbolize the whole South American continent.

Photo: E. Fodor

Tiles and tropical fading mark most of the continent's old churches, as this one at Ouro Preto.

The high altar at La Compañia in Quito, Ecuador, highlights the richest Jesuit church in South America.

Photo: *Pan American World Airways Inc.*

THE SOUTH AMERICAN MUSE

Color, Music and Daring Vision

Color, costumes and music are, of course, among South America's most unique and best appreciated attractions. The reason is that this music, this folklore and these costumes are authentic and real. They correspond to something that is alive and pays no attention to the tourist. The two great influences found here are the same ones that have played such a determining part in the forming of human categories: the Indian and the black. Music that is Indian or inspired by Indian themes runs right down the *cordillera* and overflows considerably onto the great plains of the south. Black rhythms reign all along the Caribbean and Brazilian coast. Yet, when you go from country to country, you find that these influences vary depending upon the temperament and the remoteness of the people. The famous Mexican *rancheras*, for example, are heard and highly appreciated far beyond the borders of Mexico and Central America. These *rancheras* that sound both too sad and too gay when you hear them played every evening by *mariachis* in the Mexico City suburb of Tenampa have reached Venezuela and Colombia where they are almost more popular than purely national airs like the *cumbia* of African inspiration that is played on the Colombian coast. Indian influence takes over in Ecuador, Bolivia and Peru where traditions are stronger and more deeply rooted. The same holds true for costumes. The poncho worn by the Indians of Bogota is purely symbolical. It is just a little rectangle of brown wool worn down the back and known as a *ruana*. It has nothing in common with the true poncho, so ample and so gaily-colored, worn by men and women in the three principal Andean countries. As for the derby hats worn by Indian women, they have a history and a meaning of their own. White in Cochabamba valley, they are black near La Paz and Oruro and brown in Sicuani on the high plateau sloping toward the Cuzco.

South American dances are very gay in Venezuela where the famous *joropo* recalls the *sardane* of Catalonia in some ways, but they become stiffer, more hieratic and graver in the Andean countries. There, the dancer no longer seeks amusement. He wants to forget himself, to fall into a daze by spinning and spinning until he achieves exhaustion. An Indian ceremony on the altiplano is always stupefying. These men and women who are so stingy with their gestures and so in love with silence in their daily lives are transformed for a few hours or a few nights into whirling prancing masks invoking the gods of the past and the idols of today to celebrate a birth, a marriage or a death. And no explanation of this metamorphosis can be found on these faces that hardly move and continually reflect the eternal indifference of these people from the depths of Asia who constantly seem to regret all that they have not known.

In Chile and in Argentina, folklore is already more European and less startling—even in Chile, the country which would appear to be the end of the earth by definition but which actually is one of the closest to Europe in its heart, mind and culture.

Everything changes again in Brazil, celebrated the world over for its wild rhythms, African feverishness and natural taste for the gaudy, the unusual, the absurd, the spectacular and the uninhibited. This is another world on the Atlantic side of South America, a world of *macumbas*, *candombles*, *sambas* and magic. But the magic has already been commercialized in many cases, and it takes a great deal of luck or persistence to be able to watch an authentic ritual ceremony. Occasionally, just by accident in some coastal village during the night . . . women appear as if on a stage. dressed in vari-colored skirts and with red flowers planted in their mops of curly hair. One of them might be waving a hatchet under spectators' noses, another might be holding an open bottle of rum. Or they might not be waving or holding anything. When a roll of drums draws near and the torch-bearers make their bow, then the *Pai do santo*, the father of the saint, also arrives. He is often a tall graying mulatto who stares somewhat disapprovingly at the strangers who have slipped into the first row of the audience. He is the organizer and the ruler of the ceremony. The two priestesses keep on gesticulating somewhat confusedly and it is hard to tell clearly if they are possessed by a demon or simply a little tight, judging by the snickers of the village men. Then, solemn and dressed in long white tunics, the daughters of God appear in their turn. With their eyes closed and their faces ecstatic, they clap their hands to accompany the dull pounding of the sacred drums. They make believe they are brushing their tunics as if they were flicking away imaginary specks of dust. Undulating to the steadily-accelerating rhythm of the drums, they move backwards and forwards. They seem to be riding invisible horses with their legs bowed and trembling. They moan inarticulately as they echo the guttural screams of the first two women leading the game. For this is a game and it goes on when all the village's men join the dance. Sometimes, but not always, a man or a woman may really go into a cataleptic trance, losing all control as if in the grip of a furious attack of epilepsy. Nine times out of ten, the whole thing is faked and in Bahia, for example, the police have a list of addresses where *candombles* are scheduled to be held. In other words, they are organized in advance. On the other hand, the procession at Bahia dedicated to Yemanja, the goddess of the sea, is a traditional and authentic ceremony. To get into the good graces of Yemanja, an African Lorelei who followed black slaves to Brazil, the people of Bahia make offerings to her: mirrors, cakes of soap, combs and perfume. To the beating of ritual drums on the 2nd of February every year, the priests of the Yemanja cult solemnly march into the water, climb into a boat amidst general rejoicing and head out to sea so that they will be on time for their appointment with the goddess.

As for the Carnival at Rio, it is hard to say anything that has not been said a hundred times before. It is the revenge of the black man who storms down from the *favelas* into the broad avenues in the heart of the old Brazilian capital and, every year, it sets the tone of Sambas that will be heard around the world. But the Sambas are only one aspect of this musical riot that is a religious feast, an outburst of delirium and a trance all rolled into one. It is on this occasion that every carioca leaves his everyday personality at home and chooses the disguise of the man he would like to be: a cowboy or a bandit. The dancers face each other but each is lost in an inner dream impossible to communicate.

Architecture of the Sun

Architecturally speaking, no other country has been transformed in such a short time as Brazil. Less than four centuries, in fact, have gone by from the discovery of Brazilian jungles to the building of Brasilia, that futuristic city of the year 2000. Brazilian architects who can rightfully claim some of the world's top rungs have established in the 20th century an architectural tradition that is closer to Brazilian reality and meets the requirements of soil, climate, materials, and local ways of life.

Construction of the University City and the Ministry of Education in Rio began around 1934. On the basis of the new school inspired by Le Corbusier, Gropius and Mies van der Rohe ran up a long list of achievements. Two factors have contributed to this blossoming of an original style of tropical architecture. First of all, there was the problem of the sun. While São Paulo tries to get as much sun as possible, Rio does everything to avoid it. The second factor was the use of reinforced concrete. Broad expanses of glass protected by sunbreaks, *pilotis* with open ground floors, use of azulejos of all colors (those azulejos imported by the Portuguese in the 16th century), close harmony between architectural forms and the sculpture and paintings used to decorate them . . . there you have the dominant principles of this widely-admired architecture. Naturally, it was at Brasilia, the symbol of everything Brazil would like to be, that this new school—men like Niemeyer, Lucio Costa, Rino Levi, Roberto Burle Marx and the late Alfonso Reidy—have given free rein to their imagination and talent. Seen from the air, Brasilia looks like a gigantic bird standing wings outspread on the red earth of the Goias plain. The basic plan of the new federal capital was a cross designed by Costa, but its axes have gradually curved as work went ahead. The official buildings begin on the Square of the Three Powers: the seat of government with the executive palace built on concrete colonnades, the palace of the legislative assembly where the Senate and the House of Representatives are lodged in concrete seashells, and the third power, the High Court of Justice, whose building is built in the same style. The cathedral that never fails to intrigue newcomers is built further away. You reach it through a long dark tunnel. In this city where everything is a symbol, or tries to be, the faithful are struck by light as they emerge in front of the altar. Brasilia has attempted to win the favor not only of foreigners but of Brazilians. The least that can be said today is that the actual transfer of government from Rio to Brasilia is not being carried out at the rate foreseen by Juscelino Kubitschek, who was president of Brazil from 1955 to 1961. (The transfer of the government and of foreign embassies will be completed, it is hoped, within a few more years.) A good many political and human factors explain the delay but it is doubtful that the Brazilians could change their minds at this point even if they wanted to. And the blacks of Recife sing: "If I owned Brasilia, I would pave it with diamonds so Nono could walk there . . ."

THE FACE OF SOUTH AMERICA

BRAZIL

Colossus of the Continent

BY

DAVID ST. CLAIR AND GUY LYON PLAYFAIR

(David St. Clair is a former Rio-based writer and art critic and former correspondent for Time *and* Life *magazines. He is also the author of* Macumba in Brazil *and* The Mighty, Mighty Amazon. *Music, architecture and the cinematic arts are presented by Guy Lyon Playfair, a British-born journalist and amateur musician, who has lived many years in Brazil and has written extensively on all aspects of Brazilian life.*

Editing, revision and some writing were handled by Bill Williamson, an Iowa-born newspaperman who has spent over 20 years in Brazil and since 1960 has been editor and managing partner of the Brazil Herald, *Brazil's only English-language daily newspaper.)*

"Seja bemvindo" or Welcome to Brazil.

If there is one word to sum up this amazing country it is "diversity." It is so big and covers so many square miles through all sorts of vegetation that there is nothing that is "typically" Brazilian. The tourist coming here will find everything he expected, and lots more he never dreamed existed. He will be enchanted with the natural beauties (both scenic and feminine), delighted with the friendship and smiles of the people, shocked at the poverty and ignorance, exhausted during the pagan Carnival madness and touched by the Catholic piety. He will relax on the beaches, have a nervous breakdown driving in the traffic, gain weight by eating the rich food and lose it by dancing a wild samba until dawn. He will be delighted with the "tomorrow is another day" attitude, exasperated if his airplane is hours late. He can wear heavy sweaters and eat beefsteak with the gauchos of the south, and the very next day be sweating in a pair of bathing trunks and eating alligator steak in the Amazon. He can take pictures of himself in front of colonial slave blocks in Bahia or in front of a 33-story all-glass air-conditioned office building in Rio. He can spend a week and go away satisfied that he has seen Brazil. He can live here for years and still not know the country.

Diversity is everywhere. The people are a mixture of Portuguese settlers, indigenous Indians and imported Africans. To this have been added peoples from Italy, Germany, Poland, England and even from faraway Japan. The language also has been touched by this diversity. In the south a pair of men's socks are called "capim." In the north they are called "meias."

Diversity manifests itself even in religion. The Vatican likes to call Brazil "the largest Catholic nation on earth," but a large percentage of Brazilians attend macumba or candomblé services regularly, pray to gods that are mixtures of the Christian and the pagan and wear both a cross and a voodoo charm for good luck. Children study catechism at church classes, but when they are left alone with the maid they are instructed in the age-old African rites. The diversity pattern can be seen in the larger cities with modern office and apartment buildings planted right beside sprawling favela slums of wooden shacks and tin can thatched roofs.

The tourist with a little bit of time can taste this magnificent diversity for himself. Spend a day or two in Bahia sampling the 17th-century Portuguese and African atmosphere, take a plane to Rio and savor its almost European charm. Then go to São Paulo where you dine in the very best international restaurants and live it up in air-conditioned hotels amidst the bustle of business as usual. Grab a plane headed west and have the pilot put you down amidst the primitive stone-age Indians of the Xingú river basin. You will have visited the equivalent of four different countries and spanned dozens of centuries, yet you will have been in Brazil all the time.

A Glance at Brazil's History

Brazil was discovered in 1500, just eight years after America. How Columbus missed this giant of the Western Hemisphere and touched down upon little San Salvador remains one of the mysteries of that era. Spain was badly in need of new territories and when they put all their money on Columbus they made a mistake, for Portugal was also in need and they backed a sea captain named Pedro Alvares Cabral. The Portuguese king was in a land-grab race for the new colonies with the Spanish rulers, and both of them wanted as much as they could get in the shortest amount of time. There were great things coming out of India that could be sold to fill the royal coffers, later to be converted into ships and arms and manpower to dash across the seas again and grab more land. It was a national pastime. It was a vicious circle.

When Cabral sighted Brazil he thought that he was seeing India, but upon landing and finding none of the expected Maharajas or a road clearly marked "Cathay," he reasoned that he had discovered someplace new. He thought it was an island and sent out a search party to walk around once and come back again. The party started out but whether they ever returned is not recorded in history, for what Cabral had stumbled upon was not an island, but the biggest hunk of land to be claimed in the entire New World.

The Tupi natives were friendly and naked, much to everyone's surprise and pleasure; and after celebrating Mass, Cabral left a few men to watch his new country and hurried back to Portugal with many samples.

They referred to the new colony as "The Island of Santa Cruz" (Holy Cross); later when their error was discovered they called the new colony "Land of Santa Cruz." But with the coming of merchant ships from the mother country and the vast exporting of a hard wood called "brazil," the people of Portugal began to refer to the place as "The Land of Brazil." From there it was an easy step to calling it simply Brazil.

The Portuguese Move In

The Portuguese were not harsh masters. They made friends with the Indians, and though they looked for golden temples and lost cities, they didn't start slaughtering right and left when they failed to find any. They were more interested in trade, and the long coastal lands of their new-found colony were richer agriculturally than anything the Spanish had been able to claim.

Farmers arrived from Portugal to set up huge sugar and spice farms. They plowed from the present day city of Olinda down almost to Rio. The land was rich, the nights cool, and there was lots of elbow room. But workers were scarce, and imitating their Spanish enemies, they set out to enslave the local Indians.

The Indians would have none of it and ran deeper into the jungle rather than submit. The delicate Tupis were not accustomed to toiling long, hot afternoons in cane or cotton fields and died off rapidly. So slaves from Africa were brought in. Swooping down along the coasts of Angola, Ghana and Senegal, Portuguese slave traders attacked villages, killed off the weak and shackled the strong. The trip to Brazil was long and rough and many died on the way, but those that managed to survive the voyage were brave, proud and aristocratic and accepted their condition manfully.

Soon great wealth was flowing to Lisbon, and the Royal coffers were expanding from the raw materials the Portuguese traded with the rest of Europe. So envious were the other land-hungry nations of the era that the Dutch, French and Spanish all tried to encroach on Portugal's claim. Much of her new wealth was spent in keeping the intruders at bay.

While riches were being reaped from the soil in the northeast, other riches were being dug up in the mountains to the south. No sooner had the present site of Rio de Janeiro been put on the map than thousands of fortune hunters poured through it on the way to the mines of Minas Gerais. Here were what seemed like entire mountains of amethysts, aquamarines and diamonds waiting to be scooped up. A procession of miners and trouble makers took over an area many times bigger than Alaska and in comparison made the Gold Rush of '49 look like a Girl Scout outing. For along with their thirst for gems they brought with them a taste for the better things in life. Wealth made them remember how the nobility had lived back home, and as soon as a miner had enough to live, he wanted to live well. By the boat-loads from Portugal came carpenters, stonemasons, sculptors and painters to build churches, palaces and cities in the Brazilian wilderness. Up went such architectural treasures as Ouro Preto and Diamantina. There were gas lights and golden horse-drawn coaches in the streets and gem-studded and silver ornaments in the churches. Lace came from Europe to adorn milord's cuffs, and actors and musicians brave enough to make the trip from Portugal had diamonds tossed to them after their performances.

The Flag Bearers of Empire

Other men were busy too. A hardy group of adventurous, bloodthirsty crusaders banded together near what is now São Paulo and set out to find more diamond mines and more riches. Carrying the flag of the new colony, these "Bandeirantes" (Flag Bearers) pushed out in all directions, claiming each new step for Portugal. There had been a treaty of Tordesillas signed between Portugal and Spain in the year 1494. It was the idea of Pope Alexander VI, who wanted as little blood spilled in the New World as possible. Both sides agreed to the dividing of the southern continent in a straight line from what is now Belem on the Amazon River to a little east of Porto Alegre. Everything to the west belonged to Spain, everything to the east to Portugal.

Fortunately for modern Brazil the Bandeirantes knew nothing of this treaty, or else didn't have a compass. For they spread out over thousands of miles, planting their banner on the banks of the Amazon to the north, Paraná to the south, and on the Paraguayan and Bolivian frontiers to the west. Spaniards, so busy with wars and Indian enslavement, hadn't any idea what was going on in the heart of their lands. When they finally woke up it was too late, for the Brazilians had claimed it all.

Brazil was ruled by Portugal for many years; then when Napoleon captured Portugal, the royal family fled to the new colony. It was like a shot in the arm for the New World. At once the exiled royal family opened the ports of Brazil to trade with some European nations, especially with Napoleon's enemy, England. Then when the French were defeated, the king, Dom João VI, went back to Portugal and left his young son Pedro I to govern. But Pedro had ideas of his own and did away with a number of reforms his father had set up. He proclaimed Brazil's independence on Sept. 7, 1822. As a new nation, Brazil had a long way to go and a lot to learn; but the royal family lived well in a series of palaces heavy with silver chandeliers and brocaded chairs. So unsure was the nation and so ineptly governed, that after a series of costly wars with Argentina and Uruguay, Dom Pedro I stepped aside in favor of his son Pedro II, who was only five years old. A series of regents then came into power and managed so badly that parliament finally decreed Dom Pedro II "of age" when he was just 14.

Then came almost half a century of peaceful and fruitful ruling on the part of the Western Hemisphere's only Emperor (if you don't count the short reign of Maximilian in Mexico), who mingled with his subjects, made a trip to the United States and declared that he would rather have been a school teacher than an emperor. Under his constant vigilance the nation prospered, trade agreements were signed, an attempt by Argentina to take control was put down and slaves were freed. But a democratic movement was brewing in the military, and in spite of progress and prosperity the army took over and banished Pedro and his royal family back to Portugal. On November 15, 1889, the Republic was born.

Thankful for the Nighttime

From here on out, Brazilian history grows dull with the parade of easily forgettable presidents and minor revolutionaries. There were all sorts of problems that needed to be solved, and very few able men around to solve them. Brazil stuck mostly to what the U.S. was doing politically, while staying close to France for its cultural instruction. Politicians made a number of efforts to gain power at the expense of the nation but the proud giant, in spite of them, kept growing. A popular Brazilian saying is "We must be thankful for the nighttime, because God makes the politicians sleep and keeps them out of mischief."

Brazil has had very few actual internal wars and has never had a real, bloody revolution à la Spanish-American style. There have been some skirmishes among the gauchos in the south (blame it on their Spanish blood), and once in 1932 the state of São Paulo took on the rest of the nation. It lost.

Getulio Vargas was a strongman who took over in a military coup in 1930. The country was horrified, but soon liked the idea of having one man in charge and did very little except grumble against him. When he was deposed by another military coup in 1945 he sat out his exile on his home ranch in Rio Grande do Sul and prepared for the elections. In 1951 he was elected—legally this time—president of the Republic and right beside him rode his protegé João "Jango" Goulart, later to govern the nation. Vargas tried to be more democratic this second time around and supported labor unions and the like, but still that old obstacle, Latin military, was against him. After a long period of interoffice fights and counter charges, the tired old man put a pistol to his heart and pulled the trigger.

After him came President Café Filho, and then the dynamic spendthrift Juscelino Kubitschek. Kubitschek built Brasilia from a dream into a multimillion dollar reality and put industry and commerce on a fast pace to compete with the rest of the world.

His immediate successor was Janio Quadros, a thin man with a thick moustache who insisted that everything be done exactly his way. He wrote little notes that became law, and tried to squeeze the growing giant of a nation into a special form that he never quite defined. Under some pressure, he suddenly resigned one day in August 1961 and threw the nation as close to a civil war as it has ever come.

The successor to Quadros was leftist-leaning, rabble-rousing Jango Goulart, the old pupil and confidant of Dictator Vargas. The military wanted little of Jango and his friends, and above all did not want the plans and mass platitudes of Vargas back again. In a dramatic ten days, the military kept Jango—on his way home from a trip to Red China when Quadros resigned—out of the capital and virtually a prisoner in his home state of Rio Grande do Sul. Congress hastily voted in a Parliamentary system, drastically curtailing the President's powers, and Jango finally took office, managing to persuade the people to vote the old presidential system back the following year.

Under Goulart the country seethed with strikes and instability. Prices soared to an all-time high and red-tinged politicians were appointed to key positions all over the nation. Goulart himself became swayed by ambitious leftists and many Brazilians feared for their country as never before. Then on March 31, 1964, Goulart was overthrown by the military. As before, the revolt was virtually bloodless, and while Goulart and his family fled into exile in Uruguay, the army clamped down and installed one of their own men, General Humberto de Alencar Castello Branco, as president. Again, Brazil had a military government, but this one was different. The Army seized Brazil by the scruff of its neck and shook it—hard. Sweeping reforms paid dividends as inflation began to drop, exports to rise, and overall growth to move out of the red where Jango had left it to a steady 10 percent within 5 years. Hundreds of old-time politicians lost their political rights, and two new parties replaced the countless former ones. In 1967, Castello Branco handed over the presidency to Marshal Costa e Silva, who closed Congress and made things difficult for dissident students and labor leaders. Upon his death in 1969 he was replaced by General Emilio Garrastazu Médici, who continued the Army's reform policy, strengthened the economy, waged war on illiteracy, and initiated bold development plans for the Northeast and Amazon regions.

Médici was succeeded in 1975 by retired General Ernesto Geisel, son of German immigrants and Brazil's first Protestant president. Geisel, who was previously head of the state petroleum enterprise Petrobrás, maintained most of the policies which brought about Brazil's "economic miracle" at the same time he tried to bring more political liberty and equitable distribution of wealth.

Brazil Up to Date

When you stop and remember that most Brazilians in the cities have an education that goes only to the eighth grade and that many in the interior who have but three or four years are considered "educated," you will marvel that anything has been done to improve the country at all. Ill-housed and ill-fed people cannot be depended upon to worry about anything but themselves. Give these people jobs and a sense of dignity and they will start to be concerned with their problems.

In spite of its backwardness, its communication and transportation difficulties, the Brazil of today is on its way up. It has shown more gains in manufacturing, exports, agricultural and educational improvements than any other nation in Latin America. Above and beyond the desire to put everything off until tomorrow and go to the beach today, there are many men who are doing things for their country.

The population of São Paulo is now over 8 million and Rio around 7 million inhabitants. Industrially speaking São Paulo is now the heartbeat of Latin America economy. It has few unemployed, and an intelligent system of social services and public improvements. Across the nation highways are being cut through jungles and over mountains. Twenty-five years ago the road between the two cities was unpaved and impassable during the rainy season. Today, there is a double-lane toll freeway, partly financed by U.S. aid. But although highway construction has been a top priority of all post-1964 governments, there are still only about 42,000 miles of paved highway in the whole country, little more than the U.S. had in 1840.

In order to manufacture, Brazil needs power and lots of it. In the past few years she has built huge plants in the Paraná River area that service São Paulo, one in the interior of Minas Gerais and two others in the northeast. The mighty Urubupunga will be the second-largest hydroelectrical power plant in the world. With this energy, Brazil manufactures enough plastics, textiles, automobiles, toys, canned foods, cement and chemicals to satisfy the home consumer without importing. But she must import some steel, wheat, rubber, petroleum, some paper, tractors and machinery for both light and heavy industry. Economists predict, however, a likelihood of her becoming self-sufficient in food and many other critical resources by 1978. The country continues to hope enough oil will be discovered offshore to bring self-sufficiency in that area too. The petroleum crisis caused a drastic slow-down in Brazil's "economic miracle," and for the first time in decades the national oil monopoly Petrobrás invited private foreign companies back to search for oil under risk contracts.

With respect to health, the government has been busy with the eradication of malaria, and today the mosquito is to be found only in the remote regions and not in the cities. Efforts have been concentrated in Belem and Manaus to stamp out the dread Chagas disease that comes from the bite of little beetles. The Butantan Snake Farm in São Paulo has been doing great work with venoms from snakes, spiders and scorpions making antidotes for the bites and supplying them free of charge to doctors and interior clinics. Hospitals are being built all over the nation, but the problem of persuading doctors and nurses to leave the big cities to staff them remains. Almost every town has a free clinic that is open day and night for anyone who needs attention; they do everything from set broken legs to deliver babies.

Many efforts have been made in recent years to update the country's education system on all levels, starting with a nationwide literacy campaign and ending with university reforms. Secondary education has been restructured to stress the practical arts and sciences more heavily than preparation for university; previously, the system turned out a huge surplus of poets and politicians, but too few plumbers, scientists or computer programmers.

Brazilians are eager to learn. Private courses proliferate everywhere. Under the government-sponsored Rondon Project students are visiting remote areas of Brazil and finding out what makes their country tick—or what failed to make it tick in the past.

Geographically Speaking

Brazil is just too big to generalize. You can't say she is flat, or that she is hilly, that she is covered by jungles or that she is dry desert. You can't say she is, yet neither can you say she isn't. She is, in one part or another, all of these geographical things, and as she can be different in her food, her customs and even her people, so she can be different in her land make-up.

People get set ideas of Brazil's geography either from seeing too many picture postcards or remembering too many Hollywood films. Actually a great part of this enormous nation consists of hilly uplands, plateaus and low mountains. There is a vast plain that stretches far into the Amazon region and another that spreads out through the Mato Grosso and into Bolivia and Paraguay. The Brazilian highlands that meld politically to become the Guiana highlands are some of the oldest geological formations anywhere on earth. These hills are granite and other tough stones that are heavily veined with gold, diamonds and a variety of semiprecious stones. The Serra do Espinhaço ("Spiny Mountains") that run from northern Minas Gerais to Bahia also contain iron ore, gold and manganese. Here the highest mountain in central Brazil can be found, old Pico da Bandeira ("Flag Top"), which stands 9,482 feet. Two more recently discovered peaks in the state of Amazonas are even higher—Neblina (Haze) reaching 9,889 feet. One of the world's largest lava plateaus is to be found in the south of Brazil. Termed the Paraná plateau, it is covered with dark, purple-colored soil that is excellent for raising coffee. Along the coast rich deposits of oil have been found.

The eastern side of the Brazilian highland descends abruptly into the sea and has been given the name "The Great Escarpment." There is no coastal plain but a sloping and a series of steppes that continues far out into the water. All along this there is a series of small rivers and sandy beaches. Wide expanses of white sand reach from way above Recife down past the Uruguayan border. Some beautiful, unspoiled beaches can be found in the far north and the far south. The sands in the states of Paraná and Santa Catarina, for example, are solid and pure. The lack of tourists and year-round dwellers keeps them that way. This combination of sand and escarpment has given Brazil some of the finest natural harbors in the world. Rio is perhaps the best known, but the harbors at Santos, Bahia, Recife, Sao Luis, Vitória and Ilhéus have contributed greatly to the wealth of the nation.

All That Water

Brazil's rivers are some of the longest and deepest in the world. For scientific study, they've been broken into three major systems which drain the country's highlands. The first, in the north, is the mighty, almost unbelievable Amazon River, which accepts the waters that pour down through jagged peaks, lush jungles and rich plateaus. Its tributaries sound and look exotic and offer the visitor who is not afraid of discomfort some of the most unforgettable experiences in Latin America (see the chapter on Exploring the Amazon). There the great Tocantins and the Araguaia flow. There are the mysterious and unexplored Xingú, the rubber-laden Tapajós and the Madeira. To the far west runs the impressive, and almost unknown, Rio Negro.

The second river system gathers the waters from southwestern

Minas Gerais and empties them into the placid yet treacherous Paraná. The water on the western slope of the São Paulo Escarpment flows until it reaches the sea by joining the Rio de la Plata near Buenos Aires.

The third system is that of the largest river wholly within Brazil, the almost legendary São Francisco. Beginning in the plateau near Brasilia it flows northward for over a thousand miles until it pours into the sea between the states of Sergipe and Alagoas. Navigable and studded with power plants, the São Francisco has been the main artery to the heart of Brazil for generations.

Visitors come here expecting to suffer from the heat, and when they don't it is always a pleasant surprise. The Amazon area usually hovers around 80 degrees Fahrenheit, but the humidity-filled atmosphere makes it seem higher. In January of 1963 the thermometer recorded the hottest day in Rio's weather history: 104 degrees in the shade. And this was exactly the same time that the United States was freezing with temperatures of 25 to 30 degrees below zero. Rio usually has a soft warm 73 degrees all year round. The seasons are just the reverse of what they are in the United States and Europe. The cold days in Rio (average temperature 65) come in June and July; the hot days from January to March. In the south of the country a yearly frost is common, and in some parts of Santa Catarina and Rio Grande do Sul snowfalls have been recorded.

Rains should give the tourist nothing to worry about. They come up quickly and go away just as fast. In the Amazon it rains every afternoon for an hour or so from January to June. In the northeast it seldom rains, but when it does it really pours. In Rio a steady, all-day drizzle is more likely in the months from December to April (but not *every* day so don't plan your trip around the rains) than the rest of the year.

The vegetation in Brazil is of many sorts. In the Amazon Basin and those places along the coast where the rainfall is very heavy, there is a tropical rain forest where broadleafed trees and shrubs grow to gigantic proportions and as many as 3,000 different species of trees have been catalogued within a single square mile. Through these tall shady trees very little sunlight manages to filter down, and consequently the ground is rich in decaying foliage and industrious bugs and small animals. In the northeast, lack of rain has produced a parched desert of hundreds of square miles, where cattle and humans die together in their search for water. In the south huge stands of pine trees grow wild and are used in the manufacture of paper. There are open prairies that start in São Paulo state and run down into Argentina to form the Brazilian pampas. In the northeast rain forests stand the huge Jacaranda trees and the very wood that gave the nation its name, the Brazil tree. The Jacaranda is a hard, beautifully grained dark wood almost like mahogany. Most of the fine colonial furniture that one sees in the antique shops was made from this wood. Durable yet attractive, it is one of the most sought-after materials in use today.

King Coffee

That a country as big as Brazil used to be a "one crop" country was always amazing to outsiders. They looked at the hunk of land that dominates the Latin American map and tried to imagine the entire United States living from an economy of tomatoes or cucumbers. Yet Brazil, with all her size and with all her population, has managed to do just that until recently. Her economic history has been a succession of various agricultural "kings."

First there was King Sugar. He was the earliest to establish himself on the new lands. The Portuguese crown eagerly awaited the money that he gave to the Royal coffers. The climate along the coast, from far below Bahia to way above Recife, was perfect for his growth. It was hot and muggy with abundant rainfall. It added to the nation's prosperity, population and culture. Then other empire builders like Great Britain and France began to plant and sell sugar on the world market. The Brazilians had to lower their prices and improve their quality to meet them. But the English-speaking and the French-speaking peoples preferred their own sugar, put high tariffs on the Brazilian product and almost drove it completely out of competition.

Fortunately King Rubber was just coming into his own in the Amazon. There were all sorts of uses being made from him in the United States and in Europe. Once it had been discovered that rubber could be vulcanized for longer lasting and more efficient service, there was almost no industry that didn't want and need Brazil's crop. The town of Manaus grew to international importance. Jenny Lind came to sing there. Men lit their cigars with ten dollar bills and housewives sent their laundry to be washed and ironed in England. Supporting all this luxury were thousands of Indian, black and white day laborers, working deep in the malarial jungles under slavelike conditions. The rubber trees grew wild and had to be worked where they were found. Planting them produced no rubber at all. Then an Englishman visited the interior and smuggled out a few hundred rubber seeds which he took to Indonesia and cultivated. There the trees flourished, and in seven years Indonesia was competing with Brazil. The Brazilians, proud and overly sure of themselves, refused to lower their prices to meet the new competition. Buyers flocked to Indonesia and almost overnight King Rubber was dethroned.

But the throne wasn't vacant long. First in the State of Rio de Janeiro, then in São Paulo, Coffee declared himself King. Coffee had become an important cash crop in southern Brazil, and with rubber out of the way, all energy was devoted to increasing coffee production. São Paulo had the ideal climate of chilly weather followed by warm and rainy days. There was fertile land that was more European in makeup than in Bahia or other places. There was also the added advantage of Italian and German immigrants who wanted to be farmers and raise a cash crop. With everything working smoothly, coffee soon became the most important national product and Brazil depended heavily on it.

Coffee actually built the gigantic industrial city of São Paulo. With the money the growers got from the exports and the taxes the state got from the growers, new industries were started and new ideas tried. There were even many small industries that sprang from the by-products of coffee. The protein in coffee is used to modify certain oils and tars. The carbohydrates are used in the making of cellulose, dyestuffs and plastics. The coffee bean oil is used in dozens of varied industries. While production has increased elsewhere, particularly in Africa, Brazil remains the world's biggest coffee grower. Surpluses have disappeared, due in part to controls imposed by the International Coffee Agreement, and more recently because of the severe 1975 frost that destroyed much of the following two years' crops. This resulted in the big increase in world coffee prices (proportionately greater in Brazil, perhaps, than abroad) and brought King Coffee back from less than 25 percent of Brazil's export income to more than one-third in 1977.

If Brazil is a country of contrasts in its geography and its peoples, it's also a contrast in its economic levels. Though it has a large and rapidly growing middle class it is still a country of the very rich and the very poor.

The visitor is very much aware of the slum shacks. You can't help being. At first glance the favela slum sections in Rio, nestling into the mountainsides in the south zone seem to be pastel-painted, enchanted summer cottages with magnificent views of the ocean. Then on closer inspection you can see that there is no enchantment, just bleak despair and resignation.

The favelas themselves began back in the year 1897 when soldiers of the new Republic, having put down a revolt of the Monarchists in the state of Bahia, suddenly found themselves without a cause, without money and without a place to live. They had been encamped on a hill they named Favela because of the abundance of a wildflower with the same name. So when they arrived in Rio, they called their first settlement of shacks "favela" too. The soldiers assumed they had the right to any land that wasn't being used, and once their shacks were built there were few politicians willing to incur their wrath by driving them off.

The years from 1920 to 1940 saw the favelas grow alarmingly. Brazil was entering into world trade and needed more coffee, cocoa and fruit to export. Workers deserted the cities for the farms, cultivating the land and shipping the produce to the coast. Then prices began to fall and with the fall the workers returned to the cities, along with other peasants who had lost their jobs. They took up residence in the favelas. When Dictator Getulio Vargas set the wheels of industry into motion, he made great promises to the Brazilian people. More flocked to the cities to work. From the north, truckloads of "nordestinos" converged upon Rio, anxious for the easy money but unlettered and untrained in mechanics. They found little work and much misery.

As Rio expanded her metropolitan area, cut through roads and erected new buildings, the poor were routed and tenements demolished. Land was plentiful in the far suburbs, but the working groups (maids, bus drivers, washerwomen) could not afford to live away from the centers of activity. Transportation was sporadic and expensive. The free schools and clinics were in town, not in the outlying suburbs. They were not truly free to move to the fresh air of the distant suburbs, for necessity bound them to the favelas.

The racial mixture of the favelas has been classified by the Census Department as 28 percent white, 36 percent black, 35 percent mulatto and 1 percent oriental.

Although some major favela eyesores have been entirely removed in the last few years, many still remain and nearly a fourth of Rio's population still lives in them.

The choice sites in any favela are at the bottom near the road and water supply. Many times there will be just one pump for hundreds of people, and those living at the top have to fill empty cans with water and carry them on their heads to their homes.

Sanitation is almost unknown and garbage and slops are simply tossed out of the window. Here dogs and pigs root, flies breed and children play barefoot. Worms and parasites infect them all and early deaths are common. Hands are seldom washed as they take a grimy plate filled with rice and black beans. Cooking is done on tiny wood-burning stoves in the centers of one-room shacks. When it rains the water pours in through the cracks in the wood slat walls or down across the flattened tin cans used on the roofs. Many times a family of ten will share one of these cubicles.

Work in Rio has been slow due to the large number of people to be rehabilitated. Welfare groups have been active in building better housing and in giving free lessons in mechanics, carpentry and the manual arts. A number of the poor of Rio have been moved into individual concrete houses, financed originally through the Alliance For Progress but now under projects financed domestically. Unfortunately, while these moves have solved some problems, they have created others. Many ex-favelados now live up to 25 miles out of town, making transportation a heavy expense, and although they are being encouraged to buy their new homes on the instalment plan, many cannot afford the low monthly payments and once again face eviction.

THE BRAZILIAN WAY OF LIFE

What is a Brazilian?

The people of Brazil are a symphony in colors. There is no other nation on earth where such a wide spread of skin tones from whitest white to yellow to tan to deepest black are all grouped under one nationality.

The pride and joy of this gigantic nation is that it has less racial prejudice than other countries with a significant mixture of colors. The "black revolution" currently going on in the United States could almost never happen in Brazil, even though it has a large number of blacks with most of them living under very bad financial and educational conditions. A man may be black but he rides anywhere on the bus that he likes. A black woman may be in rags, but if she is ahead of a well-dressed white woman in a shop, the ragged one will usually be attended first, the well-dressed one will wait her turn. The clerk in the shop would probably never think of passing the colored one to favor the white.

This relatively happy mixture that makes Brazil and Brazilians really began way back in the colonial days when the first Portuguese sailors were left to manage the new land. They were sailors and they were men, and like all sailors and men they felt the need of feminine companionship. They took to calling on the local belles in the nearby Indian villages, found them most friendly and cooperative and when the Portuguese ships came back to the new land for them, there was a whole crop of babies at the dock.

These babies were looked upon as the rightful heirs of their white fathers and shared every legal status that the fathers had.

There was never any question about it. "Miscegenation" (a word coined by Americans in 1863) started right from the first.

When the black slaves were brought into the Bahia and Recife areas to work the cotton and sugar fields, no one thought anything about it when the white master took up "friendly relations" with one of the more comely African women. When she bore his child, the child bore the father's last name. There was even a law that when a child of a slave and the owner was baptized, the father could declare the child and the mother freeborn during the ceremony. The father knew that the mother would stay on and work for him and that she needed a place to rear the child. Making her free just made her more attached to her benefactor, and she raised the child teaching him to respect and be grateful for the "patron" that gave him his birthright.

In the old plantation houses it was quite common for a man to have both a white wife and a colored one, both sets of children growing up free and equal in the eyes of the father. Many times the mulatto son turned out to be the smarter and more gifted, and it was he who inherited the lion's share of the plantation on his father's death.

This mixture of white and black and Indian today forms the base of what is simply called the "Brazilian race." There is no hesitancy on the part of any Brazilian to declare that he has black blood.

In spite of the many thousands of African slaves imported over the years, it's very difficult to find a "pure" black. The inter-marriage has been so easy and so complete that no one thinks anything of it. To see a light-skinned girl walking arm in arm with a dark-skinned man in Rio is not out of the ordinary. There are no taboos, nor even snickers or shocked stares, though there might be an adverse reaction in more conservative parts of the country.

Indians and Immigrants

It is easier to find a pure Indian. In the center of Mato Grosso and in the Amazonian states, tribes still roam along the watersheds and the deep jungles exactly as they did thousands of years ago. Very little is known of their origins. They seem to have none of the ability that the Indians of Peru or Mexico had in pottery or painting but bear remarkable resemblance to the tall proud Poly-nesians. Theories abound as to their origin, many people having the idea that they drifted over the Andes from Peru about the same time that other Peruvian Indians were taking boats for the South Seas. Others say they were always in the heart of the jungle and have been flushed out because of the scientific light of the 20th century. Still others hold them as remnants of the original peoples from the lost continent of Atlantis. Whoever they are, and wherever they came from, they make up one of the most interesting segments of the Brazilian population.

Immigrants also make up a large percentage of Brazil's populace. And once they have become established they are considered Brazilian and no longer as "foreigners." Of all the countries Portugal still sends the most immigrants per year. There are a great number of Italians (especially in the industrial São Paulo area) and many Germans and Poles in the rich agricultural south. A current and very important immigration to Brazil are the Japanese. Many of them came before the Second World War, and a great many more followed. Because of special treaties signed between Brazil and Japan they were given land, special farming equipment and special considerations. What they have managed to do with the land, especially in the Amazon area where they've filled local markets with fruits and vegetables hitherto unknown, is truly impressive. Two Japanese-Brazilians have served as cabinet ministers, and in large measure it is the baseball-loving Japanese immigrants who are responsible for the São Paulo ball team reaching championship level.

All of these races and nationalities have managed to get stirred together in Brazil's melting pot. The country has never known a race riot, or even the slightest unpleasant public incident.

Of Differences and Samba

The Brazilians are a relatively happy people and unlike their Spanish neighbors would rather sing than cry, rather dance than fight. To a Carioca from Rio, everything is a wonderful joke and nothing is really too serious to laugh about. It's even better when a song can be made up about it.

Brazilians are Brazilians and want visitors and the rest of the world to remember that. They are not "Latin Americans" (a term they intensely dislike), they do not speak Spanish (although they understand it), and their capital city is not Buenos Aires (though some tourists seem to think it is).

Their differences all stem from the fact that it was the Portuguese and not the Spanish who discovered and civilized the land. They try so hard to be apart from the rest of the nations on the big leaf that is South America, that sometimes the effect is exaggerated. Their main cultural iron curtain is their language. They are proud that they speak Portuguese and are not at all upset that the rest of the world has yet to master it. They polish their language, write excellent novels and poetry in it, and never bemoan the fact that outside of Brazil, Portugal, Angola and Goa none of it can be understood without a translator.

Brazilians don't like revolutions, wars and fast deaths. They've never had a bloody uprising, don't get overly concerned about politics, and rather than stage bloody riots over food shortages are content to stand patiently in line and wait their turn.

They did not have capital punishment until 1969, when it was introduced for acts of political terrorism that result in death. But so far there have been no executions under the law. Most murderers spend no more than 14 years behind bars for their crimes. While crime exists in Brazil as elsewhere, there have been almost no cases of guerrilla terrorism, kidnapping, hijacking, or assassination in recent years.

The Church of the Spirits

Brazil is officially a Roman Catholic country. The Holy See in the Vatican likes to boast that it is the "largest Catholic country in the world," and at first glance it may appear to be, for there are beautiful churches and cathedrals ranging from the colonial to the baroque to the modern all over the nation. The church owns huge parcels of choice lands in Rio and São Paulo; and in interior towns long-robed fathers and nuns can be seen everywhere. When a president takes the oath of office there is always a priest and a Bible close at hand. Children study catechism, are baptized with the names of saints and attend Catholic schools. Everybody wears a religious medal or two. Taxi and bus drivers have prints of St. Christopher prominently placed, and in June the two biggest winter celebrations are reserved for St. John and St. Peter. To the tourist, overcome with the gold and gems of Bahia's São Francisco church or the impressive concrete modernism of the cathedral designed by Oscar Niemeyer in Brasilia, Catholicism and allegiance to Rome seem to be everywhere. Actually, most of this is on the surface. The real church of most of the Brazilians is the church of the spirits.

The Portuguese brought their religion all ready made to the new colony and planted it right along with the rows of cotton and sugar cane. The Indians had their own gods whom they worshipped and, even when driven into slavery, refused to relinquish. When the African blacks were beaten and chained aboard stinking slave ships bound for the new world, they may have been forced to leave their families and their possessions behind, but they brought along their gods. And what an impressive array they were.

Foremost among them was Iemanjá who while she had been in Africa was the goddess of the rivers and water. There was also Oxalá who was the god of procreation and harvest. Exú was a wicked spirit who could cause mischief or death. There were others of lesser rank, but all powerful, like Ogun, Oxôssi, Xangó and Yansan. They arrived in Brazil together with the slaves who, when things were going badly, turned to the gods of their homeland.

The Catholic Church was naturally against this, threatened excommunication to the whites who did not control their slaves' religious outbreaks, and threatened corporal punishment to the slaves themselves if they continued to believe in their old gods. The slaves, most of whom came from the very best and aristocratic native tribes, were smart enough to realize they couldn't fight the priests but would have to compromise. So they took on all the ritual of Rome but didn't take their old gods from the high places.

Many times all they did was give the African god a new Christian name. Thus Iemanjá became the Virgin Mary and was queen of the heavens as well as queen of the seas. Oxalá, already most powerful in Africa, became the most powerful in Rome, Jesus Christ. Exú, full of evil to begin with, became Satan. Ogun became St. Anthony, Obaluayê became St. Francis, Yansan, St. Barbara, and Oxôssi was turned into St. George. On their altars along with the sacred white feathers, the magical beads and the bowls of cooked rice and cornmeal were placed plaster statues of the Virgin, Christ and gleaming crosses. The Roman Church was content to let matters lie, hoping for an eventual dying off of African tradition over the years and a strengthening of Christian beliefs. Which hasn't been the case.

Bahia is still the stronghold of the voodoo religion, which they prefer to call "Candomblé." Rio holds second place with its powerful "Macumba" and Recife is third with its spiritist doctrine called "Xangô." Visitors to all three places—as well as almost any small town across the nation—can witness a voodoo ceremony. All it takes is an arrangement with someone who knows the right time and place, and the patience and good manners to sit through the ceremony once you get there.

Rites on the Beach

There is no stranger, more pagan sight in all Latin America than that which takes place on the sands of Copacabana Beach each New Year's Eve. Travelers who have seen things all over the world still stare at this with fascination and disbelief. For under the warm, tropical sky with the tall modern apartment buildings for a background, literally thousands of voodoo worshippers meet to pay homage to Iemanjá, the goddess of the sea.

The end of the old year is a time for thanksgiving and the beginning of a new year the time to ask for the things that will make you happy for the next twelve months. From all over the city stream the faithful, determined to start the new year off right. They are of all ages, both sexes, and all colors and economic brackets. Armed with fresh flowers, candles and cachaça cane alcohol, they invade the beach around ten P.M. and get ready for the stroke of midnight. Some draw mystic signs in the sand. Others lay out a white tablecloth loaded with the gifts that a proud, beautiful woman would like to receive. There are combs, mirrors, lipsticks, hair ribbons, perfumes and wines. Around this offering they set a chain of lit candles and chant and sing over it. Some of them bring bouquets of flowers with notes asking for special favors tucked in among the blossoms. Even whole spiritist temples show up in full force, with their white costumes, their drummers and their altars. They rope off a section of the beach, light candles and begin to dance. Others bring a live chicken or a goat that will be sacrificed to the goddess.

By 11:20 p.m. the six-kilometer-long beach is a mass of white-dressed bodies and flickering candles. From a distance it looks as if it has been invaded by millions of fireflies. Amid the worshippers, the curious and the tourist may freely wander, if he is careful not to step on an offering or to offend the goddess in any way.

At exactly midnight, fireworks, sirens and bells can be heard from all parts of Copacabana, Ipanema and Leblon beaches. Now the festivity reaches its maximum. Shrieking, sobbing and singing, the mass of humanity rushes into the water carrying the flowers and gifts for the goddess. Others stay patiently on the shore waiting for the third wave after the stroke of midnight to come up and claim their offering. Be it hypnotic suggestion or whatever, the waves suddenly seem to grow in size and come slapping onto the sand with a new fury. Once the water has carried the gift into the sea, the giver relaxes and goes home, for this means that the goddess was satisfied with what he gave and has promised to grant his wishes. If the ocean should throw the offerings back, this is considered an ill omen.

Legends and Folklore

In a country like Brazil that is composed of so many different ethnic groups, whose history is filled with pirates, African slaves, wild Indians, gold and rubber fever, and strange primitive religions, there is bound to be a rich supply of legends and folklore. The tales of ghosts, witches, special cures and magic words stretch from the cattle country of the south to the cobra country of the Amazon.

Most popular is a little fellow named Saci-Pereré. He is a small black who wears a red nightcap and hops around on one leg. He is typically Brazilian in his sense of humor, his ability to get himself into and out of trouble, and his habit of playing jokes on unsuspecting stuffed shirts. Normally found in the forest, he has come with modern times to the city as well and stirs up problems while continuing to smoke his long-stemmed pipe. He can make food burn in the pots, frighten cattle, and startle lonely travelers on dark roads. Sometimes he makes himself seen, but most of the time he is invisible. Brazilian children, in order to escape the blame of a bad deed, tell their parents that "Saci did it."

If you go treasure hunting in Brazil and your soul is not clean, the only thing you'll find for your efforts will be lumps of coal. And pregnant women should be careful of an Amazonian demon called Caruara who shoots arrows into their backs and makes them suffer until the baby is born.

There's another more dangerous creature roaming the Amazon

forests called the Capelobo. It has the body of a human but is covered with long, silken hair. In place of a face it has an anteater's head, and when it comes across a man wandering in the jungle it grabs him, crushes him with an embrace and sucks the victim's brains out. The whites in the area say it is the spirit of an Indian. The Indians claim it is the spirit of a white.

November 2nd is a religious day, consecrated by the Catholic Church, corresponding to Memorial Day. A devout Brazilian would not hunt or fish on this day but would visit the cemetery, buy flowers, light candles and pray that all the spirits that are set free just for that day won't harm him. He must also stay out of places where a man was killed or where someone died, for the first place the spirit returns is to the scene of his death. Should it have been a murder the spirit will strike down the first living person he sees there to avenge himself. Needless to say the cemeteries in the backlands (as well as in the cities) are crowded on that day.

The Figa

The one folklore item that every visitor notices almost immediately upon arrival in Brazil is the *figa*. It is a hand, usually the left hand, with the thumb sticking up between the first and second fingers that have formed a fist. It is probably one of the oldest amulets against the evil eye in the Western Hemisphere. It symbolizes fertility, passion and good luck, wards off envy and jealousy and keeps wicked spirits at bay. They are made of almost anything from wood or plastic to turtle shell and even gold, silver and precious stones. They also come in sizes so small that they can be hidden behind a gold cross on a necklace or as big as a real human fist. Because it does so much good, you can't just go out and buy one for yourself. Someone has to buy it and give it to you as a present. Many tourists buy them for their traveling companions, and the companion turns around and buys one for the first purchaser. If you have no one to buy one for you and you want to wear one, go ahead. It won't bring you bad luck, but it won't bring you good luck either. Another important thing: if you lose your figa, do your utmost to find it; because while it's not on your person all the bad luck that it has warded off will come crashing down on you.

The Brazilians are great holiday lovers. They use any excuse to take off a day from work, close the banks, stop the wheels of industry and just stay home doing nothing. They take full advantage of every religious holiday and celebrate all the civic ones as well, both state and federal. All in all they have 10 days set aside as official holidays. (Americans working in the Embassy or Consulates get another nine because they celebrate their country's holidays as well!) Christmas Eve is celebrated by decorating the house with a manger scene, putting up a small imitation pine tree and enjoying a midnight supper. On Christmas Day, however, everyone relaxes. Gifts are given out on Christmas Eve, but another bunch are handed to the children on January 6th which is the Day of the Three Kings.

Good Friday is celebrated all over Brazil with masses and candle-lit parades through the streets. Usually the most prized figure of Christ is taken out and put in the center of a procession, draped in black. While a chorus of the faithful (in some interior towns it is the entire population) follow behind chanting funeral dirges, the image is carried up one street and down the other and later returned to the church. When Easter morning dawns, it is just like any other old Sunday. There are no special celebrations, no Easter finery, but families go gather for luncheon.

Dia de São João

One of the most popular days of the year is June the 23rd, the feast day of São João (St. John). Everywhere his birthday is celebrated, both in the cities and the interior towns. He is considered one of the nicest saints in the heavenly collection and enjoys good music and a good drink just like his earthly believers do. Because he sleeps all day, the Brazilians make huge bonfires at night and send up fireworks to explode in the sky. This will wake him up and he will come down (in spirit) and join in the fun. Streets are roped off and people dress in backlands clothes. A mock marriage is performed, complete with drunken priests and an irate father holding a shotgun to the groom's back. Single women leave a pan of water outdoors the night before and on St. John's day will see the face of their husband-to-be reflected in it. Also if a spinster puts two needles in a pan of water the night before and wakes up to find them together on the saint's day that means marriage is not far off. Another way is to write the names of various possible husbands on pieces of paper, roll them up and drop them into a bottle filled with water. On St. John's day, the name that is unrolled will be the future husband.

The Flamboyant Fine Arts

Art in Brazil is as varied, far-flung and exotic as the country itself. There is nothing that can be labeled "Brazilian art," in just the same way that one can't say "Brazilian climate" or "Brazilian scenery." The distinct mountains, rivers, desert areas and jungles have separated artistic endeavours into regional groupings as they have separated the people themselves. The lack of communications as well as the lack of an understanding, culture-conscious people has kept almost all art forms identified with regions rather than with the nation as a whole. Those artists (i.e., painters, sculptors, writers) who have managed to create some ripple on the national scene soon find that only a small percentage of the people are interested in what they have produced. These people tend to be the intellectuals, upper and café society of large cities, and critics of daily newspapers. Consequently, and perhaps unknowingly, the artists strive to please this small percentage and end up by conforming to their wishes.

It's difficult to say who is the "best" Brazilian painter today. A number of artists have risen to the top fast, been declared "King" and then suddenly died. Perhaps the man most revered by the nation, and whose canvases now sell for small fortunes, was Candido Portinari. He was the first one to paint his way to international fame. Coming from a small coffee plantation in the interior of São Paulo, he experimented with Brazilian themes and colors and was never really satisfied with the results of his labors. Once he sent for 60 pounds of earth from different areas and mixed the black, purple, reddish and yellow dirt with his paints. Because of this his whites were more brilliant and his shadows had more depth, which served perfectly to portray the humble people he captured on his canvases. Being the first man to paint backlands scenes in addition to the glamor that the art world attached to his just being Brazilian, soon made Portinari world famous. He did such an expert job on the murals for the Brazilian Pavilion at the 1939 World's Fair that American art critics insisted that he send an exhibition to the United States of his other works. It toured 200 cities and encouraged the University of Chicago to publish a book on him. In 1962 Portinari died, the victim of slow lead poisoning from the very canvases he made live. The entire nation went into mourning. His old house in Brodosquy, where he was born, is now a national museum of his works.

The current "king" of the nation's art world is a rotund, white-haired beatnik, now nearly 80 years of age, named Emilio di Cavalcanti. A born Bohemian, he came from a family of poets and generals, yet caroused in the underworld of Rio with prostitutes and professional thieves. He painted only what he felt like —which was usually seductive mulatto women—and scorned upper society. After he and a group of friends startled the Brazilian art world in 1922 with an exhibit of French impressionists and cubists he went to Paris and drank with Picasso, Ernst and Chirico. On his bright canvases, everything he has lived through is applied. In vivid tones of green, yellow and red, surrounded by thick black outlines, he paints full-blown black women or a smirking cat with all-knowing eyes.

Clay Into Art

Regional art is varied, interesting and unfortunately breakable. The best things being done are the ceramic jugs, dishes, plates, statuettes and nativity scenes from Bahia northward. Most of the village markets are full of earthenware products, made in the region for use right at home. People adapt themselves to their locale, and in areas where there was good rich clay, it was quickly molded into kitchen utensils. While not so elaborately painted as the Mexican ware nor with a tradition so far back as Peruvian pottery, Brazilian ceramics can definitely stand on their own merit. In the north most items are molded into pleasing shapes, be they animal, human or just spheres or cubes, and fired to a bright red color. Then they are hand painted with white floral and abstract designs.

Music

Brazil is one of the world's most musical countries, and talent flourishes in the tropical climate as exuberantly as the exotic creepers that grow two inches a day. Brazil is well known for having invented the samba and bossa nova, but just take a look at the list of "serious" musicians Brazil has also given the world in this century: composers Heitor Villa-Lobos, Claudio Santoro, Camargo Guarnieri and Marlos Nobre; pianists Guiomar Novais, Ophelia de Nascimento, Jacques Klein, Roberto Szidon, João Carlos Martins and Nelson Freire; singers Bidu Sayão, Maura Moreira, Maria d'Apparecida, João Gibin and Maria Lucia Godoy; guitarists Eduardo and Sergio Abreu; conductors Eleazar de Carvalho and Isaac Karabtschevsky, early music specialist Roberto de Regina and ballerina Marcia Haydée, to mention only a few.

The four musical centers of Brazil are Rio, São Paulo, Salvador and Curitiba. Salvador has the best music school, where many rising young composers have learned their trade from a German-influenced faculty; Curitiba presents an annual music festival that puts anything similar in South America to shame, while both Rio and São Paulo offer a musical season that can match that of many a European capital in quality.

Rio's musical life, like the city itself, is essentially cosmopolitan, with fine musical performances. You never know whom you might discover for yourself at Rio's Teatro Municipal or Sala Cecilia Meireles (a rare example nowadays of a cinema's being converted into a concert hall). One advantage is that you can usually get a ticket if you show up half an hour before the concert, unless a major international star is appearing, in which case book a few days in advance.

Architecture

Brazilian architecture, though it has not fulfilled the bright promise of the thirties, has much to offer both architecture student and amateur photographer. The most striking modern building in Rio, the Palace of Culture, completed in 1945, is now protected as a national monument. When started, it was one of the most revolutionary buildings anywhere in the world, being one of the first to be built on *pilotis*—huge concrete pillars that leave almost all the ground level of the site free for patios, plants and parking areas.

Le Corbusier, a long-time friend of Brazil, was largely responsible for the design, ably assisted by the brilliant Brazilian Lucio Costa, the man who planned Brasilia and the Barra de Tijuca suburb of Rio. Take a stroll among the pillars and gardens of the Ministry for a glimpse of what 20th-century city planning could be like if visionaries like Le Corbusier and Costa had their way. The block it occupies is an oasis of civilized urban delight in one of the world's most overcrowded and underplanned cities. (Students of population explosion may like to study the average Copacabana residential street, where the cars park on the sidewalks and the children play ball in the street, and draw their own conclusions.)

Equally delightful is a stroll around the Rio Museum of Modern Art, designed by the late Affonso Reidy, whose exuberant use of concrete is matched by his structural daring; the whole floor of the Museum's main wing is one single slab without divisions or central supports, and all around are the splendid gardens laid out by Roberto Burle Marx, one of the outstanding landscape gardeners of our time.

From the air, São Paulo looks as if a child had flung all his bricks onto the floor at once, but from closer up you can see that some sort of order is at last being introduced into its chaotic sprawl. Fine new buildings surround the Praça Roosevelt area, near the Hilton Hotel, and a drive through some of the smarter suburbs will show you private Brazilian house design at its best.

For architects, though, Brasilia is the real thing. Despite its many problems, it is here to stay and is a truly great place to visit, wander around and photograph. The air is fresh and unpolluted, the traffic well organized by Brazilian standards, and many of its buildings, like the new Foreign Ministry, are outstanding—though it should be added that Oscar Niemeyer is the most unpredictable of architects, and many of his buildings are considerably worse than outstanding.

Contemporary Scene

The "hippie" generation of Rio and São Paulo offers an interesting and colorful counterpoint for tourists. A hippie art fair is held on Sunday in Rio, at Ipanema's Praça General Osório, and in São Paulo, at Praça da República. Local paintings, sculptures, wood carvings, articles of leather, textiles, jewelry, etc. can often be purchased at bargain prices.

Even more eye-catching are the young surfers on Ipanema beach and around the Castelinho, where the smallest bikinis imaginable are worn by virtually every Carioca girl. They are called "tangas" in Portuguese (from the Indian word for loincloth) and in 1974 were launched in the English-speaking world as "the string."

FUN-LOVING BRAZIL

Girls, Beaches, Carnival and Food

Take the grace of a tall palm tree, add the zest of a breaking wave, put in the sparkle of glistening sand, the brightness of a tropical sun, the softness of a jungle flower and the smouldering fire of a leopard, and you will have the recipe for the girls of Rio. Sugar 'n spice 'n everything nice may be what little girls are made of in Des Moines, Calcutta or Vienna, but when you come to Brazil throw away your set formulas and your preconceptions. It may be a "man's world" but those few square miles that are Rio de Janeiro are definitely woman's domain.

Rio itself is feminine. She lies invitingly curled around a deep blue bay, her body a collage of black and white mosaic sidewalks, tall apartment buildings and tree-covered hills. Her movements are slow and easy, unperturbed by hurrying people or rushing vehicles. Her breath is heavy, sweet and warm. Her eyes are the bright lights that flash out over the ocean and then, as the night grows on and you get to know her better, take on a soft, seductive glow. By day, fleecy clouds and multicolored birds adorn her hair. At night for ornamentation, she uses the stars and the illuminated Christ of Corcovado.

Sitting at sidewalk cafés, strolling along the vast expanses of beach or smiling at you across a room are the girls that dwell in this enchanted city. Exotics, blondes, brunettes, cream colored, browns and ebony blacks, they fill the city with their charm and grace. They tempt you, they promise you and they fascinate you. You can never explain exactly what it is that all of them have that makes them so compelling. It bothers you at first, then you accept it, finally you relax and enjoy it.

Getting to Know Them

How does a guy meet a girl from Rio? The beach! The ardent visitor, his American-style bathing trunks down to his knees (advice: girls think U.S. suits laughable, and want to see all the masculine merchandise packed into a European-style suit) arrives on the beach looking pale but eager. He sits down next to a group of pretty girls, smiles at them and shortly tries out one of the phrases he learned in his Portuguese-English dictionary. This will bring more laughs but there will always be one girl who will want to try out her classroom English. Once this beachhead on a beachhead has been established, it is up to private initiative to take over from there.

For the man who can't find a girl of his own, there's always the oldest profession. On Rio's Avenida Atlantica or Ipanema beaches he doesn't have to look for it, it comes to him. It is nothing for a "touristy" looking man to be accosted five times in five blocks while walking alone. Most of these women are those that are no longer admitted to the regular prostitute hangout bars (of which Copacabana has aplenty and all are within walking distance of the swank hotels) and who must ply their trade on the streets. They'll offer all sorts of pleasures, and any number can play.

International experts all agree that Rio women know how to dress. There are many small, inexpensive and rather elegant shops in Copacabana where a girl can get the very latest French or Italian design in a blouse or skirt. Rio girls wear a lot of sports clothes, and since most of them have maids ($60 a month will get you one) their clothes are always freshly washed and ironed.

Rio women also look good in evening wear. Those that can afford it have their gowns flown over from Dior or Balenciaga. Lately many local dress designers have become internationally famous. Some of the most important are Guilherme Guimarães, Denner, Zuzu Angel, José Ronaldo, Hugo Castellana, Clodovil and Hugo Rocha.

Rio girls are very culture-conscious and love good symphony music, an opera or a ballet. They traditionally would flock to the old Municipal Theater in the heart of the downtown business district—a quarter-scale model of the Palais de l'Opéra in Paris. With this landmark now closed for renovations many today go to the smaller Sala Cecilia Meireles for cultural events. Into this Old World setting come the dark-eyed, raven-tressed daughters of the New World. On gala opening nights, ensheathed in silks of red and gold, their hair in the latest European fashions and tastefully adorned with diamonds or pearls, they sit in the curving gilded balconies and offer a spectacle better than the one being played

ENJOY *RIO!*

1978 TOURIST CALENDAR

JANUARY   Pre-Carnival Festivities Brazilian
                   Car-Racing Championship

FEBRUARY   Carnival
                   1978 Carnival Champions-Parade

MARCH   413th Anniversary of the City
                   of Rio de Janeiro Festivities

APRIL   Orchestras Meeting

MAY   Brazil Travel Mart – BTM RIO-78

JUNE   Launching of 2nd Fabulous Samba
                   Contest Carnival Winner's Night

JULY   2nd City of Rio de Janeiro's
                   Bycicle Tournament Cup

AUGUST   2nd Fabulous Samba Contest.
                   Tourist Folklore month.

SEPTEMBER   Finals of 2nd Fabulous Samba
                   Contest. Rio Tourist Week.

OCTOBER   Theater Fortnight.
                   1st World Festival of Clowns.
                   Flowers Fair

NOVEMBER   Super 8 – Film Festival

DECEMBER   Christmas Celebrations

RIOTUR
Empresa de Turismo do Município do
Rio de Janeiro S.A.
Rua São José n.º 90 – 8.º andar Brasil

WORDS TO THE WISE

A Few Useful Travel Hints

Whether you are on holiday or have important business to do, after a flight through several time zones give your body's clock a chance to catch up. It is easy to underestimate the effects of jet-lag.

Don't carry all your cash, travellers' checks, passport etc. in the same place, spread them around a bit – and never carry your wallet in your hip pocket.

Experienced travellers travel light. Don't forget that the hand luggage you carry with you onto the plane is a vital part of your travel equipment. Make sure you have your essentials in it, not in your other baggage.

With strikes and the cost of excess baggage always in the background, you would be sensible when flying not to take more than you could comfortably carry yourself – in a pinch.

Don't leave already exposed film in your pockets or in any hand luggage while passing through airport X-ray machines. The process can sometimes fog the film and you may find a whole trip's photographs ruined. Put the film on one side while passing through.

Never make long-distance phone calls from your hotel room without checking first on the likely price. Some hotels have been known to mark up the cost of a call as much as 200%.

Several airlines will provide a cardboard carrying box for any loose items you might arrive clutching at the checking-in desk. It saves leaving a trail of last-minute purchases all the way to the plane.

You would be amazed the amount of free information that you can get from National Tourist Offices to help you plan your trip – all the way from brochures to movies.

Put a tag with your name and address on it *inside* your suitcase as well as outside. It will greatly help identification if the case goes astray.

Never leave valuables in your hotel room – put them in the hotel safe.

on the stage. At intermission time they stand in the open terraces drinking black demitasse cups of hot coffee or cold lemonade. When the opera is over they meet to converse in little groups on the black and white mosaic sidewalk in front of the theater and make dates for the next night before getting into their cars or taxis. If the bachelor tourist on vacation has the inclination for a little culture, as well as an eye for a pretty woman, he will not go away disappointed.

And when the tired, satisfied traveler is once more in a modern jet speeding away from Brazil and toward the responsibilities and conformity of his own land, he will look back at his days spent with the girls of the *cidade maravilhosa* with pleasure and bitter-sweet sadness. If he is wise, he won't try to figure them out. He won't attempt to compare them with other girls that he has known or classify them all under one heading. For years to come he will remember the warm smiles, the exciting personalities and the genuine enthusiasm for being alive of the girls of Rio.

Cult of the Beach

Visitors to this country are always surprised to see how important the beach is to the Brazilians. Not just for those who live in the coastal cities, but even for those who live deep in the interior. Copacabana Beach or the fashionable "Arpoador" section of Ipanema Beach are focal points of life in Rio. From São Paulo, people go down the mountains to Santos to the beach. Gauchos in Porto Alegre fill the beaches during the summer months and the newcomers to Brasilia built their own beach.

Copacabana Beach has no private cabanas, no rest rooms, no place to change clothes. You either arrive in your suit at the beach or else you peel off your clothes right there with your bathing suit on underneath. There is no color line drawn, the rich lie on the none-too-clean sand with the poor, as fruit and soft drink sellers walk over them equally. As one upper-crust American tourist once put it: "It is probably the most democratic beach in the world."

Brazilians begin their beach life early. It is not at all unusual to see tiny babies in wicker baskets soaking up the sun alongside their bikini-clad mothers. When they get old enough to walk they are usually accompanied by a maid who hovers over them and many times gets her aproned uniform soaked when she has to dash into the water to pull them out. Once they are able to leave their maids they go to the beach with their friends. The boys learn to play soccer and to surf, while the girls have fashion shows with their dolls. Later on, these same children will do their homework on the beach, listen to rock music on the beach, meet a "steady" on the beach, show off their engagement rings on the beach and when the cycle is completed bring their newly born babies to the beach.

Almost anything goes there. Early in the morning you can see old men still trying to keep young by a sunrise dip or jogging. Muscle boys cavort there. Bums urinate there. Crooks steal there and politicians even used to campaign there.

Many business deals are closed there too. Often a weary executive won't want to go to all the trouble of putting on a white shirt and tie and will tell a client to meet him at the beach. The client also shows up in a pair of trunks rather than a dark suit and brings his briefcase. In spite of the sand, the fleas and the noise of the shouting people, they manage to get their business done.

There are also many things to buy on the beach. A short list would include Coca-Cola, beer, ripe coconuts, skewered bits of filet mignon, salted peanuts, air-filled crackers, fresh oranges, candy-coated grapes, pineapple slices, bright-colored kites, melting ice cream, sunglasses, beach umbrellas and ladies' bathing caps. The salesmen wander among the bathers and call attention to their wares by blowing on whistles, shouting, singing, beating a small drum or whirling a metal thing that clatters loudly. Keep your eye on your belongings. There may be fast-working kids around, ready to snatch the unguarded purse or camera.

Another annoyance that Brazilians take for granted is the volleyball games that seem to spring up just as you have gotten comfortable and drowsy on the sand. From out of nowhere will appear eight to a dozen young men, their arms loaded down with poles, nets, rope and a leather ball. They plant the stakes, string up the net and mark off their boundaries in a matter of minutes. Many times the unsuspecting beachgoer, when he opens his eyes, will find himself in the middle of the playing field and must make a hasty retreat before the ball starts bouncing. Even those at the boundary lines aren't safe, for more often than not the ball comes sailing out into the crowd, hitting first an umbrella, then a stomach and finally a reposing face. Brazilians, with a disinclination for trouble, just pick up their towels and move elsewhere; it is the foreigners who get furious and threaten to take on both sides of the team at once. There have been laws passed that say a volleyball game cannot be played in certain sections of Copacabana Beach or started before 2 p.m., but they are frequently ignored.

At night the beach takes on a different character. Midnight swimming and fishing is allowed. When the sun goes down, fishermen throw their lines there, prostitutes ply their trade there, lovers sit and talk there, pretty girls stroll by there, fences receive their goods there and maids have sex there. By two in the morning the movement has slowed down and the beach heaves a sigh of relief. There is no one on it except some favela poor covered with newspapers or pieces of cardboard who have no place else to sleep. And far out over the quiet sands, into the pitch blackness of the sea, the lights of a luxury ocean vessel can be seen flickering.

Carnival ! ! !

Then there is Carnival: that fast-moving, mad, unbelievable, music-filled, sleepless time when the entire nation rockets off into orbit and doesn't come back to earth for four days and five nights.

The official season is actually the Saturday night before and the days leading up to Ash Wednesday, but in practice the action starts Friday at 11 p.m. when the first "bailes" (balls) begin. Usually this period falls in February but can also come in March; however preparations are going on months before.

The visitor to Rio will start hearing the strains of Carnival in late December. At first it's nothing more than the gentle throb of drums from the hillside shanty towns, mingled with the ordinary sounds of the city at work. At night the drums get louder and voices are added, chanting a fast, spirited refrain. Soon the visitor notices little dark children parading through the streets, beating on old tamborines, tin cans or the hoods of parked automobiles. Their naked feet dance in the dust of the streets and the sands of the beach. In front of the hotels they go through the motions of a fast Samba looking not only for tips and praise but also for a good time. Then, as the actual season draws closer, their parents and older brothers and sisters will parade through Copacabana in a cacophony of drums, whistles, triangles and a weird, yelping instrument called the *cuica*. They will actually block the entire avenue, causing traffic to come to a halt while people hang out of their apartment windows and encourage them. The police do nothing to set the flow of cars in motion again, for usually they have left their posts and are dancing right in the midst of the revelers.

Stores that normally sell pens, books and ink blotters suddenly deck their windows with coils of serpentine streamers and bags of confetti. Fabric shops, their wares spilling out onto the sidewalks, are crowded with men and women buying bright-colored silks and cottons. Other shops sell laces, stiff crinolines, masks, gold and silver chains and decorated hats. Seamstresses double their prices and sew into the dawn, and all through the city runs an electrifying current of excitement. It affects not only the young but the oldsters as well, not only the Brazilians but the visitors.

Samba Schools Get Ready

This is a good time for the tourist to arrange for a visit to a Samba school, for they are at the peak of their practice sessions and admit anyone who is willing to pay a small admission and sit on a hard bench. The school usually belongs to a certain favela slum, and most of the dancers in it live right there. They rehearse after work far into the night or on Saturdays and Sundays. Each Samba school also has a theme. And the rules of the Carnival commission insist that the theme be Brazilian.

Because they live in poverty throughout the year, they want to "act rich" during the throbbing night of glory; they pick a theme from the days of Brazilian colonial rule so that they can dress in fancy laces and expensive satins, wear powdered curled wigs and billowing hoop skirts. Their theme chosen, they then choose a specially written Samba to represent it and work out a complete dance routine to its rhythm. A Samba school can have as many as 3,000 people in it, each with his own job to do in the over-all pageant.

Such an organization costs money—in any country—and the poverty-wracked members show great ingenuity in scraping up the needed funds. Costumes alone can cost as much as $1,500 apiece which is a lot of money to anyone, especially for a man who earns but $60 a month. The top group of Samba schools parading on Sunday night is the single greatest show of the entire Carnival. Because of traffic problems and subway construction, and most important the need for more bleacher space, the location has changed several times. In recent years, the parade has been on President Vargas Avenue, where bleachers are built over an open drainage canal. For the best seats, in covered areas of the specially constructed stands, order from your travel agent well in advance. Once Carnival starts they are difficult to come by, even at inflated black-market prices. Official costs in 1977 were $20 to $30 for the open bleachers, $40–50 in covered areas reserved mostly for foreign tourists. But many visitors paid $100 for the show and considered it money well spent.

The parades start around 8 p.m. (though scheduled for 6) and end at 10 or 11 the following morning, sometimes even later! Bleacher tickets are good for the other Carnival nights as well, to parades of "blocos," "frevos" and "great associations." If you don't get tickets, the Brazil Herald will tell you where the "secondary" Samba schools fighting to win a place in next year's top 12 will parade. You can watch these for nothing.

The schools have their one night of glory as they vie with one another for the top prize offered by the Carnival commission. To win that top prize is just as important for them—and they practice just as hard—as any U.S. baseball team that wants to win the pennant.

Days of Delirium

Comes the weekend before Ash Wednesday and the city goes insane. Samba is everywhere. Down from the hills stream the poor of Rio, gaudily bedecked in satins and tinsel, their faces powdered or smeared in paint. Out of swank apartment houses come the rich in their costumes costing many hundreds of dollars, laughing and embracing everyone they meet. Entire streets are blocked off from traffic, and Samba bands play twenty-four hours a day for anyone who wants to dance. And everybody does.

The Carnival Samba has no rigid routine of steps that one must follow. The feet move fast, the body shakes from the hips up and the arms are thrown overhead in complete abandon. The music penetrates to the very bones of the Brazilians, and they give themselves to it much as a canoe gives itself to a river's rapids. The tourist seeing this for the first time is aghast; but as his foot starts beating out the music, he discovers himself trying some of the steps he sees around him, and then he is carried by the crowd into the very midst of the laughing, sweating bodies. By this time all reserve is gone, and only hours later, when he has collapsed onto the moonlit beach, does he realize how far away from home he has really come. The next day, now bitten by the bug, he goes completely native.

Carnival is for every man at every level. The poor have their street dancing and their parties in wooden-walled, tin-roofed shacks. The middle class give blow-outs in their apartments or visit a friend who has a home in the suburbs with a backyard to expand in. The rich have their parties at their sumptuous homes in the surrounding hills or go to one or all of the fancy dress balls.

These balls give the visitor a true and intimate picture of the Brazilians at play. Crowded, hot, reeking with perfume and whisky, they are one never-ending confusion of noise, music and bare flesh. Tickets should be purchased in advance from hotels or tourist agencies rather than taking a chance of buying them at the door. For those who don't wish to go to the expense of a fancy costume, black tie (frequently overlooked) is the rule. Business suits and ordinary dresses are not permitted at the better balls. Either you enjoy yourself in a loose costume or you swelter in European formality.

Carnival's Lavish Balls

One of the most exclusive Carnival balls is the "Hawaiian Night" at the Rio Yacht Club. It is held one week earlier beside the swimming pool under the tall palms—and the pool is where most of the sweating bodies end the night's festivities around dawn. Tickets here cost about $20 for members; for guests prices are $30 for ladies and $60 for men (but after the music started last year the latter rose to around $125).

Saturday night's official Carnival ball is the "Baile da Cidade" (Ball of the City) at the mammoth Canecão nightclub, which can pack in up to 6,000 persons. Individual tickets cost about $60— or for a mere $2,500 you can get a box for 10 persons. This includes dinner, which many people don't stop dancing to eat, but drinks are separate; at the Canecão last year they cost from $1.25 for a glass of beer to a little more than $4 for a Scotch. This lavishly decorated "happening" features two orchestras playing non-stop on a revolving stage, and brings out the Governor, Mayor and all the famous visitors to the city. But it doesn't live up to the traditional ball of the Municipal Theater it's supposed to replace, while that building is closed for repairs.

Other leading balls last year included those of the Flamengo Club on Thursday, the Rio-Sheraton Friday, the Hotel Nacional Monday, and the Monte Libano and Hotel Inter-Continental Tuesday. But every night there are dozens of less expensive balls at other clubs—all open to the public and equally crowded and frenzied.

To these balls flock the beautiful women of Brazil. Dressed in costumes that give them a personality as well as the absolute minimum of coverage, they come as Egyptian slaves (short white tunic and silver chains), alpine peasants (thin white blouse and short green shorts), sultans' favorites (gold brassiere and panties with flimsy silk trousers) or one of a thousand other ideas that are guaranteed to display their charms. They may come with a date, but that doesn't mean they will dance only with him. Once onto the crowded floor it is everyone for himself and strangers dance wildly together for a minute then move on to another stranger. Kisses are given freely, seductive glances flashed frequently and passions aroused. Affairs of the heart are started quickly during such dances and end just as quickly once the merriment is over. Cariocas refer to them as "Carnival romances."

When the dawn of Ash Wednesday finally comes to put an end to the revelry for another year, Rio looks as if it has been attacked by Roman hordes. Sleeping bodies lie everywhere. Drunks sit on curbstones holding their heads. Arabs wander dazedly down the center of the avenue accompanied by exhausted clowns, dishevelled Pierrettes and stumbling African slaves. Couples are found in all stages of dress and undress under bushes, beside staircases and in doorways. And while an army of street cleaners start sweeping up the tons of debris, somewhere a never-say-die Samba band can still be heard playing.

Some advice to the inexperienced attending Carnival balls and processions: Leave your inhibitions at home or at the hotel. Dress lightly. Be sure your shoes or slippers are comfortable. Leave papers (except Passport) and your "14 karat hardware" in the safe! Take along only as much money as you intend to spend and your credit card.

And remember: the normal Carioca girl, even though she dances seductively and has only five percent of her total surface area covered, is not—repeat not—necessarily asking for amorous advances. That is one point some newcomers to the scene find hard to understand. So, take it easy, have a good time, and "paciência."

Food and Drink

In any other South American country the tourist can sample one or two plates in a restaurant and say that he has tasted the "national dishes." But just as Brazil is different from the rest of the continent in so many other ways, so is she different when it comes to food. It is good food and in most restaurants it is usually appetizing. What it is, though, is completely strange in comparison to what North American or European are used to eating. Tourists who are finicky eaters probably won't go for Brazilian food. But those who are ready to face anything that offers the challenge of a new gastronomical experience will have a field day here.

A word of history must be inserted if you are really to appreciate the local food. Like the plum pudding and roast beef of England, Brazil's food is also tied up in tradition and happenstance. The food of Bahia is as different from the food of Rio de Janeiro as the food of Rio Grande do Sul is varied from that of the Amazon region. All of it has a reason. Most of it is simply delicious.

Bahian cookery to many people seems to be lots of little things clinging to one another in a rather oily sauce. In the early slave days the Africans were treated none too well as far as food was concerned. Their capturers had told their new masters that the African tribesmen knew nothing of steaks and chops and would eat almost anything. The master usually saved the scraps from the table or leftovers from the previous day to give to his slaves. Some slaves were allowed to fish, and others had permission to look for shrimp and clams. Consequently the black woman had to take advantage of every little scrap of food she could get her hands on. She remembered her cooking-pot training in Africa, put the bits together, added the milk of coconuts or the oil from the dendé palm and fed her family. Over the years these catch-as-catch-can meals took on a regular form, recipes were worked out and names given. Today it is called Bahian food.

Some of the delicacies that are served nowhere else but in Brazil (and no place better than right in Bahia itself) are:

Vatapá, pieces of shrimp and fish, mixed with palm oil and coconut milk, pieces of bread and served over white rice.

Sarapatel, with the liver and hearts of either a pig or a sheep, the Bahia women mix fresh blood of either animal, add tomatoes, peppers and onions and cook it all together.

Caruru, takes lots of fresh shrimp, bright green okra bulbs, onions and red peppers to make it, and lots of courage to eat it.

In Rio Grande do Sul the *churrasco* is the big dish. It is pieces of beef skewered on to a metal sword and roasted outdoors over hot coals. This is served by sticking the sword point into the table and each diner cutting off a hunk with a sharp knife. There is a tomato and onion sauce to go over it if you wish. The gauchos of the interior will barbecue an entire steer this way. There is also a delicious dish called *galleto al primo canto*, which is a rooster of two months old that has crowed for the first time. Cut into pieces, it is placed on a spit, basted with white wine and oil and served crispy and brown. This washed down with a bottle of red wine satisfies any diner's appetite.

Near the mouth of the Amazon a favorite dish is *pato no tucupi* which is pieces of duck in a rich sauce that's loaded with a wild green herb that tingles in your stomach hours after eating. There's also a thick yellow soup called *tacaca* that's laced with dried shrimp and garlic and served on street corners. Once your nose gets used to the strange smell, you'll enjoy this filling and nourishing bowl.

In the northeast, where refrigeration or even ice isn't found very often, leather-clad cowboys have been eating dried meat with beans or some green vegetable for generations. After killing the steer, the meat is heavily salted and hung over fence posts or on sticks out of the dogs' reach to dry in the sun. When the woman wants to make a meal, she lets the meat soak in water overnight and the next day it's ready for frying or boiling.

In Rio de Janeiro the favorite dish is *feijoada*, and no visitor to the city should go away without trying it, unless here in the hottest days of summer, when it is not normally served. It is a thick soup made from black beans and garnished with such delicacies as chunks of beef, pork, sausages, chops and sometimes pigs' ears and tails. This is put over white rice and garnished with a bright green boiled leaf called *couve* and slices of oranges. Originally a dish of the poor folk and those of the interior, *feijoada* has come into its own in Rio. The best day to eat it is Saturday because after one sitting you'll have no energy to do anything but sleep for the rest of the afternoon.

The Brazilians are not vegetable eaters. They live mainly on rice and potatoes are rarely served. They like olives, especially the big black ones from Portugal, radishes and carrots for appetizers. Beans are another staple, as are squash, cabbage and a strange, pale green thing called *xuxu*. Eggplant is served fried, broiled, baked, stuffed and in cracker crumbs called *milanesa*. Unlike the rest of South America very little corn or corn products are used. Hearts of palm are inexpensive and used in salads, soups and baked dishes. In the States a can of them is so dear that they are considered a delicacy. In Brazil *palmitos* are like any other vegetable, even though they have to chop down an entire palm tree to get at the white veined heart in the center.

Vitamins and Alcohol

Nutritionists visiting here often tear their hair in despair at the way a Brazilian meal is planned. There is no regard for what's good for you, or even for whether it looks good heaped together on a plate. Tourists are dismayed to find such combinations as rice, sweet potatoes and macaroni served as a full meal. Other times a bit of fish, a leg of a chicken and a small steak are piled high on one plate. And it is not just the interior that is guilty of these offenses, but some of the best restaurants in the coastal cities as well. For some reason vegetables don't seem to have the same vitamin value that they do in northern climates. A meal of carrots, peas and rice may be filling but is not very nourishing. Brazilian cooks have been accused of boiling the good out of their vegetables, but agricultural experts claim that a tropical soil is weaker in minerals than that in northern climates. Whatever the reason, Brazilians have to depend a great deal upon vitamin tablets and specially enriched powders. Drug stores are crammed from floor to ceiling with pills, syrups and vials to supplement the vitamin and mineral lack in the nation's food. Of course food is not entirely to blame. More likely, bad eating habits and poverty are also big, important reasons for malnutrition.

On the drinking side of the ledger, let it go on record that the Brazilians like to. They manufacture almost every well-known alcoholic beverage and with the same ease drink all of them freely. Their beer is probably the best in the entire Western Hemisphere. Experienced world travelers and beer drinkers give first prize to Brazil all the time. There is no other nation that makes such highly alcoholic and highly palatable beer as Brazil. The brew in Mexico, Colombia and Peru is good, but when taken beside a bottle from Brazil it just can't stand up under the comparison. And the light-colored water that they sell as beer in the United States should not even be mentioned in the same breath. Most of Brazil's beer fame comes from the fact that for generations there have been expert Germans and Dutchmen watching the processing and heading the manufacturing of all the major companies.

There is also a powerful clear liquid made from fermented cane alcohol called *cachaça*. It smells foul, and to the inexperienced palate it tastes foul. But mixed with the juice of a lemon or the orangish fruit *maracujá*, it becomes a *batida* and is used before meals to pep up the appetite and after meals to settle the stomach. A Rio *feijoada* should never be eaten without a *batida* beforehand. Because of its cheap price, *cachaça* is the whisky of the poor. When you see bartenders in the little coffee shops shake up a plain bottle and pour out a couple of fingers of some strange looking liquid—and see the customer gulp it down and then spit on the floor—you'll know you are seeing *cachaça* being consumed. Because it is manufactured by over 2,000 independent little distilleries across the nation there is no uniform taste, and there are no special brands to recommend. The only sure way to find the one you like best is just to keep sampling. But be careful of your liver, your wind-pipe and your stomach lining. It wouldn't be at all surprising if the secret liquid fuel used at Cape Kennedy in the space rockets isn't really just plain Brazilian *cachaça*.

In the south of the country some of the best wines in Latin America are produced. While travelers rave about the wines of Chile and Argentina, few of them know about the wines of Brazil. There are all kinds, from mild rosé to deep burgundies to dry white wines that when chilled rival anything being bottled in the Hemisphere. And that includes the wines of the United States as well. They even make champagne in Brazil. A lucrative but little-known sidelight to the Brazilian wine industry is its exporting. Every year huge, unmarked wooden barrels of local wine are shipped to France and Italy where they are mixed with the best grapes of those lands. Rebottled and relabeled, the wines are exported all over the world as "genuine" French or Italian products. Brazilians know this and drink the homemade stuff with pleasure, letting the unsuspecting tourist pay three times as much for a bottle of the same wine dressed up in a French label.

PRACTICAL INFORMATION FOR BRAZIL

Because Brazil is a continent within a continent and is much too big to write about as a single entity, at least as far as practical information is concerned, we are not presenting all the facts and figures on Brazil in one *Practical Information* section. Most of the details you're looking for, such as listings of hotels and restaurants, will be found within separate subchapters for the major regions of the country, following. A few paragraphs on items of general interest are in order, however, and we'll lead off with them:

CAPSULE COMMENTS. *Physical Features.* A giant country larger than the continental United States, Brazil includes the great Amazon basin at the equator, a vast subtropical central section, and the temperate mountain regions of the southern coast. It occupies over half of South America's land mass.

Climate. Rio is always pleasant with days and nights very much like summer in the midwestern U.S.A. São Paulo also has a mild climate. The vast Amazon rain forest and tropical section are hot and humid all year.

Population. 110,000,000. Rio 7,500,000. São Paulo 8,500,000.
Language. Portuguese (not, repeat *not*, Spanish!).
Archeological Attractions. Lagoa Santa, Sambaquis, Marajo.

FESTIVALS AND SPECIAL EVENTS. *Carnival In Rio* is world's gayest. Costume balls, big club balls, gala street dances, lavish costumes, fireworks and fun. Rio de Janeiro. Begins Fri. night before Ash Wednesday, lasts four days. Carnival in Salvador (Bahia) rivals that of Rio and is less crowded with foreign tourists.

Other world-famous religious festivals in Bahia are those of the *Patron Lord of the Sailors* (Jan. 1–4) and *Our Lady of Bomfin,* which combines Catholic and African rites (Jan. 17–20).

Holy Week Celebrations throughout Brazil. Particularly notable in Ouro Preto, Minas Gerais State. March or April.

Biennial Art Exposition, São Paulo, brings together renowned international artists in Brazil's most important exposition. Odd-numbered years in September.

Grand Premio Brasil Horse Race. Rio de Janeiro. Aug.

Commemoration of Independence Day, Sept. 7. *Feira de Providencia* (annual 3-day charity event), Rio, Sept. *International Piano Competition,* Sept. *Rio Circuit,* Santos-Rio Yacht Races, Oct-Nov. *Proclamation of Republic Day,* Nov. 15.

Macumba Ceremonies. Semi-religious Afro-Brazilian rites, exotic and unusual, often on sightseeing tours. All year. In Bahia they are called *Candomblé.*

 HOW TO REACH BRAZIL. By air: From the U.S. to Rio and São Paulo there are smooth jet flights (including some nonstop 747s and DC-10s) on five airlines: from New York, Miami, Los Angeles on *Avianca, Argentine Airlines, Braniff International, Pan American* and *Varig*; from Dallas-Houston on *Braniff* and *Pan American.* From New York to Brasilia on *Pan American,* from Miami to Brasilia on *Pan American* and *Varig,* to Manaus and Belem on *Varig.*

From London to Rio and São Paulo: *British-Caledonian* (some flights stop in Recife), *Varig* (some stop in Bahia), and main European and South American airlines from other principal capitals on the Continent.

From South Africa: *Pan American, South African Airways* and *Varig* have flights from Johannesburg and/or Cape Town.

From the Pacific, Australia and New Zealand: *Qantas* through Tahiti to Acapulco and Mexico City, changing for South American destinations, or *LAN-Chile* from Fiji, Tahiti or Easter Island through Santiago.

From the Orient: *Varig* from Tokyo, or other airlines, changing for South America on the U.S. West Coast.

By sea: Passenger accommodation on freighters from the U.S. is offered by *Columbus Lines, Torm Lines Holland-America, Ivaran Lines, Hamburg-Sud, Moore-McCormack Lines,* one-way or round-trip cruises. *Lloyd Brasileiro, Brodin Line, Prudential-Grace Line* cruises call at Rio, Santos and Paranagua. *Sunline* cruises at: Rio, Santos, Vitoria, Salvador and Recife. From Europe by: *Lamport and Holt Line Ltd.*

TEPSA buses connect with several countries and operate within Brazil.

PASSPORTS AND VISA. Passports are required, and visas, except for citizens of the USA and Canada visiting Brazil for 30 days or less. If you like Brazil very much, you can extend your 30-day stay another 30 days at any immigration office in the country. For citizens of other countries and for Americans and Canadians desiring to stay more than 60 days, a tourist visa is required. This is valid for 90 days and can be obtained free at Brazilian Consulates (3 passport photos needed). Visitors need a valid smallpox vaccination certificate. Regulations change often, so check entry requirements just before departure. Airport tax on international departures is around $5.00 from most Brazilian airports.

CUSTOMS. Travelers from abroad may bring duty free to Brazil the following items: clothing; jewelry for personal use; personal books and magazines; articles for personal consumption, i.e., beverages, eatables, tobacco, cigars, cosmetics, restricted to a total of $25; and domestic professional objects or souvenirs, excluding domestic electric appliances, to a total value of $100.

WHAT TO WEAR. Although not too many years ago men were required to wear coats and ties to take a streetcar or go to a movie in Rio, today informality is the keynote—fortunately, considering summer (December–March) temperatures occasionally reach a humid 40°C. (104°F.). Now one seldom sees a tie at Copacabana restaurants or nightclubs. Ironically, jackets and ties are needed daytimes at some of the better downtown luncheon clubs where bankers and businessmen gather. A hat may be needed only on the beach or golf course.

Slacks and pantsuits are acceptable for ladies, and hats and gloves are never worn—not even to weddings. Shorts are rarely worn, but female beachwear is about the skimpiest you'll ever see. You might want to buy a Brazilian "tanga" (the "string" originated in Rio) to shock your friends back home. In wintertime (summer in the Northern hemisphere), there can be chilly days (in the lower 50s, F.), so a sweater or wrap is a necessity. As a general rule, dress in Rio as you would in Miami, but with seasons reversed.

In São Paulo, weather is cooler and dress more formal. Sports wear is enough for a Brasilia sight-seeing trip of a day or two; if you stay longer or have diplomatic contacts, more formal clothing will be needed. But a man will rarely need a dinner jacket in Brazil—unless he wants to swelter at one of Rio's gala Carnival balls rather than wear a costume (a common, simple one consists of bright shirt, Hawaiian leis, captain's cap and shorts).

During winter (May to October), you will need warmer clothing in the South, whereas in Bahia, the North and Northeast, climate is humid and tropical year-round. Sun glasses and a light raincoat or umbrella are good items to have along when visiting anyplace in Brazil. In some areas outside Rio and São Paulo, an insect repellent may be needed; "Off," "Autan" or "Super Repelex" sprays—all available locally.

CURRENCY. Inflation is still a problem, although the government has slowed it down considerably. But the *cruzeiro* still is subject to fluctuations. Inflation used to work to the advantage of the tourist because it kept prices comparatively low, by hard currency standards. Do not change too much of your hard currency at one time. The old *cruzeiro* was replaced by the *cruzeiro novo* in 1968, 1,000 of the former equaling *one* of the latter, though some old-timers still talk about "1,000 cruzeiros" when they mean "one cruzeiro." Foreign currency or Travelers Checks are changeable into cruzeiros at official places: banks, and exchange shops marked "Cambio." At press time, approximately Cr. $13 = U.S. $1, Cr. $24 to the pound sterling.

TIPPING. At restaurants and nightclubs, when 10 or 15% is added to your bill, you usually add 5% more. In hotels, 10% is usually added to your bill as a service charge. However, you will find that porters, doormen, elevator operators and chambermaids are accustomed to getting a small tip for their services, either at the time the service is performed, or when you check out. If a taxi driver helps with your luggage, a small tip of about 10% of the fare is expected. At the barbers or beauty parlor, a 10–20% tip is expected. Cinema and theater ushers do not expect tips. In general, tip washroom attendants, shoe-shine boys, etc., about what you would tip at home. At airports, tip the last porter who puts your bags into the cab; they work on a "pool" system and all earnings go into a general kitty.

GETTING AROUND. There are four major commercial airlines (*Varig*, *Cruzeiro do Sul*, *Vasp* and *Trans-Brasil*), which together fly over 3 billion passenger-miles a year. The airline companies take good care of their planes, have top flight mechanics, and first-class pilots, and crews who refuse to let a plane go up unless they are absolutely certain it is ready to fly. The service is nothing short of excellent and full course meals are the rule rather than the exception. On many flights there is free Brazilian whisky or wines, and always many cups of the ever-present black coffee.

Their plane scheduling is fairly imaginative and is designed to meet both passenger needs and the competition. One of the most successful and most used of all the airline services is the popular "air bridge" between Rio and São Paulo. In 1959, the four air companies pooled their forces to set up a system to keep both passengers and planes constantly flowing between the two major cities. The traveler does not even need to buy a ticket or make a reservation in advance, he just shows up at the airport and gets aboard the next plane. During the rush hours there is a plane leaving every 30 minutes, and every hour on the hour up to 9 p.m. from Rio, 10 p.m. from São Paulo. The air bridge has been a success since its inauguration, carrying more than 2,000 passengers a day. If you want to leave on a specific flight, it's possible to make a reservation.

So successful was the Rio-São Paulo bridge that in 1962 air-bridges were inaugurated to Belo Horizonte and Brasilia. The flights are not so frequent, because the distances are greater, but the regular commuters who use it seem more than satisfied. Planes tend to fill up on weekends; book well in advance if you plan to fly anywhere on a Friday, especially to or from Manaus or Brasilia.

Even though the airlines make attempts to keep on schedule, exceptions can occur. Many people have spent nights in strange towns because their connecting flight left without them. In the interior, the wise passenger is at the airport at least half an hour before takeoff time, for many pilots anxious to get back to the cities spend only the barest minimum of time in the local fields.

 RAIL SERVICE. Train service between Rio and São Paulo is comfortable. There is excellent regional service from São Paulo on the Paulista and Sorocabana lines and 24-hour service from São Paulo to Brasilia. Also from Rio to Belo Horizonte. Most service to other areas of Brazil is inferior to air travel. Travelers save both time and often considerable trouble by avoiding long rail journeys in Brazil.

HOTEL COSTS. See *Rio* chapter, *Hotel* listings.

 **SPORTS.** Soccer, called "futebol" and pronounced fut-tea-ball, is as much a national heritage for Brazilians as wine is for the Frenchman and snow for the Eskimo. They wouldn't know how to live without it. They would fight to the death to keep it. They were, after all, three times World Soccer Champions.

The soccer the Brazilians play is a fast game, almost like a ballet, that begins when little boys take their first ball to the beach or into the middle of a vacant lot. You can see them bouncing the ball off their knees giving a backward kick with a bare foot and sending it to a buddy who butts it with his head. In Brazil as well as the rest of the international playing world, only the goalkeeper is allowed to touch the ball with his hands.

If you like sports at all and are in Rio on a Sunday when two of the major Rio teams are playing each other, you should visit the huge Maracanã soccer stadium. (It's hard to say how many people it holds, since they oversell the stadium for really big games and announce tickets sold rather than the number who actually managed to get in and see the game; but it is well over 100,000.) The four main Rio teams are Flamengo (Brazil's most popular team, somewhat comparable to the N.Y. Mets), Vasco (chiefly identified with the Portuguese colony in Rio), Fluminense (the high society team), and Botafogo (the least definable in personality). If you try to go, talk it all over ahead of time with someone at the hotel who can tell you how to get there, when to go, how to buy tickets, and so forth. Unlike baseball, U.S. or Canadian football, rugby, cricket, and the like, soccer is easy to understand even if you've never seen it before. Not being an aficionado and not rooting for a particular team, you won't get so excited as the rest of the crowd. But even if the game doesn't turn you on, the stadium is impressive, and the crowd itself is half the spectacle. Soccer crowds in the British Isles and northern

Europe can be extremely surly; and in the Mediterranean and other Latin American countries (as well as most of Brazil), they can be dangerously passionate. But the Maracanã crowd is unswervingly good natured, and the stadium is exceptionally safely constructed, so don't worry about stories you may have read about soccer disasters. For one of the big games between two of the major local teams, large numbers of the rooters bring huge homemade flags, featuring the team's colors in a variety of designs made up themselves, and they wave these flags when their team comes on the field or makes a goal. Another feature you are not likely to encounter at the World Series or the Super Bowl is that drums start beating in various parts of the stadium well before the game and maintain their tom-tom rhythm without a break right through to the end. All in all, the crowd is one of the most colorful and exciting spectacles in sport. If you go, try to buy the highest-priced reserved seats. If you want to be with "the people" in the "arquibancada," be advised that it is plain concrete bleachers, so be sure to buy foam rubber pads to sit on before you go into the stadium.

Capoeira and More. Another sport that is purely Brazilian, not to be found anywhere else in the world, is the Capoeira. It is a fight, a dance and a bit of judo all rolled into one. In the early slave days there were constant fights between the blacks, and when the owner caught them at it he had both sides punished. The blacks considered this unfair and developed a smoke screen of music and song to cover up the actual fighting. When a pre-arranged battle was to be fought, the natives brought their "berimbau," a bow-shaped piece of wood with a metal wire running from one end to the other, where there was a painted gourd. Using an old copper coin the player would shake the bow, and while the seeds in the gourd rattled he would strike the taut string. The effect is like background music for a Hollywood monster film. There would be a chorus chanting a fast song and the two fighters would get in the center and slug it out, primarily with their feet. Whenever the master came into view the fighters would do an elaborate pantomime of slashing the air with their fists and kicking out so as to miss their opponent. Over the years this was refined into a sport that is practiced in Bahia and Recife until today. Both cities have their champions and there are many *capoeira* houses where the tourist can go to watch these dances. In Salvador (Bahia), they may be seen on any Saturday morning around the Modelo Market. The idea is to swing and kick to the mood of the music but without either man touching the other. The back-bending all the way to the floor, the agile foot movements to stay clear of a gleaming knife, and the strange African music make it a sport that needs great dexterity to play but is fascinating to watch.

There is also a mountain climbing society in Rio as well as a spelunking society that are happy to welcome experienced tourists on their weekend outings. If your meat is climbing up the pitted side of Sugar Loaf or delving deep into a grotto in Minas Gerais, any tourist agency can make the necessary introductions.

Water skiing and underwater diving are also practiced by sports-men in clubs all along the coastline. Brazilians are a very club-conscious people, and almost everyone you meet will be a member of something and will be able to take you to his particular club and introduce you around. They love to show off visitors and most clubs can only be entered with a member. Once you are inside you'll find the frendship and generosity for which the Brazilians are famous.

Horse racing is also immensely popular. The Grande Premio Brasil held first Sunday in August highlights the racing season. *Golf* and *tennis* in all leading cities. Two golf clubs in Rio, where you can play by invitation only. *Yachting* extremely popular in Rio. *Surfing* on the beaches.

For those who like to fish, Brazil can be a surprising wonderland. Many tourists try for some marlin fishing off the coast of Rio, and others go to the magnificent Foz do Iguaçu to try their hand at dorado. In the Amazon River there are monstrous fish called Pirarucú that reach up to 280 pounds each. The nation's rivers and streams are filled with a variety of game fish. No license is needed and no limit set.

If you have a taste for bigger game, you're out of luck today, because the government recently outlawed the hunting of big-spotted jaguars, wild boar, fleet-footed jungle deer, moss-backed turtles and dozens of other animals which were once considered fair play. But a camera safari into the Mato Grosso or Amazon jungles can still be an adventure. Most travel agencies can tailor a program to suit you.

 THE LANGUAGE. A prime rule to remember for anyone visiting Brazil is that the national language is Portuguese and not Spanish. There is nothing that annoys a Brazilian more than to have a visitor make that mistake. They are extremely proud of their language and the literary and musical heritage that goes with it. They are not proud of Spanish. They have no reason to be.

Those visitors who have been traveling through other countries in Central or South America before coming to Brazil will have their ears tuned to the music of the Spanish language. Arriving and hearing Portuguese will be a shock. For there is nothing that sounds so strange to the ear as a beautiful woman speaking Portuguese after listening to other beauties in Spanish.

Portuguese is a nasal and a guttural language that is a mixture of Latin and Spanish with a heavy emphasis on Arabic vocabulary. Centuries ago the Arabs ruled Portugal as they did Spain and left their influence in the architecture, the music and the language. Spain managed to shuffle off most of the Arabic words, but the lackadaisical Portuguese kept them on. The Brazilians have great contempt for Spanish anyway, saying that "Spanish is merely Portuguese badly spoken."

Yet there exists a difference between the Portuguese of Brazil and the Portuguese of Portugal. It is a little like the differences between the English of the United States and the English of Great Britain. The Brazilians talk more slowly and distinctly than their relatives in Lisbon, and because of all the new situations faced in the making of their nation they had to coin many new words or take words directly from the Indian vocabularies. Names of rivers, many states and innumerable cities are in Tupi or Guarani, just as *Dakota* and *Mississippi* came from the Sioux and Ojibway languages.

But don't get discouraged right away. If you can speak Spanish you can get around in Brazil. You won't understand them but they will usually understand you, and the Brazilians will not despise you for speaking it. But if you take the trouble to learn just a few Portuguese words to sprinkle in your conversation you will win your listeners over almost immediately. They like someone who has the interest to try their language and will make great efforts to understand you no matter how badly you mangle it. The statement that you read in many tourist folders, saying that everyone speaks English in Brazil and therefore you'll have no trouble, is pure fiction. There are many Brazilians who do speak or understand English, but the majority of the people the visitor comes in contact with—waiters, taxi drivers, hotel clerks, sales girls, etc., away from major hotels and nearby shops—won't be able to understand anything you say in English. Therefore a few minutes spent in brushing up on some Portuguese will pay big dividends.

The accents and other curlicues you find above or below the letters of many words actually make pronunciation easier. For instance the word for coffee is café. When you see this acute accent at the end of a word you accent that syllable and it becomes ca-FAY. That strange word for saint as in Saint Paul (São Paulo) or Saint Francis (São Francisco) is pronounced SOWN (as in "down"). When there is a little curlicue mark under a "c" in a word like Braço (meaning arm), you pronounce it like a soft "s" and it comes out bras-so. If the "c" doesn't have the added appendice you usually pronounce it hard like a "k," as in buscar (bus-kar), to look for. Also "q" in a word is pronounced like "k" and most "x's" have a shhh sound. Because of this you will run into many English words that look like your hometown product but have been twisted around by the Brazilians. The gasoline company Texaco comes out tay-SHA-ko and X-ray has been converted into a raio-sheesh. Other words borrowed from English that you may (or may not) recognize in Brazil are *lanche* (a quick lunch), *time* (a soccer team but pronounced tea-me), *football* (pronounced foot-tea-ball) and *cinema* (here it is sea-NAY-mah).

There are a number of words that are the same or just about the same as in English. Words like *hotel, telegrama, restaurante, whisky, auto, possivel* and *impossivel, envelope, taxi, okay* and *romantico*.

See Vocabularies at the end of the book for some useful words and phrases.

 AMERICAN EXPRESS AGENTS: South American executive offices of American Express are located in Rio (phone 266-0900). However, all travel related services (mail, travelers checks, credit cards, etc.) are handled exclusively by *Kontik-Franstur* ground operators, who can also provide you with transfers, city tours and other services in ten major Brazilian cities. *Rio de Janeiro:* Av. Almirante Barroso 91, 7th floor, P.O. Box 2952. *São Paulo:* Rua Marconi 71, 2nd floor. *Salvador, Bahia:* Praça da Inglaterra 2, P.O. Box 973.

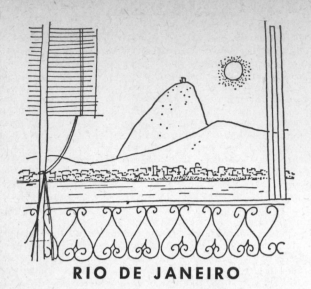

RIO DE JANEIRO

The Cidade Maravilhosa

(The Practical Information section of this chapter was prepared by Bill Williamson of the Brazil Herald *and Andre Fodor, South American representative of the Fodor guide organization.)*

Rio de Janeiro has been cited by many experienced travelers as the most beautiful city in the world, with a natural setting surpassing even Hong Kong and San Francisco. It has everything. There are long stretches of soft sandy beaches and lines of tall palm trees. There are mountains covered with deep green untouched jungle and birds, butterflies and flowers in profusion. There are great fleecy clouds floating lazily over the ocean, pushing in cool breezes and an occasional rain storm. There are warm days and cool nights and starlit skies and huge full moons.

What nature has given, the Brazilians have embellished with their own personalities. Along the black and white mosaic promenades walk some of the loveliest women in Latin America. The men, well built and tanned from hours on the beach, add their note of masculine grace. Colonial buildings vie for space with modern air-conditioned skyscrapers. There is music everywhere, from the honking of taxi and automobile horns, to the soft singsong voices of the blacks from the *favela* hillside shacks. There is an excitement in the air, curiously mixed with the tropical languor of let's-do-it-tomorrow.

But Rio is more than an eye and ear pleasing pastime. It is a city that boasts its own ballet company, magnificent opera house and dozens of cultural centers. It is a mecca for artists and the enterprising businessman. It also calls the international drifter, the expatriate and the fortune hunter. And in very recent years, with the construction of many luxurious, new hotels, it is becoming South America's tourist capital as well.

EXPLORING RIO

Rio stretches out along the sandy shores of the Atlantic Ocean like a beautiful woman basking in the sun. Her head forms the downtown section with her full hair streaming into the north zone. Her curved body makes up the residential areas of Flamengo, Botafogo and Copacabana, while her legs, doubled at Arpoador Beach, reach out to create the neighborhoods of Ipanema and Leblon.

São Sebastião do Rio de Janeiro is 15 miles long and varies from 2 to 10 miles wide. Nestling between the tall blue-green mountains and the deep blue-green sea, the city offers a breath-taking sight, by day or night. During the day the sun plays on the sand and palm trees, and the white buildings with their red tile roofs serve more to ornament its natural beauty than to detract from it. At night the city wears strings of glowing lights, that give the impression that strands of diamonds have been lazily entwined around the buildings and the mountains by some benevolent giant.

The most obvious attraction for the visitor is the beach. Just the name Copacabana inspires romantic images, and rare is the tourist who doesn't arrive in Rio and immediately unpack his bathing suit. Rio has 16 different beaches, scattered from the international airport in the north to the other side of the mountains in the south. Most popular is the one at Copacabana. There are no bathing fees for any of the beaches. Oceanfront hotels provide cabanas, towels and soap. Waves at the beach come in hard and fast most of the time, so don't expect to do any swimming, just a lot of splashing. Also be prepared to confront lots of people on the weekends and keep an eye on anything valuable.

Assuming you've had enough sun and that you want to see some of the city itself, here is a good plan:

Take a taxi or a bus marked Urca (a 15-minute ride from Copa-cabana) to the little station where the cable cars start their trip up to the top of Sugar Loaf. It is advisable to get there early for there are usually many people who want to make the visit and the cars move slowly. Once you are being borne upward you'll have the pleasant sensation of space all around you and a vivid panoramic display of Rio and her natural beauties below. The car makes a half-way stop on Urca mountain, where there is a pleasant restaurant, and you can either linger if you wish or transfer to another car to go to the top. There you have the city at your feet and can

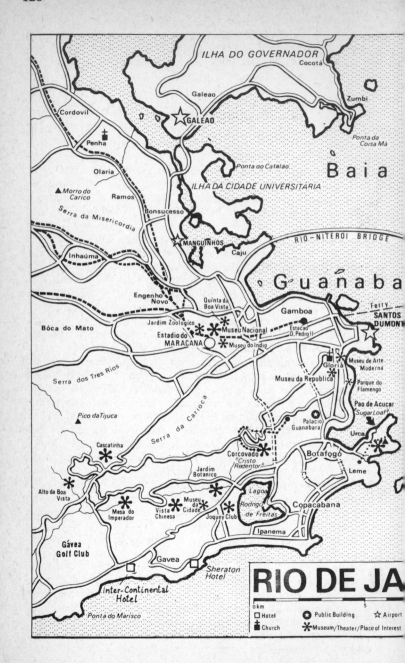

ILHA DO GOVERNADOR
Cocotá
Galeao
Zumbi
Cordovil
Ponta da
Coisa Má
Penha
Olaria
Ponta ao Catalão
Morro do Carico
Ramos
B a i a
Serra da Misericordia
Bonsucesso
ILHA DA CIDADE UNIVERSITÁRIA
Inhaúma
MANGUINHOS
Caju
RIO-NITEROI BRIDGE
Engenho Novo
Quinta da Boa Vista
G u a ñ a b a
Ferry
SANTOS DUMONT
Jardim Zoologico
Gamboa
Bôca do Mato
Museu Nacional
Estacao D.Pedro II
Estadio do MARACANA
Museu do Indio
Museu de Arte Moderna
Gloria
Serra dos Tres Rios
Museu da Republica
Parque do Flamengo
Pico da Tijuca
Pao de Acucar "Sugar Loaf"
Palacio Guanabara
Cascatinha
Serra da Carioca
Corcovado "Cristo Redentor"
Urca
Botafogo
Jardim Botanico
Leme
Alto da Boa Vista
Mesa do Imperador
Vista Chinesa
Museu da Cidade
Lagoa Rodrigo de Freitas
Copacabana
Joquey Club
Ipanema
Gâvea Golf Club
Gavea
Sheraton Hotel
Inter-Continental Hotel
Ponta do Marisco

RIO DE JA

0 km   5
□ Hotel   ● Public Building   ☆ Airport
■ Church   ✳ Museum/Theater/Place of Interest

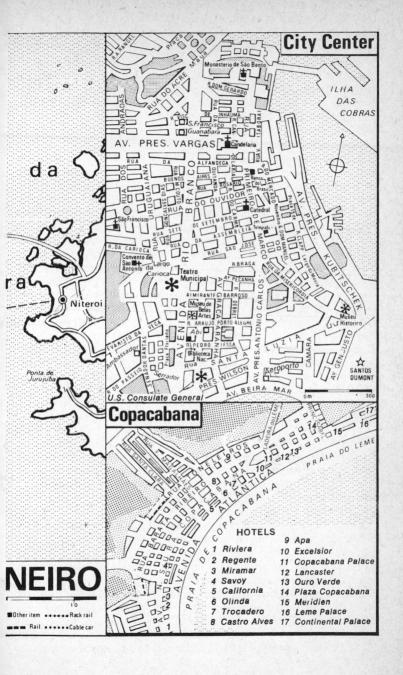

City Center

ILHA DAS COBRAS

Monasterio de São Bento

R.A. RANGEL
RUA DO ACRE
R. DOM GERARDO
R. VISC. DE INHAUMA
S. Francisco
Guanabara
AV. PRES. VARGAS
Candelaria
ALFANDEGA
RUA DOS ANDRADAS
RUA DA
BUENOS AIRES
RUA DA QUITANDA
RUA URUGUAIANA
RUA GONÇALVES DIAS
RIO BRANCO
RUA DO OUVIDOR
ROSARIO
Banco do Brasil
São Francisco
RUA SETE DE SETEMBRO
RUA DA CARIOCA
RUA DO LARGO
Catedral
ASSEMBLEIA
RUA SÃO JOSE
R. DA CARIOCA
Convento de São Antonio da Carioca
Largo da Carioca
Teatro Municipal
R. BRAGA
AV. PEÇANHA
ALMIRANTE BARROSO
Museu de Belas Artes
R. ARAUJO PORTO ALEGRE
AVENIDA GRAÇA ARANHA
Abi
R. PEDRO
Biblioteca Nac.
EVARISTO DA VEIGA
Ambassador
Praça Floriano
Serrador
R. DO PASSEIO
SENADOR DANTAS
Rua SANTA LUZIA
AV. PRES. WILSON
AV. PRES. ANTONIO CARLOS
RUA DA MISERICORDIA
CAMARA
AV. GEN. JUSTO
Aeroporto
AV. BEIRA MAR
SANTOS DUMONT
Museu Historico
AV. PRES. KUBITSCHEK
R. CLAPP
LARGO MANUEL
MERCADO
NOVEMBRO E DOM MANUEL
Teleporto
Praça XV
Teleférico

U.S. Consulate General

0m   300

Copacabana

PRAIA DO LEME
AV. ATLANTICA
PRAIA DE COPACABANA
RUA SANTA CLARA
FIGUEIREDO MAGALHÃES
BARATA RIBEIRO
RUA NELEROS
RUA DE
LADEIRA DO LEME
PRINCESA

14
17
16
15
13
12
11
10
9
8
6
5
4
2
1

NEIRO

1 0

■ Other item   •••••• Rack rail
━ ━ Rail   •••••• Cable car

Ponta de Jurujuba

Niteroi

d a

r a

HOTELS

1	Riviera	9 Apa
2	Regente	10 Excelsior
3	Miramar	11 Copacabana Palace
4	Savoy	12 Lancaster
5	California	13 Ouro Verde
6	Olinda	14 Plaza Copacabana
7	Trocadero	15 Meridien
8	Castro Alves	16 Leme Palace
		17 Continental Palace

identify the other points of interest that you must see before you leave. The top of Sugar Loaf (1,200 feet) has a restaurant crowned by a television transmitter. It is best to visit Sugar Loaf *before* you visit the Corcovado Christ statue, or you will remember Sugar Loaf only as an anticlimax. A nice "family" way to sightsee is on a "Bateau Mouche," which cruises Guanabara Bay. You get a different view of Sugar Loaf and a glimpse of Jurubaiba Island.

There are taxis waiting at the platform where you will return and ask the driver to take you—slowly—to the Gloria Church (Igreja da Gloria). On the way down Avenida Pasteur you will pass the high-walled Yacht Club (admittance strictly to members only but you can peer over the chain-barred entrance-way) and the pink-painted colonial buildings belonging to the Brazilian University. Coming out in front of the new tunnel of Pasmado, you'll go along Botafogo beach and after going around a bend you'll be in the Flamengo beach district where a major face-lifting has taken place. Here they have built the largest public park in Latin America on land reclaimed from the sea. Every ounce of earth was carted in by truck. The planting was done by master landscape gardener Roberto Burle Marx. Thanks to the Flamengo *aterro*, as it is called, you can now drive to and from Copacabana in a matter of minutes. The park is a delightful place for a late afternoon stroll. You can also explore it by tractor-drawn mini-train, and if you have small children with you, there is a fine playground, complete with a real DC-3 to explore and a special space for model aircraft enthusiasts. Be sure to use the overpasses and underpasses to cross the main freeways; accidents are frequent on the *aterro* as just about everywhere else in Rio.

Favorite Church of the Imperial Family

The driver will turn off and climb a steep hill that is lined on both sides with houses harking back to the days of the Portuguese colonials and will let you off in front of the big wooden doors of the Gloria Church. Built in the 18th century it was the favorite spot of the Imperial Family and contains many fine examples of art from both the old and the new world. The site of the church was once the hut of a hermit who in 1671, with the help of two mysterious youths (angels), sculptured a beautiful statue of Our Lady of Glory. Seventeen years later, when the image had been accredited with miraculous powers, the hermit returned to Portugal, taking the image with him. But the ship sank into the ocean, and the statue washed ashore at Lagos, Portugal. In 1924 a copy was enshrined in its place in the Gloria Church. The Brazilians still want the original image returned. On August 15, the church is lighted up like a baroque birthday cake, and silhouetted against the dark sky and the palm trees it is one of the loveliest sights in Brazil.

Walk down the street you drove up and then along the Praça (park) Paris. Laid out by a French architect a good many years ago, it reminds many Parisians of home, with its marble statues, trimmed hedges, reflection pools and water fountains. On the opposite side of the avenue you'll see the contrast in the ultramodern Monument to the Brazilian Dead of World War Two. Brazil sent troops to fight in Italy and suffered heavy losses. Much of this area has recently been torn apart to make way for Rio's long overdue and highly controversial Metro. Despite a series of financial crises and floods, the thing is being built at last, though nobody expects to be able to ride on it in their lifetime.

Museums and Historic Sites

Have lunch in the area, then pay a visit to the Museum of Modern Art, which opens at noon. Here you will be able to see many fine canvases of Brazilian modern painters and also representatives of the modern European and American schools. A monstrous canvas by Mathieu dominates one entire wall. He painted it in front of a mob of curious Cariocas in one hour while a samba band gave him inspiration. There are two restaurants in the museum; upstairs is the leading lunchtime spot for executives and politicians, downstairs a snack bar whose prices are more accessible to the tourist.

Crossing the avenue at a left angle and passing over the cement platforms where the buses stop, you will enter another park called Passeio Publico. It is the oldest public park in the city. Filled with tall shade trees, small lagoons and rustic bridges, it is a pleasant place to get in out of the sun. It also has its share of tramps and beggars and a large collection of alley cats.

Leave the park by the upper right-hand sidewalk and keep walking right over to Rio's main commercial heartline, Avenida Rio Branco. Walk up to Rio Branco avenue and you will pass the National Library (worth a visit) and the Museum of Fine Arts (also worthwhile) on your right and the Municipal Theater on your left. If this theater looks familiar, it is because it is an exact one-quarter scale copy of the Opera House in Paris. At present closed for complete interior remodeling, it should be reopened by 1978. Two blocks farther down the Avenue on the left rises the 34-floor, air-conditioned, glass-paneled Edificio Avenida Central, once Rio's tallest building, though higher still skyscrapers are now under construction.

If you walk through the arcades to the other side of this modern building and look across the street, you'll see the old Convent of Santo Antonio. Built between 1608 and 1619, it contains aside from priceless colonial art objects, the tombs of Leopoldina, the first Empress of Brazil, and the Infante Dom Pedro de Bourbon. Beside the convent is the richest little church in Rio, the São Francisco da Penitência. Its interior is completely hand sculptured and covered in gold foil. It also has a remarkable altar and sacristy. The climb up the hill is worth it.

The former hill of Santo Antonio was removed, its earth used to form the Flamengo *aterro*. The site was transformed to a double avenue bordered by new buildings. These include the cone-shaped Metropolitan Cathedral—still unfinished and being used as a parking lot—the aluminum-block headquarters building of Petrobrás (the government oil monopoly) and, across the avenue, the high-rise headquarters of the National Housing Bank. Behind this modern setting you will see the colonial arches built in 1723 to carry water down to the city.

Go back down Rio Branco, until you come to Rua Ouvidor. There are no automobiles permitted on this street and it buzzes like an over-active beehive. Don't be dismayed or taken in by the infected beggars or mothers with sickly children you see asking for alms in this area. Most of the sores are painted on and most of the children are rented out for the day. Of course there are some who are genuine, but the majority are not. The city has tried to clear the downtown streets of these pathetic cases, but they keep coming in from the interior faster than they can be sent out.

Five blocks from Ouvidor is the overly wide Avenida Presidente Vargas. Be careful crossing the street here, because Brazilian drivers are notorious for disobeying traffic lights. To your right is the squat and attractive Church of Candelaria. The inside is vast, dark and relaxing after a walk in the sun.

Continuing downward on Rio Branco you will come to Praça Maua and the beginning of miles of docks that have made the city such an important world trading center. Praça Maua is peopled by all sorts, with heavy emphasis on foreign sailors and the women and con-men who make their living from them. Now take a bus marked Copacabana and go back to your hotel and have a tall, cool drink. You've earned it today.

The Mother of Palm Trees

Another full day could start with an hour at the beach, a shower, and then a taxi ride to the Botanical Garden on Rua Jardim Botânico. Don't try to take a bus, or you'll get lost. The garden is one of the best in the world, say noted horticulturalists, and is carefully kept up. Covering an area of 567,000 square meters there are over 135,000 plants and trees. There are 900 varieties of palm tree alone. Founded in 1808 by the prince regent Dom João, there stood near the entrance gate the famous *palma mater* transported from the West Indies and planted by the monarch. There is also a strikingly beautiful avenue of palms that is 740 meters long and comprises 134 royal palms. Also be sure and see the bronze fountain dating back to 1820 and the mammoth Victoria Regia water lilies that measure 21 feet around. There is also a peaceful jungle atmosphere, lake and waterfall, a small greenhouse filled with flesh-eating Venus Flytrap plants, and some rare trees from Indonesia whose huge roots spread atop the ground like writhing cobras.

From there take another taxi to the Laranjeiras Palace, the residence of the President when he is in Rio. You probably won't be allowed past the guard, but the drive through the Guinle Park and past the luxurious private apartment houses that line it is worthwhile. Now still in your cab, take a quick look at Catete Palace on Rua Catete, Praia do Flamengo. Built of granite and rose-colored marble in 1862 by a wealthy coffee baron, it was purchased 32 years later by the federal government and used as the Foreign Office. Dictator Getulio Vargas, when he returned to power as duly elected President of the Republic, insisted on living there rather than at the other palace where he had been tossed out. It was also at Catete that he killed himself in 1954. The palace, with its magnificent gardens, was converted into the Museum of the Republic when Brasilia was inaugurated.

Now you can have lunch downtown (perhaps at Le Tour revolving restaurant which opened in 1977) and hop into another cab for a better look at the old aqueducts, over which little trolley cars cross on their way to the lovely residential area of Santa Tereza. You saw these arches from the other side yesterday, remember? Now, however, you will be standing in the newly renovated Lapa district. The parks and fountains inaugurated in 1975 are on a site which was once the center of Rio's bohemian nightlife and samba. Many of the surrounding buildings have escaped the march of progress; indeed, some have been protected as examples of Rio's architectural history. Look for the Automóvel Club, the Sala Cecilia Meireles music conservatory and the large white Convent of Santa Tereza, built in 1970 and now the home of a Carmelita order of nuns who have no contact with the outside world.

Now for a visit to one of the most charming corners of the city, the Largo do Boticário just off Rua Cosme Velho. Everyone will tell you it dates from colonial times, whereas in fact only one of its houses dates from earlier than the 1920s. Anyway, it is a pleasantly shady spot, one of its attractions being an English-owned antique store.

Now comes the treat, Corcovado. You can do one of two things. Continue in your taxi to the top of the mountain, which will give you a slow, unwinding, breathtaking view of all angles of the city, or go to Rua Cosme Velho 513 and take a tiny cogwheel train to the top. Trains leave every half hour and the ride is almost straight up through dense jungle. When you arrive you'll have to climb a number of stairs to get to the base of the statue. The statue is impressive up close and the view from the top simply indescribable. The statue, inaugurated in 1931, has a height of 100 feet and weighs 700 tons. The head alone weighs 30 tons, each arm weighs 30 tons and each hand 8 tons. The statue was designed by Frenchman Paul Landowski and paid for by contributions of the people of Rio.

The best time to visit the statue is in the late afternoon about one hour before sunset. The effect of the reddening sun against the buildings and the sea far below will leave you gasping. Then wait patiently and one by one the lights of the town will start to come on, like fireflies awakening for the evening. Within half an hour the city will be dressed in sparkling diamonds and silhouetted against the dark shapes of Sugar Loaf and the blackening waters of the bay and ocean. Warning: the last trolley leaves at seven p.m. and is always crowded. If you go up in a cab have him wait.

The third day's outing will give you time on the beach (be careful you don't get burned), then go to the Indian Museum which opens at 11:30 every morning except Saturdays and Sundays. Located in an old home on 127 Rua Mata Machado, it is a storehouse of Indian art work (feathers, ceramics, stone and weaving), as well as a growing archive of films and recordings made of the indigenous people's way of life and music. Some of the guides are themselves full-blooded Indians, and there is always a possibility that you will see some visiting tribesman around the grounds.

Almost across the street is the Maracanã soccer stadium, the biggest in the world. Built in 1950 for the World Championship Games, it can hold—and has held—as many as 150,000 people at one time. While the designers looked after the comfort of the spectators, they also considered the players, and there is a wide moat around the field to protect the poor athletes should they lose.

Within walking distance is the Quinta da Boa Vista Museum, a beautiful old pink and white building that used to be the Imperial Family's Rio palace, in a gemlike setting of landscaped parks, lakes and marble statues. The museum opens from noon to four p.m. every day except Monday and is filled with traces of Brazil's past, both historical and archeological. There are Indian funeral urns, reconstructed fossils, a fine collection of Amazon reptiles and insects, and one of the best collections of birds in the world. It is probably one of the best museums of its kind in Latin America.

Right beside the museum is the zoo. Open all day every day, it keeps most of its more important animals in unwalled natural settings. Be sure and note the colorful Amazon parrots as you go in (their squawking for attention will force you to notice them) and the hungry leer on the face of the jungle jaguar. Also don't miss the shaded jungle pool with the colorful red cranes and little white scavenger birds. The monkeys have an island of their own, as do the Amazon boa constrictors and the alligators. Take your camera along, and for a tip you can even get the guards to wrestle with a constrictor while you snap away. Somehow, it just doesn't feel like a zoo.

Now here you need another cab for a long ride out to the north zone to visit the Church of Penha just as the sun goes down. Perched high atop a mountain with 365 steps, it is a favorite place for repentant pilgrims to crawl on their knees. The inside is hung with crutches and silver charms representing parts of the body that were cured thanks to the intervention of Our Lady of Penha. The view from the top is superb.

The Emperor's Picnic Table

On the fourth day, call another cab (fortunately they're not expensive in Rio) and make the voyage to the Tijuca Forest. On leaving Copacabana, you will pass through the neighborhoods of Ipanema and Leblon, climb higher to go around the Two Brothers mountain on Avenida Niemeyer and go past the Gavea Golf Club and several new restaurants selling coconuts and fresh oysters at São Conrado. Have your driver stop at the Emperor's Table (Mesa do Imperador). Here is a mammoth concrete picnic table where the Emperor used to bring his royal court to dine. It has an unequaled view of the south zone of the city. Nearby is the Chinese View (Vista Chinesa), which also is impressive.

The forest itself was once part of a private estate belonging to the Baron de Taunay and is studded with exotic trees, thick jungle vines and a delightful waterfall. Also be sure and see the tiny little Mayrink Chapel with an altar painting by Brazil's famed Candido Portinari. This chapel is very popular with Brazilians and, in spite of its cramped quarters, has seen many society marriages.

EXPLORING AROUND RIO

The main attraction for visitors in Petropolis, after the elaborate Quitandinha Hotel, is the Imperial Museum, located in an ornate old palace once the summer home of the Emperor and his family. Dom Pedro II liked the climate and fresh air of the area so much that he ordered a residence built in 1845 and sent for German emigrants to found a city around it. The Germans liked the land as well as the monarch did, and their guttural language can still be heard in the streets today. The museum, open every day but Monday from noon to five p.m., contains clothes, jewels, silver- and gold-plated items that the Imperial Family used. The rooms are as they were during the occupancy, and the Brazilian Imperial Crown with pearls and 44 diamonds is quite spectacular. Because the authorities do not want the inlaid wooden floors marred, you must put on a pair of soft cotton slippers over your own shoes. There is a cathedral nearby, begun by Pedro II, where the benevolent monarch and his wife Dona Teresa Christina now are entombed.

Teresópolis, an hour's drive from Petropolis past wooded hill-sides and lovely homes and farms, belonged at one time to an Englishman named George March. In 1855 he sold his ranch to the government who cut it into lots and encouraged immigration. The town gets its name from the Empress Teresa, the same way Petropolis took its name from Dom Pedro. Most memorable thing about Teresópolis is the string of mountains it's on called the Serra dos Orgãos, which became a national park in 1939. Here is the 1,650-meter Finger of God pointing straight to Heaven, as well as the Finger of Our Lady, the Fish Mouth and the Priest's Nose. Tallest of them all is The Rock of the Bell which towers 2,263 meters above sea level. Alpinists climb these mountains every weekend, and if you're interested, ask your travel agent to put you in contact with a group.

Nova Friburgo came into being by command of the Imperial Family, but years before either Petropolis or Teresópolis (in 1818 to be exact). Most of the newcomers were either German or Swiss; the man responsible for laying out the city with its parks and beautiful homes was the Count of Nova Friburgo. The three main squares are symphonies in marble, eucalyptus and bamboo. Be sure and visit the park of São Clemente with its pools and wide shaded paths.

Cabo Frio has wide white sandy beaches, long enough and hard enough to drive on. It is studded with architectural relics from the colonial days like forts, a 17th-century Franciscan convent and an ancient cemetery. All places are open to the public and tourists can wander around undisturbed to their hearts content. If you like water skiing or fishing, make friends with someone from Rio who has a boat, or else convince a salty old fisherman that he should rent you his. You might also visit the little fishing village of Barra de São João and watch the men working with their long woven nets. The thatched roof cottages are mixed with modern summer homes of Cariocas who have discovered it as a weekend spot. Seven miles south on the beach is the fishing village of Arraial do Cabo. Here scores of Japanese fishermen live and bring in giant whales during the cold months from June to September.

Paquetá Island is the most beautiful in all Guanabara Bay. There, without benefit of automobiles or trucks and forced to use an antiquated ferry boat to come and go, live some 6,000 Brazil-ians who wouldn't live anywhere else. When you visit it, you'll understand why. There is a calmness that is most inviting, after the hectic madness of Rio. There are soft sandy beaches and some interesting rock formations along the coast. Territory of the Tamóio Indians, it was later taken as a private vacation spot by the king, Dom João VI who arrived in Brazil in 1808. The cannon that was fired as a salute to the monarch each time he arrived is still there near the boat docks. Here you can rent a bicycle and go all around the island.

PRACTICAL INFORMATION FOR RIO

WHEN TO COME? Almost any time is a good time to visit Rio, for the climate is not that variable and there is something interesting going on almost all the time. The hottest months of the year are January to March when the temperature has risen to a sweltering 104 degrees in the shade. But these months are also the months with the most rain, and even though the rain's cooling effects lessen as the water evaporates, the sudden showers do give pleasant respites. The beaches are heavily populated during these months, and the sun can be unbearably hot for white-skinned tourists after 10 a.m. The coolest months of the years are July and August, when there is occasionally a gray cast to everything and the ocean comes crashing up over the sidewalks and fills the main avenue with sand. At this time Brazilians stay away from the beaches in droves, wear heavy Italian sweaters and complain of the cold. Visitors from more northern climates find the air comfortable and many even prefer it to the blistering heat of January.

Of course the big event in the Rio calendar is Carnival, that impossible spectacle of madness that takes place from Friday night to the morning of Ash Wednesday. Since the date for Easter Sunday varies from year to year, the date for Carnival does too, and visitors would be wise to check their calendars before planning to jump into the fun. Carnival can be as early as the first week in February or as late as March. These are the hot months, remember, so come prepared to sweat while you samba. Make reservations well in advance.

The cultural year begins in April with stars of international magnitude drawing capacity audiences during concert seasons for performance after performance. This is also the beginning for the artists and the galleries and hardly a week goes by without an important new showing of Brazilian painting or sculpture. Movie houses show many European art films, but remember that the movies are in their original language with Portuguese subtitles.

ARRIVING IN RIO. In this modern age almost everybody is in a hurry, and most tourists choose jet planes to make their arrival into Rio. The international airport is called Galeão, and the first building of the new terminal opened in 1977. This is the most modern in South America and replaces the inadequate building where travelers formerly had unpleasant memories of waiting in long, hot lines to get passports and health certificates stamped and have baggage inspected. The drive from the big international airport to the downtown area doesn't take more than a good half-hour's traveling. To go by bus to the downtown Santos Dumont domestic airport costs only about 75¢. There is, luckily, a taxi service (called Transcopass) that charges you a flat fee, depending on your destination. This is paid at the airport (in front of the taxi stand) in advance (about $5.50 to downtown, $7 to Copacabana, $10 to Leblon and São Conrado where some of the new hotels are located). You pay your driver nothing when you reach your destination, but it's customary to give him a tip. If you take a regular taxi, be prepared to argue the price beforehand. If you don't settle on a price in advance, be ready to pay more and even to be insulted if you don't give in easily. This is not meant to frighten you away from coming into Rio, but only to prepare you for what can happen.

If you have taken a ship you may either dock in Rio itself, or else in the city of Santos. The Customs shed is inside the Touring Club in the heart of downtown Rio, and taxi drivers and porters there are a little more honest than at the airport. If you arrive in Santos, you will have to go through Customs, then take a bus or a taxi to São Paulo (hour and 15 minutes drive), then take another bus (6 hours) or a plane (one hour) to Rio.

 WHAT TO SEE? Rio is divided into zones of North, Central and South. The city is not so big that the area can't be covered in a nonstop two-hour taxi ride if traffic is light, but there are so many things to see that one day is not nearly enough, and one week is more like it. The North zone is the poorer area, with the lower economic classes and small individual homes. Away from the breezes of the ocean it can also be sticky hot. But it does have interesting and important spots to visit like the Church of Penha; the Museu Nacional, in the former Imperial Palace, Quinta da Boa Vista (Tues.–Sun., noon–4:30); Maracanã (world's biggest soccer stadium); the Zoo; and the Indian Museum, Rua Mata Machado 127 (Mon.–Fri., 11–5).

The central part of the city is the commercial area, with bustling Avenida Rio Branco and the overly wide Avenida Presidente Vargas. Here are all of the banks, important department stores and office buildings. Here also is the Museum of Modern Art, Av. Infante dom Henrique (Mon.–Sat., noon–7 p.m., Sun. 2–7 p.m.), with a fine restaurant and cafeteria, daily film showings, and a lovely garden; the badly-in-need-of-reforms Museum of Fine Arts (Belas Artes), Av. Rio Branco 100 (Tues.–Sun., noon–9); the National History Museum, Praça Marechal Ancora (Mon.–Fri., noon–5:30 p.m., Sat.–Sun., 2:30–5:30 p.m.); the classic Municipal Theater; all the old Congress and Supreme Court buildings from when Rio was the nation's capital; and an area with movie houses called Cinelandia. Radiating from the center is the Roman-styled aqueduct built by the colonial Portuguese, a piece of the Old World remaining intact called Largo de Boticario and the world famed Corcovado mountain with the mammoth Christ statue.

Other museums in this area: Museum of Geology and Mineralogy, Av. Pasteur 404, Brazilian gems and semiprecious stones; Museum of Geography, Av. Calogeras 6-B (Mon.–Fri., 11–5:30), landscapes, maps; Museum of Pictures and Sound, Pca. Marechal Ancora (Tues.–Sun.); Museum of the Mentally Disturbed, Hospital D. Pedro II, Engenho de Dentro, over 50,000 works of art by the mentally disturbed; Museum of Sacred Arts, Praça Nossa Senhora da Gloria, a fine collection in one of Rio's most beautiful colonial churches; Museum of the Republic, Rua do Catete 153, the former Presidential Palace (Tues.–Fri., 1–7; weekends 3–7); Museum of Villa-Lobos, Rua da Imprensa 16, memorabilia of the famous composer.

The south of Rio is the more chic, more expensive, more comfortable place to live. Here are the best hotels, restaurants and beaches. Here is Copacabana and its sister neighborhoods Ipanema and Leblon.

A little farther are Avenida Niemeyer and São Conrado beach, where the newest and best hotels are located. Here also is the beautiful Lagoa (lagoon) Rodrigo de Freitas, the traditional Jockey Club, the calm and well-kept Botanical Gardens, Presidents' and governors' palaces and, rising from the bay's blue water, Sugar Loaf.

Out of town via private car or taxi you have the junglelike Tijuca forest with its Emperor's Table, Chinese View and impressive waterfall.

HOW TO GET ABOUT. At the airport vouchers are issued at set prices for taxis, depending on your final destination. Inside Rio, taxis are the best way to travel. Your hotel can arrange with *Avis, Nobre* or *Hertz* to rent a Brazilian-made Volkswagen beetle for as little as about $35 a day. Most accept your home state drivers license and credit cards. Rio taxis have meters that start at around 50 cents as we go to press. Between 11 p.m. and 7 a.m. the number 2 on or above the meter indicates the higher night fare. This fare is also charged for driving you up steep hills, such as to the Corcovado, although Rio taxi drivers are uncouth and often refuse to climb hills.

Bus travel is cheap and easy and, except at rush hours, fast and convenient. To go from Copacabana to the center of town, look for one marked *Castelo, E. Braga* or *Estrada de Ferro*. For the journey back to Copacabana, take any bus labeled *Forte, Copacabana, Ipanema* or *Leblon*. Much confusion is caused by the so-called "circular" buses. For instance, a bus marked *Gloria-Leblon via Copacabana* means that it goes to Leblon through Copacabana, but comes back a different way, known as *via Jockey* (or *Joquei*). So if you want to get to the Jockey Club or the *Jardim Botanico* from the Gloria area, take the bus marked *via Jockey*, remembering that it comes back the other way. The trick is to remember that if you are in Leblon and want to get to Copacabana, you must take the *via Jockey* bus, because that is the way it came, not the way it is going.

You get onto a bus at the rear and leave at the front, paying the conductor as you go through the turnstile. Buses only stop if you pull the cord by the side windows. Most bus fares are around Cr $1.20 (12 cents U.S.), and it is wise to have change ready. They won't change anything over Cr $5, and often they have no change at all. So keep plenty of coins handy for bus fares. New air-conditioned buses, called "frescões" (big fresh ones) go to most sections of the city, at fares ranging from 30 to 50 cents U.S.

If you want to take a tram ride, go to the station just off *Largo de Carioca*, take the tram marked *Dois Irmaos* and enjoy, for Cr $1.50 (about 12 cents U.S.), a breezy, rattling tour of the hillside Santa Teresa suburb, where many foreigners live. At the end of the line, you can take a bus on to *Silvestre*, have a cool beer and snack at the bar there, and come back the same way.

For intercity travel from Rio, avoid trains, except to São Paulo, Brasilia or Belo Horizonte. By air, flights leave daily to most major cities. Some internal flights leave from the international airport, and so details should be checked carefully.

For a glimpse of the real Brazil in comfort, take an intercity bus trip. Deluxe coaches are now available on a few main routes, and bus travel in general within Brazil is fast, reliable and cheap. Book well in advance, however, and check your reservation. The main bus station, known as the *Rodoviaria*, is five minutes from Praça Mauá by taxi.

A hydrofoil goes across the bay to Niteroi (50 cents), or drive across the impressive new bridge, paying a toll of $1.30 each way. There are ferries to Paqueta and other islands. You can also take a boat tour of Guanabara Bay, with lunch included.

TRAVEL AGENTS. For all kinds of national and international travel contact the American Action Service Agency, owned and operated by U.S. citizens.

SPORTS. In Rio, of course, getting a suntan is the major sport of the entire population. Copacabana Beach is the focal point of this mania and is always crowded. It is not the cleanest beach in the world either. There are other beaches in nearby Ipanema or Leblon that have fewer people. For more solitude with your sun, go on out to São Conrado, Barra da Tijuca, Recreio dos Bandeirantes, Prainha or Grumari.

Yachting is also a major sport in Rio and there are two yacht clubs in the Botafogo area that lies halfway between Copacabana and the center of town. Most exclusive and interesting is the Rio Yacht Club, where high society makes it a point to congregate. Clubs are open to members only and gate crashing is not easy.

Tennis is popular. See the manager of the Rio Country Club or the Caiçaras in Ipanema or the Paissandu Club in Leblon for special permission to play. Only hotel with courts is the Inter-Continental.

Surfing is popular at Copacabana Beach, Ipanema's Arpoador beach, and at Praia dos Bandeirantes. The sea is rough and dangerous.

Golf hasn't really caught on in Brazil as yet, but the two clubs that exist for it are stunning, beautifully trimmed places in the hills of Gavea. The Gavea Golf Club has many American and English members and a number of foreign firms keep memberships for their executives. The tourist can visit the club and admire the majestic scenery without being accompanied by a club member, but to play you must be invited. The Itanhanga Golf Club is nearby.

Ocean fishing goes on all year round, and if you don't know someone who has a boat you can always rent one. There are marlin as well as other ocean gamefish awaiting either your hook and sinker or your spear. No license is needed and the fish are so big that you won't have to throw any of them back.

Horse racing events are held Thursday nights and weekend afternoons at the Jockey Club. An impressive place with excellent grass and dirt tracks, it runs the best horses in the nation for your pleasure. Betting is not only permitted, but encouraged, and when you do win (with the inflation as it is) you may need a basket to carry away your money. The first Sunday in August is reserved for the Grande Premio Brasil, which draws the finest bluebloods from all over Latin America. It is also an occasion for ladies to wear elaborate hats and gowns and for the top brass, from the President on down, to show up glittering in medals.

Soccer rules supreme in Brazil, and will remain so for years to come. The best players in the world (this is no exaggeration) are on

ONCE UPON A TIME..

Once upon a time the best hotels in Rio were in Copacabana. In fact, the best of Rio was there too. But Rio grew more sophisticated, more exclusive, and in need of a true resort hotel, near but far enough from the hustle - bustle of Copacabana. That was when the Hotel Inter - Continental opened in Gavea. Adorned with mountains, overlooking the greens of the Gavea Golf Club and the beautiful beaches of São Conrado and Gavea, the Hotel Inter-Continental Rio offers you the best of two worlds. No parking problems no noise, uncrowded beaches, the most beautiful swimming pool in Rio, 2 tennis courts (two more to be built this year) and the international know-how of inter-Continental Hotels.

500 air-conditioned rooms with color tv and frigobars. Two fine restaurants. Pool terrace barbecue. Two snack bars. Discothèque. 24 hour room service. Two bars, a sauna and turkish baths, shops and boutiques, a Bank, a travel desk, an airline desk, hairdresser salon and convention facilities for 10 up to 1200 persons.

**WE WELCOME AND HONOR
AMERICAN EXPRESS CARDS**

HOTEL INTER-CONTINENTAL RIO

Rio: Av. Litorânea, 222 tel. 399-2200
Reservas: São Paulo: 257-5430
B. Horizonte (PANAM) 24-6348
Brasília (PANAM) 23-2000

SÃO PAULO

SALVADOR BAHIA

RIO DE JANEIRO

OTHON - IN THE TRADITION OF THE WORLD'S FINEST HOTELS

BELO HORIZONTE

BAHIA OTHON PALACE HOTEL - (Salvador, Brazil) - Deluxe resort hotel on Ondina Beach. 301 luxurious rooms and suites, pool, tropical gardens, nightclub, restaurant, coffee shop, sea view bar, and shopping arcade. Fully air conditioned. Convention facilities for 600. Tel. 71-044.

RIO OTHON PALACE HOTEL - Rio's most fabulous new hotel on Copacabana Beach. 606 luxurious rooms and suites. Rooftop pool, nightclub, restaurant, bars, coffee shop, Convention facilities for 700, shopping arcade. Fully air conditioned. Tel. 255-8812.

BELO HORIZONTE OTHON PALACE HOTEL - On the most sophisticated avenue of Belo Horizonte, overlooking Municipal Park. 317 spacious rooms, restaurant, pool, bar, coffee shop, shopping arcade, fully air conditioned. Convention facilities for 700 people.

OTHON PALACE HOTEL (São Paulo) - In the heart of São Paulo. With Presidential Suites. 253 deluxe rooms with air cond. Two restaurants, luxurious bar, conference and banquet rooms. Rua Libero Badaró, 190. Tel. 239-3277.

LEME PALACE HOTEL (Rio) - On Copacabana Beach. 194 air cond. rooms. Modern decor, deluxe and Presidential suites. Restaurant, beauty parlor, panoramic bar, coffee shop. Av. Atlântica 656, tel. 275-8080.

HOTEL TROCADERO (Rio) - On Copacabana Beach. Near shopping, movies, nightclubs and theatres.. Air conditioned. 15 minutes from downtown and domestic airport. 120 spacious comfortable rooms with bath. Av. Atlântica 2064, tel. 257-1834.

SAVOY OTHON HOTEL (Rio) - In Copacabana. Near the fashionable shops and 15 minutes from downtown. 156 air conditioned luxury rooms. Restaurant, bar and coffee shop. Av. Copacabana 995, tel. 257-8052.

HOTEL CALIFORNIA (Rio) - On Copacabana Beach. Near to nightlife and shops. 122 air conditioned rooms with bath. Sidewalk Café and pleasant bar and restaurant. Av. Atlântica 2616, tel. 257-1000.

HOTEL OLINDA (Rio) - On Copacabana Beach. 102 delightful rooms. Air conditioned. Sidewalk Café, spacious lobby with ocean view, bar and restaurant. Close to nightlife and shops. Av. Atlântica 2230, tel. 257-1890.

HOTEL LANCASTER (Rio) - On Copacabana Beach. 74 pleasant, spacious rooms with air cond. and bath. Handy to commerce, nightlife. 15 minutes from downtown and domestic airport. Av. Atlântica, 1470, tel. 257-1840.

HOTEL CASTRO ALVES (Rio) - One block from beach, in the heart of Copacabana. 76 rooms with bath and air cond. 15 minutes from downtown and domestic airport, walking distance to shops, nightlife. Av. Copacabana 552, tel. 257-1800.

AEROPORTO HOTEL (Rio) - Comfortable downtown hotel, five minutes from domestic airport and city's business center. 80 rooms with view of Sugarloaf and Guanabara Bay. Restaurant and bar. Av. Beira Mar 280, tel. 232-4280.

HOTEL SÃO PAULO (SP) - Comfortable and convenient hotel, in heart of business center. 178 rooms all with outside view and bath. Popular restaurant serving international cuisine and Bahian specialities. Praça das Bandeiras, tel. 239-1388.

OTHON HOTELS

CENTRAL RESERVATIONS OFFICES:
Rio de Janeiro: Telex - 2122655 - Cable Address: RESERVOTHON
São Paulo: Telex - 1121674 - Cable Address: HOTELOTHON
Bahia Salvador: Telex.- 711217 - Cable Address: BAHIAOTHON

H. Stern
Jewellers

Genuine Brasilian Gemstones
of breathtaking beauty,
fashioned into exquisite jewelry,
designed and produced by
South América's leading jewellers.

hand to delight the visiting soccer fan. Rio's top clubs have top players and any game that has teams like Vasco, Flamengo, Botafogo or Fluminense can be counted on for top excitement.

 SHOPPING. The best buy in Brazil today is precious and semiprecious stones, and there are a number of honest, integrity-minded shops where you can buy in confidence, sure that you are getting your money's worth. Top gem seller is *H. Stern*, Av. Rio Branco 173/177, Av. Atlântica 1782 (next to the Excelsior Hotel), a new branch at Ipanema's 113 Rua Garcia Davila, Galeão Airport (Exit Hall, Transit Hall and Domestic Terminal), downtown Santos Dumont domestic airport, the Touring Club, Hotel Sheraton, Intercontinental Meridien, Othon Palace and many other principal hotels. They offer one-year refund guarantee and world-wide service along with the largest selection in town at reasonable prices, from low-priced pieces to fabulous creations.

The leading specialists in emeralds are *Amsterdam and Sauer*. They have their own mines and shops at Av. Rio Branco 156, and Av. Atlântica 1782, in Copacabana. For fine jewelry, there are: *Roditi* at Av. Atlântica 2364, Copacabana, and Av. Rio Branco 133, as well as at the Copacabana Palace and Nacional hotels (they have a one-year guarantee and refund branch in New York). And *E. Simon*, Av. Copacabana 339-C; *Thompson*, Av. Copacabana 371-A; and *Star Jewelry*, Rua Duvivier 24. *Thompson Jewelry, Av.* Copacabana 371/A.

Maximino has its head office at Av. Rio Branco 25, as well as two branches in Copacabana: at Rua Santa Clara 27 and at Rua Figueireido Magalhães 131. Exclusively designed jewels and original watches by Piaget and Boucheron can be found at *Natan*, next to the Copacabana Palace Hotel, and at *Lucien* on the Av. Atlântica. *Zitrin*, at Av. Atlântica 1536, has superb jewels and curios. Also, a new branch on Ipanema's Av. Ataulfo da Paiva. Between Rua Rosario and Rua Buenos Aires are some excellent shops: *Schupp*, Rua Gonçalves Dias 49; *Ernani and Walter*, Praça Olavo Bilac 28, 2nd floor; and nearby, *Krause* and *Gregory and Sheehan*, both around the Flower Market. At Av. Copacabana 346, is *O. Lange*, a small shop where prices are low and quality is high. *Burle Marx*, right around the corner from the Copacabana Palace Hotel, specializes in unusual shaping of semiprecious stones placed into one of a kind settings. He designs necklaces and bracelets that have won prizes for their good taste. Another fine jeweler is *Ziemer*, who for 60 years has specialized in deep blue aquamarines and tourmalines from its own mines. Warning: stay away from anyone who tries to sell you a gem stone on the street. Unless you really can spot a good jewel from a worthless piece of glass, take your purchase problems to a reputable jeweler.

Indian artifacts and folklore items, like butterfly trays, wooden statues, cowboy hats and stuffed snakes, can be found in profusion in many shops downtown and in Copacabana. Highly recommended: *Liane*, Av. Rio Branco 25, and at Santa Clara 27; *Casa de Folklore*, Av. Rio Branco 173, 2nd floor and *Macumba Souvenir*, near the Excelsior Hotel Copacabana on Rua Fernando Mendes 28; *New-Copa Souvenirs*, Av. Copacabana 98-H/I; and *Casa Hugo*, Rua Buenos Aires near the Flower Market. *Joe and Jack Band*, Rua Barata Ribeiro 157a, heads Rio's exclusive antique stores, offering European and Brazilian items and specializing in silverware, furniture and fine Brazilian gems and jewels.

For embroidered handbags, see *Zita's* collection at the Touring Club and at their shop in Copacabana. For articles made of alligator skin, look for the specialty shop, *Souvenir do Brasil*, on Av. Rio Branco 25. For beautiful leather handbags visit *Rozwadowski*, Av. Rainha Elizabeth 152, suite 101. *Copacabana Presentes*, Av. Copacabana 331-A, specializes in leather and crocodile items, stones, skins, rugs, handbags and belts. *Copacabana Couros e Artesanatos*, nearby at Rua Fernando Mendes 45, also features crocodile goods and has exclusive designs for handmade bags and belts. Brazilian artistic wood carvings and native paintings by *Batista and Mady* are excellent souvenirs; visit their studio on Rua Pacheco Leão 1270 in Ipanema.

 HOTELS. Construction of fine, new international hotels and the ASTA (American Society of Travel Agents) convention in Rio in October 1975 have had marked effects on the city's hotel business. Older hotels have been remodeled or redecorated, and increased competition has made for improved service in nearly all. But even with four big hotels opening more than 2,300 deluxe rooms on the beaches (Sheraton and Inter-Continental in 1974, Othon Palace and Meridien in 1975–76), choice space is still scarce during Carnival, Gran Prix week, or when large conventions are taking place. So it is wise to book well in advance.

Hotel rates are comparable to those found in the U.S. At a *deluxe* hotel: single $25–$50, double $30–$60; *first class* hotels: single $18–$45, double $20–$45; *moderate* hotels: single $9–$20, double $12–$25. Nearly all hotels are European plan, but most serve an ample Continental breakfast at no additional cost.

VIDIGAL-SAO CONRADO (GAVEA)
Deluxe

Three deluxe hotels which started Rio's hotel boom are located beyond the end of Leblon on beaches called Vidigal or São Conrado (Gavea) away from the city. All have shuttle buses to Copacabana; they are:

RIO-SHERATON. Av. Niemeyer 121. This imposing complex is the only hotel which can claim a near-private beach, with no street to cross to bathe in the Atlantic surf; in addition, it has its own fresh-water pool and filtered salt-water lagoon. Rio's first international luxury-class hotel, it opened in August 1974 with 617 rooms, five restaurants, featuring Brazilian and international cuisine, one of Rio's most popular nightclubs

for dancing, outdoor amphitheater, health club, tennis courts, shops. *H. Stern* store.

INTER-CONTINENTAL RIO. Praia da Gavea 222. Opened its 500 air-conditioned rooms overlooking the beach and golf course in October 1974. Among its many attractions are a rotisserie, brasserie, snack bar, two cocktail lounges, lighted tennis courts, highly original discotheque, swimming pool with underwater bar stools, convention rooms. Convenient parking. *H. Stern* store.

NACIONAL-RIO. Av. Niemeyer 769, also on Gavea beach. First to be built in the area, this tower has 520 wedge-shaped rooms, all with phones in bedrooms and bathrooms, as well as 25 luxury suites and one floor of presidential suites. Five restaurants serve Brazilian and international specialties, and the nightclub usually features an excellent Brazilian samba floorshow. Across from lobby is Rio's biggest convention center (ASTA convention headquarters), theater, shops, heliport. *H. Stern* store.

COPACABANA
Deluxe

On the beach:

RIO OTHON PALACE. Av. Atlântica 3264. Opened in 1976, this hotel soars 30 stories above the center of famed Copacabana Beach and combines traditional Brazilian charm with the latest advances in hostelry. Largest in the beach area, it has 606 air-conditioned rooms, two presidential suites and a variety of other luxury suites. Rooftop bar and pool with panoramic view, international restaurants, bars, nightclub, banquet facilities for up to 700, shopping gallery, beauty parlor. *H. Stern* store.

MERIDIEN-RIO. Av. Atlântica 1020. A late 1975 inauguration, this one near the beginning of Copacabana; its 36 floors make it the tallest building on the beach. It counts 552 rooms, including two presidential suites, 130 more in the luxury class and 29 cabanas. Panoramic rooftop restaurant and rotisserie serving international and French cuisine, pool, bars, nightclub, sauna, shops, beauty parlor. *H. Stern* store.

COPACABANA PALACE. Av. Atlântica 1702. The best known of Rio's hotels and the oldest in the deluxe category. Recently renovated again. 400 rooms, 2 restaurants, 24-hour service, a sidewalk cafe with view to the beach on one side and pool on the other, theater. *H. Stern* store.

LEME PALACE. A posh establishment at Av. Atlântica 656 in the Copacabana Beach area known as Leme. 194 rooms, good restaurant and sidewalk bar, cozy rooftop bar. Entirely air-conditioned, and site of leading supper club, *Sacha Rubin's Balaio.* *H. Stern* store.

OURO VERDE. Av. Atlântica 1456. One of 8 hotels in the world which retain the "discreet charm of the small hotels," according to *Fortune* magazine, this 66-room Swiss-owned and -managed jewel enjoys international prestige. Exquisite decor, all-round comfort and courteous service. Renowned gourmet restaurant, bar with garden, classic hospitality. *H. Stern* store.

First Class

On the beach:

Excelsior, Av. Atlântica 1800. 220 rooms, fine restaurant and bar with ocean view. Rates include one meal in addition to Continental breakfast.
Miramar, Av. Atlântica 3668. Restaurant, rooftop bar, marvelous view. Reasonable.

Regente, Av. Atlântica 3716. Reasonable, recently renovated.
Luxor, Av. Atlântica 2552. Recently redecorated. Terrace restaurant.
Debret, Av. Atlântica 3564. Air conditioned, ocean view.
California, Av. Atlântica 2616. Modern rooms, bar, restaurant.

Trocadero, Av. Atlântica 2064. Fine Brazilian restaurant, *Moenda.*

Lancaster, Av. Atlântica 1470. Family atmosphere.

Olinda, Av. Atlântica 2230.

Just off the beach (not more than a block) and first-class are:

Savoy Othon, Av. Copacabana 995. 160 rooms, fine restaurant and bars. *H. Stern* store.

Continental Palace. Rua Gustavo Sampaio 320, in Leme.

Moderate

Two smaller and more moderate hotels located on Copacabana Beach are:

Riviera, Av. Atlântica 4122, at far end of the beach.

Praia Leme, Av. Atlântica 886, at the beginning. Cozy.

One or two blocks off Copacabana:

Toledo, Rua Domingos Ferreira 71.

Castro Alves, Av. Copacabana 552.

Canada, Av. Copacabana 667.

Plaza Copacabana, Av. Princesa Isabel 263.

Biarritz, Rua Aires Saldanha 54.

Apa, Rua Republica de Peru 305.

Acapulco, Rua Gustavo Sampaio 854.

Angrense, Trav. Angrense 25.

Martinique, Rua Sá Ferreira 30.

IPANEMA
Deluxe

On Ipanema Beach:

ARPOADOR INN. Rua Francisco Otaviano 177. At the beginning of the beach. Casually elegant, with 50 air-conditioned rooms and restaurant.

SOL IPANEMA. Av. Vieira Souto 320. Restaurant, bar, beauty parlor, sun deck and children's pool on roof.

First Class

Near the beaches in the Ipanema and Leblon areas:

Everest-Rio, Rua Prudente de Morais 1117. Opened April 1975; this 22-story hotel has 176 rooms and everything to make guests comfortable.

Vermont, Rua Visconde de Pirajá 254.

Carlton, Rua João Lira 68. Quiet surroundings.

San Marco, Rua Visconde de Pirajá 524.

DOWNTOWN
First Class

GLORIA. Praia do Russel 632. In Flamengo not far from the city's center, it has 730 new or recently renovated deluxe and first-class rooms. Fine colonial-style restaurant, bars, pool, terrace with view. Convention center. Far from beaches. *H. Stern* store.

Moderate

Other hotels, downtown or between the beach area and the center:

Center, Rua Teófilo Otoni 82, downtown. Opened late 1975. Air-conditioned, with refrigerator-bar in each room.

Flamengo Palance, Praia do Flamengo 6. 60 rooms, opened in 1975.

Empire, Rua da Gloria 46. Fine restaurant on top floor with magnificent view of the bay.

Novo Mundo, Praia do Flamengo 20. Restaurant, bar. *H. Stern* store.

Serrador, Praça Mahatma Gandhi. 14. In "Cinelandia," Rio's downtown movie house district.

São Francisco, Rua Visconde de Inhauma 93. Air conditioned, restaurant.

Guanabara Palace, Av. Presidente Vargas 392. In banking district. Restaurant, bar.

Regina, Rua Ferreira Viana 29.

Florida, Rua Ferreira Viana 75. *H. Stern* store .

Argentina, Rua Cruz Lima 30.

Paissandu, Rua Paissandu 23.

Ambassador, Rua Senador Dantas 25.

Grande Hotel OK, Rua Senador Dantas 24.

Aeroporto, Av. Beira Mar 280. Near city airport.

Presidente, Rua Pedro I 19.

Nelba, Rua Senador Dantas 46.

Itajubá, Rua Alvaro Alvim 23.

 RESTAURANTS. Typical Brazilian food is varied, unusual and delicious, but one of the biggest troubles for the tourist is trying to get some of it. Almost all the good restaurants in Rio serve international-type food only and shy away from the home product. Why? Because when the Brazilian goes out to dine, he wants to eat something different from what the wife or the maid gives him every day. Try at least one *feijoada, vatapá* or the mouthwatering *muqueca de peixe*. A meal with beer or wine will cost about $10; more at hotels.

Typical Brazilian Dishes

Moenda, at the Trocadero Hotel, Av. Atlântica 2064. Nice atmosphere. Seafood specialties.

Chalé, Rua da Matriz 54. A converted colonial home, decorated with Brazilian antiques. Dinner only. Closed Sunday.

Sinhá, Rua Constante Ramos 140.

Oxalá, Rua Francisco Serrador 2.

Tabafé, Rua da Matriz 62.

Another worthwhile place is the *AlbaMar* at the former Mercado Municipal. Try deviled crabs, fish chowder or fish filet in black butter. It's downtown and crowded at lunchtime, they close at 9:30 p.m. Nice view of Guanabara Bay.

The Brazilian "barbecue" restaurant is called *churrascaria*. The tab for 2 will run about $10.

Top honors go to the *Gaucha* on Rua Laranjeiras 114, off Largo do Machado. Their branch on Ipanema Beach is *Barril 1800*, Av. Vieira Souto 106. With an open patio is the *Jardim* at 225 Rua Republica de Peru in Copacabana; *Parque Recreio*, Rua Marques Abrantes 96 in Botafogo; *Las Brasas* at Rua Humaita 110, also in Botafogo; *Rincão Gaucho*, Rua Marques de Valença 83; *Carreta,* in Ipanema, Rua Visconde de Pirajá 451 (Austro-Hungarian dishes, too); *Leme*, near Copacabana Palace, on Rua Rodolfo Dantas 16; *Majorica*, Rua Senador Vergueiro 11/15; *Roda Viva*, Av. Pasteur 520, at the funicular station to

Pão de Açucar. Try the *churrasco mixto*, pieces of beef and pork, or a *lombo de porco* (pork roast), filet mignon or T-bone. *Chamego do Papai*, downtown at Av. Erasmo Braga 64, in front of the "Palace of Justice," where lawyers and judges go for barbecued baby beef specialties.

French

Some of the best French restaurants are: *Le Relais*, Rua General Venancio Flores 411, in Leblon; *Le Bec Fin*, Av. Copacabana 178A. *Les Templiers*, Av. Borges de Medeiros 3207; *Monte Carlo*, Rua Duvivier 21; *Michel*, Rua Fernando Mendes 25 (very expensive); *Bistro*, Rua Fernando Mendes 7; *Ragout*, Av. Bartolomeu Mitre 366, Leblon; *Castelo da Lagoa*, Av. Epitaçao Pessoa 156. *Le Provence*, Rua dos Jangadeiros 10-A, Ipanema; *La Potiniere*, Rua Montenegro 288; *La Guillotine*, Rua Barão da Torre 422.

Chinese

China Town, Rua Barao da Torre 450. *Shangri-La*, Rua Almirante Guilhelm 74. *Oriento*, Rua Bolivar 64. *Chon Kou*, Av. Atlântica 3880. *Chu's*, Rua Souza Lima 37. *Great China*, Rua Siqueira Campos 12.

Swiss

Le Mazot, Rua Paula Freitas 31-A, Copacabana; *Le Chalet Suisse*, Rua Xavier da Silveira 112, Copacabana; or *Swiss Club*, downtown, Rua Cândido Mendes 157 (lunch or dinner, closed Mon.).

Miscellaneous

Russian food at *Doubiansky*, Rua Gomes Carneiro 90. Japanese dishes at *Miako*, Rua do Ouridor 45, downtown, or *Akasaka*, Av. Copacabana 1391. Very expensive for what you get.

Danish dishes at *Helsingor*, Rua Garcia Davila 77. Mexican food at *Lagoa Charlie's*, Rua Maria Quitéria 136. For Spanish food, *Rio Xerez*, and *El Faro*, Av. Atlântica 3808, or *Don Paquito*, Rua Dias Ferreira 233.

Fish

If fish is what you crave, then have lunch or an early dinner (they close at 8:30 p.m.) downtown at *Cabaça Grande*, Rua Ouvidor 12. Try the *muqueca* or a filet of white fiish in shrimp sauce. Inexpensive, it's crowded at lunch time and no reservations are taken over the phone. (P.S. Don't be shocked by the rundown neighborhood it's in.) *Principe Real*, with good seafood, Av. Atlântica 947, Leme.

Take a taxi to Leblon and try the *Cavalo Marinho* (Sea Horse) at Dias Ferreira 147. Clean with good service; their shrimps on a skewer or filet of white fish can't be beat. They close at 1 a.m. Also good are *Real*, downtown at Rua Pharoux 3 and at Av. Atlântica 514A; *Bar dos Pescadores*, Estrada da Barra da Tijuca 793; and *Ancora*, Av. Sernambetiba 18151.

COPACABANA

Here are some of the gourmet restaurants in Copacabana. Small and expensive: at Ouro Verde Hotel, one of the finest hotel dining rooms in Latin America, with impeccable service, a first-rate menu, and haute cuisine; *Bife d'Ouro* at Copacabana Palace; the new *La Fourchette*, an international restaurant at the Leme Palace Hotel; the *Saint-Honoré*, on the 37th floor of the Hotel Meridien; and the dining rooms of Excelsior and Miramar hotels.

Portuguese

Popular is the *Adega de Evora* on Rua Santa Clara 292. Try their grilled *bacalhau* (dried cod fish) moistened well with olive oil. *Fado; Lisboa A Noite*. overlooks Copacabana. Very expensive.

Another place worth your visit is the *Taverna O Galo* on Rua 5 de Julho 312. Decorated like a cave, it's painted white and studded with multicolored Portuguese ceramic roosters. Good steaks and pale pink wine from Portugal. Slightly expensive.

International

For international dishes, try *Antonio*, Av. Bartolomeu Mitre 297C, Leblon; *Antonino*, Av. Ataulfo de Paiva 528 (American bar); and *Berro d'Agua*, Rua Alberto de Campos 12 (open for lunch Sat., Sun., closed Mon.). *Castelo da Lagoa*, Av. Epitacio Pessoa 1560. International cuisine on Rio's sleepy lagoon. *Open*, Rua Maria Quitera 83, Ipanema. *De Encontro*, Rua Barato Ribeiro 750-B. *Nino's*, Rua Domingos Ferreira 242-A. *Concorde*, Rua Prudente de Morais 129.

A new landmark opened in downtown Rio in 1977: *La Tour* —South America's first revolving restaurant, at the top of the 34-story Aeronautical Club building at Rua Santa Luzia 121, half a block from the American Consulate General. Spectacular view of the entire city. Open for lunch and dinner.

Italian

Good are *LaFiorentina* and *Sorrento*, both located on the beach on Av. Atlântica Leme. Try the pizza and green lasagna. Also *Forno e Fogão*, Rua Souza Lima 48A; *Pappagallo*, Av. Prado Junior 237, Copacabana; and *Cesare*, R. Joaquim Nabulo 44-B, Copacabana. Also *Mafia*, new, sophisticated and elegant, at Rua Joaquim Nabuco 53, *L'Amore*, Rua Visconde da Pirajá 514, and *O Pirata*, Rua Carlos Gois 83, Leblon.

German

Alt Berlin, live music, R. Visconde de Pirajá 22, Ipanema. *Lucas*, Av. Atlântica 3744. Pig's knuckles and sauerkraut in the tropics, with Brazil's own beer. *Alpino*, Av. Epitácio Pessoa 40.

HERE AND THERE

While you are downtown, you might try *Mesbla Department Store* (Rua do Passeio 42), which also has an economy-priced cafeteria on the first floor; Museum of Modern Art (Avenida Dom Henrique), lunch only; *Maison de France* (lunch only), Av. Antonio Carlos 58 for French food, and *Mosteiro*, 13 Rua São Bento, for classic Portuguese and Brazilian cuisine.

For the economy minded, *Bucsky*, a popular Hungarian specialty restaurant, Rua Rosario 133; *German Ernesto*, Rua Buenos Aires 100; *Casa Westfalia*, Rua Assembleia 37 and 73 (all for lunch only). *Confeteria Colombo*, 36 Gonçalves Dias, in the heart of the shopping district. Good lunch, reasonable. Art nouveau decor.

In Botafogo, stop at the *Sol-e-Mar*, a seafood restaurant open for dinner and a bar and terrace open for lunch, where you can enjoy a magnificent view of Guanabara Bay. Sightseeing launches leave from here several times a day.

Others in Leblon: *La Mole; Baco; Le Figaro; Miramar; Rick; Churrascaria Brasao da Torre*, Barão da Torre 218. *Bulldog*, Dias Ferreira 571.

Rio's beaches are dotted with snack bars and walk-in sandwich stands. Among the best are *Castelinho* in Ipanema, *Bob's*, and *Gordon's*, an ever-growing chain of American-style hamburger stands, serve good snacks and ice cream. McDonalds has plans of opening in Brazil also, and the first may already be operating in Copacabana by the time you get here.

 NIGHTCLUBS. The legend of gay Rio is very exaggerated—there are almost no places which one could compare with the *Lido*, the *Folies Bergères*, or a really top New Yorker-type nightclub. What there are are a number of small little *boîtes* where the customer can buy a drink and listen to a jazz combo or a bossa nova singer. Most shows start after midnight. For excellent Brazilian folklore shows, there are the nightly "Brazilian Follies" dances with dinner at the Hotel Nacional Rio.

Sacha Rubin's *Balaio*, Avenida Atlântica 565 (Leme Palace Hotel) is a perfect supper club-cocktail lounge. No cover, no minimum, seats only about 60. Better make reservations.

Sambao, in Copacabana, is the place to go for the samba beat. For the young, discotheque set, there's the *New Jirau*, Rua Siqueira Campos, 12; the nearby French-owned *Le Bateau*; *Katakombe*, Av. Copacabana 1241; *Flag;* Rua Xavier Silveira 13; *Pussycat*, Rua Belfort Roxo 88-B; *Lisboa a Noite*, Rua Francisco Otaviano 21; *Sachinna* (Rua Antonio Vieria 6-A); *Le Bilbouquet*; *On the Rocks* in the Panorama Palace Hotel and *Zum-Zum, New Kilt Club, Boite* restaurant dance, (Av. Copacabana 266) all in Copacabana. A number of new night places, some with shows, opened recently in the fashionable Ipanema and Leblon districts: *Number One*, Rua Maria Quiteria 19. Ipanema. *Open*, restaurant bar. Rua Maria Angelica 83; *Pujol*, Rua Anibal Mendonca 36. *Oba Ôba*, Rua Visconde de Pirajá 499. *706*, Av. Ataulfo de Paiva 706. Good late-night Carnival Samba show at *Sucata*, next to Leblon's drive-in cinema.

Local food and samba are offered at *Las Brasas*, Humaita 110, and *Sinha*, Constante Ramos 140.

Downtown: *Assyrius*, a sophisticated strip-show boîte, Av. Rio Branco 277.

Similar skin shows in Copacabana at *Erotika*, Av. Prado Junior 63 and *La Corne*, Av. Copacabana 73.

For more taxi girls, go to *Barmen's Club* (Lido Square), *Bolero*, Av. Atlântica, and to small boîtes around the Rua Rodolfo Dantas.

For live music, visit the *Crazy Rabbit* bar, the *Saloon* (closed Sun.). Men's bars are *Piper* and *Big Al's*.

Making a big hit with Brazilians and foreigners alike is the *Lord Jim Pub*, which opened in 1975, with imported British decor at Rua Paul Redfern 63 in Ipanema.

For drinks, snacks and girl-watching in Ipanema: *Castelinho*, Av. Vieira Souto 100; *Lagoa*, Av. Epitacio Pessoa 685 (quiet, with a view over the Lagoa); *Varanda*, Praça N. Senhora da Paz (a restaurant for Bohemians).

The less expensive, German-type beer halls are popping up all over. The biggest, with 2500 seats, is *Canecão*, Rua Lauro Muller 1,

Botafogo, top-name floorshows (cover charge $4). Others, smaller but fine for dancing, are *Bierklause*, Rua Ronald de Carvalho 55; *Schnitt,* Rua Volun- tarios da Patria 24; *Hoffman's*, Rua Ronald de Carvalho 55-C. All serve dinner. *Special*, night club of the jet set, Rua Prudente de Morais 129.

 ART GALLERIES. Rio is very art conscious and supports a number of very good galleries. Prices are high but the following are the most reputable, with high quality national or foreign works.

Bonino (Barata Ribeiro 578) great selection to offer, *Vernon* (Fernando Mendez 18B and 28B) primitives only and *Petite Galerie* (Praça General Osorio 53 in Ipanema) lean toward the younger generation's more inventive newcomers. *Relevo* (Copacabana 252) has a good assortment of primitives as well as more formalized national painters. Others: *Ambiente Spazio* (Rua Barata Ribeiro, 200), *Guignard* (Rua Barata Ribeiro, 529/C), *Debret* (Avenida Copacabana, 331/B), *IBEU* (Avenida Copacabana, 690), *Piccola* (Avenida Copacabana, 690), *Meira* (Avenida Copacabana, 1063), *Dezon* (Avenida Copacabana, 1133), *Decor* (Rua Toneleros, 356), *Nagasawa* (Rua Constante Ramos, 43), *Modulo* (Rua Bolivar, 21), *Exclusividades* (Rua Xavier da Silveira, 19/A), *KASA* (Rua Almirante Gonçalves 4-A), the only store authorized by the National Indian Foundation to sell indigenous art and handicraft, *Varanda* (Rua Xavier da Silveira, 59), *Cantu* (Rua Barão de Ipanema, 29/A), *L'Atelier* (Rua Barão de Ipanema, 110), *Giro* (Rua Francisco Sá, 35), *Goeldi* (Rua Prudente de Moraes, 129), *Santa Rosa* (Rua Visconde Pirajá, 22), *Meia Pataca* (Rua Visconde Pirajá, 47), *Morada* (Avenida Ataulfo de Paiva, 23), *Escada* (Avenida General San Martin, 12–19), *Montparnasse* (Rua São Clemente, 72).

MUSEUMS. See *What to See?* section at beginning of *Practical Information for Rio*, earlier.

 TOURS. *Yacht Turismo do Brasil*, Avenida Reporter Nestor Moreira, Botafogo, offers tours of Guanabara Bay, aboard the *Bateau-Mouche* which has a good bar and English-speaking guides. Morning, afternoon and all-day tours are available at prices ranging from about $12 to $24, including snacks or cold buffet. City tours are possible through several agencies. Sample prices (furnished by *Brazil Safaris & Tours*, Rua Cosme Velho 103, and in the Sheraton and Inter-Continental lobbies): Corcovado $10, Sugar Loaf $12, Niteroi Bridge $9, Paquetá Island $19 including lunch. *Istur Tours and Travel*, Rua São José 90, Suite 1206, specializes in tours to Salvador, Manaus, Iguaçu Falls. *Acquatur Serviços de Turismo* offers yachts to rent for deepsea fishing and for short or extended bay or ocean cruises. *Marlin Tours,* Av. Copacabana 605, Suite 1203, offers day-tours among primitive tropical islands in Sepetiba Bay aboard a luxurious native schooner.

 MEDICAL SERVICES. Since the closing of the Strangers' Hospital in 1967, English-speaking doctors can be contacted by calling the U.S. Consulate-General at 252-8055 or Dr. Roger Smith at Clinica Sorocaba, tel. 226-5531.

The *International Association for Medical Assistance for Travelers* (*IAMAT*), Av. Princessa Isabel 323, Apt. 1113, Rio de Janeiro. Tel. 225-3443.

USEFUL ADDRESSES. American Consulate, Presidente Wilson 147. British Consulate, Praia do Flamengo 322. Canadian Consulate, Av. Presidente Wilson 165. American Express, Repr. by Brazil Safari Tours, Av. Rio Branco 156, Room 3119. Wagons-Lits Cook, Av. Rio Branco 156, loja 126. Guanabara Tourist Office, Rua Real Grandeza 293. Automobile Club of Brazil, Rua do Passeio 90. Lions Club, Rua Senador Dantas 74. Rotary Club, Av. Nilo Peçanha 26, 12th floor. American Chamber of Commerce, Av. Rio Branco 123. The Union Church, Rua dos Oitis 63 in Gávea, interdenominational, English-language services. Our Lady of Mercy Chapel, Rua Visconde de Caravelas 48 in Botafogo, is the American Catholic Church. Anglican Church, Rua Real Grandeza 99. Synagogue, Rua Tenente Possolo 8. Brazil Herald, daily English newspaper, Rua do Rezende 65, Sightseeing excursions: USE, Av. Rio Branco 9; Breda, Av. Rio Branco 257. American Society and the American Club, Av. Rio Branco 123. Touring Club of Brazil, Praça Mauá, downtown. Avis, Rua Bolivar 17-A. American Rent-a-Car, Rua Laranjeiras 147B. Hertz, Praia do Flamengo 244. Nobre, Rua Gustavo Sampaio 826. BL Rent-a-Car, Rua Arnaldo Quintela 10.

PRACTICAL INFORMATION FOR RIO REGION

WHAT TO SEE? Watch for the strangely shaped rock called the Finger of God on your drive up to the mountain cities. Be sure and visit the Hotel Quitandinha in Petropolis, if only to just wander for hours among its many salons, and the Imperial Palace, now a museum, with intimate objects that belonged to South America's only royal family. In Teresópolis if you're lucky you may witness a fleecy cloud snuggling right in the middle of the main street. Well beyond Teresópolis is an impressive high-in-the-air Swiss and German colony called Nova Friburgo that contains excellent hotels and offers peace and quiet for those desiring it.

Along the beach northward from Rio is Cabo Frio where there are white painted forts originally built to chase away French pirates and deserted beaches. Leaving the city in the other direction are the white sand, unspoiled beaches of Barra da Tijuca, now a virtual suburb of Rio, and Recreio dos Bandeirantes. This area is crowded on weekends and holidays, when thousands visit the newly constructed clubs and international restaurants famed for seafood.

If you keep going in this direction, down the new Rio-Santos Highway, you will come to the resort areas of Itacuruçá, Angra dos Reis and Parati, with their hundreds of beaches and islands as well as relics and monuments dating from colonial days.

And way up in Rio's Guanabara Bay lies the island of Paquetá, where automobiles are forbidden and inhabitants ride about in horse-drawn carriages or on bicycles under flamboyantly flowered trees.

HOW TO GET ABOUT. Regular buses leave from Estação Rodoviária every half hour or so for the towns of Petropolis and Teresópolis; the ride takes slightly more than one hour and costs about 85 cents to the former, $1.25 to the latter. Most of the tourist agencies have special excursions there as well.

Nova Friburgo can be reached either by going there after you've seen Teresópolis or by taking a 3-hour bus trip from the Estação Rodoviária. Price is about $1.75.

Cars can be rented in Rio, São Paulo and Brasilia. There is a new highway to Salvador, capital of the State of Bahia, on which the tourist can drive to the mountain resorts of Nova Friburgo, Teresópolis and Petropolis, and many beach resorts can be reached down the Rio-Santos Highway.

Paquetá Island can only be reached by ferry boat, from Praça Quinze, with boats leaving regularly every hour starting from six a.m. The last boat to leave the island on the return trip to Rio is at nine p.m. The trip takes almost two hours and the boats are not too uncomfortable.

HOTELS. There are still no big hotels on the Barra da Tijuca or Recreio dos Bandeirantes, but there are plenty of small motels and clubs, used principally on weekends.

PETROPOLIS. Landmark is *Quitandinha*, built as a super gambling casino with dozens of richly appointed rooms. There are an excellent restaurant and bar, ice rink, indoor and outdoor pools, tennis and squash courts, roller rink, billiard rooms, stables and riding facilities. Landscaped garden has a pretty lake where you can scoot around in a pedallo boat. The hotel supposedly is for members who have purchased shares. Your travel agent may be able to get you in.

Other good hotels with restaurants: *Pousada da Serra*, Rua Olavo Bilac 467; *Margarida's*, Rua Monsenhor Bacelar 274; *Amob-Tour*, on the highway coming in from Rio; *Casablanca Center*, Rua General Osório 28.

TERESÓPOLIS. No deluxe hotels. You won't go wrong staying at the *Pinheiros,* in Quebra-Frascos suburb, the São Moritz, way out on the road to Nova Friburgo, *Residência* on Avenida Feliciano Sodre 930, the *Phillip* on Jardim Europa, *Le Magourou* on Avenida Delfim Moreira 439 or *Higino Palace Hotel* on Avenida Oliveira Botelho 328. Also recommended: *Teresópolis*, Avenida Dr Oliveira Botelho, 647.

NOVA FRIBURGO. It's a toss up as to whether the *Park* (São Clemente 140) or *Bucsky* (Ponto da Saudade) is the best. The latter has a definite European atmosphere and beautifully tended grounds. Other good hotels: *Le Chalet Suisse* in Alto Mury; the *Fazenda,* back in the hills out of São João (charming); *Floresta*, next to Olifas; *Repose*, Ladeira Rebaday 6; *Schumacher*, Praça Suspire, 114; *Granja São Bernardo* (bungalows only); *Garlic,* in Mury on the highway; *Sans-Souci* (Jardim Sans-Souci) and *Olifas* (Parque Olifas).

ARAURAMA. *La Gondola* and the *Parque.*

CABO FRIO. Best stopping places in this colonial beach town are: *Malibu Palace* on the Praia da Barra, *Helena* on Rua Mario Quintanilha 62 with the *Lido* in second place (Praia do Forte) and the *Cabo Frio* and *Colonial* a very close third (Porto Rocha

160). Other new hotels are *Acapulco; Motel Cabo Frio Sol; Ogiva; Portofino; Palace; Residência; Cabanas.* All have good restaurants, meals included in the room price.

BUZIOS (CABO FRIO). The "Côte D' Azur"—like the fashionable summer resort of the international jet set, among others Brigette Bardot. The best hotels are: *Hotel dos Avellandeda, Pousada dos Buzios* and *Biba's.*

PAQUETA. The *Fragata* on Praia Grosso 58 is not even a good second-class hotel. Its rates are a little too high and the restaurant leaves much to be desired. The *Balneario Lido* on José Bonifacio 59 or the *Miramar* on Domingos Olimpio 12 are not much better.

ITACURUÇA. Two hotels are located on tropical paradise islands in this area about 55 miles west of Rio. Newest is the *Jaguanum,* on its own beach on Jaguanum Island, about 30 minutes by launch from the Itacuruçá pier. Luxurious apartments and bungalows, deepsea fishing. European management. Book in advance in Rio.

AGUAS LINDAS is nearer, in a cove where many of the wealthy have weekend cottages, on the island of Itacuruçá. Thirty-two rooms and bungalows overlooking the beach.

ANGRA DOS REIS. Make this your headquarters for visiting some of the 300 islands in the Ilha Grande Bay, staying at the *Hotel do Frade* on a beach 18 miles from town, at the *Hotel da Praia,* eight miles out on Ipirapuã Beach, or at the *Londres,* Av. Raul Pompéia 75, in the heart of this village settled in the 16th Century.

PARATI. Leading hotels in this colonial city surrounded by beaches, rivers and islands are the small but picturesque *Coxixo,* Rua Tenente Francisco Antonio 62; *Pousada Pardieiro,* number 74 of the same street; or *Hotel dos Candeeiros,* Rua Dona Geralda 25.

RESENDE. 143 kms. from Rio, is an excellent vacation spot in Itatiaia Park. Among its attractions: Agulhas Negras Peak; Funil Dam—a Finnish settlement; Blue Lake waterfalls; Agulhas Negras military academy. The best hotel is *Simon,* at Itatiaia; *Repousa Itatiaia,* Tyll.

RESTAURANTS. In Petrópolis you might try *Chaillot* and *Chez Henri* for very good French cuisine; *Myrthes Paranhos, Bauemstube, La Terrine, Buon Giorno* are also well recommended. On Paquetá, the *Netuno* on Rua José Bonifacio has some very good seafood. At Barra da Tijuca be sure and have either lunch or dinner at the *Bar dos Pescadores.* Reasonable prices, fast service, and the decoration is one of dockside simplicity. *Recreio dos Bandeirantes* has the *Ancora* Restaurant. Prices are rather high but the food is good. In Cabo Frio, try the assorted shrimp specialties or the mullet steaks served at *Dom Bosco* on the town square; *Toni, Palace, Lido* on the beach.

In Teresópolis look for *Taberna Alpino, Bife Grande, Palhota, Cremaillere, Chalé do Alto.*

In Buzios (Cabo Frio), the best restaurants: *Piscis; Spelunk; Bar do Tião; Pousada do Sul; Joaquim Maia; Palato; Bibas; Le Pirate, Igrejinha* and *Area Alex.*

INDUSTRIALIZED BRAZIL

São Paulo and the Progressive South

No matter how well you've studied Latin America and boned up on Brazil, the city of São Paulo will come as a startling surprise. There is nothing like it in any other South American nation, no other place that can come close or that even hints of coming close. It's the richest area in South America, the fastest growing and the pride of all the Brazilians.

When you approach the city from the air, it looks like Chicago or Detroit. There are towering skyscrapers—many of them—lining double-lane highways and avenues, where thousand of cars, buses and trucks stream by. More than eight million people call it home. At night the city lights up like a Christmas tree in swirls of neon and fluorescent bulbs, while advertising slogans, weather reports and the latest news is flashed to the busy Paulistas from the tops of tall buildings. The city boasts the best restaurants in Latin America, the most comfortable movie houses and some of the best schools. Up higher than Rio and away from the coast, it also has a cooler climate that is conducive to work and study. Here sweaters are the rule rather than the exception.

The state of São Paulo is a fit setting for its active, pulsating capital city. With some of the richest farmland in Brazil, it supplies almost half the nation's coffee, cotton, fruits and vegetables. The fertile land is crisscrossed by an excellent system of railways and modern highways, which the industries scattered in the small towns use to their advantage.

Whenever the Paulista needs to get away from the routine of making money, he takes an hour's drive down from his lofty

154

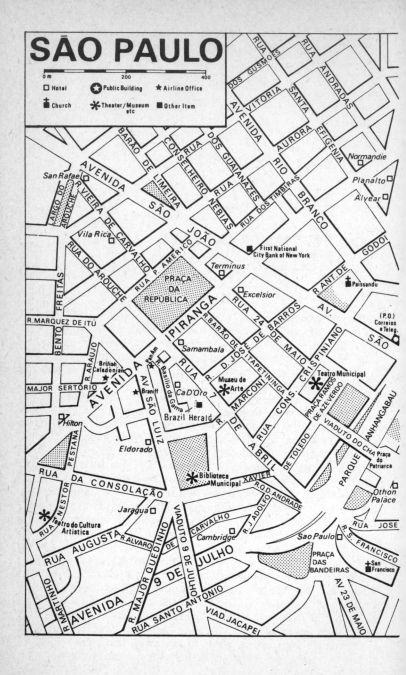

SÃO PAULO

0 m   200   400

☐ Hotel   ★ Public Building   ★ Airline Office
☗ Church   ✳ Theater/Museum etc   ■ Other Item

RUA DOS GUSMOES
RUA
RUA ANDRADAS
AVENIDA VITORIA
AURORA
SANTA EFIGENIA
RIO BRANCO

Normandie
Planalto
Alvear

San Rafael
AVENIDA
LARGO DO AROUCHE
VIEIRA DE CARVALHO
BARÃO DE LIMEIRA
RUA CONSELHEIRO NEBIAS
RUA DOS GUAIANAZES
RUA DOS TIMBIRAS

Vila Rica
SÃO JOÃO
RUA P. AMERICO
RUA DO AROUCHE
RUA DE FREITAS

First National
City Bank of New York

GODOI
R. ANT. DE
Paissandu

Terminus

PRAÇA DA REPÚBLICA

Excelsior

R.MARQUEZ DE ITÚ
BENTO FREITAS
IPIRANGA
R BARÃO DE I.
RUA 24 DE BARROS
DE MAIO
CONS. CRISPINIANO
AV. SÃO
(P.O.) Correios e Teleg.

Samambala
R. DOS ITAPETININGA

R. ARAUJO
Pan Am
British Caledonian
Basilio da Gama
Braniff
Ca D'Oro
Brazil Herald
Museu de Arte
Teatro Municipal
Praça Ramos de Azevedo

MAJOR SERTÓRIO
AVENIDA SÃO LUIZ
RUA DE ABRIL
RUA MARCONI
RUA CONS. CRISPINIANO
DE TOLEDO
VIADUTO DO CHÁ
ANHANGABAU
Praça do Patriarca

Hilton
PESTANA
Eldorado

RUA DA CONSOLAÇÃO
XAVIER
Biblioteca Municipal
R.Q.D ANDRADE
Othon Palace
RUA JOSE

Jaraguá
VIADUTO DE
CARVALHO
R. J. ADOLFO
Cambridge
Sao Paulo
R.S. FRANCISCO

Teatro do Cultura Artística
RUA NESTOR
R.ALVARO
9 DE JULHO
PRAÇA DAS BANDEIRAS
San Francisco

RUA AUGUSTA
R MARTINHO
R. MAJOR QUEDINHO
9 DE JULHO
RUA SANTO ANTONIO
VIAD. JACAPEI
AV 23 DE MAIO

AVENIDA

155

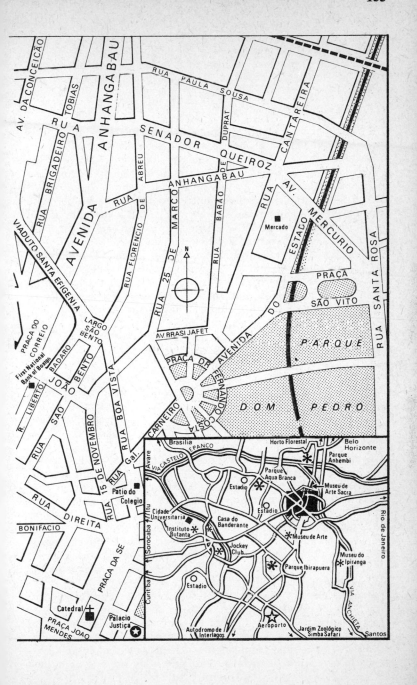

plateau to the equally active, but decidedly tropical seaport city of Santos and the nearby island paradise of Guarujá. Here he goes to the beach, relaxes in nice hotels and gets his suntan.

The Paulistas say that their area has everything, and they really don't need the rest of Brazil at all . . . except as cash customers.

Gaucho Country

The land of the gauchos is almost fabled. The flat pampas grasslands stretching as far as the eye can see, the spirited proud horses, the women in their skirts and their multicolored petticoats, the thousands of grazing cattle, the lonely nights, the full moon, and the gaucho lament plucked softly on a guitar.

The home of the Brazilian gaucho begins at the border with Uruguay and Argentina and stretches up as far as the state of São Paulo, but the color and the legend, the clothes and the individualism have become centered in Rio Grande do Sul.

Gaucho country has other things to offer as well. There are the old mission cities, now in splendid ruin, built by the Jesuits in the 1600s. There is the rich grape growing area where the best wines in Brazil are produced. And, there is that magnificent wonder of nature, the powerful, unforgettable Iguaçu Falls.

EXPLORING SÃO PAULO

São Paulo is a cosmopolitan city that owes its progress to people from all nations, the richness of the soil and the temperate climate. It is a never ending source of investigation and amazement on the part of sociologists and a richly rewarding experience to those Brazilians who feel their country is capable of becoming an important world power.

From a sleepy little Jesuit colony founded in 1554 it has grown into a metropolis almost five times the size of Paris, with a population increase of 150,000 a year and an industrial district that swallows up mile after mile of surrounding land per annum. There is a violent energy in the air and none of the sentimentality that binds the rest of the nation to the past. For São Paulo there is only the future. The Paulistas like to say that "São Paulo can never stop." And from the way it has weathered every political crisis and change and steered its way through inflation and depression, it looks as if it never is going to stop.

But it is not an inhuman city of robots, concrete and machines. It is a city of people who have come looking to better themselves from every nation on the globe. They are individuals who desire better living conditions and are willing to work for them. The Paulista asks nothing from anyone. He has two hands and uses them to get what he wants. Sometimes his attitude is rather

Texan, in that he thinks the world comes to an end at the state's boundaries. His capital city is self-contained and thrives on the manufacture of textiles, clothes, paper, pottery, chemicals, leather, rubber, timber, cement, iron and steel. There are few unemployed there.

The city was first with enough cheap electrical power to handle any industry that was interested in building there. It also offered a direct railway connection to the seaport town of Santos, and its early governors encouraged immigration of industrial workers rather than farmers. Those Europeans who couldn't take the climate of Rio or Bahia thrived in São Paulo, built their homes there and encouraged their children to stay on and handle the family businesses. The result is that today the city counts a number of millionaire families who are third and fourth generation Paulista, and they are proud to tell the visitor the way their grandparents worked their way up from steerage class to the mansions along Avenida Paulista, which are rapidly being replaced today by ultra-modern bank and office buildings.

The Times Square of Brazil

Probably the best place to "feel" the pulse of the city is right in its heartbeat, the bridge over the vast Avenida Anhangabaú. It leads into the Praça do Patriarca. Just stand there and observe the autos and people hurrying below you in what appears to be organized confusion. This is the Times Square of Brazil. Now look at the buildings that flank each side of the bridge and note especially the squat white granite, solid looking one that is partly below the bridge and partly above it. It is the Matarazzo Building, former headquarters of the most powerful family in Latin America. The first Matarazzo came to Brazil as an immigrant and arrived dripping wet when his boat overturned going to the shore and he lost every one of his possessions. Undaunted but broke, he started in to buy and sell pork fat door to door. Soon he had a small lard company and this he parlayed into a canning factory. Not long afterward there was nothing that he wasn't manufacturing or operating. Today the Matarazzo empire is run by his son and grandsons. The exact amount of money they have is a mystery to the outside world, but it's believed they would put the Fords or the Rockefellers to shame. To their credit the grandsons have been active in social welfare and treat their thousands of employees in Brazil with careful consideration. It is to families like this one that São Paulo owes its present-day wealth and stature.

Now walk up Rua Barão de Itapetininga (Paulistas love to give their streets difficult Indian names) across the Praça Ramos de Azevedo along the front of the majestic Teatro Municipal and four blocks to Av. Ipiranga. Here is the center of the man-in-the-streets haunts, with the huge movie theaters, the elegant and well-kept Praça da Republica and the sidestreets leading off to shops and specialty stores. Most of the tourist and souvenir shops are in this area as well as the airline company offices and better bookstores.

On the corner of this avenue and Av. São Luiz you'll see the graceful, serpent-shaped apartment and office building designed by famed brasilia builder Oscar Niemeyer, across the street from the São Paulo Hilton. Turning from Ipiranga and walking down São Luiz, which leads to the Hotel Jaraguá, you'll see new office buildings with shops, theaters and luxury stores that have sprung up in the past three years. São Paulo is like New York in this respect; wherever you look there is an old building coming down and a new one rising in its place.

In 1888 the state government purchased an old farm house and turned it over to a scientist who had some crazy notion that snake serum could be used to save the life of someone bitten by a snake. His first patients were the horses of the Paulista cavalry, and he had 64 snakes to work with. Today the Instituto Butantan is the largest snake farm in Latin America, counts more than 16,000 live snakes in its collection as well as thousands of spiders, scorpions and lizards. It extracts their venom regularly and processes it so it can be flown anywhere in the country when it's needed in a hurry. The institute is open daily from 8 a.m. to 5 p.m. and its guards are very cooperative with visitors. Be sure to see them milking the snakes between 10 and 11 a.m.; it's quite a sight. You can take a bus from Praça da Republica or, of course, a taxi, for it's quite a distance from the downtown area.

Within walking distance of the snake farm is the House of the Flagbearer (Casa do Bandeirante). An old ranch house that goes back to the golden age of the colonials, the building was completely restored in 1954 and decorated with priceless furniture and pottery of the period. Even the outside buildings like the corn crib and the mill are authentic down to the last detail. If you are interested in the antiques of this era, you'll love the place. It's open every day except Monday from 12 to 5:30 p.m. There is a guide there with all the explanations. Entrance is free.

Ibirapuera Park is perhaps the biggest one of its kind in the world. It covers two million square meters, is decorated with natural lakes and rolling, well-watered lawns and contains ten modern exhibition halls where one thing or another is being shown. The entrance to the park is dominated by a statue containing 36 figures of the pioneers, Indians, their women and horses who braved the unmapped lands and carved out a new empire. The statue, the work of Frenchman Victor Brecheret, is 50 meters long and has been given the rather affectionate if irreverent name of "Don't push." Inside the park you'll be able to visit the Japanese Pavilion which is an exact reproduction of the Katura Palace in

Japan and is kept up by donations of the Japanese colony. There is also a windowless dome of cement called the History Pavilion. Here are the museums of Science, Aeronautics and Technical Arts. In the Pavillion Pereira, the world-famed Bienal art exhibits are held. The greatest display of contemporary art in Latin America, the show attracts painters from all over the globe who compete for top honors in the art world. The Planetarium is also in this park and is rated the best in South America. Complete, absorbing shows are given each Saturday, Sunday and holiday at 4, 6 and 8 p.m., and Tuesdays and Thursdays at 8 p.m. Tickets at the door cost about 65 cents. There is also a radio-telescope (the only one in Brazil) that lets you "listen" to the stars, as well as an interesting corner where telescopes are assembled. Take any bus marked Ibirapuera.

Along the banks of the Anhembi River, at the entrance to the São Paulo-Rio Highway, is Anhembi Park, whose exposition hall is the world's largest aluminum structure. The roof is supported by 25 light columns and the hall is illuminated by 200 aluminum globes. Right beside it is a modernistic convention hall seating 5,000 persons. A 453-room hotel is also under construction nearby and should be finished during 1977.

The Zoological Park is located on Avenida Miguel Estefeno. The largest in the world, it displays over 400 animals and 600 birds. There are few fences or cages and Paulistas dot the lawns on Sunday afternoons with their tablecloths and picnic baskets. It is open daily from 9 a.m. to 6 p.m., and adult admission is about 80 cents.

Near the zoo, on the same avenue, is the orchid farm where there are over 35,000 species. The force of so much beauty is overpowering at times. You may visit the orchids and the zoo by taking a number 546 bus from Praça da Liberdade or Anhangabaú.

If you are interested in collecting stamps or coins, then a must on your itinerary is a visit to the center of downtown Praça da Republica on a Sunday morning. There collectors and dealers traditionally gather to talk, swap and sell. But today they are outnumbered by "hippies" selling their handicraft—leather goods, furniture, paintings and trinkets made of glass, straw, metal.

Three museums should be on your list of "musts." The first is the Museum de Arte de São Paulo, on Avenida Paulista. Open free of charge from 2 to 6 p.m. daily except Monday, it is the only collection in South America that shows a panorama of Western art from the Gothic Age to the present. Here hangs Rafael's famed "Resurrection," painted when he was just 17 years old. There is a Rembrandt self-portrait, three Frans Hals, 13 Renoir, 10 Toulouse-Lautrec and many others. There is a section of 19th-century and contemporary Brazilian painters, a selection of Gobelin tapestries and a collection of early Italian majolica.

The second important museum is the Museu de Arte Contemporánea located in the Pereira Pavillion in Ibirapuera Park. There are over 1,650 works by such modern masters as Kandinsky, Leger, Carrá, Portinari and various cubists of the pre-World War One era. Open every day but Monday from 2 to 6 p.m. Admission is roughly 40 cents.

Third is the Museum of Brazilian Art on Rua Alagoas 903. Here are copies of all the monuments and statues in the parks and buildings of Brazil including copies of the famed Prophets of Aleijadinho. Free admission Tuesdays through Fridays from 2 to 10 p.m.

EXPLORING SOUTH OF SÃO PAULO

If one cannot understand the "Paulistas" contented "I want to be isolated" attitude from studying their capital city, then it will certainly become apparent when the rest of their domain is seen. The area has everything from sandy beaches to lofty mountain plateaus, from colonial splendor to ultramodern health resorts. To see all of it you need time, much more time than most tourists have to devote to an area. That is one of the problems of visiting Brazil. There is so much to see that it's absolutely impossible to crowd it all in one visit.

The State of São Paulo itself is about the size of Great Britain and Northern Ireland put together, covering 95,800 square miles. Slow to catch a hold (the first colonies founded by the Jesuit fathers were complete failures), São Paulo didn't really start to grow until the coffee plant was introduced in the early 1800s. The product found a ready market, and when in 1847 a landowner near Limeira brought over a colony of Germans to work his fields, the area was on its way at last. The demand for coffee grew and more and more immigrants came from Europe to try their hand with the new plant. From Italy alone came a million people. Portugal sent half a million and Spaniards and Japanese many hundreds of thousands. From the sale of coffee came money enough to start factories, install electrical power, build railways and clear rich forest land.

Santos is another pride of the Paulistas, for aside from having the biggest dock area in Latin America, it also has a tropical climate and some beautiful beaches. Apart from the basilica of Santo Andre which faces the beach and the row after row of modern apartment buildings, the city has little to offer the tourist except her beaches. They are different from the ones in Rio, the sand being darker and harder.

The nearby island of Guarujá is lush, green and lined with towering palm trees. Still amazingly unspoiled, considering its proximity to Santos and the number of weekend visitors it receives, it offers a pleasant visual and mental change from the hustle of the city. A trip around the island by automobile can be made in an hour, for the roads are paved and in good condition.

The coastal village of Paratí was founded way back in the early 16th century. Its calm, natural little harbor was the perfect jumping off point for adventurers looking for the gold and precious stones in Minas Gerais. For decades the town flourished while it catered to the needs of the miners and helped them spend their money. But the boom calmed down, Santos rose in importance because of its superb harbor, and over the years Paratí was forgotten. Then just a few years ago, the Paulistas rediscovered this colonial village (actually located in Rio de Janeiro state), and the government declared it a national monument whose architectural style must be preserved. Today it is important as a tourist center. With the Rio-Santo Highway passing close by, traffic jams became so great that cars are now banned from most city streets. Those who have taken the time to visit it come back with glowing tales of baroque churches, charming squares and an unspoiled old-world charm. Many houses have been restored by private parties and the tendency is to preserve as much of the original flavor as possible.

The various spas and hot spring resorts radiate northward into the higher country, away from the capital city. Most of them have a large German or Swiss population and will remind the traveler more of Europe than South America. High in the air and richly gifted with mineral waters, the villages of Aguas da Prata and Caxambú offer the tired tourist rest and health. Every hotel has its own doctor, and some people actually find it fun to get up around six a.m. for a walk to the spring for their first glass of water that day. Brazilians, like the French, blame every ailment on the liver and they constantly bathe this organ in mineral waters, either bottled or *au naturel*. Many of the waters are radioactive.

The hot springs attract an equal number of visitors, who go there to sit in the warm, swirling (at times rather smelly) water, rather than drink it. Campos do Jordão, Poços de Caldas and Serra Negra all have dry climates and their waters are famous for treating such diverse ailments as rheumatism, skin diseases and fatigue. Clean and nicely landscaped, these villages are as pleasant to the eye as they are to the skin.

EXPLORING THE LAND OF GAUCHOS

Porto Alegre will surprise you. One of the most up-to-date and fastest growing cities south of São Paulo, it has modern buildings, amiable people and well-stocked shops. Lying as it does at the junction of five rivers, it has become an important shipping port, and much of the state's leather, canned beef and rice are freighted from here to destinations as far away as Africa and Japan. The Lagoa dos Patos on which the city nestles is the largest freshwater lagoon in South America.

The old residential part of the city is on high ground with

delightful views all around. It is dominated by the Governor's Palace (where soldiers crouched with machine guns both when "Jango" Goulart came back as President in 1961 and when he left in disgrace in 1964). Nearby there are an imposing stone cathedral, recently completed, and two high white towers of an old church called the Lady in Pain. The streets of the city wind in and around and up and down, and one of the best ways to enjoy Porto Alegre is to get out and walk; head toward the prisons and the electrical energy plant on General Salustiano. The huge, green-grassed park of Farroupilha is the site of a zoo and botanical gardens and on weekends and holidays is also the scene of folkloric dancers.

The best Brazilian wine is produced in the area round Caxias do Sul, home of Italian immigrants who transported the art from their native land. Today 28 different companies work at growing, selecting and bottling the juices from thousands of tons of grapes grown in this region. In March the entire city stops work to celebrate the "Festival of the Grapes."

Farmers arrive to show off their products, visitors come from all over Brazil as well as France and Italy and regional folk dances are held. There is also more beef eaten than can be imagined and more wine drunk than should be. The owners of *Michielon* (Avenida Michielon 136) welcome visitors to their bottling plant from 7:30 to 11:00 and 1:30 to 5.

In the first years of the 1600s, the Portuguese domination of Brazil didn't go farther south than Laguna in the State of Santa Catarina. Below this was Spanish territory, and it was here that the Jesuits came from Spain to build a series of missions. They managed to win the confidence of the Indians and soon had them making and laying bricks. The Indians stayed near the missions for protection. Then the Portuguese "flagbearers" from São Paulo came rushing south. Enemies of the Spanish, they killed the priests, enslaved the Indians and destroyed the mission cities. What is left today—towering walls, delicately curved arches, carved angles and cornices—stands in mute testament to the grandeur that the Jesuits tried to implant on Brazilian soil. The Cathedral of São Miguel, roofless and overgrown with grass, is probably the most impressive ruin remaining. There is a museum beside it with some of the wooden images and iron bells that were salvaged from the Cathedral. Other ruins, all reachable in one day, are at São João Velho, São Lourenço das Missões and São Nicolau. At this last ruin the legend still holds that the Jesuits buried a treasure chest before the Portuguese arrived.

All through this area and especially near São Borja, the home of both Presidents Getulio Vargas and João Goulart, you'll see the gauchos and their horses. They still wear the bright-colored shirts and neckerchiefs, the balloon pleated trousers, the creased leather boots and the flat chin strap hat. They will stop and talk to you and may even offer a taste of their chimarrão, the traditional gourd of hot mate tea.

Another unforgettable day will be spent at Iguaçu Falls. Eleanor Roosevelt remarked that: "After seeing Iguaçu Falls, it makes our Niagara Falls look like a kitchen faucet." The water comes from the joining of some 30 rivers and streams from the interior of Paraná, and as it rushes toward the 200-foot precipice, it foams and carries huge trees it has uprooted. The volume of roaring, earth-shaking water has been estimated at 62,000 cubic feet per second. During the flood months of May to July the water plunges over at 450,000 cubic feet per second.

Both the Brazilians and the Argentines have made a national park of their side of the falls and views from both countries are spectacular and different. Your hotel will take care of transportation to Argentina and all the necessary customs paperwork. You will be impressed by the Devil's Throat Falls which must be seen by taking a highly adventurous (not for the weak hearted and elderly) outboard trip across the rapid currents to a trembling but secure little island. Don't wear your good clothes. The spray of this breathtaking portion of the falls is thrust 500 feet into the air.

Curitiba is a busy city of one million inhabitants standing some 3,000 feet above sea level on the plateau of Serra do Mar. For over a century, its bracing climate and picturesque location have attracted immigrants of Slav, German and Italian origin, who have imparted a few European characteristics to its buildings and surroundings. Formerly best known as the center of the *herva-mate* industry, it has now acquired much greater importance as the capital of a flourishing and progressive state which derives its economic prosperity from extensive coffee plantations in the north and vast timber forests in the southwest, as well as fertile areas that produce abundant crops of cereals and other foodstuffs. In addition to being the capital of the State of Paraná, it is the headquarters of the Fifth Military Region and therefore the residence of many officers and their families, and there are barracks for infantry and artillery regiments. There is also a modern and well-equipped military air base. The University of Paraná attracts thousands of students from all over the states of Paraná and Santa Catarina as well as from more distant states of the union.

Places of interest include: the Coronel David Carneiro Museum, with a unique collection of objects of historical interest; the Graciosa Country Club, and others. Also worthy of note are the modern buildings, especially the Civic Center, which houses in one homogenous group the Governor's Palace, State Secretariats, House of Assembly, Treasury, Law Courts, etc. There are two modern theaters (one for plays and revues, one for concerts and ballet) and a library in the center of the town. By bus along a paved road to São Paulo (250 miles) takes eight hours; the daily train takes 24 hours.

PRACTICAL INFORMATION FOR SÃO PAULO

 WHEN TO COME? The weather information for Rio is also good for São Paulo, except that when it is cold in Rio, it is twice as chilly here. Since the city sits 820 meters (2,665 ft.) above sea level, it is prey to the variable winds that come northward from cold Argentina as well as those breezes coming from muggy Mato Grosso jungles. It is a stimulating climate, one that does not sap the energy of the visitor. There are no big events taking place in the city but rather a continuing series of interesting things like museum openings, art exhibits, industrial fairs, sports programs and the like. There is always something going on, and the visitor will not have to worry about killing time, in spite of the lack of sandy beaches.

 ARRIVING IN SAO PAULO. Most people visit here after they have been in Rio. Easiest and most comfortable way to come is via the ultramodern, ultra-efficient *Ponte Aérea* (Air Bridge). It is a constant arrival and departure of airplanes between Rio's Santos-Dumont airport and São Paulo's Congonhas field, four-engine turboprops leave every half-hour from 6 a.m. till 9 p.m. Reservations aren't needed, unless you want a certain plane. You just show up and take the next plane. It is a good idea to book in advance for a weekend flight, especially Friday evening. Tickets: about $35 one way.

Most international flights land at the Viracopos international airport in Campinas, a two-hour bus or taxi ride from São Paulo. Try to avoid it. PanAm and Varig, however, have shuttle flights on 727s to Congonhas connecting with most of their international flights to Rio.

The city can also be reached by first-class buses which leave Estação Rodoviária every half hour and make the 253-mile trip in five-and-one-half hours on an excellent highway with one rest stop. Either Expresso Brasileiro or Viação Cometa will give you more than satisfactory service.

If you arrive by ocean liner in Santos, then arrange for an automobile-bus with Expresso Luxo or Expresso Zephir; they have scheduled trips hourly at $2.25 per person. There are also deluxe buses, leaving Santos every fifteen minutes or so on the Expresso Brasileiro or Cometa line, costing a little more than $1. You can also take a taxi direct for about $30.

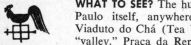 **WHAT TO SEE?** The hustle and bustle of busy São Paulo itself, anywhere in the downtown area. Viaduto do Chá (Tea Viaduct) over Anhangabaú "valley." Praça da República (hippie fair Sunday mornings). Avenida Paulista, the history and future of the city in a nutshell, where old coffee barons' mansions mingle with modern skyscrapers. São Paulo Museum of Modern Art (Av. Paulista). Ibirapuera Park (Av. 23 de Maio between downtown and the city airport) on whose spacious grounds are the Museum of Contemporary Art (2 to 6:30 p.m. Tues.–Sun.) and the Museum of Modern Art (2 to 6 p.m. Tues.–Sun.). Butantan Institute, snake farm and museum. Nearby the 400-year-old House of the Flagbearer (Casa do Bandeirante) at Praça Monteiro Lobato (noon to 5:30 p.m. Tues.–Sun.). Campus of the University of São Paulo, Brazil's largest. Anhembi Park, exposition hall and convention center.

HOW TO GET ABOUT. At Congonhas city airport, the regular taxi stand is located at door of the domestic wing. A trip to your downtown hotel costs about $4. Air-conditioned "luxury" taxis outside the international wing cost double. Contract with driver of the latter there or alongside Hotel Hilton for a day (around $60) to tour the city in comfort. Avis, Hertz, L'Auto and American rental cars available, but São Paulo is a difficult city for the nonresident to get around in. Most cab drivers don't know many streets. City buses are cheap, but lines are long at rush hours. New subway crosses city from north to south for 20 cents. Ask your hotel porter for information. Tours can be arranged with American Express representative, Kontik-Franstur, Rua Marconi 71, 2nd floor. Tours also arranged by Brazil Safaris & Tours, Rua Barão de Itapetininga 221, seventh floor, or in the Hilton lobby. Another good agency is Agaxtur, Rua Maroni 31, mezzanine, or Av. Paulistana 2001, shop 42.

SHOPPING. The best shops for both men's and women's clothes are in São Paulo. Here quality and not quantity are stressed. The elegant Rua Augusta and Av. Paulista are lined with dozens of interesting establishments and many clerks speak English, French, Spanish and Italian as well as their own Portuguese. This same street also has some of the finest antique shops in Brazil. Among the internationally known shops here are *Karitas Antiguidades* (Augusta 2725, also in the Hilton Arcade) for antiques, crystal and fine semiprecious stones. *Cristais Prado* (Augusta 2487) for crystal and pottery, which is also found at *Marcob* (Augusta 2284). At *Majo* you can find watch specialties (Alam. Jau, 1529 at the corner of Augusta). For fashions: *Rue de la Paix* (Augusta 2607) and *Mayflower* (Augusta 891). Leatherwares: *Supercouros* (Augusta 2032), and *Germonts* (Augusta 2566).

For precious and semiprecious stones, *H. Stern* has branches at Augusta 2340 (also at São Paulo Hilton, Iquatemi Shopping Center and Praça Mauá 3, Santos), with the largest selection in town, multilingual salesgirls and air-conditioned comfort; own office in New York, besides world-wide service. Emerald specialists are *Sauer Jewelers* at Praça Republica 36; *Amsterdam Gems,* Praça Republica 64. *Santos Stones,* Rua Xavier de Toledo 114, Suite 502, brings stones directly from their mines to their own workshop. Other shops are: *Simon* (Praça Republica 146), *Charles* (Praça Franklin Roosevelt 128), *Casa Indra* (Rua J. Nascimento 391), *Birskawa* (Rua Barão de Itapetininga 167), *Mimosa* (R. J. Nabuco 304), good for souvenirs, as are *Dourado Souvenirs,* Rua Braulio Gomes 115, across from the Eldorado Hotel and *Roval,* Av. São Luiz 153, shop 43, in the Galeria Metrópole. The *Casa do Folklore* at Praça Republica 242 has the best collection of Brazilian handicrafts, reasonable prices; also for folklore is the *Tenda da Bahia* on Rua Barão de Itapetininga 255.

HOTELS. Booming São Paulo is a city of international businessmen and their customers; so it is only natural that the city is preparing to take care of them. There are many good hotels in town, and rates are about what they are for similar accommodations in Rio. Warning: bring earplugs with you (they're almost impossible to buy in Brazil) for this is one of the world's noisiest cities.

Deluxe

SAO PAULO HILTON, the leading hotel whose 391 rooms, 24 parlors and 24 suite combinations rise towerlike. Located in the center of the downtown area on the spacious Avenida Ipiranga 165, its 34 stories command a sweeping view of the world's fastest growing city. Air conditioned and heated. Parking, 24-hour room service and coffee shop. Grill, bar, rooftop supper club and cocktail lounge. On the 10th floor there are an outdoor pool, sauna, medical facilities, barber and beauty shops.

OTHON PALACE, Rua Libero Badaró 196. It rises majestically with 277 deluxe apartments right off busy Avenida Anhangabaú and has a very good restaurant, a popular bar.

ELDORADO, Av. São Luís 234. New and elegant small hotel (157 rooms) with heating and air conditioning. Terrace coffee shop with view of the busy avenue, fashionable. Pool, nightclub, convention hall, international cuisine.

BRASILTON SAO PAULO. In the center of shopping and entertainment district. 250 rooms, swimming pool, grill room and cocktail lounge, garage. Opened in 1977.

First Class

SAO PAULO CENTER, Largo Santa Ifigênia 40. A traditional building recently redecorated in modern style a few blocks from the heart of the city. 111 air-conditioned rooms.

GRANDE HOTEL CA D'ORO, Rua Avanhandava 308, is luxurious, and peaceful. Italian restaurant, bar, parking, pool on 23rd floor.

JARAGUA, on Rua Major Quedinho 44. 240 rooms, ranging from super-deluxe suites to pleasant bedrooms. Centrally located, it has excellent international cuisine and a popular bar. Recently redecorated.

PAMPAS RAMADA, Av. Barão de Mauá 71 in the neighboring auto factory city of São Bernardo do Campo, has restaurant, nightclubs, and heliport for busy executives.

HOLIDAY INN, first in Brazil, at Campinas, 8 miles from airport. 103 rooms. And now a second, with 220 rooms, in the industrial São Bernardo do Campo suburb.

CA D'ORO, Rua Basilio da Gama 95. Small. Good Italian restaurant, run by Grande Hotel Ca d'Oro. Air conditioned.

SAO PAULO, Praça das Bandeiras 15, with its new, typically Brazilian restaurant *Acaraje*.

SAMAMBAIA, on 7 de Abril at Praça da Republica, right in downtown area. It's small but has excellent service and cuisine.

EXCELSIOR HOTEL, Avenida Ipiranga 770, has 180 apartments, a low-priced restaurant and an old-world charm as does its across-the-street neighbor the *Marabá*.

HOTEL VILA RICA, Rua Vieira de Carvalho, provides good service in a colonial atmosphere. International restaurant.

SAN RAPHAEL, Av. Sao João 1173, has well-appointed apartments to rent, complete with well-stocked refrigerators.

CAMBRIDGE, Av. 9 de Julho 216. Fine restaurant and cozy music bar. Travel desk.

DOMUS, Rua Aurora 409. Quiet street downtown.

Moderate

Good hotels are the *Lord Palace* on Rua das Palmeiras 78; the *Amazonas* on Rua Vieira de

Carvalho 32; *Normandie* on Av. Ipiranga 1187; the *Danubio* on Av. Brig. Luiz Antonio 1099; the *Comodoro* on Av. Duque de Caxias 525; *Alvear*, Av. Gaspar Libero 65; *Planalto*, Av. Gaspar Libero 117; *Delphin*, Av. Castro Ribeiro 133. All Paulista hotels serve Continental breakfast free of charge.

 RESTAURANTS. Gentlemen, loosen your belt and the first button on your trousers. Ladies, leave your girdle in the hotel bureau drawer and prepare yourselves for some of the finest international eating delights on the continent. It is difficult to choose the best when every one is so good. Your dining should not be confined to the following list, as it is merely the *crème de la crème* of the Paulista restaurants. Look around and experiment. The most luxurious place is still the one-priced, very expensive *Maria Fulo*.

For good *Brazilian* food, don't ignore *Rodeio* on Rua Haddock Lobo 1498, where you can enjoy the best steaks in town in a typical Gaucho ranch-style atmosphere. Other recommended churrascos are: *Rubayat*, Rua Vieira de Carvalho 134; *Dinho's Place*, Largo do Arouche 246; featuring Santa Gertrudes beef; *Ao Franciscano*, Rua da Consolação 257; *Chave de Ouro*, A1. Santos 2393; and *Rebouças* (dinner), Rua João Moura 257, which boasts of its pizza pies.

Portuguese food is served best at *Abril em Portugal*, Rua Caio Prado 47. Inside this restaurant waiters serve mouthwatering *bacalhau Maria Rita* (dried cod fish with a special sauce) and *pescada a moda de Vigo* (a Portuguese version of bouillabaisse). Start your meal with a bowl of *caldo verde* (green broth) and finish it with a dessert called *neves de serra*.

Try also the Restaurante Mansão Portuguesa at Rua Marquês de Itu 449, where you can enjoy a typical Portuguese cuisine in an atmosphere of candle-light and live music.

Feel like going *Spanish?* Then have dinner at *Don Emilio* (Rua 7 de Abril 425) where the *paella*, *langosta real* (lobster royale) and *pulpos* (octopus) *al salpicon* are just plain fabulous. Also to be recommended is *Don Velasquez*, Av. Brig. Faria Lima 2182, and *Don Curro* on Rua Alves Guimarães 230.

There are many excellent *Italian* restaurants here. Best is the deluxe *Ca d'Oro* on Rua Basilio da Gama 101. Some of their specialities are huge raviolis (*casoncelli*) filled with meat and dried grapes, *amaretti* (fluffed-up dough with peanuts), chicken in the pot with *polenta*, and even pheasant. Their wines, cheeses and smoked sausage come right from the old country. Open every day for lunch from 11:30 to 2:30 and dinner from 6:30 to 10:30. Other good Italian restaurants are: *Trastevere*, Alameda Santos, 1444; *Picolomondo*, Rua Romilda Margarida Gabriel 142; *Circolo Italiano*, Av. São Luis 50; and *Gigeto*, Rua Avanhandava 63.

If you're in the mood for *Rippchen mit Sauerkraut* and other *German* dishes, try the *Wonder Bar*, Praça do Arouche 207. *Koblenz*, A1. Barros 703, offers such specialties as *Stubenkuken Vierlander Mastente* and the sailors' favorite *Labskaus*.

For an evening of family dining, the *Don Fabrizio*, on Alameda Santos 65, is highly recommended for *Italian* and *international* cuisine. The *Terraco Italia*, on top of the Edificio Italia, has a fabulous view of the city and also serves international food.

The *French* are well represented with *Le Casserole* at Largo do Arouche 346. Air conditioned and with music from a hi-fi, the elegant atmosphere is so Parisian that you are sure you are on the Champs-Elysées as you sample their *boeuf bourguignon*, their duck *à la française* or their omelet with truffles. Open for lunch and dinner every day but Monday.

Noubar, Rua General Deodoro 236, Santo Amaro, offers Swiss and French cuisine with fondue a house specialty, while *Maison Suisse*, Rua Caio Prado 183, has the finest selection of Swiss and French cheeses in the city.

Le Tabarin on Largo Arouche 330 offers as its specialty shrimp in coconut milk that fills the eyes and the stomach. Their snails are perfection, as is their rabbit. They are proud of their stock of Chateau d'Yquem wine. Closed Sundays.

Other French and international deluxe restaurants include the *Bistro*, Av. São Luiz 258, mezzanine; *Chamonix*, Rua Pamplona 1446; *La Cocagne*, Rua Jerônimo da Veiga 358; *La Toque Blanche*, Av. Lorena 2019-Cerqueira César; *Le Flambeau*, Rua Pamplona 1704, Jardim América; *Paddock*, Av. São Luiz 258, mezzanine; *Viela*, Rua Amauri 265. You won't go wrong at any of these.

There are many fine *Japanese* restaurants in São Paulo, and if you are looking for good food as well as company then pay a visit to the *Heike* at Avenida Paulista 2064, Loja 24, the *Yaohan* in the new department store of the same name at Rua Teodoro Sampaio 2400, or the *Akasaka* on Rua 13 de Maio 1639. Run by

Senhora Yuki, who was a geisha in Japan for ten years, the restaurant has five young and comely geishas to help you eat your *tempura* (with shrimp), *sukiyaki* (made right at your table) or *yakitori* (chicken). For dessert try *yokan* (made from beans). Be prepared to spend a little money here. There's also *Enomoto*, Rua Galvao Bueno 54.

Another favorite is *Restaurant Suntory*, which serves the finest in meats and seafoods. Located on Alameida Campinas 600, the place offers diners a view of a Japanese garden.

Bahian specialists: *Maria Fulo,* Rua São José 563, out in the Santo Amaro suburb.

The Paddock, Rua São Luiz 258, serves a good international menu in comfortable surroundings. Try their steaks. Also good for steaks is the Galpão, Rua Augusta 2640, small and rustic.

Massimo, Alameida Santos 1826, features an American Bar, restaurant and barbecue. *A Tocha*, Av. Santo Amaro 2554, serves international cuisine, plus a typical Brazilian "feijoada" every Wednesday and Saturday.

Both the *Hungaria*, A1. Joaquim Eugenio de Lima 766, and the *Kakuk*, A1. Glete 1023, offer good menus, their own ensembles.

Also good: *Diogenes*, a *Greek* restaurant, on Rua Atica 80.

For *Chinese* cooking try the *Palácio Imperial*, Rua Capitás Antonio Rosa, near Av. Rebouças 2552; the *Genghis Khan*, Av. Rebouças, or *Kin Kon*, Av. Paulista 1963; or the *Sino Brasileiro*, São Paulo's oldest Chinese restaurant, Rua Dr. Alberto Torres 39.

Dishes from Peking and Shanghai are available also at the *Restaurant Peking*, Rua Alvaro Rodrigues 143, in the Brooklin district.

The *Ancoradoura do Queijos*, Rua Princesa Isabel 121, boasts of its delicious cheese soufflés and other good cheese dishes.

NIGHTCLUBS. Surprisingly enough, there are better clubs and bars in São Paulo than you'll find in Rio. The Paulista enjoys going out after a day in the office and seems to have more money to spend on night time playing. There are none of the big girly shows that other metropolitan centers offer however, for the Brazilian prefers to listen to a slow samba or a *bossa nova*.

One of the best night spots is the *Baiuca* at Praça Roosevelt 256. Always with a top trio in the bar and good food in the connecting restaurant, the place is considered "tops" by local society. The music goes on till 4 a.m., and if you sit at the bar there's no cover charge.

The Blow Up (Rua Augusta) features dinner and floor show every night against a psychedelic background.

The young in heart make their way to the *Beco* on Rua Bela Cintra 308 for the nightly floor show—one of the best in Brazil —and international cuisine.

The *London Tavern* in the basement of the São Paulo Hilton is a real English pub, open for tea and cocktails in the afternoon, and dinner and disco-theque dancing until 4 a.m. Fridays and Saturdays. Very popular with Brazilians and foreign residents.

Brazilian music, dinner and drinks are the fare at the *Casino Royale*, Av. Santo Amaro 5291.

For hot samba and bossa nova try the *Telecoteco na Paroquia*, Rua Santo Antonio 1015; *Sumbão do Shalako*, Rua Joaquim Floriano 82; *Kurtisso Negro*, Rua Almirante Marques Leão 500; *Fina Flor do Samba*, Rua Major Sertorio 763.

A place called *Tonton Macoute* (Nestor Pestana 109) throws together a show of some 40 people with a heavy accent on samba and sequins.

Quitandinha (Rua Marquês de Itú 182) presents an all black show that is very Brazilian.

Other small *boîtes* called locally *inferninhos* are *Urso Branco, Playboy, Tao Bar. Club de Paris* has nightly shows, and *La Licorne* many young taxi-girls. Other favorites of the young set are: *Bambu, Monami, Holiday, Stardust, Djalma, New Diana, Moustache, Mao-Mao, Casino Royale, Hulla-Balou, Le Batuk, Michel.*

 MEDICAL SERVICES. There are English-speaking doctors and nurses at the *Hospital Samaritano* at Rua Conselheiro Brotero 1486, tel. 51-2154. Also, the English-speaking house doctor at the Hilton can probably suggest a doctor for you.

 USEFUL ADDRESSES. American Consul, Rua Padre João Manuel 20. British Consul, Avenida Paulista 1938. Wagon-Lits Cook, Rua Marconi 101. American Express (Represented by Brasil Safari Tours), Rua Barão de Itapetininga 221. Turistur, Rua Bráulio Gomes 107. Tourservice, Rua 7 de Abril 176. S.C.T.T., Rua 7 de Abril 270. Also Spark Turismo on Rua Bráulio Gomes 37 and Exprinter, R. Barão de Itapetininga 255. (All good tourist agencies.) Brazil Herald, Galeria Metropolitano, Avenida São Luiz 153. American Chamber of Commerce, Rua Formosa 367. Braniff International, Av. São Luiz 116. Pan American Airways, Av. São Luiz 29. British-Caledonian, Av. Ipiranga 318. Avis, Rua Consolação 204. Metropolitan Transport, Av. Luis Antonio 54. Anglo-American Home and Art Agency, Rua 7 de Abril 277.

PRACTICAL INFORMATION FOR COASTAL SAO PAULO

 WHEN TO COME? It depends on where you are going. Because of the varying altitude of the region, which ranges from sea level to 9,000 feet above, it can be hot in some places and cold in others at the same time. If you want the seashore, then the months of December to March are the best, especially for the beach towns of Santos, Paratí and the island of Guarujá. Those same months can be chilly in the mineral water spas and hot spring resorts. If it's coffee you are interested in, then the picking and drying season from June to August is the best time for a visit.

 HOW TO GET ABOUT. From Rio to Santos—until completion of a new coastal highway between the two—it's best to go via São Paulo. This has been described in the section "Exploring São Paulo." From Santos to Guarujá, there is a new highway link, or you can take the ferry boat at the end of Avenida Almirante Saldanha da Gama, which is the final stop along the beachfront. The boats leave every fifteen minutes or so on a first-come, first-serve basis. They handle cars as well as people and the trip takes 15 minutes. On the other side there are buses waiting to transport passengers to the various beaches. A word of warning: the ferry boats to Guarujá and back on the weekends are very busy, and the highways up the mountain to São Paulo from Santos frequently have bumper-to-bumper traffic Sunday evenings.

 WHAT TO SEE? The beaches of Santos, Guarujá and Paratí. The docks in Santos that make this city the most important harbor in South America and the leading coffee port in the world. In Paratí almost everything in this old colonial city is worth seeing, especially the churches and the brightly tiled commercial buildings. At the spas and hot springs you just relax.

 HOTELS. The spas and hot spring hotels are open all year round and are usually crowded during the months of December to March. It's best to have a travel agent make reservations for you, because many of them have special "pull" with the management. The seaside hotels are also crowded at this time, and during Carnival almost impossible to get into without advance reservation.

AGUAS DA PRATA. Probably the best at this mineral water spa, is the *Grande Hotel Prata* on Avenida Washington Luiz 9. Good restaurants and all meals are included in your room rate. *Ideal*, Rua Gabriel Rabelo de Andrade 79.

ARAXA. Famous mineral spa. Best hotel is *Grande Hotel de Araxa*. Suggested side trips to springs at Barbeiro, Osario, Cascatinha Gruta de Monje, and Historic Museum of Dona Beja.

AGUAS DE LINDOIA. *Tamoio* at Rua São Paulo 622 and *Hotel* *das Fontes* on Rua Rio de Janeiro 267 are considered the most comfortable hotels here.

CAMPOS DO JORDÃO. This popular hot springs resort has many hotels. All of them are comfortable but probably the top are the *Vila Inglêsa* on the street with the same name, the *Refúgio Alpino* on Vila Capivari, *Toriba* on Avenida Ernesto Diederichsen, and *Grande* on Avenida Januario Miraglia and the *Balonjha*. They have good restaurants and serve three meals daily to guests.

CAXAMBU. Very popular mineral water resort across the border in Minas Gerais. Recommended: *Gloria*, Camilo Soares, 590; *Lopes*, Rua Constantino 48; *Grande*, Rua Dr. Viotti 438; *Palace*, Rua Dr. Viotti 567; *Avenida*, Avenida Camilo Soares, 648.

Recommended side trips to Parque das Aguias, Colina de Santa Isabel, Chacara Rosalan, Chacara das Ucas, São Tome das Letras, Corcovado Morro do Caxambu.

GUARUJA. Among the many fine hotels is *Jequitimar*, on Pernambuco Beach. Make reservations at Lojas Cristais Prado, Rua Augusta 2487, São Paulo. *The Delphin*, Av. Miguel Estefno 1295, is luxurious, air conditioned. Pool. Convention facilities *Casa Grande*, Av. Miguel Estento 999; *Ferrareto*, Rua Mario Ribeiro 564; *Gavea Palace*, Rua Marechal Floriano Peixoto 3112; *Strand*, Av. Prestes Maia 385; *Ancora Praia*, Jardim Virginia.

Best restaurant: *Sobre as Ondas*, Av. Mar. Rondon 30.

LAMBARI (Minas Gerais). *Parque*, Rua Americo Werneck 48; *Itaici*, Rua Silviano Brandão 321. *Rosario* on Rua Tiradentes 265.

POCOS DE CALDAS. Also in the nearby state of Minas Gerais, this hot springs is probably the best one in Latin America. It boasts of 37 hotels but try and get into the sumptuous *Palace* on Praça Pedro Sanches. Built by the state government, it has up-to-date facilities for treatment of rheumatic, skin and intestinal diseases. *Minas Gerais* on Rua Pernambuco 615.

Suggested side trips are to Cascata das Antas, Veu da Noiva, Fonte dos Amores, Morro de São Domingos.

SÃO LOURENÇO. *Primus*, on Rua Coronel Jose Justino 681; *Brasil*, Praça João Laje; *Negreiros*, Rua Veneceslau Bras 242.

SANTOS. Hotels and boarding houses on every corner. Best: *Universo Palace*, on the sea at Av. Presidente Wilson 143; *Indaia*, Av. Ana Costa 431-Gonzaga; *Ritz*, Rua Mar. Deodoro 24-Gonzaga; *Praiano*, Av. Barão de Penedo 39; *Maracana Santos* (beach), Av. Pres. Wilson 172; *Comodoro*, Rua Jorge Tibirica 44.

SERRA NEGRA. Best hotel: *Grande Hotel Pavani* on Bairro das Palmerias. All others are definitely second class in comparison.

 RESTAURANTS. In the spas and hot springs, you'll dine at your hotel, because you'll probably be on some special diet and won't want to experiment outside (providing there is some place to experiment, that is).

In Santos you have a choice of a number of fine eating places. On the beach are: *Atlantico*, Av.

Ana Costa 574; *Belem* (seafood), Av. Vicente de Carvalho 30; *La Reuda* (seafood), Av. Vicente de

Carvalho 35; *Fifty-Fifty*, Av. Bartolomeu de Gusmão 119; *Vasco da Gama* (seafood), Alm. Saldanha da Costa 33; *Dom Felipe* (barbecue), Av. Bartolomeu de Gusmão 45; *Chuleta* (barbecue) Av. Bartolomeu de Gusmão 7; *zi Tereza* (Italian), Av. Bartolomeu de Gusmão 39; *Brumar*, Av. Pres. Wilson 100. *Vista ao Mar*, Av. Bartolomeu de Gusmão 68.

PRACTICAL INFORMATION FOR THE GAUCHO COUNTRY

WHEN TO COME? Try not to come in the winter months from June to August, for cold winds from the south whip across the pampas and leave your skin chapped and sore. Almost any other time is good, and the spring (October-December) is especially enchanting with the fresh green grass, the new wildflowers and the young calves and lambs.

HOW TO GET ABOUT. There are regular plane connections from all large cities to Porto Alegre, which should be your starting point. You can take buses all over the area. Since the land is flat, the highways run smooth and buses stick to a tight schedule that is bound to please. Automobiles can also be rented in Porto Alegre and Varig airlines has regular service from Porto Alegre to many small towns in the interior that can be explored on foot.

HOTELS

CAXIAS DO SUL, capital of the wine country. Good hotels are: *Alfred Palace*, Rua Sinimbu 2302, and the older *Alfred* next door at 2266; *Samuara*, 12 miles from downtown on the Parque do Lago; *Volpiano*, Rua Ernesto Alves 1462; *Cosmos*, Rua 20 de Setembro 1563; *Itália*, Av. Julio de Castilhos 3076; *Real*, Marquês do Herval 606.

CURITIBA. Numerous fine hotels here include the *Iguaçu*, Rua Cândido Lopes 102; *Del Rey*, Rua Ermelino de Leão 18; *Lancaster*, Rua Voluntários da Pátria 91; *Mabu*, Praça Santos Andrade 830; *Presidente*, Rua Des. Westphalen 33; *Caravelle Palace*, Rua Cruz Machado 282. Also the *Colonial*, Rua Comendador Araújo 99; *Curitiba Palace*, Rua Ermelino de Leão 45; *Guaira Palace*, Praça Rui Barbosa 537; *Ouro Verde*, Rua Dr. Murici 419; *Plaza*, Av. Luiz Xavier 24; *Tibagi*, Rua Cândido Lopes 318; *Tourist Universo*, Praça Osório 63, and the new *San Martin*, Rua João Negrão near Rua XV de Novembro.

PORTO ALEGRE. Best in town are *Plaza São Rafael* on Av. Alberto Bins 514, its 218 rooms, air conditioning, bar, nightclub and central location, making it the ideal spot while in the Gaucho capital; the *Porto Alegre City* on Rua José Montauri 20; the *Plaza* on Rua Senhor dos Passos 154; the *Everest Palace* on Rua Duque de Caxias 1357; *Alfred Executivo*, Av. Otávio Rocha 270; *Lido*, Rua Andrade Neves 150; *Umbu*, Av. Farrapos 292; *Embaixador*, Rua Jerônimo Coelho 354; *Rishon*, Rua Dr. Flores 27; *Savoy*, Av. Borges de Medeiros 688; *São Luiz*, Av. Farrapos 45. More modest and with no restaurants are the *Hermon*, Av. Vigário José Inácio 541; *Palácio*, Av. Vigário José Inácio 644; *Metrópole*, Rua Andrade Neves 59, and *Presidente*, Ave. Salgado Filho 140.

FOZ DO IGUAÇÚ, city of the falls. Absolutely tops, even from the international tourists' point of view is the government-owned *Hotel das Cataratas*. The food is good and they've guides with automobiles to take you to the falls. It's best to make a reservation with a Rio travel agent or wire ahead for rooms. Other good hotels are the *Salvati*, Rua Rio Branco 951 in town, and—out of town on the Cataratas Highway headed towards the falls—the *Bourbon, Carima, San Martin* and *Panorama.*

SANTO ANGELO, the mission stopoff. Best in town are the *Maerkli*, Av. Brasil 1000, and the *Debacco*, Av. Borges de Medeiros corner of Rua Marechal Floriano. Simpler are the *Brasil*, Rua Marechal Floriano 1400, and *Avenida*, Av. Brasil 1256.

FLORIANOPOLIS. (Sta. Catarina). *Oscar Palace*; Av. Hercilio Luz 90; *Querência*, Rua Jeronimo Coelho; *Royal*, Rua João Pinto; *Bruggemann*, Rua Santos Saraiva 300; *Swenson Palace*, Rua Santos Saraiva 300; *Ivoran*, Av. Hercilio Luz 66.

 RESTAURANTS. It's an iron-clad, proven rule that you can't go wrong anywhere in the Gaucho country if you eat in the local *churrascarias*. Here you can be sure—and in any town—that the meat is fresh, the rice fluffy and delicious.

CURITIBA. Dining rooms of the better hotels and the following: For churrasco—*Pinheirão Campestre*, Rua Vítor do Amaral 1010, and *Xurrasko*, Rua Jacarezinho 721; German foods—*Matterhorn*, Rua Anita Garibaldi 1, and *Schwartze Katz*, Rua Franco Torres 18; French and international dishes—*Frau Leo*, Rua Visconde Guarapuava 4069, and *Ile de France*, Praça 19 de Dezembro 538; seafoods—*Bierklause* (in spite of its name), Rua Mateus Leme 429; Italian—*Bologna*, Rua C. Carvalho 150, and *Palazzo*, Rua XV de Novembro 3119. Also numerous fine Italian restaurants in the Santa Felicidade area, such as *Madalosso, Veneza, Pinheirão Colônia*.

PORTO ALEGRE. Probably the best beef in all Brazil is served in this town. In most churrascarias, you slice your own steak off the sizzling skewer, and eat it with a salad of lettuce, tomatoes and hearts of palm—washing it all down with an inexpensive pitcher (caneca) of *vinho*

verde. Start with a *salsichão grosso* (grilled sausage), then move on to filet, *picanha* or *lombo de porco* (pork loin). There are just too many good spots with this mouth-watering specialty grilling over smouldering charcoal to list all, but start with the *Mosqueteiro* near the Olímpico Stadium; the unpretentious *Churrasquita*, Rua Riachuelo 1331, *Farrapos*, Rua Andrade Neves 97; *Bom Gosto*, Dr. João Inácio 917; *La Cabanha*, Praça Maurício Cardoso corner of Félix da Cunha, or *Treviso* at the Public Market.

In the unlikely event you tire of the succulent beef, try Italian food at *Don Nicola*, Av. Getúlio Vargas 577, or the *Trattoria D'Italia*, Rua Andrade Neves 107; French and international at the panoramic *Everest Roof*, Duque de Caxias 1357, or *Le Bon Gourmet*, Rua Alberto Bins 514; German at the *Ratskeller*, Rua Cristóvão Colombo 1564, or *Franz*, Rua Protásio Alves 3250 in Petrópolis; Japanese at *Sakaes*, Rua Vigário José Inácio 787.

CENTRAL AND NORTHEAST BRAZIL

Brasília, the Mining Region and Salvador (Bahia)

To visit Brasilia is more than a step into the future, it's a head-long leap into the 21st century. For there, rising amid the scrawny jungle of the high red earth plateau, stands one of the most unusual, most strikingly different, most beautiful cities in the world.

There is nothing outdated about Brasilia. In fact everything there, architecturally, is far in advance of its time. Like something out of Buck Rogers, the city's administrative buildings spread out along the ground, coil around, then leap up in a shaft of white marble to capture the rays of the sun and the light in the onlooker's eyes.

It was a city "they" said couldn't be done, but others, more dedicated and more determined, went ahead and did it. With a rare thrust of Brazilian energy, a city rose in just three years, in the very spot where once the jaguar roared.

The city represents many things to the Brazilians. It first of all awakens a sense of pride, that their nation called "underdeveloped" by so many could have such a capital to work out of. To others, Brasilia is an affirmation of what they, the Brazilians themselves, are capable of doing. To some Brazilians the city is a polished jewel that they are happy to show tourists and visitors who think that their nation is all old buildings, beaches and samba rhythms, and, to a few others, Brasilia remains a national disgrace, a city that should never have been built, a city that ruined the national economy and now refuses to function.

No trip to this magnificent and confusing country is complete without a visit to this city. It's not quite the same as visiting Italy and not seeing Rome—but almost.

Yet all around this spanking new wonderland of modernity, nestles the old Brazil. The land of coffee bean and beef cattle, of palm trees and sluggish rivers, of shoeless peasants and Indians.

While it would be unfair to say that the area neighboring the new capital hasn't progressed with the city, it is a gross exaggeration to say that it has greatly changed. Belo Horizonte, the most important interior city after São Paulo, has taken advantage of the geographical fact that almost everyone and everything traveling by highway to the new capital passes through it. It was a bustling and prosperous town before Brasilia, as its steel mills and hundreds of factories attest. Goiania, a vibrating little town that has sprung up in just the past four years, was doing all right before Brasilia was even thought of. But it has managed to cash in on the boom.

One city, in the Brasilia area but far enough away from any national progress not to be tarnished, is Ouro Preto. The sleepy, colonial prize still rings with the sound of hooves on its cobblestone streets, the sound of Latin chants coming from its thick walled churches and the sad plaintive notes of a lover's guitar being strummed beneath a balcony. The city at one time (the 1700s) was a bustling state capital with gold, silver, diamonds and slaves. But hemmed in by tall, almost impassable mountains, it slowly strangled in the commercial competition of the 20th century. In 1897 it lost its status as capital city of Minas Gerais, and Belo Horizonte came into prominence instead. Preserved by the National Patrimony, it stands as a proud reminder of the glory that was once Imperial Brazil. Here, too, are many works by Brazil's greatest artist, the sculptor Aleijadinho.

Building Brasilia

Brazil has had three capitals—Salvador, Rio de Janeiro and, since 1960, the new city of Brasilia. The reason for the move from Salvador to Rio was that the Portuguese court wanted to be near the center of all the mining and exporting activity. The reason for the move from Rio to Brasilia was that the nation had stagnated for too long along the coast and wanted the center of this sleeping giant to be awakened.

It was not a new idea. As far back as 1808 newspapers were clamoring that Rio was not an adequate place for a capital and were proposing the construction of a city in the interior where communications could be made with the rest of the country. "Our present capital is in a corner of Brazil, and contacts between it and Pará or other far removed states is extremely difficult. Besides Rio subjects the government to enemy invasion by any maritime power." In 1892 Congress authorized a special expedition to go into the backlands and study the terrain in the center of the nation where "a city could be constructed next to headwaters of big rivers and where roads could be opened to all seaports." After a three-month overland trip they decided on the planalto area of Goias. They turned in their report and nothing was done with it.

It took a sharp politician named Juscelino Kubitschek to bring the idea into reality. He needed a campaign platform when he was running for President, and one night at a rally someone shouted to him about building a new capital. Immediately he took up the idea as his own and as soon as he was installed as President he set the wheels in motion.

It was a monumental undertaking, one without equal in the modern world. What had to be done was to build a totally new city that would become the center of government for the biggest nation in the Western Hemisphere—with all the conveniences of light, power, telephones, sewage, housing, streets, police protection, fire protection, schools, hospitals, banks, industry, commerce, ministries, churches, theaters and all the necessary buildings needed by the Congress, Supreme Court and the President to govern the country. Brazil was in debt to everyone. Her exports were woefully out of balance with her imports. Her people needed a thousand and one reforms in health, nutrition and education; nevertheless plans were rushed through and the new capital became a reality.

In the very beginning there was nothing there but scrub trees, red dust and wild jaguars. President Kubitschek flew there, had Mass said, stayed the night, and set up a long list of work committees. Chief of one of these was Oscar Niemeyer who was ordered to design every building needed; of another, Lucio Costa who was to lay out a plan for the city; and of another, Israel Pinheiro, who was to get the city built. Money came from all over the world in the form of loans and government grants. The Brazilians pushed the button on their printing presses and turned out billions of cruzeiros that inflated their economy (from which they still suffer) as never before.

Very few of the raw materials needed for such a grandiose enterprise could be obtained in Brasilia and so had to be contracted from outsiders. In the months of September to November 1958 alone, over fourteen million dollars in steel tubing, wire, power equipment, telephone trunk lines and dam construction materials were ordered. Airplanes flew in continually from Rio and São Paulo, loaded with steel bars and bags of cement. The roads to the new capital were still under construction, and so all this heavy equipment had to arrive by air.

From the northeast of the nation came literally thousands of unskilled, uneducated workers who needed money and were willing to face any hardship to get it. They learned fast and worked hard. Living in wooden shacks and working as much as 15 hours a day, they built Kubitschek's dream city. For months on end the noise of hammering could be heard 24 hours a day as swing-shift crews worked on. At night, what visitors thought to be fireflies were really red hot rivets being tossed through the darkness from man to man. Holes were dug quickly, foundations laid in record time and entire buildings seemed to grow from the soil. Many times workers would have to wait until the draftsmen gave them the designs of the next floor. And overseeing it all was President Kubitschek, who would arrive suddenly from Rio, hop into a jeep and climb over girders to see that progress was being made. He was a true "man of the people," and the unschooled workers loved him. He would sit down with them at meal time, open his own lunchbucket and talk to them about their families and their jobs. Wherever he went he left a trail of friends, and after one of his visits the men worked twice as hard.

Back in Rio, opposition to the new capital was loud and heated. Debates in the senate turned into fistfights, and investigating committees were formed to see where all the money was going. Very few people wanted to move to Brasilia and they complained bitterly about the "lack of everything" there. They said their children would not have the proper schools, that they would be unable to pay the high prices that the artificial city was commanding and that they would be separated from their families and friends. Actually most of the big politicians were unhappy about being away from the beach and afraid that their investments in Rio apartment buildings and commercial shops would suffer once the city ceased to be the nation's capital. Kubitschek's government countered this with special inducements to civil servants of a 100 percent increase in salary for working in Brasilia, special tax considerations, and an earlier retirement age. He also promised free transportation of government workers and their household effects, commissioned furniture factories to manufacture modern styles to be sold to workers at wholesale costs and put rentals on new houses and apartments at ridiculously low rates.

Those who came in the first few waves were either very brave or else went back to Rio fast. There was not a blade of grass or a tree anywhere to stop the monstrous billowing clouds of red dust that rose from the bulldozers and moving trucks. Businessmen had to change their white shirts at least three times a day, and the dining room of the completed and swank Brasilia Palace Hotel was filled with men in rough, mudcaked boots and dust-stained workclothes.

A Bit of Wild West

Over at "Freetown," where most of the construction workers lived, a city of over 100,000 had sprung up. It was a rough, sprawling, dirty, vice-ridden place, where anything went as long as there was money to buy it. It was straight out of Hollywood. There were wooden store facades with false second stories. Instead of horses, men parked their jeeps in front of the hundred and one bars. Two movie houses did a roaring business, and the far end of town was devoted strictly to the oldest profession. On pay night there were so many men and so few prostitutes that they formed a line in front of each girl's house. Anyone who tried to sneak to the front of the line was beaten back. Most of the girls made so much money in a month or two that they were able to go back to their hometowns and open up respectable dress shops or restaurants of their own.

Kubitschek had set the date for the inauguration of the city for April 21, 1960, and in spite of all odds it was ready. The inauguration itself was a memorable day that began with a Mass in the uncompleted cathedral and ended with fireworks and the name Juscelino Kubitschek burned in letters 15 feet tall. Guests came from all over the world, as did newspaper reporters and television men. There were few accommodations available to them, and many slept on the floors of unfinished apartment buildings or slung hammocks in the nearby woods. One man made a fortune selling straw-stuffed mattresses for $15 apiece (they sold for $2 in Rio) then going back after the festivities and collecting them all. There was not enough food to go around, and those thousands who hadn't been invited to the sumptuous government lunches and dinners fought it out in the town's three restaurants or roasted sides of beef Indian-style on the lawns of the Ministry buildings. The one hotel was booked so solidly (guests unwilling to vacate for invited diplomats were physically tossed bag and baggage into the dust) that even famed hotelman Conrad Hilton was offered a cot in the barbershop when he showed up unexpectedly. At the Grand Inaugural Ball in the Planalto Palace, costly gowns and striped trousers were spattered with red mud; the Japanese Ambassador fell into a pothole, and the U.S. delegation slept all night in a Boeing jet.

For all of the troubles and haste and bad feelings that Brasilia generated, it is today a modern, functioning capital city. The people living there are happy and comfortable, and it offers many things of interest to the visitor (see the chapter on exploring Brasilia) aside from its architecture and feeling of unreality. It has already started to do what those journalists of 1808 wanted. The area around the capital is being opened and a new era of pioneering and colonization has started. There are roads (the Brazilians call them highways) that stretch outward from the new capital to far off Acre, upward to the coastal city of Belém and others in construction to Fortaleza and Salvador, Bahia. All along these roads, families are coming in, clearing the land and raising their children. Little communities are forming, and the poor of the big cities are finding out how much nicer life can be in the country than in a cramped favela slum. It will be a long time before the city really "works" or the interior of the country is really settled—maybe another hundred years—but that Brasilia has kicked off the much-needed social improvement, there is no doubt.

EXPLORING BRASILIA

Brasilia, in spite of its world fame and the fact that it is the capital of South America's largest nation, is still a small city, with a population around 500,000. The tourist can see it all in one day, if he is pressed for time, or two days if he is interested in the various architectural wonders as such or in studying more closely the mode of life of a group of people who have all been recently uprooted from their original environment.

Most visitors to Brasilia plan to take an early plane from Rio—there are flights from 6:30 a.m. onward—land in Brasilia before noon, take a sightseeing tour around the main buildings and have lunch at one of the two good hotels; in the afternoon they continue their tour, this time visiting the old "free city," and are delivered to the airport in time to catch a flight back to Rio and dinner.

If you are a fastidious sightseer, this could still fit into your plans, for seeing Brasilia in one day does not carry the stigma that seeing the Louvre in 20 minutes does. The main points of the city can all be taken in from the back seat of an automobile, and the buildings with the more interesting interiors (provided that they are open for visitors that day) can easily be visited in 15 minutes or less.

There is one treat that the linger-awhile type of tourist gets that the one-dayer doesn't. That is to see the city illuminated at night. There is probably no lovelier urban sight in all Brazil than the federal buildings, all white marble with reflecting glass windows, shimmering under dozens of huge superbly placed spotlights, while the stars shine brightly out of a jungle sky of black velvet. As one old peasant woman told her daughter after she made the trip to the new capital in the back of an open truck: "It looked like I always expected Heaven to look at night. It was difficult to tell where the building lights ended and the stars began. They seemed to be put there to show off the other."

Another thing you'll notice about Brasilia is the sky. Bluer than the sky in Rio, it turns purple. There are always fleecy cloud formations decorating it. No matter how bad a photographer you are, your pictures will look great because of the "professional" sky you'll catch in each one. Another noticeable item is the red earth of the city. Not unlike the red soil of Georgia, it has stained the bases of the buildings, has tinted the carefully planted grass and,

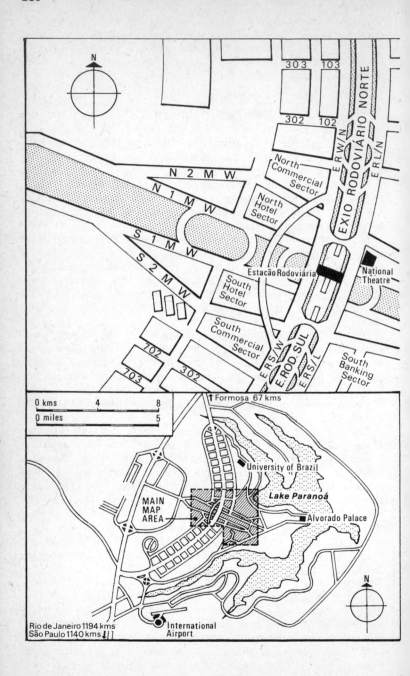

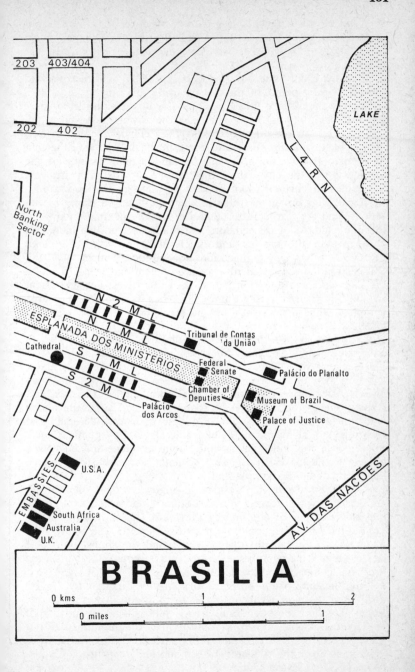

203 403/404

202 402

LAKE

L 4 R N

North
Banking
Sector

N 2 M L
N 1 M L

ESPLANADA DOS MINISTERIOS

Tribunal de Contas
da União

Cathedral

S 1 M L

Federal
Senate

Palácio do Planalto

S 2 M L

Chamber of
Deputies

Palácio
dos Arcos

Museum of Brazil

Palace of Justice

U.S.A.

EMBASSIES

South Africa
Australia
U.K.

AV. DAS NAÇÕES

BRASILIA

0 kms   1   2

0 miles   1

in a sudden gust of wind, is just as liable to coat your face and clothes with a fine red powder. Minerally, the earth is very poor; artistically, it looks as if it had been placed there on purpose for contrast.

Those with only one day to spend should be able to cover the most important points of the city by using this itinerary.

Leaving the airport, take a taxi (or if you prefer to drive yourself there are automobiles available at the airport too) and watch for the white arrow-shaped signs saying "cidade" (city). If you turn right, take a dip curve and come up again to where the sign says "Eixo Rodoviario" you will be on the main avenue of the south wing of the city. Along this avenue the luxury apartments are built, and since all rooms have huge plate glass windows onto the street, the Brazilians refer to them as "the Candango's television," and the workers do spend a great deal of time looking up into the windows of the senators and ministers who live there. It's cheaper than the movies and much more eventful! The area through here has been planned into Super Blocks (Super Quadras) and each block was designed to be a complete unit in itself. There are high-class apartments in front, then middle-income apartment buildings in the rear. Each Super Block has its own shopping area complete with supermarket and barber shops, etc., as well as a Catholic chapel. There is also a primary school for almost every Super Block so that the school-age children would not have to cross streets coming or going to class.

Brasilia, if you glance at a map, is in the form of an airplane, a fitting symbol for a city in this space-minded age. The two "wings" are for commercial and residential areas. The fuselage, from propeller to tail blades, is for government, communications and transportation centers. The city highways are so designed that there are almost no red lights or traffic signs. City planner Lucio Costa's wife was killed in an automobile accident and he vowed that he would make Brasilia as "accident free as possible," which it is, compared to Rio or São Paulo.

As you go down this residential highway, turn off beneath another sign which directs you to a Super Quadra and explore the internal workings of community life there. Then, heading in the same direction, you'll come out onto Avenida W3, the commercial main street of the capital. Here you'll find the shops, both chic and mundane, the good restaurants, a movie house, the banks, the telephone company and the post office.

After heading south on W3, turn around and go to the far north and, turning right onto the main highway by the Hotel Imperial, follow the directional arrows that will take you in front of Hotel Nacional, down a ramp under the monumental bus station (with music, shops and perhaps some visiting Indians riding up and down the escalators), then another right turn and you'll be on the Three Powers Square.

First building of importance you'll pass is the national Cathedral, with clasped fingers of concrete reaching prayerfully to the sky. Worshippers go in underground and come out to hear Mass in the center under the fingers, protected from the elements by huge panes of glass. Check with your hotel to see if there is a Mass on the Sunday or holiday you're visiting.

Besides the Cathedral, on both sides of the square, like huge glass-plated dominoes, are the various ministries. Everything from Air Force to Mines and Energy are in these 18 buildings. Functional, but with a tendency to absorb the hot sun's rays, they serve the place of literally hundreds of scattered offices used when Rio was the capital.

Beyond the last building on the right is what many claim to be the most beautiful building in Brasilia, if not in all Brazil—the Ministry of Foreign Relations, with its water garden and soaring concrete arches. Despite its extravagance—those arches support nothing but themselves—it's a must for the amateur photographer.

Congress in Two Orange Halves

Across the way, almost floating on air and the shallow reflection pools, is the magnificent Congress building with its twin, 28-story towers where senators and deputies have their offices. The two orange halves, sitting on each side of the towers, are the Senate Chamber and the House of Deputies. The Senate is the smaller inverted one. Completely air conditioned and perfectly illuminated within, there is no reason for any one to feel the lack of fresh air or sunshine. The building can be visited, but permission must be obtained from the blue-uniformed guard at the desk just across the ramp on the upper level. If either of the houses are in session, the Brazilian flag is flying from either of their flagpoles.

Continuing down the plane's nose, you'll see the small but perfectly balanced Supreme Court on your right with a modern statue of Blind Justice in front.

There is a plump, oblong cement box, with a huge head of Juscelino Kubitschek in its courtyard: that is the Brasilia Museum.

Directly facing the Supreme Court is probably one of the most beautiful of all the buildings, the Planalto Palace, where the president has his offices. Guided tours can be arranged, and be sure to see the luxurious Hall of Mirrors where state receptions are held, the severe but lovely room to the right where the President holds open conferences and the sun-illuminated interior corridors on the second and third floors, where lush green tropical plants grow in profusion.

Head east now, toward the lake, past what seems to be miles of modern lamp posts, until you come to the exclusive Alvorada Palace, the president's residence, at the "propeller" of the airplane. This was the first administrative building ready and the most expensive. Every inch of cement, all the steel girders, the pipes, the glass, tiles, everything had to be flown in, because there was no way to reach Brasilia by land. The inside with its glass walls, panels of gilded tile, and rosewood floors is just as exquisite. Beside this jewellike palace is a small circular chapel, where the presidential family attends Mass.

The long, low building nearby is the Brasilia Palace Hotel, described elsewhere, another of Oscar Niemeyer's prides and joys.

After lunch, you will still have some three hours to see the other less important things or to go back for a closer look at what you saw that morning. You could visit the handsome national theater, a pyramid of weathered concrete near the bus station, head off in the same direction for the Yacht Club (where you get an interesting side view of the Three Powers Square) or continue way out on the as yet almost deserted North wing, and arrive at the other side of the lake, where many expensive homes have been built or are going up.

For a sharp contrast of a "satellite city" to modern Brasilia—from the "architecture" of a dust town to the year 2,000—take a 20-minute drive beyond city limits to one of the communities settled by the Brazilian builders. You may want to hire one of a group of American guides, right opposite the Hotel Nacional.

If you will have an hour or so before your plane, take a quick look at the wild-west, clapboard satellite town called Free City. Though the bulk of Brasilia's working class now lives far out in the satellite towns of Gama or Taguatinga, the *Cidade Livre* (Free Town) still stands as a monument to those hardy northeasterners who built the 21st-century capital city.

EXPLORING THE MINING REGION

Belo Horizonte is the leading city in the Brasilia region because of its 1,100 factories, skyscrapers, good climate and friendly people. It gained international attention a few years ago when a group of atomic scientists called it one of the safest spots in the world in case of an atom bomb war between Russia and the United States. Apparently it lies at just the right longitude and latitude and is caressed by certain winds that would carry the barest minimum of radiation down upon the people. After this report, real estate agents did a whopping business selling land—unseen—to overseas buyers.

Belo Horizonte is a very young city. In fact it only celebrated its 75th birthday in 1972, but already it has a population of well over a million and is one of the fastest growing metropolises in Latin America.

There are many things for the tourist to do. One of them is to stroll along the shady downtown streets and watch the new buildings going up all around. Another is to visit the municipal park located in the heart of the business area. Town fathers planned well, for should you become tired of cement and commerce, you can cross over into the well-kept park, with its tree-lined walks, its small lakes, its rustic bridges and red flowered bushes. There is something going on there almost all the time, and it is a favorite spot for lovers, nursemaids and photographers.

Another interesting place is the Minas Tennis Club, one of the biggest sports arenas in the state. Extremely modern in design, the gymnasium can hold 10,000 people. Its swimming pool is Olympic size and its separate courts for volleyball, basketball and tennis have caused favorable comment from many international sports-minded figures.

Just as modern, but much more controversial, is the oddly shaped church at Pampulha, just outside the city. Designed by famed Brasilia builder Oscar Niemeyer, the church, once constructed, was refused consecration by Catholic authorities because both Niemeyer and Portinari (whose frescoes adorn it) were known Communist sympathizers. The battle raged for a number of years until the people of Minas put pressures to bear on the Bishop and the church was blessed.

The Tassini Museum has a collection of maps, crystal, lamps, work tools, photographs and general miscellanea collected over a 30-year span by one Raul Tassini and donated to the city. It is devoted strictly to objects that figure in the history of Belo Horizonte and the early diamond mining days. Well worth a visit, it is open every day except Monday.

Ouro Preto (Black Gold), for its type, is possibly one of the most interesting cities in Brazil. Little known outside of the country, it is revered by Brazilians the way Italians revere Venice or the Americans, Williamsburg. Founded in 1711 with the name Vila Rica (Rich Village), it soon became the center of the gold, diamond and semiprecious stone trading in the colonial era. So much gold came from the hills around Ouro Preto that the area was named simply "minas gerais" or "general mines."

It became *the* place to live in those days, and the rich built fine houses and palaces, donated gold to construct churches and hired the very best artists to decorate them. One of the most famous names to come out of this period was a crippled mulatto sculptor called Aleijadinho, which means "Little Cripple." The man could do no wrong when he was working with wood or stone, but his inherited diseased blood and his own sexual escapades turned him into a monster. His facial features became so deformed by disease that he put a sack over his head so that no one could be frightened by his ugliness. His legs refused to coordinate and his fingers and hands became so contorted that his assistants used to tie his hammer and chisel to his wrists with leather thongs so he could work. What he did with the beauty inside him is in evidence in

Ouro Preto and the surrounding area and is part of the rich Brazilian cultural heritage.

The Glorious Churches of Ouro Preto

The best place to see Aleijadinho's artistry is the Church of São Francisco, located just down the hill to the left from the Praça Tiradentes. Note the twin towers in an almost salt and pepper shaker form. Be sure and inspect the huge soapstone medallion high up over the front door, as well as the intricately carved doorway. Inside, the main altar with cherubic faces, garlands of tropical fruits and allegorical characters is still fresh with the original paint. Also note the twin soapstone side altars. Just doing one of them is enough for a man to be hailed as a genius, and he did two for this church alone.

His work can also be seen in the impressive Monte do Carmo Church, in whose tall towers hang two bells that weigh 7,000 pounds. The altar which dominates the church of São José was also done by Aleijadinho.

There are eleven churches in this one town in the Brazilian hills. If any were in Europe, they would be international "musts" on any tourist itinerary, but hidden away as they are here, they have preserved their charm and offer a new delight to the tourist with spirit enough to come this far to see them.

While in Ouro Preto don't fail to take a slow tour of the Museum of Inconfidência. Housed in an impressive baroque building that was started in 1748 and concluded in 1846 it was at one time the home of the Municipal Congress. It was here that the first Brazilian rebellion against the Portuguese was started and here that the first rebel, a white-bearded martyr nicknamed "Tiradentes" (tooth puller), was captured, then taken to Rio and brutally executed. The museum is full of clothes, children's toys, slaves' manacles, firearms, books and gravestones of the turbulent era. The director, who speaks English very well and is proud of his Brazilian past, will be delighted to show you around personally. Admission is free.

Many people stay two days in Ouro Preto savoring the winding old streets and the colonial buildings and dodging the donkeys and horses and carts that still move among the automobiles. Ever since 1933 when the entire city became National Patrimony, not a thing has been changed, and it is to the Brazilian's credit that many things have been restored and cleaned up. The second day, you might hire a taxi and travel a few miles to the sleepy village of Congonhas. Main attraction there is the Church of Bom Jesus de Matosinhos where Aleijadinho sculptured 12 life-sized statues of the Prophets and placed them outside at the front entrance.

These works, breath-taking in their exact details and expressive faces, have been called "a genial mixture of Quasimodo, Beethoven and Michelangelo." Aside from a number of statues inside the church, he did the Stations of the Cross in life-size, using sixty-six different figures that are housed in 6 separate buildings. Rarely visited by the Brazilians themselves, these figures are "finds" for the really discriminating tourist.

Aleijadinho, deformed and crippled though he was, got around. His works can be seen in the churches of the nearby towns of Mariana and São João Del-Rei. Baroque lovers should also visit the churches of Sabará.

Diamantina took its name from the diamonds that were extracted in great quantities from its soil in the 1700s, and even today the mines still supply gold, iron ore and rock crystal. It was here also that the famous Chica da Silva lived, the mulatto slave who captured the heart of the wealthy Portuguese mine owner. He showered her with gold and precious stones, built her a palace with hanging gardens and even transported a sailing yacht overland for her pleasure. Then he turned around and dug her a lake to sail it in.

The city looks very much like it did in the days of Chica. Be sure and note the covered overhanging roofs with their elaborate brackets.

BAHIA, THE COAST AND THE INTERIOR

If you have only time to visit two Brazilian cities, make them Rio and Salvador, usually referred to as Bahia, the name of the state of which it is capital. Salvador has all the ingredients of a South American town. There are the red tile roofs tacked atop white plaster walls. There are palm trees, baroque architecture, an abundance of churches and happy carefree people. These are the expectable things. Then there are the thousands of black faces, with bodies swathed in cloth of neo-African styles. There are dishes of hot strange foods that are prepared nowhere else in the world. There is a strange drum beating voodoo ritual that mingles the best of the African and Christian ideals into a powerful, frighteningly personal religion. There is a fight dance called Capoeira that originated in Bahia and is only practiced here. There are modern automobiles vying for traffic with plodding donkeys. There are sumptuous mansions vying for a place in the sun with mud-thatched shanties.

If you stay there for awhile, you'll find Salvador is not just a city but an entire way of life, where the arts and the human personality are more important than money or political ambitions. The city has been called the "Renaissance of Latin America" because of its attitudes towards beauty and self-expression and the number of artists from all over the nation (and the world) who have gone there for inspiration. But this does not mean that Bahia is all siestas in the sun. Far from it. One glance at the dozens of new office buildings and the hundreds of modern apartment houses will dispel that idea. It is simply that the Bahianos have found a way to live with the best of both worlds, and, like their hybrid religion, their city has become a surprising, fascinating experience.

Bird's-eye View of the Northeast

The area the Brazilians call the Northeast is that part of their nation that bulges out into the Atlantic Ocean up north. It is composed of ten states: Sergipe, Alagoas, Pernambuco, Paraiba, Rio Grande do Norte, Ceará, Piauí, Maranhão, Bahia and part of Minas Gerais. All of them are backward, underdeveloped and plagued by innumerable ills. They are as different from the south of the country as Paris is from Algiers. The same language is spoken and the allegiance to the same flag is taken, but nature has made sure that inequality is the rule.

When the northeast is not parched and dying from droughts (that come about every three years), then it is inundated by rains and flash floods. The land along the coast is fertile in places. Inside the country there is less water than in Israel. Educationally and politically the area has been neglected by the rest of Brazil. Those trying to improve their lot have gone south. Few of them return.

For the tourist this offers some of the most picturesque sights in the country. There are the jangada fishing boats along the coast, the forts and churches, the women weaving fine lace, the leather-clad cowboys and clay sculptors. Crushing poverty, barefoot children and full graveyards are also picturesque to some. Beyond Bahia, very little has been done to encourage tourism in this area. Going there, be prepared to rough it.

EXPLORING SALVADOR (BAHIA)

Salvador was the first city built by the Portuguese when they colonized Brazil. That was in 1549. Today this city spreads around the bay of Todos os Santos, and so wide is this bay (1,052 square kilometers) that it is claimed it could hold all the ships in the world. Salvador was built by the early settlers to keep the Spanish, French and Dutch away from the new colony belonging to King Dom João III. The administration buildings and residences were built on the hills, the forts, docks and warehouses on the beaches. To this day it is still divided into upper and lower cities. From 1500 to 1815 Salvador enjoyed being the nation's busiest port. The sugar from the northeast and the gold and diamonds from the mines in the south all passed through this town. It was a golden age for Salvador when magnificent homes and richly decorated churches were built. Its churches have no rivals anywhere in the world. Thanks to a federal commission called The National Historic and Artistic Patrimony Service, created in 1941, many of the city's old churches are the same today as they were the day they were built. Entire squares such as Largo do Pelourinho, hundreds of private homes and even the hand-chipped street paving bricks have been preserved. Salvador counts 97,000 buildings, and about 20,000 of them are over 250 years old. Yet there are brand new buildings going up everywhere to meet the living requirements of the progressive citizens of today.

Salvador (called by the Brazilians simply "Bahia") can be seen, if necessary, in three days. Save time for some shopping and maybe an extra day to go back for a closer look at some of the things seen in passing.

The first day. Start out on foot from the Tourist Department at Praça da Sé. They have English-speaking guides if you want one. Ladies should remember to wear low-heeled shoes but not low-cut dresses or slacks. The people of the town don't like slacks, and many churches won't admit a woman who is wearing them. To the left of the Tourist office is the Archbishop's Palace, built in the 18th century and today used as the Catholic Law School. On the other side of the Tourist office is the 18th-century Holy House of Mary church. Walking up Guedes de Brito street, right at the start you'll see Saldanha Palace with its impressive gateway. The School of Arts and Crafts is there now. As you walk up Bispo Street you'll pass São Damaso Seminary, built in 1700, and will come to a little square and the Church of São Francisco Convent. It is one of Brazil's most famous and undoubtedly one of the most beautiful in the world. Hand carved in every nook and cranny and then covered with shining gold, it is so impressive that many tourists stay around all day just watching the play of lights on the walls. It is especially beautiful during a High Mass. The image of St. Peter of Alcantara on the lateral altar on the right is so well done that church authorities had a battle with Emperor Dom Pedro II, because he wanted it for his private chapel. Only the men can visit the blue-tiled cloisters of the convent; women must be content to peer through the grillwork. There are Franciscan fathers there who will show you around. When you leave drop some money into the poor box, for the church does an impressive job three times a day supplying warm meals for the poor. Right next door is the church of the Third Order of São Francisco. Inside there is a room full of life-size statues that is worth seeing. The intricate façade was carved in 1703 but hidden for many years by a thick coat of plaster. It was a major art find when it was uncovered recently. Now to the square of Terreiro de Jesus with the 16th century Basilica Cathedral, the church of the Third Order of São Domingos (1731) and the church of St. Peter of the

Clerics. From here, up Alfredo de Brito Street you come to the architectural spectacle of the Largo do Pelourinho. It was here that thousands of slaves were chained together and sold on that platform on the right side of the street. Note the typical old balconies, the tiles and the people who look as if they've stepped from a Debret engraving. Walk slowly down to Taboão Square where five streets cross and then up the Ladeira do Carmo. Now take a quaint flight of steps that leads to the Church of the Passo and continue to the top of the street. Here the Carmo Convent and the Church of the Third Order of Carmo stand side by side. The church is famed for its image of the crucified Christ. To enter the convent, you have to know the way. Beside the biggest door in the room hangs a cord. Pull it and from somewhere inside a smiling guard appears to escort you about. Be sure and tip him when you leave. Going up the Ladeira do Carmo there is a corner of blue-tiled houses. You must be tired, so call a taxi now.

Tell the driver to take you to Baixa do Sapateiro, a street filled with shops and private homes that time has somehow forgotten. Afterward look at the Convent of the Desterro (1678), where the sisters have a well-deserved reputation as candy makers. It is Brazil's oldest and most beautiful convent. Go up Avenida Joana Angelica to the Tororó steps. Below them lies the Dique, an artificial lake made in the 17th century as part of the city's defense system. You can go for a ride in one of the boats if you wish. Now back to your hotel, for you must be starving and don't forget there is still the night to enjoy.

Coconuts and the Great Outdoors

The second day. This one will be devoted to beaches and outdoor scenery. Get a car for the day and tell the driver to go *slowly* towards the Lagoa do Abaeté. The first impressive building you will pass is the white columned University Rectory. If you want to, you can go in and see the blue tiles and the reconstructed auditorium. On Avenida Oceanica you'll go for about 20 miles past fishermen's houses, beaches, palm trees and little boys selling fresh coconuts. If you stop for one, watch how deftly he nicks off the top with his wicked knife. The milk is warm and sweet. Ask him to split open the coconut and then go on and eat the soft white meat with your fingers. You will pass famed Itapoã Beach with its tall coconut trees and finally reach the lagoon. Brazilian composers have written dozens of songs about this strange inland lake with its contrast of white white sand and black black waters. Native women wash their clothes here, and there are some good restaurants in the area for lunch or a cooling drink. Take your bathing suit too, for you might like to sample one of the beaches on the way going or coming.

Arriving back in the city, you'll pass the Barra lighthouse and the fort, built in 1598. Drive along Avenida Sete (7) de Setembro and stop to look at the fort of Santa Maria, built in 1650. A little farther on is the fort of São Diogo. It was on this spot that Tomé de Sousa landed in 1549 to found the city. The avenue then passes the church of Santo Antonio de Barro and the church of Victoria built in the 16th century and restored in 1809. Now let's take Rua da Graça and visit the Igreja da Graça, the first church built in Bahia. It was constructed by Catarina Paraguaçu, the Indian wife of the first white man to settle there. Now if there is not a capoeira exhibition at the Tourist Office that evening, then go back to your hotel, have a fast bite and try to see a candomblé that evening. Remember not to take photos unless the permission of the Mãe de Santo (priestess) is given. Be prepared to be separated from your friends once you arrive there. They will tell you where to sit and its always men on one side and women on the other. There is nothing to be frightened of either, but don't be surprised to see the Brazilian beside you suddenly become "possessed" by spirits, fall onto the ground, roll his eyes and then dance in a contorted, uncomfortable position. When you leave (sometime after midnight) show your appreciation by placing some money at the feet of the chief drummer.

The third day. Now you'll visit the other end of the city on the Itapagipe peninsula. If you leave about 9 a.m. from the Tourist Office, the car will go down commercially busy Rua Chile to Castro Alves Praça, then down the Ladeira da Montanha (where many accidents have happened when the brakes didn't hold) and reach the lower city. That big column of white cement rising to the upper city is the Lacerda elevator and is used to join the two levels of Salvador. Imagine if you had to walk up and down those steep hills every time! Taking Avenida Frederico Pontes, you'll pass the attractive Fort of Lagartixa and the Noble House of Jequitaia built in the 18th century and now used as an army officers' school. Continuing you'll come to the sprawling Agua de Meninos market. Inside there is everything that the citizen of Bahia needs to keep alive. Be sure to see the stalls filled with brightly colored fresh tropical fruit, the other stalls with freshly caught fish and the other, less agreeable ones, with hunks of bloody beef or pork hung on iron hooks and covered with flies. Most tourists like to wander through the pottery section, and you'll be amazed how inexpensive some of this art-handicraft is. The market is being cleaned up and even paved in some places, but the stench and the ankle deep mud has kept more than one sensitive tourist out.

If you take Rua Barvão de Cotegipe you'll be able to visit the Fratelli Vita glassblowing plant, where some of the finest crystal in the world is made. If you've never seen this art up close, it's well worth a stop now. Ask your driver to go to the Bonfim church, and on the way you'll pass the 18th-century Archbishop's summer palace which is connected to the Penha church by a very interesting passageway. Now at Bonfim church, you are really in Bahia, for this church is to the people of Salvador what St. Peter's is to the Romans. Yet it is not ornate or covered with gold, but just a simple building with years of tradition among the faithful. It is said that the Lord of Bonfim never fails anyone and the room of miracles looks as if that might be so. Here you'll see wooden, silver and plaster reproductions of parts of the human body hanging on the walls. These are there in gratitude for cures worked through prayers to the Lord of Bonfim. Almost always the cures are said to be miracles, as the many inscriptions indicate. It is here, on the Thursday before the third Sunday in January, that thousands of black women dressed in their colorful regional dress and carrying pottery jugs with flowers and water come to symbolically wash down the church steps. It is one of the most time-honored fiestas in Bahia. The view from atop this hill is really spectacular.

Back in the car, go to the Fort of Mont Serrat. Its white walls rising from the seacoast, this 16th-century building looks like a giant bird ready for flight. There is the Mont Serrat Church nearby with its renowned carving of the Repentant St. Peter. If the church is closed, call the guard who lives at the back, and even though he grumbles, he'll show you the tiny jewellike interior. A tip calms him down amazingly. Now you can go to the Cacao Institute where pictures and graphs tell the story of the chocolate industry from the planted seed to the finished foil-wrapped bar. More than $100,000,000 of cocoa is exported annually from Bahia's ports. Now onto the crowded-with-everything Modelo market. It's cleaner than the other one because it's under a roof, but the smells are there. After shopping for regional articles here, take a boat at the Cairu docks for a quick look at the Fort of São Marcelo right in front of the market in the bay. It was built in 1650 and kept invaders away. Then it was used as a prison and now serves more for curiosity than anything else. Back in your car, go to the lovely Museum of Sacred Art on Ladeira de Sodré. You'll be impressed with the tiles and the silver altar. It is unquestionably the most beautiful museum in all Brazil. Then, if there is still time, visit the Museum of Modern Art in the Castro Alves theatre.

You have seen Salvador. It wasn't just three days spent looking at "things," but three days of a most unusual, most unforgettable experience. You'll be back.

EXPLORING THE NORTHEAST

Recife has been called the "Venice of Brazil" because it is a city built on three rivers and connected by many bridges. It is the third largest city in the nation with a population of over one million.

The city got its name from the reefs that line the coast and make the beach of Boa Viagem an unusual place. Those who come here as tourists are always impressed with the beach. In the morning when the tide is in the waves come up almost to the road, then as the tide recedes, the rocks of the reefs slowly appear. Depending on the time of the day, individual swimming pools are formed, fish flap around the bathers and the hidden rock formations dry into odd colors in the afternoon sun.

Another sight to see along this beach is the leaving (about 6 a.m.) or the return (about 2 p.m.) of the *jangadas*, those crude, log rafts with the beautiful sails that local fishermen take out onto the high seas. Many stories and legends have been written about them, and they are as dangerous as they look. Only an expert navigator and swimmer should try one. It looks easy for the sunburnt men of Recife, but they have been working on them all their lives.

There are many old churches in this town. Most impressive are the São Pedro dos Clerigos (for its beautiful sculptured front, 1782), Conceiçao dos Militares (unusually fine ceiling, 1708), Madre de Deus (altar and sacristy, 1707) and the Convento de São Francisco (its interesting Portuguese tiles, 1606).

Olinda is a small colonial city, five miles to the north of Recife, that can be reached by a bus which leaves from the front of the Governor's Palace. Go to the end of the line and walk across the street and up the hillside. Here you will see old houses, monasteries and the mayor's office, which was once the home of the Viceroys. The city was built by the Dutch who controlled Recife in the late 1600s. Many of the houses still have the original latticed balconies, the heavy doors and the pink stucco walls.

You will notice small clay statuettes in the shops for sale. Almost all of these are made in the interior town of Caruaru. Reached by daily bus or special taxis on Wednesdays and Saturdays, the days of the fair, the trip is well worth it. Not only will you be able to see a very colorful interior market place, but you'll be able to rub elbows with the leather-clad cowboys of the harsh dry region, see the way the people live on the parched soil and be entertained by strolling musicians and dancers. Allow one full day for this.

In Fortaleza, the beach is the main attraction, but the old lace makers are in close second. Aracati is the town that contains most of the artisans. There you will see little girls of three years learning to thread a needle and unravel snarled thread, as well as old grandmothers almost blind from the years of close, delicate labor.

A new highway (BR-010), cut through the jungle between Belém and Brasilia, connects 32 new cities and villages. Daily motorcoach in both directions is available. The voyage lasts 3 days and is well worth the cost of $30 (approx.) if you are the adventurous type.

PRACTICAL INFORMATION FOR BRASILIA

 WHEN TO COME? The best months are probably the summer months, from November to around the middle of April. It gets chilly in Brasilia. Because the city is on a high plateau, some 3,500 feet above sea level, and in the direct path of winds from the moist warm jungles as well as those from the colder south, its climate is variable and invigorating. Sweaters at night during the winter months are almost a necessity, and no matter what the season, you'll probably want to sleep under a blanket.

 WHAT TO SEE? Everything. The two presidential palaces (the Alvorada where the man in power lives and the Planalto where he works), the twin-towered Congress building, the domino-placed Ministry buildings, the crown-shaped cathedral, the national theater, the modern spacious apartments and the bustling—almost small town —atmosphere of the business district. A visit should be paid to the yacht club and the area known as Embassy Row. A visit to the shrine of Dom Bosco is also in order, not just to pay him homage, but to get an over-all, complete view of the city. There are no museums as yet of any importance, nor any special collections of things. The exteriors of the buildings are more interesting than the interiors (with a few exceptions mentioned already), and don't forget to take note of the way the highways and by-passes have been laid out. Also study the faces of the "candangos," the dusty but courteous immigrant workers who built the city with almost nothing but bare hands and determination.

 HOW TO GET ABOUT. Take a taxi. Many people prefer to have a guided tour by one of the registered agencies. If you only have time for a once-around-lightly view of the city then *Ciclone-Hinterland Turismo* on Avenida W3, Quadra 5, or *Trips*, located in the lobby of the Hotel Nacional or *Ypê* at Super Quadra-106, bloco 13, apartment 607 will give you the best service. They have their own cars, usually Brazilian-made Volkswagen "Kombi" station wagons, and their drivers speak English as well as half a dozen other languages. Prices are moderate but a little higher than in Rio for the same service.

You might, just for the fun of it, get on any of the buses that leave from the street level platform at the centrally located Highway Terminal ("Estação Rodoviaria") and stay on it till it takes you back to the terminal again. No matter which line you take, you'll get odd and interesting angles of the city that other tourists don't catch from the guided tour. But it's best to do this after you've seen Brasilia the regular way, so you can appreciate what you are seeing even more.

 SPORTS. In Brasilia, there is such an exodus of governmental workers, especially such important types as congressmen and ministry directors, that weekend activities are limited. Focal point is the *yacht club*, on the artificially created Lake Pinheiro. Only open to members, your travel agent or almost any Brazilian citizen can get you in. There is a nice big pool, a small but more than adequate restaurant, and if you look sad and wistful, some friendly Brazilian is bound to ask you if you'd like to take a ride on the lake in his "yacht."

People do go fishing, some as far away as on Bananal Island. Check with your tourist agent in Brasilia about this and see if they can arrange a two-day trip to the Carajá Indians who will act as your guides. There is a hotel there; it was called the *Juscelino Kubitschek* until the latter's political disgrace, whereupon it became *John Kennedy* (same initials!). Don't go there without a reservation.

HOTELS. A number of new hotels are in various stages of study, planning or construction, by such chains as *Inter-Continental, Holiday Inns, Sheraton* and *Hilton*, among others. Still one of the most popular is the *Nacional* (phone 25-0050 or 25-1050), situated in the heart of the city with an incomparable view of the Congress, Ministries and the banking section. Ten floors of comfortable apartments each with bath and telephone. Off the spacious lobby is an excellent restaurant where one of the daily specialties is a long smorgasbord table with 100 different dishes to choose from. The wine cellar is excellent and the European-trained chefs add a Continental touch. There is a small bar done in beautiful jacaranda wood paneling, and a pool outside open to guests of the hotel. The basement is equipped with modern Finnish-style sauna as well as steam bath and massage parlors. For evening entertainment, one of the best nightclubs in town is on the ground floor, alongside a patio *churrascaria. II. Stern* store.

Another good hotel is the *Eron Brasília* (24-7080)—200 rooms with refrigerators, TV and FM music in each. Central air-conditioning, panoramic-view elevators up the side of the building, a small pool, bar and nightclub. *H. Stern* store.

The first hotel in the city was the *Brasília Palace*, away from the center of things near the beautiful Alvorada presidential palace. Designed by Oscar Niemeyer, the hotel has been photographed and written about in books and magazines all over the world. The one solid wall of glass disks is especially noteworthy. There is a very good restaurant and bar, with a dance combo on the weekends. The modern lounge has television, and there is a small outdoor swimming pool. Best to have your reservations before arriving.

Other hotels that can be recommended are the *Alvorada Hotel*, 23-3050; *Torre Palace*, 25-3360; *Bristol*, 25-2010; *Das Nações, Diplomat, Itamarati Parque, Planalto, Brasília Imperial.*

RESTAURANTS. Brasilia does have some good restaurants and most of them are in the area around the street known as W3. Getting off W3 Avenue, a small German place called *Colibri* near the supermarket at Super Quadra 305 does things with fried chicken and fried potatoes that deserve a medal. Wash this down with some of their ice-cold white wine. You won't regret it.

For good solid Brazilian beef, done "churrasco gaucho" style, pay a visit to the *Churrascaria do Lago*, on the banks of the lake, in walking distance of the Hotel Brasilia. Their specialty is a "mixto," which is a little bit of everything, both beef and pork, served with rice, manioc flour and a special barbecue sauce of raw onions, tomatoes and vinegar.

At Super Quadra 114 a recently opened place called *Cravo e Canela* serves Bahian-type cooking. Almost as good as you'll get in Bahia itself. The women in the kitchen are all from up north and got their cooking practice serving three meals a day to their families.

Other restaurants are: *Tabu*, behind Hotel Nacional; *Firenze*, Super Quadra Sul 104; *La Chaumière*, Comércio Local Sul 40-B; *Au Bon Gourmet*, Super-quadra Sul 106; *Bon-apetit*, Comercio Local Sul 203; *Xadrezinho*, Av. das Naçoes; *Panela de Barro*, Setor Hoteleiro Sul; *Diplomat*, Setor Hoteleiro Norte; *Panorâmico*, Torre da TV; *Stalão*, Setor Hoteleiro Sul; *Bier Fass*, Centro Comercial Gilberto Salomão; *Bologna*, Comércio Local Sul.

USEFUL ADDRESSES. United States Embassy, Avenida das Naçoes 3. British Embassy, Avenida des Naçoes 8. National City Bank of New York, Avenida W3. Quadra 2A. For sightseeing tours, contact the *Excelsior Agency*.

PRACTICAL INFORMATION FOR MINING REGION

Like the rest of the country, this area is no exception when it comes to distances. Belo Horizonte is 453 miles from Brasilia, but that doesn't stop people from Brasilia going there to do their shopping. Ouro Preto, the living museum city, is a full 75 miles away from Belo, but the people in the state capital consider it "a suburb." And Diamantina (another colonial jewel in the Minas hills), is 180 miles away, but citizens in Belo will calmly tell visitors who have nothing to do for the day, "why don't you run over and see Diamantina?"

Fortunately , there is regular train service between Belo Horizonte and Diamantina, and a new all paved road from Belo to Ouro Preto. Taxis will drive you there and back for $25 or so and a regular bus line charges about a dollar for the same service.

HOTELS

BELO HORIZONTE OTHON PALACE. Av. Afonso Pena corner Tupis e Bahia, newest, biggest and most luxurious in the city, with 317 air-conditioned rooms, rooftop pool and bar, international restaurant, coffee shop, sauna, conference facilities for 800 persons. Overlooking trees and lakes of Municipal Park. Opening mid 1977. *Hotel Del Rey*, Pça Afonso Arinos 60, one of the best downtown, 270 non-air-conditioned rooms, private bath, 24-hour room service. The *Normandy* on Rua Tamoios 212. Service is very good; the rooms large and airy; modern restaurant and bar are fine. Located in the center of the city's business district, it is one of the most popular meeting places. Insist on an outside room. Other hotels: *Excelsior* (250 rooms), Rua Caetés 753; *Serrana Palace,* Rua Goitacases 450; *Plaza Palace,* Rua Rio de Janeiro 147; *Financial,* Av. Alfonso Pena 571.

The Amazonas, on Avenida Amazonas 120, is new and small but service is very good. Excellent restaurant on the 11th floor.

OURO PRETO. Colonial art treasure city. Most modern and with best view of the red tile rooftops is *Grande Hotel* on Rua Rocha Lagoa. Built by Brasilia designer Oscar Niemeyer, the hotel is comfortable even if its style is in shocking contrast to the rest of the city. Good restaurant.

Pouso do Chico Rei is an old restored home that is one of the most charming and "typical" hotels in the entire town. Located on Rua Brigadeiro Musqueira 90, it has very few rooms so service becomes a personal thing. Telephone 333 for reservations in advance.

Palace, Praça Tiradentes 4, is new but in a very old building that easily dates back to the middle 1700s. While the walls have been replastered and the structure reinforced, the doors, floors and ceiling beams are of huge slabs of wood with the rough edges where the colonial axeman's blade struck still showing.

Other hotels, all small and modest, are the *Pousada Ouro Preto*, Rua Alfredo Baeta 16 (run by Luxor chain in tastefully-restored colonial mansion; gourmet restaurant); *Pilão*, Praça Tiradentes 57; *Colonial*, Travessa Camilo Veloso 26; *Toffolo*, Rua São José 76.

CONGONHAS DO CAMPO— *Cova de Daniel,* small but quaint combination of inn, restaurant and antique shop flanking the church of Our Lord of Matosinhos, which features great masterworks by South America's Michelangelo, a crippled mulatto who lived in the 17th century known as "Aleijadinho". His 12 Biblical prophets sculpted in soapstone and the 66 figures of the passion drama of Christ carved in cedar wood are well worth the hour-and-a-half drive to Congonhas do Campo from Belo Horizonte. More of "The Little Cripple's" great works are to be seen in Ouro Preto, especially the Church of St. Francis of Assisi, and in Sabará, close to Belo Horizonte.

DIAMANTINA. Colonial mining town. Best hotel in this old-world village is the *Tijuco*, located on Rua Macau do Meio 211. It adheres faithfully to the historical atmosphere demanded by the visitor.

Roberto, with 24 rooms, on Travesa do Carmo 73, is equally delightful and romantic. Has a good restaurant, too.

RESTAURANTS. While you are in this area be sure and try some *carne desfiado com tutu*, which is dried jerked beef torn to shreds, fried with onions and served with mashed black beans. This dish is also referred to as *roupa velha* (old clothes).

Belo Horizonte has the best places to eat in the area. In the other towns stick with the food served in the recommended hotels. If you are very brave and adventurous, you might eat at some small, not too clean place you'll discover on a side street. It can lead to all sorts of gastric disturbances, but can also be fun.

BELO HORIZONTE. Most popular place in town, where the steaks are thick and the cheesebread a specialty, *Camponesa* at 36 Rua Goitacazes, in walking distance from your hotel. Clean, well managed and moderate in price, you'll soon see why all of its many tables are occupied.

Other good restaurants; *Nacional Clube*, Rua Josafa Belo 100; *Elle*, Rua Fernandes Tourinho; *Mangueiras*, Pça. São Francisco 30 in the Pampulha suburb; *Casa do Baile*, Av. Otacílio Negrão de Lima 31; *Dona Derna*, Rua Tomé de Souza 1380. A touch of old Germany is the *Alpino* on Rua Tupinambas 173, with its ice-cold draft beer, its homemade black bread and such items as *Hasenpfeffer* and *Konigsberger Klops*. But check beforehand, as sometimes they are out of their specialities.

Most popular night spots, which also serve meals or specialty dishes, are *Chorare*, Rua da Bahia 1450, with good music; O *Papa Papatutti*, Av. Getúlio Vargas 823, for good pizza and beer; *Casa Grande*, Av. Getúlio Vargas, corner of Rua Maranhão, for samba dancing or relaxing on covered terrace outside. Other nightclubs are *Estilingue*, *Xamengo*, *Cavalo Branco*, *Braga's Scotch Bar*, *Chat Noir*, *Tele Telo*, and *Wood Face*.

PRACTICAL INFORMATION FOR SALVADOR (BAHIA)

 WHEN TO COME? Because of its consistently warm climate, almost any time of the year is a good time to visit Salvador. But there are certain events that will make this attractive city even more interesting if you plan your trip to coincide with them.

January 1 has the celebration of Our Lord the Good Jesus of the Navigators. Hundreds of boats float offshore, decorated with flags and streamers. Then later there are exhibitions of drum beating and capoeira fighting. January 1, Festa de Nosso Senhor dos Navigantes takes place at Monte Serrat. January 6, Festa dos Reis is celebrated in all parts of the city.

February 2 is devoted to Iemanjá, the goddess of the sea, who is also the Virgin Mary. In Rio Vermelho and Itapoan, celebrants make offerings all along the shores, and boats are gaily decorated. Festa de Rio Vermelho, in honor of Saint Anne, is held two Sundays before Carnival. Carnival itself is celebrated as in Rio and all business stops for 4 days. Must be experienced to be believed.

May 10 has the procession of St. Francis Xavier, a feast day in honor of the city's patron saint, held ever since 1686.

In *June*, twelve days after the Holy Ghost, there is a Christian procession. At the same time candomblé worshippers hold services to Oxosse, the African God of the Hunt. Festa de Santo Antonio, a religious feast, takes place in June, while the 24th has the Festa de São João, a popular festival with local dances, entertainment and fireworks. On *June* 29 a twelve day and night voodoo celebration honors all the gods.

July 2 is devoted to the heroes of Brazil's fight for independence. Aside from parades, there are folklore dances and candomblé ceremonies.

The second Sunday in *September* has an impressive procession to the sea of Our Lady of Monte Serrat, while on the 27th the twin gods Cosme and Damião are honored with banquet tables loaded with rich regional cooking.

October, all month long, is devoted to the African gods Exú, Iabás, Ogum, Omulu and Oxum.

December 4 is the Festa de Santa Barbara. Three days of festivities at Saint Barbara's Market, Daiza dos Sepateiros. *December* 8 has the celebration of Conceição da Praia, held in front of Our Lady of Conceição Church and includes candomblé, capoeira and folksingers. *December* 13: Festa de Santa Lucia, in front of the Pilar church.

ARRIVING IN BAHIA. Salvador's *2 de Julho* airport was classified as one of Brazil's international fields in 1975 and anticipates increased international travel in the near future. But today, unless you come in on *Varig*'s weekly flight from Madrid, you'll probably be coming from Rio on one of several, daily 90-minute flights (round trip costs about $275). There are also frequent flights from Brasília and, of course, cities in the Northeast. Alternatives are driving or taking a 27-hour bus trip ($20 one way, or $30 on a "deluxe sleeper") up the new highway from Rio, or calling on one of the cruise or cargo ships that stops here.

WHAT TO SEE? Spread out over the length and breadth of this intriguing city are dozens of things that belong on your itinerary. The most important are: the Modelo and Agua de Meninos markets, steep streets of Pelourinho and Baixa dos Sapateiros, the Praça Terreiro de Jesus artisans market Sundays, the Lacerda elevator between the city's upper and lower levels, the harbor filled with multicolored sailed fishing boats, the lighthouses and the old forts, the churches with special emphasis on São Francisco and Bonfim, the museums of Modern Art and Sacred Art, the beaches with the fishermen and their nets, the lagoon of Abaeté, the artists at work, a capoeira fight and most definitely a candomblé ceremony.

HOW TO GET ABOUT. Buses are overcrowded, dirty and never on schedule. Taxis are plentiful and cheap but bargain first if you're going to use one by the day. There are tourist agencies with cars for hire, and your hotel can usually supply you with a limousine and an English-speaking driver. But the best way to see most of the city is just to get out and walk around the old streets. Nothing will happen to you. You're a lot safer in the back streets of Brazil than you are in New York or London. You can hire an air-taxi from Milton Pinto (Rua Belgica 1. tel. 2-2600) and get a spectacular view of the city. Rates are by the hour, reasonable and the Cessna 170 holds three passengers. You can charter a native schooner for a day's cruise of the bay for $200 to $300, from either *L.R. Turismo* at Av. Sete de Setembro 540 or *Panorama Turismo*, Rua Marquês de Caravelas 110.

HOTELS. Outside Rio, Brazil's biggest spurt in construction of tourist-type hotels has taken place in Bahia. Big *Hilton* and *Quatro Rodas* hotels are under construction, but the pace has slowed because, except for peak season (Carnival) the city is overbuilt. Biggest and best for visitors today are the luxurious *Meridien* and *Bahia Othon Palace*, which opened in 1976 and 1975. Alternate choices are the charming little (70 rooms) *Pousada do Convento do Carmo* downtown or the 164-room beach-front *Salvador Praia*, both opened also in 1975.

BAHIA OTHON PALACE, Av. Presidente Vargas 2456 on Ondina Beach. Built in a "Y" shape, with all 301 rooms facing the ocean. Swimming pool, nightclub, convention hall, sauna, and everything you'd expect in a modern new hotel. Pride of the Othon chain and one of Brazil's best.

MERIDIEN BAHIA, Rua Fonte do Boi 216. Overlooking the ocean, 30 minutes from the airport, 15 minutes from downtown Salvador, deluxe class, 502 rooms including 2 deluxe suites, 77 suites and 27 cabanas. Conference and banquet facilities. Congress hall equipped with audio-visual aids and for simultaneous translation; 5 meeting rooms. Panoramic restaurants and bars at the top. Discothèque, beauty parlor, sauna, solarium, sea- and fresh-water swimming pools, tennis, marina, boutiques.
POUSADA DO CONVENTO DO CARMO, Largo do Carmo, in the heart of the old section of Salvador. A restored former convent whose cells have been made into hotel rooms with wooden floors and ceilings lighted by rustic lanterns. Small swimming pool in inner courtyard. Chapel and art gallery in same building. Lots of atmosphere.

SALVADOR PRAIA, Av. Presidente Vargas 2032 (Ondina Beach). Pool, bar, restaurant, convention rooms. Mural by famous Brazilian painter Caribé and sculpture by Mario Cravo dominate the lobby.

PELOURINHO, Rua Alfredo de Brito 20, in the old quarter of the same name. 40 rooms in restored colonial mansion with magnificent view of the city and the bay. Reasonable rates. Bahian cooking.

Older hotels, also recommended:

Hotel da Bahia, Av. 7 de Setembro at Praça 2 de Julho. Formerly Salvador's biggest (180 rooms), and focal point of social life. Pool, bar, restaurant and good service.

Grande Hotel da Barra, Av. 7 de Setembro 491. Beachfront at harbor entrance. Calm waters for swimming. Air conditioned.

Ondina Praia, Av. Presidente Vargas across from Ondina Beach. Modern, with pool, bar and restaurant.

Plaza, Av. 7 de Setembro 210, near Hotel da Bahia. Well run, preferred by some executives when visiting branches of their industries.

Vela Branca, Av. Antonio Carlos Magalhães on Pituba Beach. Modern, motel-type accommodations with bar, restaurant, pool.

Others: *Baía do Sol,* Av. 7 de Setembro 238; *Armação,* Av. Otavio Mangabeira, Piatã Beach; *Costa Azul,* Av. Otavio Mangabeira, Pituba Beach; *Acacia,* Rua Carlos Gomes 21; *Hotel Casa Grande,* Av. Sete de Setembro 357; *Hotel Oxumare,* Av. Sete de Setembro 22/4; *Solar da Vitoria,* Largo da Vitorio 7; *Villa Romana Hotel,* Rua Lemos Brito 14, Barra; *Themis Hotel,* Praça da Se 9.

Pensions: *Pensão Anglo-Americana,* Av. Sete de Setembro 329; *Hotel Caramuru,* Av. Sete de Setembro 258.

 RESTAURANTS. If you want to sample local dishes ask for: *Acaraje, abara, vatapa, caruru, ximxim de galinha, muqueca de peixe, camaroes a bahiana frigideira de camarão, efo, sarapatel, cocada, quindins de vaya,* and the leading alcoholic drink, called "a batida."

Salvador has a wide variety of restaurants. The following seem to appeal most to American tourists:

For regional food, *Maria de São Pedro* and *Camafeu de Oxossi,* share the 2nd floor of the Mercado Modelo and are good. *Coco e*

Dende, on corner Av. Princesa Isabel and Almeida Antunes, in Barra Avenida, has more elegant but less picturesque setting.

SENAC, the national commercial training school on the Ladeira do Pelourinho, offers one of the best bargains in the city; self-service restaurant with over 40 typical dishes, folkloric shows in open-air bar-arena, air-conditioned theater featuring plays by Bahian playwrights, museums, exhibits and an artisan shop.

Don't fail to try a *muqueca mixta* (mixed seafood dish) at the *Lampião* at the Bahia Othon Palace, or almost any dish at the *Forno e Fogão* at the Pousada do Carmo. *Solar do Unhão*, on the shoreline off Av. do Contorno and expensive, was originally a slaves' quarters in the 18th century, and is worth a visit.

Others: *Chez da Gamboa*, Gamboa de Cima 51, is excellent. Dinner only. *Chez Bernard*, Rua Newton Prado 11. One of the oldest and best. French cuisine; dinner only. Also *Chez Suzanne*, Forte de São Diagol in the Barra. *A Moenda*, on the shore road beyond Pituba, in Armacão. Rustic atmosphere, samba show. Lunch, dinner: *Casa da Culinaria*, Av. Princesa Leopoldina 54, Barra Avenida; *Dona Flor*, at Travessa Corneta Lopes 4, also serves fondue; *La Gondola*, Rua Orlando Moscoso 25; *Porão Italia*, Av. Presidente Vargas 15; *Taverna Romana*, Rua Lemos de Brito 14, for Italian dishes.

Churrascaria Alex, at the Boco do Rio, for outdoor barbecue specialties. *Perez*, in the "Passeo publico," behind the Governor's residential palace. Also: *Casa da Praia*, Av. Otavio, Mangabeira 66; *Riviera*, Pça. Da Amarelina 4.

 MUSEUMS. *Museu de Arte da Bahia.* Located in a restored mansion at Avenida Joana Angelica 198, Nazare. Ceramics, chinaware, ornamental tiles, antique furniture. *Museu de Arte Sacra.* Rua do Sodre. An outstanding collection of figures of saints and other religious art. *Museu Carlos Costa Pinto*, Av. Sete de Setembro 389. Antique furniture, Baccarat crystal, jewelry, china, silverware and paintings. Also collection of "balangandes" (silver charms). *Museu de Arte Moderna*, at the Solar Unhao. Expositions of paintings only when announced—no permanent collection. *Museu do Carmo.* Located in the Convento do Carmo. Vestments and other religious art objects. *Museu do Reconcavo Wanderley Pinto.* About an hour's drive from the city, not far from the port of the Industrial Center of Aracatu. Engravings, old maps, historical notes. *Musea da Cidade,* Pelourinho 3, has an interesting collection of figures of Orixás or deities venerated in the *Candomblé* rites with their costumes and weapons; also the world's largest collection of ceremonial women's headgear of African origin.

 OTHER ATTRACTIONS. *Candomblé* is the term adopted in Bahia for the religious ceremonies of African origin, which in Rio de Janeiro are called "Macumba," and "Xango" in Recife. In Salvador these cults have been preserved in almost original form and are a vital part of the culture. Ceremonies honoring the various divinities, called "orixas," are held in temples called "terreiros." These consist of a large room for public ceremonies, with various smaller rooms or huts for other ceremonial purposes. Visitors may attend the public ceremonies, which are usually held on Sun. nights around 8:30 p.m. Some of the most important "candomblé" terreiros are: *Engenho Velho, Voo Afonja, Menininha do Gantois, Olga do Alekato.*

Folklore shows are very worth while for the visitor because they include examples of several dances typical of Bahia, such as "samba-in-a-circle," the "maculele" (rhythmic jousting with sticks and knives), which originated in the interior of Bahia, the "dance of the fishermen" pulling in the net, "capoeira" and scenes or dances from the "candomblé" ceremonies. These shows are presented daily at 9 p.m. at the *Centro Folklorico da Bahia* at the Praça Castro Alves. During the tourist season (June, July, Jan., Feb.) additional shows are given at the *Teatro Castro Alves.*

SHOPPING. The most typical souvenirs of Bahia are the "balangadas," similar to a giant charm bracelet of silver, in tin and silver alloy, or in a silver-dipped metal base. Also typical are the many items carved from "jacaranda," the Brazilian rosewood. For these try: *Mercado Modelo* at Praça Cairu in the lower city. *Gerson Artesanato de Prata Ltda.*, ground floor of the Convento do Carmo. *Penitenciaria do Estado*, Lemos Britto (State Prison), located in Mata Escura do Retiro, accessible by car or taxi only. All prices are clearly labeled at the *Instituto Maua*, Av. Sete de Setembro 261, while bargaining is widely practised at other places. For antiques, wooden figures of saints, furniture, etc., walk along Rua Ruy Barbosa off Avenida Sete de Setembro, near the Cinema Guarani and the "A Tarde" building. Especially reliable are: *Casa Moreira*, Rua Visconde do Rio Branco 1, behind the City Hall, *Jose Pedreira*, Alameda Antunes 7, Barra Avenida, or any number of shops along Rua Ruy Barbosa, roughly between numbers 30 and 65.

USEFUL ADDRESSES. U.S. Consulate, Edificio Fundação Politecnica 4th floor of Bloco A at Av. Sete de Setembro 73/79 in the upper city. In addition to the consulate there is a U.S. Information Service Office in the Edificio Casa Blanca, Av. Sete de Setembro 333. The American Society of Bahia, tel: 8-0073. Police; Radio Patrol: Dial 190. Medical facilities: Pronto Socorr, tel: 5-0000.

Bahiatursa (Bahia State Tourist Board) has several information booths and its main offices are at Rua Mariscal Floriano 1, Canela. Telephone 5-4002 or 5-4594 (Salvador).

ART AND ARTISTS. *Atelier Renot*, Av. Sete de Setembro 437, Barra. Tapestries. *Galeria Canizares*, Av. Araujo Pinho 15, Canela. Works by students and other artists. *Kennedy Galeria de Arte*, Av. Sete de Setembro 283. Tapestries by the Chilean-born Patrick Kennedy and paintings by other artists. *Sue Galeria de Arte*, Av. Sete de Setembro 30. Works of touristic subjects.

Many artists in Bahia maintain exhibits at their studios. Before visiting these artists, please phone for an appointment. A number of them speak English. *Betty King Almeida*, 2nd Travessa da Rua Visconde de Itaborai 52. An American, who works with metal and plastic to produce murals, doors, panels, jewelry. *Carybe*, Rua Medeiros Neto 9, Brotas. Drawings and paintings. *Emanuel Araujo*, Ladeira do Desterro 19. Engravings. *Fernando Coelho*, Parque Florestal, Brotas, Rua Waldemar Falcao. Paintings. *Floriano Teixeira*, Rua Ilheus 33,

Rio Vermelho. Paintings. *Hansen-Bahia*, Jardim Jaguaripe, Piata. Woodcut engravings. *Jenner Augusto*, Rua Bartolomeu de Gusmao 7, Rio Vermelho. Paintings. *Mario Cravo Jr.*, Rua Caetano Moura 39, Federacao. Sculptures in metal and plastic. *Mirabeau Sampaio*, Rua Ary Barroso 12. Sculptures and drawings. *Walter Sa Nenezes*, Av. Tiradentes, Roma. Paintings.

SPORTS. Salvador has miles of beautiful beaches. The cleanest and most attractive tend also to be the most distant, located beyond the district of Pituba. Because it is ideal for children, "Pla-K-For" is a favorite of Americans. This beach, like others, is reachable by bus. With luck you many see fishermen pulling in their big nets at beaches named "Praia Chega Nego," across the Aero Clube, "Piata" and "Itapoa.'

Capoeira, originally an African way of fighting with the feet, was developed in the days when slaves were forbidden to use their fists or to carry weapons. Now it is preserved in a very acrobatic form of dance, accompanied by the typical instrument known as the "berimbau," tamborines, drums and other percussion instruments. Shows are given by the following "schools" under the direction of the Master, whose name the school bears: *Mestre Bimba* (located in the Nordeste de Amarlina) on Tues., Thurs. and Sat. at 8 p.m. *Mestre Gatto* (located at "Bogun," Rua Apolinario Santana 154) on Mon., Wed. and Fri. at 9 p.m. and Sun. at 3 and 5 p.m.

PRACTICAL INFORMATION FOR THE NORTHEAST

HOW TO COME? By plane from almost any city in the country. Each capital has its own airport, and most of them are equipped for jet traffic now. *British Caledonian* has two flights weekly that stop here on their way from London to Rio, São Paulo, Buenos Aires or Santiago. There are buses that run from state to state in the northeast, some of them comfortable. *Lloyd Brasileiro* runs periodically a first class steamship between Rio de Janeiro, Salvador, Recife, Fortaleza and Belém. Food and service are good.

HOTELS

RECIFE. If you are mainly interested in the delightful beaches, where the reefs form warm pools of still water at low tide, then you'll want to stop at one of the hotels on Boa Viagem Beach. They are about a half-hour from the downtown area, but the cool breeze and pleasant atmosphere make it well worth the ride. Hotels in Boa Viagem, on or near the beach:

Miramar, Rua dos Navegantes 363, newest and most modern, has 120 air-conditioned rooms, swimming pool, bar, restaurant, nightclub; *Mar*, Rua Barão de Sousa Leão 451, also has its own pool; *Boa Viagem*, Av. Boa Viagem 5000, oldest hotel on the beach (ask for a front room with balcony); *Côte d'Azur*, Av. Boa Viagem 3402; *Casa Grande e Senzala*, Av. Conselheiro Aguiar

5000; *Colonial*, Av. Boa Viagem 4020; and *200 Milhas*, Av. Boa Viagem 864.

If in Recife on business and you want to stay in the heart of town, your best bets are:

Grande, Av. Martins de Barros 593, comfortable, old-world charm with good restaurant and air conditioning; *São Domingos*, Praça Maciel Pinheiro 66; *Guararapes*, Rua da Palma 57; *Quatro de Outubro*, Rua Floriano Peixoto 141; or *Central*, Av. Manoel Borba 209.

FORTALEZA. Most comfortable for the tourist is the *Beira-Mar*, Av. Presidente Kennedy 3130 on the beach, or the smaller *Iracema Plaza*, at 746 on the same street. Downtown the best is the 12-story *Savanah*, Rua Major Facundo 411 at Praça do Ferreira. Others nearby are the *San Pedro*, Rua Castro e Silva 81; *Premier*, Rua Barão do Rio Branco 829; *Excelsior*, Rua Guilherme Rocha 172; and *Lord*, Rua 24 de Maio 642.

MACEIO, Alagoas. Only hotel with international standards is the *Luxor*, opened in 1975. It has 112 rooms, all facing the front; pool, bars and restaurant. Acceptable older hotels in the city are the *California*, Rua Barão de Penedo 33, and *Beiriz*, Rua João Pessoa 290.

JOÃO PESSOA, Paraiba. Best here is the *Tambaú*, 110-room circular hotel built into the sea at Av. Almirante Tamandaré 229. More modest are the *Aurora*, Praça João Pessoa 51, and the *Paraíba Palace*, Praça Vidal de Negreiros, downtown.

NATAL. Here you'll want to stop at the *Reis Magos*, half a mile from downtown on Av. Café Filho, on Praia (beach) do Meio. Pool, nightclub, good restaurant. Acceptable downtown hotels are

the *Samburá*, Rua Professor Zuza 263, and the *Tirol*, Av. Alexandrino de Alencar 1330. There is a 16-room *guest house* on Ponta Negra beach, nine miles from town.

TERESINA, Piauí. In 1975 the old *Hotel do Piauí* was completely remodeled and reopened as the *Luxor Hotel do Piauí*, Praça Marechal Deodoro 310. It now has swimming pool, bar, restaurant, full air conditioning. Other downtown hotels include *Teresina Palace*, Rua Paiçandu 1219; *Lord*, Rua Alvaro Mendes 1223; and *Royal Palace*, Rua 13 de Maio 233.

SÃO LUIS, Maranhão. The newest (1976) and probably best hotel for the tourist is the *Quatro Rodas* on Calhau beach, with 112 air-conditioned rooms, pool, tennis courts, bars and restaurants. Best downtown hotel is the *Selton*. The traditional downtown hotel is the *Central*, Av. Dom Pedro II 258. For more economy, *Lord*, Rua Joaquim Távora 258.

VITORIA, Espírito Santo. Beach hotel in this port city is the 45-room *Camburi Praia*, Av. Dante Micheline 1007. Recommended downtown are the *Cannes Palace*, Av. Jerônimo Monteiro 111; *São José*, Av. Princesa Isabel 300; *Helal*, Av. Jerônimo Monteiro 935; and *Estoril*, Praça Presidente Roosevelt.

GUARAPARI, Espírito Santo. In this city famous for its magnificent beaches of monazitic sand, best hotels are *Beira-Mar*, Rua Joaquim da Silva e Lima 96; *Coronado*, Av. Desembargador Lourival de Almeida 312; *Thorium*, Praça Floriano Piexoto downtown; *Novo Hotel Vieira*, Rua Joaquim Silva Lima 310; *Miramar*, Ladeira São Luís; *Radium*, Rua Ciríaco Ramalhete 52; and *Atlântica*, Av. Edésio Cirne 332.

RESTAURANTS. There is a lack of good restaurants all through the northeast. Most recommended hotels have average restaurants. Try the lobsters and shrimp, filet of white fish and fresh coconuts.

RECIFE. Most interesting from the local color point of view is the *Buraco de Otilia* on Rua Aurora 1231. Run by a fat mulatto woman named Otilia, she has moved from her shanty where her cooking made her famous and taken up residence in an old house in the center of the town. While you sample her lobster in coconut milk or her chicken in blood sauce, she will be staring either at you or the blaring T.V. set. Prices are reasonable and the food is very good.

Adega da Mouraria, Rua Ulhoa Cintra 40; *Cote d'Azur*, Av. Boa Viagem 3402; *Leite*, Praça Joaquim Nabuco 147 on the river; *Costa Brava*, Rua Barão de Sousa Leão 698; all have good international food. *Barril*, Av. Boa Viagem 4712, and *200 Milhas*, Rua dos Navegantes 64, for sea food. Brazilian specialties at *Senzala*, Av. Conselheiro Aguiar 5000, and *Le Mazot*, Av. Boa Viagem 618.

FORTALEZA. One of the best restaurants in town is at the *Ideal Club* on the beach. Its old-world charm, with white columns and dark carved wooden balcony overlooking a grove of palm trees is excellent eye appeal to go with the excellent food appeal. The restaurant is part of the ultra chic Ideal Country Club. Another private club worth seeing which has a good restaurant is the marble *Nautico Beach Club*, Av. Abolição 2727.

The *Lido Restaurant*, on the beach and across the street from the Iracema Hotel. Rain comes in through the roof and strolling vendors sell everything from hammocks to ship models, but the food is quite good. Lobster here is a specialty as is their fried chicken.

Other good restaurants: *Panela*, Av. Pres. Kennedy 746. *Sandra's*, Av. Pres. Kennedy 3520. *Cacarola*, Av. Bezerra de Meneses 811. *Bem*, Av. Pres. Kennedy 4492; *Ideal*, Av. Mons. Tabosa 1381. *Rincão Gaucho*, Av. Pres. Kennedy 3996. *Rincão das Pampas*, Av. Pres. Kennedy 4012. *Alfredo* (seafood), Av. Pres. Kennedy 4606. *Expedito* (seafood), Av. Pres. Kennedy 4320. *Trastevere*, Av. Pres. Kennedy 2666.

SHOPPING. In Fortaleza be sure and buy some of the intricate lace work made by women in the interior of the state. Best place to shop first is the public market near the Praça de Sá. There you have a complete collection of hammocks, lace blouses, tablecloths, embroidered skirts and other items at such unbelievably low prices that you'll end up by buying articles for every person on your list. There is also a shop for regional articles owned by *Joe Ney*, at 376 Rua 24 de Maio. Also see what *Casa Humberto* on Rua Liberato Barroso 222 has to offer in the line of off-beat souvenirs. In Recife, don't miss the Artene store run by the government. You will be surprised by both the high quality and the low prices of the regional goods sold there. Good native handicraft in ceramics and leather can be found around the Patio de São Pedro and also Boa Viagem beach.

THE AMAZON

Most Romantic of Destinations

(*Up-to-date* Practical Information *and much of the background text were provided by Richard Brill, our Editor for the Amazon Region, who has led travelers into the area for the past 25 years.*)

The Amazon region has figured so frequently in novels and films that few come to see it without some preconceived notion of what they will find. Most often they expect a kind of primeval forest, a sinister jungle where Nature at her most primitive reigns supreme, where the waters are infested with piranha and alligators and the land with wild beasts and uncivilized Indians.

The first Europeans to explore this country made their own contribution to this impression. When Francisco de Orellana, a Spanish Conquistador, sighted the river in 1592, so taken was he by its vastness that he called it Río Mar, the River Sea.

To descend this river from Peru to the Atlantic, a distance of 3,000 miles, was an unbelievable task. These early Spaniards, traveling by canoe, wore suits of armor and had to endure in this inappropriate dress the additional hardship of oppressive heat and humidity. As they forged their way through unknown territory, they encountered and fought what they thought was a race of women warriors whom they called Amazons. Whether they actually believed they were face to face with something out of pagan mythology is not known; but it is easy to imagine that they felt the name and its implications were pointedly appropriate to this hostile land, and this name came to refer to the entire region: Amazon.

The Amazon River system, though parts of it remain uncharted and some tributaries probably still remain to be discovered, has been extensively surveyed. Crossing from the Pacific to the Atlantic, the river itself is approximately 3,900 miles long and, if its 10,000 tributaries are included, covers an area of 3 million square miles. Among its tributaries are many which exceed 1,000 miles in length, including the Purus (2,190 miles), the Negro (1,500 miles), the Tapajos (1,300 miles) and the Madeira (2,000 miles). Its width varies from a meager one inch at the source to over 200 miles at its mouth at Belem. Ocean-going vessels find navigable waters all the way to Iquitos, 2,700 miles up the river.

Although most of the Amazon region remains unexplored, it provides the world with 40 percent of its oxygen and with 25 percent of all the fresh water. It may prove to be the breadbasket of the world, for of the 22,000 known species of plants, over 18,000 are found in the Amazon Basin; of 2,000 species of fish, 1,600 are found here. The region is rich in gold, diamonds, lumber, rubber, oil and jute, among other products. And for all its wealth, it has a population of fewer than two million people, although it is the size of the continental United States.

The region is becoming increasingly open to tourism. Amazon Explorers, Inc., an American travel firm, began to make it more accessible in 1956. Now such cities as Belem, Manaus, Santarem, Porto Velho, Leticia and Iquitos are easily reached by air and offer fine hotels, good food, excellent services and fascinating sightseeing. The sights which so impressed Francisco de Orellana in 1592 are still to be found; only now it is possible to see them in modern comfort.

EXPLORING THE AMAZON

The main attraction in the Amazon is the jungle. You can fly over it for hours and not see anything but a carpet of green trees so closely knit that the ground never gets a chance to see the sunlight. Rivers and streams bisect the forests, and every now and again a lone fisherman's or rubber tapper's palm shack will appear in a clearing on a river bank. One word of warning, do not try to go into the Amazon alone. It is one thing to be able to get around your local woods or country club golf course without assistance, but the Amazon is deceiving. Only venture in with an experienced guide and be sure to mark your way carefully. Not even the best maps of the area are always accurate.

The city of Belem is the gateway to the great Amazon River. Some 90 miles from the open sea, this handsome city of white buildings with red tile roofs and broad avenues is set in the midst of tropical foliage

A tour would include the Praça da Republica, which contains the municipal theater, some Victorian marble statues and a children's playground. You are also liable to find sellers of such contraband items as whisky, French perfume and transistor radios.

The Goeldi Museum is almost better than exploring the Amazon itself, for in addition to an extensive collection of Indian artifacts, stones and excellent photographs, there is a zoo with many local animals in their natural surroundings.

The Jungle Park is a public garden where a large area of virgin jungle has been preserved. Trails cut into the dense foliage lead to unexpected reflection pools with huge water lilies.

An old rubber plantation in the vicinity makes an interesting visit, and at the Agricultural Institute rubber and Brazil Nut trees are cultivated.

The port of Belem can be toured by motorboat. The docks at Ver o Peso Market are worth seeing and photographing, if only for the multicolored sails on the fishing boats. The best time is 5–10 a.m.

Jaguar Island, accessible by boat across the Para River, is one of the most primitive islands on the upper Delta. Luxuriant vegetation and an array of birds are seen along the only river cutting through this island, and native huts and fishermen's canoes are passed along the tributaries. It is also possible to visit a local school in a native village.

The Island of Marajó can be reached by air from Belem. One of a great number of islands which make up the estuary of the Amazon, it is bigger than Denmark. Its two, almost distinct, zones of vegetation, forest and grassy plains, account for the principal industries of cattle raising and lumber.

The cattle are a special breed, born of a cross between those originally brought by the Portuguese settlers and the buffalo and brahma later brought from India. Some of the cowboys in this area use saddle oxen instead of horses.

Practically all transportation on the island is by water through the numerous lakes, rivers and tidal creeks. These waters are alive with the dreaded piranha, those aggressive and voracious fish, schools of which can devour even large animals in little time. There are also alligators and water birds and in the forests, jaguars, parrots and macaws.

Beyond Marajó is Macapá, a neat little town of 33,000. Here there are huge herds of water buffalo, some of which are wild. Hunting is good, and local transportation is by horse or even tame water buffalo. The city lies exactly on the Equator, and so you can stand simultaneously in the Northern and Southern hemispheres.

Among the worthwhile places on the Para sides of the highway are: Paragominas, with its modern motel, and Imperatriz, a town which grew from 80 to 64,000 inhabitants since the highway started in 1969. Porto Franco and President Kennedy villages—(among many others)—provide good, clean accommodations.

Halfway between Belem and Manaus lies the city of Santarem, now enjoying an unprecedented boom due to the discovery of gold. Originally settled by American Civil War Confederate soldiers, the town boasts names like Higgins, O'Malley and McDonald, common among the Indians even today. The Confederate flag is widely used.

Manaus

Manaus is a magnificent city built in the midst of the dense jungle 1,000 miles up river. You will find such vestiges of a prestigious past as the famous Opera House, completed in 1910 just after the collapse of the rubber boom. Here Jenny Lind once sang and the Ballet Russe once danced for wealthy rubber barons, but it has never been used for grand opera; still, this opulent blue building containing works of art, chandeliers, French ironwork and Chinawear is a startling sight in the middle of the jungle.

The Custom House and Lighthouse originally stood in England until they were dismantled to be reassembled in Manaus. They rise now beside the floating docks, built especially to accommodate the annual 40-foot rise and fall of the river.

No tour of the city would be complete without a visit to the bustling City Market Building, where merchants sell caged animals and parrots alongside fruits and vegetables.

Manaus was the first city in South America to have streetcars and the people were so advanced that they sent their laundry to London to be washed rather than do it themselves. Now a modern, cosmopolitan city, it has 11 skyscrapers and four TV stations, numerous hotels and excellent restaurants, and a brand-new airport, about 45 minutes from the city and about 10 minutes from the Hotel Tropical. Of interest are: the Credilar Teatro, an imposing retail store built of native redstone and glass and—for contrast—the little Church of the Poor Devil (Pobre Diablo) in the suburb of Cachoeirinha. Built by one poor worker, it is only 12 feet wide and 15 feet long. Visits can be arranged to a rubber- or nut-processing plant.

On the outskirts of the city visit the Salesian Mission Museum, where you can see a complete documentary of the now vanished "Floating City," once part of the itinerary, and the Indian Museum of Arts, operated by the same order. Beautiful Taruma Falls may be reached by a new highway being built into the jungle

One highlight of any jungle trip is a boat cruise on the Rio Negro. Descending the river by motor launch, you will enter the dense jungle via a small tributary completely covered over by a green umbrella of giant trees and vines. Colorful tropical birds are everywhere, and wild monkeys can be seen in the trees. With the aid of an Indian guide, you can venture more deeply into the jungle in canoes. Collectors of tropical fish will be amazed to see rare specimens swimming around their canoes. Natives supplement their incomes by catching snakes, crocodiles or these rare fish. A dramatic end to this cruise is a visit to the Wedding of the Waters, where the coffee-brown Amazon River meets the inky-black Rio Negro. Their waters do not mingle, and the line between them can be seen for miles.

Among other places worth a visit along the Amazon in Brazil are:

Tefe, the center of the Brazil Nut industry, is surrounded by large plantations. This is also the hub of the region's fishing industry. Flower enthusiasts will delight in the unusual species of orchid which grows around the city.

Carauari, a small settlement run by Dutch missionaries among wild Indian tribes, is accessible once a week by Cruzeiro DC-3. *Pension Cruzeiro do Sul* is delightful. No private facilities, but this is the heart of the jungle on Rio Jura. A day with three meals costs about $10—and for prices like that, you must be in the jungle. Reservations can be made through *Amazon Explorers*, who also arrange visits to Monkey Island, the natural habitat of over 20,000 squirrel monkeys, center of a good fishing area and base for visits to nearby Indian villages.

Porto Velho, capital of the State of Rondonia, lies deep in the jungle. It is famous for the Jungle Railroad, built in 1905 at a cost of 10,000 lives, which was never used.

The Ticuna Indian village and Yaguas may be reached by motorboat from Leticia.

Sightseeing in the fascinating city of Leticia, deep in the heart of the Amazon jungle, on the Colombian side of the river, is a most unusual experience. The flora and fauna are incredibly rich and offer a veritable paradise for the botanist and the wild game hunter or fisherman. A kind of catfish called bagres reaches 300–400 pounds in this region. And outside Leticia is the Ticuna Indian village. Tabatinga, Brazil, across the border from Leticia, can be reached by a 10-minute taxi ride. Tabatinga is the headquarters of the Brasilian Army of the Solimones; it is a thriving community with complete Zoological gardens containing the flora and fauna of the region, all under the auspices of the Army.

Across the river from Leticia, a two-hour trip, is Benjamin Constant, an outpost practically on the border of Peru, Colombia and Brazil. Noted for its local pottery, the city is reached by local Amazon River ferries from Leticia/Tabatinga.

On the edge of the jungle lies the Amazon River port, Iquitos, in Peru. Here you can visit the floating town of Belem, wild animal markets, the aquarium, and the native section, or take a full-day's motorboat excursion to the Yagua Indian village. (See also Peru chapter.)

PRACTICAL INFORMATION FOR THE AMAZON

 HOW TO GET THERE. International flights to Manaus and Belem now come from Miami, Mexico City and Bogotá by *Varig*; *Avianca* from Bogotá to Leticia and Iquitos; *Cruzeiro* from Bogotá and Iquitos to Leticia and Manaus; *Faucett* from Lima to Iquitos.

 WHEN TO COME. Since the Amazon Valley lies close to the Equator, winter and summer in the usual sense DO NOT OCCUR. High humidity is common only in the deep jungle, not in the cities or on the river. Average temperature is 80°. Nights are always cool. Rainy Season—April to November (High Waters). Dry Season—November to April (Low Waters). Travel in both seasons is good—in rainy season the water is high. (And the jungle is in full bloom).

 WHAT TO TAKE. Light summer clothing. Drip dry shirts and khaki slacks for the men. Cotton dresses for the ladies or skirts and blouses. Pants and pant-suits for women are also acceptable. All shirts and blouses should be long-sleeved. All colors may be worn with the exception of green. Very comfortable shoes are a must, and sneakers or tennis shoes will come in handy. In addition, for its jungle tours, *Amazon Explorers* (see below under Useful Addresses) has the following suggestions and comments: (1) Rubber boots (high) for walk through the jungles. A must. (2) Hat or head cover. *FLASHLIGHT*—Since electricity is limited. (3) Insect repellent (for overnight trips a mosquito net will be supplied). (4) Knife, scissors, first aid kit, toilet paper, sewing kit, sunglasses. (5) Camera and *plenty* of film. Plastic bags to store exposed film. (6) All medications as needed. (7) Walking stick if needed will be supplied. (8) For fishermen: please bring variety of hooks and line. Poles are not required. (9) Binoculars—good quality binoculars for bird and animal watching—500 varieties of tropical Amazon birds are constantly around you. (10) As the life on the Amazon is much more relaxed and primitive than anywhere else in the world, you must be prepared for constant changes, delays, or cancellations of flights or steamers according to the moods of the river. Should such changes occur while traveling, your guide will notify you immediately and make new arrangements accordingly.

 HOW TO GET ABOUT. There are regular plane services that take you into Belem, the capital of the State of Pará on the mouth of the Amazon River. To get to Manaus, the capital of the state of Amazonas, you must go by plane. It is the only capital city in the world that is not accessible by highway. *Cruzeiro* flies from Iquitos to Tabatinga, Brazil, which is reached by car from Leticia; also to Manaus from Tabatinga, with flights in both directions. *Varig* and *VASP* fly from Rio and Brasilia to Manaus.

The best way to travel on the Amazon itself is to take one of the E.N.A.S.A. line diesel boats, which sail from Belem to Manaus and return, but on such an irregular schedule that dates and times are obtainable only in Belem or Manaus. Rate: $120, with meals included, first class; $80, second class; $30, third, with hammocks for sleeping.

One of the most exciting trips on the Amazon is an over-night excursion by motorboat to Monkey Island, where the traveler stays in a rustic jungle lodge. Monkey Island is the natural habitat of over 20,000 squirrel monkeys. It offers unlimited fishing and visits to nearby Indian Villages. The total trip including all meals, motorboat transportation, overnight accommodations, and all side excursions, is $65.00 per person. Reservations are made in the United States through Amazon Explorers, Inc., Professional Building, Rt. 9, Parlin, N. J., 08859.

SPORTS. Most popular sports in this area are *hunting* and *fishing*. The American firm, *Amazon Explorers*, has an office at Avda. Presidente Vargas, Belem, P.O. Box 1159 and *Amazon Explorers* and *Selvatour* provide all services in Manaus. They are experts at arranging jungle expeditions.

SHOPPING. The streets of Belem have a number of shops that sell jungle items; but remember that live animals or birds may not be imported into the U.S. Skins of protected animals such as alligators or crocodiles, or shoes/handbags or other articles made of these skins, are also not allowed into the U.S. and will be confiscated by the U.S. Customs.

Manaus, a free port, has hundreds of shops, stocked with goods from all over the world. *House of the Hummingbird*, which is owned and operated by Richard Melnyk, features rare and unusual artifacts handcrafted by Indians, Caboclos (half-breeds) and regional artisans. Will ship anywhere without service charge.

HOTELS. Once a wilderness area as far as hotel accommodations were concerned, the Amazon has now thoroughly acceptable, even luxurious, lodging. Our price categories for this region are as follows: *Deluxe* is $40 and up for single, $50 up double; *First Class*, $30 up single, $40 up double; *Moderate*, $20 up single, $25 up double; and *Inexpensive* is less than above. These rates are based on hotels in Manaus; other hotels along the Amazon are somewhat less expensive.

BELEM

First Class

EQUATORIAL PALACE. Av. Bras Aguiar 612. This is the best in the city, with a bar, pool, and restaurant; the rooms have bath, air conditioning, telephone, TV and refrigerator.

EXCELSIOR GRAO PARA. Av. Presidente Vargas. Rooms have bath, air conditioning and telephone; bar and restaurant.

REGENTE. Av. Governador Jose Malcher 485. Rooms with private bath, air conditioning and TV.

SELTON BELEM. Av. Julio Cesar (airport). Rooms have private bath, air conditioning, telephones and TV; bar, restaurant and pool.

Moderate

CENTRAL. Av. Presidente Vargas 290.

VANJA. Rua Benjamin Constant 1164. Rooms with private bath, air conditioning and telephone.

BENJAMIN CONSTANT. *Pension Fernando Braga.* Rua Getulio Vargas. 7 very primitive rooms with no private bath. Moderate.

LETICIA
(Colombia's Amazon Port)
First Class

ANACONDA. This new hotel overlooking the river offers 56 deluxe, air-conditioned rooms; swimming pool and cabanas; dining room, night club.

PARADOR TICUNA. 13 cottages, some with air conditioning. A delightful pool and good restaurant in typical Amazon surroundings.

TICUNA ANNEX. The newest, most modern hotel in Leticia. Same management as the Parador Ticuna. 20 air-conditioned rooms.

RESIDENCIAS ALEMENAS. Immaculately clean; best buy in Leticia. 12 rooms, 8 with private bath. Run by Germans.

LA MANIGUA RESIDENCIAS. Nice, clean, small hotel. 18 rooms with private bath.

Moderate

PENSION CANO. 11 rooms, some with private bath.

MANAUS
Deluxe

AMAZONAS. Praça Adalberto Valle. Located in the center of the city, this 10-story building has 214 air-conditioned apartments and 2 elevators. All rooms have private bath, hot and cold water and telephone. Permanent buffet service. Swimming pool.

TROPICAL. Built and operated by Tropical Hotels, a subsidiary of Varig, on good beach overlooking the Rio Negro. 341 air-conditioned rooms, swimming pool, excellent restaurant, night club. About an hour from the airport and 45 minutes from town.

First Class

CENTRAL. Rua Dr. Moreira. Centrally located, this 50-room, 3-story hotel has air conditioning, private baths and telephones.

FLAMBOYANT. Av. Eduardo Ribeiro. Mid-town, the 23 rooms all have private bath and telephone. Bar and swimming pool. Near the Opera House.

IPANEMA. Rua Jose Clemente 500. Downtown, this hotel has 42 rooms with private bath, telephone and air conditioning.

LORD. Rua Quintino, Bacaiuva 217. In the center of the city, this 6-story hotel has 53 apartments all with private bath, hot and cold water and telephone. Restaurant.

RIO SALOMAO. Rua Dr. Moreira 119. In the center of the city, these 28 apartments have air conditioning, private bath and telephone.

SAO FRANCISCO. Av. 7 de Setembro 1273. These 41 apartments all have air conditioning, telephone and private bath.

Moderate

LOBO D'ALMADA. Rua Lobo D'Alamada 181-A. Mid-town, with 26 rooms with air conditioning, telephone and private bath.

NATIONAL. Rua Dr. Moreira 59. Also downtown, this small hotel has 16 rooms with private bath.

In addition to the hotels listed, there are a number of small Pensions offering rooms for $15–$25 per day. However these are not recommended unless you are desperate.

SANTAREM. *Tropical.* Av. Mendonca Furtado 114. Offers 120 air-conditioned rooms with refrigerators. First class, one of finest hotels in the region. *Nova Olinda.* Av. Adriano Pimental 140. A small hotel with local flavor but no air conditioning. Moderate.

TEFE. *Grand.* 20 rooms without air conditioning. Moderate.

 RESTAURANTS. The favorite regional dish is *pato no tucupi*, which is duck in yellow soup with a herb that tingles all the way down the throat and long after it's in the stomach. Ladies on the street also sell *tacacá*, a hot nourishing soup, that is served in decorated gourds. An average lunch or dinner will cost $7.00 to $18.00 per person; there are however, numerous coffee shops and cafeterias where a meal may be had for as little as $3.00.

BELEM. For international food try *Tuna Luso Brasileiro,* Av. Almirante Barroso 4110, *Marisqueira do Luis,* Av. Senador Lemos 1063, *La em Casa,* Av. Governador Jose Malcher 982, *Tenis Clube do Para,* Rua dos Mundurubus 2300, and *Jockey Club,* Av. Governador Jose Malcher 352.

Maloca, Praça Kennedy, serves fine regional food.

For barbecue, *Garrafao,* Av. Serzedelo Correia 75, *Gaucha,* Av. Governador Jose Malcher 2731, and *Adegao,* Rua 28 de Setembro 284, can all be recommended.

Other specialties: Japanese food at *Miako,* Rua Caetano Rufino 82, and Portuguese food at *Santa Rita Casa Portuguesa,* Rua Manoel Barata 897.

LETICIA. It is best to eat at the hotels, but if you wish to experiment, many local restaurants serve meals from 20¢ up to $1.50.

MANAUS. For French cooking sample the menu at *De Paris,* Blvd. Amazonas 1538. *Chapéu de Palha,* Rua Fortaleza 619, and *Tucunaré,* Estrada de Flores 3000, serve fish, especially the rare, local fresh-water specialties, the *pirarucu* and *tucunaré.* Steaks and barbecues are available at *Acapulco,* Rua Recife 142. *Kavaco,* Av. Sete de Setembro 987, has pizza, and for Arabic food go to *Beirute,* Rua Joaquim Sarmento 26.

 NIGHTCLUBS. Though not abundantly, this region does have nightclubs, at least in the larger cities like Belem, where you'll find *Carimbo,* Rua Benjamin Constant 1164, *Caverna,* Av. Senador Lemos 574, *Papa Jimi,* Av. Presidente Vargas 648, *Portao,* Av. Presidente Vargas 762, and *Aquarius,* Av. Senador Lemos 1063.

USEFUL ADDRESSES. Travel agencies include: Amazon Explorers, George Pickerell, P.O. Box 1159, Belem; Selvatur, Av. Eduardo Ribeiro 355, Manaus; Amazon Explorers-Manaus Ltda., Edificio Hotel Lord, P.O. Box 474, Manaus, Amazonas, Brasil; and Amazon Explorers, c/o Mike Tsalickis, Hotel Parador Ticuna, Leticia, Amazonas, Colombia.

FRENCH GUIANA

Land of Wild and Primitive Beauty

Like so many of France's overseas possessions, French Guiana is a country whose tourism is on the agenda for future development. The forest, dense and mysterious, is watered by a fan of rivers spreading out from south to north: the Maroni, the Mana, the Sinnamary, Mahury, Approuague and Oyapock. A trip up any of these rivers by motorized dugout canoe is far from a luxury cruise, but it's a travel experience that's hard to beat for sheer exoticism.

Some of the greatest explorers of history reconnoitered along the Guiana coast. Columbus was here in 1498. So was Alphonse d'Ojeda, Jean de las Cosa, and that Italian navigator whose name came to stand for the whole New World: Amerigo Vespucci. Such soldiers of fortune as Sir Walter Raleigh and Laurence Keyms penetrated the steaming jungles of Guiana in search of a legendary El Dorado. In 1598, the latter found not gold—but the French, already ensconced and extracting dyes from the dark trees of the tropic forest.

In 1604 the French contingent was reinforced by de la Ravardière and a group of colonists. Several other French companies followed, leaving the province of Normandy for richer virgin territory between the Orinoco and the Amazon. There *was* gold in the soil of Guiana, though no golden city existed, and there was sugar, spice, bauxite and endless stretches of forest whose trees promised an inexhaustible supply of timber, oil of rosewood and other gums.

The rich land was coveted. The Dutch grabbed it from the French, but Admiral d'Estrées recaptured it for France in 1676. Although the French had to give up the rich prize between the Amazon and the Oyapock by the treaty of Utrecht in 1713, they held onto what is now French Guiana, the coastal arrondissement of Guyane, facing the Atlantic between 54 and 56 degrees longitude west, and the interior arrondissement of Inini, stretching south to within two degrees of the Equator.

The promise of French Guiana's joining the mainstream of international tourism may be more imminent than was believed possible a few years ago, when its image was equated with that of the Devil's Island prison complex.

The *department*—originally a colony—is the site of a two-phase development boom. It started in 1964, when France established headquarters of her space exploration program on the sandy coastland of Kourou, 26 miles northwest of Cayenne, the capital. An instant town was created here, with ultra-modern facilities. The site was ideal for rocketry because it is less than 5° north of the equator (as against Cape Canaveral's 28°) which means the rotating speed of the earth is much faster, so the same propulsion will lift 24% more hardware than in Florida. Visitors can arrange excursions to the space center; inquire at the Syndicat d'Initiative (address below) about this and about excursions to the Isles du Salut as well. In Kourou there is a good restaurant operated by A. Vande, an ex-convict and local character, worth a visit.

Then during the last three years the French government has launched a plan for the economic development of French Guiana, with various income-producing programs, such as cattle raising, commercial fishing, forestry and ore prospecting included.

There are approximately 55,000 French Guianese, predominately in young age groups. The majority live in the coastal capital city of Cayenne. The population is composed of French officials and businessmen, indigenous Guianese, French creoles and a smattering of the ubiquitous Chinese. French culture has flourished under the hot equatorial sun, and the government boasts that French Guiana has the lowest illiteracy rate in South America, a claim also made by Venezuela.

EXPLORING FRENCH GUIANA

Approaching by air or sea, you will sense grandeur as soon as you glimpse the Iles du Salut and the verdure-clad crags of the island of Cayenne, in the midst of whose luxuriant vegetation rises a touch of metropolitan France, the territory's capital. This city of 30,000 has been laid out with that unerring French instinct for urban planning, which has resulted in the handsome promenades of the Place des Palmistes and the Place des Amandiers. Curiosities of the capital include the official residence of the Prefect, built in the 18th century by the Jesuit fathers. Also, not far from the island's Rochambeau Airport, is found one of the most exotic small zoos in existence, noted for its collection of magnificent tropical birds. A taxi will take you along the coast for an interesting tour of the summer homes of Cayenne's leading citizens, and it is just a few miles to the jungle where superb groves of bamboo meet overhead to form cool archways of golden green.

Cayenne is the hub of all activity, center for sea bathing, cockfighting and fishing and point of departure for hunting safaris. The local museum is worth visiting, as are the Botanical Gardens, a wonderful place to study the flora of the equatorial jungle. Speaking of which, you will notice the giant double palms of the Place des Palmistes. These are a specialty of French Guiana, not found elsewhere.

There are a number of interesting excursions from Cayenne. Fort Diamant, built in 1652, is the New World's best-preserved example of a genuine feudal castle. Fort Trio with its double tower is another monument of European military architecture transplanted to America.

The "Tour de l'Ile" excursion will enable you to appreciate the magnificent scenery of French Guiana's rugged coast, swift rivers and dense forests. The Montagne de Mahury provides hikers with a rare opportunity to climb among the orchid-draped trees of an equatorial forest to the three lakes of Mount Rorota. Most impressive—and most rugged—of all are the river trips into the heartland of the luxuriant interior province of Inini. On the river trips, you can make overnight stops in rustic shelters in the jungle. Splendid for pioneering types. Inquire at the Hotel Montabo for details.

You may visit Iracoubo with its melancholy tombs of France's political deportees. Then there are the lovely Iles du Salut and Devil's Island, which brings us back to the spectre which still haunts French Guiana.

PRACTICAL INFORMATION FOR FRENCH GUIANA

CAPSULE COMMENTS. *Physical Features.* A tropical forest of the Amazon jungle, French Guiana extends 400 miles into the almost impenetrable jungle and is sparsely populated. The rugged land is blessed with several waterways. Most of the country's population lives along the 200 mile low lying Atlantic coastline.

Climate. Hot and tropical. Two distinct seasons: the dry from July to December and also March; the rainy from December to July. Average temperature in Cayenne is in the low 80s the year round.

Political System. Since 1946 an Overseas Department of France. A Prefect named by the French ministry and a 15-member Council General, elected by the people, administer.

Population. 55,000. Cayenne 30,000.

Language. French.

Principal Industries. Gold, sugar, coffee, rum, cacao, forestry.

 WHEN TO COME? Best weather is from July to December. There are short rain showers Dec.-Feb.; drizzles in Mar. and heavy, long rain storms Apr.-July. Average temperature is only 80 degrees, but the humidity makes it rather more sticky than this would indicate.

HOW TO GET AROUND. Rental cars and taxis are available in Cayenne. The hotels or the Syndicat d'Initiative can help with this. Small buses operate along the coast. Into the interior one travels by plane or dugout canoe.

 HOW TO GET THERE. There are air services to Cayenne's airport by *Air France. Pam Am* flies from New York to Port of Spain, Trinidad and Georgetown, Guyana where you can pick up local connections. *Air France* has an average of 3 flights per week, starting from one or the other of the islands—Martinique or Guadeloupe, which can be reached year-round from Miami on the airline, and winters-only from New York.

Cayenne is a port of call for ships of the *Compagnie Générale Maritime.* A car links Surinam from Marowijne River to St. Laurent.

Kourou may be reached by frequent daily ferries or buses.

 PASSPORTS. A valid passport without visa is required for stays under 3 months, return ticket (or Certificate of Exemption from Prefect), smallpox vaccination certificate. Airport departure tax.

CURRENCY. At press time, 1 French franc = approximately U.S. 20¢.

BANKS are open weekdays 9–12 and 3–5.

WATER from the tap is safe only in the main cities. Bottled water from France is advisable; available in the hotels.

WHAT TO TAKE. Definitely not the most revealing sort of beachwear; some prudery is discernible here. Do take sunglasses, a sun hat, mosquito repellant, an umbrella. If you plan to go into the forest: body-covering clothing, comfortable walking shoes or preferably boots (there *are* snakes as well as insects). Camera-toters should include zoom and flash in their gear, for shooting in dark-shadowed jungle.

ELECTRIC CURRENT is 110 and 220 volts.

CINEMA. There are 3 movie theaters in Cayenne and one in Kourou.

MEDICAL ATTENTION. There is a hospital in Cayenne and one in St. Laurent du Maroni, several dispensaries in other towns.

HOTELS. Cayenne. The leading hotel is *Hotel Le Montabo*, perched on a hilltop overlooking the town. The open-air lounge has a view of the sea. Pool and restaurant with European cuisine. 60 air-conditioned rooms with telephone, showers and their own balcony. Also in Cayenne; *Neptima*, town center, 21 Rue Félix Eboué; 15 air-conditioned rooms (3 with bath), moderately priced. *Kime Lone*, which has a restaurant. *Ket Tai*, 30 air-conditioned rooms, Chinese restaurant, nightclub. *Les Palmistes* and *Rochambeau*, near the airport.

Kourou. *Hôtel des Roches*, 90 air-conditioned rooms, restaurant, pool, tennis, beach. *Albia*, 40 air-conditioned rooms, 20 overlooking the sea.

Saint Laurent du Maroni. *Prévost*, 12 rooms, and *Peslier*, 20 rooms, both air-conditioned but without hot water. *Barcarel*, 8 rooms. All inexpensive.

RESTAURANTS. Cayenne & Ile de Cayenne. Outside the hotels try: *La Rôtisserie*, 5 Place de Grenoble (second floor); *Brasserie Provençale*, Place des Palmistes (near the Eldorado cinema); *La Gaîté*, 33 Rue Lt. Brassé, European cuisine.

Dragon d'Or, 39 Ave. de Gaulle, Chinese; *Le Viet Nam*, 16 Rue Félix Eboué, Vietnamese; *La Baie d'Along*, Route de Mont Joly, Vietnamese.

Creole specialties at: *Le Tatou*, Rue Chaussé Sartines; *Le Snack Créole*, Ruc Félix Eboué; and *La Bonne Cervoise*, Route du Gallion.

Kourou. *Le Mandarin Chinois*, at the junction of Rue du Bourg and Rue du Site; *Le Village, Rue Girot*, charcoal-grilled specialties; *Chez Vaud* and the restaurant of the *Hôtel des Roches*.

Saint Laurent du Maroni. *Le Toucan*; *Le Mikado*; *Chez Nam*, Vietnamese.

Saint Georges de l'Oyapock. *Chez Modestine*, Creole cuisine.

Sinnamary. *Eldo Grill*; *Chez Papa Chef*, Indonesian cooking; *Chez Tinrin*.

SHOPPING. Within the past two years a great many new boutiques have opened, offering a wide range of merchandise. Good buys are butterflies, many of which are unique to this area; basketry; hammocks, pottery and wood sculpture; gold jewelry.

FOR THE SPORTSMAN. Firearms brought in by visitors must be declared at Customs and a permit secured. Canoes may be rented for hunting waterfowl along the rivers. There is fishing in the ocean from rocks or canoes. Swimming around Ile de Cayenne. For visiting the interior, a guide is a must, and also required is a special permit from the Prefecture in Cayenne.

USEFUL ADDRESSES. *Air France*, 5 Place de Grenoble; *TAAG* (Transports Aériens Antilles-Guyane), Rochambeau Airport; *Syndicat d'Initiative*, tel. 919; *Institut Pasteur*, Av. Louis Pasteur. *Police*, at Prefectural Office, *Botanical Gardens*, Av. André Aron at Av. de la Republique.

SURINAM

From Dutch Dams to Wild Jungle

BY

ALBERT HELMAN

(One of the best-known Dutch novelists, Albert Helman is from genuine Surinam stock. He has published a large number of books and articles on the Guianas and the Caribbean region.)

Between the wide curves of two of the world's most impressive rivers, the Orinoco and the Amazon, in the north-eastern part of South America, is a vast territory called Guiana. Surinam is the heart of this region. Although it was discovered by the Spaniards as early as the end of the 15th century, it took about a hundred years more before the Dutch settled on what they used to call in those days "the Wild Coast". The old colony often changed hands between the French, the English and the Dutch, but has remained exclusively Dutch since 1816. Many are the characteristics which the Dutch impressed on this otherwise typical part of tropical America, and these characteristics are still there, in spite of the fact that Surinam has an exceptionally cosmopolitan population and is now an independent country (as of November 25, 1975).

Mostly known as "Dutch Guiana", its ancient and official name is "Surinam", an Amerindian word, meaning "Rocky Rivers", a most appropriate designation. Its capital, Paramaribo, is also of Amerindian derivation, as are most of its rivers, animals, plants and popular implements. It remains essentially "the Wild Coast", a partly unexplored country, covered by virgin forests, dense and mysterious, sometimes almost impenetrable, but always luring the hunter, the fisherman, those who love unconventional adventure, and especially the curious who are eager to meet the last representatives of some of the strangest people on earth.

Only a very small part of the country, the coastal belt in the north, is inhabited. There you will see neat Dutch polders, surrounded by high tropical forests. There too you will find the old plantations, haunted by whisperings from the past, and everywhere you will meet a mixed rural population: Blacks and Creoles, East Indians and Javanese, each retaining their ancestral ways of life, and striking attire, but living together in harmony and peace.

In the coastal belt too is the capital, Paramaribo, on the banks of the wide, impressive Suriname River. More than a third of the entire population of the country live in this picturesque city, heart and brain of a nation living on agriculture, forestry, and bauxite. A 2-2½ hours' drive inland, will take you to the main mining-town, Moengo, a modern American creation, not far from the French border in the east and from the lovely little village of Albina. There is much activity going on in the southwestern part of the country (District of Nickerie) on the part of the Government. A new community will be established near the site of hydroelectric power dam constructions. While all these places are accessible by river, the usual ways of getting there are by air (flights of ½ hour or an hour) and by road.

Slaves That Got Away

When in the course of almost 300 years many thousands of blacks were brought from Africa to supply the labor refused by the freedom-loving Amerindians, the recalcitrant slaves regularly escaped to the forests and settled in almost inaccessible places above the rapids and in the river-laced depths of the jungle. These "Bush Negroes" still inhabit the same places, which only recently have become accessible without real danger to the traveler. They live according to their age-old African traditions, a sturdy and good looking people with no inclination whatever to hide their physical beauty. Open, friendly and talkative, they appreciate the benefits of western culture, without being influenced in their primitive way of life. Many of their huts display the fine wood carvings for which they are famous and which also adorn their furniture, implements and boats. They have a special skill in felling and burning out big trees, and their boats made in this way are strong and reliable, especially in the rapids, where they exhibit a rare ability as boatmen and conquerors of the wilderness.

The Bush Negroes also carve their drums—never to be touched by any female—and as soon as the sound of a drum or rattle is heard, their feet start to move in a most dexterous way. Most dance feasts are competitions between men or between women, where they try to out-dance each other, accompanied by the songs and the rhythmic noises of the onlookers. For gaiety, wit and practical jokes, they are unsurpassed by any of the other native groups.

At night, even in your hotel, you may hear from afar the mellow sounds of metallic music. This is the famous "gamelan", played by the Javanese. By day you will see everywhere their slender, elegant women, often still wearing sarongs as in Indonesia and ready to greet you with a lovely smile. You will meet the Chinese in many shops, and if you are interested in dry goods, you certainly will have a good talk with some of the Lebanese merchants who have brought the color of the Near East to this part of America. The main ethnic groups of Surinam are: Creole, Hindustani, Indonesians, Europeans, Chinese, Bush Negroes and Amerindians, of a total population of roughly 400,000.

The important thing is that all these groups, while retaining so many of their proper characteristics, nevertheless intermingle well in all commercial and industrial activities, as well as in daily life. As there are no real minority problems and no major sources of friction, they are growing closer and soon will become completely unified, a necessity in this young but growing country with its old and diverse components.

Food

Surinam, with its varied population, offers a good variety of dishes, and adventurous visitors should not pass up the opportunity to try the Indonesian "Rijsttafel", with rice, boiled and fried, as a main course and a fairly large number of spicy meat and vegetable side dishes; "Nasi Goreng", Indonesian-style fried rice and "Bami Goreng", Indonesian-style fried noodles. Creole dishes, such as "Pom", poultry and ground tayer roots; "Pastei", a chicken pie with various vegetables; and "Peanut Soup", a tasty broth made from ground peanuts, are excellent. Indian dishes, such as "Roti", a dough pancake with curried chicken and potatoes, and Chinese are also available. Apart from the standard dishes, such as chowmein and chop suey, a local favorite is "Moksie Metie", a mix of various meats, normally served on rice.

Of course the hotels serve American and European dishes. Rice, however, is the basic food in Surinam, except for the Amerindians and Bush Negroes, who make Cassave their main diet.

EXPLORING SURINAM

Paramaribo, a city of approximately 160,000 people, has an extensive surface, hugging the left bank of the Suriname River, where it nears the Atlantic Ocean after confluence with the Commewijne River. From the harborside, where the Central Market is a daily meeting-place, the town expands in all directions, leading to the poorer outskirts with their slums and to the richer residential and villa districts with their flowering gardens and white-washed dwellings.

North of the port area is the oldest part of the town, with its typical buildings adorned with stilted balconies, constructed of hardwood and painted in bright colors. From the spacious Onaflankelijkheidsplein (Independence Square) you may continue in the direction of the river to see old Fort Zeelandia, established about 1650 by Francis Willoughby, Lord Parham, (rebuilt 1667). It now houses the Surinam Museum.

Fifty steps farther to the north is the old "Barracks 1790", a typical colonial building of stone imported as ballast by the sailing vessels of the old West Indian Company. Opposite, there is an entrance to the peaceful Palm Garden, from which you can reach again the Onaflankelijkheidsplein at the beginning of one of the oldest and principal streets, Gravenstraat. Flanking this street are centuries-old buildings: the Roman Catholic Cathedral, a wooden construction, and in the section shaded by mahogany trees, the old Portuguese Sephardic Synagogue and the Government Hospital. Continuing up this street, you'll find the Art Centre (C.C.S.) with its Library, well provided with English books. Opposite is the old Oranjetuin Cemetery with its historic tombs.

Parallel to Gravenstraat are a number of other picturesque tree-shaded streets: Herenstraat, Wagenwegstraat and Keizerstraat. Their cross streets all lead to the commercial district of which Dominéstraat is the busiest, and its parallel, Maagdenstraat (Virgin street), most picturesque with its high palm trees in two rows. Never ask why the latter street leads to the point where Heiligenweg (Saint's Road) and Knuffelsgracht (Petting ditch) happen to meet! Protestant churches of different denominations rise amidst this shopping center, whilst at the end of the Jodenbreestraat, connecting the afore-mentioned streets with the harbor, is a second large Synagogue, that of the Ashkenazi community.

From here the city fans out, ending in Zorg-en-Hoop, where the Museum of Natural History is located. It also houses an art gallery and library with historical documents, engravings and rare books about the country. In the same area large modern school buildings and three new churches (Catholic and Protestant) show a growing taste for the latest fashion in architecture. Three new, modern hospitals are now in operation: the University Hospital, government owned and largest in the country, Deaconesses Hospital, and St. Vincentius Hospital (Roman Catholic). The older "Lands Hospitaal" still exists and is located on Gravenstraat. There is also a Military Hospital, located opposite the University Hospital.

In the outskirts of Paramaribo, both to the south and to the west, are agricultural districts, mainly occupied by Hindustani and Javanese peasants, cultivating rice, citrus, and vegetables. A long road, following the Suriname River upstream, passes the lovely settlement of Domburg, leads after about 20 miles to Paranam mining settlement of Alcoa, and to the interesting mining center of the Billiton Company. On both banks of the river, old plantations, still active, can be visited by boat, either from the capital or from Paranam where bauxite is shipped to Trinidad for trans-shipment to the US. and Canada.

Opposite the capital, on the right bank of the Suriname River, accessible by hourly ferry boat, a series of plantations can be reached, as well as the open-air museum New Amsterdam with its old fortresses, strategically erected at the confluence of the Suriname and Commewijne Rivers. Fifteen miles away is the sugar estate of Marienburg, gateway to many sugar and coffee plantations and the hinterland hunting grounds.

Jungle Cruise

Several of the reliable local tour operators can arrange sight-seeing trips into the jungle interior. English-speaking guides are provided. Among the tours which are available are a one-day tour by car to Albina on the Marowijne river, which forms the border between Surinam and French Guiana, a boat trip to some Amerindian and Bush Negro villages on the river, and a day's trip to Afobakka, site of the new hydro-electrical works of the Suriname Aluminum Company, as well as Brownsberg Nature Park. Most tourists prefer the river trip, past the Bush Negro villages and into the heart of this strange and primitive land seeing the Djukas, often without benefit of clothes, paddling their canoes, dancing on the river banks, and living the ancient tribal life they brought with them from the jungle of Africa to the jungle of Surinam.

If you have the leisure for it, the most rewarding voyage of all is the four-day tour of Stoelmans island, in the Marowijne, largest river in Surinam. You travel by plane and by *corjaal* which your boatman brings through the rapids with the greatest of ease. From this point a half-day trip can be made to the Granholo Falls in the Tapanahony river. It is an unforgettable, exotic voyage. SLM-Surinam Airways also has a package tour of Stoelmans island in conjunction with their regularly scheduled flights leaving Zorg and Hoop airfield on Mondays, Wednesdays and Fridays.

PRACTICAL INFORMATION FOR SURINAM

CAPSULE COMMENTS. *Physical Features.* A complete tropical country divided into three areas. The coastal lowland; next, a narrow belt of sandy soil that rises to the interior highlands; and finally, a dense, almost impenetrable, overgrown tropical forest of hills, mountains, many streams and large rivers.

Climate. The climate is warm and tropical. Nights are often pleasantly cool. Rainy months are May, June and July. Dry months are September-November. Surinam is a pleasant country to visit anytime for Paramaribo's hard-working inhabitants have built air-conditioned, modern hotels with comforts that rival any area in the world.

Population. 400,000. Paramaribo 160,000.

Language. Dutch, local vernacular, called "Sranan Tongo", referred to as "Taki-Taki". English widely spoken.

Religion. Christian, Moslem, Hindu.

Principal Industries. Rice, bauxite, plywood, fruit, coffee.

 HOW TO DRESS. In the past few years (and especially since independence) there has been a tendency to do away with formality in dress. The jacket and tie have lost out to the "guayabera" or the so called "safari outfit." Nevertheless, it remains proper to wear jacket and tie when visiting authorities and on special occasions.

Ladies have always been a bit more liberal in their attire, and unless otherwise specified, they may wear either long gowns or cocktail dresses in the evening. Slacks are recommended for ladies on trips into the interior.

Visitors in general are advised to take along light wash-and-wear summer clothes.

 WHEN TO COME? Dec. to April is most agreeable, Jan. is the coldest month, Sept. the hottest. Although the climate is tropical, it is cooled by the north-east trades, and monthly mean temperatures range from only 79 to 83 degrees. Even in the wet season, showers are interspersed with long periods of sunshine and every year it gets harder to figure out just when the "rainy season" is.

The major national holiday is Independence Day, Nov. 25, which is combined with a Trade Fair and Sports Week, featuring local and foreign participation and entertainment. Almost the whole year there is occasion to assist at some native festivity—in the capital the frequent *Ferjari-oso*, or birthday celebration; some Javanese *Slamatan* in the outskirts, with genuine Indonesian dances and gamelan-music; or a Hindustani wedding, very ceremonial, with display of gorgeous costumes and sometimes stage-plays. In the interior the Bush Negroes easily arrange a dance-feast at night for generous visitors.

 HOW TO GET THERE. *By air.* KLM and its partner ALM, have flights from New York and Miami to Curaçao. From there ALM/SLM fly jets almost daily to Paramaribo. KLM/SLM fly from Amsterdam via Lisbon to Paramaribo. AIR FRANCE flies from Paris, New York, Puerto Rico, Guadeloupe and Martinique to Paramaribo. SLM (Surinam Airways) flies from Cayenne and internally. Cruzeiro do Sul flies from Belem (Brazil). Check with your travel agent for the latest airline schedule. Airport departure tax 5 Surinam Guilders.

 BY SHIP. KNSM-Royal Netherlands Steamship Company operates freighter travel with limited passenger accommodation every other week from New York to Paramaribo, returning to New Orleans, and from New Orleans to Paramaribo, returning to New York.

For information, contact Lislind International, general passenger agents for North America. The Surinam Navigation Company (SMS), has sailings from New Orleans. For information, check with Hansen & Tideman in New York and New Orleans.

 PASSPORTS, VISAS. All aliens should have a legitimate identity card, photo affixed, or current passport. Valid passport required for visitors from Eastern European countries, the Chinese People's Republic and Hong Kong. All temporary visitors should also have a smallpox vaccination certificate (not more than three years old) and a through or return ticket. Yellow fever vaccination certificates required for arrivals from infected areas.

CUSTOMS. Permits needed for shotguns. No other restrictions on a reasonable quantity of limited personal effects.

 CURRENCY. The Surinam Guilder (also called a Surinam Florin and abbreviated Sfl.), is the legal tender here. It is divided into 100 cents. At press time, 1 guilder = U.S. 57¢. Hotels and many shops accept U.S. currency and travelers checks. The American Express card is also accepted in the better hotels, many stores and restaurants.

 TIPPING. As a rule, hotels include a 10-15% service charge. Some restaurants may also add 10% to the bill. Other tipping is left to the discretion of the individual.

 HOW TO GET ABOUT. Plenty of taxis available in Paramaribo. U-drive cars offering more independence in getting around, can be hired.

For special temporary licence take your international driver's licence to the Police Traffic Office. Surinam traffic drives on the left. Bus transportation in the city is cheap. There is good transportation to the interior by Surinam Airways' Twin Otters (seating 17) between Paramaribo and Nickerie, and Stoelmans Island. Other points in the interior can also be reached by plane. Train excursions are organized on Sundays—but not on a regularly scheduled basis—between Onverwacht and Brownsweg.

HOTELS
(All hotels add 10-15% service charge.)

PARAMARIBO

SURINAM TORARICA. This 135-room deluxe hotel is best. Near the river not far from the center of town. Its elegant facilities include a swimming pool, an attractive dining room, a night club and a gambling casino. All rooms, private and public, are air-conditioned. Single: $25-$35; double: $30-$36, suites: $70-$100, EP.

SURINAM PALACE, Independence Square 6. 32 rooms with or without bath. Air-conditioned. Facing splendid main plaza, with a night club, dancing, good bar and casino. Food is American and European. Single: $8.50-$17; double: $15-$22, EP.

RIVER-CLUB HOTEL MOTEL.
New, approx. 7 mi. from Paramaribo at Leonsberg, near Suriname River. Air-conditioned cottages with kitchenette, pool,
snack bar. Ferry to Ft. Nieuw
Amsterdam. Single $15, EP;
double $18.

KRASNAPOLSKY PARAMA-
RIBO, connected with the old
Kersten Hotel. A new 85-room
hotel with swimming pool,
barber/beauty shops, restaurant,
supermarket, gift shop. Single:
$21-$26; double: $27-$32, EP.
Suite $35-$47.

There are also several smaller guest houses and pensions in Paramaribo but it is advisable to check on them with the tourist office.

OUTSIDE PARAMARIBO
MOENGO, mining center on
the Cottica River. *The Government Guest House,* 3 rooms (with
private bath) $5.75 each or +
$8.50 each (air-conditioning); 14
rooms (without private bath) in
annex, ± $4.75 each EP.

ALBINA, border town, opposite St. Laurent (French Guiana)
on the Marowijne River. *Government Guest House,* Colonial-
style, overlooking the river, 9
rooms, from $4.75 each EP. (add
$5.75 for 3 meals). *Marowijne,*
15 rooms, $4.50 each EP. *Happy
Day Inn,* 7 rooms, $7 each +
10% service charge CP. *River-
view,* 11 rooms, from $5.75-$7.75
each + 10% service charge CP.

STOELMANS ISLAND, on Lawa
River. *Stoelman Guest House,* 9
rooms, $6.25 each EP. (add $2
for breakfast and $3.25 for each
hot meal).

TOTNESS, town in Coronie
District, center of coconut plantations area. *Government Guest
House,* 7 rooms, from $4.75-$7
each (without bath), from $8.50-
$9.25 each (with bath, air-con-
ditioning), AP.

BROKOPONDO, on Suriname
River. *Brokopondo Guest House,*
11 rooms, from $10-$14.25 each,
depending on availability of private bath and air-conditioning.
AP.

Nw. NICKERIE, capital of the
Nickerie District, the most Western of Surinam, known as the
rice district. *Nickerie Guest
House,* 13 rooms, no private
baths, from $10-$14.25 each, AP.
Dorien, 10 rooms, $13-$17 each,
depending on whether with private bath. CP. *Sjiem Fat,* 10
rooms, $10-$13 each, AP.

WAGENINGEN, rice cultivating
settlement on Nickerie River. *De
Wereld,* 15 rooms, bar and discothèque. $13-$15.75 each +
10% service charge EP.

RESTAURANTS. Due to its varied population, you
can find here Indian, American, Creole, Chinese
or Indonesian food. Meat, poultry, fish and vegetables are the foundations of most dishes, and rice
in different forms will generally be a substantial part of the menu.
Creole dishes like *pom* (poultry and ground tayer-roots) or *pastei*
(poultry and vegetables) are recommended, as well as the Indonesian
rijsttafel (boiled rice with 10-20 spicy meat and vegetable side dishes)
and *nasi goreng* (fried rice with chicken). As preparation of these
dishes is elaborate, order in advance. Recommended: *Het Park* (Independence Square 10), *Roline's* (Weg van Ma-Retraite 23), for Creole,

Iwan's (Grote Hofstraat 6), *Jie Foek Sang* (Kleine Waterstraat 15) for Chinese; *Summer Garden* (Molenpad 92) Javanese; *Deli* (Saramaccastr. 34), *City Fountain* (Gravenstraat 37), and *Indian Dining Room* (Hotel Midnight) for Indonesian, *Tajmahal* (Watermolenstraat 39) for Indian; *Orlando's* (Kerkplein) sidewalk cafe and American coffee shop; *Plantation Room* (Torarica Hotel) French. Besides, there are some cafeterias, such as: *Lunchroom* (in the Krasnapolsky Hotel), *Soda Fountain* (Spanhoek), *Jolly Fountain* (Keizerstr. 46) and *Y.W.C.A.* (Herenstr. 14). For Chinese food another good bet is *Lucien's*, Gravenstraat 163 and for European cooking *Fajalobi* in the Krasnapolsky. *Riverclub Hotel-Motel* at Leonsberg has good Continental fare.

SHOPPING. There is a duty-free shop at Zanderij Airport. Amerindian and Bush Negro crafts are found in the villages and in Paramaribo. Popular items: hand-carved and hand-painted trays and gourds; bows and arrows, cotton hammocks, and wicker and ceramic objects; Javanese bamboo; wickerwork articles and batik. The Chinese stores carry imported jade, silks, ivory and glass (A. Fung Kon Jin, Wong San Tsoi & Co.). For film and camera equipment try Prolasco, Steenbakkerijstraat 31; Kersten in the department store on Domineestraat; or the foto shop of *Hagemeyer-Wijngaarde*, distributors for Kodak, at Keizerstraat 43. Also *Fotohandel Jong Tjien Fa* at Wagenwegstraat 57. The Ministry of Social Affairs, Wanicastraat 182, sells dolls, needlework, wall decorations.

Women's dresses and men's suits are found in local department stores or made to order by the dressmakers and tailors of Paramaribo. Dress material is plentiful, varied and of good quality, and a local seamstress can reproduce any item from a fashion magazine or as the customer wishes (Ramdhanie, Ramakers, Fashion House, Lincoln & Kersten's). There is a good number of boutiques also for the latest women's fashions. Some of the best are: *Ma Chérie* (Kerkplein 9), *Intermode* (Steenbakkerijsts 43), and boutique *Kersten,* in the new Krasnapolsky Hotel.

Locally made, good quality gold and silver jewelry can be bought at bargain prices. Also novelty jewelry of bauxite, koebiestones, gold nuggets, and cow-eye seeds. (Try *Torarica Boutique*, Hotel Torarica; *Max Chin-A-Sen*, Steenbakkerijstraat 39; *Hendrik Lieuw*, Wagenwegstraat 18; *B. Ramoedit*, Klipstenenstraat 12.) Good local paintings can be bought at Varekamp.

ENTERTAINMENT. *Torarica Hotel's Plantation Room* offers elegant dining. Its exotic *Saramacca Bar* has music and dancing nightly. Casino, too. The *Palace Hotel* provides both Continental cuisine and native dishes. It has a nightclub, dancing and gambling casino. Among discothèques can be mentioned: *River Club Hotel/Motel* at Leonsberg; *Tik-Tak*, Middenpad van Kwatta; and *Numero Uno*, 19 Malebatrum St. (guest membership available). The *Park Club* (introduction is necessary) has fine food. In general, it is a good idea to stick to the hotels for entertainment unless accompanied by local people who know the other night spots' reputations—in particular those far from the heart of town. Several movie houses, including a new drive-in, show

American, European and East Indian films. "Local Events Bulletin" (available at your hotel) lists all current activities and religious services.

 SPORTS. Swimming and tennis can be arranged through introduction at *Oase, Dolfin, Witte Lotus* and *Kwie Kwie*, four private clubs. There is also a public pool, *Parima*. An 18-hole golf course is located three miles from Paramaribo on the airport road. Hunting for tapir, deer, pingo and pakira (wild hogs), alligator (season: May 1-Dec. 31) and birds (Sept. 1-Apr. 30) is one of the big attractions of Surinam. Hunting permit required, costs *f*10 (approx. $5.80). Rifles and pistols not allowed, but shotguns may be brought in for 3 months. Gun license *f*5 (approx. $2.90). Make arrangements through local tour operators. Fishing for tarpon and the voracious but tasty pirên (piranha) is another specialty. Lawn tennis is popular. Soccer and Basketball in *Surinam Stadium* and *Sportshall*, respectively.

 MUSEUMS. The *National Museum* is located in the old "Fort Zeelandia", which played a very important role in the history of Surinam and was the scene of fighting between the English and the Dutch, in the 17th Century. The *Surinam Museum*, located on the Commewijne Street, in the section of Zorg & Hoop, houses a library, many interesting prints, drawings, and artifacts.

The *Open Air Museum Nieuw Amsterdam*, located across the river from Paramaribo at the confluence of the Surinam and the Commewijne rivers. It used to be a fort, known as "Fort Nieuw Amsterdam", built around 1750 and containing numerous relics from that period, colorful Bush Negro huts, an old light-ship and a small zoo. It can be reached by bus and ferry.

 USEFUL ADDRESSES. *American Consulate General*, Hakrin Bank Building. *British Consulate*, van 't Hogerhuysstraat (United Building); *Rotary Club*, Torarica Hotel; *Lion's Club*, Park Club. *Tourist Board and Information Office*, 10 Kerkplein, tel. 73733. *Surinam Tourist Bureau*, 1 Rockefeller Plaza, N.Y., N.Y. 10020.

AMERICAN EXPRESS AGENTS: Paramaribo, *C. Kersten and Co.*, Hotel Krasnapolsky.

GUYANA

Land of Six Peoples

BY

PETER SIMMS

(Familiar to our readers of Southeast Asia, *Peter Simms is a world traveler and reporter on foreign affairs. He recently completed a long assignment in Guyana.)*

How would you like to visit a place where gold is so common that it is used for paving stones? Where jewels, especially diamonds, are there for the finding? If it interests you at all, you belong to the famous company of men led by Sir Walter Raleigh, who first came sailing along the coastlands of the Guianas at the end of the sixteenth century. Raleigh was searching for the fabulous city Manoa where the gilded king, El Dorado, once ruled. Manoa, and its Lake Parima, were thought to be somewhere in the territory that is now Guyana. Raleigh's failure to discover them contributed to his long imprisonment and eventual beheading.

Guyana (pronounced GUY, not GEE) is an Amerindian word meaning the "land of many waters." Columbus is said to have sailed along these coasts in 1498, but he did not land. Many others came, but the muddy waters and the mangrove swamps did not appear tempting. It was the Dutch who first saw their possibilities. They sailed up the rivers some twenty to thirty miles to ground that was above tidal level and there set up flourishing armed trading settlements. Spanish records contain many references to the "Dutch infestors" and some bloodthirsty accounts of "clearing them out." The most famous Dutch fort was Kijkoveral (Overlooking All), the remains of which can still be seen today.

The Dutch were followed by the French, who left little other than some place names, such as Versailles.

The new country of Guyana is often called the "Land of Six Peoples." The first of these, certainly in time of arrival, are the Amerindians who now number some 33,000 out of a total population of 763,000. There are two villages near the airfield that can be visited in a day, but if you wish to meet them in more normal surroundings you should allow three to five days and go into the northwest or up into the interior where many of them live semi-nomadic lives in the rain forests or on the savanna.

In the towns you will notice a preponderance of blacks who are descended from the slaves brought from Africa, the horrifying "Middle Passage," or from plantations on the West Indian islands. In 1834 slavery was finally abolished and many blacks left the plantations either to set up "free" villages, some of which still exist, or to move into small shopkeeping and life in the towns.

When the plantation owners found they had lost their labor force they began to import indentured laborers. The East Indians (from India) proved to be the most resilient and suitable for agricultural work. They now form the largest racial group in the country, about 377,256.

Many other peoples were also imported including Americans, Germans, English ploughmen (complete with ploughs and horses), Portuguese and Chinese. It is these last two who form separate but relatively small parts of the population. Both races moved away from the plantations and set up in trade or became technicians. The sixth group are the British.

In recent years this former British colony was in the news because of political unrest, due mainly to Dr. Cheddi Jagan, the Marxist-leaning premier. But in December 1964, Jagan fell from power, and black attorney Linden Forbes Burnham took over, picking up the pieces of his country and welding them back together in a coalition government, which lasted until the latter part of 1968. In November 1965 Great Britain gave the go-ahead sign, and on May 26, 1966, British Guiana became independent, naming itself Guyana. General Elections in December 1968 ensured Prime Minister Burnham an over-all majority in the national assembly. A cooperative Republic since February 1970 with a Chinese, Arthur Chung, as President, it remains in the Commonwealth and was a founder of the Caribbean Free Trade Association—CARIFTA, now called CARICOM, for Caribbean Community Secretariat. Guyana is the only English-speaking democracy in South America.

EXPLORING GUYANA

The center of Georgetown is the best-preserved Georgian city in wooden architecture anywhere in the Caribbean, and it boasts the

second-highest wooden building in the world, St. George's Cathedral, whose spire rises over 132 feet above the ground. (The
Great Buddha Hall of Todaiji in Nara, Japan, is 161 feet in
height.) The beauty of this garden city of some 195,250 inhabitants is due largely to the Dutch, who laid out wide avenues with
canals down the middle as a reminder of their homeland. Now
many of the canals have been filled in, making tree-lined walks
between the roads. On each side are cool wooden houses, their
walls painted a sparkling white and their carefully designed shut-
ters a brilliant green. Even though the sea is safely at bay, the
town can still be flooded when heavy rains coincide with high seas,
and most of the houses are built on stilts some eight to ten feet off
the ground—a reminder that Georgetown was once known as the
capital of "Mudland," from the swamps around it and the brown
alluvial-laden sea water. However, within sight of the cathedral
two large fires in recent years have burned out a large part of the
business area; this has now been rebuilt with fine concrete buildings and provides excellent shopping. The real life of the city's
marketing is in Stabroek market, where the people and their wares
are equally captivating. The City Hall is just a few hundred yards
from the cathedral.

The 180-acre Botanical Gardens have an exceptionally fine collection of tropical flowers and palm trees. Look for such rarities
as Guyanese Victoria Regia water lilies, the world's largest-
leafed aquatic plant. According to legend it can easily support a
five-year old child on its fronds, but this is not recommended if
you want to be certain of keeping your offspring dry. Another
rarity are the manatees, gentle seacows, who, so it is said, were
first mistaken by sailors for mermaids. They spend much of their
time submerged on the bottom of the ponds, but at a shrill whistle
will emerge and expect a handful of grass which they'll munch
contentedly. One should also visit the Museum with its fine collection of Amerindian arts and crafts, its birds, specimens of electric
eels, sting rays and other dangers of the jungle.

The Coast

The narrow coastal belt—often below sea level—and *empold-
ered* in the Dutch manner is scenically the least interesting part of
the whole country. For mile after mile the road is lined with
houses, one village running into the next, all remarkably similar
and dull. It is however in this area that over 90 percent of the
more than 763,000 inhabitants live, working on the sugar estates
and on their own farms growing rice. If you want to see the area
at its best, take a drive a few miles along the coast towards
Rosignol. It is worth taking a day-trip by the new highway to
Mackenzie where you can see the impressive bauxite mines and the
giant excavators that dwarf the humans who operate them. There

is a good hotel and swimming pool run by the company, and a Tour Centre nearby where visitors are given a comprehensive tour of the Guyana Bauxite Co. (Guybau) operations. Arrangements can be made with Guybau's head office in Georgetown.

The Savannah Country

The Rupununi savannah is an outdoor man's paradise, and any woman's too if she likes good simple food, beautiful wide-open spaces and people who have placed their bets on the future. Once it used to take six or more grueling weeks to make your way up the cattle trail, but nowadays it is just an hour and a half by Dakota. We recommend you stay on a fine ranch near Lethem (Mrs. Orealla) and you'll be able to have dream fishing for the giant arapaima (or if you aren't interested yourself watch the Amerindians shoot him with a bow and arrow), the lukanani and a host of others. But look out also for the perai, the six to nine inch monster that goes mad if it smells blood in the water, for he and his friends can get through a whole cow in virtually no time. So when you bathe take advice. Also remember to ask about sting-rays and the electric eel (with its 500 volt shock).

There's a sparse Amerindian population consisting of the Macushi, Wapishiana and Wai-Wai tribes. The latter are hardy, remote and primitive people. Hunting dogs play an important part in their lives and are treated with great respect. The Indians rest and sleep in hammocks that can spread out to incredible size, owing to the way they are woven. Part of the hammock folds over the sleeper in lieu of a blanket. These cleverly woven "beauty rests" impressed Columbus. They are wonderful souvenirs, but it's extremely difficult to get a genuine Guyanese Amerindian ham-mock. They take an enormous amount of work and the average Amerindian who can still make them is just not sufficiently inter-ested in money to sell what has been to him a labor of love and imagination; so most of the hammocks you find will have been imported from Brazil.

The Guyanese Amerindians, as well as having considerable experience as trackers and hunters and general lore about the wildlife, are often something of linguists, since many of them learn Portuguese through their visits to Brazilian markets and to their relatives who live across the border.

Rain Forest and Kaieteur Falls

While at Lethem you must take off time to visit the Kanaku mountains with their curiously shaped hills. You'll find a wealth of flowers and other flora as well as animal and bird life that will delight you. It's rough, of course, but along with the pleasure of gliding all day down the river, with frequent stops for porterage, or else shooting the rapids, you'll see life as you'll perhaps agree afterwards it should be lived. Manari Ranch Hotel will organize trips to the surrounding Rupununi Savannas.

In the very heart of Guyana is one of the wonders of the world, Kaieteur Falls, terrifying in its grandeur, fascinating in its beauty, five times the height of Niagara (822 feet in two falls of 741 and 81 feet, respectively, versus Niagara's 193 feet). Proud locals call it "the world's highest major waterfall." Its greatest attraction is the ever-changing clouds of prismatic hues. And if you are lucky you will see the Kaieteur martin birds and swallows flying home to the undershelves of rock behind the curtain of water. Kaieteur is a corruption of native words meaning "Old Man's Fall." A local ballad tells of an old chieftain who offered himself, for the good of his tribe, to Makonaima, the Great Spirit. This he did by paddling his canoe over the mighty waterfall. His craft, turned to stone, may be seen at the foot of Kaieteur whenever a drought has reduced the volume of water. Day-trips run every Sunday by Guyana Airways cost G\$35. June, July and December are the best months in which to see the falls at their most powerful. There are over 100 varieties of plantlife unique to this area, and we really mean unique—they are found nowhere else in the Western Hemisphere.

Farther on, some 190 miles from Georgetown, are the Orinduik Falls on River Ireng at the Brazilian frontier. You can reach this beauty spot by Guyana Airways Corporation's plane which takes you there for a weekend outing in less than two hours. There are more falls and rapids on the Essequibo River, not far from Bartica where three great rivers meet. This attractive little town is the base for visiting the gold and diamond mines that Raleigh missed. Important timber operations also go on here. Camping facilities on Aratack Island; good game fishing.

Within easy access of Bartica are the ruins of Kijkoveral, the look-out island fortified by the Dutch in the 17th century, and Fort Island, sighted about ten miles upstream from Georgetown.

PRACTICAL INFORMATION FOR GUYANA

CAPSULE COMMENTS. *Physical Features.* The word *Guiana* means "land of water," and the name was well chosen for there are over 600 miles of navigable rivers in the small 83,000-square-mile country in addition to towering Kaieteur Falls and a 206-mile coastline. Most of the country is a thick, hilly jungle-land sloping toward the Atlantic. A large savanna area lies beside the Venezuelan border. Formerly British Guiana.

Climate. The weather is decidedly tropical and hot but healthy. Two distinct rainy seasons—from April to August and again from November to January. The sea breeze cools Georgetown. Best months to visit are August to March.

Population. 763,000. Georgetown 195,250.

Language. English.

Religion. Christian, Hindu, some Muslim.

Principal Industries. Gold, sugar, bauxite, rice, diamonds, manganese.

 HOW TO GET THERE. *By Air.* Air schedules have a nasty habit of changing, but one can be certain that about twice a day there is a flight in and out of Timehri International Airport (25 miles from Georgetown). *Pan Am* has flights from New York via Port-of-Spain. *Air France* has flights from New York (winter only), Miami, San Juan and Paris, via Martinique or Guadeloupe. *KLM* has flights from Amsterdam and New York; *ALM* from the Caribbean via Curaçao; *British Airways* has flights from London. *BWIA* has flights to Trinidad (for connection) from New York and/or Miami. *Cruzeiro do Sul* flies from Brazil. *Guyana Airways* serves the interior. Should an overnight be necessary in Trinidad, stay at the Bel Air or the Pan American Guest House near the airport, unless you have a whole day to spend, then it is better to go into Port-of-Spain. A taxi from airport to Georgetown is about G $20; sharing allowed. Airport departure tax: U.S. $1.50 for adults.

By Sea. The *Royal Netherlands Line*: every few weeks from Europe, fortnightly from New York and New Orleans. If you are a student or adventurous there are numerous schooners that ply between Guyana and the West Indian islands—schedules are non-existent, and length of voyage uncertain, but it's cheap.

 PASSPORTS, VISAS, CURRENCY. Citizens from the United States and Commonwealth countries are permitted to enter Guyana without visas for a period not exceeding one month. The only requirements are the possession of a valid passport or a return or onward ticket and an international smallpox vaccination certificate. Visitors from other places must apply for visitors' visas. Permission must be obtained from the Ministry of Home Affairs before visitors are allowed to travel to any interior spot except on excursions and tours operated by recognized travel agents and airlines. The Guyana dollar is legal tender (approximately U.S. 50¢ to Guyana $1.28), but U.S. and Canadian dollars are readily accepted by all banks and authorized dealers. The U.S. visitor will not have any trouble because the system is metric. Visitors may bring in as much foreign currency as they wish but must on entry make out a written declaration, and can then take out up to the same amount. An oral declaration of personal effects is required; 200 cigarettes allowed.

 HEALTH REGULATIONS. This is the only country in South America which is free from yellow fever and malaria, and so no shots for these diseases are required if you enter Guyana from the north. But if you enter from a neighboring South American country (Surinam, French Guiana, Brazil, etc.), you will need a yellow fever shot. A small pox vaccination is required of all visitors, however.

SPECIAL EVENTS, *Eid-Ul-Ahza.* Muslim, sacrificial holiday, celebrating Abraham's willingness to sacrifice his son for the Almighty One. Usually in early Jan. *Phagwah,* a joyous Hindu celebration of the triumph of good over evil, noted for throwing of perfume and water. Usually ends Feb. or early Mar. *Republic Day,* Feb. 23, flag raising and report to the nation by the Prime Minister, and *Mashramani time,* generally marked by street tramping. *Easter Monday,* traditional day for kite flying. *Youman Nabi.* In early Apr. the Muslims celebrate the Birth of the Prophet Muhammad, although it is actually the date the Holy Prophet died. At the end of Oct. or early Nov., there is a Hindu religious festival of lights (*Deepavali*), to celebrate the return of Lord Rama after 14 years' exile.

 CLOTHING. Temperatures in Georgetown range from 75° to 85° all the year round but are tempered by fresh sea breezes. Light tropical clothes for both sexes. Not-too-provocative shorts and slacks may be worn by women. Informality is keynote; however for evening wear Shirt Jacs or lounge suits are recommended. If you are planning to travel in the interior wear field-trip clothes (Khaki). A light raincoat and insect repellent are also recommended.

 **HOW TO GET ABOUT.** Most existing roads are asphalt. A new highway connects Georgetown with Mackenzie. Car-hire rates: G$15 daily. Be sure to agree on rentals beforehand. Contact Harold Mitchell Service Station, Georgetown. Usually G$1 is charged per trip in town. To or from the airport is G$20 for a taxi, or G$3 each for the minibus. No tip necessary. All rates may increase because of rising gasoline prices, which were $2.35 (G) an imperial gallon at press time. There is a steamer from Georgetown to Vreed-en-Hoop and a road from there to Parika on the Essequibo River. From Parika you can go to Bartica on the confluence of the Essequibo, Mazaruni and Cuyuni (along this last are some large gold fields waiting to be found). Good swimming, fishing, a rest house and an easy trip into the "White sands area"—recommended only for those who will accept simple living.

Guyana Airways Corporation has numerous flights into the interior. Places of interest:

(1) A one-day trip to Kaieteur Falls at a cost of about G $35 per person. These trips are run every Sunday by the corporation's Twin Otter Aircraft. You can leave at 9 a.m., spend 2 hours at the falls and be back by 1:30. On the 4th Sunday of the month, there is a tour to both Kaieteur and Oronduik falls, including lunch and carfare to and from the airport, for about G $60;

(2) Air/overland trip to Kaieteur Fall, three days at G $80 each;

(3) Three-day trip to Imbaimadai. The cost of G $150 includes air flight, meals, accommodations, and trip by boat to Maipuri Falls and Tramen Cliffs to see cliff paintings by extinct Amerindian tribes;

(4) A one-day or overnight trip to Mackenzie, the large bauxite mines and processing plant;

(5) A three, or more, day flight to Lethem in the great savannah land where you can fish, ride, swim and see Amerindians. Price: about

The faces of South America will fascinate you, as much for their beauty as for their character. Here, a Bolivian girl poses beside a temple wall face at Tiahuanaco and an Argentine gaucho looks you straight in the eye.

Photos: Braniff International (top) and Pan American World Airways, Inc.

Descendants of the first inhabitants, the Amerindians of Surinam produce pottery and beadwork, some of which is on sale in Paramaribo's Central Market.

Devil dancers, allegedly from deep within Bolivian mines, cavort on festival days throughout the land.

Photo: Braniff International

Patriotism and religion have reacted in different fashion on the South American continent, dividing it into many countries and uniting it so far as formal religious belief is concerned (though sects outside the church continue to flourish). Above, the Independence Monument in Caracas' Parque los Proceres; below, a stylized version of the candomble rite of Bahia.

Top photo: Pan American World Airways, Inc.

US $110. (Write to Mrs. Orealla, Manari Ranch, Manari, Rupununi, for comfortable guest house);

(6) Fishing at Aratack Island on the upper reaches of the Essequibo River. This island is owned by Joe Young; accommodations are in tents. Rates: G $15 per day with meals;

(7) Matthew's Ridge-Northwest District and Mabaruma, in the same area, offer superb scenery. At Mabaruma a huge, luxuriously furnished plantation house has been converted into a guest house. Rates: G $15 per person per day with full meals.

If you are on a ship or have only two or three days then there are: (1) Georgetown, its Museum, Botanical Gardens, Stabroek Market, and Muslim mosques and Hindu temples, the latter of greater sociological than architectural interest; (2) a trip to an Amerindian village, Santa, and a jungle picnic (one day); (3) St. Cuthbert's Amerindian Mission, at the back of the Mahaica River. Day trips are arranged for visitors. New tourist sites near Essequibo Lakes, in the Rupununi District and on Kaieteur Top are planned.

You can charter a Britton Islander airplane all day from *Guyana Aviation Group*, Georgetown airport, for about G $600, pack in 9 passengers to share the costs, and fly up to Kaieteur Fall for lunch and leisurely exploration of the flora and fauna.

To organize any trips outside Georgetown or obtain general information, contact: Tourist Division, Guyana State Corporation, Brick Dam & Ave. of the Republic, Georgetown.

Those who have serious, repeat serious, scientific interests should write to *Mr. Adrian Thompson*, 19, Pere & David Streets, Kitty, Georgetown, who knows where rare flora and fauna exist only a few hours drive outside the town.

 SPORTS. *Fishing.* There are few sports in Guyana; there is *one* in which it excels. One enthusiast has described the opportunities as "the best fresh water fishing in the Western Hemisphere." The rivers and the interior abound in game fish: the best known, though least enticing, is the man-eating *piranha* (called locally perai), but the most sought after by sportsmen is the *lucanni*, a fish similar in appearance and feeding habits to the large mouth bass—it can be caught on bass flies.

Most of the interior rivers are difficult to get to if you are a casual visitor, but provided you have booked, only a few hours' flight will take you to the largest fresh-water fish in the world, the *arapaima*, weighing about 250 lb.

Some of the coastal rivers within reach of Georgetown are also good for fishing, although usually it is wise to spend one night in the fishing grounds, as the best are 4–5 hours' drive from the city. Fishing licenses required. *Shooting* does not come up to the same high standards, but night hunting from boats is often a feature of coastal river fishing, and small local deer, capybara, occlots and jaguars are often encountered —as well as alligators. License for use of firearms and ammunition must be requested 1 mo. before arrival (Shotgun, G $4; Rifle, G $5). *Racing.* Guyana Motor Racing Club holds international motorcycle and car races each March and Oct. *Riding.* There's a pony club in Georgetown; and horses are available at Manari Ranch in the Rupununi Savannahs. *Cricket* and *hockey* are popular.

SHOPPING. Georgetown's most colorful sight is Stabroek Market, where you can see all of Guyana's six races, and a few more, haggling over their transactions. But it's an experience not to be missed as you can find local straw hats, baskets, clay goblets, jewelry. But if you don't like to argue over prices go to *Margarita Gift Shop* in Middle Street, *Scandinavian Shop* or *Oleander Boutique*, both on Main Street, for Amerindian bows and arrows and rather expensive hammocks, pottery and salad bowls. Be sure purple-heart bowls are treated to prevent salad oil stains. Local rum or, as it is better known, Demarara rum is world famous and it is worth taking home a bottle or two of either Russian Bear Black Label, X.M., Eldorado, or Booker's Daiquiri Rum. Booker's also has wide selection of stuffed alligators. Duty-free shop at Timehri Airport has one or two good buys.

HOTELS AND DINING OUT. Food in the hotels and restaurants is tasty and varies from European and American dishes to local dishes which have their origin in the mixed races of Guyana. From India come curries—especially mutton, prawn and chicken—and from Africa has come *foo-foo* (plantains made into cakes) and *metemgee* (edoes, yams, cassava and plantains cooked in coconut milk and grated white of coconut). Try Portuguese garlic pork and Amerindian pepperpot. On the menus of hotels and restaurants you'll always find chicken, pork and steak and, most of the time, shrimp.

GEORGETOWN HOTELS

Deluxe

PEGASUS. 109 air-conditioned rooms, swimming pool, cocktail lounge and pub on ground floor. Restaurant features dishes of country's six major races. Name band Sat. nights, dancing Wed. nights. Singles about $25 U.S., doubles $33.

First Class

TOWER, 74 Main St. 90 rooms have private baths, air conditioning; swimming pool. Dancing on weekends at the Cactus Club restaurant.

PARK, 38 Main St., Cummingsburg. 46 rooms, $14 U.S.-$20, with a decidedly Somerset Maugham atmosphere, has a large square veranda where you can sip your drinks under a giant cupola.

Moderate

WOODBINE is the haunt of a number of Guyanese politicians, newspapermen and anyone else who likes to argue about events.

Inexpensive

BELEVEDERE HOTEL has a good band on Saturday nights and is becoming increasingly popular.

There are also Guest Houses: *Esplanade, Rima, Trio La Chalet* and *Le Grille,* all inexpensive.

COUNTRY HOTELS

BARTICA. Bartica is best served with hotels: *Marin,* one block from ferry terminal. Also, *Moderne, Berner's, Croft* and *Karia.* All inexpensive.

LINDEN has the *MacKenzie Hotel.* On river bank, 25 rooms with bath. Inexpensive.

NEW AMSTERDAM. The *Penguin* has had a face lift and is now an extremely modern, comfortable hotel. Rates on request.

LETHEM, in the Rupununi region, has a Government *Rest House* which, with the District Commissioner's blessing and if there are rooms available, will accept you as a paying guest. The enchanting *Manari Ranch Hotel,* 6½ mi. away, is surrounded by mountains. Good game fishing. Both inexpensive.

Near Wichabai, at *Dadanawa Ranch*, the Rupununi Development Company has a guest house; by invitation only.

RESTAURANTS. All hotels in the country have restaurant services and bars. There are a few other places in Georgetown, however, where one can eat in pleasant surroundings, the *Palm Court* among them. In the evening one can sit here in the small paved garden and have steaks: but they are only grilled on Saturdays; on other days they are fried. *Club Diabolique*, on Church St., has elegant French food, with an appropriate atmosphere. Non-members must pay G $2 cover charge. Best Chinese food in the country is in Georgetown's *Chinese Dragon*, where locals believe downstairs is better than upstairs.

USEFUL ADDRESSES. Embassy of the U.S.A., 31 Main St.; British High Commission, 44 Main St.; Canadian High Commissioner's Office, Bank of Guyana Bldg., 2nd floor. All in Georgetown.

VENEZUELA

Where the Andes Greet the Caribbean

BY

PENNY LERNOUX

(The author, a long-time resident of South America, covers Venezuela and neighboring countries for several U.S. publications, including Newsday, and has long specialized in reporting Latin America to the rest of the world.)

Venezuela has long been a land wealthy in beauty and contrast, from her Caribbean beaches to dense jungle rain forests to villages set high in the snow-capped Andes. But now, bolstered by a multi-billion dollar petroleum windfall, this richest of South American nations has even more means to measure her prosperity: lavish restaurants and resorts, exuberant architecture and a freeway system to rival California's all attest to her new-found wealth.

For all their new riches—and responsibilities—there is nothing stuffy or pompous about the irrepressible Venezuelans. Quick to anger and just as quick to smile, they approach life with an open casualness. Like all the Caribbean coastal peoples, the Venezuelans speak a staccato Spanish liberally laced with such American words as "drink," "snack" and "lunch," and all foreigners are called "musiues," a corruption of the French "messieurs." Unlike their more traditional neighbors, the Venezuelans are willing to try anything once, including the world's highest cable car and ski resort (at the staggering height of 16,000 feet).

Caracas, Venezuela's dynamic capital, shows all the advantages and disadvantages of an oil boom, including the continent's worst traffic jams and some of its best art galleries. A provincial back-

water only three decades ago, Caracas now attracts world conferences (the United Nations' first Law of the Sea Conference was
held here), Arab potentates, the best popular and classical artists,
foreign businessmen selling everything from jet aircraft to hamburger stands, and swarms of foreign tourists. The Caraqueños,
as the capital's inhabitants are called, treat all these changes and
invasions as a natural outgrowth of their petroleum wealth. The
city has also developed a tradition as the country's melting pot,
welcoming wave after wave of immigrants, from the Spanish Civil
War, from war-torn Europe and, more recently, from the political
upheavals in other Latin American countries such as Chile.

With each new wave of immigrants (the city also is a magnet
for rural peasants), Caracas spreads farther east and west along a
narrow nine-mile-long valley, climbing over the southern hills and
spilling into the adjoining valleys. Only the very wealthy and the
very poor reside in single-family homes; the rest of the city's
2.5 million residents live in a forest of apartment buildings that
rises beside the freeways. Either they cannot afford rents of
$1,000 a month and upward for a house in the valley, or they
could not put up with conditions in the hillside slums that overlook
Caracas.

Venezuelans are among the most mobile people in Latin America due to the excellent network of freeways that crisscrosses the
coastal lowland where most of Venezuela's 12.5 million inhabitants
live. Branch highways also run south to Ciudad Guayana in the
east and Mérida in the west, cities as unalike as Pittsburgh and
Williamsburg.

Industry and Resorts

The capital of Venezuela's booming steel industry, Ciudad
Guayana, is a brash new metropolis rising out of the dusty
Guayana Highlands. To the south lie Angel Falls, the world's highest waterfall; the rose-colored lagoon of Canaima Falls; and the
little-traveled Orinoco rain forests, where primitive Indians still
hunt with bow and arrow. Mérida in the western Andes is a world
away in time and space with snow-capped mountains, poncho-clad
Indians, Spanish colonial architecture and conservative traditions.

Headquarters for Venezuela's petroleum industry, Maracaibo
also boasts a distinctive personality, a mixture of nomad Guajiro
Indians, U.S. oil executives, Arab traders and on-the-go Venezuelans. Perched on the narrow neck that bottles Lake Maracaibo
and its forest of derricks, the city is the gateway to the harshly
beautiful Guajira Peninsula, where Indian women in long, flowing
mantles herd goats across the dry brushland and flamingos fly
in scarlet clouds among the quiet lagoons.

All along the 1,750-mile coastal ribbon that stretches from
Maracaibo to Caracas and east to Cumaná are dazzling, picture-

CARACAS

0m	500	1000	

□ Hotel ★ Public Building ■ Other Item

✝ Church ✳ Museum/Theater etc •••••••• Cable car

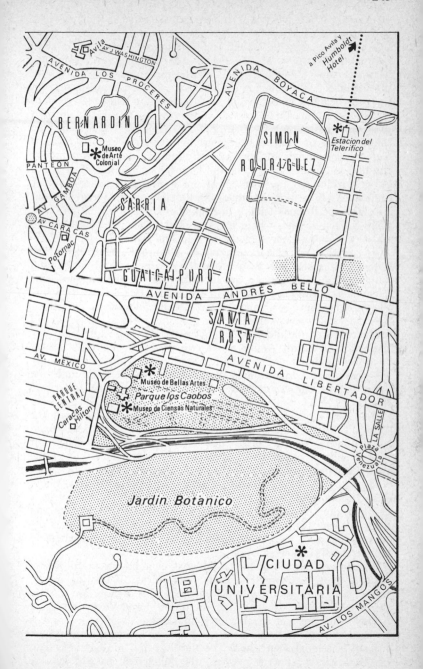

postcard beaches, from the coconut groves between Chichiriviche and Puerto Cabello to the aquamarine cove at Cata and the pearl fisheries of Margarita Island. Twenty minutes east of Caracas' international airport at Maiquetía rise the towers of Macuto, Marbella and Naiguatá in some of the most luxurious resorts on the Caribbean. Caraqueños spend their weekends here, lazing on the wide beaches, skiing, sailing, snorkeling and fishing. Red Snapper, mackerel, marlin and snook crowd the coastal waters, but the prize catch, attracting international tournaments, is the giant blue sailfish. East of Naiguatá lies another, very special resort, Los Caracas, a complex of apartment buildings, restaurants, outdoor theaters and what is said to be the largest swimming pool in South America, built for the workers of the Venezuelan Labor Confederation. A short flight north of Maiquetía, or an overnight boat trip, are Los Roques Islands, a necklace of coral formations with palm-fringed beaches where it is possible to island-hop at low tide by simply walking through the translucent water.

Flocks of lugubrious-looking pelicans share the Macuto beaches with the tourists, but to glimpse the more graceful heron and flamingo it is necessary to travel farther east to the marshes near El Hatillo and the red beaches of Colorado. For those with a historical bent, there is Cumaná, east of Colorado, where a fortified Spanish castle, San Antonio, and graceful colonial houses recall the heritage of the oldest city in Venezuela—some historians say the oldest in South America. At twilight when the coastal heat subsides, Cumaneros, in a time-honored custom, promenade along the tree-shaded Manzanares River that meanders through the town. Unlike Caracas or Maracaibo, no one here seems to be in a hurry.

A short ferry ride from Cumaná, skirting the salt flats of the Península de Araya, lies a favorite Venezuelan resort, the island of Margarita, where Christopher Columbus long ago fished for pearls. Hills of oyster shells surround the fishermen's huts at the end of long expanses of white beach (although many of the pearls sold locally are actually artificial Japanese). Blessed with a richly varied flora and fauna, Margarita also boasts some splendid colonial churches and castles from a colorful past of pirates and Spanish dons. The sleepy fishing villages that cluster along the northern part of the island might be mistaken for somewhere in the southern Mediterranean.

In contrast, no visitor to the "llanos" ever doubts the distinctly South American character of the horizonless, undulating plains. Stretching across southwestern Venezuela, the "llanos" are a 20th-century Wild West, where tough "hombres" brave floods, a blazing tropical sun, mosquitos, sting rays, snakes and other wild animals to herd their Zebu cattle across a land that is unmarked except for an occasional Jeep track. The hardiest and most independent of Venezuela's different peoples, the "llaneros" have given the country some of its most colorful legends and exciting music and dances, including the "joropo," a spur-clacking cowboy stomp.

Here, as in many other areas of Venezuela, traces of Indian influence can be perceived, if only in the stern visages of the "llaneros" themselves. While it is true that Venezuela possesses none of the great pre-Columbian monuments of the other Andean countries, its Indian tribes have contributed to the country's social make-up, folklore and art. Most of the fierce Carib Indians who inhabited the coastal lowlands were exterminated by, or inter-married with, the early Spanish settlers, but even they left their mark on Venezuelan customs. María Leonza, an Indian fertility goddess, is still worshipped with a pantheon of lesser notables in a national park near Maracay west of Caracas in a mixture of Roman Catholicism and pagan rites. In Caracas she pacifies both the jilted lover and the enraged motorist from her flower-strewn pedestal on the dividing line of one of the busiest freeway stretches, near the national university. Riding a tapir and carrying a man's pelvis aloft, the enormous, naked Indian princess is an unforgettable apparition looming out of the city haze.

Venezuelans also honor their Indian heritage in a popular con-temporary series of gold coins depicting the heads of the eighteen Indian "cacique" chieftains who fought the Spanish. But it is in the art of weaving that the country's surviving Indian tribes have con-tributed most to Venezuelan culture, from the glorious, neon-bright tapestries of the Guajiro Indians to the king-sized fiber hammocks of the Waraos, as beautiful in their simplicity as they are enduring in their sturdy workmanship.

The range of Indian cultures is as varied as Venezuela itself, the socially sophisticated Guajiros contrasting with the fierce Montilones, who still occasionally attack white men along the Venezuelan-Colombian frontier, and the peaceful Indians of Curiapo who dwell in houses built on stilts in the Orinoco Delta.

Colonial History

Similarly fashioned Indian huts along Lake Maracaibo prompted the New World's most famous map maker, Amerigo Vespucci, to call this wild land Venezuela, or Little Venice, after the narrow canals and floating houses of the Italian city. Vespucci sailed to Venezuela on an expedition headed by Alonso de Ojeda a year after Columbus had claimed Venezuela for Spain on August 1, 1498, during his third voyage to America. The expedition traveled far beyond the Orinoco Delta, which Columbus had explored, to the Gulf of Venezuela on the northern coast of Lake Maracaibo.

During the first 30 years after the discovery of Venezuela there was little effective exploration or colonization by Spain. The explorers' activities were confined primarily to the search for gold and pearls and to hunting for slaves on the northeast coast. A few settlements were established but promptly abandoned when they became unprofitable. The first extensive explorations were made by Germans when in 1528 Charles V mortgaged Venezuela to the German banking house of Welser. The Germans were primarily interested in gold, and they spent the next generation in a hopeless search for mines, rich cities and the legendary land of El Dorado, the Golden One. Sir Walter Raleigh, the piratical consort of England's Queen Elizabeth the First, also explored Venezuela in the vain hope of finding El Dorado. The Welsers established a settlement where Maracaibo, Venezuela's second largest city, is now located, but eventually the venture was abandoned and their grant canceled in 1556. With no large gold or silver deposits to exploit, the Spaniards eventually turned to farming, subjugating the fierce Indian tribes as slave labor for large haciendas. By the end of the 16th century, 20 cities had been established along the coast and in the Andes, the most prosperous of which was Caracas, founded in 1567 by Diego de Lozada.

While Spain treated Venezuela as an afterthought for most of the colony's first 200 years, other European nations, such as Britain and France, developed a thriving contraband trade while the Dutch supplied the Venezuelans with black slaves in exchange for cacao and tobacco. The Africans intermingled early with the Spanish Creoles and Indians, producing a racial fusion that is apparent in two-thirds of today's population. Runaway slaves also set up their own communities east of Caracas in what is today known as the Barlovento region of Miranda State, preserving language and musical traditions into the 20th century.

The Venezuelans developed independent habits early. Administered by remote control, first under the Audencia of Santo Domingo in the Dominican Republic and then under the Viceroyalty of New Granada at Bogotá, the provincial government in Caracas ran its affairs pretty much as it pleased. Similarly, the six other Venezuelan provinces paid no attention to Caracas' supposed juridicial supremacy, and the local municipalities administered by their own "cabildos" resisted any interference from provincial officials. Attempts by Spain to bring the colony to heel in the 18th century through the political and economic dictatorship of the Spanish-controlled Caracas Co. only served to encourage Venezuelan resistance, and there were uprisings in 1749, 1797 and 1806 in reaction to the harsh Spanish rule. The Venezuelans also were deeply influenced by the new liberal intellectual movements in Europe and the successful French and American revolutions.

Most of the revolutionary activities in the early part of the 19th century were directed by Francisco de Miranda, son of a Caracas merchant. An idealistic patriot, Miranda finally brought his people to independence in 1811 when the confusion in Spain caused by Napoleon's invasion allowed the Creoles in Caracas to depose the Spanish governor. These were immediately joined by leaders from the other provinces, and together they set up a National Congress which declared Venezuelan independence on July 5, 1811. Though this first republic was short-lived (it lasted less than 10 months), July 5 is still celebrated as Venezuelan Independence Day.

Bolívar

After the collapse of the first republic, the leadership of the revolutionary movement passed to Simón Bolívar, Venezuela's greatest hero and the Liberator of Peru, Bolivia, Ecuador, Colombia and Venezuela. Simón Bolívar was born in Caracas of wealthy Venezuelan parents in 1783. Orphaned at an early age, he spent many years studying and traveling in Europe, where he was inspired with a mission to liberate his people from Spanish rule.

Bolívar played an active role in the 1811 independence and was second in command to Francisco de Miranda under the first republic. There followed years of war and frustration for Bolívar. Though he finally managed to liberate five Latin American countries, his great dream of uniting Venezuela, Ecuador and Colombia into "Gran Colombia" was a failure. Regionalism triumphed with the determination of the local elite to rule their own countries. Bolívar died a disillusioned man in Santa Marta, Colombia, on December 17, 1830. Venezuela remained a separate state.

Foundations of a Modern Democracy

Venezuela did not really achieve independence for another 125 years since it was ruled by a succession of unsavory dictators and a small landed aristocracy. There was almost no economic or social development during the 19th century. Not until oil was discovered in the Maracaibo region did the economy begin to prosper. From 1908 to 1935 Venezuela was governed by the most bloodthirsty dictator of them all, Juan Vicente Gómez, a semi-literate bandido known as "El Benemérito." It was during the brutal Gómez tyranny that the first generation of modern Venezuelan statesmen, known as the "generation of 1928," rebelled against the government's long repression. Jailed and then exiled, these young rebels returned to Venezuela after Gómez's death to become an important political force during the transitional period under Eleazar López Contreras and Isaias Medina Angarita, who opened the door to a modern democracy. Medina was ousted in a popular revolution in 1945 headed by Rómulo Betancourt and other leaders of the 1928 generation in cooperation with a group of young military officers. Founder of Acción Democrática (AD), one of Venezuela's two most important political parties, Betancourt was strongly influenced by the country's leading social novelist Rómulo Gallegos, author of *Doña Bárbara*. Gallegos was named president in the wake of the 1945 revolution and a series of far-reaching reforms were undertaken by AD.

The military had not lost its taste for power, however, and three years later, on November 24, 1948, the government fell. Yet another dictator, Major Marcos Pérez Jiménez, stepped forward to claim the Gómez mantle. A spendthrift who used Venezuela's oil wealth to build some of the continent's flashiest public works, including a mountaintop hotel perpetually shrouded in mist, Pérez Jiménez jailed or exiled most of the country's democratic leaders. His rule lasted a decade until he was overthrown in 1958; Venezuela at last was able to establish sound foundations for a modern democracy.

Rómulo Betancourt was elected president for a five-year period. He served his full term, and for the first time in Venezuelan history, in March of 1964, a democratically elected president delivered the reins of government to another freely elected president, Raul Leoni. AD was defeated in 1969, and the Social Christian Party COPEI took over, electing Rafael Caldera, a lawyer, as the new president of Venezuela. In 1973 Carlos Andres Pérez, the AD candidate, was elected to succeed Caldera.

Industrial Development

Betancourt's protégé, President Pérez is embarked on an audacious foreign policy to encourage other Latin American nations to follow the example of the Organization of Petroleum Exporting Countries (OPEC) in forming coffee and banana cartels. OPEC's chief architect, Venezuela has followed a strongly nationalistic oil policy since 1958, leading the Arabs in abolishing concessions and demanding a bigger share of the foreign oil companies' profits. The world's foremost petroleum exporter during the sixties, Venezuela has since fallen to third place in reducing production to 2.2 million barrels per day because of diminishing reserves. It continues to supply the United States with eight percent of its oil imports, mostly for consumption on the East Coast.

Because reserves will begin to run out in the mid-1980s, the Venezuelans are anxious to diversify their economy (oil exports still finance 86 percent of the national budget), and to that end the government is expanding iron, petrochemical, steel and hydroelectric output. In 1976, Venezuela nationalized the $4.7 billion foreign-owned oil industry.

Diamonds are another gilt-edged export. In 1976 Venezuelan diamond production was 849,572 carats, mostly from the Guayana Highlands. An estimated 10,000 prospectors have rushed to the Guaniamo River south of the Caicara del Orinoco, where they have staked out 107-square-foot claims, digging through six feet of mud each day in the hope of striking it rich. These miners account for 95 percent of Venezuela's diamond production, roughly a quarter of which is gem quality.

Social Problems and Cultural Diversions

Like the Spanish conquistadores who preferred gold mining to farming, Venezuela's new generations have deserted the countryside for the cities, lured by the promise of black gold. Massive migrations from farm to town have swollen the cities and reduced agricultural production to the point that Venezuela must import 50 percent of the food it consumes. Forty-one percent of Caracas' inhabitants live in slums, and public services and job opportunities are not keeping pace with a population explosion of 3.4 percent per year. Although the government devotes one-quarter of the national budget to education, three million children are not attending school.

Many of these problems can be traced to the long reign of dictatorships which squandered the country's wealth with no thought for schools or hospitals, even as late as the 1950s. But possibly because the Venezuelans have learned to value freedom so dearly, theirs is one of the most stable democracies on the continent despite these many social problems. Every five years the country goes on an enormous political binge to elect a new government in a six-month-long carnival in which every political persuasion, from the extreme right to the extreme left, campaigns freely. Over 90 percent of the voters turn out for these elections, standing in line all day if necessary in order to cast their ballots.

After politics, the Venezuelans' favorite sport is "beisbol," which is played on the beaches, in the parks and to packed stadiums. Bullfighting, "bolas criollas," cockfights, horse racing and dominos also are popular while soccer and jai-alai have a large following among the Spanish, Italian and Portuguese immigrants.

No matter what the Venezuelan is doing, watching a baseball game or standing in line for a bus, he keeps up a nonstop flow of conversation, jabbing the air and his neighbor to emphasize points which always are preceded by that hallmark of Venezuelan speech, "Mira, chico" (Look here, boy).

The exuberance of the Venezuelan's conversation spills into an innovative young theater and into his newspapers, which offer some of the best and liveliest reporting on the continent. But it is in the arts—painting, sculpture, architecture and music—that the Venezuelan best expresses the dynamism of a young nation on the move. Caracas' prize-winning Parque Central, for example, is not only a novel experiment in urban renewal but also an open-air museum of modern art, a city within a city where 4,800 people live, work and play among waterfalls and airy sculptures, hanging gardens and colorful murals. Designed by the young architects Siso, Shaw & Associates, Parque Central attempts to bring some order out of the city's Los Angeles-like sprawl. It also reflects an earlier, equally successful experiment in integrating the arts: Caracas' University City, designed by Carlos Raul Villanueva.

Due to its rapid growth, Caracas is a hodgepodge of styles. The modern architecture is often innovative, as in the twin-towered Simón Bolívar Center atop a minifreeway; fanciful, as in the 457-foot-wide "polyhedron" geodesic dome at La Rinconada racetrack; or plain silly, as the never-completed "helicoide" shopping center that curls around a hill like some crazy white snail. There is some neoclassic architecture, such as the Congressional Palace and the Church of San Francisco, and some heavy neogothic. But little is left of the colonial period except in the downtown section around the Plaza Bolívar and in La Pastora. (The best colonial architecture is located in other states.)

Colonial art is well represented in church altar pieces, such as Domingo Gutiérrez's work in the church of San Francisco and the parish church of Santa Lucia in nearby Miranda State. The colony also boasted some skilled gold- and silversmiths who melted down Mexican silver exchanged for Venezuelan agricultural produce. Among the best are Sebastián Ochoa, whose work can be seen in the church of San Francisco, and Domingo Vicente Núñez, who did the beautiful Eucharist in the church of Coromoto in Guanara, Portuguesa State.

Federico Brandt, a turn-of-the-century landscape painter, introduced French impressionism to Venezuela, and the school of Arturo Michelena, whose work is on exhibit in a colonial house in the La Pastora section, popularized the neoclassical style. But it was Armando Reverón, Venezuela's most beloved painter, who gave impressionism a peculiarly Venezuelan flavor by incorporating tropical light and color into his canvases in such a way that objects and people seem to float in a warm haze.

In the past three decades Venezuela has produced an amazing number of new artists and sculptors whose work has earned international acclaim. Venezuelan interest in the plastic arts stems in part from the cultural explosion that followed Pérez Jiménez's overthrow, but it also is due to the keen interest of individual Venezuelans, such as the Boulton family, who have amassed some of the finest art collections on the continent, including the best from Europe and Latin America. With discerning patrons who can afford to pay New York and Paris prices, it is no wonder that Caracas boasts so many outstanding galleries with stables of first-class artists.

From the "generation of '42" came free forms and kinetic and neofigurative art, as in the work of such top artists as Jesús Soto, Marisol Escobar, Carlos Cruz Diez and Alirio Palacios and, in sculpture, Francisco Narvaez, who uses local seashells and woods in his work. Alejandro Otero, Venezuela's leading abstractionist, is now into giant sculptures composed of such fragile materials as aluminum sheaves that change with light and wind, while Pedro Briceño is known for his heavy metal sculptures and Gego for her light metal mobiles. Tecla Tofano, Cristina Marchan and Seka

Severín have become famous for their delicately textured ceramics; Harry Abend carries on the colonial silversmith's art, but in modern sculpture and jewelry. Carlos Prada is best known for his figurative sculpture, and Hector Poleo continues the figurative tradition in painting. Among the best "naive" painters are Bárbaro Rivas, Feliciano Carvallo, Victor and Carmen Milláns and Elsa Morales. The newest sensation in the Caracas art world is Cornelis Zitman, who sculpts sultry, sensuous female nudes.

Some of Venezuela's most original new art comes from the Guajira Peninsula. Genius in residence is Luis Montiel, a local hero symbolizing a Guajiro renaissance whose work is represented in the museums of three continents. Discovered by the Venezuelan public after a one-man show in Caracas in 1969, Montiel weaves blazing tapestries that catch the peninsula's incandescent sun. His latest work, a 22 by 50 foot tapestry curtain, which hangs in Maracaibo's Theater of Fine Arts, is a major tourist attraction.

Venezuelan Food

Venezuelan food, contrary to expectation, is not fiery hot. Cumin and saffron are used in many dishes, but the distinctive and delicate flavor of most of the popular dishes comes from the use of local roots and vegetables. Though the tourist in Venezuela may dine on anything from *filet mignon* to American hot dogs, he would be wise to treat himself to some of the following local specialties:

Tequeños—a popular hors d'oeuvres; thin dough wrapped around a finger of local white cheese and fried crisp.

Arepas—the native bread; a primitive cornmeal bun made of ground corn, water and salt. (Arepas date way back to the Indians, but typical of modern life anywhere, there is an "instant arepa mix" on the market.) Arepas are prepared differently in various parts of the country, but generally they turn out crisp on the outside and mealy-soft on the inside. They are often made with cheese inside. They are always served hot.

Tostadas—tostadas are arepas used for sandwiches. The mealy center is removed and the crisp shell is filled with anything from ham and cheese to spiced meat, chicken salad or cream cheese.

Guasacaca—a semi-hot relish used mostly with grilled meats. Made of chopped tomatoes, avocado, lime juice, onions and other spices.

Pabellon Criollo—a sort of hash made with shredded meat and served with fried plantains and black beans on rice.

Hallaca—this is a very popular local delicacy, eaten year-round but a traditional food at Christmas and New Year. It is a cornmeal mixture—the cornmeal is combined with beef, pork, ham and green peppers, onions, chick peas, raisins, olives, spices, etc., wrapped in individual pieces of banana leaves (tamale style) and cooked in boiling water. There are also chicken and turkey hallacas plus or minus some of the other ingredients. Hallacas vary widely, many cooks boast their own special recipes.

Parilla Criolla—beef, marinated and cooked over a charcoal grill. Traveling "restaurateurs" set up grills on street corners and serve this meat with yuca, all cut up bite-size, toothpicks as utensils. This meat is usually quite delicious.

Hervido—a soup made with chunks of beef, chicken or fish and native vegetables or roots.

Sancocho—quite similar to hervido but thicker in consistency. Not quite as thick as a stew. It is eaten with a knife, fork and spoon. The meat is cut into big pieces. The vegetables used are auyama (a local version of pumpkin), tomato, cabbage and whole sections of corn on the cob. The roots are ocumo, ñame, batata and yuca.

Purée de Apio—one of the more exotic local roots, boiled and puréed, salt and butter added; tastes something like chestnuts.

Other interesting dishes are *empanadas* (meat turnovers), roast *lapa* (a succulent, large rodent), *chipi chipi* soup (made from tiny clams), *mondongo* soup (a soup-stew made from tripe and vegetables).

Tropical fruits include lechosa (papaya), pineapple, guayaba, guayábana and mango.

EXPLORING VENEZUELA

Caracas, Venezuela's capital, is located about 12 degrees north of the equator. Founded in 1567 by Diego de Losada, it was christened Santiago de Léon de Caracas, after its patron saint.

The hub of business, cultural and every major activity in the country—except the oil industry—the capital is nestled in a long, narrow valley in the coastal mountain range just nine miles from the sea as the crow flies. At 3,164 feet above sea level, Caracas has one of the world's best climates. Springlike the year around, the temperature averages 68 degrees with a high of 85 degrees during April, May, September and October during the day and a low of 56 degrees at night during January and February. The rainy season is May through November. The rest of the year is usually dry.

The population of Caracas is cosmopolitan, the result of heavy immigration since World War II. There are now about 2,500,000 inhabitants in the metropolitan area, and the faces of Italians, Spanish, Portuguese, central Europeans and North Americans are as familiar a sight as those of the criollo on the streets of the city.

Modern architecture has brought about a change in the character of the city. Apartment buildings now outnumber the old colonial house, fast disappearing. Four- and eight-lane speedways cut the length and width of the valley and Caracas, which 15 years ago enjoyed sedate pleasures and an unhurried existence.

Due to its topography, the visitor will find that Caracas is bordered to the north by a high, green chain of mountains that run the length of its long, corridorlike valley and to the south by lower hills. The original center of Caracas is still the center of town, both geographically and commercially, and retains much of its colonial flavor.

Driving from the airport on the $6 million-a-mile *autopista*, the tourist enters Caracas through its western industrial area. Riding along the Avenida Sucre, he joins Avenida Urdaneta at Miraflores Palace and the Secretariat Building, Venezuela's seat of government, and will find himself on a modern thoroughfare lined with new office buildings.

To the north, in the shadow of tall blue mountains, lies the old colonial section called San José and La Pastora. Its narrow, sloping streets lead down to the heart of the city at Plaza Bolívar, a beautiful square shaded by tall trees and flanked by the old cathedral, the archbishop's residence, the historic *Casa Amarilla*, where the foreign ministry is located, and the municipal council building. Off to one corner is the capitol building, built in 90 days by President Guzmán Blanco in 1873 and used today entirely by Congress. This splendid building with its golden cupola has a beautiful tropical patio with orchids hanging from the trees. Don't miss the murals of national battles by Tovar y Tovar in the Salón Elíptico.

Sharp Contrasts in Caracas

Contrasting sharply with this colonial scene are the twin towers of Centro Simón Bolívar rising 30 floors above the street. This building complex, costing over $180,000,000, is a mammoth commercial and business area, crisscrossed with underground ramps for automobiles and pedestrians, shops, restaurants and recreational area. A large seven-block commercial and residential development flanks this area, replacing what must have been the world's worst slums.

Several blocks north of the Plaza Bolívar, the National Pantheon rises in tribute to the heroes who have found their final resting place therein. It is here that the remains of Bolívar are entombed.

Leaving the colonial center of the city, the tourist becomes aware of the ultramodern development of Caracas. Through San Bernardino, he heads east along Avenida Andres Bello, winds through the Country Club and enters La Castellana, Altamira and other sumptuous residential areas. Returning back along the Avenida Francisco de Miranda, he will find himself in a smart shopping area and, leaving this, he will see Plaza Venezuela, where new skyscrapers are rapidly being built, even taller than the

Centro Simón Bolívar. South of the plaza is University City, a 400-acre center of learning dotted with futuristic buildings, halls and student residences. West of the plaza is Parque Los Caobos, a bower of mahogany trees that once gave shade to coffee when it was a plantation. The museums of fine arts and science are located at the western end of this park.

Undergoing its tremendous transformation, Caracas presents a startling and often bewildering picture to the tourist. In the eastern part of the city, where peons drove cattle just 20 years ago, sophisticated Caracas residents now sip coffee and cocktails in chic sidewalk cafés in the best Continental manner. The hillsides are filling up with fine homes as dozens of new developments cut into the mountains.

A complete bird's-eye view of the valley of Caracas can be had from the heights of Mount Avila just behind the city. It can be reached by cable car from the city and from Macuto. The tourist will find a large dining room and recreation center at the top, an ice-skating rink, a luxury hotel and swimming pool. Paths winding down into cloud-forest country lead to the community of Galipan, Caracas' flower-growing center just a mile or two away.

Other Spots of Interest

Casa Natal—Simón Bolívar's birthplace and family home. A charming colonial residence in the heart of Caracas. Many historic relics from his childhood, his youth and military life are preserved here. He was baptized at the fountain in the center of the indoor patio. Some of the house's walls are decorated by Tito Salas, famous Venezuelan painter. They celebrate various aspects of his military campaigns and his private life. This National Monument is located between the street corners of San Jacinto and Traposos. Open every day except Monday.

Bolivarian Museum, located alongside the Casa Natal, preserves the relics of the Conquest, Colonial and Independence epochs. Also open every day except Monday.

Colonial Art Museum. The former suburban residence of Marquis del Toro. It is located on the Avenida Panteon in San Bernardino, a few minutes from the center of town. Situated high on a hill, this huge colonial mansion withdraws from the modern world around it. Within its walls the tourist will find a vast collection of Venezuela's colonial past in oil paintings, furniture, oratory chairs, tapestries, books, etc. These relics are not from the original house, but from the era. The house itself with its red tile floors, its indoor gardens, its private patios is a sight the tourist won't want to miss.

The Cathedral, first built in 1595, was reconstructed in 1876. Situated in front of the Plaza Bolívar, it is of a plain colonial style, but the interior is imposing. Paintings by Rubens and Michelena.

Quinta Caracas, across from Congress, where painters work at easels in a colonial patio. The Venezuelan Tourism Corporation sponsors arts and crafts exhibitions here, also an office that provides information on free cultural activities in the city.

St. Francis Church, constructed in 1574. It has three magnificent naves with carved wood altars. It was in this church in 1813 that Bolívar had the glorious title of "Liberator" bestowed upon him.

National Library, located in front of the Capitol on the new University Avenue. It has large and diverse collections of over 300,000 books and publications, many from the 16th, 17th and 18th centuries.

Parque del Este, located in the eastern end of the valley of Caracas. Acres of beautiful tropical trees and plants; orchids hanging from the trees, artificial lakes (one for boating, the others smothered with water lilies), a zoo, an excellent aviary, playground areas, baseball and soccer fields, snack bars, etc. A little surrey-topped train winds through the park on weekends.

El Pinar Park, situated at Cota 905 in El Paraiso, is worth a visit. Rustic kiosks and winding footpaths transform this part of the city into a very pleasant promenade area. There is a very fine zoo in this park.

El Calvario, located on Calvary Hill. It has at its entrance the Arch of the Federation constructed under the administration of President General Joaquín Crespo. The park has a zoo and botanical gardens and overlooks Caracas and the El Silencio section.

University City. Architect Villanueva designed the UCV complex in flowing concrete. The 400 acres were a plantation 30 years ago; the sugar mill and Ibarra hacienda remain on the hill. Look for works by Laurens, Arp, Pevsner and Leger and for the giant Calder floating discs in the Aula Magna theater. Some 50,000 people come to the campus daily. Beside, but not part of, the university is the 175-acre Botanical Gardens, with paths winding among desert, marsh and savanna gardens to a forest where vanilla orchids climb giant trees.

Agustín Codazzi Aquarium. Fine collection of river fish, caribes and electric eels set in a garden of birds in Urb. Colinas de Carrizal on Los Teques Highway. There is also a train to the park with stations decorated by Cruz Diez.

Cable Car. In 12 minutes the "teleférico" lifts you from Maríperez Terminal to Mt. Avila, 6,925 feet above sea level. A round trip costs Bs. 4, and there is service from 7 a.m. to 11 p.m. except during annual overhaul June–July. The longer coastal teleférico takes you in a stunning descent to Galipán, San José and El Cojo; Bs. 8 round trip and service until 10:30 p.m. The combined system covers 6.5 miles and was built at a cost of $24 million. There are many fun, informal fish restaurants near the beach terminal.

Banco Central Coin Collection. The history of Venezuela through Spanish pieces of gold. Royalist coppers, patriot silver coins and modern "doblón." On Esq. Carmelitas.

Concejo Municipal. Historic City Hall, Plaza Bolívar south. Venezuela's independence was declared here. See Tovar's famous painting of same. Also the flag Pizarro took to Peru and a collection representing turn-of-the-century Caracas in humorous, miniature figures in Museo Criollo Santana. Open daily 9–12 and 2–6.

Military Circle. There is an interesting cloverleaf drive in the form of the initials of ex-dictator Perez Jimenez. Swimming pool, lake, theater, gym and stables are open to civilians. Tourists pay Bs. 1; guided groups, $1.50 per person by arrangement. Los Proceres esplanade with fountains, statues is dedicated to the Founding Fathers.

Cuadra Bolívar. This is the beautifully restored home of the Bolívar family where the young Simón read, conspired with friends and rode by a pristine Guaire River. The tamarind tree in the garden comes from the Santa Marta hacienda where Bolívar died in 1830. Six blocks south of Centro Simón Bolívar, Piedras a Bárcenas. Tues.–Sun., 9–12 and 3–6.

IVIC. To see the hilly hideout of the national scientific research station, call Sra. Marina, 69-19-41, for a visiting day pass (first and third Saturday of every month). Besides reactors, there are art works by Soto, Marisol, Otero, Valera. Los Teques Highway, Km. 11.

Miraflores Palace. Built by Gen. Jaoquín Crespo in the 19th century as a residence, Miraflores is now used as the president's office. Lovely interior patio. Call 81-08-11, Ext. 235, for Sunday visiting pass (1–5 p.m.)

La Casona. Residence of Venezuela's president, it is open for visits on Wednesday afternoons. Call 361261 for appointment to see this lovely restored hacienda house in La Carlota. Excellent collection of Venezuelan art and magnificent gardens flanked by towering palms.

Transport Museum. Treasury of trains and vintage cars across the bridge at Parque del Este. Wed., Sat., Sun. and hols., 8–6.

La Rinconada Racetrack. Reputed to be one of the world's most luxurious tracks. Racing Sat., Sun. and national hols. begins at 1 p.m.

Excursions from Caracas

La Guaira. Ten minutes from Caracas' international airport at Maiquetía, Caracas' busy port also is a colonial treasure house steeped in history. Plaza Vargas, with its statue of José María Vargas, a Guaireño who was Venezuela's third president, is a good place from which to begin explorations. It is bounded by Calle Bolívar, which runs between the principal highway and the mountain. Lined by the cool and cavernous warehouses of another century's trade on one side and by the one- and two-story houses with their colonial windows and red-tiled roofs on the other, the street funnels the sea breezes like voices from a more gracious age. In 1969 Calle Bolívar and Calle León, a narrow street descending from the mountain to join Calle Bolívar a block east of Plaza Vargas, were repaved, the houses repainted and restored.

Behind the 17th-century Customs House rises Casa Boulton, a tall house with generous wooden beams and an ample balcony jutting over the narrow street. Inside is a treasury of maps, paintings, pistols, documents, pottery and miscellanea pertinent to the life and history of the port since its founding in 1589 that have been collected by the Fundación John Boulton. The early 18th-century house has been occupied for more than 140 years by the Boulton family. A young Englishman from Lancashire, John Boulton came to Venezuela at the age of 20 in 1826 and was soon in business in La Guaira exporting coffee, cacao, tobacco and indigo and importing flour, oil and brandy. Sometimes ships arrived to pick up cargo and not having a full load brought a ballast of stone from Scottish quarries. The floors of the old Boulton house, as well as a number of other colonial buildings, are paved with partly Scottish stone which has been smoothed by generations of users.

Ships of the Boulton-Dallet line (the Red-D Line), first sailing ships and then in the 1880s steamships, helped to make La Guaira the country's richest port. The Dallets were the Philadelphia partners of the Boultons.

Beach Resorts at Macuto, Marbella, Naiguatá and Los Caracas.

Colonia Tovar. Forty miles from Caracas over the mountains lies a bit of Bavaria at Colonia Tovar. With a cool spring climate year round, this is a favorite weekend spot for Caracas lowlanders. Settled by German immigrants in 1843, the village was isolated for most of a century and thus conserves old German customs. Alpine gardens, excellent German food and handmade ceramics.

Miranda State. Named for the Independence leader Gen. Francisco de Miranda, this state curves east around the Federal District to the sea, holding the capital like a cup and including a large slice of greater Caracas. Once a village, Chacao has long been part of the city, and every year new suburbs grow up around Petare, Baruta, Sartenejas and El Hatillo, spreading the urban boundaries of metropolitan Caracas.

Industry takes advantage of the nearby city and rural space to build plants in Los Teques, Guarenas, Ocumare and Charallave, but on the whole Miranda is an agricultural state. In

Guatire, Santa Teresa, Caucagua, Ocumare and Cua, the crops
are cacao, citrus fruit, pawpaw, avocado, pineapple, bananas,
coffee and sugar cane.

There are two roads to Los Teques—the fast Panamericana,
leading from the Autopista del Valle; and the old road, reached
by the Autopista to Caricuao and Antimano. Hacienda Macarao,
the colonial farmhouse once belonging to Antonia Bolívar, sister
of the Liberator, still stands among the cabbage patches outside
the little village of the same name. Turn right at Las Adjuntas,
3.3 miles from Antimano to visit the INOS reservoir and 50,000-
acre wooded tract. To enter the forest you must bring a written
pass from Caracas (INOS, Edif. La Paz, Av. Andres Bello).

Los Teques, 30 miles from Caracas, is the capital of Miranda
and the site of many historic battles. Artist Arturo Michelena lived
on Ayacucho Street, where he painted his famous "Last Supper."
Today, artists and many people who work in Caracas prefer to live
in the cooler, hilly towns of Los Teques and neighboring San
Antonio and San Diego de los Altos. Knoop Park on the grounds
of the old railroad station has swings for children and trees and
tables for picnickers and a Casa Cultural museum.

Retracing the Panamericana, you come to Carrizal on a turnoff
3.3 miles before Los Teques. Follow the picturesque road to San
Antonio de los Andes, a flowering Andean village, and stop at the
Murano glass factory, a New World branch of the famous Italian
glassblowers.

Forty miles southeast of Petare, at the eastern end of the
Caracas valley, is Guatopo, Miranda State's national Park. Heavily
forested, Guatopo's slopes rise to almost 5,000 feet, giving birth
to countless streams that feed the Guanapito and Lagartijo reservoirs. The Ministry of Agriculture has built a nucleus of facilities
at Agua Blanca, where an old sugar mill still stands. There are
shelters, bathrooms, picnic grates and bathing pools. For bird
watchers, botanists and bug hunters, this is a favorite sanctuary.
Beyond Agua Blanca lie the ruins of an old hacienda called
Casupito, on the river of the same name, and Santa Crucita, where
tourists can picnic and camp beside a lagoon. Information about
points of interest and hikes to the Morro de Apa lookout can be
obtained at the Park headquarters and guest house 50 miles from
Santa Teresa on the Altagracia road which starts at Petare.

Los Llanos

Venezuela wears its major cities like a string of pearls along its
coast. It is in this area that the majority of Venezuela's citizens
live, and it is here that most of the industry, agriculture and commerce is carried on. Nevertheless, the criollo proudly points west,
south and east and declares that "this is the real Venezuela."

The city of San Juan de los Morros, gateway to the *llanos*

(plains) lies about 84 miles southwest of Caracas. The typical llanos lie in the State of Guárico but spread over into the states of Barinas, Portuguesa, Cojedes, Apure, and even Miranda (Hotel Campomar located here).

The national dance of Venezuela, the *joropo*, is from the llanos. The locale of Venezuela's most famous novel, *Doña Bárbara* by Rómulo Gallegos, is also laid here. Skilled horsemen ride its 108,989 square miles just as they did during the wars of independence. Stoutly independent, the *Llanero* (plainsman) has persistently remained outside the influence of the currents of progress. His life is cattle raising. Hardened by outdoor life, he rises before dawn and, with only a cup of black coffee in his stomach, spends the day in the saddle until sunset, when he climbs into his hammock to sleep after a spartan evening meal.

The Llanero has two enemies. The first is the capricious weather with its alternate floods and droughts and the second is *el tigre*, the jaguar which stalks his cattle. Naturalist Ernst Schaeffer says ". . . the jaguar is the classical animal of the llanos. I know no other one that excites the same way and causes so much terror among young and old, among brave and cowardly. He is not spoken of in other than the singular as If one were dealing with one of those ancient Indian gods that has retreated before the invasion of unbridled greed, riotous music of the radio and the reek of gasoline into the heart of the deep jungle . . ." The Llanero frequently hunts the jaguar with only a shotgun.

The Llanero shows his horse-riding prowess during frequent rodeos. The chief event is called *toros coleados* in which a Llanero on horseback gallops past a steer, grabs it by the tail and flips it off its feet. Rodeos are accompanied with huge *parrillas* or *asados* (barbecues) with dancing to joropo music. The typical dress of the Llanero on these occasions is the white linen *liquiliqui* (pronounced leeky-leeky), a simple two-piece suit with military collar and studs, a Stetson-type hat and low-heeled boots. The music is played by a *conjunto* composed of *cuatros* (four-stringed instruments half the size of a guitar), a harp (miniature, without pedals) and maracas.

No other landscape in Venezuela seems to produce such a profound impression on the imagination as do the llanos. From the road are visible strange rock formations, now national monuments. Here also are the country's largest marble quarries.

Los Andes

The Venezuelan Andes rise like islands out of the tropical lowlands that surround them. Located in a northwestern part of the country, no other place in Venezuela offers such an opportunity to see varied landscapes in such strong relief.

This region of snow-capped mountains, sparkling rivers and high lakes makes up the states of Táchira, Mérida and Trujillo. In the state of Mérida, which produces the best coffee in Venezuela, the leading and largest city is its capital, also named Mérida. This city of tiled roofs is a colonial gem which houses the University of the Andes, founded 170 years ago. Jají, a colonial town 30 miles from Mérida, is worth a visit.

Lofty Pico Bolívar pushes its white summit 16,427 feet into the sky. It is the highest point in Venezuela and, along with a half dozen other peaks over the 15,000-foot level, forms the Sierra Nevada National Park in the heart of the Venezuelan Andes. You can ski here from June through November at an altitude of 14,000 feet—for the hardiest only!

Folklore of the region is maintained in the colorful clothing of the Andean farmers which they use during yearly festivals. The "Andino" (Andean) is astute, tenacious and a hard worker. He is strong because his environment will not allow the weak to survive and he is either a friend or an enemy because he is straightforward and does not split loyalties.

Nearby in Estanques in the lagoons, fishing is nearly an obligation. Most of these lakes are easily accessible and offer excellent trout. One of the best is Mucubaji Lagoon. Camping facilities are available at Mucruba on the shore of a crystalline river.

In the spa area near the Colombian border is San Cristobal, site of one of the largest bull rings in South America. Many festivals are held here.

Local delicacies include Saint Benedict Pie filled with meat, trout, milk candies called "brillantes" and wheat arepas. Try the local drink, "mistela," made from honey and spices.

Western Venezuela

Western Venezuela holds the pot of "black gold" that brought wealth to the nation. Its largest city is Maracaibo, capital of the State of Zulia and oil capital of the country. It is located on the shores of Lake Maracaibo, which is not so much a lake as it is a river, according to geophysical experts. Hundreds of rivers drain from the Andes in the south and the Sierra de Perija in the west and settle in the lowest part, forming the huge body of fresh water. This water flows northward and drains into the Caribbean. The water around Maracaibo itself is slightly brackish. Gen. Urdaneta Bridge overlooks 10,000 oil towers on the lake's surface.

Maracaibo received its name, according to legend, after a battle between the Conquistadores and an Indian tribe led by their chief, Mara. Upon defeating Mara and his tribe, the Spaniards jubilantly cried out "Mara cayó" (Mara has fallen) which finally became Maracaibo. The name is today synonymous with oil.

The "Maracucho" (slang name for a native of Maracaibo) does not apologize for his weather. It is hot, very hot. But he likes his city and state. Despite the heat, the Maracucho is active and aggressive in business, preferring to make money rather than to dabble in politics. He loves sports, is an avid baseball fan and fond of giving his children elaborate names. Maracaibo is now famous for its Prieto quintuplets.

Not far from Maracaibo are two of the most fascinating Indian tribes in the country. They are the Guajiros, a nomadic, cattle raising tribe, and the Motilones, fierce killers.

The Guajiros, maintaining a thin veneer of Spanish Catholic teaching, are a nation, with more than half of the people living on the Colombian side of the Guajira Peninsula. They are of medium height, copper complexion and have jet black, straight hair.

When dressed for visiting, the male wears a large, many-folded breechclout, a bright mantle, immense sash, a necklace and headband of feathers. The woman wears a "manta," a black or printed cotton dress which reaches her ankles, and a "puna," long strings of colored beads that pass over both arms and cross each other on the breast and back. These are held by a "sirapo," a belt of black beads. They paint their faces various hues to protect them from the sun and mosquitoes.

The Motilones have been hostile to the white man almost since the first Conquistador pushed back the Indians' territory. For centuries they were constantly at war with encroaching colonizers, and not more than a dozen tribes are reported to be in existence now. They made frequent retaliatory raids on white attackers who burned their villages, and the name "Motilon" became synonymous with any wild Indian of the region. During oil explorations, more than one geologist succumbed to their arrows. Recent efforts to pacify the Motilones have met with considerable success, and even tourists may now see Motilones at the Tucuco Mission near Machiques, a three-hour drive south of Maracaibo. Thirty miles north of Maracaibo at Sinamaica Lagoon, another Indian tribe, the Goaro Indians, live in primitive lake dwellings much the same as those observed by the first conquistadores.

Maracaibo is bounded by beaches and modern resorts. Among the most popular are Caimare Chico, 53 miles from Maracaibo; Las Palmas and Santa Fé, where native dishes made with fish are served; Las Mercedes, a short distance from Maracaibo; Lago Mar Beach; and the lovely islands of Toas and San Carlos.

Eastern and Southern Venezuela

This, the biggest and most sparsely populated area of Venezuela, represents what many believe to be the economic future of this already wealthy nation. Made up of five states (Anzoátegui, Monagas, Sucre, Nueva Esparta and Bolívar) and two territories (Delta Amacuro and Amazonas), the area covers some 206,000 square miles of plains, seacoasts, jungles, savanna and highlands—59 percent of the total area of the country.

It was here that Columbus first landed and the Spanish made their first settlements. Today's principal seaport is Puerto La Cruz, the gateway to Eastern Venezuela. The beaches along this coast are unexcelled. Dotted with islands and inlets, the water is incredibly blue, and the sands on the beaches range from pure white, through pink to golden and black. Other coastal cities are Cumaná, founded in 1521, the first Spanish settlement in America (then called Nueva Granada), and Carupano, established in 1647. Cumaná is a seven hours' drive from Caracas and may also be reached by air. Among the city's many colonial attractions are San Antonio Castle, a classic 17th-century fortification; Santiago Castle, completed in 1625 near the Araya salt mines to defend them from pirate attack; Santa Inés Church with a statue of Cumaná's patroness; Quinta San Isidro, where Bolívar lived; and the "Correo del Orinoco," where one of South America's first newspapers was published.

Northeastern Venezuela has become a highly popular tourist area, with good hotels in Cumaná (Comanagoto, Los Bordones), Carupano (Copey), Puerto La Cruz (Meliá) and Barcelona (Neverí). In Monagas, Guacharo Cave offers the adventurous great underground beauty. The nearest hotel is in Caripe (Guacharo), 30 miles away. You may want to experiment with some of the local dishes: Cumanese Pot, box turtle in a garlic, spice and pepper sauce; Carúpano mussels; "empanadas de cazón," pies made from small shark; and pickled coastal fish.

Margarita Island

Margarita Island is the principal island in the island-state of Nueva Esparta and lies 18 miles off the coast directly north of Cumaná. (There are daily ferry connections with Cumaná, Puerto La Cruz and Guanta. Bs. 40 per car and Bs. 20 per passenger.) The other two islands of this group are Coche and Cubagua. On Cubagua are found the ruins of *Nueva Cadiz* destroyed in 1550. Margarita is on the way to becoming a tourist attraction in the Caribbean. Settled by the Spaniards in the 1520s, the towns of Pampatar, Porlamar, Asunción, Juan Griego and El Tirano sprang into being. It was a haven for pirates along the Spanish Main and several well-preserved forts remain as silent witnesses to the island's historic past.

Lack of natural water, except for some springs, long limited the growth of the island, until an 18-mile undersea aqueduct was inaugurated to bring water from the Carinicuao River in the State of Sucre. Half a dozen new hotels have been built, and more are coming. The island has been turned into an International Free Port Zone. After a three-day stay you can buy a $1 permit, allowing you to purchase up to $200 worth of merchandise.

Margarita is the home of pearl fishing in the Americas. Its people have plied this trade for almost 500 years. Today, however,

Japanese cultured pearls have found their way into many shops here. Fishing is the only other important industry, plus limited salt processing. All of the salt in Venezuela comes from the sea and is harvested in Araya, Coche and Margarita. There are nice beaches at El Morro, Moreno and Pampatar.

Bolívar and the Orinoco

The capital city of the State of Bolívar is Ciudad Bolívar. Located on a mound of boulders, which form the heart of the old city, it lies 240 miles upstream from the mouth of the Orinoco River. It was formerly called Angostura because this is the narrowest part of the lower Orinoco, only two-thirds of a mile wide but over 300 feet deep. Much Venezuelan history was written in Angostura, once the capital. It was also the original home of Angostura Bitters, which later moved to Trinidad where, in the early days, it was easier to do business. The Angostura Bridge, longest suspension bridge in South America, opened here recently.

Ciudad Bolívar today is still politically the capital of the state, but industrially the booming city of Santo Tomé de Guayana, better known as Ciudad Guayana, is stealing the thunder. Founded only a decade and a half ago, the city is planned around the towns of Puerto Ordaz and San Félix at the confluence of the great Caroní River and the Orinoco. In the region are a hydroelectric plant, the gigantic Guri Dam project, an aluminum plant, the Orinoco Steel Mill (government owned), and the mill's river docks. Ore comes by train from the fabulous mountain of iron, Cerro Bolívar, 85 miles to the south.

In the dry season when the rivers in southern Bolívar state go down, gold and diamond free-lancers prospect feverishly, panning river beds. The most famous diamond found here was the Barrabas, a 155-carat stone discovered in 1942 and sold for $200,000.

Perhaps the most romantic part of Venezuela is found in the Gran Sabana, a tropical highland that begins midway down the state and runs to the Brazilian frontier. It is dotted with small communities with Indian or Spanish names among them Santa Elena, Icabaru, Kanavayén, Paraitepui and Uríman.

Truncated mountains rise from 7,000 to 10,000 feet like giant sentinels from the rolling savanna. One, Roraima, became the setting for Conan Doyle's famous novel "The Lost World." But the more famous one in recent years is Auyantepuy, from which drops the world's highest waterfall (3,212 ft.), over twice the height of the Empire State Building. These falls, discovered in the early 1930s by an American bush pilot, Jimmy Angel, are called Angel Falls.

Green Mansions of the Amazons

Puerto Ayacucho, the capital of the territory of Amazonas, still retains a frontier spirit found in very few towns today. Located near the northern extremity of the territory on the east bank of the Orinoco River, it is the typical tropical town that foreigners expect to see.

While the Government has constructed modern administration buildings, a hospital, school and a hotel in recent years, the remainder of the town is built in the traditional fashion that characterizes the region. Despite its location in the deep tropics, the town is clean, the water is good and its people are healthy. Malaria, yellow fever, smallpox, etc., have been completely eradicated.

Puerto Ayacucho is the gateway to the land of "Green Mansions" typified by Hudson and made into a moving picture which was filmed in part on location here and in Canaima. A well-surfaced dirt road leads south to a town called Sanariapo where it ends some 40 miles distant. From that point on, the more hardy visitor may engage canoes and continue on to Brazil through a joint waterway called the Casiquiare Canal which empties into the Rio Negro which, in turn, flows into the Amazon River. This canal was first recorded by Alexander Humboldt, the famous German explorer and naturalist.

Just outside of Puerto Ayacucho is a settlement of Piaroa Indians who live in typical "churuatas" or community houses made of palm fronds. A Franciscan mission nearby also tends several communities of Indians of various tribes, and Protestant missions dot the interior of the area.

For the angler, fishing in the upper Orinoco and its tributaries is superb. Indians use the net and with a single throw can take from one to two dozen fish of as many different varieties. There is a new river spa sponsored by the Venezuelan Tourism Corporation near Puerto Ayacucho called Pozo Azul.

The hunter will also find an interesting field for deer, lapa, tapir, jaguar, nutria and, if he chooses, boa constrictor and anaconda.

It might be well to advise the stranger that dangers in this area, as depicted in moving pictures, are greatly exaggerated.

Central Venezuela

Returning now to the central part of the country, in the area of Caracas, we find many beaches and resorts, easily accessible and enjoyable. West of Caracas, along a super highway, are the cities of Maracay and Valencia. Maracay, the capital of the State of Aragua, is primarily an agricultural community. In late years, however, it has become the principal training center for the air force. There are three airports in this fast-developing area.

Near Maracay, a paved road takes the visitor high into the maritime mountains to the north and into one of the most fascinating areas of the country from the scientific point of view. The Henri Pittier National Park, named for the naturalist of the same name, covers 210,000 acres of mountain forest land. It can be divided into three sections: rain and cloud forests, jungles, and wastelands. In this area are found the largest variety of insects, flora and fauna as well as ornithological specimens of any similar area in the hemisphere. At the end of the road lies Cata, a small, emerald bay that perfectly complements the rain forests.

Farther west, and skirting the shores of Lake Valencia, one reaches the city of Valencia, capital of the State of Carabobo and center of Venezuela's growing industry. The port for Valencia is Puerto Cabello, near which the nation has developed a petrochemical industry, a major dry dock and thermoelectric complex for central Venezuela. It is also the hub of a new railroad system and highway network. A $47 million highway to the coast links Valencia and Puerto Cabello, 22 miles away. There are many fine beaches nearby, such as Patanimo, Ganango and White, only 2⅙ hours from Caracas by car.

West of Caracas on the Caribbean coast, Coro is one of the oldest cities in the Western Hemisphere. It is developing into a tourist attraction with ferry connections to the Dutch islands of Curaçao and Aruba. Apart from its many colonial buildings, there are sand dunes on the outskirts of town.

South and west, along the Pan American Highway, are the towns of San Felipe, Barquisimeto and Carora all engaged in agriculture and cattle ranching.

For hunting, bird watching, nature tours or safaris inquire at the Venezuelan Government Tourist Office or at your local hotel.

Wherever you go in Venezuela, you will be constantly pleased by the contrasts—of mountain and sea, of Spanish traditions amidst futuristic cities and of primitive Indian villages only minutes from the continent's most modern petroleum industry. A 20th-century El Dorado where Jaguars zip along the superhighways and jaguars stalk their prey in distant jungles, Venezuela is a place of dramatic variety, discovered long since by tourists but still only half-explored.

PRACTICAL INFORMATION FOR VENEZUELA

CAPSULE COMMENTS. *Physical Features.* Four distinct geographical areas: the dense jungle lowlands surrounding Maracaibo, the high mountainous region covering the country's north and west, the unexplored Guayana highlands, and the flat grasslands beside the Colombia border running to the sea. In addition, and to the delight of visitors, Venezuela offers a 1,750-mile Caribbean coastline.

Climate. Caracas is pleasant to visit the year 'round. The weather is always springlike. Coolest months are December-February and many claim these are the most delightful. The lowlands are hot and the rainy season is from May to November. In the rest of the country—climate depends upon altitude.

Area. 352,150 square miles—6th largest in South America.

Rivers. Orinoco River, 1,600 miles long, is one of the world's largest in terms of water volume. Venezuela has more than 1,000 other rivers.

Waterfalls. Angel Falls—3,212 feet high is the highest in the world.

Peaks. Pico Bolívar, Sierra Nevada in the State of Merida is the highest peak in Venezuela. It is 16,411 feet high.

Population. 12.5 million. Caracas about 2,500,000.

Language. Spanish.

Archeological Attractions. Lake Valencia, Maracay Region.

Principal Industries. Petroleum (world's 3rd largest exporter), coffee, mining, agriculture, cattle, food processing.

WHAT WILL IT COST? You'll find some things, such as dining out, relatively less expensive than they are in the U.S., Canada or Britain; others, like French wine, more expensive. Just for the sake of comparison, here is a sample of some daily needs:

VENEZUELAN PRICE SAMPLER	
1 150-gram jar instant coffee	U.S.$1.99
1 lb. butter	1.12
1 head lettuce (imported)	2.00
1 dozen eggs	.86
1 bottle beer	.37
1 bottle Scotch	8.97
1 bottle local rum	3.88
1 lb. sugar	.13
1 snack-size cup of ice cream	.11
46-oz. can orange juice	.58
1 qt. fresh milk	.41
2½-lb. can SMA baby formula	3.54
Small jar of U.S. baby food (locally produced)	.15
1 tube of U.S. toothpaste (locally produced)	.78
1 box Kleenex	.43
1 bottle good wine, 720 ml.	12.54
Hair cut	2.32
Shampoo and set	4.65
One cinema ticket	2.32
Telephone call, local, 3 minutes	.10
Coca Cola	.22
Color film, 20 exposures	2.35
Picture postcards, each	.11
Air mail postage per letter	
inside Venezuela	.08
to U.S.	.17
Gallon of gasoline	.28
Package of cigarettes	.27

WHEN TO COME? There is very little variety in the weather in Venezuela, and so any time is acceptable for a pleasant vacation. There is a rainy season which lasts from about May through December, but the rain showers are usually brief and the countryside is splendid in its lushness. Temperature changes are due to altitude not to seasons. January through April is the most popular tourist season.

 FEASTS AND FESTIVALS. Every village and town in Venezuela celebrates the feast of its patron saint with typical dances, fairs, bullfighting, cockfights and sack and candle races, often in a week-long binge of drunken merriment. It is here in these provincial festivals that the tourist can best enjoy the colorful folklore that goes back in time to pre-Columbian Indians, African slaves and Spanish colonists. Among the outstanding:

January 1 and 2. Mérida, Mérida State. The Feast of the Birth of the Christ Child is celebrated in solemn religious processions, the singing of verses, local dances and much drinking of wine.

January 2. Coro, Puerto Cumarebo and Punto Fijo, Falcón State. A life-sized dummy called "Anacleto" is the principal attraction during celebrations of the "Day of the Businessman." Seated on a donkey, "Anacleto" is accompanied through the streets by costumed merrymakers who urge their fellow merchants to close shop and join the dancing and singing. Such typical dishes as cocuy (a type of hamster), tripe and goat are served during the festival.

February or March. Carnival (week prior to Ash Wednesday). All of Venezuela goes on a week-long bash that includes beauty queens, parades, floats and costume balls. This is not the time to come to Venezuela on a business trip. Caracas holds the wildest celebrations with balls in hotels, private clubs and public plazas in a true recreation of the Middle Ages' "dance of the flesh." It also is a festival in which the woman traditionally takes the initiative. Dressed as "Negritas," they are covered from head to foot in black—black leotards, black sweater, black gloves and black mask, on top of which are worn wigs, jewelry, gaily colored short skirts and bright scarves. Unchaperoned and unidentifiable, the "Negritas" move from party to party, circulating around the uncostumed, unmasked men. There is at least one suicide or crime of passion each year when wife or sweetheart insists on donning the "Negrita" costume. A less amusing carnival custom is balloons containing foul-smelling substances which are thrown at passing cars. A more traditional carnival is held in Carúpano, Sucre State, with parades, allegorical floats and a typical band called "Cachuchín Florido."

March 29. Le Cejita, Trujillo State. La Cejita is famous for its Good Friday procession called "Brotherhood of the Penitents" in which more than 300 hooded participants march through the town holding lighted candles.

Holy Week. Celebrated throughout Venezuela on Easter Sunday, the Burning of Judas Iscariot is a deep-rooted, often colorful custom. It usually is preceded by a religious procession, one of the most famous of which is Caracas' Nazarene of San Pablo, which begins and ends at the Santa Teresa Church next to the Centro Simón Bolívar. In another district called La Vega, a procession escorting the figure of Christ with hands tied to a column goes from the church to the office of the local prefect. After the priest knocks three times on the prefect's door, a prisoner from the local jail appears bound in chains in the role of the "thief." He is told that because Christ has singled him out, he is to be freed. After his chains are struck off, he joins the procession in repentant gratitude.

Judas has no such luck. A life-size doll dressed in the throw-aways of the local inhabitants, Judas often resembles some unpopular political figure or is accompanied by a female Judas. Seated on a street corner, he is villified throughout the afternoon, after which he is taken by donkey or bicycle to his pyre to the accompaniment of music. But before he is burned in a festive bonfire, there are contests, dancing and a "testamento," a poetry reading in which Judas and other unpopular persons are derided amidst much hilarity.

May 15. Bailadores and Lagunillas, Mérida State; Bocono and Jajo, Trujillo State. San Isidro is honored by the local peasants who build floats and arches adorned with native fruits. Venezuela's famous Maypole dances are performed by colorfully costumed men. Large quantities of "chicha," a local corn brew, are consumed.

Corpus Christi. Naiguatá. A beach resort east of the international airport at Maiquetía. Men of the village who wish to repay a favor dress in brightly colored costumes and wear grotesque masks as the "Dancing Devils of Naiguatá," shuffling, wheeling and jumping through the streets to the beat of accompanying drums.

San Francisco de Yare, Miranda State. This is one of the most colorful festivals celebrated near Caracas with costumed townspeople dancing in front of the church in an old Spanish tradition known as the "Dancing Devils." The locally made masks are delightful souvenirs that can be purchased from the dancers at the end of the ceremony.

June 24–25. Curiepe and Guarenas, Miranda State; Naiguatá and Caraballeda, Federal District; and Puerto Cumarebo, Falcón State. John the Baptist is honored in wild street dances accompanied by drum and "curveta" in a tradition that can be directly traced to Africa. (Many of the people who live in these towns are descendants of escaped slaves.) In the Miranda State towns, John the Baptist celebrations sometimes are accompanied by voodoo rites performed by Zombielike villagers who walk on broken glass or burn themselves with cigarette butts. In Naiguatá the "Drummers of Saint John" accompany dancers moving from house to house. In Puerto Cumarebo, all young women of marriageable age rise at dawn in order to break the white of an egg into a glass of water, a type of sorcery through which they expect to read their future. They also cut their long hair and bathe in the rivers or the sea in the belief that this ritual will improve the strength and quality of their hair.

June 29. Guatire, Miranda State. In the "Revel of St. Peter," the townspeople dance through the streets led by a man who is dressed in women's clothing and who carries a rag doll in a musical recreation of the legend of a Negress slave, Rosa Ignacio. The other dancers wear black sweaters with floor-length skirts, or "pumpá," with white handkerchiefs around their necks. They beat the ground to the rhythm of the music with "chapaletas," leather straps attached to their "alpargatas," or sandals.

July 14–17. Feast of the Virgin of Carmen. Celebrated with processions, folk dances and fairs in Mérida, Zulia, Trujillo, Guárico, Barinas and Falcón states. One of the most colorful festivals is held at Altagracia de Orituca in Guárica State, where costumed men, their faces painted black, dance to the rhythm of the drums.

Last week of August. Ciudad Bolívar, Bolívar State. Week-long festival including the Orinoco Fair, a five-nation Bolivarian singing contest, industrial and livestock fairs, contests for water skiing and trotting horses, calypso bands and local dances.

September 8. Margarita Island. This is a week-long festival honoring the Virgin of Margarita with religious processions and folk dances.

September 23–24. Maparari, Falcón State. Descendants of the Ayumán Indians honor Our Lady of Mercy in a half-pagan, half-Christian ritual known as the "Dance of Turas." The "Tureros," or musicians, play deer horns, flutes made from wild sugar cane stalks known as male and female turas and pierced maracas, which sound high and low notes in an act of exorcism.

November 1–2. Cumaná, Sucre State. An unusual game called "La Maluca" (The Afflicted One) is played by the populace in the local cemetery on the nights of All Saints and Souls Days. The game involves a type of punishment inflicted by a man with a towel rolled into a whip. As the singing begins, the man inside the circle of participants tries to slap with the twisted material whoever intervenes in the game. Local food and drink are sold near the game site.

November 18. Maracaibo, Zulia State. Agriculture and livestock fairs, religious processions and regional songs called "gaitas" in honor of the Virgin of Chiquinquirá, the patroness of Maracaibo better known as "La Chinita," or Young Girl. Humorous verse comments on current affairs sung to ukeleles and drums, the "gaitas" are played through January 6 in contests for the best songs.

December 16. Caracas. The streets of Caracas hum with the sound of roller skates from the first Mass of the Christmas season. Counterpoint carols are sung in the plazas, and the typical Christmas delicacy, "hallacas," is sold at corner stands. On December 24 all but the most infirm rollerskate to midnight Mass.

December 27. Naiguatá, Federal District. Men and women form two carousels representing "government" and "revolution" to do battle to the beat of music. The battle is concluded with an enormous dinner of regional dishes.

 HOW TO COME. When traveling to Venezuela, there are several air and steamship lines to choose from. The international air traffic may be appreciated by the fact that in a recent year more than 400,000 passengers entered or left Venezuela.

By air: VIASA flies Super DC-8 jets to Maiquetia (nonstop) daily except Mondays from New York, Miami, Washington and San Juan; flights from Canada anticipated. *Pan Am* flies from Los Angeles, New York, Miami, San Francisco; *Varig* from Rio and Miami; *Air Panama* from New York and Miami; *Delta* flies to Caracas via Maracaibo from Las Vegas, Dallas, New Orleans. *Iberia* from San Juan; *Avianca, AA, Iberia, VIASA* and *Lufthansa* from Colombia; *BA* and *VIASA* from Barbados.

From Europe: *KLM* from Amsterdam, Frankfurt, Lisbon, Madrid,

Zurich; *VIASA* from Amsterdam, Lisbon, Madrid, Milan, Paris, Rome and Beirut; *BA* from London; *Lufthansa* from Frankfurt.

BY SEA. From the U.S.—*Prudential-Grace Line*; *Royal Netherlands SS Co.* From Amsterdam, Le Havre or Bilboa, *Royal Netherlands SS Co.* From Mediterranean ports—*Italian Line, French Line* and Spanish ships "Cabo San Juan" and "Cabo San Roque." Margarita Island, Puerto Cabello and La Guaira have become popular cruise ports, with the following making recent visits: out of New York— *Holland American Line, Incres Line, Swedish American Line;* out of Florida—*German Atlantic Line, Costa Line, Norwegian Caribbean Lines* and *Sunline;* out of the West Coast—*German Atlantic Line. Chandris Line* out of Curaçao; *Cunard Adventurer* and *Ambassador* out of San Juan. *Linea "C"* and *Diamonaco Line* serve Trinidad-Caracas.

There are ferry connections between Falcón State and Curaçao and Aruba on the Swedish "Almirante Luis Brion," which carries 1,200 passengers and 40 cars the 100 miles in 3½ hours. The ferry leaves the Muaco dock near Falcón's capital, Coro, at 2 p.m. Tues.–Fri., returning the next morning. From the Guaranao dock in Punto Fijo, Falcón, at 2 p.m. on Sat. and Sun.

PASSPORTS, VISAS. Documents required are (a) valid passport, (b) ticket to destination outside Venezuela, (c) international smallpox vaccination certificate. *Tourist Cards:* Valid for 30 days, they can be extended to 90 days. They are issued to most nationalities through carrier airlines and steamship companies duly authorized by the Ministry of Development and International Affairs. Application forms and further information may be obtained from airline or Consulate office or the Venezuelan Tourist Office, 485 Madison Ave., New York 10022. Tourists arriving by ship and staying less than 24 hours do not require a passport. Tourists should NOT get a visa since a tax certificate will then be necessary to leave the country, a difficult procedure.

CUSTOMS. Tourists may bring in duty free their personal belongings, professional instruments, a typewriter, a camera, cigarettes and liquor for personal use in limited quantity and an automobile or motor cycle. Tourists bringing a car into the country should notify the Venezuelan Consulate. Visitors over 18 years of age may use their own country's driving license or an international license.

WHAT TO TAKE. If you are planning a trip only to Caracas, take the type of clothing you are accustomed to wear in spring or early summer. Caracas is a sophisticated city and does not look willingly on clothes generally described as "cruise line." If your trip takes you to the beaches, the latest in beach wear is in order. Shorts are not worn outside bathing areas. Slacks are worn during the day; pant suits are acceptable at dinner time, but long, California-style dresses are more fashionable. For dining out in the evening men should stay on the safe side and wear coats and ties.

On trips to Maracaibo and other coastal cities take light summer clothing.

If you are going to rough it in the interior, then bring along leather boots and khaki breeches, long-sleeved shirts or blouses, a sun helmet or rag hat, rain gear, mosquito netting, insect repellent. The rest you can obtain locally.

If you like golf, bring clubs. Anglers will find plenty of equipment here if anything goes wrong with their own. Hunters and fishermen may bring in equipment declared on arrival and taken with them on exit.

 HOW TO GET AROUND. Buses serve all of Caracas for 5–10¢ and run almost 24 hours a day. Buses are nearly every color of the rainbow and each color represents a different route. *Por puestos* (jitneys) cover most Caracas areas for 11¢–24¢; from airport to city, about $2.50 each, but you must wait until the cab is filled. Minimum taxi fare about $1.50; from airport to Macuto city, about $2.50 each. Taxi fares double after 10 p.m. Taxis charge a minimum of approximately $1.50; from airport to Macuto about $10. No tipping. But since they have no meters, arrangements should be made before entering. Taxi rates are posted at the airport.

There is daily service by Avensa and Aeropostal to major cities. "Sky Buy" gives tourists 17-day unlimited air travel within the country for $80.

Drive yourself cars are available from *Fiesta Car Rentals, Avis, Corporacion Venezolana del Motor* (VW) or *Hertz* for about $9.36 per day plus 9¢ per mi. Weekly $56.16. No tax.

Ferries now link Puerto La Cruz and Margarita Island. The run lasts 2 hrs. 45 min.; costs $4.50 deluxe, $2.50 tourist.

 MONEY. The monetary unit is based on the bolívar (Bs.) representing 100 céntimos. At press time, Bs. 4.30 = US $1. Hotels pay slightly less. Bs. 10.3 equals £1 sterling. Paper money comes in bills of: Bs. 5, 10, 20, 50, 100 and 500. Coins are as follows:

5 *céntimos*—a nickel coin about the size of a U.S. dime. Commonly called a *puya* or a *centavo*.

12½ *céntimos*—a nickel coin about the size of a quarter. This is called a *locha* or a *quartillo*.

25 *céntimos*—a nickel coin smaller than a dime, it is called a *medio*.

50 *céntimos*—a nickel coin about the size of a dime. It is called a *real*.

1 *bolivar*—a nickel coin about the size of a quarter, with milled edge and a portrait of Bolívar.

2 *bolivares*—a nickel coin slightly smaller than a U.S. half dollar.

 TIPPING. Tips are usually left to the client's judgment, but in the majority of restaurants and soda fountains 10 percent is added to the check. It is customary to leave another 10 percent on the table. Tip bellboys, chambermaids. In Caracas hotels tip as in the U.S.; less elsewhere. Taxi drivers are not tipped, unless they carry suitcases (2 for Bs. 4.50), while gasoline station attendants are.

HOTELS. The visitor has a choice of various first-rate hotels strategically located throughout the city and on a par with good U.S. hotels. In view of increased tourism, small hotels are cropping up throughout Venezuela like mushrooms. 10% increase in rates can be expected.

Rates given are for double room EP (room only), unless otherwise noted. In Caracas: *Deluxe* $29–$40; *First Class* $15–$20. Outside: *Deluxe* $20–$35; *First Class* $14–$20; *Moderate* $10–$14; *Inexpensive* $8–$10.

CARACAS

Deluxe

TAMANACO. Urbanización Las Mercedes. Located on the southern side of the Valley of Caracas; 600 rooms, pool, nightclub, restaurant, grill, bar, shopping and social centers. Cabaña club, pitch and putt golf, steambaths, gym. Golf, tennis at the hotel. Several rooms and suites have private, flower-decked terraces. This is one of the pearls of the Inter-continental chain.

CARACAS HILTON. A 426-room, 16-story jewel in the crown of that famous chain, on 7 acres. Among the many customary Hilton amenities are specialty restaurant, a terrace cafe, a rooftop supper club with entertainment, dancing, large pool, lively atmosphere. Underground parking, shopping arcade. Connected to Parque Central. The *Anauco Hilton*, an annex in Parque Central, offers 317 apts. ranging from day studios at $20 a day to 4-bedroom apts. at $43 a day.

AVILA. 122 rooms with phone, TV. Many with balconies; some with private garden. A quiet deluxe hotel in Urbanización San Bernardino decorated in elegant colonial style in the shady, wooded hills of the Valley of Caracas. One of the most charming hotels in South America. Formal dining room, bar with music, sun terrace, swimming pool. Golf privileges. Barber, medical services.

HOLIDAY INN. 200 rooms near Tamanaco. Pool, nightclub, restaurant, excellent shopping arcade.

EL CID. 52 air-conditioned efficiency rooms. Car park.

First Class

EL CONDE. Esquina El Conde in the heart of downtown Caracas. Businessman's hotel with 130 rooms with or without air conditioning. Bar.

CRILLON. Newer, 13 stories. Some handsomely furnished suites with terraces. 80 air-conditioned rooms, car park.

LA FLORESTA. Av. Avila, Plaza Sur, Altamira. 83 air-conditioned rooms. Restaurant, bar, swimming pool, car park.

RESIDENTIAL HOTEL MONTSERRAT. Plaza Sur Altamira. 64 clean efficiency flats near U.S. Embassy.

Moderate

CONTINENTAL ALTAMIRA. Convenient location for after dark fun. High-rise, terraced, 80 air-conditioned rooms. Cocktail lounge. Restaurant. Good value.

LAS AMERICAS. Calle Los Cerritos, Bello Monte. 72 air-conditioned rooms. Restaurant, bar, car park. Rooftop pool.

Inexpensive

KURSAAL. Calle El Colego, Esq. Casanova, Sabana Grande. 90 rooms, restaurant, bar.

LUNA. Calle El Colegio, adjacent to Kursaal. 82 air-conditioned rooms.

BROADWAY. Av. Casanova, 1 blk. from Centro Comercial Chacaito. 40 air-conditioned rooms, restaurant, bar, car park.

VEROES. Av. Urdaneta. 115 air-conditioned rooms in downtown area.

DEL COMERCIO. Esq. Pte. Soublette. Centrally located with 152 air-conditioned rooms.

Plans are under way for a 1,000-room *Hyatt Regency* on Av. Libertador, next to Centro Comercial Libertador. The Spanish *Meliá* chain also is constructing a 620-room hotel on Av. Casanova.

BEACH (LITORAL)

Deluxe

MACUTO-SHERATON. This luxury hotel has 541 balconied, air-conditioned rooms, a beach; 3 swimming pools and smart cabañas, golf and marine facilities at the adjacent Caraballeda Golf and Yacht Club, a rooftop nightclub, 3 dining rooms and 4 bars and the grandest ballroom in Venezuela. Completely refurbished.

Moderate

BAHIA-BY-THE-SEA. Los Corales. 42 air-conditioned rooms with swimming pool.

MACUTO. Simple accommodations, good restaurant, pool. Convenient to airport.

ROYAL ATLANTIC. Caraballeda. 20 rooms. Small, intimate Italian restaurant. Sheraton beach and pool privileges for small fee.

The *Melia* international chain should open by 1976 a 300-room luxury hotel in Caraballeda, next to the Macuto-Sheraton.

LOS LLANOS

BARINAS (Barinas). *Cacique.* 40 air-conditioned rooms. Restaurant, bar, pool. First class.
The government hotel chain Conahotu is rebuilding the *Hípico Llano Alto* to add 70 rooms. Moderate.

SAN FERNANDO (Apure). *La Torraca.* 42 air-conditioned rooms. Inexpensive.

WESTERN VENEZUELA

MARACAIBO (Zulia). *Del Lago.* Equipped with a healthy slice of the lake and a pool. Privileges at nearby golf club and adjoining yacht club and marina for water skiing, sailing and fishing. Coffee shop, terrace dining room, bar and Caroni Nightclub. 250 rooms. Deluxe.

KRISTOF. *Kristof.* In town. 170 air-conditioned rooms, poolside cabaña club, restaurant, bar and shops. First class.

CORO (Falcón). *Miranda.* 66 air-conditioned rooms, nightclub, pool, restaurant, bar and shops. First class.

MÉRIDA (Mérida). *Chama.* Central location, very well kept, beautiful surroundings. 58 rooms, restaurant, bar. Only Spanish spoken. Moderate.

La Pedregosa. 10 min. from city. One of the newer hotels. 144 rooms with bath and 25 chalets. Restaurant, bar, discotheque, beauty shop, boating, horseback riding, pool. Deluxe.

Prado Rio. At the foot of the Sierra Nevada near the picturesque city, 5,280 feet above sea level. Ranch style with 13 rooms in the main building and 43 single and double cabins. Swimming pool, playroom for children, soda fountain and bar. International restaurant. Bull ring. Fishing. World's highest cable car to nearby Pico Bolívar, temporarily closed however. Deluxe.

SAN JAVIER DEL VALLE (Mérida). A lovely valley with religious retreat 4 mi. outside of Mérida. *Valle Grande*, pleasant hotel with 37 rooms and cottages. Moderate.

SANTO DOMINGO (Mérida). *Moruco* is 7,000 feet high in the Andes, with an impressive mountain view, a cool, refreshing climate year around. Attractive rustic architecture, on the Swiss chalet style. Secluded, quiet. Excellent French cuisine. Trout fishing, riding and many open-air sports. Glass-enclosed swimming pool. 21 rooms with bath, fireplace and bar. Deluxe.

TOVAR (Mérida). 60 mi. from Mérida, the town has many charming colonial churches and, on outskirts, old sugar mills where the juice of the sugar cane is made into "papelón," or cones of brown sugar. *Hosteria Sabaneta* offers comfortable cottages. 28 rooms. Inexpensive.

SAN CRISTOBAL (Táchira). *El Tama.* Largest Andean city hotel, 1,000 feet above sea level. There are 313 rooms, all with private bath and terraces and 15 suites. Dining room specializes in Venezuelan and international cuisine. Bar-discotheque. Snack bar. Children's area, baby sitters. Private bull ring. Their large Olympic pool meets all standards for official swim meets. Special interest tours to where native handicrafts are made. Deluxe.

URENA (Táchira). *Aquas Calientes.* Located near Colombian-Venezuelan frontier. Ranch-style hotel with delightfully relaxed air, where birds fly in from the gardens to share the breakfasters' sugar bowl. Thermal pool and patio in each of the 30 air-conditioned rooms. Hotel uses cool, rock-spring water which also fills the hotel pool. Restaurant, soda fountain. Baby sitting. Free parking. Moderate.

BARQUISIMETO (Lara). *Hosteria El Obelisco.* 65-room motel with pool and convention hall. Moderate.

GUANARE (Portuguesa). *Coromoto.* 76 air-conditioned rooms, pool. Centrally located. Inexpensive.

TRUJILLO (Trujillo). *Trujillo.* Most peaceful hotel in small town, 3,300 feet above sea level. Built in 1955, the 42-room hotel is well appointed with bar, grill, dining room, swimming pool, shops and a handsome park. Children's playground.

CENTRAL VENEZUELA

VALENCIA (Carabobo). *Intercontinental.* City's newest. Boasts 173 air-conditioned rooms, 2 pools, convention hall and night-club. Deluxe.

Le Paris. Centrally located, with 120 air-conditioned rooms. Moderate.

PUERTO CABELLO (Carabobo).
Charming beach resort. *Balneario Guaicamacuto.* 12 air-conditioned rooms on beach. Moderate.

Balneario Canaima. 37 air-conditioned rooms and cottages; with pool, restaurant and bar. Moderate.

MARACAY (Aragua).
Conahotu's *Maracay*, with 178 air-conditioned rooms, large swimming pool, nightclub, shopping arcade and lovely tropical gardens, is an ideal place to relax. First class.

CHORONI (Aragua).
Lovely beaches and good fishing. *Alemania.* Small, German, good food. Inexpensive.

CATA (Aragua).
The most beautiful bay in Venezuela, 36 mi. from Maracay through orchid-strewn rain forests of Henri Pittier National Park. Cata. Family-style cabins; restaurant and bar. Launch rentals. Make reservations with any travel agent in Caracas. Moderate.

COLONIA TOVAR (Aragua).
Delightful mountaintop village settled by German immigrants in 1943. Descendants have preserved customs and language, food and Bavarian architecture. Pleasant weekend outing from Caracas.

Selva Negra. Black Forest architecture and blooming gardens. 35 rooms, pension style. Nightclub. First class.

Edelweiss. Small, 9-room hotel; good plain German food. First class.

Freiburg. 14 rooms, pension with meals. First class.

SAN JUAN DE LOS MORROS
(Guárico). Interesting hill formations and thermal baths. *Santa Monica* at entrance to town has 45 air-conditioned rooms, restaurant, bar, swimming pool and convention hall. Moderate.

HIGUEROTE (Miranda).
Wide beaches with an abundance of chipi-chipi (small clams) that make delicious soup; lovely parks and canals with interesting bird life.

Campomar. 22 air-conditioned rooms near beach with pool, restaurant and bar. Inexpensive.

EASTERN AND SOUTHERN VENEZUELA

PUERTO LA CRUZ (Anzoátegui).
Meliá Puerto la Cruz. Caribbean star of the Spanish chain, with tennis courts, golf facilities at Country Club and Yacht Club. 250 rooms, beaches, pool. Deluxe.

A $50 million tourist complex is being constructed between Barcelona and Puerto La Cruz on El Morro Peninsula. It is composed of Aquavilla, a sea-level area interlaced with canals, and El Morro, a peninsula with villas, aparthotels and a hilltop hotel nucleus with 1,200 rooms. A 1.3-mile cable car links El Morro with parking and transportation near the marina club on the coast and Bahía de Pozuelos, one of the world's largest natural bays, protected by a ring of islands that form part of the national parks system. The ruins of La Magdelena Fortress, an 18th-century Spanish castle on a hill west of El Morro, are being restored as a colonial museum, which also will be served by cable car.

PUERTO PIRITU BEACH. (Anzoátegui). Lovely beach resort near Barcelona. *Casacoima.* Inexpensive and charming, with 25 air-conditioned rooms.

CUMANA (Sucre). Colonial port founded in 1521. Oldest city in Venezuela. *Cumanagoto.* Conveniently located five minutes from airport and connected to Caracas by excellent roads, the hotel has 89 rooms, own beach facilities nearby and a pool and children's wading pool at the hotel. All water sports. Restaurant, coffee shop, snack bar, discotheque. Tours arranged into Cumaná. Fabulous beaches. Deluxe.

CARUPANO (Sucre). Beautiful beaches and famous carnival. *Playa Copey* with 28 beachside, air-conditioned rooms, bar, restaurant and nightclub. Moderate.

PORLAMAR (Margarita Island). *Club Puerto Esmeraldas* at Playa Moreno with 120 suites and swimming pool.
Bella Vista. The island's best. Informal. Wonderful location, adjoining art center. Protected beach, two fresh-water pools, all water sports. Two-wing building with 155 rooms overlooking bay. Patio restaurant. Deluxe.
Guaiqueri. Near Bella Vista. 70 air-conditioned rooms. Water sports equipment for rent. Pool and beach. Good bar, restaurant. Moderate.
El Cardon. Modern motel with 51 rooms on beach near airport. Inexpensive.

JUANGRIEGO (Margarita Island). Quiet fishing village with picturesque bay, flaming sunsets and nearby ruins of the Galera. *Motel Posada del Sol.* 12 cabañas. Call 2082 in Porlamar for reservations. First class.

Hyatt is planning an 80-room aparthotel and luxury hotel with shopping center, theater and convention hall at Porlamar. *Meliá* is completing construction of *El Morro Hotel.*

MATURIN (Monagas). State capital and departure point for Caripe Valley, where Chaima Indian descendents live near spectacular Guácharo Caves. Ritz 42 air-conditioned rooms, centrally located, nightclub.

CIUDAD GUAYANA, formerly Puerto Ordaz (Bolívar). *Intercontinental Guayana.* Overlooking La Llovizna Falls, 206 rooms fully air-conditioned; restaurant with music, dancing; cocktail lounge, informal restaurant, outdoor dining terrace. Pool, beauty shop, barber. Deluxe.

CANAIMA FALLS (Bolívar). One of the most beautiful expeditions in the world is accessible to the camper who travels to Venezuela. It is a week-long trip to the base of Angel Falls, whose waters drop more than twice the height of the Empire State Building off Auyantepui table mountain. By outboard launch up the Carrao River from Canaima, the trip is arranged by Dutchman Rudy Truffino (write c/o Avensa, Apartado 943, Caracas, or telephone 45-52-44). Rudy makes up his party of bearers from native Indians in the region. The usual price is $500 per person in parties of four or more.
Canaima. For those who want to enjoy the almost perfect beauty of the seven Hacha falls and the lagoon fringed with pink sands and palms (and, on the way there, fly past Angel Falls), but who cannot stand the strain of a safari, the camp at Canaima offers rustic but comfortable accommodations. All-inclusive

weekend, flight from Caracas and return, is $160. An experience not to be missed.

This area is accessible to the tourist by air from Caracas via Linea Aeropostal Venezolana. Round trip is approximately $100.

CARACAS RESTAURANTS. Caracas has a large variety of restaurants for all tastes and pocketbooks. It can be generally said that the price of food in Caracas is similar to that charged in New York, Los Angeles or Washington. In addition to restaurants, good food can also be had in the dining rooms and grills of several hotels, among which are the *Tamanaco*, *Avila*, *Hilton*, and *Potomac* in Caracas, the *Macuto-Sheraton*, the *Maracay* in Maracay, the *Del Lago* in Maracaibo and all the *Conahotu* hotels.

The Tamanaco's weekly poolside buffet is one of the best gourmet bargains in Caracas. Continental breakfast $1.90; American breakfast $3. Drinks start at $1.65. The most popular dining hours are between 9 and 11 p.m. Hotel baby sitters charge about $2 an hour.

Outside Caracas, stick to the hotels, or inquire of the front desk for their recommendations.

Best

TONI'S '65. Av. Miranda near Cine Lido. One of the best restaurants in South America. Patterned after New York's Club 21. Small menu, excellent food and service and beautifully appointed, Toni's is considered Caracas' tops. Specialties include smoked salmon and roast beef. Average meal costs $10 and up.

IL PADRINO. Plaza Altamira. Delightful Italian restaurant named for "The Godfather," with hand-painted tile staircase listing Mafia families. Italian combo plays everything from tarantellas to tangos. The antipasto is the specialty here. All pasta dishes are good. Average $8.50 per person. Wine is $14–$20 a bottle.

LA ESTANCIA. Av. Principal de la Castellana and Calle Urdaneta. This Argentine steak house occupies an old home built around a central indoor patio. Small bar popular for before dinner drinks. Fine Argentine cuisine; try "empanadas" to begin. Steaks are brought to your table sizzling on small charcoal braziers. A typical meal should cost $8.50 per person.

PETRONIO in the Air France Bldg., Av. Francisco Miranda, Chacaito. Charming, small restaurant with cocktail music. Excellent French cuisine. A specialty is fresh asparagus. $10 and up per person.

PORLAMAR. Edif. Blandín, Plaza Chacaito. Charmingly decorated fisherman's shanty with excellent seafood. Particularly popular at lunch. Average meal around $7.

LAS QUINCE LETRAS. Macuto Beach. Informal restaurant built on the sea. Shrimps barbecued in garlic sauce are best in South America. About $7 per person.

DA FRANCA. Primera Av. Los Palos Grandes. Another good Italian restaurant and favorite lunchtime rendezvous. Average $8 per person.

LA BELLE EPOQUE. Av. Leonardo da Vinci, Colinas de Bello Monte. French restaurant popular at lunch and dinner. Evening entertainment includes Caracas' best saxophone player. Specialties range from escargots to fresh asparagus and steak Tartare. Average $10 per person.

LEE HAMILTON'S STEAK HOUSE. Av. San Felipe 30, Castellana. Good steaks and luscious lettuce heart salads grown especially for the restaurant, and American dry martinis. Average price per person: $5.50.

EL PORTON. Av. Pichincha No. 18, Esq. Calle Guacaipuro, El Rosal. Caracas' best creole restaurant, specializing in typical foods. Decorated with Venezuelan handicrafts. Excellent meat, arepas and white cheese, but very noisy. Average meal costs $5.

HECTOR'S. Once Caracas's best French restaurant, Hector's has moved to the Piccadilly Pub in Parque Central. Good food and amusingly decorated. Popular at lunch. Average meal around $7.

ALVAREZ, Veroes a Jesuitas 29. Old, established downtown restaurant popular with executives at lunch time. Reasonably priced.

EL DRAGON VERDE. Bello Monte near Sears. Excellent Chinese food in pleasant surroundings. Sweet and sour pork spareribs recommended. Average meal around $5.

LE DRUGSTORE. Centro Comercial Chacaño. A copy of the Paris original with a Venezuelan touch, it offers smart boutiques, a sophisticated bar and a restaurant serving 2-ft-long hot dogs, gigantic goblets of beer and an excellent selection of sandwiches. Caracas' most popular evening rendezvous.

Typical Venezuelan Food

MARIA GUEVARA. Av. Luis Roche in Altamira. Specializes in typical fish dishes from Margarita.

EL PALACIO CRIOLLO. Av. Olimpo, Palacio de las Industrias, Gran Avenida, large and loud.

LA ATARRAYA, Plaza Jacinto, next to Casa Natal in downtown Caracas. Colonial atmosphere, balcony serenades.

Argentinian

EL ALAZAN, Av. Francisco de Miranda, Esq. Calle Santa Ana, next to Cine Car. The best bargain; here you can get a mixed "parrilla," or barbecue, for only $3.50.

Italian

CARUSO. Av. Tamanaco 36, El Rosal.

ROSSINI. Av. Los Jabillos, La Florida.

EL CID, Ave. San Felipe, La Castellana.

Spanish

LA CIBELES. Edif. El Recreo, Sabana Grande.

LA TASCA. Av. Solano Lopez, Sabana Grande. Specializes in paella and shrimps barbecued with garlic.

LAS CANCELAS. 2a. Calle de Bello Monte, Edif. Campero, Sabana Grande.

Vegetarian
EL BUFFET VEGETARIANO. La Florida, Av. Los Jardines.

Bargains

One of the best is a whole barbecued chicken at *Restaurant Tropical Room*, Av. Casanova, for only $3.50.

Also try the local *areperías*, serving delicious stuffed arepa "sandwiches," and the many low-priced pizza parlors.

NIGHTLIFE. Caracas nightlife is loud, brassy, flashy and vigorous. At the Tamanaco Hotel's *El Toledo*, for example, there are frequent shows by Flamenco dancers and Spanish entertainers as well as U.S. stars such as Eartha Kitt and Sammy Davis, Jr. Cover charge varies, but the evening adds up to about $35. The Hilton's *Cota 880* restaurant-nightclub offers two bands and a superb view of the city.

Other evening spots are meccas for dancers who love rhythm. Most popular are: *Eva*, Centro Comercial Chacaito, Local 25, with shimmering nudes and a flashing screen that produces psychedelic effects; *Hipocampo*, Centro Comercial Chacaito, with swinging music; *Blow-Up*, where dancers really do, Av. Avila, Sur Altamira; *The Flower*, Av. Principal la Castellana, Plaza Castellana, with floor shows; and *El Hipopotamo*, large and loud, Centro Comercial El Parque, Av. Francisco de Miranda.

Montmartre and *Discotheque La Pelota* are both also good fun. For a romantic evening in an intimate atmosphere, try *Mon Petit*, Edif. Auto Comercial, Plaza Sur Altamira, which offers excellent jazz as well as dance music. *Juan Sebastian Bar*, Ave. Venezuela, El Rosal, is popular with the chic young.

ENTERTAINMENT. There is always some sort of worthwhile event in the concert or entertainment field taking place in Caracas. The Nacional and Municipal theaters house a continuous stream of concerts, ballets, plays, operas, operettas and other types of attractions, with both local and imported talent. The Caracas Theatre Club presents English drama, comedy, musical comedy. The Ateneo de Caracas in the cultural center on Plaza Morelos presents plays, classic films and concerts. Art films are shown at the Cinemateca at the Museum of Fine Arts every evening at 9 p.m. sharp except Mondays. (Entrance fee: 94 cents.)

There are a series of open-air entertainments (band concerts, puppet shows, etc.) every Sunday in the Plaza Bolivar, a tree-shaded square inhabited by black squirrels, pigeons and friendly sloths. Some very good plays in Spanish at Teatro Alberto de Paz y Mateos, Cine Teatro Chacaito and Sala Juana Sujo. In addition to the Ateneo, concerts are given at the Music Hall in University City, an acoustic gem, and the Iglesia Cathedral.

MUSEUMS. Not to be missed are the *Colonial Art Museum*, a cool, tranquil 18th-century house that belonged to the Marquis of Toro. Shaded gardens, antique furniture and sunken bathtub. Panteon St.

and Av. Gamboa, San Bernardino, Wed-Thurs. and Sat. 9–12, 3–5; Sun. and hols., 9–6. *Museum of Fine Arts*, with a great variety of international and Venezuelan art, including gardens with windmills by Otero and a new Villanueva wing. Plaza Morelos. Tues.-Sat., 9–12 and 3–5:30; Sun., 10–5.

Museum of Contemporary Art, a split-level museum in Parque Central with pop art. Tues.-Fri., 12–7; Sat., 11–9; Sun., 11–7.

Also worth a visit: *Michelena Museum*, the colonial studio of Venezuela's renowned painter. Esq. Urapal, La Pastora. Tues., Thurs., Sat. and Sun., 9–12 and 3–5. *Museo Criollo Raul Santana*, miniature slice-of-life scenes. Esq. Las Monjas, Palacio Municipal. Tues.-Fri., 9–12:30 and 2–9; Sat., Sun. and hols., 10–5. *Museo Emilio Boggio* for paintings. Esq. Las Monjas, Palacio Municipal. Tues.-Fri., 9–12:30 and 2–9; Sat., Sun. and hols., 10–5.

And at the beach, *Castillete Museo Armando Reveron*, showing the work of Venezuela's favorite painter. Las Quince Letras, Macuto. Tues.-Sat., 9–12 and 4–7; Sun., 9–12. *Museo Fundacion John Boulton*, Calle Bolivar, La Guaira. Tues.-Sun., 9:30–1 and 3–6.

Private art galleries usually are open from 10–1, 4–7 except Monday and 11–1 on Sunday. Among the best are *Sala de Exhibiciones*, Fundacion Mendoza, Edif. Las Fundaciones, Av. Andres Bello. Contemporary artists, group shows, Venezuelan and international. Twice yearly auction. Non-profit gallery. *Conkright Gallery*, Edif. Galipán, Av. Fco. Miranda. Very small with excellent taste, linked with New York gallery of same name. Rachel Conkright, agent, has stable of top Venezuelan painters. *Estudio Actual*, Centro Comercial Chacaito. Spacious, very modern establishment with branch in Valencia, Estudio 2, and shows in Maracaibo. Shows Soto, Escobar and other outstanding artists. *Arte Contacto*, Av. Libertador near Estudio Actual. Very good paintings and graphic arts.

Not quite so good but still worth a visit are *Galeria Acquavella*, Edif. T. Bosque, Av. Principal del Bosque. Oldest gallery in Caracas with paintings by Poleo and occasional impressionist shows. *Maison Bernard*, Centro Comercial Chacaito. Fashionable and expensive. *Galeria de Arte Moderno*, Av. Tamanaco No. 9, El Rosal. Run by the Denis brothers with Paris connections. And for Haitian paintings, *Haitian Art Gallery*, 3ra. Av. Los Palos Grandes between Transv. 6 and 7.

SPORTS. Caracas has South America's largest, most modern and most expensive race track. Called "La Rinconada," it sports everything from an air-conditioned box for the President to a swimming pool for horses. Escalators take spectators to their stands each Saturday and Sunday as fans pack in to play the pari-mutuel or the "five and six." This latter game began in Venezuela and has spread to Colombia and Puerto Rico. It consists of a betting system wherein should the bettor correctly pick the winners out of five or six races listed, he will be awarded a slice of the pot. The amount varies from very low to very high depending on the number of winners, but it is not uncommon for a bettor to parley a four-bolivar (93 cents) bet into hundreds of thousands. The highest single winning bet on record was slightly under Bs 1,120,000 ($260,000).

Hunting and Fishing. All hunting has been prohibited for the past two years, but if the ban is lifted the visitor to Venezuela can enjoy some of the best hunting in this hemisphere. There are jaguar, deer, quail, duck, wild turkey, cayman and alligator. Arrangements for expeditions can be made with expert guides in interior towns. Trout fishing in the Andes and river fishing for delicacies such as the large fighting *pavon* of the Orinoco are considered the best in the world. Deepsea fishing off the Venezuelan coast in the Caribbean is tops and boats can be chartered at Hotel Macuto Sheraton. (Fishing season, Mar. 16–Sept. 30.) In Sept. near La Guaira, the International Light Tackle Fishing Tournament takes place.

Jungle trips and off-the-beaten-track expeditions can be arranged through: Sidney Coles, Apartado del Este 60182, Caracas; and *Promociones Turisticas Intercontinentales*, Walter Albrecht, Aptdo. 61355, Caracas (tel. 715275). Albrecht flies groups to Puerto Ayacucho, then takes them up river to San Fernando de Atabapo, where there is a thatch-roofed camp. Excursions to Esmeraldas on the Orinoco River. About $600 per person per week, all expenses included. Coles runs a small tourist camp at El Dorado in the highlands of Roraima overlooking the Yuruan and Cuyuni rivers. Excellent fishing, unforgettable views of the fabled table mountains of Venezuela's grassy savannahs (tel. 2833288 in Caracas).

Amazonas Villa-Selva, C.A., Aptdo. 61355, Chacao. Tourist camps at San Fernando de Atabapo and La Esmeralda.

Captain Jorge Arostegui. (Tel. 71-82-32 or 72-37-61 in Caracas.) Arostegui is a pilot with a camp on the Asisa River, up the Ventuari, at the foot of Mt. Parú. A-frame tepees of cane and thatch, crystalline waters, Indians, dantas, etc. Twin-engine Beechcraft from Caracas. About $740 per person for a week.

Pan Turismo. Centro Comercial Country, Piso 2, Chacaito. Trip up the Orinoco River from Puerto Ayacucho to San Carlos de Rio Negro. Weekend tours to Amazon Territory with visits to primitive Piaro Indians and beautiful Cuao rapids.

Watersports are available less than an hour from Caracas on the Caribbean, where there are several excellent beaches: Catia la Mar, Macuto, Naiguata and Los Caracas. Facilities include dressing rooms, restaurants, cafeterias, soda fountains, first-aid stations, picnic areas, children's pools, parking, boardwalks, music. Snorkeling off Margarita Island; skin-diving, water skiing at Chichiriviche and Cata Bay. Sailing, yachting regattas, skin diving, water skiing at Macuto.

Bullfighting in season is another popular spectator sport. The season usually runs from November through March and world famous matadors perform in Caracas, Valencia and San Cristobal bull rings. Prices for a bullfight in Caracas run from $8 in the sun, higher in the shade. Tickets in Valencia from $3. Bullfights in Merida take place Dec.–May.

Boxing, Baseball and Soccer are the most popular spectator sports in Venezuela and can be seen the year round. The winter baseball leagues feature many young U.S. baseball stars. Wrestling (called *lucha libre*) is a weekly event.

Skiing season is May through October. For the hardy skier (no lifts) Mérida's best skiing is July-Sept., but very few try skiing here.

Cockfights are popular in the smaller villages and towns.

Golf. Valle Arriba Golf Club; Caracas Country Club; and Lagunita Country Club, a challenging 18-hole Caracas course, which was once a coffee plantation.

 SHOPPING. Caracas. When in Venezuela you are bound to do some shopping, but apart from the normal run of goods to be found in the shops you are likely to be interested in typical souvenirs of your trip. The city's new shopping centers, known as "centros comerciales," are particularly worth a visit, with some of Caracas' most sophisticated shops and restaurants in an imaginative architectural setting with hanging gardens and modern sculpture.

Fine Gems and Jewelry at H. Stern, Tamanaco and Hilton hotels, Caracas. Known for their worldwide service and reputation. Also Cacique coins and Cochano gold at very reasonable prices.

Cacique Coins. Beautifully fashioned gold coins with the heads of the eighteen Indian chieftains who fought against the Spanish Conquistadores in the 16th century. These coins are available separately or in series of eighteen and in five different sizes. The smallest coin, a little smaller than a U.S. dime and weighing 1.5 grams is Bs. 14. The largest coin, slightly larger than the U.S. fifty-cent piece is Bs. 163, weighing 20 grams.

The Caciques can be found in most jewelry shops set into cuff links, tie pins, bracelets, pendants and pins. The prices depend on the settings. Ask for one which corresponds with your birthday.

Hand of Fatima. A little carved black fist, mounted in a gold collar with a loop for hanging from a chain. Made of ebony (azabache), it is a charm to avert the evil eye.

Gold. A yellow, rough-textured gold is found and worked in Venezuela. Miniature guitars, maracas, burros, alpargatas, oil wells, etc., fashioned from Cochano gold are available for charm bracelets. But by far the most popular Cochano gold item is the orchid (with a tiny pearl from Margarita in its center). This orchid is found in all sizes from tiny earrings to enormous brooches. *Panchita Labady*, who originated the gold orchid, can design anything in gold. Calle Real de Sabana Grande, 98, Caracas.

Pearls. From the waters of Margarita Island come pearls, most of them baroque, but a few symmetrical and of excellent color. Baroque pearls are relatively inexpensive and quite beautiful.

Alpargatas. The traditional local footwear of the *campesino*. They are stiff leather-soled shoes with woven string tops, in rather somber shades. However, alpargatas, sequined and brightly embroidered, are turned out for the tourist trade.

Pompom Slippers. Another type of shoe, worn by the Guajira Indian women. These slippers, known as *cotizas*, are flat leather sandals with huge, brightly colored wool pompoms on top. Guajiro rugs and tapestries, on sale at Tamanaco and Holiday Inn, average $100 a meter. Also available at *El Taller de la Esquina* in the new Holiday Inn shopping center, Paseo Las Mercedes.

Chinchorros. Local hammocks, available in all sizes, colors and designs. The chinchorros on sale in the cities are the same as those used by the *campesinos.* By far the most handsome and most intricately woven are those made by Margarita islanders and the Goajiros in cotton or palm fiber in their natural color. The Warao Indians in the Orinoco Delta send wooden animal toys, enormous "moriche" fiber hammocks and miniature Indian villages, complete with hammocks and fishing baskets, to *Artesania Riolama,* their principal Caracas outlet, 4 Trans. between Av. Andrés Bello and Av. Jahn, Los Palos, Grandes.

Rugs. Brightly dyed sheep or goat's wool rugs (plaid, striped or unicolored) come in various sizes and are popular as throw rugs, wall hangings and bedspreads.

Seed Necklaces. Unusual seeds from the interior of Venezuela are dried and strung into fascinating, inexpensive necklaces.

The Maquiritare Indians and *Piaroas* up the Orinoco River make baskets, hardwood paddles and low jaguar benches out of a single log, beautifully designed, hard to get and normally expensive unless purchased at *Riolama* (see above). Other shops with good selection of native crafts are *El Caribe, Calle el Recreo, Sabana Grande,* and *Yakera,* Ave. Andres Bello between 1 and 2 Transversals, Los Palos Grandes. Avoid *Palacio de las Industrias,* an enormous junk shop crammed with clay Venuses and plastic piranhas.

Shoes and handbags made to order and the ones in the shops in Sabana Grande in Caracas are a good buy. Excellent Venezuelan hairpieces. Also small selections of Dior, Chanel, Pucci, etc., available at lower prices than country of origin.

Maracaibo. A favorite tourist souvenir, in addition to Guajira crafts, is the delicately spun sun of white lace known as "soles de Maracaibo," which have been made for generations in neighboring villages, particularly Santa Cruz de Mara. Here, in the light of the same barred windows their grandmothers sewed by, girls learn how to crochet the circular designs, progressing as they acquire skill to more complex patterns. Originally made for mantillas and kerchiefs, rectangular soles are now prized as table decorations (prices range from Bs. 30 to 80). Beginners' work may be sold as simple coasters for Bs. 3 or 5 The easiest way to wash a sol is to shake it in a bottle of soapy water. The old-fashioned trick of ironing it with a zapote seed coated in wax is not, perhaps, the easiest pressing method today.

These and many other crafts may be found at the *Ministry of Development Shop,* No. 93–25, Av. El Milagro in Maracaibo. For 30 years it has acted as a non-profit exhibition room for local artisans, selling work without commission, thus benefiting both craftsman and buyer.

If you want to see how Maracuchos shop, browse around the *Central Market* and nearby *La Marina Market,* where you will find yourself on display as well, besides stalls of fruit, chickens, sandals, pots and pans, herbs and magic potions and, of course, Hong Kong trinkets.

Mercantil del Trópico, a crowded and dusty souvenir shop in downtown Maracaibo, is also worth a visit. Calle 100, No. 9–41, between Av. Miranda and Milagros.

Guapira mantles make a superb gift, as do the Indians' tightly woven wool sashes, or "fajas," which cost from Bs. 30 to 50. The Guajiros also make chinchorros woven of thread and superb macana fiber hammocks. Some take up to three months to make and are consequently priced at Bs. 180 to 500. The *Airport Tourist Office* has a varied and colorful display of Guajira crafts.

The Yukpa Indians of Tucuco Mission make bows, arrows, mats, pipes and baskets for the souvenir market. Venezuela's typical 4-string guitar, the cuatro, is another good, inexpensive buy since they are made here. Lowest price: Bs. 40.

 TELEPHONES. Fully automatic, although somewhat reluctant, phones are available wherever you need them. Pay phones (25 céntimos) are installed through Caracas and Maracaibo. For long distance within Venezuela call 100 (center and western areas) and 106 (east); for international, call 122. (The time in Venezuela is the same as that in the Eastern zone of the U.S.) There is direct dialing between most important cities, see phone book for area codes. You will usually find an English-speaking operator. 103 is for information.

ELECTRICITY. Electric current in Caracas and elsewhere is 60 cycles, 110 volts A.C.

 MAIL. Mail is rapid to the United States and Europe. A 5-gram letter to the United States is 70 céntimos and to Europe around 95 céntimos. Urban mail delivery in Caracas usually takes 2–10 days.

 USEFUL ADDRESSES. Embassies in Caracas: U.S., Avenida Principal La Floresta. Great Britain, Avenida La Estancia 10, Ciudad Comercial Tamanaco; Canada, Avenida Estancia, Ciudad Comercial Tamanaco.

The *International Association for Medical Assistance for Travelers* (*IAMAT*), Centro Professional del Este, Calle Vilaflor, Caracas. Tel.: 710907-331334. *All American Cables* has offices in Caracas, La Guaira, Puerto La Cruz and Maracaibo.

Additional information on Venezuela can be obtained from the Venezuelan Embassy in Washington or the Venezuelan Consulates in the following cities: Baltimore, Chicago, Houston, Los Angeles, Miami, Mobile, New Orleans, New York, Philadelphia, Portland, San Francisco, Savannah and San Juan, Puerto Rico.

Also the Venezuelan Government Tourist Bureau, 485 Madison Avenue, New York, New York 10022. From VIASA in the following cities: Chicago, Detroit, Houston, Miami, Philadelphia, Toronto, Boston, Washington, D.C. and New York; in Europe: in Frankfurt, Amsterdam, Madrid, Paris, Rome, Milan, Lisbon, London. From *Venezuela Panorama*, 445 Park Avenue, New York, N.Y. In Venezuela, call *Corpoturismo*, tel. 7818311.

AMERICAN EXPRESS AGENTS: Caracas, *Turismo Maso Internacional*, Hotel Tamanaco, Las Mercedes.

COLOMBIA

Emerald of the Spanish Main

BY

BEATRICE DE HOLGUIN

(Mrs. de Holguin, a New Yorker married in Bogotá, has fre-quently contributed magazine pieces on Colombia to several U.S.A. publications.)

This beautiful country, the only South American republic with a sea view of the Pacific and the Caribbean, never fails to dazzle visitors with its soaring green mountains, lush jungles and fertile deltas, its quiet Indian villages and bustling ultra-modern cities. It has beaches on both oceans, water-skiing on tropical lagoons and snow-skiing in the Andes, fishing in mountain lakes or in the deep blue sea. Colombia is big vertically as well as horizontally and its altitude range from sea level to 18,000 feet offers a cor-responding scope of tourist pleasures. Within a few days, one can enjoy deep-sea fishing, Andean mountain climbing, swimming, snorkeling, a visit to the heart of a tropical jungle.

Even Europe would be hard put to match the 16th-century walled city of Cartagena that combines the charm of quaint nar-row streets and balconied houses with the amenities of a glittering beach resort. But if you tire of the lazy life under the palm trees, Bogotá, Colombia's exhilarating 8,700-ft. high capital, is less than one hour away by jet. Yet in contrast to this modern sophisticated capital, there are Amazon villages where primitive Indians con-tinue to practise age-old rites. And the contrasts of Colombia's weather run from equatorial jungle heat to the eternal snows of mountaintops with a broad span of temperate climate in between.

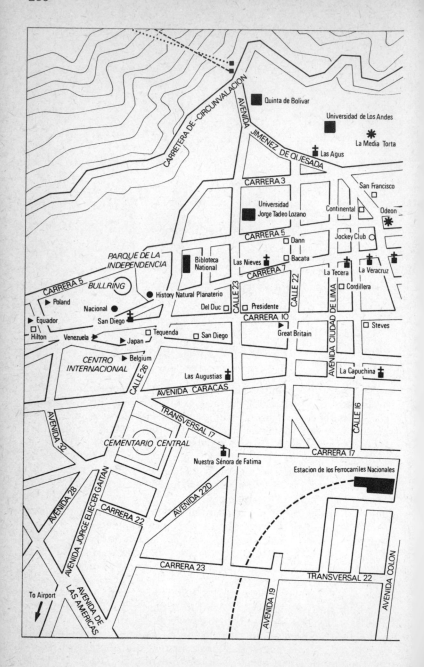

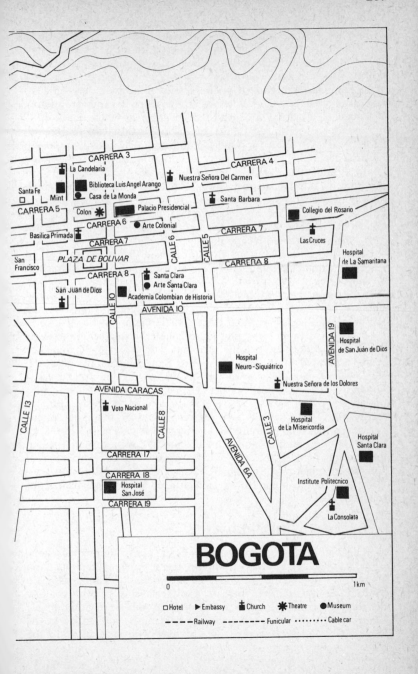

CARRERA 3
La Candelaria
Biblioteca Luis Angel Arango
Santa Fe
Mint
Casa de La Monda
CARRERA 5
Colon
Basilica Primada
CARRERA 6
Arte Colonial
CARRERA 7
San
Francisco
PLAZA DE BOLIVAR
CARRERA 8
Santa Clara
San Juan de Dios
Arte Santa Clara
Academia Colombian de Historia
AVENIDA 10

Nuestra Señora Del Carmen
Santa Barbara
CARRERA 4
Collegio del Rosario
CARRERA 7
Las Cruces
CARRERA 8
Hospital
de La Samaritana

CALLE 6
CALLE 5

CALLE 10

Voto Nacional
AVENIDA CARACAS

CALLE 13
CALLE 8

CARRERA 17
CARRERA 18
Hospital
San José
CARRERA 19

Hospital
Neuro-Siquiátrico
Nuestra Señora de los Dolores
AVENIDA 19
Hospital
de San Juán de Dios

CALLE 3
Hospital
de La Misericordia

AVENIDA 6A

Hospital
Santa Clara
Institute Politecnico
La Consolata

BOGOTA

0   1km

□ Hotel   ▶ Embassy   ♱ Church   ✳ Theatre   ● Museum
− − − Railway   − − − − Funicular   ⋯⋯ Cable car

There are over 28 million Colombians, mostly of European stock, with a strong Indian mestizo flavor. The country is intensely Spanish, inhabited by a people of deep and ancient culture and proud that its capital is known as the "Athens of America". It's an Athens for learning and a Mecca for shopping because the quality of merchandise is high and prices, thanks to a favorable exchange rate, are low. Bargains in emeralds and gold jewelry are astounding.

Since Colombia has a centralized government whose main institutions are concentrated in the capital, all roads lead to Bogotá. Along them travel visitors and Colombians alike intent on seeing historic sites linked to the birth of the country. Bogotá is the home of the Presidential Palace where Bolívar once lived and the Casa del Florero, now a national shrine. This is where the Colombian mutiny against the Spaniards began. It all started when a haughty Spaniard broke a valuable vase rather than let it be used in a Creole celebration, whipping the Creoles into a fury that did not abate until they gained freedom.

But all roads lead out of Bogotá as well. They enable you to trade the capital's climate of a year-round April for July warmth on the Caribbean coast or in low-lying towns along the Magdalena River. If you prefer winter to spring, there are the snow-covered slopes of El Ruiz near Manizales. If you prefer the past to the present, then it's not far from Bogotá to Tunja in old Boyacá, once the seat of Indian empires rich in gold, emeralds and huge temples and later a center for colonial art that was expressed in magnificently-decorated churches. Or to the San Agustin archeological zone, where sporadic government-sponsored digging has revealed hundreds of monolithic statues (some humorous, some grim) dating from 555 B.C. If you prefer wilderness to civilization, try the primitive beaches of San Andres Island or the great plains known as the *llanos* spreading out from Villavicencio. Or if you just want to go hunting and fishing, there is Leticia in the Amazon jungle and Tumaco on the Pacific coast. For loftier forms of amusement, there are the film festivals, fairs . . . and beauty contests . . . that can be found in Cartagena, Cali, Manizales, or Ibagué.

Capsule Colombian History

Long before the discovery of America, the Colombia territory was inhabited by natives of different races, temperaments and languages. Among the principal groups were the Chibchas, who lived in the mountainous interior, and the Caribs, who lived along the northern coast. Most advanced of Colombia's pre-Columbians, though, were the Chibchas, excellent goldsmiths and skilled in the arts of weaving and pottery. It was they who gave birth to the legend of El Dorado—the "gilded one"—with their custom of anointing their chief every year, and rolling him in gold dust which he then washed off with a ceremonial bath in Lake Guatavita.

The Chibchas had given up this custom long before the first Europeans landed on the shores of what is now Colombia, but the legend lingered on. It drove a host of adventurers to the New World and, while they did not find El Dorado, they founded New Granada, a colony that once comprised the territory of what is now Colombia, Ecuador, Panama and Venezuela. They included the Spanish and Italian sea captains—among them Columbus, Alonso de Ojeda, Juan de la Cosa, Rodrigo de Bastidas and Amerigo Vespucci—who sailed into the Caribbean during the late 15th and early 16th centuries. These and other explorers founded the coastal cities of Colombia and those of the interior which still exist and thrive: Santa Marta in 1525, Cartagena in 1533, Bogotá in 1538 and others. An effort had been made by Ojeda to found a settlement at Cartagena as early as 1500 but the Spaniards were driven off by fierce Indians and the effort was abandoned.

From the 16th century to the beginning of the 19th, Spain governed Colombia through a system of viceroys, *presidentes* and *oidores*, but as early as 1781 movements toward independence from the mother country were under way. The seeds of revolt were first sown in the Santander town of Socorro and the Spaniards had to give way to demands for tax reform that led to the face-losing flight of the Spanish "royal visitor" from Cartagena. They came into full harvest when declarations of independence from Spain were made in Bogotá on July 20, 1810, and in Cartagena on November 11, 1811.

But declarations were not enough. Unable to raise troops in Cartagena, Simón Bolívar left for Jamaica in 1814 and the city fell to the Spanish after an epic siege. Five years went by before Bolívar dealt a crushing blow to the Spaniards of New Granada at the decisive Battle of Boyaca on August 7, 1819, when he donned a tattered uniform to lead two thousand patriots to victory. The Spanish viceroy fled Bogotá when news of the defeat reached the capital 75 miles away. The life of the new republic began under the presidency of Bolívar, the great Liberator, and the vice-presidency of Francisco de Paula Santander, revered as "the man of laws". But Santander was far more popular than the Liberator and Bolívar was discredited. He was forced to leave his Bogotá palace and go into hiding under a bridge. Dampness and discouragement aggravated the tubercular condition that already plagued him and finally caused his death in Santa Marta. This marked the end of *Gran Colombia*, a union of Colombia, Venezuela and Ecuador that broke up in 1830. Colombia suffered another territorial loss in the 20th century when Panama was established as a separate republic in 1903.

Following the gaining of independence, a number of civil wars broke out in Colombia during the 19th century for administrative, political and religious reasons. This often blood-drenched period saw a continuous struggle for power by the Liberal and Conservative parties. The Conservatives finally gained power in 1880 and held it until 1930, a period of unbroken rule that did little to allay the bitterness of the Liberals when it was their turn to take over. Political strife in Colombia was not limited to the harmless "palace revolutions" that occurred elsewhere in Latin America during this period. In 1948, for example, a civil uprising broke out in Bogotá triggering sporadic nationwide violence for 10 years. The police fought the army and farmers streamed into the capital to pillage and burn, leaving much of the city in ashes.

Perhaps the Colombians have recognized that politics in their country is too deadly a game to be played as it is elsewhere. The political and administrative features of the government were consolidated with the Constitution of 1886, since amended several times. The last amendment, in 1957, established a unique system of alternating the presidency and all other elective and appointive offices in the nation on a 50-50 basis between the Liberal and Conservative parties for a period of 16 years. This agreement led to a four-year term for Alberto Lleras Camargo, one of the leading figures in the Organization of American States, who then stepped aside for a Conservative, Guillermo Leon Valencia. Carlos Lleras, a Liberal, was President for the 1966-1970 period; and Misael Pastrana, a Conservative, held the office until 1974. In that year, the 16-year period came to an end, and a straight election was held, won by the Liberal candidate, Alfonso Lopez Michelsen, a law professor. The system of parity in appointing ministers to the cabinets, as well as governors and mayors, will continue until 1978, so this unique system will still be much in evidence for a while.

Coffee and Riverboats

Against this turbulent political background, the Colombian economy has developed steadily. Coffee is still the mainstay of the nation's export trade, for the high quality of Colombian coffee—the country ranks second only to Brazil as a producer—keeps it in demand. But it is emerging from this old neo-colonial way of economic life. Colombia exports consumer goods such as textiles and manufactures cement and pharmaceuticals. Heavy industry took a big stride forward with the building of a steel plant at Paz del Rio during the 1950's. At the same time, the once-inextricable problem of Colombian transportation is being solved by new highway and railroad construction and by a tremendous increase in the use of air travel (Avianca was the first airline to be founded in the Americas and the second to be founded in the world).

Though the country is industrializing, it has not turned its back on the arts. From prehistoric times to the present, there have been artists in Colombia. The first ones carved the shapes of birds and animals into the rocky sides of mountains and painted on the walls of caves. Later other unknown civilizations carved great stone statues to honor departed leaders. And the Chibchas on the plateau of Bogotá fashioned hammered gold breastplates, necklaces and diadems that are still marvels today. Then European influence was injected into this pre-Columbia art and, during the colonial era, rococo churches sprouted in the country's principal towns and cities with frescos by painters like Arce y Ceballos.

The 19th century saw a flowering of Colombian painters and sculptors with Epifanio Garay, Andres Santamaria (who had an El Greco touch), Eugenio Zerda, Domingo Moreno Otero, and Roberto Pizano, an interpreter of charming local scenes, among the former. Major sculptors included Romulo Rozo, Tobon Mejia, Ramon Barba, Hena Rodriguez, Josefina Abarracin and Archila.

Painters of Satyrs and Martyrs

Colombian art, however, has come into its own particularly in these modern times that the country is living so intensely. Sculpture and painting are combined by Ramirez Villamizar, for example, who uses layers of plywood to paint in bas-relief. Among the modern masters are Santiago Martinez Delgado, whose Bolívar mural in Bogotá is worth seeing, and Gonzalo Ariza. Ariza studied in Japan with Foujita and he has used Oriental style to interpret local subjects. Proudly nationalistic, he even stirred *campesinos* in country villages to create original ceramics.

As far as major painters are concerned, Colombia's Big Three today is made up of Alejandro Obregon from Barranquilla, Enrique Grau from Cartagena and Fernando Botero of Medellin (it's no accident that they come from three of the country's most interesting provincial cities).

Obregon first rocked into the limelight several years ago when he painted a huge mural devoted to the labours of the working class in the Hotel El Prado in Barranquilla. The setting was none too apt; the controversy stirred by this painting ended only when it was painted over. But Obregon remained close to the roots of Colombian life with his scenes of *corridas*, the Andes and harbor life. One of his most famous works is a painting of a pregnant woman killed during a political riot.

Grau began at the same time as Obregon in the early 1950s when he fell under the influence of Bernard Buffet's school of sordidness and lost hope. Since then, his palette has brightened in his paintings of life a generation ago that are highly appreciated by Colombians.

Youngest of the trio is Botero who paints satyrs and madmen in a style reminiscent of Goya's later years. But his still lifes of Colombian fruits are more pleasant and there is a particularly famous one in Bogotá's Jockey Club.

In sculptors, Alicia Tafur is the latest talent worth watching and she has decorated some of South America's most exciting new buildings with her skeletal spires. Feliza Burzstyn has recently shown a group of sculptures in an unusual combination of light, sound and movement.

Music and the Dance

Music and dances are as ingrained as art into Colombian life. Dance rhythms vary as one moves around the country. Melodious African-style *porros* and *merecumbés* on the northern coast are part of Caribbean tradition, but these dances are more stately than those of the Dominican Republic or Jamaica, perhaps because the influence of Africa is felt less strongly. In the Andes to the south, music descends from the mournful airs of the Incas, but here again, there is a distinct Colombian quality in *bambucos*, *joropos* and *guabinas* flavoured by a Spanish spice. Most popular of all Afro-Colombian music and dances is the *cumbia*, in which the girl holds a lighted candle while dancing. The cumbia is also popular in the Chocó region but with a slightly different rhythm.

Villancicos, Christmas carols sung everywhere during the nine days of *novena* parties that traditionally precede Christmas, are closely related to the songs sung by medieval Spanish troubadours. Carols are heard in pageants, on the street, in churches and around Christmas cribs in homes where the holy family is always shown in a *pesebre*, a home-made moss-covered mountain scene of tiny villages, magi on camels, shepherds and flocks. And it's hard to forget the piping voices of Colombian children caroling:

"Ven a nuestras almas, ven no tardes tanto."

(Come to our souls . . . and don't be late.)

Recently some folk dance troupes have gained prominence and the best are those headed by Delia Zapata, Sonia Osorio or Hernando Monroy. They perform at coffee, sugar and tobacco festivals where they rely heavily on frequent changes of costumes (this is a good opportunity to see some of the most picturesque native styles of dress, hats and hairdos). Delia Zapata is from Cartagena and specializes in coastal dances. Her *cumbia* is very well done, for she manages to catch both the spiritual and earthy aspects of this dance. Sonia Osorio was born in Barranquilla, became a ballerina in Vienna and now interprets everything from *bambucos* to *mapalés*.

Colombian dances are likely to be accompanied by orchestras playing instruments you have never seen before. Around Tolima, there are unusual violins and guitars with the most popular being the *tiple*, a many-stringed kin to the guitar, that is played in the coffee fields. Its softness and sweetness make it a favorite of serenaders for it adds a gentle, though primitive, quality to their music. All professional local bands use the Indian flute or *flauta* because it is part and parcel of Colombia's best loved dance: the Caribbean *cumbia*. They also never fail to have a *raspa*, a grooved gourd that can be rubbed, scratched or simply rapped. Marimba virtuosos are scarce, but there are still enough to keep local marimba music alive.

We mentioned serenaders and you are bound to hear them in Colombia where they usually work in groups of two or three.

There are also several large local groups and the most famous one is attached to the Tolima Conservatory. It moves around the country to most of the good festivals and its songs are quite original.

Food and Drink

At principal hotels, nightclubs and leading restaurants the menu is international. Regional dishes can be obtained in all typical hotels and restaurants. An average meal per person, without drinks, will cost in a first-class restaurant from $4.50 to $9. American cocktails run about $1.50–$2.00; local beer about 30¢. Many restaurants offer good local fare for as low as $1 per meal. Menus and prices are to be posted on the outside of all restaurants by the time this guide is published.

Colombians rarely drink wine with dinner; they prefer beer or fermented cane juice, *guarapo*. But there are several good wines produced in Colombia: *Santa Helena*, a full-bodied red wine, and *Vino Moriles*, a Chianti-like wine made locally under a Domecq patent.

The Colombian liquors are "aguardiente" and rum, both extracted from sugar cane. "Viejo de Caldas", "Buc", "Medellín", and "Cundinamarca" rums are worth mentioning.

While you should avoid eating unpeeled fruit, uncooked vegetables and salads, be sure to try some of the following regional dishes:

Viudo de Pescado (fish stew), cooked in holes dug in the ground, and covered with hot rocks.

Frijoles (kidney beans) prepared in Antioquia and Caldas; *Arepas* (corn griddle cakes) of common use in Antioquia, Caldas, Santander and Valle. *Peto* (soup) made out of a special white corn with milk. *Lechona*, a special dish prepared with suckling pigs, principally in warm climates. *Tamales* is a preparation of corn dough, meats and vegetables cooked and wrapped in banana or wild leaves that give it a special taste. *Tortoise* and *iguana eggs* are considered a delicacy all along the Caribbean Coast. During the season (May–July), *Muelas de Cangejo* (crab claws) are favorites in Cartagena. The Bucaramanga area, in the state of Santander, offers fried and jellied ants as an exotic appetizer.

The rolls served with dinner are unique and excellent in Colombia. *Mogollas* are whole-wheat muffins with raisin-flavored centers. *Roscon* is a sugar-sprinkled bun filled with guava jelly. *Almojábanas* are corn muffins that are enriched with cottage cheese. *Yuca* bread is made with yuca (cassava) starch and cottage cheese. *Garullas* are made with flour and egg. *Obleas* are like giant Hosts, an unsalted wafer spread with the sugar-and-milk paste called *arequipe*. *Empanadas* is pastry folded to hold a paste of chopped meat, egg, and capers. Tiny salted baked "creole" (yellow) potatoes are favorite appetizers, and highly-peppered mashed avocados served as a dip. With breakfast there are buñuelos, golden balls of maize flour and cheese.

EXPLORING COLOMBIA

Anyone who still thinks of South America in terms of siestas and sombreros had better check his ideas at his port or airport of embarkation before he comes to Bogotá. Lying though it does only a few degrees from the Equator, Colombia's capital can take on the air of a northern city. It is steeped in history under the roof of perpetually grey skies that provide natural air-conditioning.

Politically, numerically, commercially and culturally, it is the first city of Colombia. It lies 750 miles inland from the Caribbean in a long flat valley surrounded by the peaks of the eastern Andes at an altitude of 8,660 feet. Over four million people (as compared to 325,000 right after World War II) live in Bogotá's Special District (similar to the District of Columbia).

Civilization came to this valley long before the arrival of Europeans. Originally, the valley had been covered with the waters of a lake which disappeared in prehistoric times leaving rich bottom lands that supported the farming communities of the Chibcha Indians, some of the greatest craftsmen of early South America.

The Chibchas' fame as goldsmiths had spread far beyond their lofty plateau and, by the time it reached the lowlands, it became another version of the legend El Dorado. It was in pursuit of this legend that Gonzalo Jimenez de Quesada set out from Santa Marta, on the northern tip of the continent, in 1536. At the head of a Spanish army and eager to duplicate the prowesses of Cortes in Mexico and Pizarro in Peru, he decided to thrust his way into the heart of the continent along the Magdalena River. Though he lost half his army at the start when his rafts overturned, he was determined to continue. He marched a ragged crew hundreds of miles along the river's banks through jungle terrain, harassed by Indians and plagued by insects. The decimated army was near desperation when it encountered some Indian salt traders and Jimenez de Quesada realized that his goal was near. He climbed the Andes and reached the plateau shortly before the arrival of two other bands of European adventurers. He outparleyed them both, and then took on the Chibchas who were no match for him. On the 6th August, 1538, he named his conquest Santa Fe de Bogotá, in honor of Bacatá, the Chibcha Indian village which the conquistadores discovered on the spot.

And then Gonzalo Jimenez de Quesada, who is believed by some authorities to have served as a model for Cervantes' Don Quixote, set about to build a city. While he was not up to the standard of Pizarro in Lima as a town planner, he did seek beauty. He picked the site for his city, nestling against the Andes for protection against the wind, and he encouraged colonists.

Yields on the rich lake-bottom land of the plateau were high enough to enable hacienda owners to accumulate enough wealth to lure some of Spain's greatest artisans to Bogotá. When a farmer received a land grant with the seal of the King of Spain, a skilled carpenter or cabinetmaker would accompany him on his trip. As a result, fine architecture sprang up very quickly after the Spanish conquest and Bogotá homes were aristocratically furnished.

The results of this workmanship are visible today in the architecture, carved altars, statues of saints and oil paintings in Bogotá's older churches. While there are several churches going back to the early 17th century, few homes and haciendas of that period have survived. However, there are several 18th-century houses: the manor house of Santa Barbara hacienda in Usaquen, the Marques de San Jorge mansion and the house standing at the center of the Los Laureles hacienda. These buildings all display the hand-carved ceiling beams and the sculptured doorways that marked the great architecture of colonial New Granada. Then, after independence, 19th-century romanticism took over and left Bogotá with Greek columns and cornices. The next stage in the 1880's was gingerbread Victorian and some quaint examples remain. By the 1930's, Bogotá was in early modern and then it switched to the California split-level ranch house current today.

All this can be viewed from the Hotel Tequendama or the Bogotá Hilton, between the uptown and downtown sections. Here, the city's architectural layers are within easy distance, beginning with the charming San Diego Church which is nearby. And the view is certainly one of contrasts. Before 1948, Bogotá was not much more than a large town. Today, its growing pains are illustrated by narrow colonial streets running parallel to four-lane thoroughfares and glass-sheathed skyscrapers rising beside one-story shacks. Yet, while the center of Bogotá is a jumble of styles, contemporary city planning becomes apparent in its outlying sections. Working-class districts and factories are concentrated in the south while the better shops and the homes of the more moneyed are spread out in the north. Embassies and private mansions line the terraced sides of mountains along the main road running north out of Bogotá toward Venezuela. These residential districts are worth seeing if only for their gardens that flourish in this climate of a perpetual spring.

The Plaza Bolívar, around which the original town of Bogotá grew, is at the heart of the city and around it spreads what is left of the old quarter with its narrow streets and massive mansions boasting barred windows, carved doorways and tiled roofs extending over the sidewalks. Worth the visitor's attention in this area are: the Colonial Museum, with numerous paintings and sculptures by masters of the Spanish Colonial period (open Tues.–Sat., 10–5:30; Sun. and hol., 2–5); Presidential Palace (if only to enjoy its handsome exterior and the colorful changing of the guard, daily at 5). Collectors would be interested in the coin museum (Casa de la Moneda) located in one of Bogotá's most beautiful examples of Spanish-American architecture. Among its

coins are some, used during the colonial period, in the shape of
bars bearing the royal seal. There are coins whose gold content
was secretly reduced by the King of Spain, and some made by
revolutionaries from empty cartridges. Most unusual of all are
coins for use in leper colonies. (Open Mon.–Fri., 8:30–12, 1:30–
4.) The Luis Angel Arango Library and Chamber Music Concert
Hall is a striking example of modern architecture and a leading
cultural center of the city, with art exhibits, concerts and lectures
(daily, 8 a.m.–9 p.m.; Sun. and hol. 9–7); Mansion of the Marquis of San Jorge, a museum of pre-Columbian pottery; Museum
of Popular Arts and Traditions, a restored former cloister, with
courtyards, fountains and arches; Santa Clara Church and Museum, 17th century, with Spanish-Moorish style altars and ceiling;
the Cathedral and El Sagrario Chapel, containing one of the
country's leading collections of paintings by Gregorio Vasquez de
Arce y Ceballos.

On leaving Bolívar Square walk along Carrera 7, which will
bring you to the 16th century San Francisco Church, with an
incredibly elaborate main altar, La Tercera Church, mid-18th century (with all altars carved in natural mahogany), and finally to
the highlight of any visit to Bogotá—the Gold Museum. All that
glitters . . .

The collection is housed in an especially designed building, a
fine example of contemporary Colombian architecture. There are
some 25,000 pre-Colombian gold pieces, including anthropomor-
phic stylization, necklaces, pendants, nose rings, diadems, pector-
als, as well as such utilitarian items as needles, ceremonial objects,
etc. By weight alone the collection is worth some $65 million. You
will be overcome by the dazzling finale to your tour! Upstairs is
Colombia's most valuable collection of emeralds, among them
the world's largest unpolished gem-type stone. (Tues.–Sat., 9–5;
Sun. and hol., 10–1. Entrance fee: $10 pesos.)

Next, visit the Quinta de Bolívar, the Liberator's country estate,
now converted into a museum preserving the relics of his gentle-
man-farmer life here. You will see the tiny bed where he slept,
and the small furniture used by this mighty but delicately-boned
man. Of especial interest to the ladies will be a combination sewing box/miniature piano. Surrounding the building is a lovely
garden. The paved walk to the house is outlined by shinbones of
countless cattle, to prevent slipping when it is raining. The museum
is an ideal spot to see the gracious way of life enjoyed by upper-
class Bogotános in the beginning of the 19th century. Just past the
villa is the station of the Monserrate funicular and cable-car, linking the city with the summit of the mountain, affording splendid
views of the city. (Cable car daily, funicular Sun. and holidays
only.)

Continuing in the same direction, you can visit the recently
opened Planetarium, and Museum of Natural History. You can
attend demonstrations of celestial phenomena and visit the six halls,

containing a collection of Colombia's flora and fauna. Close by is the Bullring and Bullfight Museum; San Diego Church, a fine example of colonial architecture; Museum of Modern Art, with an excellent permanent collection and temporary exhibits of the works of Colombian and foreign modern artists (daily 10–6); and, finally, the National Museum, housed in a 19th-century fortress/prison. This museum has archeological, ethnographic, historic and artistic collections. They include huge statues carved by the mysterious Indians of San Agustin, an exhibit of elements in the daily life of the Choco Indians, the work of Colombian painters and mementos of Colombia's independence era (Tues.–Sat., 10–6; Sun. and hol. 10–2. Free Sat.).

Also housing interesting collections but not museums in the precise sense of the word, are the Hierba Buena Literary Museum with a display of manuscripts tracing Colombia's literary movements and Theological Seminary Museum grouping works of religious art; the former was a hacienda until very recently and its fields have been worked for centuries. As an added attraction it has a ghost. As for the Theological Seminary Museum, it is a modern brick building with a tranquil view of the Bogotá *sabana* and a collection of ornate, heavily-gilded church ornaments of solid silver and portraits of early bishops painted by the great artists of their day. Both these buildings lie on the northern edge of the city.

As one roams the city, its human landscape becomes apparent as well. During its early years, Bogotá's population consisted of Indians, Spaniards and mestizos, whose differences were easily distinguishable. Indian women wore long black skirts, fringed shawls, rope-soled shoes and braided hair while men dressed in calf-length white trousers, Panama hats beribboned in black, and blanket-like capes known as *ruanas*. They still do in the country.

While these costumes may occasionally be worn by visiting villagers even today, most Bogotanos are as conformist in their dressing as New Yorkers. Men wear London-inspired dark suits and light raincoats while women copy Paris, Rome, New York. Influenced by what they see on local TV programs, the Bogotanos have lost much of their aggressive individuality of the past. Though the old Indian-Spaniard mix has seen the addition of new ingredients from as far afield as Africa or Sweden, the more pronounced types tend to disappear. There is a process of Bogotanization pouring newcomers into some sort of giant mold that seems to turn out neat and fashionably-dressed citizens. At the bullfights, at concerts or plays in the Colón Theater or at the soccer stadium, Bogotanos display their fashion consciousness. On weekends sportswear takes over and women of all ages stroll along Bogotá's downtown streets clad in many-hued slacks. They also display it in the architecture and decoration of their homes whether in the working-class south or the aristocratic north of the city.

Side Trips from Bogotá

Bogotá is also the starting point of a number of side trips. The shortest and most famous is a trip from the eastern edge of town by funicular railroad or cable car to the venerated shrine on the peak of Monserrate. The church there is not much to look at, despite the effort that went into its building, but there is a splendid view of the city and the valley in which it lies.

Half an hour to the south are Tequendama Falls where great plumes of beige-colored water spurt through a sundered mountain landscape somewhat reminiscent of the Grand Canyon. There is a grim tradition here: it is the country's most "popular" suicide spot. There is truly something of Inferno about Tequendama Falls when mist steams up from rocks hundreds of feet below. Unfortunately, when a nearby, recently installed hydro-electric plant needs to provide emergency power to Bogotá, the water is diverted from the falls, leaving only a trickle most of the time. During the rainy season, sometimes, the plant's engineers allow the torrent to renew its former might.

The Salt Cathedral of Zipaquira is forty minutes to the north by car and it is probably the favorite tourist spot in the country surrounding Bogotá. It lies in the depths of a salt mine worked far beyond recorded history by the Chibcha Indians. Upon this mine an empire was built, as the Chibchas used their salt monopoly to dominate neighboring tribes in this inland region weeks away from the sea. And they converted this salt into gold. A morning's visit to the Salt Cathedral can be terminated with luncheon at the *Liberator Inn* just outside the mine or at the *Funzipa Restaurant*, located in an old salt-processing plant. The stately cathedral, where 10,000 people can worship, is well worth the effort.

Or else, forty minutes to the west, there is the Archeological Park at Facatativa, fortress of the Zipa Indians, who left a number of still undeciphered hieroglyphics inscribed on boulders in caves.

Two or three-day tours by fine highways can be made out of Bogotá into the beautiful State of Boyacá. One covers Tunja-Sogamoso-Lake Tota and the Spanish colonial villages of Tópaga and Mongui, plus the mineral springs of Paipa and the native handicraft centers at Duitama, Nobsa and San Luis de Ucuenga. The second includes the above, plus the Castille-like valley of Leyva, the Sáchica olive groves, the 16th-century monastery of Santo Ecce Homo, and Ráquira with its traditional pottery makers and other craftsmen. There's an interesting market in Sogamoso on Tuesdays.

Beyond this, there are interesting trips to be made to a number of small towns and villages on the way to the *tierra caliente*, the hot country along the Magdalena River or to the bucolic valley of Tenza in southeastern Boyacá. Visitors may arrange trips to a ranch where fighting bulls are bred.

Exploring the Caribbean Coast

The Caribbean coast of Colombia stretches from its juncture with Panama on the Gulf of Darién eastward to its boundary with Venezuela on the Peninsula of Guajira—approximately 1,200 miles of deeply-indented coastline, curving sand beaches, modern port cities and fishing villages. Beginning with the trio of cities which dominate the north coast, the visitor finds himself deep in an atmosphere reminiscent of the Spanish Main, the Inquisition and the 19th-century wars for independence.

Fascinating Cartagena

One of the most fascinating cities of the Western Hemisphere, Cartagena de Indias, to give it its proper name, lies 15 minutes by air or two hours by highway west of Barranquilla on the Caribbean coast. A city of 650,000, Cartagena deals largely in platinum and timber from the headwaters of the Atrato and San Juan Rivers, coffee from the Sierra Nevada and oil products piped from Barrancabermeja, 335 miles up the Magdalena. An important industrial center is developing around the Mamonal area and its petro-chemical plants.

But it is not commercial Cartagena that interests the tourist but rather the city founded in 1533 by Don Petro de Heredia, which still largely remains locked behind its massive walls on what once was an island. Actually the city is no longer an island since one of the two original entrances into its bay—Boca Grande—was blocked up by the Spaniards after the attack by Sir Edward Vernon in 1741. The other entrance—Boca Chica—is now the only passage into the bay from the sea, guarded by two ancient and derelict forts, San Fernando and San José. During the days when pirates of all nations harassed the Spanish Main, Cartagena was guarded by a massive chain stretched between these two forts. Launches run regularly to San Fernando where facilities for picnicking and sea bathing exist.

Towering over all of the many forts which guarded the approaches to Cartagena is the powerful fortress of San Felipe de Barajas, 135 feet above sea level. Begun in 1657, it was captured and destroyed by the French in 1697. Between 1762 and 1769, it was converted into the impressive complex that it is today. A "sound-and-light" spectacle depicting the often-bloody history of Cartagena is presented on Tues. and Sat. nights against the backdrop of the fort.

After the interior of the country was settled, wealth of all kinds flowed into Cartagena for shipment to Spain, wealth which soon invited pirate attacks in spite of the sturdy defenses of the city. Cartagena was sacked by Martin Cote, by Sir Francis Drake and by other freebooters, but an imposing fleet and powerful British army under Admiral Vernon failed before its stubborn resistance in 1741. Vernon was accompanied by a half-brother of George Washington in this attempt; Mount Vernon is named in his honor.

During the wars for independence, Cartagena was captured by Spanish loyalist troops under Pablo Morillo after a prolonged siege in 1815 which gained it the title of "the Heroic City" or, as Colombians refer to it, "La Heroica". Simón Bolívar used Cartagena as his base in the Magdalena campaign in 1811.

Cartagena is divided by 17th-century walls into the "old" and "new" city. In the "old" city houses are in the Iberian style: thick walls, high ceilings, central patios and gardens, and balconies. The streets are narrow and crooked for protection during assault.

Other sites of interest to the visitor to Cartagena include the Paseo de los Mártires, a wide promenade flanked by busts of nine patriots executed by Morillo after he took the city; the Plaza Bolívar with an equestrian statue of the Liberator in the center and flanked by the Palace of the Inquisition, a good example of colonial baroque architecture, which was built in 1776. It has a small Colonial Museum. Also noteworthy are the Cathedral, (1575–1612); the Jesuit Church of St. Peter Claver (a well-to-do Spaniard who devoted his life to caring for the sick and aged among the black slaves imported from Africa to work on the construction of walls and forts) in which the body of the saint lies in a chest under the main altar; the restored 17th-century monastery of La Popa from which the best view of Cartagena is obtained; the bulwarks of Las Bovedas, wide enough for automobile use in sightseeing tours, and the colorful and noisy market surrounded on three sides by the waters of the bay.

November 11, the anniversary of the city's declaration of its independence from Spain, is the city's principal celebration and the population parades the streets in fancy dress and masks. Another feast of great popular participation is that of the Virgin of la Candelaria (Candlemas) on February 2 when pilgrims troop up the 500-foot height of La Popa bearing lighted tapers.

Excursions from Cartagena

A short distance southwest of Cartagena, reached in about one hour by launch from the city, are the *Islas del Rosario*, a cluster of small islands where many residents of the coast and the interior have built villas and summer homes. Among the attractions of the archipelago are beautiful coral reefs and colorful tropical fish.

One hour north by jet from Cartagena are the Colombian islands of San Andres and Providencia, possibly visited by Columbus on one of his voyages, popular among Colombians and other tourists because of their status as duty free ports, beautiful white beaches, rolling surf, and relaxed, informal atmosphere. The frequent *puentes* (holidays of three or more consecutive days) find hundreds of highland dwellers taking advantage of air excursion rates to visit them.

The island of San Andres was originally settled by Pilgrims at the same time another group landed at Plymouth Rock. The San Andres Pilgrim's ship was the *Seaflower*.

Sixty-five airline miles directly south of Cartagena, reached by a passable highway (130 miles) or by combination of plane to the town of Sincelejo and by car the remaining 25 miles, is Tolú, a small fishing town on the handsome Gulf of Morrosquillo. Lodging in Tolú is not deluxe but perfectly acceptable to the traveler looking for an out-of-the-way spot where he can fish, swim in warm, blue tropical surf and invite his soul in peace and comfort. South along the gulf beach, within sight of Tolú is Coveñas, the Caribbean terminal of the trans-Andean oil pipeline from Colombian fields on the Venezuela frontier.

Barranquilla: The Crazy City

Barranquilla is a modern industrial city of over a million inhabitants and Colombia's second port, although in recent years silting of its Magdalena River entrance has caused concern to port authorities. But this is now being solved by breakwaters and steady dredging at Bocas de Ceniza, where the Magdalena River joins the Caribbean Sea. The city, founded in 1721, is located ten miles from the river's mouth on the west bank of the Magdalena and is the principal port of entry for visitors arriving either by plane or ship from the north. The city also boasts five universities.

Barranquilla normally holds little of interest for the tourist beyond hunting or fishing, of which there is an abundance in the area, or observing the busy port and lively activity in the streets. An impressive, modern cathedral is almost completed. It has walls of stained glass, doors with aluminum and brass, and will seat 3,000. The municipal market, on the Caño de las Compañias, a side channel of the Magdalena, is vivid and noisy. There is also a zoo with an interesting collection of Colombian species.

Normally a lively, happy city, Barranquilla becomes in the week before Lent each year what its inhabitants call *una ciudad loca*— a "crazy city", in which crowds fill the streets day and night dressed in exotic costumes and masks. There are parades of floats and folklore dances and music, a battle of flowers, beauty contests, an aquatic festival and finally the night before Ash Wednesday, the burial of "Joselito Carnaval", the spirit of the celebration, for another year. Also observed by the *Barranquilleros* is the annual feast of San Roque on August 16.

Fifteen miles from Barranquilla eastward to the Caribbean shore is the beach resort of Puerto Colombia. Once used as the port of Barranquilla when the Magdalena became heavily silted, Puerto Colombia now serves only for the recreation of residents and visitors. Other nearby bathing resorts include Pradomar, Salgar, Sabanilla, Galerazamba, Santa Veronica, Puerto Caiman, and Punta Rocas. Bajo de Caja (20 miles from the city) has good fishing, miniature golf and a beach restaurant with regional food and *cumbia* performances. Torchlight illumination at night. 18 miles southwest are the excellent thermal springs of Usiacuri.

Pearl of the Americas

Fifty airline miles northeast of Barranquilla—15 minutes by plane or one hour and a half by highway—is Santa Marta, the "Pearl of the Americas", which was founded in 1525 by Rodrigo de Bastidas, an early *conquistador*. Santa Marta lies on a deep bay protected on both flanks by ancient forts. In spite of these however the city was sacked by pirates in the 16th and 17th centuries.

Santa Marta, with its deep water allowing ocean-going vessels to lie alongside its docks, is increasing in importance as a commercial port. Its principal export is bananas, brought to dockside by a railway from the widespread plantations of various fruit companies spread along the base of the Sierra Nevada de Santa Marta.

This compact range of mountains, highest of which reaches 19,500 feet, is snow-covered the year around. Coffee plantations which grow a fine grade of mild coffee are found on its flanks. It is possible to reach the summit but it is advisable to use local guides.

It was to Santa Marta in 1830 that Bolívar, the liberator of half the countries of South America, came penniless and broken in health on his way to voluntary exile after his dream of a *Gran Colombia* had shattered on the petty political machinations of his colleagues. He was given refuge at the plantation of the Marquis de Mier y Benítez, called "San Pedro Alejandrino", where he died on December 17 at the age of 47. The plantation, now a national shrine, no longer shelters the hero's remains, which were removed to Caracas in 1842, but the simple room in which he died and his few pathetic belongings may still be seen. The plantation is three miles southeast of Santa Marta on the road to the Sierra Nevada.

Aside from the beautiful Bay of Santa Marta, points of interest in and near the city are Tayrona National Park (1 hour away), with a spectacular, tropical beach, a marine biology center at Punta de Betin, the Rodadero and Gaira beach, the fishing villages of La Concha and Taganga, the Cathedral and the Church of San Francisco. El Rodadero is a modern city, with high rise condominiums, shops, casino, a branch of the famous *Unicorn* nightclub, and a tree-lined promenade along the beach. You can charter fishing boats here, snorkel, water-ski, enjoy pedalo boats and bowl. The Aquarium features sharks, sea lions and large tropical fish. The Museo Arqueologico del Magdalena is new.

Medellin: Orchids and Industry

The Caribbean coast and Bogotá usually are the main reasons
for a trip to Colombia. But they certainly should not be the only
reasons. During the nation's history, its spiny mountain topography
led to the flourishing of cities that developed a character of their
own, isolated as they were as if on mid-ocean islands. These days,
airlines and new roads and railroads have leapfrogged travel problems of the past, but town and cities have retained much of their
character. Since there is no stopping the steamroller of 20th-
century life, it might not be a bad idea to see them before it is too
late.

Colombia's second city has traditionally been Medellín, though
it is now neck-and-neck with Cali for the title as both their populations hover over the million mark. It lies in a mountain valley
at 5,000 feet where airliners fly in and out in spectacular spirals.
Though Medellín in central Colombia is the country's leading
industrial beehive, you would never know it. Its prosperity is not
expressed in soot and reeking chimneys but in clean streets,
flower-bedded boulevards and magnificent residential quarters. It
is the only city in Colombia with a Convention Bureau, intent on
promoting Medellín as "Latin America's Convention Capital".

Medellín is a sober, hard-working city that lets down its hair
once a year during its annual flower festival when it is turned into
a bower while striking beauties are paraded through the streets
under floral arches. Then Colombia's leading orchestras are flown
in to keep staid Medellín dancing until all hours.

The best view of the city is from *Nutibara Hill*, which also has a
restaurant. In 1972 the International Orchid Conference was held
in buildings that are now a part of the Botanical Gardens. Over
150 years old, the buildings are being carefully reconstructed and
house a reference library. The gardens exhibit a large variety of
orchids and native flora. The Cathedral, built of 1,200,000 bricks,
is considered the third largest brick building in the world. Near the
Inter Continental is the ultra-modern San Diego Shopping Mall,
with quality shops. University City (for about 12,000 students)
has some interesting art works and an Anthropological Museum.
La Macarena, seating 10,000, has bullfights in Feb., on Sat. and
Sun. You will find the most complete collection of orchids in the
world at *El Ranchito*, 10 miles from the city. The *Museo Folklorico Tejicondor* has exhibitions of handicrafts, costumes, rare
musical instruments, frequent folk concerts, dance groups. Free,
but check hours. "El Castillo" Museum, in the suburbs of El
Poblado, is considered the most elegant place in Medellín. Beautiful gardens. Daily 1–5 p.m. Free. *Hacienda Fizabad*, about one
hour's drive out of Medellín, is the recreation of a colonial village
with magnificent gardens and an *hacienda* house which is a veritable living museum. A favorite vacation spot for Medellín's large

families is the fishing village of Tolu on the sparkling Morrosquillo Gulf. The fishing and swimming are wonderful . . . if you like children.

Turantioquia, the helpful local Tourist Information Office, operates delightful hotels outside of Medellín. En route to Cartagena in Caucasia, is the *Hosteria Horizontes*, a small hotel with pool, typical food and excellent service. *Santa Fe de Antioquia*, 47 miles from the city, is a colonial jewel. Of interest also are the open-air regional markets held on Fri. and Sat. You can stay at the *Mariscal Robledo*, a lovely colonial-style hotel. In La Pintada, 50 miles from the city, is the *Farrallones Motel*, a charming inn with a restaurant, pool, and spectacular views of the river, mountains and valley.

Medellín is within easy striking distance of Manizales, a town that offers an electric range of pastimes. There must be few places in the world that can display waterskiing, snow-skiing and bullfighting in such a short radius. The skiing goes on at nearby El Ruiz, a peak 18,000 feet tall, and the road up from Manizales through green coffee plantations is an experience in itself. By the time you reach the snow line, the air has become quite rarified and skiing is an Andean sport here. Manizales also boasts an exciting *feria* whose biggest attraction is its program of bullfights when the world's greatest *toreros* come to the city.

The Ranchhouses of Cali

There's another *feria* between Christmas and New Year's Day at Cali and this is the best time to visit Colombia's other big city. Despite its size, it has not forgotten that it was once the heart of a colonial ranching economy and it has the grace of all cities built along rivers. The old life can be seen at Cañasgordas, a colonial ranchhouse, where relics of Cali's last Royal Sheriff are preserved. Visitors can still see high canopied beds reached by ladders, a Hapsburg-style altar in a private chapel where a resident priest said masses a century ago for the Royal Sheriff's family, and an intriguing Moorish system of rainwater canals that surround the house and supply both water and air-conditioning somewhat in the way of the Alhambra in Spain. You can visit the 150-year-old *Hacienda El Paraiso*, a romantic museum, formerly the home of the author of *Maria*. There is a changing exhibit of local artists in the *Museo de la Tertulia*, near the Inter Continental. The *Museum of Natural Sciences* might also interest you. But Cali's best-known attraction is its women, the descendants of those old ranching families, who are some of the most exquisite in all South America.

Nature is rewarding around Cali and offers a large variety of tropical birds in their natural habitat, including the *mirla* that has the power of looking glum and talking. Bird-hunting instead of bird-watching can be handled by the local Club de Caceria that helps in arranging licenses.

There are two charming towns, Buga and Palmira, near Cali in the Cauca Valley. Buga is a tranquil little place tucked away in blue hills with a hospitable population that delights in opening its homes and gardens to visitors. Palmira offers the attraction of a green sea of sugar cane at harvest time when it draws its visitors.

Then, on the rail line from Palmira, there are the red-tiled roofs and white-domed churches of Pereira (it can be reached by car, too, over a spaghetti of turns, but it's best to fly). Pereira is a young town as Colombian cities go—it is only a century old—but it has grown rapidly.

East of Cali to the Magdalena River country, there is much more ancient Neiva, founded in 1550 by *conquistadores* who came for its gold. Today, it raises cattle instead and comes to life very local-colorfully during its four yearly fairs: January, April, June and October. Travelers to colonial Neiva use it as a base for a trip that leads to one of Colombia's most memorable experiences: a visit to the San Agustin Valley where heroic-sized statues are strewn across what must once have been sacred ground in a forgotten empire. These statues share some Mayan characteristics and one theory holds that they were the work of Mayans who emigrated to the south. But the statues also have some kinship with the mysterious giants of Easter Island and their enigma makes them all the more impressive. Besides, a trip to San Agustin's Archeological Park also offers an excursion to "El Estrecho" (The Narrows), a source of the Magdalena and to a town that makes an ideal return address for letters home, called Hobo. Also in the area, at Gigante, is a giant ceiba tree covering the central square, supposedly over 1,000 years old. About an 8-hour drive on an unpaved road from San Agustin, or 4 hours from Popayan, is located the archeological site known as "Tierradentro", with its interesting necropolis of geometrically painted underground tombs.

Holy Week in Popayan

Wandering south in the direction of the Ecuadorean border, you encounter another impressive heritage of the past at Popayan, an early center of Spanish-American culture and learning. Plan your visit to Popayan during Holy Week when scions of leading families shoulder heavy platforms bearing antique statues resplendent in jewels and velvet and strangely lifelike in their candlelit setting. Dressed in the robes of medieval penitents, the men parade past the torches of spectators in processions that end in colonial-era churches. There, in the yellow glow shed by hundreds of candles, the statues are returned to their niches lined with flowers. In some churches, the flowers are replaced by young wheat sprouts symbolizing resurrection and new life. Bucaramanga, to the northeast, is a provincial capital in a spectacular site hemmed on one side by sheer cliffs crumbling in great chunks that add to the spice of life here. Bucaramanga was settled in the early days of Colombian colonization and the soldiers who accompanied the German adventurer Nikolaus Federmann on his search for El Dorado passed through. They get credit for the high proportion of blond, blue-eyed citizens seen here today. The men of Bucaramanga are tough hombres who keep their pistols at the ready and their women at home. Colombians say that anyone can tell whether he is in Cartagena, Bogotá or Bucaramanga by looking at checkrooms: in Cartagena, men check their coats; in Bogotá, they check their books; in Bucaramanga, they check their artillery.

An archeological museum, housed in a building where Bolívar lived for two months, contains excellent pre-Colombian pottery, jewelry and textiles that lead some scholars to presume that the Incas reached this area. Then there are the oil paintings and wood carvings in graceful churches . . . and there are also murals in the Bucaramanga city club where an artist placed the faces of several well-known society ladies above the figures of lightly-clad nymphs.

Bucaramanga's eating habits are equally picturesque. One local specialty is fried or jellied ants: fried, they come in paper bags and one crunches them like peanuts; jellied, they resemble caviar. Another is *tinajo*, a seal-like animal that tastes like pig when roasted. Finally, there is armadillo, tasting somewhat like chicken.

It's worth noting that tourists are welcome to Bucaramanga's country club. There's golf and tennis during the New Year season, and a nationally-celebrated costume party.

Our next stop on this ramble around Colombia is a fascinating one: old Tunja, the capital of Boyacá, steeped in Indian lore. This pre-Colombian civilization was deeply religious and transformed its ample supply of gold and emeralds into idols. Then the Spaniards came to the blue mountains of Boyacá under Captain Gonzalo Suarez Rendon and ordered the Indians to collect their precious idols inside their temples. The story goes that one temple chockful of gold was burned when two Spanish soldiers upset a torch, touching off its straw.

Boyacá boasts the greatest emerald mines of the Western Hemisphere at Muzo, Coscuez, Chivor and Somondoco. According to another local legend, the Indians hid one mine from the Spanish for a hundred years. Then a Castillian horseman found a green rock under his horse's hoof. It turned out to be emerald matrix and he was able to trace it back to the secret mine. But Boyacá has other gems as well: colonial churches and shrines, great haciendas, fruit plantations, trout-filled lakes, and Shangri-la valleys covered with wheat fields, olive groves and willow forests.

You can take an 8-hour tour out of Bogotá to Colonial Tunja

and the Boyacá Battlefield, lunch included. Consult Allen & Mary Lowrie Travel Ltda.

Tunja, as we said, was an Indian religious center and it clung to its sacred role as it moved into the colonial era. Among its outstanding churches and seminaries are San Laureano, begun in 1566, the College dating back to 1612, and the Tunja Cathedral that bears the date of 1598. Rendon built a home and settled in Tunja; this home is now open to the public, (daily except Mon. 9–6), as is the home of the King's Scrivener Don Juan de Vargas (daily 8:30–12:30; 1:30–6). San Ignacio Church is an important museum of religious art.

Swim Suits of Gold Dust

Around Boyacá, there are other charming colonial towns besides Tunja. You reach them on roads that run through ranchlands and past lakes where the Indian kings are said to have created the El Dorado legend by diving into lakes clad only in gold dust. Along the roads, you also see Boyacá women weaving straw hats or the wool *ruanas* worn by most Colombian mountaineers and made famous by Avianca Airlines' hostesses. A magnificent church with onion-shaped towers and a mosque-like cupola awaits you in Duitama. Sogamoso has a museum that stands in the site of a great Temple of the Sun overlooking the Conchucua Spring used by Indian priests in their rituals. Mongui offers a temple and an old convent with paintings by Arce y Ceballos, one of Colombia's greatest colonial artists. As for Chiquinquirá, its basilica and shrine draw thousands of pilgrims, for the Virgin is said to have appeared here. Villa de Leyva, a gem of colonial architecture, is located in an arid valley whose olive groves, wheat fields and pepper trees are reminiscent of Spain. Boyacá also lures visitors with its hot sulphur springs at Paipa and its Lake Tota with boating and trout fishing.

A line drawn southeast of Tunja passes through Bogotá, worth a chapter in itself as we've seen, and then to Girardot, a favorite river vacation spot with its passionately tropical atmosphere punctuated by flamingo trees and blooming bougainvillca.

Across the Magdalena River at Girardot, is Flandes, a Tolima town, and many visitors make the crossing for a shot of Tolima rum that is more like a cannon shot in its impact.

Around Melgar, there are a number of resorts up in the cooler coffee country in the hills. Melgar is tiny but delightful, and a favorite weekend spot for Bogotá's diplomatic colony. Then there is Fusagasuga which also has a big Bogotá clientele, but the climate here at 6,000 feet is cool and can be rainy. Yet Fusagasuga is a good starting point for excursions by car, into the Andes 11,000 feet high. On the road, giant ferns soar to twenty-foot heights and then you climb into eternal mists brightened only by the candles placed by truck-drivers in roadside shrines. A splash of color is provided on this trip. by the orchid-like blossoms of *siete cueros* trees. Great bird watching here, too!

Skipping back to Girardot and then to the northwest, there is Ibagué, best known as Colombia's music center and the home of a handsome modern country club considered an architectural gem. There are fine choral groups in Ibagué which also offers a folklore festival with excellent orchestras. Out of Bogotá, Lowrie's has a 3-day, 2-night trip that visits the Magdalena River Valley, Central Cordillera of the Andes, Manizales, Pereira, Armenia, Ibagué, Girardot and Tequendama Falls.

On the eastern fringe of this part of Colombia, there is a unique experience awaiting the traveler who ventures over the mountains to the great plains known as the *llanos*. The capital of this region is Villavicencio, three hours by car or half an hour by air from Bogotá. Villavicencio is cooled by nearby mountains in the evening but the days are well-nigh equatorial. The great Orinoco has its source in this region and the handsome Guaitiquia adds its waters, too, to the beauty of these endless seas of grass.

The *llanos* are good hunting country, abounding in jaguar, boar, alligator, deer, puma, tapir and enticing birds. Safaris here should be carefully and competently planned so that the hunter does not become the hunted with venomous snakes or carnivorous piraña fish doing the stalking. Those piraña fish can strip a steer to a skeleton in minutes and hardbitten *llaneros* always take due precautions before driving a herd across a river (they send their least valuable animal in first). The *llaneros* of Colombia belong to the same race as cowboys anywhere. They can ride hard all day long and dance their *joropo* all night. The best time to see them is in December when Villavicencio stages a song festival and a cattle fair.

Pacific Surfing and Giant Shrimp

Colombia changes when one moves from these inland regions across the Andes to the Pacific Coast. Midway along this coast lies Buenaventura, the country's busiest harbor, which is mainly a port of entry. There is not much to induce a traveler—unless he's a commercial traveler—to linger here.

Near the Ecuadorean border on the Pacific, Tumaco is still undeveloped, but has long beaches of fine sand equipped with a steady supply of Pacific breakers for surfing. Besides swimming and surfing, the Pacific offers superlative off-shore fishing and the big marlin are out there waiting the fisherman who is man enough to take them. Boats capable of reaching deepsea grounds can be hired but it would be wise to bring your own gear. Tumaco itself is one of Colombia's newest towns because it was rebuilt a few years ago after a fire had destroyed it. Gourmets know it for its giant shrimp, best eaten around a bonfire by moonlight on the beach with dinner music supplied by a local *murga*, a band of serenaders. That's the kind of tropical night that takes a long while to forget.

Pasto is also near the Ecuadorean border but inland. Therefore it doesn't have the Pacific but it does have Galeras, an active volcano, and the usual bargains found in frontier towns. It also offers unique woodwork: hand-carved tables, chairs, trays or plates that are embossed with a latex-like sap that is dyed red or green then glued to an ivory or black background. The resulting geometric designs come from ancient Indian styles. And there are some modern Indian tribes in villages near Pasto. They wear conical saucer hats that resemble those worn by Vietnamese farmers . . . and help support the Kon-Tiki theory of the origin of South American Indians.

Still further south and looking right into Ecuador is Ipiales in a valley bordered by three volcanoes. It draws pilgrims to its church, the Sanctuary of Our Lady of the Stones, perched seven stories above a gorge with a Gothic tower, arches and buttresses in a tropical setting. Another local landmark is the Rumichaca Bridge, the feat of Inca engineers.

The valley around Ipiales is another stretch of Colombian cattle country. Here, the vaqueros dress in straw hats, cotton ponchos, leather chaps known as *zamarros* and rope-soled sandals.

And now we have circled around most of settled Colombia. But there is still unsettled Colombia: the Amazon. Leticia, a river port, can be reached by plane from Bogotá in less than two hours and planes have transformed it from a junglebound trading post to an international tourist center. Brazil and Peru are within easy distance here and Lowrie offers a trip to the river Atacuari, the natural border between Peru and Colombia, devoted to setting up temporary living quarters and camping with the Yagua Indians, observing their weapons, customs and general living habits. Minimum 3-day stay.

The *pièce de resistance* of a stay in Leticia is a trip on the Amazon, preferably with a good boat. This may show you the manatees, aquatic mammals native to tropical Atlantic coastal waters, as well as the unique birds of the Amazon. Descriptions and rates for tours available on request from Lowrie's.

Even if you don't see anything more exciting than parrots or monkeys on your river trip, you will not go home empty-handed. For in Leticia in the heart of the jungle . . . there's a zoo. It's run by an American of Greek origin as a living warehouse of animals in demand in the United States for zoos, film sequences or collectors. And there are others who will also supply you any variety of local fauna you may wish. Some of the odd specimens here are in transit, but others are preserved against the day when they may be threatened with extinction.

PRACTICAL INFORMATION FOR COLOMBIA

CAPSULE COMMENTS. *Physical Features.* Colombia is unique in many respects. Her coasts border both the Pacific and Atlantic, and her land ranges from the tropical Caribbean to the bleak high plateau country in the interior. There are tropics along the 940-mile Magdalena River and warm, fertile central valleys. Towering rain-forests in the Amazon River basin.

Climate. Any climate one desires exists in Colombia—and when one finds it, it doesn't change. Bogotá is always springlike, with cool days and crisp nights. In the lowlands the warm summer air of the tropics prevails year 'round.

Population. 28,000,000. Bogotá 4,500,000.

Language. Spanish.

Archeological Attractions. St. Agustin Monoliths, Tayrona ruins near Santa Marta, and Sogamoso Archeological Park. Brightly painted cave-tombs in the Tierradentro area.

Principal Industries. Coffee, emeralds, petroleum, bananas, textiles, steel, paper, rice, cocoa, cattle.

COSTS. Colombia is one of the few countries in South America where costs are relatively stable. Rather than a lot of prose, we thought it would be instructive to describe some costs here in tabular form, as follows:

COSTS OF A TYPICAL DAY

1st Class Hotel (per person in Double)	$16.50
Three Meals (including service)	9.75
Four Taxi Rides	3.25
Two Drinks (imported brands)	4.00
Theater Ticket	2.25
Movie	0.75
City Sightseeing Tour	8.25
Laundry (Shirt)	0.50
Dry Clean Suit	0.70 (Dress $0.50)
Pack of American Cigarettes	0.55
Total Cost	$46.50

RESTAURANT COSTS—US$

Category	Major City	Major Resort	Provincial City	Budget Resort
Luxury	$10.00	$9.50		
First-class	6.75	6.00	$6.00	$4.50
Moderate	5.00	4.50	4.50	4.00
Inexpensive	2.75	2.75	2.50	2.25

HOTEL PRICES--US$

Category	Major City	Major Resort	Provincial Capital	Least Expensive City
SUPERIOR FIRST-CLASS				
Single	$31.00	$16.50	$22.00	$ —
Double	$37.00	$20.00	$25.00	$ —
FIRST-CLASS				
Single	$13.50	$11.00	$11.00	$ 9.00
Double	$19.00	$16.50	$17.50	$13.50
MODERATE				
Single	$12.75	$ 9.50	$ 9.50	$ 8.00
Double	$16.00	$11.00	$11.00	$10.50
INEXPENSIVE				
Single	$11.00	$ 9.00	$ 5.50	$ 5.00
Double	$14.50	$10.50	$ 9.00	$ 5.50

A DAILY MODERATE-RANGE BUDGET—US$

Moderate hotel, with breakfast, tax and service charges included, per person in a double room:	$11.00
Lunch in a middle-price restaurant:	5.00
Dinner in a middle-price restaurant:	5.50
Transportation by taxi, basic fare for two kilometers (no tipping):	0.55
Theater ticket, middle-range ticket:	2.00
One pack of cigarettes, best local brand:	0.30
One coffee in a popular coffee shop:	0.15
One beer in a popular bar:	0.35
10% for contingencies:	2.50
Total	$27.35

WHEN TO COME. Since Colombia is a tropical country with its capital lying less than 800 miles north of the equator, climate is very largely a matter of altitude. Temperatures range from an average of about 83 degrees F. along the Caribbean coast to a chilly 55 degrees F. average (in the 40's at night, about 75 degrees at noon) in the capital city, perched in the Andes at an altitude of 8,640 feet.

Although seasons as such do not exist, in general, there can be rainfall Oct.-Nov. (afternoons) and Apr.-June. The dry season is usually Dec.-Mar. In the coastal area the dry season is mid-Dec. through Apr. and July-Sept.

Rainfall, however, is never excessive, except in such coastal areas as Chocó where rainfall averages an inch a day; also in Bogotá.

Colombia celebrates the following holidays: *New Year; Epiphany* (Jan. 6); *St. Joseph's Day* (Mar. 19); *Holy Week; Easter; Labor Day*

LOCAL PRICES COMPARISON TABLE—US$ (ESTIMATED)	
150-gram jar instant coffee	$1.25
1 lb. butter	2.25
1 head lettuce	0.25
1 dozen eggs	1.00
1 large beer	0.35
1 lb. sugar	0.25
1 snack-size cup of ice cream	0.10
46-oz. can orange juice	0.85
1 qt. fresh milk	0.25
Small jar Colombian baby food	0.35
1 tube Colombian toothpaste	0.55
1 box Kleenex	1.00
1 bottle good local wine	2.00
Haircut	1.50
Shampoo and set	3.50
One cinema ticket	0.75
Telephone call, local, 3 minutes	0.10
Coca Cola	0.10
Color film, 20 exposures, Kodak	7.00
Toilet tissue, 800 sheets	0.30
Picture postcards, each	0.25
Air mail postage per letter to the United States	0.25
Cablegram (21-word minimum) to the United States	8.25

(May 1); *Ascension Day* (May 25); *Sacred Heart* (June 2); *Corpus Christi* (June 17); *Saint Peter and Paul* (June 29); *Independence Day* (July 20); *Battle of Boyaca* (Aug. 7); *Assumption* (Aug. 15); *Columbus Day* (Oct. 12); *All Saint's Day* (Nov. 1); *Independence of Cartagena* (Nov. 11); *Immaculate Conception* (Dec. 8) and *Christmas*. (Some of these dates change slightly; these are for 1978.)

The Caribbean coast of Colombia is rich in festivals of all kinds—music, folklore, sports, religious and commercial—and the *costeño* is generally regarded by his more sober brothers of the Andean highlands as rather more given to fun-making and the lighter things of life than is proper. He has been described as "expansive, conceited and vehement . . . His life opens on the limitless horizon of the sea, and his African descent confers on him the fatuity and conceit which is one of the characteristics of that race. His feelings are skin-deep, free, for he has nothing to hide and this makes him thoughtless of the future, generous and spendthrift."

Cartagena celebrates its independence from Spain on *November 11* with a week of merrymaking, parades and dancing, which ends with the election of the National Beauty Queen, who is Colombia's representative to international beauty contests. It also sponsors weeks devoted to folklore and music. Its Film Festival, held in March, is internationally recognized.

Barranquilla's carnival season, famous throughout the hemisphere, is held the week before Ash Wednesday.

International tennis matches are scheduled there in *March* and international fishing competitions are held in May and November.

In July, Santa Marta, oldest European-founded city on the South American continent, presents a "Fiesta del Mar" with regattas, beauty contests, water-skiing exhibitions and street dances. In late May or early June, the Flower Festival is held in Medellín. Medellín, incidentally, is the "orchid capital of the world."

The Folklore Festival, in Ibague, is usually held in the last week of June. This is Colombia's largest folklore event, and includes auto races, horse shows, shooting contests and art shows, as well as the traditional dance and music events.

Many other Colombian cities have pageants and parades. Manizales has its *feria* the second week of *January* coinciding every two years with its International Coffee Queen contest. Cali celebrates its fair from *December 25* to *January 1*. Sonsón has a corn festival and Neiva a *bambuco* festival.

Bogotá has bullfights most of the year but the principal season, during which outstanding Colombian, Venezuelan, Spanish and Mexican toreros appear, is in *December* and *February*. Outstanding *corridas* also take place during the Cali and Manizales *ferias* late in *December* and *January* respectively.

A national agricultural and cattle fair is held during the first week of *August*. Independence Day (*July 20*) and the anniversary of the decisive battle of Boyacá (*August 7*) are usually occasions for showy military parades.

Horse racing with parimutuel betting, on Thurs., Sun. and holidays.

Bogotá's plush Colón Theater presents *ballet*, *opera*, *drama* and *music*, with international and local groups. The open-air Media Torta presents music, plays, folk dances Sun. afternoons and holidays. Free. The Community Players of Bogotá, an amateur theatre group, give frequent performances in English.

 TRAVEL DOCUMENTS, CUSTOMS. U.S. and Canadian visitors need a valid passport, smallpox vaccination certificate and onward ticket. In addition, Canadian citizens need a visa. Foreigners or businessmen who desire to work will need a special visa given by Colombian consulates.

200 cigarettes, or 50 cigars, 2 bottles of liquor allowed duty free. No other restriction on personal effects. There is a US $10 airport tax on international flights and a 60-peso (about US $2.00) tax on domestic flights.

A 15-day Transit Card, obtained from airlines or Colombian consulates with no photographs required, permits transit through Colombia to a third destination. e.g. Miami/Bogotá/Lima. The traveler must have a valid passport in order to obtain the Transit Card.

 CURRENCY. Monetary unit is the peso, currently exchanged at approximately 37 to the American dollar, 60 to the pound sterling. This exchange rate is slowly rising. American and Canadian money is changed at hotels, banks, shops and travel agencies. There is usually a fee for such exchange. When leaving, upon presentation of official

exchange receipts, you can convert your pesos (up to U.S. $60) back
into U.S. dollars. It is illegal to exchange money at other than authorized exchange sources.

 TIPPING. Most Colombians give no tip to taxi
drivers but drivers expect one. If you want to tip
yours, he will thank you profusely. In restaurants,
10 per cent is the rule. At a favorite spot where
you want a choice table, 15 per cent is advisable. Hotel maids or
clerks are seldom tipped. Locker room attendants at private clubs do
not expect tips. At the Cartagena Country Club the suggested tip for
caddies is 20 pesos (50¢) for 9 holes, 25 pesos (65¢) for 18. Bogotá's
shoeshine boys swarm around any tourist with a kind face. They live
on their tips and a difference of one penny is important. The going
price for a shoeshine is four pesos. Give one peso to urchins who
offer to watch your car or clean your windshield. Other waifs sing
to crowds emerging from movie theaters, etc.; they expect one peso
each.

 HOW TO GET THERE. By Air. From the U.S.: To
Bogotá—*Avianca* non-stop from New York and
Miami; *Braniff* non-stop from New York, from
Miami via Panama; *Aerocondor* and *Air Panama*
from Miami; *Aerolineas Argentinas* and *Avianca* non-stop from Los
Angeles. To Barranquilla—*Avianca* from New York; *Aerocondor* from
Miami. To Cartagena—*Avianca* from New York and Miami. To Medel-
lín—*Aerocondor* from Miami; *Avianca* from New York and Miami;
SAM and *COPA* from Panama. To Cali—*Avianca* and *Braniff* from
New York, Miami and Panama; *LAN-Chile* from New York and Mi-
ami; *Aerocondor* and *Ecuatoriana Airlines* from Miami. To San Andres
—*SAM* from San Salvador, Managua and San José; *Lacsa* from San
José; *Sahsa* from Tegucigalpa and Panama. *Eastern* anticipates service
from Miami. To Providencia—*Cessnyca* from San Andres. From
Mexico to Bogotá—*Aeromexico*.

From Europe: *Air France* from Paris and Lisbon to Bogotá; *Avianca*
from Frankfurt, Paris, Zurich and Madrid to Bogotá and Barranquilla;
British Caledonian from London; *Iberia* from Madrid via San Juan to
Bogotá and Barranquilla; *Lufthansa* from Frankfurt via New York and
Kingston and from Casablanca via Caracas; *VIASA* from Beirut,
Rome, Milan, Paris, Madrid, Amsterdam and London via Caracas.

Regional: *Aerocondor, Aeropesco, Avianca, S.A.M., Satena T.A.C.*

Flying hours to Bogotá from: New York 5; Miami 2.5; San Juan 3;
Paris 11; London 12; Panama 1; Lima 3; Santiago 6; Lisbon 10;
Madrid 10; Rome 14; Quito 1; Rio 8; Buenos Aires 7.

By ship. The following maritime companies regularly serve Colombian ports with both passenger and combination passenger-freight
vessels: From U.S. Gulf ports. *Prudential-Grace Line* cruises. From
Europe *French Line, Italian Line, Pacific Steam Navigation, Royal
Netherlands SS Co.* and *Linea "C."*

Many calls have been made by cruise ships.

By car. Since the Darién Gap, which lies in southern Panama and
northwestern Colombia, still remains open in the Pan American High-

way it is impossible to drive one's car into Colombia from Panama at the present time. Vehicles must be freighted from Panama to one of Colombia's Caribbean or Pacific ports.

By bus. TEPSA buses connect with several other S.A. countries out of Pasto. There are second-class buses from Maracaibo to Santa Marta and Cartagena.

 WHAT TO WEAR. With climate in Colombia depending pretty largely at what altitude one may be, what a traveler brings with him will depend on where he intends to go in the country. On the coast the climate is tropical, averaging about 80 degrees F.; sport shirts and slacks for men and cotton dresses, pants and shorts for women are recommended. In the better hotels jackets, and ties for men and dresses for women are expected at meals. In Bogotá, the days are mild; nights chilly. Pants suits or separates, and a coat are fine for women; a fall-type suit for men. Don't forget your raincoat!

 HOW TO GET ABOUT. Colombia, faced with the extremely difficult problem of transport in a country which is almost as vertical as it is horizontal, has developed one of the best air transportation systems in the world.

Avianca, owned by private Colombian citizens, is the oldest airline in the Americas and second oldest anywhere. It operates daily flights connecting all important cities of Colombia, including those of the Caribbean coastal area.

Other airlines conducting internal flight operations: *SAM, Aerocondor, TAC, Aerocosta, Aeropesca, TARCA, Cessnica, Aerotaxi,* plus *Helicol,* an Avianca subsidiary, for short helicopter flights.

Avianca, SAM and *Aerocondor* operate daily flights from Bogotá, Barranquilla and Cartagena to San Andres island. At San Andres bicycles and dune buggies can be rented. There are boat trips to Johnny Cay and the Aquarium.

A good highway connects Santa Marta on the east with Cartagena, crossing the Magdalena River by a recently opened automobile bridge and passing through Barranquilla en route. The brand-new Trans-Caribbean Highway, four-laned most of the way, has now placed Barranquilla only five hours away from the border with Venezuela. Northeast of Santa Marta, in the Guajira Peninsula, roads are usually passable except during rainy periods. *Avis, Hertz* and *National* have car rental offices, but driving in the city is not recommended.

Highway transportation is maintained between the coastal cities and the capital and other cities of the interior, but much of the highway is rutted. Modern buses and mini-buses provide transportation between coastal towns and cities. Taxis are plentiful with rates at about U.S. $0.30 per mi.; from airport 25 pesos is added to the fare; on Sun. and evenings, 15 more, or total of 40 pesos is added. Hourly rate about 100 pesos. For the hardy traveler there are shared taxis, sold on seat availability basis. City bus fares are approximately U.S. $0.15.

The Magdalena River is the main artery of Colombia and although passenger service on it has been suspended, the traveller would be wise to inquire about it when making arrangements to visit Colombia.

We strongly urge the ladies to hold on to their purses; men, carry your wallets in your inside coat pocket. The street urchins are adept at snatching.

 HOTELS. Generally speaking, Colombia's hotel standards stand up well in comparison with those of other hotels throughout South America. A few of its top-notch establishments rival the finest on the continent; prices are relatively low, and service is excellent. In the face of constantly increasing tourist business, the hotels of the capital and the Caribbean area are often short of space. It is advisable to reserve well in advance. A five per cent tax is added to hotel bills throughout the country to help promote tourism; but with the moderate prices, this is quite painless. Living costs are still fairly low and the favorable exchange rate makes your dollar go a long way.

Hotel and restaurant rates are subject to change, but you may use these guidelines. *Superior first class* means $30 (US) and up for double; *First Class* is $20 up for double; *Moderate*, $12 up double; *Inexpensive* rates are lower. Rates quoted are for room only, no meals. There is a 5% government tax on rooms. A 10% increase in rates is expected by 1978.

BOGOTÁ

Superior First Class

TEQUENDAMA. Absolutely top flight hotel member of the Inter Continental chain. 800 rooms, 2 excellent restaurants. One on 17th floor offers entertainment, but at an exorbitant cover charge. Suggest drinks in bar opposite for the same panoramic view. 24-hour coffee shop. Good shops. Ten blocks from major business district, near park.

BOGOTÁ HILTON. Outstanding. 12 blocks from business section. 33 singles, 167 suites. The dining area overlooks enclosed, heated pool with conservatory. Popular, lavish Sun. Buffet. English "pub" bar. Gourmet supper club with entertainment on 41st floor, offering beautiful views of city. Shops, garage.

First Class

DANN. Practically next door to *Bacata*. 150 rooms. Superior, reasonably priced dining room.

BACATA. Recently enlarged. Large repeat clientele. First-class rooms. In downtown area.

EL PRESIDENTE. Fairly new. Inferior location. Good for the budget-minded. Restaurant, coffee shop, bar.

CONTINENTAL. Centrally located. First-class, commercial: 250 rooms. Good restaurant specializing in Italian food.

Moderate

SAN DIEGO. Half-block away from *Hotel Tequendama*. 34 rooms. Popular with Colombian businessmen. Good, second class.

TUNDAMA. In business district. 69 rooms. Commercial hotel.

CORDILLERA. Downtown location in center of business district. Bar. Restaurant. 103 rooms.

LAS TERRAZAS. Family-type hotel in residential area. Inexpensive. Bar. Restaurant. 33 rooms.

DEL PARQUE. Downtown, inexpensive and popular with students. Bar. Restaurant. 90 rooms.

BARRANQUILLA
First Class

EL PRADO. Oldest hotel in the Inter-Continental chain, this delightful hostelry is everything a South American hotel should be: full of Spanish colonial atmosphere, plus superlative service. 200 rooms, pool, tennis courts, tropical garden, dinner-dancing. Excellent food. Showers only.

ROYAL LEBOLO. Recently opened near El Prado area. Bar. Restaurant. Discotheque. Pool. Expensive. 74 rooms.

Moderate

CARIBANA. Good downtown location. 150 rooms. One of the best in its class. Restaurant.

CENTRAL. Handy downtown location. Bar. Restaurant. Discotheque. 90 rooms.

DORAL. New, small. Excellent location. Informal coffee shop and bar. 63 rooms.

Inexpensive

MAJESTIC. Near El Prado, handy for buses. Popular with North Americans. Restaurant, pool. 46 rooms.

ELSEWHERE

ARMENIA. *Zuldemayda.* 48 rooms. Centrally located with good food and pleasant atmosphere. Moderate.

BARBOSA. *Moncada.* Motel with 32 rooms grouped around a large swimming pool. Bar, restaurant. Inexpensive.

BARRANCABERMEJA. *Pipaton.* 40 rooms, all air conditioned. Bar; restaurant; swimming pool. Employees friendly but untrained, making service somewhat indifferent. Inexpensive.

BOYACA. Best are the *Suescun Hacienda* in Sogamosa, a comfortable hotel, very popular with high Bogotá society, and the *Rocas Lindas* on Lake Tota. The *Tisquesusa* is also on the lake. In Duitama you can stop at *San Luis de Ucuenga*, a charming little inn built in a restored colonial *hacienda*. The above hotels are all inexpensive.

At Paipa Hot Springs is the pleasant tourist hotel, *Sochagota.* Very posh, picturesque; all services. Some suites have private thermal baths. Moderate.

The *Savarita*, in Chiquinquira; the delightful *Hosteria del Molino de la Mesopotamia*, a restored 17th-century inn, and the *San Francisco.* The last two in Villa de Leyva; all are moderate.

Hospederia Duruelo, also in Leyva. Brand new and charmingly furnished and located on the brow of a hill overlooking the tile roofs of the town. Bar; restaurant; TV room; conference room. Excellent food. 62 rooms. Meals mandatory, but moderate prices.

BUCARAMANGA. *Bucarica.* Best in town. 90 rooms, inexpensive; bears the name of an Indian cacique on whose lands the city was founded.

El Pilar. Much better than the inexpensive price would indicate. So-so dining room, but the size of the hotel (15 rooms) welcomes you to a family atmosphere which is very pleasant.

BUGA (near Cali). *Guadalajara*, a quality establishment, radiant with tropical flowers. Moderate. Also *España*, inexpensive.

CALI. *Intercontinental* is best in the city. 254 rooms, 2 restaurants; rooftop supper club; pool. Golf and tennis privileges arranged with a private club. Superior first class.

Petecuy. Located in market area, so can be noisy and unsafe. 140 air-conditioned rooms. Moderate.

Aristi. Centrally located. Very good, modern. Authentic pre-Columbian idols or burial jars sold inexpensively. Moderate.

Other hotels: *Menendez* and *New York*, both inexpensive.

CARTAGENA

First Class

CAPILLA DEL MAR. Recently opened as Cartagena's only five star hotel. Excellent French dining room. Coffee shop on terrace. Beauty and barber shops. Sauna. Beach. Pool. Revolving bar on 17th floor with spectacular view of bay and ocean. Expensive. 210 rooms.

EL CARIBE. Solid structure with good flower-bordered swimming pool and dining area. All 188 rooms, in two buildings, overlook ocean. Partly air conditioned. Private beach, tennis courts. Casino, supper club with music. Sophisticated dining room being added. Shops. Good value and best location.

PLAZA BOLIVAR. 42 rooms with ceiling fans; however, air conditioning is being installed. Located in the heart of the old walled city on the square of the Palace of the Inquisition. Dining room; bar; 10 minutes by cab to Bocagrande Beach.

LAS VELAS. Recently opened; 18 floors with 120 rooms, many of them suites with kitchenettes. Good dining room; conference room; scenic swimming pool; bar on top floor offering a breath-taking view of the beach and the Caribbean.

A new apartment/hotel Don Blas (300 rooms) should be ready to receive guests by mid-1978. Located in the resort area of Boca Grande but does not have a beach.

The Hotel Cartagena Hilton is slated for opening in mid-1978.

Moderate

AMERICANO. 120 air-conditioned apartments; grill, cocktail lounge, dance floor, beach. Coat and tie required in casino. Location good but service indifferent.

FLAMINGO. 35-room, air-conditioned hotel, near beach. Better value than price indicates.

PLAYA. 60 rooms, overlooking ocean; private beach. Air-conditioned bar, terrace with snackbar. Private baths. In Bocagrande residential area. Good. Helpful management.

BAHIA. 70 rooms, private bath and telephone, air-conditioned restaurant, on the beach front and good value.

QUINTA AVENIDA. 38 rooms, all with bath and air conditioning; 13 with private terraces. Indifferent management.

RESIDENCIAS BOCAGRANDE. 40 rooms. Boarding-house atmosphere.

Recently opened hotels are: *El Dorado*, first class, with a discotheque; *El Lago* and *India Catalina*, moderate.

CUCUTA. *Tonchala.* Best hotel in town. 120 rooms, 80 air conditioned, with telephone. Bar, grill, swimming pool. Vacationers from the capital come to enjoy the near-equatorial heat. Moderate.
Rio. Third-class family hotel; private bath and air conditioning in some rooms.
Motel Bolivar. 13 double, 24 single apartments. Air conditioned. Pool. Moderate.
Vasconia. Downtown. Air conditioned. 21 rooms. Inexpensive.

GARZON. *Hosteria Ambeyma.* Only six rooms but conveniently located on the road from Neiva to the Archeological Park of San Agustín. Indifferent food; enormous swimming pool. Inexpensive.

GIRADOT. *Lagomar El Peñon.* Recently inaugurated complex offering practically anything the visitor would want. Artificial lake with water skiing and other aquatic sports; tennis; horseback riding; swimming pool; casino; good dining room and poolside snack bar. Superdeluxe, but all meals included.
Piscina, Rio, San German, family-style hotels; have local atmosphere. Inexpensive.

GIRON. *San Juan de Giron.* 28 bungalows clustered around a large swimming pool. Dining room; bar; motel atmosphere. Moderate.

IBAGUE. *Ambalá.* 140 air-conditioned rooms. Swimming pool and conference room for 210 persons. Very attractive. Moderate.

IPIALES. *Hostería Mayasquer.* Good, second class. 31 rooms overlooking Colombian-Ecuadorian border. Inexpensive.

LETICIA. *Parador Ticuna*, with 13 cottages in operation, 6 more planned. Pool. First class. Also recommended: *Anaconda.* Air conditioned; restaurant, bar. Multi-story, but no elevator. Moderate.

MANIZALES. *Europa*, inexpensive. *Las Colinas.* 65 rooms, bar, dining room with so-so food.

MARIQUITA. *Las Acacias.* More motel than hotel; has 30 rooms; large swimming pool; dining room; bar, pleasant gardens. Inexpensive.

MEDELLÍN

Superior First Class

INTERCONTINENTAL MEDELLÍN. Best hotel in the city, beautifully located. 335 rooms, 2 restaurants, pool with poolside bar; lobby shops. Public rooms air conditioned. Well managed. Bullfighting ring for bull calves.

First Class

NUTIBARA. Very good. Located in active business and shopping district. Lovely pool, dining room, convention facilities. Gambling casino.

Moderate

VERACRUZ. Recently refurbished and expanding. Small pool on the 11th floor, with panoramic view.

Inexpensive includes *Europa-Normandie, Bolivar, Residencias Nutibara, Salvatore, Horizantes* (new, small), and *Universo* (for budget minded).

MELGAR. (near Giradot). *Guadaira*, charming hotel with large pool. Moderate.

MIRAFLORES. *El Dorado Lodge.* Fishing lodge. 24 guests in cottages around main lodge. Superdeluxe prices, but all meals included.

MONTERIA. *Sinu. Moderate.* 66 air-conditioned rooms, good food and inviting swimming pool.

NEIVA. *Matamundo.* New, but resembling old colonial mansion. Flowering gardens, pool. Moderate. *Hotel Plaza.* On main square of city. Large pool, bar. Inexpensive. *Avirama* is recommended. Inexpensive.

PAMPLONA. *Cariongo.* Good, inexpensive, fairly new. 52 rooms. Excellent food.

PASTO. *Hotel Morazurco.* Two-and-one-half hour drive to Colombian-Ecuadorian border. 54 doubles, 5 suites. Tastefully decorated. Popular restaurant, bar, shops, convention hall. Moderate.

PEREIRA. *Zoratama.* 83 rooms; bar; restaurant; located on central square overlooking controversial nude statue of Simón Bolívar. Inexpensive.

PITALITO. *Calamo.* 24 rooms; bar, restaurant; swimming pool; located on central square of town and therefore noisy. Inexpensive.
Timanco. 42 rooms; bar; restaurant; swimming pool; snack bar; immense grounds with lake for boating; very friendly and helpful management. Inexpensive.

POPAYAN. *Monasterio.* An utterly charming, remodeled 17th-century convent with restaurant, bar and swimming pool. Inexpensive.

PROVIDENCIA. *Aury.* 14 rooms, only 6 with private baths. Overlooks Catalina Island. Moderate.

RIOHACHA. *Gimaura.* 42 rooms, all air conditioned. Inexpensive.

SAN AGUSTIN. *Yalconia.* The jumping-off place for viewing San Agustín's magnificent monoliths. Inexpensive.
Osoguaico. 5 rooms, none with private bath; camping facilities; good dining room, one specialty of which is baked guinea pig. Inexpensive.

SAN ANDRES ISLAND

EL ISLENO. Best on island. All 42 air-conditioned rooms have terraces overlooking beautiful beach. Attractive porch and bar. Poor food.

MALIBU. 1½ blocks from beach. 22 rooms; some small. Maintenance could be improved. Good food.

NATANIA. Half-block from beach. 33 rooms. Small restaurant with limited menu. Best bargain on the island.

ABACOA. 52 air-conditioned rooms. Nice décor. Well operated. Cafeteria. Shops.

CARIBBEAN. New. Cottages surrounding central building with dining room, bar. On beach.

CASABLANCA. Spanish style architecture; beach; swimming pool; restaurant; air conditioning.

SAN GIL. *Bella Isla.* 34 rooms; bar; restaurant; conference room; swimming pool; striking view from terrace. Inexpensive.

SANTA MARTA AREA
(No hot water unless noted.)

First Class

IROTAMA. Secluded. Between airport and El Rodadero. Lovely junior suite-type cottages and new complex of buildings (excellent for groups) a short walk away. HOT WATER. Carefully tended gardens. Gourmet, terrace and informal beach dining. Some entertainment. Repeat clientele indicates continued fine service. Splendid, large beach.

PUERTO GALEON. 120 suites; 5 minutes from airport; beach; bank; HOT WATER; swimming pool; good restaurant; bar and snack bar located in replica of old Spanish galleon. Adjoins casino.

Moderate

MARLINDO. In Santa Marta. Small, nice, clean.

TAMACA INN. Right on the beach at El Rodadero, about 15 min. from Santa Marta. 72 rooms, air conditioning. Excellent food and service. Informal atmosphere. Adjoining casino.

LA SIERRA. 34 rooms, some kitchen facilities, English-speaking personnel. Snackbar on beach. Friendly service. Better value than price indicates.

EL RODADERO. 45 modest passable rooms. Contact Allen & Mary Lowrie Travel Service in Bogotá for rental of apartments at El Rodadero, accommodating up to 6 persons.

SANTAMAR. New. HOT WATER. Pool, tennis.

REFUGIO NAUTICO BURUCUCA. Difficult access. Charming, unique, informal hideout on a rock point 3 miles from El Rodadero beach. 14 rooms, boats, water skiing, fishing, excellent seafood. Personalized service.

TIERRADENTRO. *Refugio de Pisimbala.* Only seven rooms, each with private bath; open-air dining terrace; swimming pool but climate hardly conducive to bathing; horses for rent for visiting the archeological sites. Inexpensive.

TOLU. *Morrosquillo.* 50 rooms on beach; indifferent service but a great favorite for vacationing Colombian families. Inexpensive.

TUMACO. *Boca Grande*, on beach, a few miles outside of city proper. Cabanas or cottages. Moderate.

VALLEDUPAR. *Sicarare.* 56 air-conditioned rooms; all services. Moderate.

VILLAVICENCIO. *Meta.* 38 rooms. Swimming pool. *Del Llano.* 67 air-conditioned rooms. Both moderate.

 RESTAURANTS. Bogotá. Here in the capital the hours are very Spanish indeed: you'll be sitting down to an *early* dinner at 9 p.m. There's a grand choice of restaurants.

Hotel Dining Rooms

Tequendama: Monserrate Dining Room, rooftop, provides top-notch food and music for dancing. *El Virrey* is a pleasant coffee shop. *La Cascada* coffee shop is open 24 hours.

Hilton: La Hacienda, with Spanish Colonial décor, has a daily international buffet. *Le Toit Supper Club and Restaurant*, on the 41st floor, has excellent food and a wonderful view. Coffee shop service and popular Sun. buffet in *La Orquidea Restaurant*, overlooking pool.

Bacata: Specialty: Pineapple Surprise with chicken. *Continental:* European cuisine; Italian specialties. A special treat. *Dann:* Superior international cuisine. *Presidente:* International cuisine.

Typical Colombian

Casa Vieja, Avda. Jimenez 3–73. *El Zaguan de las Aguas*, Calle 19, 5–62. Nice colonial dwelling. *Los Arrayanes,* Avda. Jimenez 3–63. Local cookery based on old recipes. *Hosteria El Brevo*, in northern residential section. Sun-filled garden and verandah dining. Great for Sun. lunch. *Los Sauces*, good food from all areas of Colombia; rustic decor; folklore dance group provides entertainment every hour on the hour. *Paletera*, menu includes both typical and international foods; best folklore dance group in town but expensive due to exorbitant cover charge. Both the above located in northern residential area.

Meson de Indias, at Calle 13 No. 5–33; typical Old Santa Fe de Bogotá food served in the charming atmosphere of one of the truly colonial houses left in the old section of Bogotá.

La Estufa. Carrera 2 between Calles 18 and 17. Located in patio of colonial church. Parrillada mixta served at your table. Patio also includes art gallery and wine bar with folk singing.

Spanish

Club La Zambra, Carrera 3, 74–32, in the basement of a medieval castle, is the most enjoyable of cabaret-restaurants serving Spanish food. Excellent *paella* and wine in a *porron*—spill wine when drinking and your tie may join those on the ceiling. Music and entertainment.

Reasonably priced and centrally located is *Tasca de Madrid*, Carrera 5 No. 20–26. Roast pigeon and kidneys in wine sauce are specialties.

As de Copas, Carrera 13, 59–24, Interior 9. Cabaret. Food

fair. *Salinas*, Carrera 11, 85–62 (uptown) and Calle 21, 6–43 (downtown). Good. Delicious food.

International

La Table Du Roi, Carrera 8-A, 15–31. Best of all downtown restaurants. Expensive. *Eduardo's*, Carrera 11, 89–43. Jet-set rendezvous. Expensive, but superb food. *Verner's*, Calle 25, 12–23. Fine European food; German specialties. *Balalaika*, Carrera 15, 32–83. Old Russian atmosphere. Delicious Beef Stroganoff and Chicken Kiev. *Au Bourguignon*, Carrera 18 No. 82–10; serves only French food; excellent.

Eduardo's downtown branch at Calle 13 No. 8–66 has same high standard. Lunch only; expensive..

Trattoria-Bistro. Calle 59 Numero 8–50. Personally run by French-Italian chef Fernando Bertagmini. Best French food in Colombia. Reasonable prices, but reservations a must.

Pimm's, Carrera 15, 82–46. Best onion soup in town. Informal. Reasonable.

La Reserve, Carrera 15, 37–15 is sophisticated, serving delicious French food.

Le Grand Amiral, Carrera 14, 90–31, specializes in sea food with super results.

Petit-Paris, Carrera 4, 74A–21. Authentic French cuisine lovingly prepared by the French chef/owner.

Cuban

Havana 1900. Calle 64 between Carreras 6 and 7.

Very Cheap, Good and Typical

El Sifón de los Montes. Carrera 3 between Calles 19 and 20. Specializes in corn empanadas and "Muchacho," beef stuffed with chopped carrot and egg.

Doña Ceila, Av. 30 No. 1A–05.

For Chinese food: *Y Yuen*, Carrera 11, 91–58, in El Chico. Good food and excellent atmosphere. *Hong Kong* is also good. *Mandarin*, Calle 100 No. 17–56; expensive, but best Chinese food in town.

Others

Cream Helado, Carrera 14, 31–49. Cozy atmosphere nice clientele. Try *arroz con pollo* or great hamburgers, milk shakes. *La Mesa Redonda*, Carrera 10, 27–27, in the Tequendama complex. Strikingly designed building. Superb steaks. *Steaks & Chops*, Carrera 10, 27–27, Interior 147. Excellent. *Refugio Alpino*, Calle 23, 7–49. Small. Good food. Plain atmosphere. *El Museo*, Calle 37, 7–49. Excellent food and exhibition of the best of Colombia's artists.

In the northern residential areas some good, but plain restaurants are: *Amberes, La Fragata* (seafood) in three locations, two downtown and one in the northern residential section, and *Sandrick's*, at two locations. Fried chicken like mother used to make.

El Portico, 10 miles from city. Charming. Excellent steaks. Playground equipment for youngsters and llama cart rides. Bullfighting ring for amateurs.

Chalet Suizo, Carrera 7 No. 21–51, centrally located, inexpensive. *Chesa*, Calle 23 No. 7–39, fine Swiss food, and the tea shop downstairs has pastries to make your mouth water.

Ranchburger, Calle 77 No. 15–28 in El Lago Shopping

Center, excellent hamburgers and snacks.

Stables of Camino Real, located on the outskirts of Bogotá in the town of Suba; great for horse lovers: as you dine, an exhibition of fine horseflesh and excellent riders is offered in, around and through the dining room.

Outside the Capital

BARRANQUILLA. Best for dining and dancing is *El Prado*. *Pez que Fuma*, serving seafood specialties, is tops in town. *Brandes* has a good French cuisine. *Monserrate* is noted for international food. *La Colonia's* specialty is suckling pig, but you can also get international food. *Biblos* serves Lebanese specialties. *Chop Suey* is a recommended Chinese restaurant. *The Steak House* boasts succulent steaks.

BUCARAMANGA. The restaurant of the *Hotel Bucarica* is fairly good.

La Carreta specializes in steaks served in an open patio under huge trees. *El Everest*, about 10 minutes outside town; magnificent views. The private-membership *Country Club* has the best food in town, served in a flower-filled garden. *El Suizo* serves international food.

CALI. The two restaurants of *Hotel Intercontinental Cali* have international and local dishes. The brand-new *El Campanario*, excellent international fare in charming atmosphere. *El Hostal* has international cuisine. *Don Carlos* is one of the best restaurants in Colombia's South, popular for Italian meals. More traditional: *Los Gauchos, La Casa de Los Mariscos*. *Toy San* is good for oriental meals. For great local fare and atmosphere,

try *Cali Viejo* or *Cequia Grande*. *La Tablita* is an intimate garden café with Argentinian and international food. Popular locally.

CARTAGENA. The *Capilla del Mar* is one of Colombia's great restaurants. Its owner, Pierre Daguet, is a French Gauguin-type expatriate painter. Try *Cazuela de frutas del mar*, a bouillabaisse of clams, oysters, squid and barracuda flavored with herbs, or lobster (Caribbean crayfish) thermidor. Closed Mon.

La Fragata, sea food supreme in restored colonial mansion in the heart of the Old City. Expensive.

Also outstanding for seafood is the *Club de Pesca*, picturesquely situated in old Fort de San Sebastian.

Restaurante Baru serves unusual seafood dishes. *Hosteria Sevillana*. Recommended charming, Spanish vine-covered arbor and dining area. Excellent *paella, sangria*. Flamenco and local entertainment. Small bull ring in rear for customers' use. *Chef Julian*. Classical colonial restaurant with garden patio in rear. Lobster and jumbo shrimp specialties, as well as char-broiled steaks. What coconut pie! *Trattoria Pietro* is the place to go for decor; also high-priced Italian meals. Daily specials. Closed Mon. *Marcel's* is a charming restaurant, overlooking the sea. Fine French cuisine, Closed Wed. *Malecon 70* offers typical Colombian food and patio or indoor dining. *Grill & Discoteque Blowup* serves good seafood on the 3rd floor. Nice view, too. Closed Mon. *El Bodegon* has outstanding soups, mouth-watering beef and sandwiches. Closed Tues.

One of the best low-priced restaurants is *Patio Italiano*,

where Venetian chef Diana serves home-made pasta and superb scampi.

Cuban Sandwich. Super submarine sandwiches for only $1 (US).

CUCUTA. *Hotel Tonchala's* dining room is very good. For fine international food served in a strikingly designed building, try *Chez Estevan.*

FUSAGUSAGA. *Los Arboles,* recently opened. Local specialties. The *Manila Hotel's* French restaurant features a delicious dish of butter-fried mountain trout, a local delicacy.

GIRARDOT. The food at the *Tocarema* is poor. In nearby Flandes there are several rustic restaurants specializing in a sort of bouillabaisse called *viudo de pescado.* The most interesting of these is the houseboat restaurant down on the shore of the Magdalena. Many roadside stands offer a wide variety of goodies not, however, recommended for tummy-pampering visitors. The three restaurants of the recently-opened *Lagomar El Peñon* are all excellent.

MANIZALES. *Hotel Las Colinas* dining room not very inspired. You'd do better at *Vitiani* (Italian dishes) and *Las Torres* (international food)

MEDELLIN. *La Posada de la Montaña* is a must for any visitor! Exquisite, old hacienda recently converted into restaurant. Roofed dining area surrounds Spanish-tiled courtyard with lovely garden, fountain. Indoor dining also. Excellently prepared authentic regional dishes served on ceramic platters and colorful straw mats. Waitresses and waiters in regional dress. Background music. *Aguacatala* is an old wayside tavern, with very good typical cuisine. At *Las Lomas* you will get excellent *paella, mariscos* and other Spanish seafood. There are three branches of *Bremen-Manhattan,* known for German food. *Piemonte* serves Italian meat dishes. *La Res* has excellent beef. *El Penasco* is for international food. *El Postillon* serves European specialties. *Salvatore* has good Italian and European cuisine. International food served in *La Tranquera* and *Les Gourmets*; *El Mirador del Aburrá* was recently opened on a hill overlooking the city and serves excellent international cuisine. For French food there is *La Bella Epoca,* located in the superb Torre Lavega estate and decorated with roaring twenties mementos. *La Madrilena* offers Spanish dishes. Its decor is great for bullfight aficionados.

The *Hotel Intercontinental Medellín* has a top-floor supper club with excellent food and a spectacular view of the valley. There is also a coffee shop with international food and poolside service. The *Hotel Nutibara* dining rooms are nice. Try also *Parador Tequendamita,* near Medellin; a small, informal inn.

Marinilla (50 minutes from Medellín) will appeal to enthusiasts of the Colonial era and its *Camino Real Inn* specializes in "paisa" dishes.

For local sausage and other regional specialties, there are several *al fresco* cafes in the main square of the village of Envigado, about fifteen minutes from downtown Medellín.

SAN ANDRES. Of course seafood is the order of the day here. *El Acuario* is tops for food and atmosphere. *Miss Bess* is small and friendly. Meals cooked to order. *La Tortuga* serves

Italian-style seafood, Italian dishes and has a pizzeria.

SANTA MARTA AREA. The *Irotama* will fill your every need. There is terrace dining, a gracious dining room and beachfront, informal patio. Some entertainment. Terrific drinks. At El Rodadero, the *Tamacá* is best, with a wide selection of food. *Capri,* on the promenade, is a gathering spot for Americans. Owner-operated, the Italian and international cuisine is superior and the drinks generous. *Los Cumbieros* serves Italian specialties. *La Casa de mi Abuela* is inexpensive for seafood and international dishes. *Los Delfines* has recently opened. Serves seafood. *La Brasa* is for typical Colombian meals. Informal. *Pan American* serves international food.

SOCIAL CLUBS

Bogotá. The best food to be had in town is found at the private clubs. The *Jockey Club* has smoked rainbow trout hors d'eouvres that are sheer delight. *Los Lagartos* offers fried butterfly shrimp that competes with the best anywhere. The *Country Club* serves an ice-cream cake topped with chocolate sauce. The new *Executive Club* offers a breathtaking view of the city and good food.

Bogotá's *Country Club* is considered to be one of the best modernistic centers in the hemisphere, and its *Polo Club* boasts some of the finest players on the continent. *Los Lagartos,* a family club, offers a most challenging golf course with hidden driving ranges perched high on hills above a sparkling lake where the younger crowd enjoy water skiing. The *Military Club* has an interesting dome-shaped glassed-in pool. The *San Andres Golf Club,* situated about one hour out of town in the precincts of a delightful colonial village, attracts the most intrepid golfers in Colombia, as it is said to be the country's most difficult course. Tennis is best at Los Lagartos, where the courts are on terraces carved out of a mountain. Bowling is available at the swank *Jockey Club* and *Country Club* upon invitation from a member. Private clubs throughout Colombia are open only to visitors presented by members. Airlines and hotel managers often supply guest cards.

Almost all Colombian cities have one or more social clubs, usually with golf and swimming. Guest cards can usually be obtained by the hotel where guests are lodged. Some of the more spectacular clubs outside the capital are listed here:

Medellín's Country Club has two 18-hole golf courses, swimming pool, excellent restaurant and flowering gardens abounding with orchids. The businessmen's Union Club has a swimming pool and well-stocked bar where the future of the town is decided over drinks.

Barranquilla has two clubs. The Country Club is located in the city with an 18-hole golf course and swimming pool. Also has a good restaurant and well-stocked bar. The Club Lagos de Caujaral is located 5 miles from town and has an 18-hole golf course and swimming pool. Greens fees at either are about 150 pesos for 18 holes.

Cartagena's Country Club offers golf and swimming; however, the 9-hole golf course is not very exciting as it is burned brown almost the year 'round due to lack of water.

Tunja's downtown Club Boyaca is very exclusive, but admittance may be arranged by applying to the Tourist Board, located on the central square. Very staid and full of authentic Colonial furniture and a venerated portrait of Simon Bolivar done from life.

The Club Popayan, in the city of the same name, is probably the most exclusive in the country with large swimming pool and excellent restaurant; guest cards very difficult to obtain but may be visited during Holy Week when the doors are thrown open to the public. The Country Club is located just outside of town in a renovated Colonial farmhouse; swimming, no golf.

Manizales. Golf is popular at the 18-hole course of Manizales' Country Club, but most visitors find golfing a pretty puffy proposition at over 7,000 feet elevation.

Neiva. Located about three miles out of town on the San Agustin road, the Country Club offers a bowling alley, an Olympic-sized swimming pool and a projected 18-hole golf course.

Santa Marta has a recently opened golf course (8 holes with another 8 holes planned) six miles outside of town in a beautiful valley filled with fruit trees, many of which have been retained and give their names to the different holes.

Cucuta's two social clubs are the Tennis Club outside of town with tennis, swimming and horseback riding and the downtown Commercial Club with swimming pool, restaurant, bar and discotheque.

Bucaramanga. Outside of town is found the Country Club with swimming pool, 18-hole golf course, flowering gardens and accommodations for eight guests lucky enough to obtain entrance. Also has downtown Commercial Club on main square of town.

Ibague's Country Club, outside the usual 18-hole golf course and large swimming pool, also has a small bull ring where amateur bullfighters cape small calves almost every Sunday.

Cali's Country Club has all sports facilities and an excellent dining room, one feature of which is an artificial waterfall covering one wall.

 NIGHT LIFE. Bogotá: *Paletera* is open nightly with an excellent Colombian orchestra and floorshow. Expensive. Brand-new, *Tierra Colombiana* (near Hotel Tequendama) offers first-class Colombian floorshow. For languid ballads of Colombian highlands played by master musicians, *Club Camucol*. *Hippocampus*, Carrera 15 No. 85–31 has excellent U.S.-style piano bar with dancing.

Hollywood Thirties, Carrera 15 No. 87–78. With *Unicorn*, the most fashionable discotheque in Bogotá.

Gayest nightspots, in addition to the Tequendama's *Monserrate Room* and Hilton's *Le Toit*, are *Mao Mao*, *La Zambra* (Spanish) and *La Pampa* (Argentine). The *As de Copas'* floorshows specialize in flamenco artists from Spain, as does *Las Cuevas de Sacromonte* near the Hotel Tequendama. *Portòn Tres* for sophisticated tangos. There are also several *discotheques*, the most famous being *Unicorn*, affiliated with same-named night spots in Lima and Panama. *Rafael* has a mariachi band, good singers and excellent Mexican food.

In Medellín, 4 good nightclubs: *Grill de las Estrellas*, located in the Nutibara Hotel, *La Hosteria*, *Piamonte* and *Fujiyama*. Discotheques include *2002*, *Ali Khan*, and *Omega*. And there is a casino in the same Nutibara Hotel. *Hotel Intercontinental Medellín* offers dining and dancing in the roof-top supper club, as does the *Hotel International Cali*.

In Cartagena: *Taberna La Quemada*, in the old walled city. A replica of a 17th-century English pub in a genuine Spanish colonial house, used in the film "Queimada", starring Marlon Brando. Terrific jazz sessions on weekends. *Zubiria* discotheque is very loud and very dark. *Hotel del Caribe* has casino with entertainment. *Grill & Discoteque Blowup* has modern American music, Latin music and great food. *Molino Rojo Disco*, at El Dorado, *Aquarius* and *La Cueva de Joe* are others.

The best discos in Barranquilla are: *La Torre de Babel*, *La Caja de Pandora*, *La Casa de la Bruja*, *Tiphany*, and *El Gusano*.

In the Santa Marta area at Rodadero there is now the exclusive *Unicorn*, and the disco-restaurant featured by Puerto Galeon resort inside a replica of a 16th-century Spanish galleon.

SHOPPING. Fine emeralds may be purchased from *Willis F. Bronkie y Cia.* (Bavaria Building, in the lobby of Residencias Tequendama, Bogotá, and at the Del Caribe, Cartagena), owned by a North American mining engineer. Inexpensive emeralds set in gold can be bought for as little as $60. You'll find them also at other jewelry shops along with wonderful trinkets in 18 carat gold and silver. The ones that are made to sew onto the clothing of a saint's statue sell for as little as half a dollar! Other fine jewelry shops in Bogotá are *H. Stern* at Bogotá Hilton, Hotel Tequendama and Airport (duty free)—ask for free local "charm" and booklet, *Joyeria Bauer* and *Joyeria Enrique Lievano*.

You'll find excellent leatherwork and all sorts of tempting items in alligator, crocodile and snakeskin. The Colombians also have a way with straw, called *toquilla* and *iraca* and with *agave*, a tough native fiber from which they make hats, shoes, handbags and even umbrellas. Particularly good ladies' shoes and handbags can be obtained in Medellín. *Artesanias de Colombia* offers a wide range of handcrafted articles in Medellin, Bogotá, Cucuta, Pitalito, and San Andres.

Men strike it rich in Colombia shops. Beautiful linen shirts are as little as $10. You can get a made-to-measure suit in silk or wool for $100 and up. Top quality shoes and hats are as low as $15. You'll find these plus accessories at the *Men's Shop* in the Hotel Tequendama, Hilton, and at *Daniel's* all in Bogotá.

The Handicrafts and Traditional Arts museum, located in the San Agustin Convent, has a well-stocked shop.

At *TAB* or *Amaral* you can find beautiful hand-woven textiles and wall hangings. One hangs in the lobby of the Hotel Bogotá Hilton.

Daniel's is also a leader for women's fashions. Which leads us to one of the unique buys of Colombia: the famous *ruana*, the striking native poncho, hand woven from hand-carded Colombian wool. An oil in the wool of native flocks makes these colorful garments well nigh impermeable to rain, and they're as warm as toast. Average price is only $15 to $20, depending on quality and style. *Almacen Tropicana* has a shop within Hotel Tequendama which offers the best buys in hand-loomed wool *ruanas* and artifacts.

In Bogotá, antique-lovers may browse in Medina's on Carrera 7 and Calle 50, at Cancino Sisters on Plaza Bolívar and at Jaime Botero's at Calle 10 No. 2-57, where both authentic antiques and reproductions are offered for sale in a lovely home called La Toma de Agua, constructed in 1650. It's one of the finest examples of Spanish colonial architecture in Bogotá.

If you're an admirer of pre-Columbian artifacts and jewelry, you'll find the real thing here along with some very skillful imitations. Don't despise the latter. Fashioned by hand, they make excellent souvenirs of this fascinating country, and you can actually find small charms and objects in 18 carat gold for $3 up. For authentic pre-Columbian artifacts, look in the shop in the Hotel Tequendama, owned by a knowledgeable Chilean, Jaime Errazuriz. If you're lucky he may invite you to his home to see his fantastic private collection of artifacts from the Tumaco culture. Genuine artifacts (complete with authenticity certificate) also available at *Galeria Cano* in the Bavaria Building and in the lobby of the Hotel Bogotá Hilton.

In Barranquilla, *Gutfreünd Ltda.* has fine handmade jewelry, rare brass stirrups and pre-Colombian artifacts. *Gerald Khon* offers much the same items. At the airport you can buy tax-free liquor. Colombia's best rum, Ron Viejo de Caldas, in a beautiful straw cover, sells for about $2.50, but this price applies only if you are on your way out of the country.

In Cartagena, we hear you can get fabulous buys in emeralds and gold jewelry at pawn shops, but be sure you are getting the real thing. It's easy to be fooled.

In Medellín the *Centro Comercial San Diego* shopping center and *Exito* department stores offer a wide range of Colombian items.

In the Santa Marta area, at Rodadero, there are two branch stores of the *Tropicana*—one next door to the Capri, and the other at the Tamacá. Both have a fine selection of handmade rugs, macramé bags, *ruanas*. At the Tamacá you will also find exquisite jewelry and pre-Colombian artifacts. *Cocodrito* and *Puerto Libre* sell local souvenirs.

Best shopping for manufactured items is the Free Port of San Andres, where Scotch whisky, Japanese cameras and British tweeds are readily available.

 SPORTS. *Fishing* is excellent the year round for marlin, sailfish, tarpon, dolphin, and tuna. A license is required, obtainable from INDERENA, the National Institute for Natural Resources (see USEFUL ADDRESSES for location). International fishing competitions are held in Barranquilla in May and November. Fishing safaris for fierce species in the huge rivers of the Eastern Plains (Dec.-Mar. only).

There is good *skindiving* at El Rosario Islands off Cartagena. Check with local authorities beforehand, since both sharks and barracuda have caused accidents. Beaches all along the north coast are of white sand shelving gently into the water and *swimming* is the most popular sport. *Fishing* and *skindiving* are excellent in the clear waters off San Andres Island and Santa Marta. *Water skiing, boating* and *pedal boats* are common pastimes at El Rodadero and Puerto Galeón.

Tennis is a very popular sport among *costeños* and an international tournament is held each March at the Country Club in Barranquilla.

Because of import restrictions rental equipment for the above sports is not readily available; visitors wanting to participate should bring their own gear.

In the field of spectator sports, *baseball* is extremely popular on the coast, and the Professional International Baseball Championships are held each October.

For the more active sportsman, the Sierra Nevada, which begins some 30 miles east of Santa Marta, offers an experience in *mountain climbing* with peaks that go up to nearly 19,000 feet.

Hunting for ducks along the coast may be arranged; however, hunting such game as jaguar, tapir and others is becoming increasingly difficult as Colombia's conservation laws become more stringent. Also available by arrangement are safaris into the *Llanos* or the Amazon basin to established hunting camps. *Jaguar Safaris S.A.*, Apartado 1280, Medellín, specializes in safaris.

In Bogotá, visitors may play *golf* at the *Bogotá Country Club* (two 18-hole courses), *Los Lagartos* and *San Andres* by arranging for guest cards at their hotels or tourist agencies. All three clubs have *tennis* courts. New *El Rincon Club*, very exclusive, with Trent Jones Course. By invitation only.

Golf is also available on presentation of a guest card at the *Cali Country Club* (18 holes), *Medellín Country Club* (18), *El Rodeo Golf Club* in Medellín (18), *El Centro Country Club* in Barrancabermeja (18), *Bucaramanga Country Club* (18), *Manizales Country Club* (18), *Cartagena Country Club* (9), *Barranquilla Country Club* (18), and *Lagos de Caujaral*, overlooking the CBB, a striking 18-hole course designed by Joe Lee. *The Gaira Golf Club* (8 with 8 more planned) 5 min. from Rodadero in Santa Marta.

Sailing and *water skiing* are practised at Los Lagartos and at the Bogotá Yacht Club on Lake Tominé near the city. *Water skiing* on River Cauca, Cali, and at Rodadero. *Hunting* expeditions and trout *fishing* in mountain lakes may be arranged locally. Spectator Sports. *Bullfights* in almost all cities, but in particular: Dec. and Feb., Bogotá; Dec. 26-Jan. 2, Cali; Jan. 1–6, Cartagena; Jan. 1–13, Manizales; Feb. 2–24, Medellín. *Cockfights:* Bogotá, Barranquilla, Cartagena, Santa Marta, Valledupar. International contests at Cartagena in early Jan.; Valledupar in late Apr.-early May; national contests in Popayan in mid-Oct. *Polo:* Bogotá, where international matches are often held. *Horse races:* In Bogotá on Thurs., Sun., Sun., and hol. afternoons, with parimutuel betting. *Soccer:* In most cities late Jan. through Dec. every Sun.

 ELECTRIC CURRENT. In all of Colombia, except the cities of Bogotá and Armenia, electric current is 110 volts, 60 cycles AC. In these two cities current is 60 cycles alternating but 150 volts. The Hotel Tequendama in Bogotá, as well as a number of other new buildings, has been converted to 110 volts. Transformers should be 110-150 volts, 60 cycles AC with standard U.S. flat plugs.

USEFUL ADDRESSES. Colombia Government Tourist Office, 140 E. 57th St., New York, N.Y. 10022. Barranquilla: Apdo. Aereo No. 36–16; Cucuta: Apdo. Aereo No. 800; Santa Marta: Apdo. Aereo No. 50–64; San Andres: Apdo. Aereo No. 110 Tourist Information Centers: Bogotá—Eldorado Airport; Calle 19, 6–68; Sabana RR Station; Carrera 9, 16–21; Cartagena—Inquisition Palace; Medellin—Turantioquia, Calle 49, 43–52.

Embassies: U.S.A., Calle 38, 8–61; *Canada*, Calle 58, 10–42, 4th fl.; *Great Britain*, Carrera 10, 19–65, 7th fl., all Bogotá. *Consulates:* U.S.A., Carrera 3, 11–55, 2nd fl., Cali; Calle 52, 49–27, 8th fl., Medellín. *Great Britain:* Calle 11, 1,07, Rm. 410, Cali; Carrera 44, 45–57, Barranquilla; Calle 52, 49–27, Medellin.

Automobile Club: Carrera 14 No. 46-64, Bogotá; AAA Representative in Colombia: Allen and Mary Lowrie, Ltda., Carrera 7, No. 19–29, 3rd Floor, Bogotá.

Travel Agencies: The most prominent, particularly useful to American visitors, is conducted by Allen and Mary Lowrie, Carrera 7, No. 19–29, 3rd Floor (tels. 432-546, 432-547, 426-827) two expatriate Americans who fell in love with Colombia, particularly the Caribbean coast. They can arrange group or individual tours; Exprinter, Cra 6 No. 14–64 (tel. 415–704;) Wagons Lits-Cook, Hotel Tequendama (tel. 419–250). *La Rana Tour Operators* Calle 27B, 6–73, specialize in exotic tours to places like Guajira, Amazon, Sierra Nevada, San Agustin/Pisimbalá.

The *International Association for Medical Assistance for Travelers (IAMAT)* is represented in Bogotá by the Clinica Samper, Calle 75 No. 7–81.

INDERENA, the *National Institute for Natural Resources*, Carrera 14 #25A-66, Bogotá.

The *Hertz Rent-A-Car* system has offices in Bogotá at the Hotel Tequendama and El Dorado Airport.

Avis has offices in Bavaria Building in Bogotá.

Protestant Churches: St. Alban's Episcopal Church, Calle 69 No. 5–33 (all services in English). St. Paul's Episcopal Church, Calle 51 No. 6–19 (all services in Spanish). Union Church of Bogotá, Cra. 4 No. 69–06 (all services in English).

Catholic Church: Colegio de Nuestra Señora del Buen Consejo, Calle 104 with Cra. 19 (all services in Spanish).

Synagogues: Ashkenazi, Synagogue Bet David Meier, Cra. 16A No. 28–33. Sefardi, Synagogue Maguen Ovadia, Calle 79 No. 9–66. Conservative, Asociacion Israelita Montefiore, Cra. 20 No. 37–54.

AMERICAN EXPRESS AGENTS: *Barranquilla*, Tierra Mar Aire, Calle 35 No. 43–43; *Bogota*, Tierra Mar Aire, edf. Bavaria, Torre B locales 1–25, Carrera 10 No. 27–91; *Medellín*, Tierra Mar Aire, Calle 53 (Maracaibo), No. 49–8; *Cali*, Tierra Mar Aire, Carrera 3a No. 8–13; *Cartagena*, Tierra Mar Aire, Calle del Colegio 34–28.

ECUADOR

Small, Rich and Majestic

BY

JAMES MONROE WOODMAN III

(A former Quito resident who has traveled extensively within Ecuador, including several months in the remote Oriente jungle, Mr. Woodman is the author of several travel books and the founding Secretary of the South American Travel Organization.)

Ecuador is a tiny land of tremendous contrasts. An amazing variety of peoples, terrains and climates has been packed within the borders of South America's fourth smallest country. Only French Guiana (34,740 square miles), Uruguay (72,172 square miles) and Guyana (app. 83,000 square miles) are smaller than Ecuador's 104,510 square miles (roughly the size of Colorado). The country's sharply contrasting topography runs from her Pacific coastline over the double-ridged Andes and down into the true headwaters of the mighty Amazon.

Geographers have divided Ecuador into three areas. First is the coastal region, a low-lying strip of land offering one of the world's narrowest zones of climatic transition. Along Ecuador's northern coast the land is covered by a dense rain forest, and moving south, as rainfall decreases, the land becomes less wooded and quickly changes into a stark desert at the Peruvian border. In the middle of this coastal strip lies the Guayas lowland, where much of Ecuador's tropical agriculture is centered, and Guayaquil, the country's largest town and leading seaport, is located here.

The next important area is the Andean Highlands—offering some of the world's most spectacular mountain scenery. This mountainous backbone of Ecuador is composed of two avenues of towering peaks including 30 volcanoes. Highest is majestic Mt. Chimborazo whose perfect cone rises to 20,574 feet, well into the zone of perpetual snow. At night the reflection of molten lava in the depth of Mt. Sangay glows against the clouds making an unforgettable panorama of spectacular peaks, fire and color. In the valleys between the giant peaks are the highland or *sierra* towns and cities of Ecuador. Quito, the Ecuadorian capital, stands in a large hollow at the foot of the mighty Mt. Pichincha.

The final geographical division is the Oriente or Eastern Amazon lowlands. Here at the edge of the Andes is the beginning of the world's mightiest drainage system—the headwaters of the Amazon. This vast, tropical rain forest has been explored, and drilling begun by U.S. oil companies, who foresee it as one of the richest oil areas in South America. Ecuador also offers an "extra" to geographers and visitors—the exotic Galápagos Islands —an area developing as an important destination for scientists as well as for international travelers. These mysterious volcanic Pacific islands, located 656 miles off Ecuador's coast, are as curiously fascinating as any place on earth with a flora and fauna unique in the world.

In a sentence, Ecuador is a small, rich, rugged land where civilizations have risen and fallen for centuries.

Capsule History

Ecuador has been continuously occupied since the dawn of recorded history. Many generations before the Inca Empire was established the Caras and Quitus civilizations inhabited the land.

In the early years of the 15th century the powerful, neighboring Incas extended their empire northward and conquered the area near present day Quito and gained control of the surrounding country. Their victory was a short one, for the *conquistadores* of Spain soon discovered South America's rich Pacific coast.

Because the Inca Empire was severely weakened by internal disputes, the newly arrived Spaniards had little trouble conquering the disorganized opposition in Ecuador. Francisco Pizarro and his bold men soon mastered the lands from Bogotá south to Lima. Ecuador's brief conquest ended, the colonial period began and Quito was formally founded by the Spanish on December 6, 1534.

Politically, Ecuador became a colony between the Viceroyalty of Peru and New Granada (present day Colombia), and almost 300 reasonably peaceful years followed as the country learned the new ways of her conquerors. Colonial customs, laws and ideas were introduced as well as cattle, swine raising and wheat. On the coast great sugar plantations were started.

Gradually Ecuador became restless under Spanish domination, and when the cry of revolution rang through South America,

334

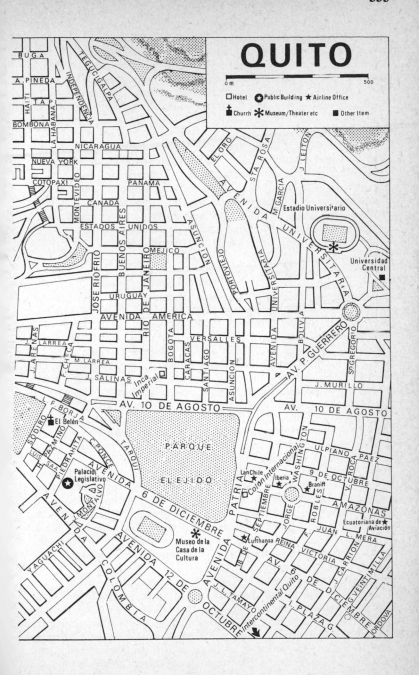

Ecuador started fighting against the Spanish on August 10, 1809. Under the able leadership of Field-Marshal Antonio José de Sucre the Spaniards were routed at the crucial Battle of Pichincha in 1822. From that year until 1830 Ecuador, Colombia and Venezuela formed *La Gran Colombia.* Ecuador pulled out of the union in 1830 to become a separate republic. Several decades of severe border disputes with both Colombia and Peru followed, and the Colombia-Ecuador border wasn't mutually defined until 1916. Difficulties with the Peruvian border exist to the present day.

Internal political unrest has troubled Ecuador seriously for the past 100 years, but conditions have improved considerably since substantial government reforms were introduced in 1946. One of the serious problems the country faces is uniting the coastal lowlanders, who are commercially active, and the self-sufficient highlanders—Indians, cholos, as well as whites—who concentrate on agriculture. Recent industrial development, oil findings and new roads are helping to bring these two groups together.

Economy of Soil and Sea

Ecuador is primarily an agricultural country. The great percentage of her coastal people are engaged in raising bananas (Ecuador is the world's largest producer), coffee, cacao, rice and sugar. The *sierra* farmers raise corn, wheat and potatoes. Cattle raising is increasing on both the coast and in the *sierra,* and a recent upsurge in the developing fishing industry is encouraging. Despite aid, Ecuador is at odds with the U.S. over fishing rights in waters considered to be within territorial limits. Shrimp and tuna processing and packaging plants are now completed and operating profitably. Balsa, the world's lightest wood, is also an important export as are rubber and kapok. Another famous export, although sales are dwindling due to high prices, is Ecuador's misnamed Panama hats. The hats, woven from Ecuador's superior *toquilla* straw, were inadvertently given the name of the country where they were first distributed in large quantities. Other typical handicrafts—rugs, blankets, shawls, ponchos and tweed-like materials—are produced in great quantities. Mineral resources are reportedly rich. Oil resources are being developed by major companies which have begun drilling on the Santa Elena peninsula, in the Oriente and at the Gulf of Guayaquil. There is some gold, silver and sulfur mining, also.

Despite the richness of the country and the industry of her people Ecuador still has all the earmarks of an underdeveloped country. Population is increasing, and there is a restricting lack of capital for development. International loans and aid programs are currently underway however, and considerable industrial progress has been made in recent years. Agriculture gets top priority, and production has increased owing to modernized methods.

The Ecuadorian Way of Life

Life in Ecuador is tranquil. There is a quiet pace about the daily routine, and many customs and traditions of Colonial days still exist. The spirit of Spain is everywhere in the language, religion and habits of the modern Ecuadorians.

As for day to day life, the majority of citizens rise at seven o'clock every morning and have a light breakfast of coffee and bread. Traditionally the business day started at 8:30 and continued until 6:30, with a two-hour midday break, the meal being a large affair usually consisting of hot soup, followed by rice and meat, salad and fruit. Now a single work session, 8–4, is being adopted. In the evening the family dinner is usually served at 7:30 and is another warm meal, usually with fish or meat and rice. There is little nightlife, except in Quito and Guayaquil, where there are excellent restaurants and nightlife attractions. In smaller towns, social life is centered in homes or private clubs. Movies are the most popular form of entertainment, and by 10 o'clock the great majority of Ecuador is quietly in bed.

Despite the Spanish emphasis, anyone traveling in the provinces soon realizes the great majority of Ecuador is Indian and Mestizo. In fact, *Quechua*, the leading Indian language, is spoken exclusively by more than 15 percent of the country's population. Life in the tiny Indian villages has changed little in centuries and is only now beginning to feel the effects of the 20th century.

For the visitor to Ecuador, both the colonial cities and the timeless, unchanging beauty of the Indian villages portray a tranquil, good life.

Food and Drink

Beer! Ecuador has South America's finest and certainly some of the world's most excellent brews. *Pilsener* and *Cerveza Andina* are the two top labels, distributed on the coast and the highlands, respectively.

Tap water is not recommended for visitors, but safe bottled water is available everywhere. Top brands: *Güitig, Mercedes*.

Put *llapingachos* on your "must" list; this mashed potato and cheese specialty is excellent. Shrimp or lobster *ceviche* make a memorable hors d'oeuvre. *Locro*, a stew of potatoes and cheese, is a popular Ecuadorian soup. Also try *humitas*, a delicately flavored sweetcorn tamale, or baked guinea pig, the national delicacy.

Another Ecuadorian delight is a unique fruit juice called *naranjilla*—an unbelievable taste somewhere between citrus and peach.

International drinks and whiskies are expensive in Ecuador. A whiskey or cocktail costs $1.50 in the better bars. Good Chilean wine is available, but for $7 a bottle; other imported wines even

more expensive. Best local drink is *paico* usually about twenty
sucres (just over 75¢). *Paico* is two parts fresh lemon and the
final part a shot of the aniselike *aguardiente*. Unlike most Latin
aguardientes, paico is not too bitter. Local wine is poor.

As a general rule avoid uncooked fruits and vegetables in
Ecuador. A great variety of exotic tropical fruit is available but
should be peeled at your table before eating. Best of the jungle
fruits is *chirimoya* with a delicious custardlike inside. Also try
mamey, which has a red, sweet, squashlike meat; *pepinos*, a sweet
white and purple striped cucumberlike fruit; the Ecuadorian
pineapples which are very sweet, juicy and large.

EXPLORING ECUADOR

Exploring the land of Chimborazo and Cotopaxi is a unique
experience. In no other small country will the visitor find such a
variety of geography, climate, flora and fauna than in Ecuador.
From the Galápagos to Guayaquil and from the colorful market
at Otavalo down the steep eastern slopes of the Andes to the
Oriente, Ecuador abounds with color and character.

Quito and Excursions

Most visitors to Ecuador start their itinerary in the capital city
of Quito (Alt. 9,250 ft., Pop. 750,000.). Quito is often labeled
South America's most historic city. The sprawling mountain capital dates back to 1534 when the Spaniard Sebastián Benalcázar
founded the city on the site of the ancient Indian town of Shyris.
Since its founding Quito has welcomed an endless pageant of the
men who created Spain's empire in the New World.

The daring expedition that discovered the Amazon left from
Quito; the first free government of the Spanish colonies was
established here, and a rich artistic tradition grew as the city
prospered. To the present-day visitor the city's historic past is
vividly reflected in the unmatched art and architecture that survives in abundance. A visitor once correctly said that Quito itself
is a giant outdoor museum.

Sightseeing is extremely well organized in Quito (*Metropolitan
Touring*, run by dynamic Eduardo Proaño, is unquestionably the
best). Most Quito tours include visits to the following sites:

La Catedral—the city's white-walled, green-domed cathedral is
a world-renowned treasure chest of great art. Marks of the city's
stormy political past show as mutilations on the outside walls, but
the ageless, classic beauty still shines through. Ecuador's national
hero Sucre is entombed here.

La Compañia—one of the New World's most magnificent churches is famous for its glittering interior coated with gold leaf. La Compañia is filled with one of the world's most outstanding colonial art collections. The church, one of 57 in Quito, is considered the richest Jesuit temple in South America.

San Francisco—this classic convent is the first great religious building in South America. Founded by a cousin of the Spanish Emperor Carlos V, the convent developed into an unrivaled example of baroque art. World famous sculpture inside attracts thousands annually. The convent also contains an excellent museum of religious art.

La Merced—a second convent well worth a visit for its idyllic cloister.

Arco de Santo Domingo—a favorite with photographers; the arch presents the classic scene of colonial Quito.

Palacio Nacional—the National Palace has been the seat of Ecuador's political power for centuries. The Palace faces the Plaza de Independencia where the visitor sees the very heart of the city. Long arcades and the Palace of the Archbishop make the plaza extremely impressive.

Universidad Central—nine faculties comprise Quito's centuries-old center of higher learning. The University traces its origin back to the Seminary of San Luis, founded in 1594. Quito's Central University, unlike most others in Latin America, has a magnificent campus of modern buildings located within a university city. Over 15,000 students attend the co-educational institution. Special courses for foreign students are offered in August and September.

Panecillo Hill—a former Inca sunworshipping site, this dramatic 600-ft. hill offers unequaled views of the city, and a new restaurant, La Fuente, where visitors can eat as they admire the sight.

Real de Lima—the former military barracks of Ecuador's revolutionary leaders in the early 1800s. The building is now the Municipal Art and History Museum containing the city's historical archives and several works by the country's top artists.

La Ronda—excellent example of the architecture of colonial Spanish America. The narrow streets of 16th-century colonial homes allow the visitor to step back generations and walk past the heavy grilled doors and the whitewashed walls of centuries ago.

San Roque—a picturesque Quito suburb whose narrow streets climb the side of towering Mt. Pichincha. Traditionally the hide-out of revolutionaries, the area is now tranquil, and its main attractions are the many small bargain bazaars.

Guapulo—a storybook town if there ever was one. This tiny

town beside Quito is encircled by mountains and trimmed by towering eucalyptus trees. The town's sanctuary is as peaceful a place as exists in today's hurried world.

In addition to the specific points of interest on any tour or excursion in Quito, the entire city itself—its atmosphere, people, and physical setting—are as impressive as any of the individual highlights. Inspiring and unforgettable views from each hill, the small plazas, the patio gardens, the municipal landscaping, and the colorful Indians walking beside the ancient buildings make Quito memorable to even the most seasoned world traveler.

From Quito a great many excursions to outlying areas are popular. Excellent tours or independent transportation is available to the surrounding sights. Most popular excursions are:

Equatorial Monument—fifteen miles north of Quito (usually an hour by car) stands the globe-topped monument that marks the equator. Although there's really nothing spectacular about the granite monument, built in 1936, or the actual spot geographers call 0° 00′ 00″, most visitors greatly enjoy the sensation of crossing the equator a dozen or so times and having their pictures taken with one foot in the northern hemisphere and the other in the southern.

Chillos Valley—this is probably the most popular excursion for residents. Most weekends find streams of locals driving from Quito through the neighboring farming villages and checkerboard, mountainside fields to the twin thermal swimming pools of the Chillos Valley, *Tingo* and *Alangasí*. At both these pool resorts there are good restaurants and public/private clubs where the visitor is given a hearty welcome and will have an unusually fine opportunity to meet and mingle with the friendly Ecuadorians.

Quito is also the departure point for excursions to Ecuador's many Indian fairs and markets.

Guayaquil and Excursions

Ecuador's largest city is the magnificent natural port of Guayaquil, claiming a population of 1 million. The city's importance is emphasized by the fact that Guayaquil is the country's commercial as well as financial center. The tropical city lies on the heavily wooded banks of the chocolate-colored Guayas River, forty miles from the Gulf of Guayaquil. The Guayas teems with ships, small boats and native dugouts. Hyacinths that drift atop the water add a dash of color to the busy river. The river, navigable for the largest of ocean vessels, makes this one of the Pacific's most important and best-protected ports. Approximately 85 percent of Ecuador's exports flow through the port of Guayaquil and on the Guayas River to the outside world.

The city itself is not attractive. Ravaged by centuries of fires, earthquakes, swarms of termites, and brutal pirate attacks, Guayaquil is just now beginning to build a degree of permanence. New cement buildings, constructed under a strict code, are at last defying termites and earthquakes. Modern firefighting equipment is well organized, and the pirates are now only legends (although a few still seem to be driving taxis). Guayaquil is progressing rapidly. The city itself is well laid out, with wide concrete boulevards and spacious parks. Best evidence of progress is the magnificent new airport that greets the arriving air traveler. Guayaquil is Ecuador's city of industry. Oil and sugar refineries, cement mills, breweries and several other factories line the crowded river banks. Spread out behind the mills and plants and rising on the scattered hills of the city are the rusting galvanized-iron roofs that still seems to be the trademark of Guayaquil's homes.

Rich in history, Guayaquil was the scene of one of South America's most historic meetings. The date was August 9, 1822, when the two greatest Latin American heroes of liberation—Bolívar and San Martín—met to decide the fate of Guayaquil. The negotiations were secret and most of what happened remains unknown to this day. After the crucial meeting San Martín left Ecuador for a self-imposed exile, and Guayaquil was incorporated into Gran Colombia.

Today's Guayaquil visitor will enjoy seeing a city that is progressing rapidly and hurrying to catch up to the 20th century. Several tours of the city are available ($4.00) which usually include sightseeing to: San Carlos fort, Municipal Tower, City Museum, Government Palace, La Rotunda (a colonnade commemorating the Bolívar-San Martín meeting), main docks, Colón Park (where the city was founded), Santo Domingo Church, and the general cemetery or "White City" which is one of South America's most striking burial grounds, with elaborate tombs and monuments.

Most visitors visit *El Mirador* for a panoramic view of the city. Tours also include a stop at the world's largest balsa wood factory and a drive through several modern residential areas.

An interesting river tour is available in Guayaquil. A private yacht, with room for eight, may be chartered for $50 per half-day to cruise the Guayas River to Daule and Babahoyo. The cruise takes the visitor along a genuine tropic shoreline where the flora and fauna are as varied and fascinating as anywhere on the Amazon.

From Guayaquil several excursions are available for the adventurous visitor seeking a resort or sporting atmosphere. Most popular nearby destination is Playas (also known as Villamil), a resort town of fine beaches, a casino and excellent fishing.

A second popular destination is Salinas, a fashionable resort located 98 miles west of Guayaquil on a half-moon bay with a magnificent sand beach, a good hotel and gambling casino. At Punta Carnero is one of the best places to stay on the Pacific coast, the deluxe, 45-room *Carnero Inn*. The blue waters abound with black, blue and striped marlin, sailfish, amberjack, albacore, corbina, wahoo, dolphin and roosterfish.

Off Manta, a port 130 miles north of Guayaquil accessible by fair road or air, big game saltwater fish are plentiful and the area is still relatively unknown to sport fishermen. Local commercial fishermen, using primitive hand-lines from small dugout canoes, annually catch thousands of marlin. However, there are several Ecuadorian and foreign companies fishing for tuna and marlin with modern boats and equipment. Accommodations as well as charter boats should be arranged in advance in Guayaquil for Manta and the other northern Ecuadorian ports and resorts.

A final port worth mentioning is Esmeraldas, reached by sea and air from Guayaquil and by road from Quito. An oil tanker and banana-loading center, Esmeraldas is gaining tourist interest because of the new *Atacames*, *Castel Novo*, and *Sua*, situated on beautiful beaches, with palm trees and meadows running down to the sea.

Comfortable motorcoaches make the 200-mile trip between Quito and Guayaquil every day. The 8-hour tour stops in San Domingo de los Colorados, where tourists may stay overnight, continuing their journey on the following day. (Fare: $5).

Train Ride to the Sky

The world's mightiest roller coaster stretches in a crazy, rollicking 288-mile ride from Guayaquil to Quito (Mon., Wed., Fri.) and back (Tues., Thurs., Sat.) via the *autoferro*, a one-car "train" which looks like (and may be) a school bus on a railway chassis, with 30 tiny, and hard, nonreclining seats. Despite the discomfort, this magnificent tour is a guaranteed highlight on any South American trip if you can take the noise, at times almost unbearable, and the lack of heat or food (pack a lunch).

If you are in a hurry to get from one city to the other you can hire a taxi from your hotel and make the trip for about $85 (for two) along the Pan American Highway (good condition) in about 7 or 8 hours.

The bumpy *autoferro* trip is not for the faint-hearted, for the switchbacks and turns are enough to take the breath away from a mountain climber. Probably the best way to give an idea of the trip is to reproduce the stations listed on the ticket, with their altitudes:

Altitude in Feet	Station	Miles from Guayaquil	Altitude in Feet	Station	Miles from Guayaquil
15	Durán (Guayaquil)	0	10,379	Luisa	142
20	Yaguachi	14	9,020	Riobamba	150
42	Milagro	21	11,841	Urbina	170
100	Naranjito	31	10,346	Mocha	178
300	Barraganeta	43	9,100	Cevallos	186
975	Bucay	54	8,435	Ambato	196
4,000	Huigra	72	8,645	San Miguel	219
4,875	Chunchi	76	9,055	Latacunga	227
5,925	Sibambe	81	10,375	Lasso	239
8,553	Alausi	89	11,653	Cotopaxi	250
9,200	Tixán	95	10,118	Machachi	263
10,626	Palmira	103	9,090	Aloag	266
10,000	Guamote	112	9,891	Tambillo	273
10,388	Cajabamba	132	9,375	Quito	288

After scanning the elevations and then examining the geography between Guayaquil and Quito one begins to appreciate the magnitude of the challenge construction engineers accepted when this road was planned. The obstacles before the builders were formidable. From the sea-level left bank of the Guayas River the track extends out 54 miles over flat savanna lands. At the 54th mile the road begins a dizzy climb to 10,600 feet within the next 50 miles. To accomplish this, the track climbs at a 5½ percent gradient along such engineering triumphs as "Devil's Nose"—a double switchback zig-zag cut out of solid rock.

After a brief stop for both man and machine to catch their breath the *autoferro* starts out again climbing even higher to Urbina at 11,841 feet above sea level. Urbina lies at the foot of snow-capped Mt. Chimborazo, which towers another 10,000 feet above the tracks and presents probably the most spectacular view seen from any train window anywhere in the world. As the journey continues, 309 bridges, tunnels, and bends are passed, and Mt. Cotopaxi, the highest volcano in the world, at 19,200 feet, looms against the bright, clear blue mountain sky. After crossing, climbing and descending these Andean ranges a final descent is made to Quito, where a tired but probably satisfied group of rail veterans disembark.

Listed below is a brief summary of the trip from Guayaquil to Quito with the most important stops identified. Best bet, however, is to take the trip in the opposite direction to get the most spectacular scenery in daylight. An advance reservation is needed because the trip is extremely popular and space is very limited. One-way fare is about $4.

Leave Guayaquil at 6 a.m. First stop is Yaguachi, a small village 14 miles from Guayaquil. First important stop is Milagro, where scores of Indian women greet the train with native fruits and *allullas* (a small, tasty, cookielike bread). At the 54th mile of the journey the train arrives in Bucay, where a larger engine is often connected for the steeper grades ahead.

From Bucay the trip becomes spectacular as the lush tropical fields pass by and the Andean ascent begins. The train climbs through the Chanchán River gorge to the small village of Huigra.

The most breathtaking segment of the journey starts an hour from Huigra. After inching along a steep canyon ledge high above the Chanchán River the engine begins the slow pull up the Nariz del Diablo (Devil's Nose), which consists of a series of zig-zags that climb 1,000 feet in the gorge above the river. Tunnels, bridges and steep cliffs highlight the arduous climb up the perpendicular ridge. The air cools and the tropics fade to a green haze far below.

Next a series of small Indian mountain villages pass by. Chanchán, Sibambe (where connections may be made for another train to Cuenca), and on to the popular mountain resort village of Alausí, where bus connections to Quito are possible.

At the 103-mile mark the train stops in Palmira, and here on the crest of the Andes, in the clear stimulating air, many of the towering peaks of the Ecuadorian highlands appear.

The rarefied atmosphere seems to put Chimborazo, Tungurahua, Sangay, Altar and Carihuairazo almost within reach. The train soon leaves for Guamote and continues past the shores of Lake Colta and into the agricultural oasis of the Cajabamba Valley.

After Cajabamba dusk usually begins to conceal the dramatic scenery and the train pulls into Riobamba. Many travelers choose to stay here the two nights before continuing on to Quito. Riobamba is the capital of Chimborazo Province and a striking city of graceful stone colonial-style buildings. At night the sky glows with the reflection from Sangay volcano and its ashes often cover Riobamba's cobbled streets. Saturday is market day, and leather goods, baskets, sandals and Indian wares are very reasonable. The tiny, intricate Tagua carvings are a favorite buy. Try the Andean specialty, baked guinea pig, at the large open-air restaurants.

From Riobamba the line climbs to its highest point, Urbina Pass, and for 26 miles crosses a succession of towering ridges to Ambato, an important town of 45,000 inhabitants, impressively situated at the base of towering Chimborazo. Ambato is an important road junction and home of one of Ecuador's best-known Indian markets.

From Ambato the line skirts the mighty volcano Cotopaxi to Latacunga, another important city of 25,000 inhabitants. Latacunga is dominated by the perfect-coned Cotopaxi, which is 18 miles from the city but still manages to dwarf everything in sight. On a clear day the sharp-eyed can see nine volcano cones from the town. Several tours are operated from Quito to Latacunga for the Saturday Indian market.

The only stop of interest after leaving Latacunga is Machachi, where one of Ecuador's top brands of mineral water is bottled. From the Machachi springs the train descends into the basin where Quito lies, and the final 25-mile run to the capital is rapid.

Bus connections for Quito can be made at either Riobamba (4 hours) or Ambato (2½ hours).

Indian Fairs

Ecuador's centuries-old Indian markets are one of the country's truly outstanding attractions. Both north and south of Quito in the high Andean valleys a series of weekly fairs attracts thousands of visitors annually, affording them a chance to buy native handicrafts and textiles at bargain prices.

Metropolitan Touring in Quito packages many fine tours all over the country. The top attractions are the weekly market days in Otavalo, Ambato, Latacunga, Riobamba and Saquisilí. Metropolitan Touring's trips to Saquisilí, Latacunga and Ambato include lunch at a *hacienda,* where tour members may enjoy horseback riding. There are also half-day tours on Sundays from Quito to Indian markets in nearby Machachi or Sangolqui, etc.

Otavalo, estimated 20,000 population, is located 70 miles north of Quito via a fair but highly scenic highway. Market day is Saturday, and the industrious Otavaleños hold probably the most colorful Indian market in all South America. The gala Saturday affair starts at an eye-opening 5:30 a.m. when the mountain Indians, brightly attired in blue, purple, and scarlet ponchos, stream into town for market. They soon fill Otavalo's steep, cobbled streets carrying large loads of their handmade wares. By 7 a.m. the market is in full swing and bargaining reaches its height.

The Otavaleños, a pre-Inca tribe with a thousand-year heritage as farmer-artisans, offer a great variety of fabrics and leather goods for sale. Most popular buy is the homespun woolen material. Embroidered women's blouses and skirts are also a good buy, as well as wallets, rope-soled slippers, filigreed silver, tapestries and brightly colored ponchos. A good souvenir is one of the stiff felt hats the women wear to market.

Because their fair starts so early most tours to see the Otavaleños usually leave Quito Friday morning for the three-hour drive north. The afternoon is spent sightseeing, and an overnight is usually arranged at one of four hotels: the Otavalo, Chipacan, Chorvali or Ajaví. Some tours put up in nearby Ibarra at the Hacienda Paradero Cusin, where there is accommodation for 30.

In *Ibarra* (pop. 25,000), some excellent wood carvings may be found in the town's small shops. After overnighting, visitors to the Otavalo fair are given an early call at five o'clock and spend the morning hours at the market. Most tours leave Otavalo by 11 o'clock and return to Quito via San Pablo lake (the country's largest) arriving back in the capital in the early afternoon. Daily tours are now offered to this area by Metropolitan Touring, and a minimarket may be easily organized for any group, any day, with the cooperation of the Otavalo Indians who live in Peguche, an attractive Indian community.

Ambato (pop. 90,000) may well be the Indian version of the Garden of Eden. Situated on the flowering banks of the Ambato River at the foot of Chimborazo, the luxuriant town's best-known attraction is the vast plaza that fills every Monday for market day.

Because the fair doesn't get under way as early as Otavalo's, visitors may leave Quito early Monday morning and arrive in Ambato at the height of the trading. The bright, noisy market offers the visitor a chance to see more than 20,000 colorfully dressed Indians spread across the vast six-square market. The most popular buy is the area's renowned "Persian knot" rugs. Best spot for lunch on market day is the Hotel Villa Hilda. After lunch, tours take visitors to the nearby Salasaca Indian territory for a look at rural Indian life in the highlands. A late afternoon return to Quito usually features a flaming sunset on Cotopaxi, the country's highest volcano.

Latacunga (pop. 40,000) offers a Saturday market and a smaller one Tuesdays, good substitutes for those who can't spare the time necessary to visit Otavalo. Latacunga is an easy 54-mile drive from Quito, and several one-day tours are available. The market is beside the rushing Cutuche River and often draws as many as 18,000 natives for the weekly trading and bargaining sessions. Native handicrafts, leather goods, and textiles are the best buys. Ten miles from Latacunga are Pujilí, with a Wednesday market, and Salcedo, with a Sunday market.

Saquisilí (pop. 8,000) is located 68 miles south of Quito and offers a colorful Indian market every Thursday that may be visited in a day from the capital The incredible scenic drive to Saquisilí is as satisfying as the market itself. Rolling meadows, valleys of tiny Indian settlements, and a drive along the very edge of Cotopaxi make the trip memorable. Also check for occasional, extremely colorful religious processions at Saquisilí.

The Galápagos Islands

Six hundred miles off Ecuador's coast a sizeable strand of isolated isles are just being developed as a major tourist attraction for visitors to Ecuador. Known as the Galápagos this group of volcanic islands have a total area of over 3,000 square miles and contain several small villages. The Galápagos hug the equator and stand beside the cooling Humboldt Current. The unique geography has resulted in a curious collection of islands that some call the world's most "zany zoo." Included in the Galápagos animal community are such outlandish animals as the blue-faced booby, the bump-head, bearded titmouse and the short-eared owl.

Recently, a reporter for the South American Travel Organization visited the Galápagos Islands and compiled a fascinating report, from which we quote several paragraphs:

"Discovered and called *Galapago* (tortoise) by the enterprising explorers of Spain in 1535, the archipelago was annexed by Ecuador in 1832. Despite their Latin lineage, the Galápagos bewitched so many British navigators and naturalists that English names are used as well as Spanish. Isabella, the largest of the atolls, for example, is also known as Albemarle, while Santa Cruz is Indefatigable, Santiago is James, Floreana is Charles, and Española is Hood.

"In the vanguard of voyagers from Britain came Charles Darwin in 1835, who summed up the setting as 'a living laboratory of evolution'. A lost Atlantis in Darwin's day, the Galápagos are now a simple and delightful trip from Guayaquil.

"Thanks to the Humboldt Current cooling the equatorial coast of Ecuador, the temperature in the Galápagos hovers around 78° F, days are sunny and nights are chilly. As a result seals and penguins from the polar regions enjoy co-existence with the most tropical of birds and beasts.

"Since the Galápagos have been declared a wild life sanctuary, the flora and fauna are now protected from pirates and poachers who ransacked the islands in the past. The giant tortoises, weighing up to 500 pounds, were a coveted catch in the old sailing days as a source of meat and oil, since they could be kept alive during a long voyage and served fresh in place of salted or dried rations.

"Despite vandals, the Galápagos still have a monopoly on weird creatures and strange vegetation. Biologists say 37 percent of all species of shore fish and 96 percent of the reptiles are found nowhere else. An astonishing 47 percent of the plants grow nowhere else on the globe but in the Galápagos.

"As the advance man for many a traveler today, Charles Darwin recorded his trip to the Galápagos in his historic *Voyage of the Beagle*. While exploring these volcanic specks, Darwin made a study of the famous finches (which come in 13 different varieties) and concluded that they had evolved from one ancestral form. He observed, too, that many of the creatures, primitive and complex, cut off from the outside world, tended to develop features, physical and psychical, to suit their environment. Such deductions, of course, served to document Darwin's *Origin of Species*.

"An El Dorado for entomologists and ichthyologists, ornithologists and herpetologists, the Galápagos, nonetheless, lure all manner of men. Anyone searching for a fresh identity with nature, rugged and raw, will find it in the Galápagos. Here and there, midst the sand dunes and lava rock are rain forests, green and lush, as unexpected as a splash of gaudy color on the craters of the moon.

"Many of the settlers on these stark shores have been as strange as the birds and beasts. Legend has it that an Irishman, known hereabouts as Oberlux, set up a colony at the turn of the 19th century by shanghaiing sailors. Following publication of William Beebe's *Galápagos: The World's End* in 1929, a wave of migrants flowed in and out.

"While the present Ecuadorian Indians are colorful colonists, the big show is the wild life of the Galápagos. No aquarium or zoo is so well stocked with fabled fauna—gobies and groupers, parrot and damsel fish, great auks and green herons, sea lions and floating snails, feather stars and flightless cormorants. No circus on earth offers such animal antics as the dragon joust of the iguana or the wedding dance of the albatross. The Galápagos are unique!"

There are now various ways of visiting the island group. A number of small yachts, accommodating 4, 6, 8 or 10 passengers, are available for full charter. The Ecuadorian Navy's passenger-supply ship *Calicuchima* takes civilian passengers on its 11-day round trip runs. The motor vessels *Iguana* and *Buccaneer* make the round trip to Baltra; and there are usually one or two cargo ships that make 12–14-day round trips from Guayaquil, on irregular schedules; or one can fly both ways; alternatively one-way by sea and the other by air can be arranged. Round-trip air fare from Quito is about $175, from Guayaquil $153. Within the islands, yachts, small local boats, buses and private cars all provide transportation, but advance arrangements are wise in season. For details, see page 355.

Santo Domingo de los Colorados

One of Ecuador's stellar attractions is the Colorado Indian territory. Located in the lowlands 85 miles west of Quito the frontier-like town of Santo Domingo de los Colorados is a curious complex of mud streets, bawdy houses and all-night taverns that create a boom-town atmosphere. However, the local attraction is not the town's similarity to the Old West, but the neighboring Indians who come to market every Sunday dressed unlike any other people in the world. The most astonishing feature of the Colorado Indians is their hair. It is plastered down and colored bright red by a paprikalike paste. Their bodies are painted with bright red stripes as a protection against evil spirits, and the women are naked from the waist up. The colorful tribe is peaceful and affords the visitor an excellent chance to observe true Indian life, and the market is a photographer's paradise.

Most tours to Santo Domingo de Los Colorados are two-day trips and include an overnight stop at the outstanding Hotel Zaracay, a remarkable jungle oasis that features a night club, swimming pool, tennis courts, and good food.

All-expense, two-day tours to Santo Domingo which include a visit to a nearby Indian village in the jungle cost $56 for a seat in a motor coach. Private cars and guides are also available. An additional highlight of the trip from Quito is the descending highway that takes the traveler from the Andean highlands through a subtropical zone and then a final descent into the true jungle of Ecuador. Hacienda Tinalandia, in the middle of the jungle, has attractive bungalows, good food and service—only 8 miles from Santo Domingo.

The Ecuadorian Oriente

The word *Oriente* often confuses the newly arrived visitor to Ecuador. The word doesn't refer to the Far East and the Orient of the Pacific, but rather to a vast, trackless, barely explored Ecuadorian territory that lies to the east of the Andes.

Over half of Ecuador's land area is included in the Oriente, but only a sparse population of an estimated 80,000 people live in the rugged, isolated jungle area. Geographically the Oriente is composed of the lower eastern slopes of the Andes and the jungle lowlands of the upper Amazon tributaries. The Oriente is laced with large, fast-running rivers that are often dangerous because of heavy, sudden flood rains, many rocks, rapids and other obstructions. The Oriente today is still virtually undeveloped and in many parts barely explored. These conditions however are changing fast because of recent oil discoveries, with a new network of roads and an airport facilitating travel into the Oriente.

Tours into the Jungle

For visitors who have only the time or the desire to sample just a taste of the Oriente, several photographic safaris are available from Quito to the jungle's edge. Tours leave from Quito via Ambato for an inspiring descent of the eastern Andean slopes through lush semitropical forestlands, the Salasaca Indian territory, deep gorges spanned by delicate bridges, past great waterfalls, fields of wild orchids and jungle flowers to the very edge of civilization and the small, prosperous town of Baños. Thriving Baños contains several small but excellent hotels certain to please visitors, especially the reader-recommended Sangay, English-operated. There, good cuisine is available and the hot springs, and swimming pools filled by cascading waterfalls, make the spot idyllic.

From Baños several morning excursions to surrounding areas may be made on tours that return the same day to Quito via Ambato and Latacunga. For the extremely adventurous and experienced traveler the lands past Baños stand as a challenge and as one of the last really wild, unexplored areas left in the world. The Oriente traveler must have plenty of adventurous spirit and be prepared for slightly difficult walking. A 5-day trip will provide an unforgettable experience. Accommodations at first class hotels and meals are included in the rates of $240–$370, depending on the number of participants. Special group rates. (Contact: Metropolitan Touring, Box 2542, Quito.)

By Plane and Canoe

ECUAVIA, TAME, SAETA and ATESA (Charters only) offer small plane service to several of the area's most important outposts. In addition there are some mission planes available for hire. Travel is also by motor canoes along the rivers.

A trip down one of the Oriente's rivers (most popular are the Napo and Bobonasa) is a fascinating adventure. Here is the true jungle with a swift, clear, fast-running river cutting into a five-story high jungle crammed with animal life and vegetation. In addition to the very comfortable *Jaguar Hotel* in Santa Rosa, there are excellent typical lodges in the area of Ahuano and Santa Rosa. New hotels planned in Tena and Coca. A few guest houses without sanitation are available at Puerto Napo and other villages. Best bets for overnight accommodation are the scattered Army posts and many riverbank settlers' homes. For the Spanish-speaking traveler a cordial welcome is always the rule along the main rivers. In emergencies an evening may be spent with the river Indians who will usually provide shelter and a hot fish stew in return for any small gift. The Indians along the main riverbanks are normally friendly, clean, honest people.

The Oriente Indians are divided into three main tribes—the Yumbos, Jívaros (sometimes Jíbaros) and the Aucas. The Yumbos are peaceful and mainly live along the larger rivers. They have been exploited by the white man and have given little resistance to the slow advance of civilization into the Oriente. Many Yumbos work for settlers along the riverbanks, pan gold, and nearly all lead quiet lives. This is not the case with the Oriente's two other tribes.

One way to "do" the Amazon in comfort is by floating hotel, the so-called "Flotel" *Orellana*. This is a kind of triple-decker raft with 22 double cabins and three four-berth ones (and even private baths!) that plies the river on 3- and 4-night cruises, starting from Coca, which is reached by air, taking jungle experts and four real (but motorized) dugout canoes along, for side trips. The tours cost from $195 to $305 per person.

A Visit to the Head Shrinkers

The Jívaros are world famous as the head shrinkers of the Amazon. The famed Jívaro shrunken heads or *tzantzas* are extremely rare. Many good imitations are for sale in almost every gift shop in Ecuador, and a good goat-hide imitation costs around $2.60.

The Aucas are one of the fiercest Indian tribes left in the world today. Not one Auca has ever become civilized, and the wild tribe made tragic, world-wide headlines in 1956 when they murdered five North American missionaries deep in the Oriente.

Limoncocha (Lime Lagoon) is a two-mile-long lake, the historic home of the Quechua Indians and the home base for the University of Oklahoma's Summer Institute of Linguistics. The two-hour flight from Quito offers an awe-inspiring panorama of jungle and mountain scenery. Within minutes by the Institute's land and float planes are the Cofan and Secoya Indian tribes, in a rich hunting area.

Safari expeditions can be arranged from Coca, Macas and Sucua.

PRACTICAL INFORMATION FOR ECUADOR

CAPSULE COMMENTS. *Physical Features.* A country of dramatic contrasts. Three distinct areas—the coastal plains, the highlands of the Andes, and the headwaters and lowlands of the Amazon. The highlands offer some of the world's most impressive scenery with 16 snow-capped volcanoes rising over 15,000 feet. One-and-a-half hours by jet from the mainland lie the primitive Galápagos Islands with a splendid climate and just now being discovered by international travelers.

Climate. Springlike days and crisp cool nights the year round in Quito. Because the equator passes 15 miles north of Quito, the sun always rises and sets at six a.m. and p.m. In the coastal lowlands it is always hot and tropical.

Population. 7,500,000. Quito 750,000.

Language. Spanish.

Archeological Attractions. Emeralds, Guano.

Principal Industries. Bananas, cocoa, rubber, coffee, balsa, textiles, oil.

HOW TO GET THERE. By air. There is excellent international air service to Ecuador. From New York: *Lufthansa, KLM* (via Curacao); from New York and Miami: *Avianca, LAN-Chile, Braniff*;

from Miami: *Ecuatoriana* (daily from New York and Miami, twice a week from Los Angeles); *Air France* from Los Angeles: *Braniff*.

From Frankfurt: *Lufthansa*; from Frankfurt, Paris, Zürich, Madrid, San Juan: *Avianca*; from Paris (via Lisbon or Pointe-à-Pitre): *Air France*; from Madrid direct or via San Juan: *Iberia*; from Amsterdam: *KLM*.

From Panama: *Ecuatoriana, Air Panama, LAN-Chile* and *Braniff*.

By Sea. Frequent steamship service calls at Ecuador's port of Guayaquil. Regular cargo-passenger service from west coast ports, *Prudential Lines*.

From Europe the *Hamburg-South American Line, Knutsen* and *Johnson Lines* offer regular passenger-cargo service, normally taking 20 to 22 days. *Italian Line* has monthly sailings from Mediterranean ports. *Royal Netherlands* from Rotterdam and Le Havre.

The entrance to Guayaquil by sea is extremely memorable, for ships first enter the 100-mile-long Gulf of Guayaquil from the open sea, proceed past Isla de Puná, and sail down the Guayas River past 40 intriguing miles of Indian settlements to Guayaquil's newly opened modern port.

BY ROAD. Ecuador's portion of the Pan American Highway is complete and bisects the country from the Colombian border at Rumichaca south to Quito and on to Riobamba, Cuenca, Loja, and ends at Macará. A road to Huaquillas on the Peruvian border is open.

TEPSA buses connect with several countries. Bus service within Ecuador is plentiful and inexpensive, although it is usually extremely crowded and often primitive. Bus service between Quito and Guayaquil and from Quito to the main cities of the highlands is good. There are reserved seats.

While many roads are still bumpy, highway construction has been extensive. There is a good network of paved roads running north-south. The oil companies are developing highways into the Oriente. The roads between Quito and Guayaquil and between Quito, Latacunga, Ambato and Riobamba are completely paved. The excellent road connecting Quito, Otavalo, Ibarra and Tulcan is now completed. Tulcan is the frontier with Colombia. A handy pocket-size card with all of Ecuador's highway routes and mileages is available in most book stores (ask for *Rutas del Ecuador*, prepared by Carlos A. Tufiño).

By Rail. There is no international railway service to Ecuador.

SPECIAL EVENTS. Highlights of an Ecuadorian visit are trips to the *ferias* or special market days. The top attractions are the *ferias* of Otavalo, Ambato, Latacunga, Saquisili, and Riobamba. Held once a week, they offer the visitor an excellent chance to observe true Indian life and pick up some excellent bargains. Full information on these colorful fairs and markets is contained in the *Exploring* section. Other special days of interest in Ecuador are:

January 1   New Year's Day

January 6   Three Kings Day

February	Carnival. The Ecuadorians begin festivities three days before Ash Wednesday. The most obvious part of the celebrations are the masked balls, parades— and unfortunately for many surprised visitors—the buckets and baloons of water that rain down on the unsuspecting from rooftops all over the country. Ambato Fruit and Flower Fair, held during Carnival
April	*Semana Santa* (Holy Week). Very colorful and moving religious services all over Ecuador. Holy Friday Processions are very impressive
May 24	Battle of Pichincha Day commemorating the victory over the Spaniards at Quito
June 5	Corpus Christi festivities celebrated by Indians in highlands. Also, commemoration of founding of Ecuador's Liberal Party
July 24	Bolívar's birthday
August 10	*Primer Grito de la Independencia* (day recalling the first cry of independence of 1809)
September	First two weeks Festival of Yamor in Otavalo—the most colorful of Ecuador's Indian celebrations. Native masks, costumes, dances
October 9	Most popular holiday in Guayaquil celebrating the city's independence. Parades, selection of the city's queen
October 12	Columbus Day
November 1	All Saints Day
November 2	*Dia de los Muertos* (Day of the Dead). All citizens honor the dead, pay visits to cemeteries, refurbish graves of loved ones
November 3	*Dia de Cuenca* (Cuenca's Day)
December	Quito Holiday, Dec. 6, preceded by Quito Fair, outstanding tourist event, bullfights, folklore exhibitions, sports events, carnival air, Dec. 1–6
December 24	Impressive Christmas Eve (*La Noche Buena*) services. Costume pageants in Quito and Guayaquil
December 25	Christmas Day
December 31	New Year's Eve.

PASSPORTS, VISAS, CUSTOMS. U.S. and Canadian tourists and all others except those from Iron Curtain countries need only a disembarkation card, which is filled out aboard the airplane or ship before arrival, proof of citizenship, return ticket and smallpox vaccination certificate. 300 cigarettes or 50 cigars, 2 bottles of liquor allowed duty free.

CURRENCY. Monetary unit is the Sucre which is currently exchanged at approximately 25 to the U.S. dollar. The Sucre is divided into 100 centavos. Bills are issued in the following denominations: 5, 10, 20, 50, 100, 500, 1,000. Nickel coins are one Sucre, 20, 10, and 5 centavos are minted. Travelers' checks and U.S. dollars are accepted for payment in most hotels and shops.

CLOTHING. Springlike weather the year 'round is the rule in Quito. Because of the capital's unique position almost squarely on the equator there is little variation in temperature from month to month. Quito's highs rarely go over 70 degrees and lows usually hover in the mid-40s. Average temperature is in the mid-50s; and these temperatures hold true for most of the country's central highland area. Best bets for clothing in the *sierra* areas are dresses and woolen suits for women, plus a sweater and fur wrap. For excursions in the highlands sports clothing is recommended. At main restaurants and hotels, a jacket is required for dinner. Men should have a woolen suit and topcoat. Raincoats are also needed in all of Ecuador. In Guayaquil, the coast, Galápagos and the jungle tropical wear is worn all year. For Galápagos comfortable, summer-weight clothing year round is the norm. For on-island touring, tough outdoor wear like denim or khakis for men and women. Shorts are sometimes okay depending on the island. The sun is strong, so bring good head protection. For walking, especially on the lava, some prefer solid hiking boots with rubber soles, others choose sneakers. And of course swimming wear. On ship, it's casual sport clothing. And for the often cool evenings, a sweater or jacket might be appreciated.

HOW TO GET ABOUT. Guayaquil and Quito are linked by frequent domestic air service by *TAME* and *Ecuatoriana de Aviacion*. 40-minute flight costs $18.00 for international ticketing. It's very dramatic! The plane takes off from sea level Guayaquil, climbs to 10,000 feet, and then lands at Quito's sky high airport. There is frequent daily service between the two cities and several on Sunday. *TAME* is run by the military and offers only local service. *SAN and SAETA* serve the main cities. A number of small airlines serve the coast and eastern part of the country.

The Quito airport is about a 15-minute drive from the Hotel Quito ($2.00 per car), and the Guayaquil airport is on the edge of town with taxis charging about $2.00 in daytime and $4.00 at night per car.

Ecuador's spectacular train service from Guayaquil to Quito (described in detail in the Exploring section) is well worth investigating. Other than this special trip the remaining rail service is not recommended for even the most adventurous.

Coastal steamers make frequent trips along Ecuador's coast stopping at Mantas and Esmeraldas.

The Galápagos Islands are both a National Park and a wildlife preserve, so tourism there is regulated by the government. The basic source of information is: Superintendent, Galápagos National Park Service, Isla Santa Cruz, Islas Galápagos, Ecuador. The principal commercial agency covering this area is: Metropolitan Touring, P.O. Box 2542, Quito, Ecuador. Access by sea is by one navy ship, two passenger vessels and a couple of cargo ships. By air there are weekly flights by TAME airline (TAME, 10 de Agosto 239, Quito); charter flights through Metropolitan Touring (see above); and weekly flights by the Ecuadorean Air Force. Within the archipelago, travel is by bus, car, tourist boat, hired yacht, and the local mail boat. All visits to any part of the National Park (90% of the land area and some marine areas too) require permits and licenced guides. Accommodations are limited; at Puerto Ayora 4 small hotels provide about 90 beds. There is one small hotel on each of the two other islands. Restaurants total about 10. There are two limited camp-grounds. Amenities such as sun lotion, film, pipe tobacco, etc. are usually not available. For complete information contact the Superintendent's office, or Metropolitan Touring (addresses above).

Taxis and rental cars are readily available in Quito and Guayaquil, as well as in other cities, for excursions to nearby areas. *Hertz* is one agency.

HOTELS. Prices are low, with the following range in our categories: *Deluxe*, $20 up for singles, $24 up for doubles; *First Class*, $16 up for singles, $18 up for doubles; *Moderate*, below these figures. All hotel prices are subject to 20 percent tax and service charge.

QUITO

Deluxe

QUITO INTERCONTINENTAL.
A modern hotel with gambling casino, pool, beautiful rooftop bar and restaurant, and a magnificent view of the city and surrounding valleys. Now being re-modeled and improved.

COLÓN INTERNACIONAL.
A newer hotel with more up-to-date accommodations and a more central location in a residential section of town. The restaurant offers fine cuisine. Sunday buffet is highly recommended. Pool and gardens. Currently expanding: 240 brand-new rooms opened Sept. 1977.

Among the smaller *first-class* hotels are *Zumag,* newest in the residential area, *Inca Imperial, Savoy Inn,* in the vicinity of the airport, and *Humboldt,* downtown.

Moderate tourist-class hotels are *Embassy, Embajador, Waldorf* and *Alcron.*

Among the pensions, *Residencial Lutecia, Naciones Unidas* and *Pension Americana* are recommended.

OUTSIDE QUITO

AMBATO. Brand new and first-class, the *Miraflores. Villa Hilda* and *Florida* are first-class moderate; meals are mandatory.

CUENCA. *Dorado* is first class, *Crespo* moderate, and *Cuenca* inexpensive.

GALAPAGOS. *Hotel Galapagos,* at Academy Bay, is deluxe in price, first class in facilities. Meals mandatory, of course.

HOTEL SIEVERS, new in 1977, with private beach and facilities for 32 people.

GUAYAQUIL. *New Continental* is a good place to eat, has doubles, suites ($26 up), rated deluxe, as is the *Atahualpa*.

New first-class is the *Grand Hotel*, centrally located, with 150 rooms, fully air-conditioned. Other first-class hotels are the Continental (old wing), which has the best food in town, the Palace and the Humboldt.

OTAVALO/IBARRA. *Hacienda Parador Cusin*, in outskirts of Otavalo, and *Hacienda Hosteria Chorlavi*, in Ibarra, are first class, and meals are mandatory. *Ajavi* is inexpensive.

Turismo and *Otavalo* are moderate; meals mandatory at latter.

PUERTO NAPO. *Anaconda Typical Lodge*, on the river, first-class moderate. Meals mandatory.

PUNTA CARNERO. *Carnero Inn* is a deluxe resort hotel, beautifully located with pool, casino. Excellent deepsea fishing, water sports.

SALINAS. *Miramar* and *New Hotel Salinas* are deluxe and first class, respectively.

Moderate hotels include *Yulee* and *Brisa*.

SANTA ROSA. *Jaguar*, in the heart of the jungle in Oriente, is first-class moderate. Meals mandatory.

SANTO DOMINGO DE LOS COLORADOS. *Tinalandia* is deluxe resort hotel, with golf course, swimming, and excellent service. *Zaracay* first class. Meals mandatory at both.

 RESTAURANTS. Quito has excellent restaurants featuring international specialties. *Chalet Suisse*, best steak house. New *Don Carlos*, and *Alexander* for international cuisine. *La Cueva de Luis Candelas*, *Centro Español* and *Tronio* are best for Spanish food. *La Casa de Italia* for best Italian dishes. Try *Moby Dick*, *La Jaiba* and *El Cerviche* for seafood.

La Choza has the best typical Ecuadorian dishes in town.

Equinoccio is a nice folkloric-style restaurant in the Equatorial Monument.

La Fuente, Panecillo Hill overlooking the city, has typical and international dishes.

Of course, very popular eating places are *El Conquistador* at the Hotel Colón and *El Techo del*

Mundo at the Intercontinental Quito Hotel.

The coffee shops at the hotels Quito and Colón offer excellent inexpensive meals and are open 24 hours a day.

Restaurant prices are very reasonable in Ecuador. Just about three dollars will buy an excellent meal in the finest places.

Nearby: Only 26 miles from Quito, in the Chillos Valley, is Sangolquí, where there are excellent restaurants and public and private clubs.

 NIGHTLIFE. People are going out more in Quito than formerly (but Paris it's not). A few night clubs offer entertainment but they are usually expensive for what one gets. The *Hotel Quito* has a casino and an elegant night club, *La Llama*. Hotel *Colón* also has a casino and a good disco.

In Quito the *Le Toucan* and the *Tally Ho* are the best local night spots but nothing to write home about. There is a variety of discotheques, good ones are the *Unicorn* at *Hotel Colón*, *Pianoteca*, *Licorne*, *Morgan's* and *Rolls Royce*.

A final word of caution—remember at Quito's high altitude a few drinks often feel like a few dozen.

 SHOPPING. Excellent bargains of many kinds are available in Quito's fascinating shops and the country's many Indian markets. Some caution is advised for one of Ecuador's most thriving industries is the creating of "colonial and medieval" paintings and carvings.

There are few silver stores in the world better than the larger ones in Quito. Vast collections of antique pieces and modern, handmade wares are available and at reasonable prices.

Native wood carvings and Indian textiles are very reasonable and make excellent buys. Woolen rugs and blankets and handloomed textiles are popular with visitors. Inquiries will uncover prizes from the Oriente country—*tzantzas* (shrunken heads), genuine aboriginal art and native weapons.

Bargaining is the rule rather than the exception in all of the country's smaller shops. A few stores around the major hotels have fixed prices—but don't be timid about attempting to lower the price anywhere.

Best bet for bargain hunters are the weekly Indian markets in the smaller towns. Prices there haven't been pushed up by too many free-spending tourists—and there are great bargains in handicrafts, woven goods and souvenirs. In Quito the best shopping areas are on Venezuela and Guayaquil streets and around the main plaza.

Most popular shop for Ecuador's unique handicrafts and Panama hats is the *Folklore* near the Hotel Quito and run by the engaging Señora Fisch. For Ecuador's antique silver the best shops are *Recalde*, Chile St., *Joyeria Bolivar*, Espejo St. and *El Poncho*, the newest, with moderate prices. For an excellent and large selection of dolls, paintings, prints, masks, jewelry and clothes visit *Akios*, Gorivar St., and *Ocepa*. Ask for Akios' catalog; it will tell at a glance what is available and how much it costs. *Artes* is a new art studio and handicraft shop specializing in modern art. *H. Stern* has a branch in the Intercontinental Hotel with a full line of locally made silver and gold jewelry. Ask for their free local "charm" and their free travel booklet.

In Bellavista is the studio and workshop of Oswaldo Guayasamin world-known painter. The paintings, sculptures and handcrafted jewelry displayed here are for sale.

In the Province of Azuay, the cities of Cuenca and Gualaceo offer a wide variety of handicrafts.

 SPORTS. *Soccer*, or *futbol*, is wildly popular in Ecuador as in all Latin America. Most towns have a team and top games are played weekends in Quito's Olympic Stadium, as well as in Otavalo. *Bullfights* are frequently featured in Quito's huge new ring. Best fights are in early December with top Mexican and Spanish stars. There are also bull rings in Ambato and Riobamba. For the visiting amateur, the new, large *Hacienda Tambo Mulaló*, which is visited during the Indian market tours, offers a very nice bull ring where he can try his cape work but no sword play on young but not-so-harmless bulls. Otavalo offers *cockfights*.

Pelota de Guante (gloveball) is a difficult national game, played with a heavy ball and leather glove. Best place to see this game is on Saturday and Sunday at *Mejia* and *Pobre Diablo* stadiums.

Swimming, golf and *tennis* are popular around Quito and on the coast at the new resorts. *Horseback riding* and *hiking* are extremely enjoyable in the *sierra country*, as are golf and tennis. There are excellent country clubs in Ancon, Quito and Guayaquil; visitors are welcome through a local member. Golf fees are about $5.

Top new sporting attraction in Ecuador is *marlin fishing*. Several other game fish abound in Ecuadorian waters. Because the north-west flowing Humbolt Current nearly touches Ecuador's coast from June to December, bringing cold water from the Antarctic, the offshore waters teem with hard-fighting, large coldwater game fish usually uncommon near the equator. In the remaining months the current flows southward and the large game fish are replaced by great numbers of smaller species. Four huge lakes in the Otavalo area yield good fishing. Fair roads lead from Guayaquil to nearby Playas (60 miles) and Salinas (98 miles). First-class accommodations are available at both towns. Close by is the new *Carnero Inn*. The depths off the Inn have already produced a 1,440-lb. black marlin, reputedly the second largest ever landed. Four new world records have already been broken here. 2, 3, 4, 5 days, leaving daily. Rates on request from Metropolitan Touring.

Photographic safaris and sightseeing trips to the Oriente are also becoming popular. Several tour operators now offer five-day (and longer) "jungle tours" from $220 ea. (groups) to $840 for a couple, by private car.

CULTURAL EVENTS. Plays, concerts and ballet are regularly scheduled in Quito's excellent Sucre Theater. All productions are in Spanish. An English-language group "The Pichincha Play House" presents plays in English several times a year. *Artes* handcraft shop also has musical performances.

Quito's museums are top attractions for visitors. The following are well worth visiting: Museum of Colonial Art, Municipal Museum, Museum of San Francisco, and Museum Jijou at the Catholic University. Visitors interested in archeology will enjoy the Christian Brothers Archeological Museum (*Museo Arqueologico de los Hermanos Cristianos*). A Museum of Natural History is also open daily at the *Colegio Mejia*, and the Musical Museum in the *Casa de la Cultura* is a must for all. Among the best is Banco Central del Ecuador's excellent Anthropological Museum with a fine collection of Indian pottery, utensils, figures and granite carvings.

USEFUL ADDRESSES. Embassy of the U.S.A., Box 538; Embassy of Great Britain, Box 314; Embassy of Canada, Box 2245—all Quito.
The *International Association for Medical Assistance for Travelers (IAMAT)*, Baquerizo 271, Quito.

AMERICAN EXPRESS AGENTS: *Guayaquil*, Ecuadorian Tours S.A., Pedro Carbo 427; *Quito*, Ecuadorian Tours S.A., Ave. Amazonas 399.

PERU

Heritage of Inca and Conquistador

BY

C. N. GRIFFIS and BARRY ST. CLAIR McBRIDE

*(Mr. Griffis is the grand old man of English-language journal-
ism in Peru, a former editor and publisher of* The Peruvian
Times; *Mr. McBride is widely known as a lecturer on South
America and is the author of* Amazon Journey. *The Peruvian
chapter of this year's* Fodor's South America *has been brought up
to date by Mr. Griffis' son, Donald Griffis, present publisher of*
The Peruvian Times.)

Peru is divided into three main areas, distinctive regions each
with its own way of life: the desert, the mountains, the jungle.
The desert stretches all along the West Coast, covering perhaps a
tenth of the area of Peru. This desert is the driest on earth and
would be forbidding but for the crossing valleys which stretch
down from the Andes, supplying seasonal streams which cut into
the desert and nurture green irrigated stretches of sugar and cotton
plantations. It never rains in this desert and this dryness has preserved intact the mummified bodies of people buried centuries ago
on the slopes just outside their valley settlements.

Look inland on a clear day and you will see the country rising
before you like a wall. Desert sand gives way to bare rock on the
hills which climb higher and higher, thousands of feet into the
Cordillera, the range of the Andes. This is the second region of
Peru, the *Sierra*, clear cold peaks which stretch away in jagged
lines like ridges on the back of a crocodile. Between the ridges lie

deep valleys with fast-flowing streams, green pastureland and little red-tiled villages of the hill Indians.

The third region of Peru lies beyond the great range of the Andes, down in the jungle. This is the *montaña*, a vast area of rain forest covering over half the area of Peru. Down here it is hot and wet, and as early morning mists rise from the rivers the jungle seems to steam. Water is virtually the only means of transport for the jungle tribes.

You won't need quinine, a sun helmet or a machete to visit Peru. But bring along a good supply of superlatives. Otherwise you'll be at a loss for words. Peru's half a million square miles make it the equal of Texas and California combined. Its vanished Indian civilizations were the oldest and the most advanced; its conquest was the most unlikely and the most unbelievable; its colonial era was the proudest and most glorious. Peru's deserts are the driest, its mountains some of the most impressive in the world.

Peru's economy has been based on everything from guano and gold to oil and fish meal. Transport in the country can be by aircraft from Lima, the biggest airport on the Pacific coast, to old steamers, manhandled in pieces up the Andes and now floating on Lake Titicaca. It has roads that would break the heart of a jeep, but it also has trans-Andean highways that would warm the soul of a Roman. Peru gasps for breath in the Andes and basks in the warmth of the Amazon. Peru makes steel at Chimbote and reed rafts at Puno. Peru builds earthquake-proof skyscrapers in Lima and lives in 18th-century manor houses in Ayacucho. Peru wears coats along its coast cooled by the Humboldt Current and sheds them a few minutes away in the desert sunshine.

Peru has been conquered and civilized by pre-Incan people, the Incas, and Pizarro and his Spaniards, but it is still open to exploration and even conquest. Something new can turn up any day. The explorers are the world's great archeologists, who make their finds with spades and radioactive carbon dating methods.

Capsule History

Thousands of years before the Spanish Conquest, the land now known as Peru was inhabited like Mexico by complex and sophisticated societies. They spread civilization through the Andes, the coastal valley lands and deserts and part of the forested foothills in the east.

Archeology tells us more and more of these pre-Inca and Inca civilizations, and the chronicles of early Spanish priests and travelers like Garcilaso de la Vega and Pedro de Cieza Leon have filled in the gaps in the story of the Incas. In fact the 19th-century historian, Prescott, whose classic *Conquest of Peru* is one of the best and most readable works on the subject, was apparently almost unaware that the Incas were only the last—and in some ways, not even the most advanced—of many different civilizations that had flourished in Peru. Some were primitive. Others, like the Chavin, Paracas, Tiahuanaco, Nazca and Chimu, were highly distinctive cultures whose stonework, pottery and textiles are now deemed among the finest of their kind in the world.

Ancient Civilizations

Despite modern techniques of statistical analysis, radio-carbon dating, and aerial photography, the picture of the sequence and character of these overlapping cultures is still far from clear. Bones and artifacts have been traced back many thousands of years, and the coastal desert is littered with shellmounds which have been dated back to 3000 B.C. They seem to have been left by primitive hunters and fishermen.

Chavin is generally considered the first Peruvian civilization to have created a complex agricultural society with outstanding masonry and stonework. There are several good examples in the Museum at Pueblo Libre (Magdalena Vieja), a suburb of Lima, although a visit to Chavin de Huantar itself, in the Callejon de Huaylas north east of Lima, is essential for anyone interested in Peruvian archeology.

Then came various stages of the *Tiahuanaco* culture, named after ruins at Tiahuanuco, near the Bolivian shores of Lake Titicaca. Coinciding with later Tiahuanaco were the coastal desert cultures of *Paracas*, famous for the quality and forceful imagination of intricately woven textiles, and *Nazca*, with pottery of brilliant color and design. Both Paracas and Nazca, are found on the southern coastal desert. *Mochica* and *Chimu* were two developed cultures on the north coast, with fine pottery, roads, forts and large population centers. One of the best examples is at Chan Chan, just outside the city of Trujillo.

All these coastal cultures had advanced irrigation systems, better and more extensive in some cases than those in use today. It is generally believed that the population of Peru's desert valleys was at least as high and probably higher than today.

The conquering *Inca* empire extended over all these civilizations or their successors. Held together by a system of roads and forts, and a well-developed administrative and communications network, it ran from present day Quito in Ecuador down through the Atacama desert into Chile. From their capital in Cuzco, Incas dominated the central Andes for approximately three centuries, prior to the arrival of the Spaniards, and have been compared to the Romans in their taste and capacity for conquest, their genius for the construction of roads and buildings, and their ability to organize and control a great empire. The Incas have left a legacy of legends of lost cities and treasures, some of which have been found, like Machu Picchu, and one more recently at Pajaten.

Discoveries and Rediscoveries

A month seldom goes by without some archeological discovery in the sands of the desert coast, among the crags of the high Andes, on the forested slopes or in the lowlands beyond the great mountains. Many of these discoveries are rediscoveries. Despite recent progress, a comprehensive archeological inventory of Peru does not yet exist and records of research are buried in scores of books and learned journals in several languages.

Relics of Inca and pre-Inca civilizations are also widely scattered in European and North American museums and private collections. Even in Lima the present archeological museum contains only part of the collections by state institutions. To remedy this situation, the government is now planning to construct a National Archeological Museum.

Among recent discoveries has been the completion of a further stage of the excavation work carried out by Japanese archeologists from the University of Tokyo at the Kotosh ruins near Huanuco in the central Andes. Here, Incaic structures had been superimposed on earlier buildings of another culture. In an older building, scientists found on the opposite walls of an otherwise undecorated room, two models, nearly identical, of human hands crossed at the wrist, worked in clay in high relief and somewhat larger than life size. Highly realistic, the hands are entirely distinct in style and execution from any previous carvings or modelings found in Peru. Japanese experts date the earlier construction as early as 2500 B.C.

Gene Savoy, an American explorer and writer who makes no claim to being an archeologist, nevertheless made archeological history during the 1960s by aerial observation and photography of the remains of ancient civilizations along the north coast of Peru and in the western Andes of the Department of Ancash and La Libertad, north of Lima. It was in this region that the conquering armies of the Incas all but obliterated traces of the coastal civilization, generally known as the kingdom of the Chimu, that had flourished here. Savoy discovered the Inca city of Vilcabamba, just north of Machu Picchu, considered an important find. He later discovered in northern Peru several pre-Inca cities including the imposing Pajaten.

At best, ancient Peru, at least prior to the Inca conquests, is shrouded in mystery. You meet an odd ceramic design that embodies a keen sense of the humor common to all humanity or a textile pattern that might claim attention in the smartest shops, and occasionally does when some present-day designer seeks inspiration from museum walls. But what the ancient civilizations were like, the daily life of their peoples, their beliefs, hopes, fears and ambitions, can only be imagined.

The Great Wall of Peru

The *Chimu* civilization is largely identified with the ruins of Chan Chan, believed to have been the capital of this kingdom. They form a vast warren of adobe walls and buildings extending over an area of 11 square miles near the present city of Trujillo. In 1931 the Shippee-Johnson expedition from the United States, made the first large-scale attempt at an aerial photographic record of the topography of Peru. They discovered in the region of the Santa River valley some 60 miles south of Chan Chan an adobe wall several yards high that ran across the desert plain and into the western Andes where the construction material changed to stone masonry. This wall became known as the Great Wall of Peru.

Very little was done to follow up this discovery until Savoy learned of it on his first visit to Peru some years ago. His research, along with fellow members of the Andean Explorers Club, which he founded, has shown it to be part of a vast defensive system running hundreds of miles along the coast to the south and linked by hitherto unreported highways into the high Andes. (Chimu was generally considered an exclusively coastal civilization.) Savoy found that there was not one Great Wall of Peru but seven. They crossed the coastal deserts in the south from points near the sea into the Andean foothills. The Great Wall in the Santa Valley region was merely an outpost of a system of scores of masonry fortresses and strong points with walls 10 to 15 ft. high that crown the crests of the mountain spurs on both sides of the valley. Finally, he learned that that system is served by a previously unknown "super-highway," about 100 ft. wide (compared to the 24 ft. width generally ascribed to Inca highways), laid down for more than 125 miles through the deserts and over the mountain spurs between the coast and the crest of the coastal range of the Andes.

Seen from the air, where it has not been effaced by the drifting sands and erosion of centuries, this highway is as sharply defined and accurately traced as though planned by a modern engineer with precise surveying instruments. Where branches intersect, the angles are sharp and true. It requires little imagination to picture a helmeted highway policeman waving traffic through—but what traffic? The highway seems far too extensive for mere ceremonial processions. If it was designed for marching armies, they must have been mighty armies. Although isolated remains had long been known in this northern region, only aerial observation has been able to link the widely scattered elements of this vast defensive system.

The whole system, in the opinion of Savoy and other competent observers, challenges the Inca ruins in the Cuzco-Machu Picchu region of southern Peru and, in many ways, surpasses them.

A strong movement with official support is now under way to

raise funds to restore the Chimu capital of Chan Chan to some semblance of its former glory. Undoubtedly, this campaign will be extended to the network of ancient roads and fortifications built to defend this kingdom.

Further south in the *Nazca* region 280 miles from Lima, there is an even more inscrutable mystery of desert archeology. There, on a section of the level pampa lying between Nazca and the village of Palpa some 30 miles to the north, a clan of astronomically minded draftsmen ages ago drew an amazing series of lines radiating apparently from a solitary hill in the midst of this waste. To the local people, this is known as *El Calendario* (The Calendar), and it is now well established that the lines have some connection with astronomical observations and the movements of the sun, moon and stars as related to the seasonal changes of the year. Besides these lines, there are figures shaped like birds, animals and flowers. Aerocondor now runs regular small-plane flights over the lines from the airport at the town of Nazca.

The Spanish Influence

Peru and Mexico, both centers of the highest civilizations conquered by the Spaniards, in turn became centers of Spanish influence in the Americas. Peru was the principal seat of Spanish power in the Western Hemisphere, the last of the Vice-Royalties to gain independence.

Francisco Pizarro, conqueror of Peru, made his first expedition down the Pacific Coast from Panama in 1527, attracted by rumors of gold to the south. He returned to Panama, raised another expedition, then set out and landed on a lonely beach on the coast of Peru in 1531. Pizarro and his men marched south and into the hills as far as Cajamarca, where they were received by the reigning Inca Atahualpa, whom they seized and held for ransom. Though the ransom—a room crammed from floor to ceiling with gold and silver—was paid quickly and in full, Atahualpa was strangled. His Inca empire had only recently recovered from civil war, and Pizarro and his 183 men easily marched south to Cuzco, defeating any opposition on the way. Pizarro then founded Lima as his capital city in 1535.

In 1541, Pizarro was murdered. Three years later, the Spanish Vice-Royalty of Peru was established, theoretically under the control of the Spanish Crown. In fact, it took over ten years for the Crown's representatives to quell rebellious Spanish leaders who wanted to keep their spoils. The Vice-Royalty was to last for nearly three centuries until 1820 when Peru was swept into the independence movement that wrested the Americas from the control of European powers.

During the colonial period the Spanish consolidated their gains, brought thousands of Indians under their sway, and mined the gold and silver that had attracted them to Peru in the first place. But

Reflecting the architecture of its Spanish founders are this grouping of buildings and the Ortiz Bridge over the Cali River at Cali, Colombia.
Photo: Pan American World Airways, Inc.

Twelve of South America's 13 nations are republics, and all have presidents, though few equal Peru in the beauty of their presidential palaces, as here in Lima.

Photo: *Pan American World Airways, Inc.*

One of the loveliest parks in the Americas is Santa Lucia, a hill transformed from a garbage dump about 100 years ago.

Photo: Pan American World Airways, Inc.

Montevideo's elegant doorways are a source of pride to Uruguayans; their cars, old by necessity, will be a source of amazement to many visitors.

Photo: Pan American World Airways, Inc.

Creoles, the locally born Spaniards who were often of as pure a Spanish stock as officials sent out from the mother country, chafed under the rule of the Crown and its trade monopoly. Freedom looked as enticing to Peru as it did to the other South American republics of Venezuela, Argentina, Chile and Colombia. Argentina and Chile were the first to declare independence, but the Viceroy's power then had to be destroyed if they were to preserve their independence. José de San Martin, an Argentine general, brought a combined Chilean-Argentine army up to Peru from Valparaíso in 1820, proclaimed the independence of Peru on July 28, 1821, and convoked the first Congress on September 20, 1822. The first president, José de la Riva Aguero, was elected on February 26, 1823. But more outside help was needed to rid the country of Spanish forces that still remained.

Peru as a Republic

Bolívar arrived in September 1823 and organized an army to attack the Viceroy and his forces in the interior. A year later, the battle of Junin was fought in the central Andes. In December the same year, the final battle of the South American Independence movement was won by Peruvian and allied forces under General Sucre on a high mountain outside of Ayacucho. The power of Spain in Peru was finally broken.

The early republican era up to the beginning of the 20th century saw confused politics and economics. Income from guano on the off-shore islands was offset by mismanagement of public finances.

In 1879-80, a quarrel that was to last many years broke out, with Peru and Bolivia on one side and Chile on the other. The Chileans laid claim to the Atacama desert region and its immense nitrate wealth. Peru was militarily weak while the Chileans had a strong army and navy, and the Chileans occupied Lima from 1881 until the Treaty of Ancon in 1883, ceding to Chile the province of Tarapaca.

Not until 1929 was the issue finally settled through the good offices of the United States and the determination of President Leguia to eliminate the principal source of discord between Peru and her neighbors. Chile ceded Tacna to Peru, retaining the province and port of Arica, to which Peru was to be allowed free access. The Tacna-Arica Treaty then signed has withstood the test of time.

In 1930 President Leguia was overthrown by a military revolt led by Sanchez Cerro. The presidents of Argentina, Brazil, Chile and Bolivia, as well as Peru, were all overthrown within a period of six months at this time, a coincidence explained largely by economic difficulties that followed the onset of the depression in the United States.

In September 1932, hostilities broke out between Peru and Colombia in the Amazon region, led by elements opposed to the terms of the boundary treaty of 1922. Hostilities were still continuing when Sanchez Cerro was assassinated in 1933. General Benavides was elected president, and one of his first acts was to terminate hostilities with Colombia. He governed until Manuel Prado, a banker and member of a prominent family, was installed as constitutional president in 1939.

The first Prado administration (1939-1945) was a period of national prosperity and large-scale public works. From the mid-1920s onward, a leftist party, founded by Victor Haya de la Torre and known as APRA (Alianza Popular Revolucionaria Americana), had been a dissident factor in Peruvian politics. However, President Prado reduced political friction within the country to a minimum. With the support of APRA a compromise candidate, José Bustamente, a prominent lawyer of Arequipa and later a member of the International Court of Justice at the Hague, was elected as his successor and installed in office in 1945.

Under President Bustamente, conflict with APRA broke out anew, and the party was again outlawed in 1948. This failed to stem political unrest. A group of army officers led by General Odria proclaimed a military revolt at Arequipa on October 27, 1948. Four days later General Odria was sworn into office as provisional president.

This military government stayed in power until 1950, when General Odria was installed as constitutional president. The period of nearly eight years during which Odria directed the destinies of Peru were years of prosperity and progress. In 1956, he was succeeded by Manuel Prado, elected for a second term with APRA support and then ousted by the military.

In the general election of 1962, Haya de la Torre was nominated as president, only to be ousted by the military. New elections in 1963 saw a contest between Haya, Belaunde Terry, a prominent Lima architect, and Odria, in which Belaunde Terry was elected president.

President Belaunde Terry's government was overthrown by a military coup on October 3, 1968, and General Juan Velasco assumed the presidency. Relations between Peru and the United States have regrettably deteriorated ever since General Velasco's junta took power. During the past seven years the military government has carried out the most radical changes in Peru's republican history. A vast, bloodless agrarian reform program is being completed, including the expropriation of the sugar and cotton barons' holdings. All communications and radio and television stations have been nationalized, as well as the daily newspapers. Foreign-owned mines, insurance companies and oil companies have been either nationalized or forced to sell their holdings to Peruvian nationals. Branches of foreign banks are allowed to operate, though with some restrictions. The government maintains that it is neither capitalist nor communist but nationalist and humanist. While there have been disputes with the United States, especially in compensation for the takeover of U.S. interests, a friendly settlement was reached in 1974. Velasco also stopped the escape of domestic capital to hidden accounts abroad and generally stole the thunder of the extremist left by his radical nationalist policies. In August 1975 General Velasco was removed from office and succeeded by General Francisco Morales Bermudez, who had been Prime Minister. This has been a change in leadership and also in policies, with more incentives for private and foreign investments.

With all these political convulsions, Peruvians remain very friendly to foreign visitors.

Spanish Arts and Indian Crafts

During the three hundred years of Spanish Colonial rule, architecture and painting were greatly encouraged, as can be seen in the remaining churches, palaces and missions with their carved doors, balconies, miradors and altars. Architects and artists were brought from Spain and copied what they had seen in the cathedrals of Toledo, Leon and Seville. Painters followed the moods and methods of those back in Europe, but gradually the free feeling of the New World had its effect on these artists and their work. Enthusiasm overtook them; they were stimulated by this freedom and readily available materials, fine woods, gold, jewels, and their work became rich, elaborate and overpowering.

These colonial workers with such incentive were not the first people to feel this way. For centuries potters and weavers and metal workers had produced exquisite and distinctive work, unique in its originality and strength of character. There are certain regions in Peru which are characterized by the artistic ability of their inhabitants. Styles and techniques, patterns and materials have remained the same through the years: *Ayacucho* produces sculptures in Huamanga stone, famous clay reproductions of the village churches and Christmas altar pieces.

Huancayo, Puno and *Cuzco* produce a variety of colorful garments, shawls, sweaters and skirts, rugs of alpaca or llama wool, and dolls dressed in their regional dresses.

Nearly all the provinces of Peru produce ceramics, figurines, *huacos* (pots) and bowls.

The fame of the goldsmiths and silversmiths of Peru is worldwide. These are the traditional metals of Peru, the metals the Spaniards came for, and you will find work of all designs, ancient or modern, from simple brooches to elaborate and heavy watch bracelets.

Peru, like other countries of the New World, has her share of novelists, poets, architects, artists and composers. The National Symphony Orchestra was founded in 1938 and plays every Sunday in summer in the open-air auditorium in Campo de Marte, Lima.

There are free seats for 10,000 people. During winter the orchestra gives popular-priced concerts weekly at the Municipal Theater.

Capsule Sociology

People. Peru has 15,860,000 people, nearly half of whom are Indians, descendants of the country's ancient indigenous inhabitants. Half the population is either white or mestizo, a mixture of white and Indian blood, and there is a small minority of black or Oriental origin.

The ruling class of Peru, originally purely white Creoles—Spaniards born in Peru—but with an increasing number of mestizos, has created the modern republic of Peru. However, their power has waned since the military took over in 1968. The military, most of whom are members of the emerging middle class, now hold most of the key positions in the government. Their civilian counterparts hold many important positions in commerce and industry which are also coming more and more under direct government control or influence. At the same time, the government is trying to break down the class differences between the very rich and very poor by agrarian reform, worker participation in and ownership of industry, and by better education, housing and job opportunities for the underprivileged.

Nevertheless, a vast gap between rich and poor remains. The rich ruling class is responsible for a country which maintains its cultural tradition, first-class hotels, museums, railways, highways, airlines, and a sophisticated approach to everyday living. The poor people are the workers, the five million Indians whose life is bound to the soil, to heavy labor and servitude. Originally oppressed and imposed upon by the Colonial yoke, subdued into a state of feudal labor on great estates, these people have gained more freedom in recent years. They are more represented, listened to and looked after than ever before, and in the main they are content in their picturesque villages, working their plantations or riding their donkeys to the fields or high mountain pastures to round up herds of llamas and sheep.

Population. The population increases very quickly at 3–4 percent annually. Birth rate is at 50 per 1,000.

Education. Elementary education is compulsory and free up to the age of 14. There are free secondary schools and private elementary and secondary schools. San Marcos, Lima, is the oldest University on the continent, one of eight State Universities, a Catholic University and several private universities embracing most faculties.

Social Security. Legislation of the Republic includes a set daily and weekly number of working hours, paid holidays, overtime pay on Sundays and holidays, and special security for children and women. Social insurances include hospital, maternity, medicines, old age pensions, disability and funeral expenses.

Religion. Catholicism has been the predominant religion of Peru since the conquest. This religion was introduced and ministered by its priests who moved into every village in the land, becoming a father to the village, and the church with its bells ringing on Sunday mornings an integral part of the Peruvian way of life. The Catholicism that has developed still maintains some of the pagan beliefs originally incorporated within it in the early days of converting the Indians, manifest in the devil masks and weird costumes worn in the fiesta processions on Saints days.

The churches of Peru are among some of the richest in South America, notably in Lima; San Pedro, San Francisco, La Catedral, Santo Domingo, San Agustin, La Merced, Jesus Maria and Magdalena Vieja.

Lima has Anglican, Interdenominational, Christian Science, Russian Orthodox, Lutheran, Evangelical, Jewish and Buddhist places of worship. Peru has had freedom of religion since 1916, and divorce has been permitted since 1933.

Language. Spanish is the language spoken in Peru. Quechua and Aymara are the predominant Indian languages, except among the jungle Indians where they speak their own tribal dialects.

English is spoken in most city hotels, banks, business places, clubs, etc.

Customs. All Spaniards are proud of their traditions and Peru maintains her inheritance from Spain. Life is conducted at a leisurely but gay pace; business achievements are made it seems with a minimum of effort. The *mañana* outlook, however, is not particularly prevalent in Peru.

One of the greatest attributes of the Peruvian people is their hospitality. Another is their *joie de vivre*, reflected each evening in the city or village plaza where everyone turns out clean and well dressed to walk and talk in the old Spanish *paseo*, to admire the señoritas and, above all, to stop and admire other people's children.

In an effort to reduce gasoline consumption, the old custom of a long lunch hour that permitted a siesta has been abolished. Most state and private offices work from 8 or 9 a.m. to 4 or 5 p.m. with a half-hour break for lunch. Stores open later, 10 a.m. or after, are open during lunch and close about 7 p.m. Cocktail parties begin at 7:30 p.m. and dinner is at 9 p.m.

Handshaking is general whenever you meet, even with close acquaintances. Gesticulation is a part of conversation.

Part of the Peruvian way of life are the internationally known dances, la marinera and the huaynito, the waltz and the polka.

Food and Drink

Despite its hot and flavored content created by that indomitable pair of ingredients—*aji* and *ajo*, pepper and garlic—Peruvian food has become celebrated at home and abroad.

Peruvians have their favorites of fruit, fish or meat. Avocado pears are plentiful. When near the coast try *ceviche*, uncooked fish marinated in lemon juice, hot peppers, corn, sweet potatoes (Peruvian potatoes are yellow), and onions.

*Anticucho*s are the shish kebab of South America: beef hearts, or chicken livers, beef or fish, skewered and broiled and served on the end of the skewer, dipped in piquant sauce.

Rice is a main ingredient of many dishes, served with beans, eggs (*arroz con huevos*), duck or chicken, or as a dessert, *arroz con leche*, cooked until soft, sweetened and supplemented with raisins, orange rind and a sprinkling of cinnamon.

All kinds of seafoods are specially prepared; shrimps or *camarones*, mussels or *choros*, and *escabeche*, a fish appetizer. Other specialities:

Sopa criolla—soup with chopped beef, noodles and spices.

Chupe de camarones—soup made of potatoes, milk, shrimp, hot chili peppers and eggs.

Tamales—corn with hot pepper, wrapped in banana leaves and stuffed with chicken or pork, eggs, olives, almonds or raisins.

Picarones—doughnuts made of *yuca*, a tropical root vegetable, flour and eggs, fried in lard and served with molasses.

Mazamorra morada—a jelly dessert of corn, flour and dried fruit.

It is advisable, everywhere in Peru, to drink only bottled water, carbonated or *sin gas*. Milk is pasteurized in Lima. Light and dark beer and wines both red and white are plentiful and good, but most famous is the pisco sour, made from a local, potent and colorless grape brandy. The recipe: 2 parts pisco, ¼ part syrup, ¼ part lemon juice, crushed ice, bitters and the beaten white of an egg. Other drinks from pisco are: *algarrobina*, pisco and algarrobina syrup; *chilcano*, pisco and ginger ale; *capitán*, pisco and Vermouth.

A popular drink with the Indians dates from Inca times when it took the place of beer: *chicha de jora* made from fermented but not distilled corn. *Chicha morada* is a red corn juice drink.

EXPLORING PERU

Travel in Peru isn't as hard as it looks on the map. The coastal desert, the great ranges of the Andes, and the jungles of the Amazon basin are all accessible by plane, road or rail. The few tourist spots without plane service, such as Huancayo and Puno, have train or road connections. There are also many difficult but rewarding ways of arriving at places like Cuzco and Arequipa—though both are only one to two hours from Lima by plane.

No one should leave Peru without seeing Cuzco and the archeological sites at Paracas, Paramonga, Trujillo, and Cajamarca, all easily accessible. *Receptour*, in Lima, can arrange tours of this area.

Travel in the provinces of Peru has been greatly improved over the last decade. The Andes, running the length of the country, present a natural barrier, but safe, efficient airline services by *Faucett* and *Aeroperu*, the new Government airline flying Jet Fokkers, have overcome this barrier. The days are over when Cuzco was five days from Lima by bus and train, and Machu Picchu was an added stretch on muleback. (Cuzco is 1 hour from Lima, and Arequipa is 1 hour, by plane.)

Most traditional Peru is south, and travel is relatively easy and comfortable. The "Southern Circuit" we describe here is the best way of seeing the south of Peru; Cuzco and its environs, Arequipa, Ayacucho, Huancayo and Puno near Lake Titicaca. A side trip through Tarma down to La Merced and San Ramon (Chanchamayo Valley), an upper jungle area, can be very rewarding.

No planes fly to Huancayo, but the train journey from Lima over the 16,000-ft. main range of the Andes is an unforgettable experience. A highway closely follows the railway, whose construction was started by the American engineer-adventurer Henry Meiggs in 1870. Take the Saturday train from Lima, stay overnight at Huancayo and shop at the weekly Indian market on Sunday, a colorful display of woolens, hides and silver. *Receptour*, in Lima, has a three-day, two-night trip to this area, which includes this thrilling train ride. From Huancayo there is an adventurous road through to Ayacucho, about 10 hours by bus, winding down to beautiful tropical Andean valleys and rising to bleak moorland. There are direct flights from Lima.

Ayacucho, halfway between Lima and Cuzco on the old direct route, was a town of considerable importance in the days of the Spanish viceroys. It has more than thirty colonial churches, among the finest in Peru, though it is only a small town today. Ayacucho itself is one of the most pleasant towns in the Andes, with a fine, dry climate, Indian country people, narrow streets, colonial arcades and courtyards. Recently, the old university, which had waned during the early Republican period, was re-established and it is now flourishing.

A side trip to the upper jungles of the Chanchamayo Valley can be made before or after a visit to Huancayo, by road through La Oroya and Tarma, to San Ramon and La Merced. San Ramon can also be reached by direct plane from Lima on the Aeroperu airline as well as by daily buses and cars. This part of the jungle is heavily planted with oranges and coffee. If you have time, it is worth pushing on to Oxapampa, a small town at the end of a rough road, where two-story timber houses reflect the influence of a large German colony that settled here in the wilderness a century ago. There are still many blond heads and German names in the area.

Or set out north from Lima, up through the Coastal desert past historic archeological sites, cotton and sugar plantations. Take your surfboard—there are plenty of waves—or just take a swimming costume and sit on the long beaches. Inland at Cajamarca is the site of Pizarro's conquest of the Inca ruler Atahualpa.

The least accessible part of Peru beyond the Andes in the green jungle woven with winding rivers, is really another world. Here there are little-known jungle tribes, missionaries, small trading settlements and oil camps. A far cry from sophisticated Lima.

Lima, The Viceregal City

A glitter of lights sweeping ten miles along the Pacific coast and six miles inland greets a traveler arriving by air at night in Lima, a city lying on a gentle plain between the foothills of the Andes and the curving shores of Callao and Chorrillos bays. Yet this metropolis of 3 million people began over four centuries ago as a tiny Spanish settlement. On January 18 in the year 1535, Francisco Pizarro founded Lima and baptized it Ciudad de los Reyes (City of Kings), for the day was Epiphany, the feast of the Three Kings. The name Lima is a corruption of Rimac, the Indian word for the shallow river that flows through the city.

The Capital. Lima was the most important city in South America for three centuries from its foundation in 1535.

Greater Lima. Includes the districts of San Isidro, Miraflores, San Antonio, Barranco, Chorrillos, Pueblo Libre, Magdalena del Mar, San Miguel, Surco, Surquillo, La Victoria, Breña, El Cercado, Lince, Jesus Maria, and El Rimac, an area of about 40 square miles.

Population. Over 3,000,000 including suburbs. Growing constantly. Fifth largest city of South America, after Buenos Aires, São Paulo, Rio de Janeiro and Santiago.

Geography. Lima lies 8 miles from the port of Callao on the Pacific Ocean and is 512 feet above the sea level. Lat. 12° 2'5 south, Long. 77° 5' west Greenwich, or on the same meridian as New York City lying directly south of that city. The magnetic equator passes near Lima.

Climate. Situated only 12 degrees south of the equator, Lima should have a tropical climate; however the cold Humboldt Current modifies the temperature. The coast of Peru is a rainless region. During the winter months (June-September) fog and mist prevail, and a light drizzle called *garua* falls.

Only two or three decades ago Lima's skyline was still dominated by the towers of its Spanish colonial churches. But since the end of World War II, a wave of industrialization, bustling business and population growth has engulfed the city, dominating the old skyline with towering modern office and apartment buildings. Lima is in an earthquake belt, but steel and reinforced concrete have enabled architects and engineers to build tall quake-resistant buildings just as in Tokyo.

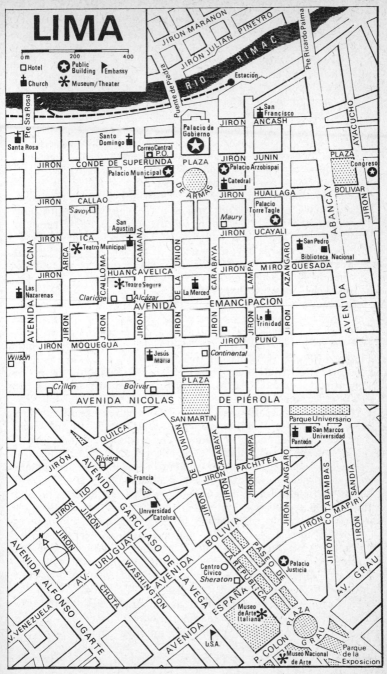

LIMA

0 m   200   400

- □ Hotel
- ✝ Church
- ★ Public Building
- ▶ Embassy
- ✳ Museum/Theater

RIO RIMAC

Pte de Piedra

Pte Sta Rosa

Puente de Piedra

Pte Ricardo Palma

Estación

✝ San Francisco

JIRON ANCASH

✝ Santa Rosa

Santo Domingo ✝

Correo Central □ P.O.

CONDE DE SUPERUNDA

Palacio Municipal ★

Palacio de Gobierno ★

PLAZA DE ARMAS

JIRON JUNIN

★ Palacio Arzobispal

✝ Catedral

PLAZA Congreso ✳

JIRON CALLAO

Savoy □

JIRON HUALLAGA

Palacio Torre Tagle ✝

BOLIVAR

AYACUCHO

JIRON TACNA

San Agustin ✝

Maury □

JIRON ICA

✳ Teatro Municipal

CAMANA

JIRON UCAYALI

✝ San Pedro

Biblioteca Nacional ■

ARICA

HUANCAVELICA

✳ Teatro Segura

Claridge □ □ Alcázar

✝ La Merced

LAMPA

MIRO QUESADA

AZANGARO

✝ Las Nazarenas

CARABAYA

JIRON DE LA UNION

EMANCIPACION

AVENIDA

□ La Trinidad ✝

AVENIDA

JIRON

J RON

JIRON

JIRON

JIRON PUNO

JIRON MOQUEGUA

✝ Jesús María ■

□ Continental

Wilson □

□ Crillon

□ Bolivar

PLAZA

AVENIDA NICOLAS

DE PIÉROLA

SAN MARTIN

Parque Universario

QUILCA

DE LA UNION

CARABAYA

LAMPA

✝ San Marcos Universidad ■

Panteón ■

Riviera △

PACHITEA

▶ Francia △

JIRON AZANGARO

AVENIDA ILO

Universidad Catolica ■

JIRON

JIRON

JIRON

COTABAMBAS

SANDIA

JIRON

AVENIDA GARCILASO DE LA VEGA

URUGUAY

AV.

WASHINGTON

BOLIVIA

PASEO DE

JIRON MAPIRI

△

AVENIDA ALFONSO UGARTE

AV. VENEZUELA

CHOTA

Centro Civico ○

Sheraton □

REPUBLICA

ESPAÑA

★ Palacio Justicia

AV. GRAU

AVENIDA

U.S.A. □

Museo de Arte Italiana ✳

PLAZA COLON GRAU

Parque de la Exposicion

P. COLON

✳ Museo Nacional de Arte

Pizarro laid out his city on the left bank of the Rimac, which can become a raging torrent during the height of the rainy season in the mountains. It comprised 117 blocks in nine thirteen-block rows. The blocks were square, usually 450 Spanish feet on each side, and separated by streets or lanes 40 Spanish feet wide that were designed to accommodate traffic of that day and age. About seven miles to the west he founded the port of Callao on the natural bay protected by two offshore islands and a narrow peninsula of land called La Punta.

Today, modern Lima has swallowed up nearly all the fields that once separated the capital from its port, as well as the farmland between the city and its residential suburbs to the south: Magdalena, Miraflores, Barranco and Chorrillos that overlook the Pacific from high cliffs. Old farm roads have given way to busy avenues and boulevards, but the business and political heart of Greater Lima is still bounded by the 117 blocks laid down by Pizarro. Just as in his day, the nucleus of the city is on and around the Plaza de Armas, the great square where Pizarro ordered the building of his own residence as the seat of government. Here too, he raised the city's first church where the Cathedral now stands.

Pizarro was slain by a mutinous band of his own followers on June 26, 1541, less than six and a half years after he planned the city. Yet his fame as the conqueror of the Inca Empire and the founder of what was to be the viceregal capital of the Spanish Empire in South America for more than two centuries, and the capital of the Republic of Peru, has lasted: the site of the house from which he ruled Peru for a few brief years still serves as the seat of government.

No replica or description exists of the original building, which must have been a primitive structure of adobe, wood and cane. Over the years, rambling additions were made around four courtyards, but the "palace" of Pizarro never attained architectural distinction during its existence, whether in its labyrinthian confines or its unimpressive two-story adobe façade. In the 1920s President Leguia had plans drawn up and work started on the construction of a new palace, finally completed in 1938.

Built at a cost of $2 million, this Palacio de Gobierno was designed with a large courtyard and an impressive façade on the Plaza de Armas. It is the official residence and office of the President of Peru. The people of Lima, though, still call their House of Government the Palacio, for they can imagine Peru ruled only from the Palace of Pizarro.

According to legend, Pizarro's remains were wrapped in a bloody shroud and buried in an unmarked grave in the church he had founded. Not until 1891 were these mummified remains recovered and placed in a glass-walled coffin in the Cathedral. Since then, they have been viewed by thousands of visitors and few tourists miss them. His body has the texture of a dried locust.

The Plaza de Armas

The new Plaza de Armas symbolizes the renaissance of modern Peru. Except for the Cathedral, which was entirely rebuilt after the great earthquake of October 28, 1746, and partially reconstructed or remodeled many times since, all the buildings which currently face the Plaza de Armas are of modern construction. The present Archbishop's Palace, adjoining the Cathedral, was completed in 1924, and the buildings opposite the Government Palace and the Cathedral were all constructed during the past twenty years.

These four- and five-story buildings are of reinforced concrete, but, by municipal decree, their façades have kept the intricately carved wooden balconies and the picturesque street-level *portales* or arcades of Spanish colonial architecture. There is a Portal de Escribanos (Scribes) on the west side and the Portal de Botoneros (dealers in buttons and laces) on the south side, named after the trades and shops that flourished here in the past.

Besides the gruesome memento of Pizarro's remains in glass, there is a spirited equestrian monument in bronze to the great Conquistador, the work of the American sculptor Charles C. Rumsey, and a copy of the original in Trujillo, Pizarro's birthplace in Spain. When it was unveiled on the porch of the Cathedral, some quarters objected to a mounted warrior with a drawn sword before a religious edifice, and so the monument was later moved to its present site in a small *plazuela* adjoining the Plaza de Armas.

Nearly all the old buildings of Lima are within a few blocks of the Plaza de Armas. The only important exception is the Real Felipe Fortress in the port of Callao. This star-shaped masonry stronghold, built as a defense against the threat of Dutch and English pirate raids on the site of earlier and more primitive fortifications, was erected between 1747 and 1772 and named in memory of King Philip V (Felipe) of Spain. Real Felipe Fortress was the scene of one famous military action, the last stand of the Spanish forces in South America. Under the command of Brigadier General José Ramon Rodil, some 2,000 Spanish royalists were besieged in the fortress for 18 months by the republican forces, capitulating on January 23, 1826. Rodil's stubborn resistance drew from Bolívar the admiring comment: "How we would have praised him had he been a patriot."

This fear of pirate raids that led to the construction of the Real Felipe Fortress had previously resulted in the conversion of Lima into a walled city. The wall, mostly adobe on a masonry foundation, was built between 1684 and 1687. Nine miles long, it had 34 bastions and five gates, later increased to nine. A traveler who visited Lima around 1840 found the wall in a ruinous state. He described it as 18 to 20 feet high, 10 to 12 feet wide at its base and 9 feet wide on top. In 1869, a contract was given to Henry Meiggs, builder of the Central and Southern Railways, to demolish the wall, which he did. Only a fragment now remains in the Jirón Commandante Espinar, between the Barbones barracks and the Rimac River.

History has been kinder to Lima's first permanent bridge across the Rimac, the Puente de Piedra (Bridge of Stone), 530 feet long, built between 1607 and 1615. Reinforced and widened sixty years ago, it carries modern traffic from the Plaza de Armas, along the west side of the Palace of Government, to the poorer section of Lima known as Bajo el Puente (below the bridge).

Across the Bridge of Stone is the Quinta de Presa, built by the Viceroy Manuel de Amat y Junient for his mistress, Micaela Villegas, an actress of remarkable character who has become a legend. He once insulted her by calling her a half-caste bitch— La Perricholi—and the name became, not derogatory, but one of admiration by her contemporaries: hence an opera by Offenbach and "The Bridge of San Luis Rey" by Thornton Wilder. Today the building is a small museum.

In 1869, President Balta ordered the construction of a second permanent bridge across the Rimac, the so-called Puente de Fierro (Bridge of Iron), but its approaches were not completed until fifty years later in 1919. Only one divided roadway crossed the old city from west to east. Its construction was ordered by President Nicolas de Piérola at the turn of the century and it is named after him, but everyone calls it La Colmena (The beehive).

Though only five blocks apart, the Plazas San Martin and de Armas are separated by centuries. Laid out in 1924, the Plaza San Martin has a fine equestrian statue of the Argentine Liberator-General José de San Martin, who proclaimed the Independence of Peru on July 28, 1821. It is the transportation hub of Lima, the principal departing point and stopping place for the main lines of buses, microbuses and *colectivos* serving the port of Callao and the southern suburbs. *Colectivos* are passenger cars operating over specified routes between the center of the city and outlying district. Rates are low and service efficient, though the visitor to Lima may find the intricacy of routes somewhat confusing.

Construction of a subway to link Lima with Callao and with its southern suburbs has been under discussion for the past decade or more; a number of foreign experts have presented plans, but none has yet been carried out.

The Glorious Churches of Old Lima

There are a number of surviving colonial structures or sites worth seeing in old Lima, apart from the Cathedral and the Stone Bridge. Among them are churches built in the 16th and 17th centuries; the Torre Tagle Palace, a colonial mansion built in 1735, now housing the Ministry of Foreign Affairs, and the building where the Court of the Inquisition sat from 1584 until its abolition in 1820.

The principal churches all have their distinctive treasures accumulated over the centuries, sumptuous golden altars, intricately carved woodwork by master craftsmen in paneling and furniture, exquisite examples of wrought iron and tile, and rare religious paintings, which would fill an antiquarian's catalogue of many volumes. They are:

Santo Domingo, one block west of the Government Palace, famous for its two high towers that have defied earthquakes for nearly four centuries. The oldest university in the Americas, San Marcos, founded in 1551, functioned here for the first twenty years. The remains of Santa Rosa of Lima, the first saint of the New World, are preserved in an urn in one of the main altars.

San Francisco, one block east of the Government Palace, has beautiful cloisters, a library of more than 20,000 volumes dating back to 1480, and three levels of macabre catacombs rediscovered in 1951.

La Merced, two blocks from the Plaza de Armas on the Jirón de la Unión, Lima's main shopping street, is dedicated to Our Lady of Mercy, who, according to tradition, saved Lima from an invasion by the Dutch corsairs in 1615. Along with its rich interior, it is distinguished by an intricately carved stone façade (restored in recent years). After being declared the patron saint of Peru by the Vice-Regal Council in 1730 and made a Marshal of the Peruvian Army by San Martin in 1823, Our Lady of Mercy was crowned by Decree of September 24, 1921. On September 24 every year, the President of Peru and representatives of the armed forces attend special services here.

San Pedro, one block south and two blocks east of the Plaza de Armas. Built by the Jesuits in the mid-17th century and long regarded as the most fashionable church in Lima. This is the richest church in South America. San Pedro is only a few steps from the Torre Tagle Palace which is now the seat of the foreign ministry. The Torre Tagle Palace, heavily reconstructed in recent years, displays elaborately carved wooden balconies, a massive entranceway that accommodated the carriages of the colonial era and a large main patio overlooked by wide verandas with richly carved columns, arches and balustrades.

San Agustin, two blocks from the Plaza de Armas with its sculptured stone façade of churrigueresque style, separated from the street by stone pillars and intricate wrought-iron fencing. In the vestry is a wood carving representing "Death" by Baltazar Gavilán, a Lima artist of the 18th century. Legend says that Gavilán was frightened to death by his own handiwork when he came upon it one night while walking through the church with a lighted candle.

The small building housing the old Court of the Inquisition is on the Plaza Bolivar. The main hall of the old court building where the Peruvian Senate met for many years has a magnificently carved mahogany ceiling. In 1939 the Senate was transferred to the modern Congress building on the same plaza which had been partially completed and occupied by the Chamber of Deputies in 1912. On this site the first Constituent Congress was held in 1822.

Across the Rimac River are the Quinta de Presa, named after a former owner, a rococo mansion in the French Provincial style of the 17th century; the Alameda de los Descalzos (Barefoot Walk), a promenade laid out in 1610 by the Viceroy Monteclaros; and the Paseo de Aguas, an aqueduct and fountain built by the Viceroy Amat (1761-1776), who also constructed the Plaza de Acho, the Lima bull ring long famous in the annals of bullfighting in South America. It still draws crowds when famous Spanish toreros visit Lima, usually during the season known as the October Fair. (Bullfights are also held during the summer months from January to March.)

Monuments to Progress

Despite these reminders of the Spanish Colonial period in South American history, present day visitors cannot fail to be impressed by the vitality of the City of Kings as an exponent of modern progress and development. Among the notable modern buildings: The Civic Center, adjoining the Lima Sheraton, with a large auditorium and the latest facilities for international meetings. A central office building, 36 floors (making it Peru's tallest structure) is now completed.

The 22-story Ministry of Education building, of monolithic functional design containing 3,000 tons of steel, faced with concrete, served by a bank of ten elevators, and completed in 1956. This building is on the Parque Universitario four blocks from the Plaza San Martin. The older two-story buildings of the University of San Marcos, the first university established in the New World by a decree of Emperor Charles V of Spain issued on May 12, 1551, also face on this park area, badly damaged in the 1967 and 1974 earthquakes. A new and modern University City is now nearly completed and in use on Avenida Venezuela between Lima and Callao.

The Central Social Security Hospital for Employees was completed in 1956. This 16-story structure with two 13-story wings, designed by the eminent North American architect Edward D. Stone, is said to be one of the largest and best equipped hospitals in Latin America.

Other modern structures of Lima of special interest are: the National Sports Stadium of reinforced concrete, occupying an area of nearly 100 acres, with seats for 50,000 spectators, built in 1952. The stadium is on a site within a mile of the center of the city, on land presented to Lima for this purpose by the British colony on the occasion of the Centennial of Independence in 1924. The Monterrico Hippodrome or Race Course of the Jockey Club of Peru, some 5 miles from the city, with grandstands seating

25,000 people. High-rise apartment and office buildings now dot the city and the residential areas of Miraflores and San Isidro.

Unidades Vecinales (Neighborhood Housing Units) is the term applied to groups of model middle-income housing units recently built by the Government. These units are excellent examples of modern architectural design and city planning. The principal groups are the Rimac, in the Rimac district; Matute, on the Avenida Mexico in Lima; Mirones and Unidad Vecinal No. 3 between Lima and Callao; San Felipe, on Avenida Salaverry; Santa Cruz in Miraflores; and Santa Marina in Callao.

Any description of present-day Lima would be incomplete without mentioning her famous *barriadas*, now called Pueblos Jovenes, or "New Towns," (slums and squatter settlements) that have grown up on the edges of the city during the past twenty years, with the phenomenal migration of the Indian and mestizo population from the provinces, especially the Andean highlands. Attracted by Lima's rapid industrialization, higher wages, better schools, and bright lights, the population of these barriadas has been estimated at anywhere from half a million to 1,000,000. Some hundreds of families make a living from collecting garbage from the city rubbish dump.

Shantytowns have appeared many times over in the development of great urban centers around the world. They are especially evident at present in South America where whole populations are moving. The desert plains and barren foothills that surround Lima form a stark and grim backdrop for these barriadas. However, government and municipal authorities are now carrying out a sweeping campaign to rehabilitate the barriadas, to install electric light and power, paving, water and sewage systems, and to construct civic centers, hospitals, churches and schools. Many of the improvements are made by the community-minded inhabitants of these barriadas (called by the Government Pueblos Jovenes— young towns).

Museums in Lima

Museum of Art, covering some 5,000 years of Peruvian culture from pre-Inca days to the present. The museum is rich in paintings of the Cuzco school and in the works of outstanding Peruvian painters of the 19th century. It is in the 1868 Exposition Palace.

Museum of Anthropology and Archeology, on the Plaza Bolivar in the suburb of Pueblo Libre. Established in 1938 it has more than 80,000 archeological objects from all parts of Peru and constantly shows new acquisitions.

Museum of the Republic, adjoining the Museum of Anthropology and Archeology in a small villa once occupied by San Martin and by Bolivar. It contains a wide range of paintings, portraits, documents, weapons and uniforms and other mementos related to the War of Independence and the early days of the Republic.

A famous private museum, which is eventually destined to

become national property, is that of *Rafael Larco Herrera*, 1515 Bolivar Avenue, Pueblo Libre. This museum is especially rich in ceramics, textiles and gold and silver objects, workmanship from the pre-Inca cultures of the north coast of Peru. Selected items from this collection have been exhibited in recent years in Europe, North America and the Far East. It also has a remarkable section devoted to early exotic art, some of it disarmingly exuberant.

Another world-famous private collection can be seen at the Gold Museum of Sr. Mujica Gallo, located in the park of his private residence in Monterrico suburb, which also houses his collection of antique weaponry and firearms.

Museum of the Viceroyalty, in the Quinta de Presa in the section of old Lima on the north bank of the Rimac. An unusual collection of paintings, costumes and furnishings of the Colonial period.

Museum of Military History, in the Real Felipe Fortress at Callao. This museum supplements the collection in the Museum of the Republic and covers the military evolution since colonial times.

Museum of Natural History, 1256 Avenida Arenales, part of the University of San Marcos. This collection presents a comprehensive survey of Peruvian flora and fauna, as well as ores illustrating the mineral wealth of Peru. Among the exhibits is a collection of flora assembled by Raimondi, an Italian scientist who pioneered scientific research in the Peruvian Andes.

Religious Art Museum. Located in Lima Cathedral, Plaza de Armes. Recently opened its exhibits, a varied collection of religious art covering three and one-half centuries.

Museum of Italian Art, Paseo de la República, the gift of the Italian colony to Peru on the occasion of the first centennial of Independence. This museum contains representative Italian oil paintings, water colors, ceramics and other works largely dating from the early part of the present century.

The October Fair

The October Fair is a series of fiestas welcoming spring in Lima, the biggest being the processions of the Lord of the Miracles (El Señor de los Milagros) on October 18, 19 and 28. Thousands of the faithful follow a heavily ornamented litter on which is mounted an oil painting, set in a gold frame, of Christ crucified. The litter is borne on the shoulders of some thirty bearers all clad in purple vestments as are many of the marchers. Starting at eight in the morning, the processions last until midnight. After nightfall, thousands of lighted candles flicker like fireflies in a vivid reincarnation of the life and spirit of the City of Kings in colonial days.

The oil painting is a copy made in 1747 of an original done in 1651 by a liberated slave on the wall of a black religious brotherhood. The survival of this wall and image through a series of disastrous earthquakes led to its veneration and incorporation within a small chapel built in 1671. The chapel was reconstructed a century later as the present-day Church of the Nazarenes.

A recent addition to the October Fair season in Lima is the biennial International Pacific Fair, held for two weeks at the end of October. This exhibition concerned mainly with commerce and trade has grown steadily in importance, and since 1961 it has had its own grounds, covering an area of 53 acres between Lima and Callao.

Limeños are lucky. They have historic buildings, fine modern ones, beaches and parks, monuments, museums and galleries and beautiful garden suburbs. Plan your visit well and be selective, for there is so much to see.

Excursions from Lima

Pueblo Libre—a suburb, part of which has retained its colonial atmosphere. Site of two important museums: National Museum of Archeology and Anthropology and Museum of the Republic.

San Isidro and Miraflores—beautiful garden suburbs of Lima.

Chorrillos—the popular beach of La Herradura. A road has been constructed bordering the sea beneath high cliffs from Chorrillos to Magdalena, opening up many miles of beaches, formerly inaccessible.

Pachacamac— in the Lurin valley, 20 miles south of Lima. This is believed to have been a sacred city dating back to about A.D. 600-900 of a pre-Inca feudal community. The city covered about four square miles and was divided into two parts, for residents and for visiting pilgrims.

The main ruin is of the Temple to the Creator God, built in terraces 400 feet long and containing special rooms for sacrificial ceremonies. The walls were covered in frescoes of bird and animal designs and doors inlaid with coral, crystal and turquoise.

The Inca Pachacutec conquered Pachacamac a century before the Spaniards arrived and erected a temple to the Sun God of the Inca people. The ruins of this temple are visible, and there are remains of remarkable irrigation works and reservoirs.

Pyramid of Huallamarca—100 B.C. With small museum. In center of San Isidro residential suburb.

Puruchucu—A.D. 1100. Reconstructed pre-Inca "palace" and adjoining small museum, where folklore open-air concerts are held. Also a corral with llamas for photographers.

Cajamarquilla—10 miles east of Lima. A great ruined city, a mystery in a lonely valley, deserted when the Incas came.

Chosica 25 miles east of Lima on the Central Highway, is a winter resort, has the Fiesta de la Cruz in May.

Ancon—the most fashionable beach near Lima, 25 miles to the north. The water is cold but the beach is the best and safest.

Punta Hermosa—a summer resort on the Pan American Highway 30 miles south of Lima.

Paracas—a resort 2,600 years old built on a well-protected bay.

Ventanilla—23 miles from Lima. A bathing resort between

Lima and Ancon with bus and helicopter terminal beside the sea.

Santa Maria del Mar—a fashionable cliff-hanging beach settlement 45 minutes drive from Lima, where there is a new 27-bungalow resort hotel.

Callao—the main port for Peru, 9 miles from Lima. It is a commercial town with a large harbor, Real Felipe Fortress, Yacht Club and dockside fish restaurants. (We recommend the chowder.)

Cuzco, Fortified City

Cuzco, the ancient capital of the Incas, is Peru's leading tourist attraction and one of the most interesting cities in the hemisphere. The town itself, with its famous remains of Inca walls, fine colonial churches, and potent mixture of Quechua Indian and Peruvian population is worth a prolonged visit. Cuzco is also the center of an archeological region of outlying villages and towns and heavily cultivated slopes of terraced mountainsides. Here can be found the homes and fields, the markets and the people who have formed the living backbone of the Andes for centuries.

Cars and taxis can be hired in Cuzco itself, either to tour the city and its immediate surroundings or for more extended trips to Pisac, Urubamba, Calca or Ollantaytambo.

Pisac has beautiful ruins and an Indian market, but we hear the market has inflated prices. Chincheros is a typical, charming town, also with an Indian market. Cuzco can easily be explored on foot, but some parts are steep and this can be tiring at an elevation of 11,400 feet. To explore the surrounding country, there are provincial bus and truck services that connect Cuzco and other towns to all outlying districts.

It is advisable to go to sleep for the first few hours you are in Cuzco. Those who don't are likely to come down with *soroche* (altitude sickness), which has spoiled many a trip to Machu Picchu.

The best time of the year to visit Cuzco or anywhere in the Andes is from April to September. May is perhaps best of all because mountain slopes are still green from the previous rainy season. From November to March is the rainy season. Warm clothing is needed in all seasons. When the sun is hidden by clouds, the normal cold air of the altitude takes over.

Cuzco was a city teeming with people and busy with commerce long before the Spaniards arrived. From here the Inca ruler controlled an empire which extended from present-day Ecuador to Argentina. He kept control by building an excellent network of roads over which he could move his runners and armies speedily.

The streets and plazas of Cuzco today are a mixture of the Inca and Spanish civilizations. Colonial buildings are based on Inca masonry foundations, and Inca descendants dressed in their poncho capes lead their llamas through the streets.

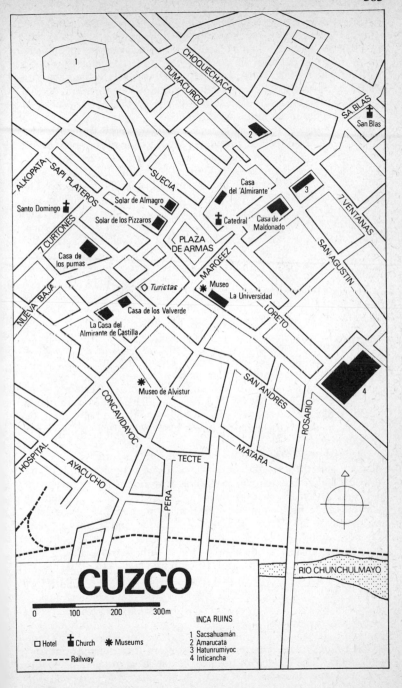

CUZCO

| 0 | 100 | 200 | 300m |

☐ Hotel   ✝ Church   ✳ Museums

- - - - - Railway

INCA RUINS

1 Sacsahuamán
2 Amarucata
3 Hatunrumiyoc
4 Inticancha

RIO CHUNCHULMAYO

The earliest arrival of the Incas in Cuzco is about A.D. 1100. There are several legends concerning the founding of Cuzco, and the favorite one tells how Manco Capac and his sister-wife Mama Ocllo were the children of the Sun who sent them down to earth with a Golden Staff. When this staff sank easily into the ground it would be the sign of fertile earth and there they were to found a Temple to the Sun. The staff sank into the ground in the Valley of Cuzco, and the Inca empire was founded.

Another legend tells how a great deluge covered the earth in a flood of water and when the water receded those few people left alive crawled out of caves near Cuzco to start the new world.

The Incas were master colonizers, treating their conquered tribes with consideration and gradually absorbing them. The empire was divided into four provinces and Cuzco, which means navel, was the center. Communities were divided into decimal units each with its officials responsible in turn, right up to the Inca. Men born in a certain trade remained in it all their lives, gradually given more land by the state as they married and had children. The land was worked on as a collective principle, one part for the owner, one for the Sun and one part for the State. There was no money. Gold and silver were purely decorative and sacred to the gods. There was no poverty; in return for a man's work he was assured of social security, food and the equivalent of an old age pension.

The Incas did not know how to write and had no idea what a wheel looked like, yet they were skillful irrigation engineers, invented the suspension bridge and the hammock; they were ingenious weavers and potters and metalsmiths. Certainly they must have had a theory of construction to beat the earthquakes which shake this part of the world—look at their fantastic masonry in the walls, carved granite blocks fitted closely together without mortar.

Cuzco was a fortified city, protected by the fortress of Sacsahuaman and the fortified outposts of Pisac, Ollantaytambo, and Machu Picchu. The temples and palaces were richly adorned with gold and silver; in place of altars were golden discs representing the sun, and the Temple of the Sun contained five great halls dedicated to the Moon, the Stars, Thunder and Lightning, the Rainbow, and reserved for the priests only. According to the Spanish chroniclers gardens were filled with flowers, shrubs and life-size figures of animals molded of pure silver and gold.

Rumors of this gold which reached the ears of Pizarro in Panama were the beginning of the end for the Incas.

Sightseeing Highlights

The Main Square was the scene of many Inca celebrations and ceremonies. The Palace of Manco Capac is a monument to the first Inca and founder of Cuzco. You'll also want to visit the famous Stone of Twelve Angles, which can be found in the walls of the Palace of Inca Roca. The famous Temple of the Sun is now the Monastery of Santo Domingo, and the foundation walls of the Convent of Santa Catalina are the remains of the House of the Chosen Women.

Such Colonial churches as La Merced, El Triunfo, Cathedral, Jesus and Maria, Santo Domingo and Jesuits should not be missed, nor should such Colonial residents as La Casa de Garcilaso de la Vega Inca, the home of the Inca chronicler; the Renaissance-style La Casa del Almirante; the 16th-century La Casa do los Marqueses de Buenavista; La Casa de Diego Maldonado (a lieutenant of Pizarro's); and La Casa de Concha, a fine 18th-century Colonial house.

Among the interesting museums are the Art, Anthropological and Archeological, Culture, Viceregal, and Larco Herrera.

Sacsahuaman

Sacsahuaman is a curious fortress of three parallel zigzag walls, now the only remaining masonry left after the Spaniards looted the stone for their own buildings. The walls contain 21 bastions, but nothing remains of the great fortified towers each of which would have held a thousand men.

The Inca reviewed his armies on the parade ground in front of the walls. His throne is still there, carved from the stone and there are rock groups covering subterranean passages said to be the abode of oracles and wherein the Incas may have buried some of their treasure.

Ollantaytambo

Ollantaytambo lies 45 miles north of Cuzco, reached by the narrow railroad which enters the Urubamba gorge and goes to Machu Picchu. The ruins were a fortress which sheltered the Inca Manco when he fled from the oncoming Spaniards.

One of the two great entrances to the fort remains, and on the terraced hillsides are remains of lookout posts. In the center of the fort are the remains of the Palace and Temple. Above on the hillside are ruins of what were once barricades for soldiers and a solar observatory.

This country has scattered remains of Inca buildings and stones and 32 miles further on one of the most significant archeological discoveries of this century was made in 1911:

Machu Picchu

The train finally stops beside the rushing brown waters of the Urubamba on its way to the Amazon. A bridge over the river leads to a steep hairpin road which climbs the 1,000-foot side of the mountain on which Machu Picchu was built. It is very easy to understand how difficult it was to explore this terrain.

Machu Picchu is a large city built on a narrow saddle in the mountains, surrounded by precipitous mountainsides which were terraced right to the edge to provide land for the inhabitants.

The town, intact but for the straw roofs which have of course rotted, is a maze of empty plazas, chambers and palaces connected by stairways carved out of solid rock. For four centuries it was hidden under ferns and bush until its discovery.

In 1962 an expedition of U.S. parachutists flew over and landed in the Cordillera Vilcabamba north of Machu Picchu. It was generally believed there may be more towns built in these unexplored mountains, but after a few days the expedition saw no sign of inhabitation either former or present; however it returned with valuable maps and information on this inhospitable terrain. Not long afterward Gene Savoy, American amateur archeologist, discovered ruins of a large Inca town in these very mountains. His book *Antisuyo* describes these hidden cities.

Bones found at Machu Picchu were at a ratio of ten female to one male, and all gold ornaments were women's. We can assume this place was a final refuge from the Spaniards for the Inca Virgins of the Sun. A sun dial, carved from massive rock, was used by Inca astronomers to mark solstices and equinox. It is still there.

South of the Capital

Arequipa is connected with Lima by a good road, the Pan American Highway—the journey takes from 12 to 16 hours. If you wish to see the coastal desert and its green valley oases, then travel by road. Otherwise take the daily *Faucett* or *Aeroperu* flight straight to the capital.

Arequipa, at an elevation of 7,500 feet, enjoys a remarkably fine climate, with sun and clean dry air the year round. The city and its valley are dominated by the extinct (as everyone hopes) volcano El Misti, 19,200 feet high and snowcapped most of the year. The cathedral and several churches are worth visiting, for the soft, white volcanic stone quarried near the city has permitted some exceptionally fine carving in the ornate Spanish Colonial baroque style. Arequipa has suffered a number of earthquakes over the years, the most recent being a severe one in 1960. There are therefore comparatively few old houses, although Arequipa is one of the oldest colonial cities in Peru. The local *picanterias*— criollo restaurants—are famous in Peru and are worth a try.

If you take the road you will pass through the oases which grow Pima cotton, sugar cane and truck crops for the Lima markets. Before we go into Arequipa let us visit some of these desert towns in southern Peru.

Ica is well known for its vineyards and its port, Pisco, has given

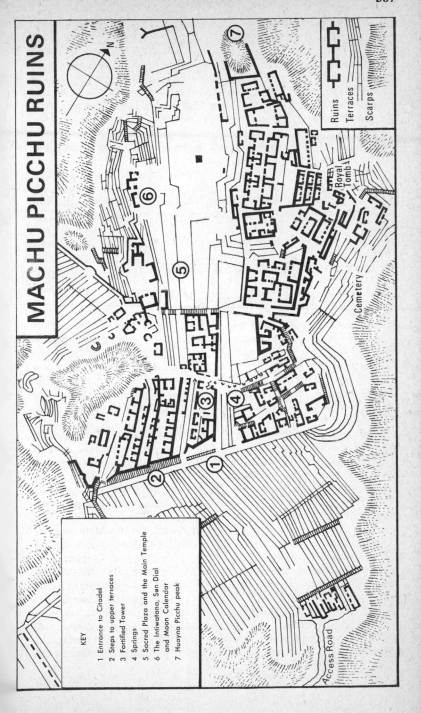

MACHU PICCHU RUINS

KEY

1 Entrance to Citadel
2 Steps to upper terraces
3 Fortified Tower
4 Springs
5 Sacred Plaza and the Main Temple
6 The Intiwatana, Sun Dial and Moon Calendar
7 Huayna Picchu peak

Ruins
Terraces
Scarps

Royal Tomb

Cemetery

Access Road

its name to the grape brandy used in Pisco sour, which one might
call the national drink of Peru.

Pisco is divided into two districts, Pisco Pueblo with Colonial
houses, patios and gardens, and Pisco Puerto, the commercial port
exporting raw cotton and lead and zinc mined inland.

Nine miles away is the Bay of Paracas where the Liberator San
Martin first set foot in Peru. On one side is a modern port and
on the other is the Hotel Paracas, an ocean-front resort. Nearby
is a fishing town.

A short distance from the hotel is the site of an old civilization.
There is a small museum at the site.

Nasca is 90 miles from Ica, center of a civilization which had its
peak in about A.D. 800 and is noted for its fine ceramics, wood
carvings and gold jewelry. Nearby is the ruined Temple of the Sun
and underground irrigation channels, some of which are still in
use.

Tacna which has been attractively modernized in recent years,
is a small town backed by the snow peaks of Tacora. Only 40 miles
further south is the international port of Arica, Chile.

Arequipa: The White City

It is a day's fast drive from Lima, south through the barren
desert to Arequipa. You will see little more on the way than people crossing the sand dunes on their donkeys, headed it seems
for nowhere in particular, and glimpses of the Pacific breakers
on the long beaches. Flocks of pelicans and cormorants circle
out at sea and the ribbon of road stretches on through the dunes
as sea breezes lift the sand and blow it in wisps of yellow across
the black tarmac.

Arequipa is the second town of Peru, situated at 7,500 feet in
the Rio Chili valley and dominated by a perfect volcano known
affectionately as El Misti, though inhabitants keep a wary eye on
its 19,200-foot peak in case it should not prove so dormant as it
looks. Arequipa is known as the white city because many of its
buildings are made of the pink or white volcanic rock quarried
locally.

In the days of the Incas Arequipa was an important staging
post on the road from the sea to Cuzco: chasqui runners carried
fresh fish in baskets to the Inca's table in Cuzco in 24 hours.

This attractive city has magnificent surrounding scenery, a
fine climate, and wealth of Spanish baroque architecture to be
seen in the cathedral, La Compañia church, and the churches of
Santo Domingo, San Agustin, La Merced, and San Francisco, and
in the colonial residences of Casa del Moral, Casa Ricketts, and
Casa Gibbs. The simple beauty of the cathedral is complemented
by the intricate ornamentation on the façade of the Jesuit
church, La Compañia across the square.

The Plaza de Armas is the center of town, filled with flowers, trees and shrubs and bounded on three sides by a Moorish arcade. Roads lead away from the Plaza between high walls with arched gateways leading to the gardens of old colonial mansions. Arequipa's main tourist attraction, the Santa Catalina Convent, a gem of the Middle Ages, is now open to the public by Papal decree after 400 years of seclusion.

The North

Most attractive areas and towns north of Lima are the Callejon de Huaylas, Trujillo and the ruins of Chan Chan, Paramonga and the ancient pre-Inca fortress (Fortaleza). Chiclayo and Piura are coastal towns with a bustling, active charm of their own. All these places can be reached by direct Faucett or Aeroperu flights from Lima.

Much of this area was severely damaged by the August 1970 earthquake, and recuperation is slow. The Chavin ruins have not suffered damage.

The Callejon de Huaylas is an 80-mile-long valley lying between the coastal range (Cordillera Negra) and the main range of the Andes (known in this section as the Cordillera Blanca). The latter range possesses a number of peaks of over 20,000 feet, including Huascarán (22,205 feet), one of the highest peaks in the Western Hemisphere.

This heavily populated valley between the two ranges is one of the beauty spots of Peru. The great snowpeaks and the green foothills and fields of the valley contain a thriving and colorful Indian population, with many picturesque towns and villages. Huaraz, the chief town at 10,000 feet is pleasant though rather cold and windy; most visitors will be more attracted by villages such as Recuay, Caraz, Carhuaz, and above all, Huaylas itself. Huaylas lies in a subsidiary valley at the northern end of the Callejon, and the village itself, its inhabitants, and the commanding views of the snows make the journey over a slightly breathtaking road well worthwhile. The Callejon can be reached in 10 hours by car from Lima, turning off at Paramonga; another way is to continue up the coast to the turn-off at Casma. There is also a pleasant ride to the northern end of the Callejon, the Santa Valley from the fishing port and iron and steel manufacturing center of Chimbote.

Cajamarca has achieved fame as the town where Pizarro and his soldiers waited all night to meet the Inca Atahualpa who wanted to see the "white god with a beard" who was walking through his land. The Spaniards prayed in the night and sharpened their swords. When the Inca came into the town on his golden litter Pizarro stepped forward with his lieutenants and the priest Valverde who offered Atahualpa a Bible, on which to swear his allegiance to the King of Spain, the Pope and Christ. Atahualpa threw the book to the ground and told them that he was God and would bow to no man; whereupon Pizarro waved a handkerchief and his cannon opened fire and his armed soldiers fell on the Inca followers, slaughtering many. The Inca was captured alive and imprisoned. Held for ransom he was eventually falsely tried by the Spanish rabble who had no sense of honor, only greed for gold, and garroted.

Places to See: Chamber of Athahualpa's Ransom, Plaza where his followers were killed, Inca stone reviewing seats on the hill, Cathedral, San Francisco church.

Cajamarca lies several hours inland from the small port of Pacasmayo; the easiest way to get there is by plane from Lima or Trujillo. Cajamarca was once one of the chief cities of the Inca Empire and also an important Spanish colonial town. Now it is the center of a vast, rugged area of Indian communities and large cooperative haciendas in important cattle producing country. Worth seeing are its Inca baths and the room where Pizarro is said to have had Atahualpa garroted. The room that is said to have been filled with gold from floor to ceiling for Atahualpa's ransom is also on show. The adventurous might press on by bus or truck to the town of Chachapoyas, the seat of a bishopric, and on round to Bagua, returning to the coast across a low pass in the mountains to Olmos on the Pan American Highway.

The principal attraction of this backwoods country, set among deep valleys and steep mountains with occasional stretches of savanna or timberlands, is its general atmosphere of a still unspoiled frontier. A 550-mile oil pipeline has been built in this area to carry oil from the jungle fields of eastern Peru to the Pacific coast. A trans-Andean highway is being driven across this frontier by engineering battalions of the Peruvian Army, from the Pacific coast to the navigable headwaters of the Marañon and Huallaga rivers, among the great western tributaries of the Amazon.

Chan Chan: The town covered many square miles. On the land side walls were constructed 50 feet high and 700 feet long as protection from invaders. Within these walls were palaces, temples, fortresses, dwellings, stores, workshops and burial mounds. The Chimú chief's Palace contained nearly 500 rooms, many believed to have been lined with gold leaf. In the 15th century the Incas conquered the city, and then the Spaniards in their eternal lust for gold wrecked and looted the gold and silver statuettes from the burial mounds. Pottery and garments are still found in an excellent state of preservation thanks to the dryness of the climate, and many objects from Chan Chan are in the museums of Lima, notably the Larco Herrera collection.

Chimbote: This town was severely damaged by the earthquake. It has a port larger than Rio de Janiero, and deep enough for ocean going ships. The Santa Valley has been industrialized, with a hydroelectric plant, steel mill, iron smelter, and chemical plant, all government owned.

Chiclayo and Piura are active coastal towns. Some of the finest deepsea fishing in the world is to be found off Cabo Blanco, further to the north. Piura is an attractive village with a pleasant hotel. Between Chiclayo and Piura is Bayovar, a new port, and the terminus of the 550-mile pipeline from the Amazon oilfields to the coast.

Drakky, the Bogey-Man

Trujillo is the third largest city in Peru. Founded by Pizarro and named after his birthplace in Spain, it is now a dignified and somewhat sleepy town. Its main attraction is the ruins of the ancient Chimu city of Chan Chan, spread over a large area just north of Trujillo. The civilization that built Chan Chan is pre-Incaic and is one of the most impressive indications that the Incas were not the only civilization in pre-Columbian Peru to attain a high level of organization and sophistication.

Traces remain on the city walls built by the Duke of La Plata to protect the town against English pirates who ravaged the Pacific coast. Drake became a legend along this coast and his name is still remembered as a particularly fearsome bogey-man; mothers reprimand naughty children with the words "If you're not good, Drakky will get you."

Places to see include churches of Santo Domingo, San Francisco, Cathedral, El Carmen, monastery of San Agustin, Santa Clara, and the residences of the Bracamontes and the Counts of Arama.

Another example of pre-Incaic building can be found right on the Pan American Highway at Paramonga, 115 miles north of Lima. This ancient Chimu fortress is in a fairly good state of preservation, and it offers a view of huge sugar plantations lying along the northcentral coast. Further north, around Piura, some of the finest cotton in the world is grown.

The arid desert north of Lima is cut by about 30 valleys which bring snow waters from the Andes and transform the desert into green oases of cotton and sugar cane. Historically this coast is important as the path of the Spanish Conquest. Pizarro landed on what is still a small deserted beach, near Tumbes, called Puerto Pizarro, inhabited by one or two fishing families.

Talara: Talara is a town on the desert coast built round the oil company tanks, center of the Peruvian petroleum industry.

Tumbes: 100 miles north of Talara, Tumbes is not far from the Ecuadorian frontier. From the attractive small main plaza buses leave for Lima, a 24-hour journey.

Fortaleza, overlooking the sea near Paramonga, is the famous Inca fortress. The well-preserved ruins consist of eight qua- drangular walls rising in tiers to the hill top. On top is a Palace of Mochica or Chimu culture.

Huaraz is on the Rio Santa, 250 miles northeast of Lima, in a wild region at 10,000 feet surrounded by snow peaks. Land is tilled on slopes as high as 13,000 feet, and Indian farmers fol- low a life which has not changed for centuries. There are a number of hill resorts and hotels scattered in the region. Se- verely damaged by the 1970 earthquake, the area is undergoing reconstruction.

Callejon De Huaylas. Leaving Lima for the Callejon the road travels north for three hours through the desert until it turns inland up the Fortaleza River, heading for the mountains. At Conococha, 13,000 feet, the air on the plateau is cool and crisp. The Andean Cordillera splits here to form the two ranges. The Conococha is a sparkling mountain lagoon which gives rise to the two rivers Fortaleza and Santa which head for the Pacific through the valleys and canyons which the road followed.

After the high plateau the road reaches Recuay, center of an old civilization, and drops down through the eucalyptus trees and cactus to Huaras. There is a Government Hotel here.

You continue past the mighty Huascarán peak, beyond the town of Carás and down through the Santa gorge and into a 10-mile stretch of forty-two mountain tunnels. The entire jour- ney from Lima takes about 3 days.

Train to La Oroya

We were now at twelve thousand feet and climbing to thir- teen thousand, fourteen thousand, higher than we had ever been and still going up to over fifteen thousand feet at Ticlio. No one said or did very much and the children either slept or stayed by the women: at that height there is no energy left for surplus movement. We kept very still and breathed in deeply to get our share of oxygen from the air until a man in a white coat came along the middle of the carriage carrying a cushion, step- ping over the bundles and baskets of chickens. (Remember this is second-class traveling where you will see more life. In first class you will see less but travel more comfortably, of course.) The "cushion" was a bag of oxygen with a tube and nozzle attached for anyone who felt faint and needed one or two pulls at the tube. It takes a lifetime to get used to living at these fan- tastic altitudes.

Each station was a thousand feet above the last, Chicla, Casa- palca, Chinchan, to the highest point on the line at 15,688 feet in a tunnel between Ticlio and Galera, the highest standard- gauge railway station in the world at 15,685 feet.

Then the worst of the altitude was over and we had no more
climbing but a long gentle downhill run all the afternoon. We
were in the center of the mountains, across the first range,
pulling into the mining town of Oroya.

From Oroya we followed the Mantaro valley to Pachacayo,
Llocllapampa and Huancayo, finding it a little hard to believe
that the Mantaro River which rushed along beside us was a
tributary of the Amazon. The valley widened into fertile farming country with lines of eucalyptus trees, Australian gums,
ploughed land and patches of maize between villages of mud-
walled houses with orange tiled roofs. Little shrines were set
into the rocks every few miles along the track.

Royal Road of the Inca Virgins

Huancayo: Huancayo is the main town of Central Peru, with
a fine climate, lying in a wide valley at 11,000 feet between
Andean ranges.

This town was on one of the old imperial highways of the
Incas and has probably always been an important center. The
main street, Calle Real, is actually part of the Inca road. The
Inca rode in triumph through Huancayo on a golden litter, preceded by heralds and musicians and attended by Virgins of the
Sun who strewed the road with flowers. Priests guarded the litter and the army marched behind, each section wearing its own
insignia, puma skins, woolen shirts and vicuña hats. Pizarro
followed this road on his way to Cuzco, and centuries later the
armies of the Liberators, Bolívar and Sucre passed on their way
to fight for independence.

Huancayo has been declared capital of Peru three times in its
history, the most important occasion in 1854 when the Abolition of Slavery was signed here by Ramon Castilla. Hotel Turistas
in town.

The Sunday fairs are the main attraction for visitors. Indians
come from miles around with laden burros and spread their
goods out along the main streets: fruit, vegetables, cotton and
woolens, furs, dyewoods, plants and herbs, and the finely
wrought silver, bone articles, gourds and dolls. An interesting
side trip is to the weavers' and silversmiths' villages of Hualhuas
and San Jeronimo. For those who cannot make it on Sun. there
is a Sat. fair at Chupaca, 10 miles from Huancayo, which is
excellent.

Ayacucho: This is the principal town on the rough road from
Huancayo to Cuzco. The road travels through places with poetic
names, Ayacucho, Andahuaylas, Abancay, small towns at 10,000
feet where the mountain scenery is some of the most beautiful
in South America. You can look down into the deep valleys and
see a small settlement hours before your vehicle actually arrives

there. The nights are cold, and when clear the snow on the
jagged cordillera stands out against a sky full of stars.

Ayacucho was built during the conquest and its 33 churches
and old houses are well worth seeing. The interiors are rich in
silver taken from nearby mines. See the Cathedral, Santa Clara,
Santa Domingo, Santa Teresa, La Merced, San Francisco de Asis,
and the Iglesia de la Compañia de Jesús; the Museo Historico,
and University. Nearby the final battle for Independence was
fought in 1824. The only hotels are the Sucre and Tourist.

The Eastern Jungles

Efficient air service has made the eastern jungle region of
Peru as accessible as the highlands. Iquitos and Pucallpa are the
main towns, with Contamana, Yurimaguas and Tarapoto as the
secondary population centers. Closer to Lima are Chanchamayo
and Tingo Maria, both pleasant areas of upper jungle and both
with Tourist Hotels. There are regular scheduled flights to all
these places (except Contamana, on the river Ucayali), from
Lima. Some jungle towns, like Iquitos and Pucallpa, have
become boom towns as oil drilling teams from various parts of
the world arrive to search the jungle for petroleum.

The 500-mile trans-Andean highway between Lima and
Pucallpa, a two-day trip in the dry season, must be one of the
great roads of the world. It starts from the coastal desert at sea
level to cross 16,000-foot Andean passes, then runs through La
Oroya and Cerro de Pasco, both important mining centers, down
to the jungles of Tingo Maria and the Amazon plain around
Pucallpa. It is a topographical cross-section of the three worlds
of Peru. From Pucallpa, a lively, ramshackle river port, there
are tugs and steamers downstream to Iquitos, four days away.
It is better to fly and spend the time you save traveling by small
boat out of Iquitos. On the smaller rivers around Iquitos, the
jungle can be seen at first hand from comfortable motorboats.
There are hunting, fishing and visits to some safe but satis-
factorily savage jungle Indians. The climate is hot and damp but
more comforable in this respect than New York in summer. Special equipment isn't necessary, but long-sleeved shirts and long
trousers and slacks are often advisable. The best season for visiting is May to September.

Yurimaguas, a river port on the Huallaga river, is a pleasant,
respectable little town. Tarapoto, which can only be reached by
air, is the center of a great area of upper jungle which flies out
its products by plane, making it one of the busiest airports in
Peru. The eastern region is warmly recommended to the visitor
who has time, a smattering of Spanish and a little initiative.
Plane travel makes it accessible, and simple accommodation is
available without difficulty. Food is reliable and sometimes very

good. It will recall for you childhood tales of the jungle; you will find it can be a friendly, beautiful place despite those terrifying stories people once told you.

In the past, difficult access into the mountainous region has discouraged tourists from visiting areas east of Lima and has kept them from visiting the Amazon region beyond. In the last few years Peru has been building roads into the remote Andean villages and down to the Amazon rivers.

The starting point for trips into the back country is Lima. An automobile trip over the Andes on one of these roads is a touring adventure hard to equal. Driving east from Lima, the Carretera Central climbs the granite-walled Rimac Valley to Matucana. From Matucana to the east, you will see Indians guiding herds of llamas along narrow trails on the steep mountain sides. Near Rio Blanco, the highway passes through potato fields so steep that, if a potato is dropped during harvest, it might roll several thousand feet to the Rimac River below.

The pass at Anticona is 16,000 feet above sea level, and the water from glaciers in the Andes travels 70 miles down the Rimac to the Pacific and 3,500 miles down the Yauli-Mantaro-Ucayali-Amazon system to the Atlantic. At Ticlio, llama trails and highway converge to go over the pass together; the railway passes through a tunnel underneath. It is an easy five-hour drive from Huancayo to San Ramon. As far as Tarma, the road winds through a picturesque stretch of treeless mountain pasture empty except for llama and sheep and on to San Ramon where the route winds down the side of a 6,000-foot canyon whose walls are covered with heavy jungle growth that is broken here and there by a waterfall.

Coffee, oranges, papayas, avocados, sugar cane, bananas and other tropical foods are produced in the valley. On the steep hillsides is the untamed jungle, with orchids and other exotic plants. Among the palm, chonta, mahogany and the Peruvian cedar trees, parrots and other colorful birds flit from branch to branch, and around the pools on the edge of the Chanchamayo River are clouds of yellow, blue, red and black butterflies. The area is a haven for photographers shooting in color. Stay at San Ramon's comfortable and modern hotel.

Another road climbs the cordillera and across the high moorland plains of altiplano to Cerro de Pasco down to Huanuco and then further down to a town with the pretty name of Tingo Maria in the Rio Huallaga valley. There is much new settlement in these valleys. Land has been cleared along the banks and stories leak out of pioneer settlers making their fortune with tobacco, cotton or sugar cane. From Tingo Maria the road climbs again through the Cordillera Azul, Blue Range, and down through the Pampa del Sacramento to Pucallpa on the Ucayali River. From here riverboats can take you to join the Amazon, the Iquitos and the Atlantic Ocean.

Pucallpa

Wild rubber, which comes in great smoke balls, is collected together at Pucallpa. This city is also the terminus for the Central Highway, which begins at Callao on the Pacific coast and crosses the Andes at 16,000 feet above sea level, and is the principal starting point for river traffic in the Amazon system. Today, as one of the centers for the search for oil in the jungle, it has become a boom town. Some eighteen companies—American, British, German, French, Spanish and Japanese—have been exploring the jungle, though negative results have caused most to leave. Two companies, Petroperu, the state oil company, and Occidental Petroleum of the U.S. have found several productive fields. The first field in this area, discovered 45 years ago by the Blue Goose Petroleum Company (which sold it to Petroperu three years ago), is small but still producing.

At Lake Yarinacocha, 25 minutes from Pucallpa, the Summer Institute of Linguistics has its main camp, first established 27 years ago. Yarinacocha has become the largest and most important missionary center in South America. In the last ten years foreign missionary families have increased from 150 to 550, most of them connected with this camp. The Institute is nondenominational and has more than 3,000 members in 28 countries. The Summer Institute has translated and given written form to 36 Peruvian Amazon dialects; the translation of the Bible into local languages is their ultimate goal. Beyond this, the missionaries—almost all Americans—have trained teachers and community leaders to make use of legal and political channels in order to protect their tribes against white settlers, merchants and poachers.

The Institute's radio network is the most effective communication system throughout Peru's vast Amazon jungle, and the six hydroplanes owned and operated by the missionaries serve to provide reliable transportation not only for the Institute's members but also for Peruvian officials, doctors, technicians and border guards.

Pucallpa has a small hospital, started some years back, which is doing good work among the Indians This is the Hospital Amazonico Albert Schweitzer, founded by Doctor Theodor Binder and his wife Carmen. On August 1st, 1957, the first brick of the hospital, fired on the site, was laid.

From the first day there was a steady stream of patients at the clinic. Most of them came from Pucallpa, but word spread about the new hospital and Indians began to arrive from their villages three weeks away by canoe. There were twenty-four beds at first but plans are to have a hundred beds, a special tuberculosis ward, and to keep Binder's former house in Pucallpa as an outpatients' clinic.

The words HOSPITAL AMAZONICO ALBERT SCHWEIT-

ZER are painted on the wall above the main door of the long
hospital building, and beneath the sign Indian men wait with their
children and women, who wear their long black hair cut in a
fringe across their eyes but allow it to grow in long strands at the
sides and back, falling down their shoulders, and who wear their
short straight skirts wrapped round like a Burmese longy and
decorated with strong black, white and brown geometric
designs. Babies are carried on the hip in a shawl slung round
the shoulder.

The Indians of the Amazon have always relied on the soil
and the river; manioc from the soil and fish from the river.
They trap animals and have developed poisons to tip their arrows
and fire at the birds, while some are cannibals and some head
shrinkers like the famous Jivaros of Ecuador. They have always
slept in hammocks or on mats and lived in palm and bamboo
huts; more permanent buildings have never been found. But in
those jungles who can tell? Within months the encroaching
foliage can hide stone walls as well as they did at Angkor Wat:
Francisco Raposo's great Lost City of Atlantis that Fawcett was
seeking may yet exist.

Pucallpa has four hotels ($5–$10 single; $7.50–$14 double).
Mr. Heinrich Maulhardt rents some comfortable bungalows with
all modern conveniences at Lake Yarinacocha. Pucallpa is really
a jungle outpost, worth a visit if you are particularly interested
in the jungle and in the characters it attracts: doctors, missionaries and oil men.

Green Mansions or Green Hell?

Iquitos is the capital of the Loreto Department of Peru and
main town for a vast region, which includes a network of
rivers, the Ucayali, Marañon, Hulluallaga, Apurimac, and the
Urubamba; and distant outposts such as Pucallpa, Yurimaguas,
and Tingo Maria. The region covers virtually a third of Peru.
Its jungles vary in character according to the visitor's point of
view: to Duguid it was a "Green Hell," to Hudson the "Green
Mansions." Iquitos is as far from the Atlantic coast (3,000
miles) as from the Pacific coast, and although Peru has no
Atlantic coast, it is here the Peruvian government maintains its
Atlantic fleet.

Once the land of the rubber boom, this country returned to its
former insignificance after the boom in the early years of this
century. Now it is growing in importance again and many consider it to be the land of the future The jungle is broken by
intermittent spaces of fertile open country and these are being
colonized. Its tremendous mineral wealth, gold, oil and iron, is
being mapped and studied and extracted. Vegetable wealth
includes rubber, quinine, and palm oil.

Iquitos is a center for small launch trips up neighboring tributaries; connection by air with Lima or by ship down the Amazon to Europe or U.S.A.

The town is but a ghost of its former self. A stone balustrade along the bluff overlooking the river is covered in the consuming vegetation of the tropics. Statues to forgotten men stand in neglected squares and few people are seen, whereas fifty years ago the streets would have been thronged. There are fine houses built during the rubber era, decorated with azulejo tiles from Spain and ironwork from England. The old market was destroyed by the river, but there is now an open-air market at that site at Belen, where the homes are built on rafts so that they can be floated from one place to another and stationed on the shores of the river. Recently the search for oil has brought some new activity, and a measure of affluence.

The city's Aquarium, under the control of the Hunting and Fishing Bureau of the Ministry of Agriculture, exhibits a collection of brilliantly colored tropical fish, and the Museum of Natural History displays specimens of the animal life found in the jungle and river.

As life has been picking up there since it has become a staging area for the oil companies, some strange little businesses, like catching tropical fish for overseas aquariums, are developing.

A new government hotel on the shores of Quistococha Lake, 15 min. from the center of Iquitos, is in the planning stages. The international jet airport should open between 1977 and 1978.

A two-day, one-night visit to the Amazon jungle, with speedboat transfer upon arrival in Iquitos direct to Amazon Lodge, a visit to the Jivaro Indians' settlement plus a visit to a nearby Yagua Indian tribe, tour of Iquitos, and transfers can be arranged by *Receptour*, leaving Lima daily. More lengthy tours are also available, where swimming, canoeing, etc., can be enjoyed.

A full-day excursion by motorboat up the Amazon and the Rio Napo from Iquitos to the village of the Yagua Indians, the famous users of the blowgun, is splendid fun. The Indians will demonstrate their hunting and fishing skills. Not too long ago, the Yaguas were feared warriors, and the Spaniards were never able to conquer them; now they are quite friendly. The Indians, both men and women, wear grass skirts and headdresses.

Puno and Lake Titicaca

From Cuzco the road and railway lead south to *Lake Titicaca* and the famous altiplano of southern Peru and Bolivia. This high, cold, windswept plateau, lying at an altitude of 12,000 to 13,000 feet with snow-capped mountain ranges on the horizon, is the home of the llama, guanuco, alpaca and the vicuña. Despite its bleakness and uncompromising climate, many areas, especially those around Lake Titicaca, are populated by the Quechua and Aymara Indians, whose homesteads are dotted over the plain. They glean a rugged existence from the cultivation of scant fields of potatoes and from their herds of llamas and alpaca. There are also great haciendas covering thousands of acres where top-grade sheep are raised for exceptionally soft wool.

The road from Cuzco to Puno is acceptable, but the journey is most comfortably made by train in eleven hours. There is an airstrip at Juliaca served by *Aeroperu* from Lima via Aerquipa, Wed. and Sun., returning the same day. Near Cuzco, the railroad passes through valleys with signs of ancient terraces along the hillsides. Many archeologists are of the opinion that the Peru of Inca and pre-Inca days was more heavily populated than it is today. The remains of terraces and of complicated irrigation systems all over the country certainly indicate that there was more land under cultivation and also suggest that the agriculture was more efficient and intensive.

Going south from the town of *Sicuani*, famous for its wool and hides, the country opens out onto the altiplano of the Titicaca basin. Juliaca is one of the principal junctions of the Southern Railway and center for much of commerce of the Titicaca region. It is one of the best places to purchase woolens and hide goods, for sale at the station when the train comes in.

Juliaca: At an altitude of 12,550 feet Juliaca is a junction on the railway line from Arequipa to Cuzco or Puno. It is the center for wool and hides. In the plaza there is an interesting colonial church. On Sunday the usual local market attracts Indians from the district. No hotels to be recommended; newest is at Puno, 30 miles away.

Puno is the capital town of the Peruvian altiplano. The streets are full of trudging Indians and women in long skirts and bowler hats. Puno is at its best at Carnival time, when the whole town whirls and dances in costume through the streets to the music of local orchestras.

Puno is one day by train from Cuzco. The best time to visit is during the dry season from May to November. Hotel reservations (*Government Tourist*) should be made before leaving Lima.

Numerous fiestas, most often associated with religious events or figures, are held during the year with processions and dancing. The two most important are February 2, when they celebrate La Virgen de la Candelaria, the patron saint of Puno, and November 1–7 to commemorate the founding of the city.

From Puno interesting excursions can be made to Lake Titicaca, to the churches of Juli and Pomata of colonial mestizo style or to the strange chullpas, stone tower tombs of a pre-Inca people at Sillustani.

Lake Titicaca: Lake Titicaca has a sacred place in Peruvian legend. According to the 16th-century chronicler of the Incas, Garcilaso de la Vega, the Incas believed that the Sun God created Manco Capac, the first Inca King, and Mama Occlo, his Queen, on the Island of the Sun in Lake Titicaca. From Titicaca, these two traveled forth and settled in the Cuzco Valley. There they established an empire which was to endure for five centuries until the arrival of Francisco Pizarro.

Titicaca is almost as legendary today to trout fishermen as it was to the Incas. Fish believed to be a cross between lake and cutthroat trout and weighing up to 30 lbs. are not uncommon. Arrangements for Titicaca fishing expeditions can be made in Puno.

From Puno and Juliaca there is train service down to Arequipa, the second city of Peru. The trip takes about twelve hours.

Sunrise over Titicaca is well worth the effort of getting up early. Excellent trout can be taken from the lake and tributary streams, and it is also possible to arrange a visit to Uros Indian communities on islands made of reeds and rushes. They have a language and a life of their own. From the motor boat, they will ferry you onto their island free of charge in their little reed boats, but you have to pay to be ferried back!

In the past the Uros Indians covered their floating islands with soil and planted potatoes and oca, a sweet tuber, to supplement their diet of fish. The floating potato fields have disappeared as the Uros have found commercial trout fishing more profitable.

On a sunny day the reed islands offer a spectacular panorama for the color photographers with the blue Andean sky, white clouds, dark blue water of the lake, yellow of the reed houses and rafts and the colorful clothes of the Uros. The Uros are somewhat shy before the camera, but this is easily overcome by a few soles.

Launches powered by outboard motors are available for sightseeing trips to the Indian islands along canals through banks of reeds. The three-hour round trip costs about $5 per person.

Lake Titicaca lies two miles above sea level, the world's highest navigable lake. It is 95 miles long, 35 miles wide and 700 (official) to 1,200 (unofficial) feet deep (about one-third the size of Lake Ontario).

From Puno one can continue on to the Bolivian port of Guaqui by lake steamers operated by the Southern Railway of Peru and by train from there to La Paz. This is the traditional route into Bolivia. The steamers were constructed in England and hauled up piece by piece over the Andes in the early years of this century. Or you can take a hydrofoil across Lake Titicaca.

Or take the hydrofoil tour for $60. You travel by car from

Puno to Ilave, Juli and Pomata to Copacabana. After lunch and a visit to the Shrine of Our Lady of Copacabana, the modern, 27-seat hydrofoil takes you to Huatajata, in Bolivia, via the Island of the Sun. From Huatajata, you progress to La Paz by car. Contact any travel agent in Lima or Cuzco or Turismo Titikaka, who represents the hydrofoils of Crillon Tours in Puno.

At Sillustani, about 15 miles northwest of Puno, are perhaps the finest examples of chullpa tombs, impressive towers of cut and fitted stones. The workmanship is equal to the best of Inca standards at Cuzco and Machu Picchu. The circular towers stand about 25 feet high, and the circumference of each is greater at the top than at the bottom. Their symmetry and beauty are a tribute to Inca architects and workmen.

The Spaniards destroyed most of these Chullpas immediately after the conquest. A drive by chartered taxi to Juliaca and then to Taraco and Huancané affords glimpses into life in the altiplano, as well as views of grazing llamas and alpacas, Indian villages and ornate old Spanish churches.

PRACTICAL INFORMATION FOR PERU

CAPSULE COMMENTS. *Physical Features.* There are three distinct geographical areas: the coast is a warm, narrow ribbon of desert interspersed with over 50 rivers that flow to the sea, making fertile lands and green oases between the sea and the Andes; the highlands or *sierra* form Peru's backbone and the continental divide with an average elevation of 13,000 feet and climbing to 22,334; the *Montaña* is Peru's vast jungle land that stretches from the eastern slope of the Andes into the unexplored upper reaches of the Amazon headwaters.

Climate. Great variations according to region. Lima is pleasant to visit all year. In Peru's winter (July-August) an almost constant fog rolls in from the ocean. Cool mornings and evenings and warm afternoons are usual in Lima the rest of the year. Best time to visit Peru is from December to April.

Population. 16,000,000. Lima 3,500,000.

Archeological Attractions. Peru is a giant outdoor museum. Cuzco, the ancient Inca capital and home of the Temple of the Sun, and Machu Picchu, "the city lost for 400 years," are world famous. New "lost cities" are constantly being discovered.

Principal Industries. Copper, marine products, silver, zinc, sugar, iron ore, cotton, lead, coffee.

WHAT WILL IT COST? Lima, like other major world capitals, is becoming expensive. The leading hotels will run US $20 and up and meals are $5 and up plus a 21% tax. The more expensive restaurants cost $10. Other hotels are available for $10 a day single.

Meals in a good but informal restaurant will average about $6 including tax. There are boardinghouses and smaller hotels where the rates are more reasonable.

In the provinces prices are less than half what they are in Lima, with the exception of cities like Cuzco and Arequipa where rates are comparable.

Air fares are standard. Round trip between Lima and Cuzco costs $80; between Lima and Iquitos, $90.

The cost of living in Peru has been increasing rapidly in the past few years. At present it is going up at an annual rate of 45%. The cost of imported articles, when they are available, is double what it is in the U.S.; on the other hand, domestic help, plumbers, painters, and the like, are readily available and very inexpensive. A sleep-in maid costs $60 a month.

 WHEN TO GO? The best time to visit Lima and the coastal area is October through April. These are the summer months for the coast but the rainy season for the mountains and jungle. From April or May to October, the mountains are clear, but the coast is often covered by fog.

Seasonal Events. Peru observes one of the most generous number of Public Holidays of any country. Invariably these holidays or fiestas are connected with religious festivals.

St. John's Day, June 24. This is a colorful Indian fiesta in Cuzco's Inca Fort Sacsahuaman in which hundreds of Indians in typical regional costumes participate. The Inti Raymi festival involves symbolic sacrifice of a virgin and a llama to the Sun God.

The October Fair. This is a traditional holiday which really lasts throughout the "purple" month of October. A procession of the Lord of Miracles takes place on October 18, 19 and 28. Bullfights take place in the Plaza de Acho of Lima. The capital takes on a festive air, and street stalls sell a national delicacy known as *turrón de Doña Pepa*— almond nougat. At *Christmas* time visit the Cathedral and Church of San Francisco to see the grand Nativity scenes.

National Public Holidays. The holiday calendar begins in Peru, as elsewhere, with a *New Year's* celebration on January 1. In March or April there is *Maundy Thursday, Good Friday* and *Easter Sunday*. Their *Labor Day* falls on May 1. June 29 is the *Feast of St. Peter and St. Paul. Peruvian Independence* is marked with celebrations on July 28 and 29. The remaining holidays are religious: the feast of *Santa Rosa* on August 30, *All Saints Day* on November 1, the *Immaculate Conception* on December 8, and, of course, *Christmas* on December 25.

Religious Fiestas outside Lima

Arequipa. New Year's Day, Pear Festival at Tiabaya; January 6, Carnival Corpus Christi; July 28, Independence; August 30, Day of the Indian; September 24, Our Lady of Mercy.

Anniversary of Arequipa: Is celebrated on August 15, with civic events and a formal dance.

Asillo. December 18, Virgin of the Star Feast Day, procession, fireworks, feasting, bullfights.

Bolognesi. November 20-21, Feast of the Pilgrim Virgin, patron of the city—folk dancing, music, fireworks.

Holy Week: Semana Santa in Ayacucho with processions on Monday Wednesday and Friday. The Ayacuchanos dress in black for the occasion and figures representing Calvary are carried on litters. On Wednesday people go barefooted their heads covered with hoods. This procession is similar to the famous one of Seville, Spain.

Cuzco. Jan. 6, Epiphany, Adoration of the Magi, Corpus Christi; Monday before Easter, Procession of the Señor de los Temblores; Sept. 24, Our Lady of Mercy.

In the Puno and Lake Titicaca area is the famous La Candelaria, one week series of festivals held Feb. 2 to 10.

Towns of the colorful Callejon de Huaylas region celebrate national holidays with parades and fireworks. Religious festivities are enlivened with processions and local fairs.

Holy Week is celebrated with daily processions and bands. Carnival in the Callejon de Huaylas is a mixture of religious and pagan; during Carnival Indians bring big crosses into the church, decorated with wild flowers which grow at an altitude over 12,000 feet.

FESTIVALS AND SPECIAL EVENTS. *Indian Open-Air Market in Huancayo.* Most striking feature is the silence since the Indians utter almost no sound. Sundays, throughout year. *Holy Week Celebrations* are most notable in Arequipa, Cajamarca, Coracora, Cuzco, Santiago de Chuco. Tarma. *Corpus Christi Celebrations.* Most notable in Cajamarca, Chiquian and Hualgayoc. *La Candelaria,* one week series of festivals held Feb. 2–10, in the Puno and Lake Titicaca area. *Inti-Raymi/Sun Easter of the Incas.* Colorful performance in honor of ancient Sun God, Cuzco. Indian Day, June 24. *San Juan de Amancaes Fiesta.* Dance and music companies from all parts of Peru compete. Lima. June 24. *Independence of Peru National Festival.* Major celebration in Lima. July 28–30. *Anniversary of Arequipa,* Aug. 15. *Bullfights* part of year in Lima. "Summertime" bullfights in March. Bullfighting "season" is October-December. *Señor de los Milagros/Lord of Miracles Festival.* Attractions include Peruvian October Fair of Purple Month and great religious procession. World's most noted bullfighters compete for "Escapulario de Oro". Lima. Oct. 18–20. *Feast of the Pilgrim Virgin,* Bolognesi, Nov. 20–21. *Christmas Season Celebrations.* Notable in Hacienda Chichu in Trujillo, also Lima and Lloclapampa. Dec. *Virgin of the Star Feast Day,* Asillo, Dec. 18.

HOW TO REACH PERU. *By air:* Lima can be reached from New York by *Braniff Airways, KLM* via Curaçao, *Air Panama, LAN-Chile, Lufthansa.* From Washington: *Braniff.* From Miami: *Aeroperu, Aerolineas Argentinas, Air Panama, Avianca, Braniff, Air France* via Pointe-à-Pitre, *Ecuatoriana* and *LAN-Chile.* From Los Angeles: *Aeroperu, Varig, Aerolineas Argentinas.* From Los Angeles and San Francisco: *Braniff.* From Canada: *CP Air.* From Europe: *Aeroflot, Air France, Avianca, British Caledonian, Iberia, KLM* (via Buenos Aires), *Lufthansa, VIASA.* From Tokyo: *Varig.* From Hong Kong and Tokyo: *CP Air* (via Montreal, Toronto and Mexico City). There are flights from Mexico, via *Aerolineas Argentinas, Avianca, CP Air, Ecuatoriana, Aeroperu, Aereo Mexico.*

BY SEA. Two regular passenger lines call at Callao, the main seaport. *Prudential Lines* sails from San Francisco and Los Angeles every 23 days for a trip around South America via the Panama Canal; these call at ports on the east coast of the continent, pass through the Straits of Magellan, and stop at Valparaíso and Callao. This is a 55-day voyage on modern vessels. From Mediterranean ports: *Italian Line*. Seaport tax: Lima—Adults, $10; children, $5.

HOW TO GET ABOUT. *By air:* Peru has two domestic airlines: *Faucett*, in the Bolívar Hotel at Plaza San Martín, Lima, and *Aeroperu*, the Government airline flying Jet Fokkers. Both airlines link Lima to Arequipa, Ayacucho, Iquitos, Piura, Pucallpa, Talara, Trujillo, Tumbes, Yurimaguas, Tacna, Chiclayo and other cities.

By rail: The highest standard gauge railroad in the world travels between Lima and Oroya with branches to Cerro de Pasco, Huancayo and Huancavelica. The Southern Railways of Peru operate between Arequipa-Puno (on Lake Titicaca) with one weekly connection (Wednesdays) by steamer across the lake to Bolivia (returning Fri.), as well as three weekly connections to Cuzco. Check schedules, the boats are often docked for repairs and railway has *summer* and *winter* schedules.

By road: The main highway is the Pan American, paved over most of the distance, running north-south through the coastal desert of Peru. Another road connects Lima, Canta, Cerro de Pasco to Huanuco and on to Tingo Maria and Pucallpa on the Ucayali River. The Central Highway connects Lima with Oroya, Huancayo, Huancavelica, Ayacucho, Cuzco, Puno to Arequipa. The grand circuit from Lima, Cuzco, Puno, Arequipa, Lima is 1,500 miles.

The *Peruvian Touring Club* helps prepare itineraries. *Hertz, Avis* and *Budget-Rent-A-Car* have offices in Lima for car rentals; *Turamerica*, opposite Bolívar Hotel, rents VW's, Peugeots; *Graf* (Avis representative) features Toyotas. All roads are served by local bus, a very cheap and sometimes rough means of travel recommended only for the hardiest, with the exception of Greyhound-type buses operated by Roggero and TEPSA along the Pan American Highway and by the latter internationally from Ecuador through Peru to Chile. *Morales, Moralitos Line* offers new Spanish buses to La Paz via Arequipa.

In the city: Taxis are cheap. Microbuses—short-bodied buses carrying 15–20 passengers—crisscross the city. Good municipal bus service is available. There are also a few colectivo lines, taxis carrying five passengers and following set routes, which are cheap. They will pick up or set down anywhere on that route. Drivers signal a vacant seat by waving their arm up and down. In Cuzco, pick up a taxi fare schedule at the National Tourist Office on the Plaza de Armas at Portal Carrizos. In Lima, a small percentage of the taxis have meters; fares "in city" are 35 to 40 soles, to an Isidro 60/80, to Miraflores 80/100. To the airport from the city should not cost more than 300 soles.

Travel Agencies in Lima: Receptour, Rufino Torrico 889 (tel. 312022). Owned by Americans.

Others: *Lima Tours, Dasatour, Sudex, Travelex, Chavez Bros., Wagon-Lits Cook, Exprinter.*

 PASSPORTS, VISAS AND CUSTOMS. *Peruvian Consulate* in U.S. is at 1700 Masachusetts Ave., N.W., Washington, D.C.; in Great Britain, 52 Sloane Street, London, S.W.1. *Consular officials* in the U.S.A. are in: Los Angeles, San Francisco, Miami, Chicago, New York, New Orleans, Baltimore, Boston, St. Louis, Portland, Philadelphia, Houston, Seattle, Honolulu and at Cristobal, Canal Zone, Mayagüez, San Juan, P.R., and Charlotte Amalie, V.I.

All travelers must carry an International Certificate of Vaccination. A visa is not needed by citizens of U.S.A., Canada, Great Britain or most Western European countries. Valid passport, smallpox vaccination certificate, and evidence of continuing transportation must be carried.

All personal effects allowed in limited quantities: 200 cigarettes, 25 cigars or ½ lb. tobacco; 2 qts. of liquor.

 CURRENCY. The Peruvian monetary unit is the *sol* which is divided into 100 centavos. Paper bills are in denominations of 1,000, 500, 100, 50, 10, and 5 soles. A sol and medio-sol, 25, 10, and 5 centavo pieces are bronze alloy coins. Tourists are requested to declare currency they bring into country, which can be changed at Banco de la Nacion at the airport. In town, money can be changed at the bank or hotel. Peruvian currency can be changed for dollars or pounds at airport upon departure. The rate is now 75 soles to one dollar, with regular mini-devaluations. Declaration of money on entering country is to allow tourist to change back surplus at official rate.

TIPPING. There is a 21 percent service charge on all bills. Additional tips of 5 percent are expected. Taxi drivers do not expect tips.

 CLOTHING. The coastal region is most agreeable from January to April. Light-weight men's suits are then the most comfortable wear. From June to November it is cooler but humidity is very high (90 percent to 98 percent) and a layer of cloud shuts out the sun. However, 25 minutes by car to the east and you are in lovely sunshine at Chaclacayo. The temperature remains between 60°F. and 80°F.— English-type summer clothing is then the best.

Women wear woolen or silk dresses in winter; dresses of cotton, silk or crêpe are more common in summer. Dinner or cocktail dresses are worn, with fur coats or wraps in cooler months. Lima has become more informal in recent years. During summer months most people wear Cuban-type 'guyaberas'. Pants-suits for women are quite common even at formal evening affairs. Businessmen still wear ties and suits, especially at evening functions, but sports shirts for men and slacks for women are quite common now, and you are likely to see more women in slacks (and especially jeans) than in skirts. Shorts are still out, except at summer resorts. Hats are rarely worn by either men or women except among the Indians.

In the Sierra take summer and winter clothing with sweaters and topcoat, and lightweight raincoat; there is a sharp fall in temperature on cloudy days and at night.

In the jungle the climate is tropical. Take lightweight clothes and extra shirts, hats and spare handkerchiefs for mopping the brow.

Sun glasses indispensable. Insect repellent necessary in the Sierra and jungle.

HOTELS. Peru has many excellent hotels where you will find a high standard of cleanliness, good food and service. Lima has the largest choice. In other towns it has been usual to find only one good hotel; government-run, these are often modern, but more frequently converted estate houses or colonial mansions. Now, as a result of tax incentives, many new hotels are being built, many of which should open during 1977, including the *Libertador Marriott* in Lima.

The *best* hotels in Lima have accommodations at $20–$40 single, $25–$50 double. Other hotels are $10–$19 single, $13–$20 double. Outside Lima, $8–$16 for double, approximately, plus 17–21% government tax. All prices subject to change.

LIMA
Deluxe

LIMA-SHERATON, in the Civic and Convention Center, downtown. New. 406 air-conditioned rooms on 20 floors. Modern, functional decor. Fine restaurants, but expensive. Outdoor pool, sauna; tennis and golf nearby. Shopping arcade. Parking facilities.

GRAN HOTEL BOLIVAR, Plaza San Martín, the oldest and best known in the country. Famed for its pisco sour. 350 rooms.

CRILLON, 589 Ave. Nicolas de Pierola, in style of traditional European palace hotels. 547 rooms and suites.

Also, *Cesar's Hotel*, Calle La Paz, Miraflores, a 17-story luxury hotel opened in December, 1976.

First Class
COUNTRY CLUB HOTEL, Ave. Golf, in San Isidro-Miraflores section, next to golf club. Exclusive, intimate and elegant. Deservedly popular.

Moderate

Maury, 201 Ucayali. 100 rooms. *Savoy*, 224 Cailloma, 225 rooms. *Alcazar*, 564 Camana. 100 rooms. *Riviera*, 981 Av. Garcilaso de la Vega. 185 rooms and suites. *Continental*, central location. 150 rooms. *Columbus*, Av. Arequipa 1421. 42 rooms.

Hostal Miraflores, 5444 Petit Thouars; *Hostal del Sol*, 388 Jeronica. *Residencia Miramar*, British-American management, 1244 Malecón Cisneros, Miraflores; *Hostal Beech*, British management, 165 Libertadores, San Isidro; *Hostal Collacocha*, Andres Reyes 100, San Isidro.

Inexpensive
Pensions include: *Pension Alemana*, 4704 Av., Arequipa; *Pension Americana*, 664 Carabaya; *Astoria*, 155 Camino Real; *Residencial Inn*, 187 Bartolomé Trujillo; *Shell*, 452 Shell, Miraflores; *La Casona*, at the corner of Cailloma and Moquegua, a rebuilt 19th century building with attractive large patio, 33 rooms; *Damasco*, 199 Ucayali; *Oriental*, 696 Cuzco; *Universal*, 754 Zángaro.

In Foothills
GRANJA AZUL INN. Located 20 minutes from Lima in the foothills of the Andes. Bungalows. 390 beds. Part of hotel consists of typical Andean village, but with all modern conveniences. Has swimming pool, golf course, tennis, riding, gym, discotheque. First class. Excellent.

KISKAS. Brand new, 60 bungalows, 60 minutes from Lima. Pleasant climate. Has a river for fishing in addition to the other recreational facilities.

The *Empresa de Turismo del Peru* (ENTURPERU), Santo Toribio 210, San Isidro (tel. 28-7815) operates government hotels throughout Peru, and all reservations can be made through the head office. They also have a booking office on Plaza San Martin, at the Aeroperu offices. There are hotels at: Ayacucho, Abancay, Arequipa, Camana, Chala, Contumaza, Cuzco, Machu Picchu, Urubamba, Chiclayo, Huancavelica, Huanuco, Tingo-María, Huarmey, Iquitos, Ica, Nazca, Piura, Puno, San Ramón, Tarma, Tacna, Trujillo, Huaraz, Paca (Jauja), Tumbes, Cajamarca, Juliaca, Puerto Maldonado, Zorritos, and Yura.

NORTH OF LIMA

HUARAZ. *Monterrey* (4 miles north of Huaraz, 253 miles from Lima, via Pativilca). The warm spring water has sedative qualities; the climate is dry and invigorating. From the valley the Cordillera Blanca and Huascarán can be seen. Inexpensive. Also an ENTURPERU hotel.

CHIMBOTE BAY. *Chimu-Chimbote* (257 miles north of Lima). Modern hotel situated on the bay, now a busy anchovy fishing port. Inexpensive.

NORTH OF CHIMBOTE

Beyond Chimbote there are ENTURPERU hotels, called *Hotel de Turistas*, at Trujillo, Chiclayo, Piura and Tumbes, all on the Pan American Highway. At Trujillo there is a new modern hotel, *El Golf*.

SOUTH OF LIMA

Santa María Beach Club Hotel (30 mi. south, off Pan Am Highway). 27 bungalow units, dining rooms, bar, discotheque "Unicorn del Mar," 3 pools, water sports. Package 1-day tour, transfers, lunch.

PISCO. *Paracas*, a luxury hotel, privately owned, on the south coast near Pisco, a few hours drive down the Pan American Highway from Lima. Moderate.

FURTHER SOUTH

South of Lima there are *Hotel de Turistas* at Ica, Nazca, Camana, Arequipa, Moquegua and Tacna, near the border with Chile. Rates vary but run moderate to inexpensive. These hotels are especially recommended.

EAST OF LIMA

TARMA. *Hotel de Turista*, on the eastern slope of the Andes, 5–6 hours drive up the Central Highway. Pleasant, with tennis courts, swimming pool. Inexpensive.

CUZCO. *Marriott Libertador. Luxury.* Built around a restored colonial mansion. Others are the *Hotel de Turistas* (ENTURPERU), in the center of town with a fine lounge with log fire, and the *Savoy*, not near center of town, but with good food.

Continental, San Agustín, Ollanta, a short walk from the Plaza, *Cusi,* are good choices. The *Virrey* is small, no restaurant. All are moderate to inexpensive.

Also: *Espinar.* Behind the Turistas Hotel, half a block from Plaza de Armas. All rooms carpeted and with private bath. No elevator. *Garcilaso.* Occupies part of the former home of the well-known chronicler of the Incas, Inca Garcilaso de la Vega. Large carpeted rooms with private bath. Both are inexpensive. In addition, there are several bed-and-breakfast type pensions, including *Leonardo's Lodgings,* Av. Pardo 820, which are run by Americans or other foreign residents.

MACHU PICCHU. *Turista* at Machu Picchu. Moderate prices. New one under construction. Cuzco-Machu Picchu, 68 miles. Daily train service. Suggestion: arrange your complete Cuzco-Machu Picchu tour well in advance.

AREQUIPA. *Internacional,* under Marriott administration, is to open in late 1976. *Presidente,* new Pierola 201, *Turistas,* Selva Alegre Park, *Sucre,* Calle Sucre 207, *Crismar,* 107 Moral, good downtown location, are all inexpensive.

IQUITOS. Best is *Turistas,* 70 rooms, some air conditioned. Splendid view of Amazon. *Imperial, Olímpico,* and *Ambassador.* Clean. All moderate.

Jungle Lodge on Rio Napo, run by Amazon Explorers, is in the heart of the Yagua Indian country. 10 rooms, no private bath. First class, meals included.

Explorama Lodge, 40 beds. Rates on request. *Amazon Lodge,* an hour downstream from Iquitos, has 14 twin rooms, 7 baths. Moderate, meals included. Yagua and Jivaro Indian tribes on 750-acre property. All inclusive tours available for $60 per night per person. Special group rates. Call Jorge Milberg, managing director, at 31-2022, Lima. Group rates available.

 RESTAURANTS. Seafood is the favorite on the coast of Peru—shrimp, clams, crabs, oysters, scallops, flounder, *lenguado* (sole bass), *corvina,* swordfish, *pez espada.* There are also good dishes composed of the more unusual squid, sea urchins or octopus. A recent regulation forbids the buying of beef for the first 15 days of each month. However, a choice of lamb, veal, pork and poultry is on all menus during such periods. Tipping is not necessary, since ten percent of the check goes to the waiter, who deserves and expects 5 to 8 percent additional tip if service is efficient. Recommended eating places include the following:

LIMA AND ENVIRONS

Tambo de Oro is a deluxe restaurant and international market in a restored colonial mansion. Five dining rooms, cocktail lounge. Very expensive.

La Chasse a la Licorne, adjoining the Unicorn discotheque (same owner), is in San Isidro. All mirror decor, excellent cuisine, very expensive.

Las Trece Monedas, 536 Ancash, an old colonial mansion where the food is good but prices high.

The best French food in Peru is found at *St. Tropez,* in San Isidro. Expensive. *Café de France,* in Lima, is more moderate.

Acquarium Room, at the

Country Club, San Isidro, has excellent cuisine, also a dance orchestra.

Hotel Crillon has a good grill downstairs, plus the excellent Sky Room. Buffet lunch served on 21st floor terrace Jan. to April.

Meson la Ronda, near the bull ring, *El Huerto de mi Amada* and *La Palizada*, in Miraflores, for Peruvian cuisine. *The Grill* at the Hotel Bolivar. *El Cortijo*, across from Hotel Bolivar, good steaks, chicken.

Chalan, Avda. Lima Tambo 3091. Peruvian dishes and creole show.

La Toscana, Jirón Cuzco, Magdalena del Mar and *Machu Picchu*, San Isidro. Peruvian dishes.

Rincon Bolivariano, Santa Rosa 285. Pueblo Libre. Special regional dishes.

Try *Chalet Suisse*, *Suizo*, *Taberna Alemana* or *Rincon Toni*, good German and Swiss food; excellent and inexpensive.

At San Isidro try *Todo Fresco*, *La Caleta* and *La Barca*. Excellent seafood restaurants. $20–$25 for two.

For charcoal grilled chicken, exotic drinks and attractive surroundings, try *La Granja Azul* of Chosica Highway, off km. 17.

Ebony 56, restaurant, cocktail lounge. Las Begonias 730, San Isidro.

Key Club, in San Isidro. Specializes in steaks and lobster. Fair to expensive. *La Caleta*, across the street from El Chalan in San Isidro, excellent airconditioned seafood restaurant. Expensive.

Las Papas Fritas. In La Colmena. Very inexpensive ($1.50 for 3 courses).

Carlín, *El Hipopotamo*, *El Periplo* (good 1900s atmosphere), and *El Bled* (Arabian food), in Miraflores. All excellent.

El Sombrero in San Isidro. 360° view of Lima, but expensive.

CUZCO

Both the *Savoy* and *Turistas* have restaurants (Savoy reputedly better). Service is poor in both. If you like roasted chicken, take a taxi to the *Balkan*, Av. Garcilaso 221. *Country Club*, Av. la Cultura and *Quinta Sarade*, typical local food. *El Bucaro*. Modern. Half-block from Temple of the Sun; 3 blocks from Plaza de Armas. International cuisine.

ORIENTAL FOOD

Peru is noted for its Chinese restaurants. Some of the best include: *Yut Kung*, in Lima; *Lung Fung*, in San Isidro; and *El Pacifico*, in Miraflores. For Japanese food try *The Mikasa* (Mi Casa) in San Isidro.

 NIGHTLIFE. Social life of the Peruvians centers mainly around the family at home. There are few nightclubs in the capital. Movies are most popular, as is the National Symphony Orchestra and Theater. Chief entertainments are the gay religious and national fiestas. Best nightclubs are the *Grill Bolivar* (see Hotel Bolivar), open from 9 p.m. for dinner and dancing, a society nightclub with two orchestras and floorshows; the *Sky Room*, in the Hotel Crillon, another attractive society nightclub, open for dinner and dancing, expensive; the *Embassy Club*, Carabaya 815, for Peruvian international shows. *El Chalan* in San Isidro specializes in creole music and floor show and creole food. Other night clubs with floor shows are *Lido's Club* above the *Chalan*; Grill Tabaris, Colmena 611, and *La Fontana*, Colmena 457, Lima. Other night spots, mostly discotheques, include, in San Isidro: *Charlie's*,

Ebony Sicodelico, Jumbo 747; Johann Sebastian Bar, in Miraflores with classical music; *Black Out*, Lince; *El Escarabajo*, and the *Palmero*. The best discotheque in town is *The Unicorn*, for members only, but invitation can be arranged through your airline or tour operator. *Sea-Going Unicorn Discotheque*, at Santa Maria Beach, about 20 mins. from Lima, is open Dec.–Apr. *Hacienda Villa*, a 16th-century Jesuit convent converted into a colonial home, on the outskirts of Lima, is now open to the public. Lunch every day, dinner on Fridays and Saturdays. Sunday lunch has a $1–$2 cover charge which includes a cockfight and a turn at the bullring.

Theaters: *Teatro Municipal*, Opera House, Ica 355, tel. 28-2303, performances 7 and 10 p.m.; *Teatro Segura*, Huancavelica 250, tel. 27-7437); *Club de Teatro de Lima*, Nicolás de Piérola 757, tel. 27-8997, amateur theater, performances 7 and 10 p.m.; *Teatro La Cabana*, Parque de la Exposición, tel. 23-0449, amateur theater; *Corral de Comedias* in Miraflores and *Teatro Arequipa* in Lima presents plays and revues; *Auditorium*, Campo de Marte, Salaverry and Plaza Jorge Chávez, open air concerts at 6 p.m., Sundays, January to April.

Movies: Lima has many movies, including internationally known films from the U.S.A., Great Britain and Europe. Films start at 7 p.m. and 10 p.m. The following are the better known moviehouses in the city: Cine El Pacifico, Alcazar, San Felipe, Tacna, Metro, San Antonio and San Martin.

 SHOPPING. Shops in Lima are open from about 10:30 a.m. to 6 or 7 p.m. The number of good shops is limitless. In the four blocks between the Bolivar and Crillon Hotels stores will sell you alpaca wool sweaters, dolls, stuffed animals, Indian masks, alpaca and llama rugs, fur slippers and attractive reproductions in gold and silver of Inca jewelry. And you can get excellent buys at Porvenir Park or La Legua peoples' market. Any taxi driver will take you to the market in Avenida de la Marina for $1–$2 fare. The main streets for shopping are Jirón la Unión and La Colmena.

Lima shops are stocked with international fashions in clothes and with a full range of other standard goods. Of far more interest to the visitor are the silver and gold and antique shops and curio stores selling textiles worked by Indians on hand looms. Silver and gold are cheaper here than in most parts of the world. You will find the occasional piece of ornate colonial silver or jewelry with ancient Inca designs and motifs copied from old textiles or pottery. There are prolific displays of modern silver- and gold-work and leather-work with silver decoration. In the antique shops are colonial silver stirrups and spurs. The jungles of Peru supply many woods for tables, caskets and frames. Peruvians make particularly serviceable and beautiful long low tables, covered with leather. Indian baskets and carved gourds and cotton or wool textiles hang alongside soft rugs of alpaca and llama fur.

When traveling in the country wander through the local markets to see the products of local handicrafts, weaving, knitting, carving, gourd decoration and silver work. The Indian fairs at Huancayo and Cuzco are famous. The best buy in Cuzco is the famed alpaca rugs. The Co-op Shop here, opened with the aid of Peace Corps volunteers, offers a variety of handmade products at bargain prices.

Silver, gold and fine gems. *H. Stern*, in the Hotel Bolivar and Hotel Sheraton (ask for free local "charm" and free travel booklet). *Casa Mas*, Unión 814 and at La Colmena. *Old-Cuzco*, Unión 835. *Welsch S.A.*, Unión 498. *Siam*, Cajamarca 559. *Camusso*, Benavides 679, Lima, silver factory, and Las Magnolias 788, San Isidro. *Peruvian*

Handicraft, next to Museum of Anthropology and Archeology in Pueblo Libre. *Vierlinger*, on Plaza de Armas, Lima has original, modern designs in Peruvian silver and gems. Also *Vasco's* in San Isidro.

Leather Goods. *Pedro P. Díaz*, Unión 315, Lima.

Rugs. *Casa Mas*, Jirón de la Unión 814.

Book stores. *Internacional*, Jirón Unión—Boza 892. *Mejia Baca*, Jirón Azángaro 722. *Librerias A.B.C.*, Hotel Bolivar, Ocoña, in the building El Pacifico, Av. *Diagonal*, Miraflores, and in "Todos" shopping center, San Isidro.

Food markets. Hours 6:30 a.m.-4 p.m. *Mercado Central*, 650 Huallaga, Lima. *Mercado Mayorista*, 400 Aviacón Av., La Victoria. *Mercado de Surquillo*, Alameda Ricardo Palma. Miraflores food market. (Watch cameras and pocketbooks.)

Beauty shops. *Elizabeth Arden Salon* in Todos Shopping Center, San Isidro and Sheraton Hotel. *Helena Rubinstein*, Alcanfores 393, Miraflores. *Robert*, Moquegua 346. Salons also in principal hotels.

MUSEUMS. Most are open 9 a.m.–12 noon, 3 p.m.–6 p.m. from April to December; January to April 1st 9 a.m. until 5 p.m. throughout—closed Mon. In or near Lima are: *Museum of Art*, (a must!), Paseo Colón. *Museum of Anthropology and Archeology*, Plaza Bolivar. *Museum of the Republic*, Plaza Bolivar. *Museo de la Cultura Peruana*, 650 Alfonso Ugarte Ave. *Museum of Viceroyalty*, Quinta de Presa (Colonial mansion). *Museum of Natural History*. Arenales Ave. *Museum of Italian Art*, Paseo de la República. *Museum of the Church of San Francisco*. *Religious Art Museum*, located in the Cathedral of Lima, exhibits religious works of art accumulated during three and a half centuries of colonial history. English speaking guides available. Open daily 10–1 and 2–6 p.m. Admission: $1, students 50¢.

Art Galleries. Museums of Reproductions, Abancay Av. Art Center, 246 Alameda Ricardo Palma, Miraflores. Artes Manuales, 805 Unión St.

Private Collections (which may be visited): Rafael Larco Herrera Museum (ceramics, highly recommended). Pedro de Osma Coll. (colonial paintings). Lavalle Collection (sculpture and Cuzcanian paintings). Casa de la Tradición (colonial patio). Sr. Mujica Gallo's *Gold of Peru* collection is now on permanent display in his residence in Monterrico. Also see his Arms collection. Hunting Pavilion, living room of his home, is seen only by appointment. Admission prices range from 50¢ to $1. Elsa Cohen's Gold Collection, Larraburrey Inanue 392, Lima. *Museo Amano*, Av. Angamos 11th block, San Isidro. 7xceptional collection of ceramics and textiles.

SPORTS. For sports and recreation Peru offers an all-year-round climate like that of California. In these conditions sport thrives.

Local people follow with typical Latin fervor the fortunes of their *soccer*, *basketball* or *volleyball* teams. *Polo* is played at weekends at Lima Polo and Hunt Club at Monterrico, 20 min. from center of Lima, June through Dec. In summer at Villa Country Club and Club Hipico Peruano, Feb. 1 through April 31 at 4:30 p.m. Sat. and Sun. *Boxing* matches are held at Luna Park, the National Stadium, in the Paseo de la República.

Bullfights with Spanish and Mexican matadores are traditionally held Saturday and Sunday, Oct. 15 to Nov. 30, in what is known as the October Fair of El Señor de Los Milagros, when the purple Christ comes out for three processions. Minor bullfights are held during the year. If interested, ask your concierge.

Cockfighting, another bloodthirsty attraction, is held Mondays, Wednesdays, Fridays, Saturdays and Sundays at the Coliseo Sandia, Sandia 150 near the Parque Universitario. Also at Pachacamac and Hacienda Villa, 20 minutes south of Lima, usually weekends between July and September.

November to May are the best months for *bathing* at the resorts of Ancón, La Punta, Miraflores, La Herradura, Chorrillos outside Lima. In the same season the *sulphur baths* near Ica are fashionable.

Golf and *tennis* facilities are excellent in Lima and suburbs. The finest course is Lima Golf Club, near the Country Club.

Horse Races are held at Lima's course on Saturday and Sunday afternoons and Thursday and Friday nights.

Riding is most popular in the mountain valleys such as the country round Huancayo in Central Peru. Good mounts may be had for sightseeing trips at nominal charges. *Receptour* can arrange for several hours horseback riding including car transportation for $15.

Duck shooting is excellent at Lake Junin in the season. The lake is twelve hours by rail from Lima at 13,000 feet.

Mountaineering. For the very energetic there are many unconquered and challenging peaks in the Andean range, some of the highest in the Americas; of these the Huascarán was climbed first by an American woman. Clubs with information on the best mountaineering areas and the local conditions are: Club Andinista Cordillera Blanca; Club Andino Peruano; Club Peruana de Alta Montaña; Club Andinista Urubamba; Club Andino Oyón.

Surfing. The beaches of Lima rank alongside the best in Hawaii or California for surfing. World tournaments are held periodically in Peru. Boards may be hired and introductions to Waikiki Club can be easily obtained from your airline.

 FISHING. Swordfish and marlin world records are held from Cabo Blanco, 750 miles from Lima, and there is good sea fishing offshore from Chorrillos, Pucusana (43 miles from Lima), and Ancón. Flounder, sole and submarine fishing off neighboring rocky beaches. Trout and salmon may be taken in Lake Titicaca and in Conococha, 194 miles from Lima, in the Llanganuco lagoons and in these rivers near Lima: Santa Eulalia (31 miles), Chillón (50 miles) and Cañete (84 miles).

Hunting. The best spots for pigeon are at Surco and Chancay, for partridge at Matucana and Caltan. Wild duck are numerous at Piura, Chiclayo, Atahuanca, San Felipe, Camaná, Sorococha and Lake Junín. Deer, vizcacha, hare, puma and bear will be found in the mountains.

Sports in the North. Tarucas, vizcachas and bears are found over 11,000 feet on the Cordillera Blanca and Cordillera Negra in the Callejon de Huaylas. Doves and partridges can generally be found. Trout and pejerrey are in large and small tributaries of the Santa River, and especially where the Santa River starts near Conococha lagoon.

For those not at all energetic we advise a small investment in the Lima-Callao lottery which is drawn fortnightly for high money prizes. The lottery is government controlled and proceeds go to national charities.

FAUNA AND FLORA. The animals, birds and plants of Peru depend, of course, on the geographical environment of the three regions of coastal desert, high sierra, and the jungle which segregate the different species very distinctly from one another.

There are few animals living in the desert, just rodents and armadillos. Otters live in the streams. There are some owls, vultures and other birds of prey.

Offshore it is a different story. Here the cool Humboldt Current is alive with fish, anchovies, cod, haddock, mackerel, sole, flounder, smelt, shrimp, lobster. Seals and whales live in this part of the Pacific. Living on the fish are thousands of birds, gulls, cormorants, boobies, terns, pelicans and penguins which flock on the islands offshore and contribute piles of white droppings which as guano fertilizer was once the mainstay of Peru's economy.

In the sierra, the animals are either fur or wool covered: the llama, alpaca, guanaco, vicuña, chinchilla, sheep. Temperate zone bird life thrives at this altitude and you will notice the robin, flycatchers, phoebes, finges, migrant duck and geese, partridges and the great Andean condor.

Animals of the jungle become too numerous to list. It is an animal paradise and all the old favorites may be seen. We say "may" because although the jungle is alive with wild life it is not always visible. The lucky will catch a glimpse of monkeys playing or the flash of a parrot or macaw.

It is very easy to describe the desert region since there is virtually no vegetation, just diminutive, lonely cacti.

In the sierra, wattle and eucalyptus gum trees grow sparsely amid the coarse grasses which give way to mosses and lichens in the higher altitude. In some of the deeper warmer valleys cactus is prolific, along with bamboo and thorn trees.

The jungle is just jungle, a matted green tangle of hundreds of different trees, wild rubber, mahogany, hard woods, soft woods, growing in great profusion and inaccessible stands draped with liana creepers. Orchids hide away in cracks on the trunks and branches.

 PHOTOGRAPHIC HINTS. The air is generally clear and bright in Peru, encouraging photography and helping you to obtain excellent results. But pay close attention to your light meter: the sun and glare and sand or snow can be misleading.

INTERNATIONAL MAIL, telegraph and telephone service is good; the leading hotels have mail service and telex, telegram and international telephone service.

 USEFUL ADDRESSES. U.S. Embassy, corner Av. Wilson & España; British Embassy, Plaza Washington, in Lima; Canadian Embassy, Libertad 132, in Miraflores.

The *International Association for Medical Assistance for Travelers* (*IAMAT*), British American Hospital, Lima. *South American Travel Org.* (*SATO*), Av. Arequipa 340, 6th floor, Lima.

AMERICAN EXPRESS AGENTS: *Arequipa*, Lima Tours S.A., General Moran 122; *Cuzco*, Lima Tours S.A., Heladeros 167; *Lima*, Lima Tours S.A., Ocona 160.

BOLIVIA

Highest Land of the Andes

BY

HENRY LEE

(*Mr. Lee is a roving, free-lance foreign correspondent in South America, contributing to several newspapers and magazines. Previously, he was a U.S. foreign service officer in Latin America for eight years.*)

Bolivia is a country of superlatives. It has the highest navigable lake in the world, the highest airport, the highest golf course, the highest ski run, the highest capital, one of the newest and wildest frontiers, one of the oldest ruins, and what is said to be the highest concentration of cosmic rays on earth. Bolivia is also a nation of contrasts, which led a French explorer-scientist to call it the "microcosm of our planet." It has every type of geologically classified land, many types of people, flora, fauna, minerals, and tropical products. Here one can view a wide range of human development—both living and dead. There are the ruins of an early, great civilization; there are live, primitive Indians with their bows and arrows.

To focus on Bolivia's diverse land it is best to start with the inland sea of Lake Titicaca (12,500 feet) and work east. The nation is developing economically and socially in that direction, much as the United States pushed its frontier westward.

Lake Titicaca is a major western boundary between Bolivia and Peru. Almost two miles in the air and stretching some 3,500 square miles, this deep (700 feet in places), clear body of water sprouts a reed that greatly influences the life of nearby inhabitants. The traditionally suspicious Aymara Indians fashion these reeds together into exceptionally strong canoes from which they land the abundant trout that sometimes weigh up to 37 pounds. These reeds also become floating and inhabited islands. The pliable but durable material breaks loose from lake beds and joins with other matter gradually to form living space for Indian tribes whose pottery alone separates them from the Stone Age. This reed is also used for building simple furniture, for feeding livestock and for making other useful products.

Lake Titicaca rests on the "altiplano" (high plane), shaped by the Andes mountain range that hunches along the West Coast of South America and slices southeastward through Bolivia. This two-pronged mountain range has formed between its peaks a rambling plain about 85 miles wide and 520 miles long that cuts through southeast Peru and southwest Bolivia. About 40,000 square miles of this bleak, cold, treeless and windswept plateau lies in Bolivia. However hostile this 30 percent of the nation's land is, it supports 62 percent of the population and houses the major cities.

Most of the inhabitants are Aymara Indians, who cluster along the few streams draining into Lake Titicaca. In the major mining centers are found many "mestizos" or "cholos" (mixed Indian and white) and European whites. The otherwise impoverished altiplano is streaked with vast deposits of tin, copper, silver, tungsten, lead, zinc, and other minerals.

For centuries the Aymara Indians have clung to this hostile land and have generally resisted efforts to be resettled on the more fertile soil that abounds elsewhere in the country. Their diet consists mostly of potatoes and a vegetable called "oca." They also grow a couple of nutritious cereals, one of which is converted into an intoxicating brew called "chicha." Drunk intemperately at festivals, it affords a brief escape from an otherwise painful environment and shields them from a world they have come to distrust. Indian festivals reveal a mixture of enforced Catholicism and deep-seated paganism; their pagan heritage bursts through the veneer of this adopted religion and manifests itself in their strange and drunken behavior.

The animal life on the altiplano is more understandable. It includes the wool-bearing sheep, llama, alpaca, and vicuna, along with the fur-bearing chinchilla and red fox. The fabled vicuna was once killed before shearing. This beautiful and delicate animal still survives, and today Bolivia is the only country in South America where you can still obtain vicuna fur and wool articles at very reasonable prices. The manufacture and export of clothes and handicrafts made from these wools are developing as important national industries.

After two years' study and with good possibilities already established, a big drilling campaign is starting on the High Plateau searching for oil. They have already found natural gas. The proximity of the High Plateau to the Pacific Ocean harbor will enable the oil to be exported easily.

At the edge of this altiplano, La Paz is encased in a basin at an altitude of about 12,400 feet. The discomfort of the thin air is more than repaid by the majestic beauty of the snow-capped mountains that encircle La Paz. Four of these peaks reach above 20,000 feet.

Spotted along the high mountain shelf southeast of La Paz are several cities whose existence can only be justified by mineral wealth. Oruro is the first city along this high crest, standing at an altitude of 12,160 feet, and most of the community's 81,000 inhabitants are employed in mining. Further south is Potosi, which retains its colonial air and art treasures from an age when the nearby Cerro Rico (Rich Hill) Mountain was one of the first great discoveries of the Spanish conquerors and which pumped some $2 billion into the Spanish treasury. The city (pop. 53,000) is at 13,340 feet.

These and smaller cities are linked by a railroad from La Paz to Buenos Aires, routed along a fairly level plateau that stretches between the two capitals. Other rail lines at Oruro connect La Paz with Arica, Chile, and Cochabamba, Bolivia's second largest city with 100,000 people. Oruro is the hub of these rail lines. There are also rail connections with São Paulo and Buenos Aires via Santa Cruz.

Creased Valleys

From this high plane, the land spills off into lush semitropical valleys to the north and east. These valleys, called "yungas," are drained by the Beni River system, which then empties into the Amazon River. This land of present beauty and future development begins about three hours out of La Paz. The mean annual temperature of this healthy area is between 60.8 and 64.6 degrees, while the rainfall is between 27 and 31 inches yearly.

The soil of the altiplano washes into the basins of this region where citrus fruits, cattle and other products are raised, much of them going to La Paz. Eventually, widespread road building and river clearing will link this region with the rest of the nation. Altiplano Indians and others who formerly lived along the routes of these roads have to some extent already been resettled by colonization projects that are introducing many to the 20th century. These resettlement projects in the Beni area and elsewhere have proved that the usually suspicious altiplano Indians can be introduced to a productive life in the subtropical valleys below. These colonists are purchasing radios, bicycles, beer, and even refrigerators with money derived from the sale of cash crops.

A new route is under construction among the High Plateau consumer areas and the productive plain of Beni which will ensure the incorporation of this jungle area into the economic life of the country.

Cochabamba, Sucre, Tarija and Caranavi are the major population centers among these fertile valleys. As the center of a colonization area, Caranavi, about 150 miles north of La Paz, has grown from four huts to about 4,000 people. Cochabamba, with an average temperature of 64.6 degrees, 8,570 feet altitude, and eternal sunshine, is described as the best living area in Bolivia. Sucre, still the nation's legal capital, has retained much of its colonial color and republican charm at an elevation of 10,300 feet. The 18,000 inhabitants of Tarija are something special. Isolated, individualistic, cultured, European and deeply religious, they have not changed much since declaring themselves an independent republic in 1807.

These valleys spread out into the tropical lowlands that sweep from the Andes foothills in the north to the southeast near Argentina and Paraguay. With much of the land but few of the people, this area is said to be Bolivia's future. Most of the area is dense tropical forests, with some rough pasture, swamp and scrub in the center. Seasonal rainfall is high and the climate is usually hot, except when a cold, Antarctic-based wind from the southern steppes strikes in the tropical east around Santa Cruz. These annoyances are called "surazo," and they strike several times yearly for two or three days.

The northern part of these tropical lowlands was widely known in the 16th and 17th centuries. The Beni area provided Europe with excellent tropical fruits, nuts and dried beef. This area fell into decay after the Jesuit priests were expelled and the trails to the outside world disappeared.

An estimated ten million semiwild cattle are said to roam the Mojos plains of the Beni area. This and other untapped resources have moved the government to chart a development plan for the Beni. The key to this development will be the linking of new roads with old rivers, thus unlocking the area's gold, sugar cane, rice, citrus fruits, Rocky Mountain coffee and oil plants. Wild rubber is plentiful both in the Beni and Pando departments.

Trinidad, Beni capital, is the only significant city of the tropical north. Until recently the only contact its 30,000 people had with the outside world was by air. This community was an important farm center in the early colonial period; some of the city's crumbled ruins remain as mute testimony to its past. But, like the rest of the Beni area, it also seems to have a future.

The Human Assortment

Bolivia's people are about as diverse as its geography. The latest census estimate claims the population to be about 5,150,000. About 75 percent of the population are Indians, 20 percent mestizo, and 5 percent white. Socially, the population is in ferment. The once stilted social structure of the nation was destroyed by the 1952 social revolution that took political control from a small white oligarchy and passed it to an Indian majority, under white and mestizo middle-class leadership. Indians are now called peasants and no longer bow or tip their hats when passing white people. Many former cholos and market vendors are apparently forming a new middle class; while labor leaders, top military leaders, and the bureaucracy are forming a new elite. Most of the old aristocracy and many of the middle class left Bolivia in the wake of the revolution's turmoil. Some of these are returning now, making their peace with the revolution or joining the opposition.

This composition of the population changes from west to east. Almost all the inhabitants around Lake Titicaca are Aymara Indians, whereas more than half in the La Paz area are Indians (mostly Aymara), and approximately half of the valley people are either mestizo or white; the other valley inhabitants are generally Quechua Indians. According to available reports, those in the tropical lowlands are mostly white, but close observation discloses that the sun or some other force has darkened the complexion of many.

This population pattern, like many other things in Bolivia, is changing. Altiplano Indians are being successfully resettled in colonization projects in the rich subtropical valleys below. These resettlement projects have succeeded sufficiently for foreign observers to come here to study the program's techniques in solving a problem that has persisted throughout world history. Anthropologists have noted that the Indians, before impervious to change, now discard some indigenous ways, adopt western dress, extend their diet and consumption habits and become somewhat sophisticated.

Bolivia's unique geography and population have shaped its distracted history, determined its depressed economy and fashioned its distinct culture. This nation, which only recently joined the 20th century, still confronts sweeping changes that shape an uncertain future. But in all its political turmoil and social change, there are indications this harried nation may in the future harness its geography, develop its people, exploit its resources, shape its national destiny and write its own history.

Much History, Little Success

Historians usually raise the curtain on Bolivia's tortured history at Tiahuanaco about A.D. 600, although dissenting conclusions date back as far as 7,000 B.C. The Aymara Indians had developed a lesser civilization early at this location between La Paz and the southern end of Lake Titicaca, but the second one was influenced by the Nazca and Chimu civilizations of Peru, and from these mixtures a truly great civilization emerged. It was characterized by great buildings, massive monuments, ornate textiles, skillful pottery and attractive metalwork.

This flowering civilization began to wither for some unknown reason. When the Quechua-speaking soldiers of the great Inca Empire of Cuzco conquered the area about A.D. 1,200, they found the Aymaras about their decaying but still impressive ruins. The Incas held all Bolivia until the arrival of the Spanish conquerors with new plans for the region.

In 1535 Diego de Almagro, Francisco Pizarro's partner in conquest, found a site near what is now Oruro. Then four years later Pedro Anzurez found a place later named Charcas (Sucre), which became the Audiencia de Charcas under the Vice Royalty of Peru in 1559.

But Bolivia's destiny was shaped in 1545, with the discovery of Potosi and the shadowing mountain of silver: "Cerro Rico." This find stirred great interest back in Spain and inspired a splendor at Potosi that rivaled the pretentious display of Lima. As the vast reserves of silver were shoveled out of the Cerro Rico Mountain, a Crown mint established locally converted the metal into coins for shipment to Spain.

While the Spanish took much out of Bolivia, they put little back in it. Metal ores were largely to shape Bolivia's unfortunate future, in which the Spanish treasury was filled by the labor of impressed Indians who were worked under the most inhuman conditions imaginable. The nation was to be described as a "beggar sitting on a throne of gold."

The well-organized social system of the Inca conquest was destroyed by Spanish oppression. Indians were pushed off fertile plains onto infertile mountainsides, or they were incorporated into a peonage system that bordered on human slavery. Spanish colonial officials took over the best lands and lived in relative luxury. Creoles, Spanish born in the Americas, also lived fairly well but resented their exclusion from high appointive offices dispensed back in Spain.

These and the mestizos were the first persons in Latin America to sound the cry for liberty from Spanish rule. The first revolt broke out at La Paz in 1661, followed by another at Cochabamba in 1730. Then the Bolivian Indians began fighting for their freedom—something that distinguished them from many other Indians and a characteristic that dominates their activity today. They revolted at Sucre, Cochabamba, La Paz and Oruro between 1776 and 1880. They held La Paz for several days in 1780 but were defeated when besieging Sucre.

The Audiencia de Charcas was turned over to the Vice Royalty of Buenos Aires (River Plate area) in 1776, which meant little in the light of the condition of transportation and communication. General Sucre, one of Bolivar's top leaders, liberated the country at the Battle of Tumulsa on April 2, 1825. After Sucre set up Bolivia as an independent nation and departed, his top general took over and proclaimed a Peruvian-Bolivian confederation in 1836. General Santa Cruz was defeated by several neighbors three years later and the confederation was dismembered.

Independence did little for the people of Bolivia, only switched political control of the nation from one greedy group to another. Instead of packing the treasury of the Spanish Crown, the new creole rulers stuffed their European bank accounts and lived lavishly from the profits of the vast but ill-used mineral wealth. Bolivia was a republic, but it was not a nation.

For about 146 years after independence, 145 revolutions seated an assortment of presidents with generally the same results: bad government. Few were educated; fewer were leaders. When elections were held, the oligarchy would arrange for the election of a weak and pliable front man. "Why, if I had known Enrique (Penaranda, 1940–43) would be president," his mother was jestingly quoted as saying, "I would have sent him to school."

Weak governments made Bolivia vulnerable to the aggressive designs of neighbors. Several border disputes have dominated the nation's history, subtracted one-fourth its territory and left it a land-locked country. Several incidents seemed to work in a pattern —a neighbor would grab a piece of Bolivian territory, then build the loser a railroad. So, Bolivia ended up with several disjointed railroads and without its most useful land. When Chile beat Bolivia and Peru in the War of the Pacific (1879–83) and took Bolivia's Pacific Coast area, the victor built a railroad from La Paz to Arica. When Argentina annexed some of the Chaco area, it too built the loser a railroad connecting the two nations. When Brazil annexed the rich Acre area in 1903, it promised a railroad (not yet completed). In the Chaco War with Paraguay (1933–35), Bolivia had to surrender a large area without the benefit of a railroad.

But this war was to influence Bolivia's future greatly. Stunned by an embarrassing defeat, young officers and indignant intellectuals began examining the nation's conscience and prescribing solutions. The result was the formation of the National Revolutionary Movement (MNR) that gained power in 1952 and launched the first fundamental reforms in the nation's history.

Social Revolution

Two events have symbolized this revolution and help explain the troubled nature of Bolivia's contemporary history. Returning from the Chaco War with an understanding of the world beyond their immediate misery, some Indian veterans began thinking about the lot of their people and ways to change it. Several veterans in the Cliza Valley, near Cochabamba, organized their fellow Indian peasants into a union and began joint efforts to build a school. When union members tried to buy this land they had tilled for generations, the planters responded by flooding the valley and destroying the humble homes. Like-minded miners at Catavi on the altiplano fared even worse. "Hundreds" were shot down by government troops while striking in 1942 for better wages and improved working conditions.

Cliza Valley and Catavi became symbols in Bolivia's contemporary history. The peasants and the miners emerged from the social revolution as the two strongest political forces, each armed and functioning as a militia because the traditional army had been destroyed in the 1952 revolution.

The peasants (151,434 family heads have been given land titles under the revolution's agrarian reform program) have tended to support the moderate MNR majority behind ex-President Victor Paz Estenssoro, who served two presidential terms before being deposed in an Army revolt on November 4, 1964. But the miners threw their support to the party's leftist sector directed by Juan Lechin, who had undertaken a number of government and political posts, including the vice presidency. This sector has supported excessive labor demands that have occasionally brought the nation's economy to the brink of disaster and incited political turmoil.

Following the 1964 coup, the MNR served little purpose, not even as a functioning opposition party. But within its ranks it has about five so-called sectors that function in at least one case as a distinct and aggressive political party of the opposition. The party's leftist sector has its own registration, membership cards, and organization (national, departmental, and provisional). Also, there is a wide assortment of ineffective opposition parties, extending from the extreme right to extreme left. The still strong Nazi influence in Bolivia is reflected by the American National Socialist Organization. The Bolivian Socialist Falange looked like it might at one time discard violent revolution and develop as an opposition force, but it, too, split into two sectors. The Authentic Revolutionary Party was organized by Walter Guevara Arce, after he split with the MNR. To the left of MNR are the small Christian Democratic Party, the loud but weak Communist Party, and the

Workers Revolutionary Party, the second largest Trotskyite party in the world and which has also split into four sectors.

A new government under Air Force General Rene Barrientos, elected President in 1966, struggled with the vast political problems of incorporating the Indian majority into the national society and economy. Gen. Barrientos died in a helicopter accident in May 1969, and Dr. Siles Salinas, his Vice-President, took his place. He was displaced by Gen. Ovando Candia in a revolution in September 1969. Gen. Ovando nationalized the Bolivian Gulf Co. and tried several social and economic reforms, with little success. Ovando was in turn displaced by a revolution on October 3, 1970, in which Bolivia changed presidents five times in a single day. General J. J. Torres became President. In only one year he practically destroyed the economy of the country. On August 20, 1971, the Bolivian army with the Falange Socialista Boliviana and Movimiento Nacionalista Revolucionario forced J. J. Torres to escape. The new President, Col. Hugo Banzer Suarez, formed a new Government with these two political forces, the army and 3 representatives of private enterprise. They are struggling to rebuild the prestige and economy of the country. In March 1972 they defeated the remaining guerrillas.

A new tourist policy is trying to open this country to visitors, and changes have been made in investment laws to draw foreign capital.

At the present time Bolivia has a military government in which no political party participates. The most Bolivians hope for is that the long-awaited program of development will be well under way in a few years' time.

Tin is Bolivia's Gold

Bolivia is still statistically a one-crop country of tin. Ninety-two percent of its exports of $76,122,723 in 1963 involved minerals, and 80 percent of these was tin. Farm products involved only 5.8 percent of these exports, and petroleum another 1.91, while the nation's essentially agricultural character remained obvious with manufactured exports at an insignificant 0.08 percent.

While Bolivia was producing these export items, it was importing machinery, manufactured goods and other items valued at $90,261,990. This imbalance of some $14 million reveals that the nation was consuming more than it was producing. Most of this gap was filled by the U.S foreign aid program. This program, which has been pumping about $40 million yearly into the nation's economy, is expected to put it in the black in the next five years

This will result mainly from diversifying what remains an essentially one-crop economy and exploiting the new wealth of the eastern frontier. Current figures already indicate this direction of the economy, which now only provides about $99 a person yearly.

To understand the importance of these increases, one should consider that in 1948 Bolivia imported 80 percent of the food it consumed. Some 10.5 percent of all foreign exchange earnings were spent on imports of sugar and rice. Surpluses in these products were expected in 1963, providing increased consumption and possible increased exports. Although some current textbooks still list sugar, rice and wool as major imports, Bolivia is now seeking markets for these products.

Bolivia's various plans for economic development indicate the direction it is trying to go. When the Alliance for Progress prescribed that each participant draft a 10-year social and economic development plan, Bolivia already had one. But this plan was found to be a little rich for the nation's financial resources; so its planners had to revise the plan to conform with what it might reasonably expect to do within the next ten years.

Bolivia was provided $80 million of Alliance funds for this small plan, which will fit into a larger 10-year one. This money will be spent for highway, education, irrigation, energy, mining, farming, housing, public works and public health projects.

Highways will link most areas of the nation in this ten-year span, or they will be under construction. Irrigation projects are to open 35,520 square acres of land, and new marketing facilities will be provided for increasing farm surpluses. One of the nation's most severe problems will be aided with adequate energy for consuming centers and the construction of two hydroelectric dams. Suitable water supplies are scheduled for La Paz, Cochabama, Oruro, Sucre and Santa Cruz. Mining is to be improved with the search for new reserves, metallurgical studies, modern machinery and reduced production costs. Health is to be improved by better prenatal care, dental hygiene, occupational hygiene (especially among miners) and the construction of six hospitals and three clinics.

Food and Drink

Bolivian food is not only distinctive but good. The most popular national food is the *empanada salteña*, a mixture of ground or diced meat, chicken, olives, raisins, diced potatoes, hot sauce and pepper, packed inside dough and baked into a crusty handful about the size of a hotdog. As one travels eastward in Bolivia, the *lomo montado* (mounted steak) is found increasingly on the menu. It is fried tenderloin with two fried eggs on top, rice and fried banana. A popular chicken plate is *picante de pollo*, southern fried chicken with fried potatoes, rice, tossed salad with hot peppers and an odd item called *chuno*, which is a dried potato. Young roast pig is, of course, fairly universal, but in Bolivia it is called *lechon al horno* and accorded special attention at important festivals.

For reasons of good health, tourists should avoid green salads and any water not known to be boiled or filtered. Mineral water and bottled drinks are available in restaurants, and filtered water may be requested at the hotels for use in the room.

EXPLORING BOLIVIA

Many people agree that Bolivia has about the greatest unexploited tourist resources in the world. But those pondering a visit there should underline the word "unexploited" and recognize that any comfortable contact with many of the nation's wonders must await considerably more development. The government is at present diverting the bulk of its limited capital to other sectors of the economy rather than concentrating on tourism. Therefore the exacting traveler is liable to be limited to a several-day visit to the La Paz area, and the cities of Cochabamba, Sucre and Potosi.

To get oriented with the complex La Paz street arrangement, one might use as a check point the wide double roadway on both sides of a grassed promenade, called the Prado or 16th of July Street. This main artery with a couple other names extends in both directions and touches or nears many of the capital's major sites. The tourist usually moves uphill from this point.

The best place to start a city tour is up several steep blocks at the Plaza Murillo. Surrounding the park are the presidential palace, legislative palace and cathedral. The two stonelike soldiers on 24-hour guard by the plaza stand by a lamp post that is one of Bolivia's more important monuments and symbolizes its tortured political history. President Gualberto Villarroel was lynched by a mob in 1946 and strung from this historic lamp post. He is considered one of the early leaders of the once powerful MNR Party. The House of Culture, with its relics from past Indian cultures and exhibits of present savage tribes, and several other attractions are found near this plaza. Down three steep blocks from the plaza, Avenida Camacho runs horizontally through the center of the shopping district. This street to the left intersects Avenida Bolivar at a block-size Indian market; the market, which sells fruits and vegetables, rests on the edge of a river that flows through downtown La Paz but is visible only at this point.

The tourist is now one block from the Prado. To appreciate all the Prado has to offer, it is best to go above the street to the big Indian market that stretches over several square blocks and probably contains more contraband goods per square foot than any area of the world. One should note the intelligent, aggressive, cruel and independent characteristics of the matriarchal market women. Their shrewd business practices enable them to help support their often inferior husbands (frequently common law) and send their children (often illegitimate) to school. Some social scientists feel that these women will emerge from Bolivia's social revolution as an essential element of the middle class.

When one of these market women went to the American Consulate, with her now famous bowler hat, to apply for a visa to visit the U.S., she was asked the customary question about a financial guarantee that she would not become a public charge. She pulled from under her several lavish petticoats a $20,000 roll of bills.

The merchandizing ability of these women is now recognized by the more sophisticated merchants of La Paz. These merchants are now said to be opening booths at the market and copying some of the techniques of these women. And these merchants report better spenders, bigger profits and lower overhead at these market stalls.

These Amazon-type women can also be skillful in warfare. They played the second most important role in the successful revolution of April 1952, which has shaped Bolivia's contemporary history. According to the plan of rebellion, especially selected market women went to strategic guard posts the first night of the revolution and offered themselves to pliable army guards. As the awkward guard would lay aside his rifle, he found himself disarmed instead of being loved. The market women would then take over the guard post.

From this market, one should re-enter the Prado (here called Mariscal Santa Cruz) as he travels back down into the center of the city. At Plaza Venezuela, the San Francisco church and monastery, built in the 16th century, still stand and are open to the public. Continuing down the Prado, one passes an equestrian statue of Simon Bolivar, several restaurants, clubs, hotels and government buildings and then reaches the tall and modern building of the University of San Andres. The National Museum can be reached by turning off the Prado at the Copacabana Hotel to Calle Don Bosco 93. The nightclubs, bars and theaters are also concentrated in this area.

Visitors are welcome at the university. Like other Latin universities, San Andres is a center of stormy political life, and it gives the visitor an opportunity to see the important function of the university in Latin life.

You can also visit the open-air museum, the collection of Tiahuanaco Arts and the Witch Doctor's Market. Visits to native dancing and music shows can be arranged for Fridays or Saturdays.

The sportsman may wish to go above La Paz to Mount Chacaltaya. Here is the highest ski-lift in the world at 17,860 feet (check beforehand if it is operating), with a ski lodge at 17,250 feet. In the same trip, one could golf at Mallasilla, where the rarified atmosphere enables one to get over 300 yards with his drives.

LA PAZ

□ Hotel ● Public Building ⊛ Cinema ★ Airline ▶ Embassy
✠ Church ✳ Museum/Theater/Market etc ■ Other item

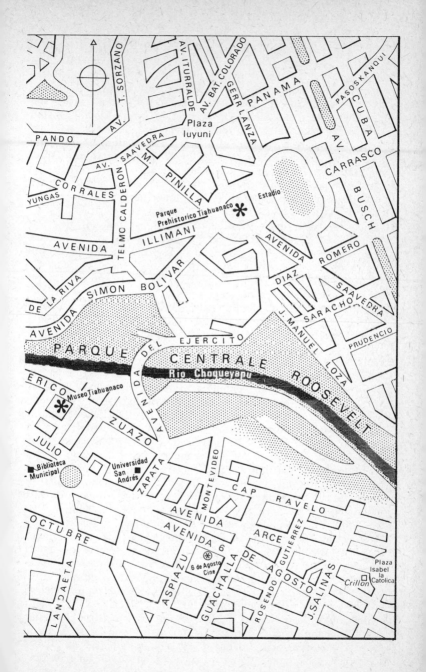

The Inland Sea

The first distant trip out of La Paz is apt to be Lake Titicaca. It is possible to do the lake area in a day and thus avoid the necessity of overnighting in a less than desirable hotel. Reaching the yacht club at Huatajata, one sees modern yachts and the famous reed boats that have come to symbolize this inland sea of deep blue water (up to 700 feet) and 51-degree weather. Then one usually travels about a mile by boat along the Tiquina Strait, that divides a small lake from the larger one. Thirty miles beyond the strait is Copacabana, a religious shrine that attracts many pilgrims to the famous cathedral and a special devotion to the Blessed Virgin. This town lies on an impressive bay.

Lake Titicaca offers what is described as some of the best trout fishing available, with catches ranging up to 37 pounds. Duck hunting is another attraction. Try the highest hydrofoil ride in the world on two-and-a-half-mile-high Lake Titicaca. Or have a picnic lunch on the Islands of the Sun and the Moon which, according to legend, gave rise to the Inca empire. Visitors may observe natives building the famous Lake Titicaca reed boats by 1000-year-old methods at Titicaca shipyards on Suriqui Island. Two native families of Suriqui Island were taken to Egypt to build the famous raft "RA II" used in an expedition led by Thor Heyerdahl to cross the Atlantic Ocean. A reproduction of this raft, built by the same families, is shown on the Island, and Crillon Tours Ltd. operates tours by hydrofoil. Another reproduction has been built in the hydrofoil harbor of Huatajata.

Tiahuanaco warrants a whole day if one has the slightest interest in archeology or human history. Located 49 miles from town on the road to the lake, the excavations have already uncovered several square blocks of ancient wonders. The exact date of this civilization is still being debated by scientists, but one of them holds it to be the cradle of American man dating back to 7,000 B.C. Anyway, the excavations have thus far uncovered vast monuments, aqueducts, temples and the impressive "Gateway to the Sun." These buildings were fashioned together in interesting geometrical designs with stones weighing up to 100 tons without the benefit of any cementing material. While these advanced Indians did not work with iron or other hard metals, they made attractive copper and tin tools which would carve granite.

A big attraction in the La Paz area is the subtropical valleys that thread Bolivia's high mountains into tropical lowlands. This trip through the so-called Yungas is sort of like a roller-coaster ride through various climates, topography and scenery. You leave 12,400-foot high La Paz, cross a mountain pass at 16,500 feet, then wind your way down a valley to an altitude of only 4,000 feet. This two-mile descent covers 60 miles of road in about three hours, depending upon your chauffeur's regard for life. A half-hour out of La Paz, you are in the midst of snowfall. After an hour, a new world begins to unfold with verdant plantations of cocoa, bananas, fruits and an especially high grade coffee called Rocky Mountain. Waterfalls and many hues of flowers make their contributions along this scenic route. Fishermen will find big and plentiful trout in the local mountain streams.

One can crowd this trip into a long day. If spread out over two days, there are adequate tourist hotels in the area's main communities of Coroico and Chulumani. Most tourists seem to prefer overnighting at Coroico, but there is now a new hotel on the road between these two towns, the San Antonio, which charges $18 a day each, with meals.

Instead of returning to La Paz, the stout-hearted and outdoor-minded may wish to continue to Caranavi, about another two hours northwards into the tropical lowlands, for camping, hunting and fishing. In the rivers and lands that fan out from Caranavi (the Alto Beny and Kikive area) are found animals, birds and fish that populate one of the great reservoirs for sportsmen. This game must be classified by the non-professional in universal terms, but there are some unique differences between Bolivian game and those accorded the same name elsewhere.

There is a large variety of fish, from really big ones to the tiny, carnivorous piranha, no more than a foot long but able with a few confederates to devour any other species in a few seconds. These tropical rivers also feature crocodiles up to 20 feet long.

The hunter can have just as much fun as the fisherman. There are 14-point deer, jaguar, ocelot, wild boar, ant eater, water wolf or londra, wildcat and flag bear up to seven feet long. Even the cattle tend to be wild in this tropical area of Bolivia; an estimated million head of wild or semiwild cattle are said to roam the Beni area of the north.

Bolivia's game birds and bird life are difficult to catalogue, for some have obviously remained unclassified by scientists. The conventional ducks and geese abound in many of the lakes and rivers. What can be regarded as marsh hens and rooster-size partridge are found in the same places. The tropical area of Bolivia, covering about 65 percent of the country, has many smaller types of game birds. All the birds are extremely fast in flight.

There is no season for shooting or worry over limits on catches. Bolivia has so much wild game, there are not apt to be any restrictions for many years ahead. Bolivia has the problem of pushing back its frontier eastward, and tourists, hunters and fishermen can only help in that direction for the time being.

Safaris can now be arranged in northern Bolivia. These are

usually based in Trinidad, capital of the Beni Department, which was famous in the early colonial era and still functions as a jumping-off spot to northern frontier outposts. In these safaris, the hunter is even equipped with a bow and arrow, along with an Indian staff including drums and hunt callers.

Primitive Indian Life

If one happens to be interested in primitive Indian life, it can be found further north in the Pando and Beni deparmtents. Some of these tribes are extremely primitive, but civilization— be it curse or cure—is pursuing them relentlessly. A young Maryknoll missionary priest organized a band of primitive Brazil nut gatherers several years ago into a producers' cooperative. Now 116 former savage Indian families have a business with capital equipment valued at $125,000 along with the best credit rating in the nation. Since these Indians are now relatively rich, they are getting ready to go to school and undertake other sophisticated habits of Western man that might be expected of primitive capitalists.

Returning to La Paz, the tourist can decide whether he wants to see more of Bolivia. Actually, he would probably thus far have seen only the usual tourist sites around La Paz and the unusual tourist attractions farther north. The Bolivia of the past and future still lies ahead in all its charm and challenge.

Bolivia is moving eastward today, politically, economically and socially, much as the U.S. moved westward. This development becomes apparent as one travels from La Paz eastward along the altiplano and through all the old historical strongholds. This eastward journey is a story in nation development, the story of how a tin-based economy is being switched to the development of tropical agriculture. It is the story of how roads are uniting a country and shaping its economy—how a nation after some 400 years of inept colonial exploitation and unhappy republican rule is at last acquiring a political consciousness and becoming a nation.

Oruro, a mining center 130 miles southeast of La Paz, is also a railroad hub. The only tourist attraction here is the dance and ceremony performed during the Devil's Festival on the Saturday before Ash Wednesday. This involves an elaborately costumed "bear" and "condor" clearing the way for a parade of equally costumed dancers. These are led by alternate twosomes of Satan and Lucifer and St. Michael the Archangel and China Supay, the Devil's wife and sexual stimulant. After a leaping and shouting parade through town, the participants crowd into the main plaza and perform dramatic rituals in which virtue, like hero over villain, prevails over sin. A mining theme is woven into the drama, in which the costumes represent a major portion of one's wealth.

The Catavi tin complex, about two hours by car from Oruro, has some historical significance and remains an emotional political symbol. It was here that several hundreds of tin miners were shot down in 1942 while on strike. This scene has come to symbolize labor as a strong political force in the social revolution and has at times stirred it to excessive economic demands. Visitors can enter the mines. If one gets into one of the communist labor leader's office, he will see on the wall pictures of Fidel Castro and Patrice Lumumba, the slain Congo leader.

Trains at Oruro connect with international trains to Buenos Aires, Argentina, and Antofagasta, Chile. A branch line continues eastward to Cochabamba, about eight hours and 127 miles away.

Cochabamba is still a city of beauty, eternal spring and sunshine, but it has been caught in the cross fire of Bolivia's political turmoil and economic change. Once the prosperous center of a rich and vast area of plantation agriculture, the social revolution's land reform program has sent many of the old planters into exile or other livelihoods, divided up the big and absentee-owned plantations among peasants and diverted other peasants to colonization projects in Eastern Bolivia. Some of the old ornate residences are falling into disrepair, and the once ornate drinking club for upper-class men has become tattered. The most important tourist attraction is the townhouse of Tin Baron Simon Patiño, which has been converted into a museum. The usual market here has the additional attraction of local Indian women with their unusual stove-pipelike hats. Newly-discovered ruins at Incallajta, about 65 miles from Cochabamba, will soon be open for tourists.

Potosi is nine and a half hours southward by train from Cochabamba over one of the world's highest railroads, reaching an altitude of 15,809 feet at the junction of Condor. One of the first great cities of the Americas with a population of about 150,000 early in the 17th century, Potosi has retained much of its colonial charm. Twisting, narrow streets pass aging mansions with colonial coats of arms, reminding one that this busy agricultural and mining center was once a majestic city. The city remains in the shadow of "Cerro Rico," which pumped so much silver into the Spanish treasury in the early colonial period and which now stands like a jilted mistress. "Real Casa de Moneda" (Royal Mint), built in 1522 and rebuilt in 1759, still stands but has been converted into a museum. Some of the old homes and churches house oil paintings of considerable merit. Some 30 churches reflect good examples of Renaissance or Romanesque architecture.

Sucre is still the big oddity of Bolivia. This city, 109 miles

northeast from Potosi, is the legal capital of the nation, but the
Supreme Court Building is the only vestige of what now unof-
ficially belongs to La Paz. La Paz became the "de facto" capital
in the wake of the mining boom. Some, however, feel that
tropical agriculture might lead Santa Cruz to do to La Paz what
La Paz did to Sucre. This historic city has an interesting display
of buildings of both the colonial and republican eras. Many
Latin American revolutionary leaders studied here at the second oldest university in Latin America. Isolation has been something of a blessing, preserving for Sucre what modernity might
have destroyed. Now the jet age has arrived, and the new airport
is open to flights by Lloyd Aereo Boliviano jets.

Island City

All these communities are joined by railroad. The only way to
get to another important community, Tarija, in the southeast of
these upland cities, is by a difficult road near the Argentine border
or by LAB. This settlement in the rich Guadalquivir River valley
was founded in 1574 and has since remained an isolated island
apart from the rest of Bolivia. Thus cut off, the people have grown
a variety of fine crops for their own consumption, developed an
individualism that has made them as much Argentine as Bolivian,
produced a supply of skillful farm hands for Argentine agriculture
and formed a pocket of advanced culture apart from the rest of
the nation.

Returning to Cochabamba, one can continue eastward into
the interior of the nation or take a river trip north to Trinidad.
This latter trip would involve traveling 120 miles by road to
Puerto Chipiriri, on a branch of the large Rio Grande. The boat
trip up this river to Trinidad would consume four days, and
the tourist could later fly back to La Paz or any other part of
Bolivia. The alternative of continuing eastward on the Cochabamba-Santa Cruz Highway opens several interesting possibilities.

The 315-mile Cochabamba-Santa Cruz Highway demonstrates
what 20th-century communication can do for a nation isolated
in the 19th century. This highway, completed in 1954 after
nine years of construction and a $50 million U.S. Export-Import
Bank loan, actually united a nation that was falling apart and
shaped an economy that was in serious trouble. There was a
strong secession movement in Santa Cruz to join Brazil. Similar
feelings were sweeping Tarija and several other communities.
But this highway helped to turn the nation's development
inward instead of outward. Unintegrated Indians began settling
in colonies and mixing with others along this road; soon, they
found themselves feeling like Bolivians instead of Indians. The
development of other roads had the same effect.

This Cochabamba-Santa Cruz Highway winds through the
Cliza Valley, where the first important modern political move-

ment among Indians began. Spurred by the 1952 social revolution, an Indian peasant union in the valley community of Ucurena demanded that a planter return land to peasants who had been evicted in the 1930s for union activity. When the planter stalled, these Indians began a march on nearby towns, and for a while civil war between rural and urban groups hovered over the nation. Politics are still tense in this valley that someday might symbolize the political awakening of Indians in Latin America.

Continuing east, the traveler can forget politics and take up geology. In the next 300 miles he will travel through all four of the classified geological areas. First, he will experience the tundra area of the valleys, with its many flowers but no trees. Then the rain forest is entered, with its mosses, ferns and damp, humid climate. Next, the desert with pipe-organ cactus, much sand and little grass. Finally, near Santa Cruz, the tropical jungle breaks out in towering and verdant growth.

"This 311-mile trip is like traveling from Ecuador to Alaska," one geologist remarked after traveling over the road and examining its specimens "Here one finds every flora zone."

Arriving at the frontier community of Santa Cruz, one can decide whether he wants more frontier or would prefer to return to La Paz. There is no tourist attraction on the road northward, only an area undergoing rapid economic growth with cattle and tropical farming and intense social change with colonization projects. If a highway survey party cuts a small path through this jungle, colonists will line it immediately and begin tilling its fertile soil. This area is truly a laboratory for economic growth and social development. The center for this area's development is Santa Cruz.

There is still plenty of unexplored frontier in Bolivia. A tourist can travel from Santa Cruz to Corumba, Brazil, by railroad and see unfurled before him the beauty of the tropics, the smell of the jungle and birdlife that at times seems to etch a rainbow in the sky. Over this 406-mile railroad, one passes villages populated by former savages, some of whom have become civilized only in the past decade. Until several years ago, uncivilized cousins of these residents occasionally attacked the communities with bow and arrow. Now the savages have disappeared further into the jungle brush to avert what they consider the annoyance of modern civilization.

They may have to keep moving if this area keeps on getting more civilized and joins the industrial revolution.

Trees and Birds

This would destroy a lot of beautiful bird life. Mahogany trees here spread skyward in majestic dimensions. These trees house what appear to be communities of many-hued birds. At times several duplexes or two-room bird dwellings can be seen dangling from a single limb. Sometimes a tree will enfold as many as 50 bird nests.

These birds often have several colors arrayed in attractive patterns. When they fly in formations against the late afternoon sky, they give you something to remember. The many types of parrots (some very talkative) often fly in groups, whereas the many big-beaked toucans usually fly in pairs.

Another interesting tree in the area is a cotton tree, that reaches some 100 feet upward and sprouts a bulb of cottonlike material as large as a cantaloupe and which can be used for making cloth. There is an abundance of other flora that—with the fauna—makes this, the heartland of a continent, something beautiful to see.

In the mid part of the train ride from Santa Cruz to Corumba, an unusual type of topography stretches over about 10 miles. Beautiful mountains rise like polished stones abruptly from what is otherwise level jungleland. These small, stonelike mountains near San Jose have several colors, which, reflected by the noon-day sun, provide another-world atmosphere.

Upon reaching Corumba, on the Paraguay River, one can take a steamer down the river to Asuncion, Paraguay, or Buenos Aires. By entering Bolivia by rail from Arica, the traveler therefore could continue crossing the continent overland by following the route outlined above. It's rough but rewarding.

PRACTICAL INFORMATION FOR BOLIVIA

CAPSULE COMMENTS. *Physical Features.* Landlocked Bolivia is a country of dramatic contrasts. The high plateau of western Bolivia, called the altiplano, is one of the world's highest populated regions, with several towns above 14,000 feet. Lake Titicaca is the world's highest navigable body of water. The remainder of the country is hot, humid low plains of luxuriant tropical vegetation and wide-open cattle ranges.

Climate. Normally very pleasant, dry, sunny weather prevails in La Paz and the surrounding highlands. Visitors often find La Paz uncomfortable at first because of the oxygen-thin air of its 12,200-foot elevation; a few days of acclimatization are often needed. December, January and February are the rainy months in La Paz. The eastern plains range from temperate, to hot and then to steamy, as one enters the lowlands.

Population. 5,150,000. La Paz 800,000.

Language. Spanish.

Archeological Attractions. Tiahuanaco, Islands of the Sun and Moon, in Lake Titicaca.

Principal Industries. Tin, silver, copper, lead, rice, coffee, cacao, rubber, oil, gas, meat, wood, cotton.

WHAT WILL IT COST? Bolivia has the least inflation of any South American country, and by 1976 no change is expected in the 1975 prices. There is free money exchange (no red tape) and what some call "fabulous" shopping, described as "several good souvenirs for US $30 or $40."

A TYPICAL DAY IN BOLIVIA

A breakdown of the average tourist's expenses in La Paz for a day and night (exchange rates *approx.*):

First Class Hotel (one person in double room)	$13.00
Three Meals (including service)	20.00
Four Taxi Rides	.50
Two Drinks (Pisco Sours)	2.00
Theater Ticket (Reserved Seat)	1.50
Movie	.60
City Sightseeing Tour	10.00
Laundry (Shirt)	.50
Dry Clean Suit	2.00 (Dress $1.00)
Pack of American Cigarettes	.50
	$51.60

WHEN TO COME? The best time to visit the capital of La Paz is in the dry season from March through November, when the sun seldom fades in the daytime and snow-capped mountains frame the distant landscape. But Bolivia has four different climatic zones. Average temperature on the altiplano is 55 degrees, and it is usually damp except in the western part from May to December. In the high valleys leading from the altiplano the average temperature is 66 degrees. In the lower valley it is an average of 75 degrees with occasional rain. In the tropical lowlands of the north and east, the average temperature is 85 degrees and rainfall is scattered throughout the year, with heavy summer rains coming from November to March.

The major festival in Bolivia occurs at Oruro the Saturday before Ash Wednesday. The major theme of this festival, stirred by colorful costumes and ancient costumes, is the victory of virtue over evil, portrayed in dances by both individuals and groups. For others see: Festivals & Special Events.

FESTIVALS AND SPECIAL EVENTS. *Alacitas Handicraft Fair.* Alacitas, La Paz. January 23–28.
Carnival. Folk celebrations throughout Bolivia.
Reed boat regattas, Lake Titicaca, May.
Corpus Christi. Religious processions, folk dances everywhere. May-June.
San Pedro Fiesta. Religious procession, folk dances in La Paz. Raftmen celebrate in Bay of Tiquina, Lake Titicaca. June 29.
Fiesta of the Virgin of Carmen. Same day as Independence Movement, La Paz. Jul. 16. *Holidays of La Paz.* Native dances in La Paz and surroundings. Jul. 15–16.

Santiago. Religious celebrations in La Paz—notable in St. Francis Cathedral—and all of the "Altiplano". Particularly interesting in Guaqui and Laja villages. Processions, fireworks, native dances. July 25.

La Asuncion de Nuestra Señora Fiesta. All Bolivia. On same date, *Virgen de Las Nieves Fiesta.* Display of native dances in Sanctuary, Copacabana. August 5.

La Natividad de Nuestra Señora Fiesta. Fireworks, native dances, "Prestes" in St. Francis Cathedral, La Paz. Bullfights in Viacha. Sept. 8.

Nuestra Señora del Rosario Fiesta. Celebrated in La Paz, in suburbs Rosario and Visperas, with fireworks, rocketry; in Viacha with native dances, games, Oct. 1. *Founding of La Paz Celebration,* La Paz, Oct. 20.

 DOCUMENTS. Tourists can enter Bolivia with passport and tourist card instead of visa, plus smallpox certificate. Free tourist card is issued free by Bolivian consuls, carriers and tourist agencies, and it is good for 90 days with an extension available for another 90 days. This tourist card enables one to depart from the country without an exit permit or the necessity of reporting to police upon arrival. All other travelers arriving in Bolivia must present their passport and other documents to both the immigration and police authorities within 48 hours of arrival. Any agency will take care of this matter in less than an hour.

HOLIDAYS AND SPECIAL EVENTS. As in other Latin nations, public holidays are frequent.

Jan. 1—New Year's Day

Feb. 2—Copacabana—Virgin of Candelaria

Carnival Week—preceding Lent

Holy Week—3 days preceding Easter

May 1—Labor Day

May 2—Lake Titicaca—Reed and canoe regattas

Corpus Christi (not set)

June 23—St. John's Day

June 29—Day of St. Peter & Paul Tiquin. Regattas, folk dancing

July 15–16—La Paz Day; Feast of the Virgin del Carmen, La Paz. Patroness of Bolivia is honored

July 21—Martyrs' Day

July 25—Interesting religious processions, native dances in Santiago, Guaqui and Laja villages

Aug. 5—La Asuncion de Nuestra Senora Fiesta. All Bolivia

Aug. 5–7—Independence Festival —nationwide

Sept. 8—La Natividad de Nuestra Senora Fiesta. Fireworks, native dances, bullfights —La Paz

Oct. 12—Day of the Race

Nov. 1, 2—All Saints Day

Nov. 17–18—Festival of the Virgin of Amparo, Amparo

Dec. 8—Immaculate Conception Christmas

 **HOW TO REACH BOLIVIA.** From the U.S.: *Braniff International* (New York, Miami, Washington; Los Angeles via Lima); *Lufthansa* (New York); *Aerolineas Argentinas* (Miami via Lima); *Lloyd Aereo Boliviano* (Miami-La Paz). From Europe: *Lufthansa* (Frankfurt); *Iberia* (Madrid). Regional: *Lloyd Aereo Boliviano* (Lima, Buenos Aires, São Paulo and within Bolivia); *Lufthansa* (Bogotá, Lima, Santiago); *Iberia* (Bogotá, Lima, Quito, Santiago); *Braniff* (Buenos Aires,

Guayaquil, Lima, Panama); *Aerolineas Argentinas* (Buenos Aires). *Cruzeiro do Sul*, from Bolivia to eastern center of Santa Cruz, on Mondays and Thursdays. *Lineas Aeras Paraquayas* from Asunción to Santa Cruz. Airport departure tax: $5. By hydrofoil from Puno, Peru.

But travel to Bolivia is especially conducive to mixing a little land travel with your air travel or even to going all the way by land or water. A favorite mode of traveling to La Paz is the air-rail-lake steamer trip from Lima with a stop-off at Cuzco or by modern hydrofoil across Lake Titicaca. Another little-known but very interesting way is to take one of the several good passenger liners to the port of Arica, Chile. A train leaves from Arica at 8 p.m., Nov.–Mar., Tues. and Thurs.; other months on Wed., traveling up the Andes and then over the altiplano to the capital city of Bolivia. This 10-hour trip in a railway bus is comfortable. One can also make an eastern approach from Rio de Janeiro by rail or air, then take the rough, two-day train ride from Curumba, Brazil, to Santa Cruz. Instead of this, a party of travelers might wish to rent a railroad automotive vehicle which will cover the 406 miles in about 16 hours. The cost, $200, with room for eight.

It is possible to reach the land-locked republic of Bolivia by water. This involves traveling up the Amazon and Madeira rivers. Rapids on the Madeira require a detour by rail before reaching the Mamore River that connects Bolivia's three major river systems. This mode of travel would open many possibilities for adventure through the continent's heartland.

CUSTOMS. Tourists may bring in canned food, camping equipment, 100 cigarettes or 25 cigars, 1 qt. liquor and other essentials for hunting and fishing duty free. The legal measure for the quantity of duty-free goods of this nature is weighed by the needs for the individuals involved and their plans. A camera, typewriter and similar articles may also be brought.

CURRENCY. Happily for travelers, the clumsy Bolivian currency was changed in 1965, with a new Bolivian peso (20 Bs for US $1) replacing the boliviano (worth about .005 of a cent). The effect of this new currency was to cut three zeros off the old, inflated currency and spare one the annoyance of taking a bulging pocket of money out for the day's needs. Exchanging foreign currencies involves few problems.

Spanish is the legal language, although perhaps the first language of a majority is either Quechua or Aymara. Hotel clerks and those engaged in the tourist business usually speak English. The casual tourist should not find any problem in not speaking Spanish.

WHAT TO SEE? There is much to see in Bolivia, and most tourists will not wish to appropriate much time to see even a small part of the offerings. Consequently, the problem of seeing is one of choice and selection. Starting from the altiplano, the first must is the Tiahuanaco ruins near Lake Titicaca, then the Islands of the Moon and the Sun on the world's highest navigable lake. In La Paz there are several museums, colorful Indian markets, historical monuments, and shops for items like wood carvings, costume jewelry and wool handicrafts. The markets are especially interesting since most of the merchandise is contraband, and the vendors are organized into a union called the "Union of Commercial Smugglers." However high La Paz is, the tourist can go up or down. He can experience exotic sports or see scientific experiments on high mountain peaks above the capital, or he can go down into the subtropical valleys below and enjoy a quiet beauty encased between high mountains. He can continue northward and experience some of the most interesting hunting and fishing in the world. Or he can go further east and find a region in ferment that may become the heartland of South America.

HOW TO GET ABOUT. *Lloyd Aereo Boliviano* connects every major urban center of the nation. This airline has improved its service within Bolivia and now provides adequate air transportation throughout the whole country. A 12-hour train ride connects La Paz with Cochabamba, passing through Oruro and other interesting places and providing uncomfortable travel but adequate for those who don't mind. Over 2,000 miles of railway link La Paz to Santa Cruz and several interior cities. Service between La Paz and Arica sector is deluxe, equals best Chilean service. The railway-lake steamer service to La Paz from Mollendo (Southern Peru) is a hard 46-hour trip. A 411-mile surfaced road connects Cochabamba and Santa Cruz, and a gravel road is being pushed north of La Paz to Santa Ana in the Beni area. Other roads are under construction that will link three of Bolivia's major river systems, thus connecting isolated but interesting parts of the nation. A new paved road from La Paz to Lake Titicaca is due to open this year. There are several small railroad lines to tourist attractions or which can be linked with bus travel. Long bus trips are not recommended. For car rentals, try *Hertz*, in La Paz, or two local companies.

CLIMATE. One could encounter so many different climates in the La Paz area within one day that it would be impossible for the tourist-class traveler to confront such changes adequately. The thing to do is to improvise. One may begin a trip from La Paz to the Yungas, for example, by wearing a sweater and carrying a coat for the high altitude and cold weather encountered in rising over high mountains. Then as one descends into the valleys and subtropical climate below within hours, he will want to shed both sweater and coat and find himself comfortable in shirtsleeves. If one is going to fish or hunt, he will want to bring along clothes suitable for such activities in subtropical climate. If one is going to ski or golf in altitudes approaching 20,000 feet, then a unique combination of clothing is indicated. If one is going into the tropical areas of the north or east, he will find that old sports wear is suitable because such primitive areas are hard on clothing. Combat-type shoes are needed for the scrub and reptiles of the tropics. Only one generality can be used in discussing clothing requirements in Bolivia: clothing demands are generally informal socially, and the tourist is seldom apt to find a need for formal clothing. A dark suit or cocktail dress, however, may become useful if one is invited to a diplomatic or other social function.

The best advice that can be given the arriving tourist is to walk slowly and eat lightly the first day. Arriving at the hotel, the tourist should rest for at least 45 minutes. Any prolonged and intensive physical activity should be avoided for the next 24 hours, and normal food intake should be stepped up gradually from such light eating as soups and sandwiches. To cushion any altitude sickness, an oxygen tank or bag, headache pills and sleeping pills should be available just in case. Altitude sickness is apt to show itself in an intense headache and perhaps stomach cramps, as well as insomnia. However most of the larger tourist hotels provide oxygen and pills to relieve the effects of altitude, and an Alka Seltzer or "Coca Mate" will bring instant relief.

 HOTELS. Based on international standards, Bolivia has no first-class superior or deluxe hotels, though a new *Sheraton* (350 rooms and convention facilities for 2,500) is about to open in La Paz and in addition two or three smaller first-class hotels should be opening within a year. In Santa Cruz the *Holiday Inn* 'Los Tajibos' is considered one of the best hotels in South America, and there are several reasonable, moderate and inexpensive hotels in La Paz and Cochabamba, but the hotels elsewhere are fairly rudimentary.

Service charges and taxes amounting to 25% are added at all hotels. Rates are for room only, except where otherwise indicated. Our rating system runs like this: *First class*: $20 and up for single, $26 and up for doubles; *Moderate*: $8 up for singles, $10 up for doubles; *Inexpensive*: $5 and up for singles, $8 and up for doubles.

LA PAZ
First Class Superior

CRILLON. Nearest approach to a first-class hotel, 5 minutes by taxi from the center. Under American management. Rooftop restaurant, fine food, nightclub.

EL LIBERTADOR. Opened 1973. Centrally located. 72 double rooms and suites. TV. Dancing in Sky-Room.

LA PAZ. Near Central Sq. Redecorated, with all modern conveniences. Among the best.

SHERATON, see above.

First Class Moderate
COPACABANA. Conveniently located facing Paseo El Prado. Excellent views. Dining room, bar.

SUCRE. 16th of July Ave. Passé elegance. Some modern rooms.

ELSEWHERE

ORURO. Inexpensive *Prefectural* and *Oruro*.

COCHABAMBA . *Gran Hotel Ambassador*, on Calle España, is good, with gardens, pool, tennis courts. The *Capitol* downtown is modern and comfortable. Both inexpensive.

SANTA CRUZ. *Motel Los Tajibos* (Holiday Inn) is one of the best hotels in all Bolivia (250 rooms). First class superior. The *Drive In Motel* and *Posa del Bato* are very good hotels with all modern conveniences. Pool. Both moderate.

SUCRE. A new motel has twin-bedded rooms, private baths. In the beautiful El Parque region, four blocks from center. Moderate.

POTOSI. The Bolivian Government hotel, *IV Centenario*, offers guests single and double rooms with baths, reasonable prices and moderately priced meals.

PUNO AREA. *Turistas*, 74 beds. *Ferrocarril*, 40 beds; both inexpensive hotels with good facilities. *Tambo Titicaca*, located 12 miles from Puno on the shores of the lake. New and modern. All conveniences. 44 beds. *Turistas—Jiliaca*. New hotel with all modern conveniences. 90 beds.

Except for pensions, other hotels in Bolivia should be considered as camping out rather than good living. There are several pensions in La Paz, Cochabamba and Santa Cruz that will provide the tourist on a budget with a reasonable amount of comfort, inexpensively.

 RESTAURANTS. A meal in a very expensive restaurant will cost approximately U.S. $10; expensive: $6–$8; inexpensive: $3–$5. All five of the hotels in La Paz have quite good food. But a little research will usually disclose a nearby restaurant that is not operating on the basis that a few expense-account or per-diem people will always be around who do not care much about the quality of food and less about the price. You can often find some thrifty immigrant who has found out about what the tourist wants to eat and has done something about it.

All the La Paz restaurants patronized by tourists are a few steps from the *Copacabana* and *Sucre Palace* hotels. *Las Vegas* is a new luxurious rooftop restaurant with beautiful view. *Los Escudos Restaurant* in Club de la Paz building offers excellent food and folklore shows on Fridays. *The Grill of Hotel La Paz* is one of the best restaurants in La Paz, offering typical and international food. The *Crillon* has an excellent rooftop dining room with a good view and fine service. *The Lobo* is one of the best restaurants—and the one with the most pleasant atmosphere—in the lower part of La Paz.

La Tropera is a popular restaurant patronized by a young swinging local crowd. You select your own fresh vegetables and meat from skewers. The *Colonial* has typical food and a nice atmosphere.

The *Daiquiri* on 16th of July Street and its parrillada grill is popular with budget-minded tourists while the *Casa Espana* offers Spanish food. *Maxim's*, also in the Prado, serves international food in a comfortable atmosphere. Reasonable prices. *Restaurant Internacional* in H. Lapaz building and *Los Escudos* in the Club de la Paz building are good, modern.

A German family has captured the imagination of young, bargain-hunting American tourists room. The *Cafeteria Ely*, continuing down 16th of July Street with an American-style lunch (many Bolivian streets have two names and this one is also called the Prado), offers good ham and eggs, steak and French fries, hamburgers, soups, sandwiches and other such nonexotic dishes in a very clean, small corner lunchroom at unusually low prices. If no table is available, just seat yourself with someone else.

The food is adequate at the two Cochabamba hotels, and there is a good Chinese restaurant and a couple of acceptable restaurants. The food at the *Hong Kong*

Restaurant, Empalizada 81, Flor-esca, in Santa Cruz is excellent. William Cheung, its owner, offers 123 Chinese dishes of fantastic quality.

 NIGHTCLUBS. The tourist is not apt to think much about nightclubs upon arriving at La Paz, which has a nightlife that is somewhat different than elsewhere and does not get underway until about midnight. Instead of planning an evening on the town, the custom here is to drop by a nightclub after dinner or after a private party in some home. Those thus disposed usually find their way to the *Club* 21, near the Sucre Hotel, which features darkness. Activity at: *Max's Place,* popular nightclub; *Moulin Rouge,* good dancing place; *El Fogón,* the former *Don Pepe.* For striptease: *Maracaibo, Soraya* and *Special.* Ask your travel agent to arrange a program of folk music or dancing on Friday or Saturday in La Paz. The Bolivian folklore is now available on Fri. and Sat. at the *Peñas Folklóricas.* These shows start at 10 p.m. and offer 3 to 4 hours of native music.

There is little nightclub activity at the decaying city of Cochabamba but much more at the wild and booming city of Santa Cruz.

 MUSEUMS. Bolivia is better equipped with museums. The National Museum in La Paz is near the Pardo at Calle Don Bosco 93 and is really a reflection of the advanced arts and crafts of the ancient Tiahuanaco civilization. Styled in the noted Tiahuanaco architecture, this building provides a capsule study of what may have been one of the first great civilizations. Another museum, still under development and housed in the House of Culture, has recovered much from Bolivia's pre-Columbian development and the life of widespread primitive life still abundant in Northern Bolivia and still existing in patches in Eastern Bolivia. The Casa de Murillo is a typical and well-preserved colonial house that shows the paintings and furniture popular in that era. The original owner of this house was Pedro Domingo Murillo, who in 1809 headed a bloody but unsuccessful rebellion against Spanish authority. The Spanish executed him, and he became Bolivia's first great hero. The Tiahuanaco ruins, 49 miles from La Paz, are still being uncovered but provide an open museum that when completed may rival some of the world's great landmarks. Excavations are proceeding slowly because the director of the project is reported to wish that only Bolivian scientists be associated with the work. The only other museum worth seeing is the old home of Simon Patiño, the so-called tin baron, in Cochabamba, which has been converted into a museum by the University of Cochabamba. As for art, one can view colonial paintings at the Pinacoteca and at the same time see the house of the Marquis of Villaverde, where the Pinacoteca is housed. Occasional exhibits of paintings may also be seen at the Salon de Exposiciones.

 WHAT TO BUY. Bolivian handicrafts are coming into increasing demand as they find their way into the world market, and local production has increased and improved. It should be remembered that the ancient ancestors of these Indian craftsmen fashioned some of the first textiles and metalworks with remarkable dexterity. The most popular of the handicrafts among tourists are the alpaca sweaters, shawls, ski caps, woolen bolts, purses, native dolls, rugs. This fine and strong wool is woven into designs recaptured from the ancient arts of the Aymaras and improved with modern wool processing. For the best native handcraft try: *Titikaka Ltd.*, Sanches Lima 2320, La Paz. Tourists may now buy the famous vicuna fur, noted for its fineness and beauty. Gold and silver (both mined in considerable quantities in Bolivia) costume jewelry is considered a good buy, while an enquiring tourist might find something particularly interesting in silver and wood antiques. The latter are more apt to be found in Sucre and Potosi. Wood carvings, often symbolizing an Indian theme, are also considered good buys for tourists who have a little more space in their luggage. While the products can be bought throughout Bolivia, the tourist may want to consider better quality and prices in certain regions. Jewelry buys are better in La Paz, while alpaca and llama buys are better in Cochabamba, and wood carvings are better in Santa Cruz. The exceptionally hard mahogany wood in this area is almost like stone and makes very attractive wood carvings.

MAIL. Air mail service to and from Bolivia is good, compared to some other Latin American countries. Delivery can be expected in three or four days. Air mail service within Bolivia is adequate in view of the isolation of many of the areas serviced. No mail should be sent surface, either outside or inside the country. Surface mail from Lima to La Paz, for example, takes up to four months, if indeed, the mail reaches its destination. Braniff International operates a special mail service out of La Paz, accepting mail between 11 a.m. and 12 a.m. on flight days and delivering it the next day in the United States and perhaps a little later to Europe. Airmail to U.S.A.: 13¢.

TELEPHONE. Bolivia has no national telephone system, only patches of small, privately operated systems scattered about the larger communities of the nation. Long distance calls are difficult, and even local calls often leave a lot to be desired. The hotel switchboard operator usually has a long list of important and often-used local telephone numbers, so ask him to get you the number and thus save time and trouble. The local telephone directory is often outdated, and residences are generally listed under the owner rather than the occupant. Your patience may be tested in this process, for the hotel switchboard operator may leave your conversation hanging for a couple of minutes. This could mean that he is attending one of his other two or three jobs, or it may just mean that a friend dropped by.

However bad the service is at present, Bolivia may become the telecommunications hub of the continent. An American firm is making a feasibility study of an international communication link-up among several of the South American nations. This firm has thus far concluded that Santa Cruz may emerge as central to such a system in the next two years. The firm bases this development on the internal growth of the continent and the shifting of populations inward.

CABLES. Adequate cable service is available out of La Paz through West Coast Cables or All America Cables to all world points. It is always wise to ask for a copy of the cable if in English so the accuracy of non-English speaking punchers can be checked. Radio-telephone service out of La Paz is very difficult, while it is impossible to get a signal of broadcast quality. The tourist should remember that cable offices close at 11 p.m.

PHOTOGRAPHY. Bolivia perhaps has the most scenic variety of all the world for the photographer in a short span of time. Within five hours, the photographer can get Indians living on floating islands just outside the Stone Age, ancient ruins, 20,000-foot snow-capped mountain peaks, famous Indian markets and scenic subtropical valleys. The tourist can bring in duty free a camera, camera equipment and film. Because of the thin atmosphere and brilliant light he should close the aperture one stop below light meter readings. Ultra-violet filters are recommended for the plateau area. Consult a local camera shop.

TOURIST TIPS. Reading can become a useful pastime in La Paz, since the high altitude tires one faster than sea level. So one might find it useful to pack a couple of paperbacks for light reading. In the larger hotels are newsstands where all the popular English-language magazines and news magazines can be bought. The U.S. Information Agency supports a good English library in cultural centers established in La Paz, Cochabamba and Santa Cruz. These centers, called *Centro Boliviano-Norteamericano*, welcome visiting tourists.

Here are some miscellaneous hints: To the 25 percent service charge added to your hotel and restaurant bill, it is customary to add another five to 10 percent as a tip; 1–2 pesos per bag to porter.

In case of a medical emergency, there is a good American Clinic in La Paz with a Harvard-educated director.

In case of a citizenship problem, call the American Consulate in the American Embassy.

There is an American School (primary and secondary) of stateside standard, near La Paz.

There is a good barbershop and beauty salon in the Sucre Palace Hotel, Hotel La Paz and Hotel Crillon.

Sometimes a taxi driver will try to overcharge you, but it is less apt to occur here than anywhere else.

U.S. appliances may be plugged into the current at hotels which is generally 110 volts, 50 cycles A.C.—but check first, since 220 volts is also in use; also, certain U.S. items, such as record players, will not function well as the U.S. is on 60 cycles 110 volt current.

Business hours are usually from 9 a.m. to 12 p.m. or 12:30 p.m., and 2 to 6 p.m.

Crillon Tours Ltda. is a top tourist agency with a fleet of good cars, competent bilingual guides, fishing, camping and hunting equipment, own boats, etc. This agency operates the Hydrofoil on Lake Titicaca and offers a variety of package tours.

SPORTS. Bolivia abounds in exotic sports for adventurous people. One can *golf* at such altitudes that the rarified atmosphere makes drives of 300 yards common. Or *ski* in April, May, September and October at the highest run in the world, 18,000-foot Mt. Chacaltaya, just 30 miles out of La Paz. Bolivia's woodlands and streams offer the sportsman a great variety of *animal* and *fish* life. World record lake-trout *fishing* is drawing an increasing number of sport fishermen to Bolivia. Record 34-pound salmon trout was taken in Bolivian waters. *Big game hunting* in the wilds of Eastern Bolivia is now convenient because of new air taxi service. *Safaris* can be arranged to suit one's individual tastes for adventure, mostly in the area stretching north of Caranavi where even the cattle is often wild. *Mountain climbing* offers particular opportunities, and several mountain climbing expeditions come to Bolivia yearly. *Soccer*, and several other spectator sports, regularly scheduled at La Paz's Miraflores stadium.

 USEFUL ADDRESSES: *American Embassy*, Edificio Banco Popular, Calle Colon, Esquina Mercado. *British Embassy*, Avenida Arce No. 2732-2754. *Braniff Airlines*, Avenida Camacho 1245. *Bolivian Lloyd Airlines*, Avenida Camacho No. 45. *Crillon Tours*, Avenida Camacho 1223. *Exprinter*, Avenida Camacho, Edificio Krsul. *Direccion Nacional de Turismo*, Avenida Camacho (telephone 7521). *Lufthansa*, Avenida Mariscal Santa Cruz 1336. *Iberia*, Avenida 16 de Julio, Edificio Petrolero. *Ministrio de Immigracion*, Avenida Arce.

AMERICAN EXPRESS AGENTS: La Paz, *Crillon Tours Ltda.*, Avda. Camacho 1223.

CHILE

A Long and Friendly Land

(Editor's note: Political developments in Chile over the past few years have been—and are still—so controversial in many parts of the world that we have tried to avoid making any value judgments about the country's political life, past or present. Therefore, we have asked a long-time British resident of the country to describe what a visitor will find, and how he can expect to enjoy his stay. The comments expressed by the author, accordingly, must be considered as his own and are not necessarily the views of the editors and publishers of this book.)

Since September 11, 1973, Chile has been governed by a four-man military Junta, consisting of the commanders-in-chief of the army, navy, air force and carabineers. The army man, as senior general, has been named President of the Republic. In the government, ministries are fairly equally divided between civilians and serving or retired officers of the services. The key posts of Economy and Finance are held by civilians.

Visitors today will receive a warm welcome to an orderly country from Chileans of all levels, who are intensely patriotic and unceasing in their efforts to ensure that visitors share their opinion that Chile is the best country in the world. During 1976, 280,000 foreign tourists visited Chile.

An Isolated Country

Modern air travel has broken down the barriers which once isolated Chile from the rest of the world: the snow-capped Andes mountains on one side, and five thousand miles of Pacific Ocean on the other. The first European invaders were the Spanish "Conquistadores", by whom the purely Indian population was forced further and further south, fighting fiercely as they went.

SANTIAGO

0m 100 300 500 700

☐ Hotel ⬤ Public Building ★ Airline Office ■ Other Item
✚ Church ✳ Theater/Museum Etc ⚑ Embassy/Consulate ◯ Stadium

DAVILA
LASTRA
AVENIDA LA PAZ
SALAS
FERIA MUNICIPAL (Central Market)
RECOLETA
Recoleta-Franciscana
CALLE ANDRES BELLO
FLORIDA
AV.
ARTESANOS
Parque Recoleta
BELLAVISTA
AVENIDA SANTA
ESTACION MAPOCHO
RIO MAPOCHO
AVENIDA PRESIDENTE
JOSE MARIA
PARQUE VENEZUELA
MARIA
GRAL MACKENNA
BALMACEDA
CARO
Plaza Ecuador
SAN PABLO
PARQUE
ROSAS
PUENTE
ESMERALDA
SANTO DOMINGO
21 DE MAYO
MONJITAS
IVER
SAN MARTIN
AMUNATEGUI
TEATINOS
MORANDE
CATEDRAL
(P.O) Correo Central
MAC
MIRAFLORES
Santa Ana
Catedral
Sagrario
Plaza de Armas
ENRIQUE
CONGRESO Nacional
City
MERCED
COMPANIA
Tribunales de Justicia
Carlos V
Lehner
Splendid
Sao Paulo
La Merced
Panamericano
★ Braniff
ANTONIO
ESTADO
Gran Palace
Kent
Ritz
Santa Lucia
HUERFANOS
SONH
BANDERA
AHUMADA
San
★ LAN
Crillón
AGUSTINAS
San Agustin
✳ Teatro Municipal
Carrera
Plaza de la Constitución
Agustinas
MONEDA
MANUEL RODRIGUEZ
MONEDA
Palacio de La Moneda
NEW YORK
Claridge
El Conquistador
Biblioteca Nacional
Emperador
Windsor
✳ Museo Historico
Plaza de la Libertad
BERNARDO
O'HIGGINS
SANTA
ALAMEDA
Universidad de Chile
San Francisco
SAN FRANCISCO
ROSA
BERNARDO O'HIGGINS
Plaza Bulnes
ARTURO
SERRANO
NOVALLE
S. IGNACIO
Ld. COCHRANE
NATANIEL COX
ALONSO
SAN DIEGO
PRAT
San Vicente de Paul
TARAPACA

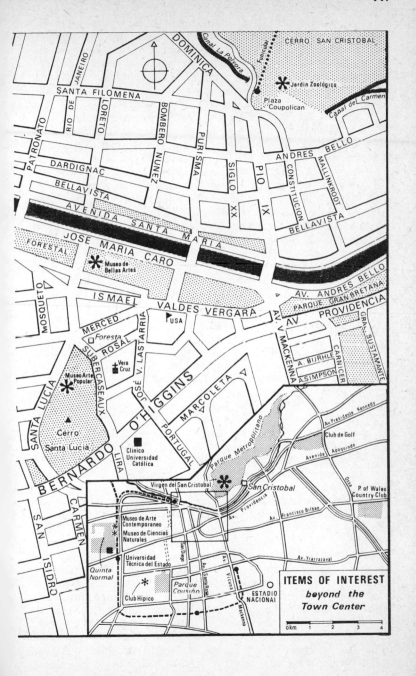

CERRO SAN CRISTOBAL

Canal La Polvora

DOMINICA

funicular

JANEIRO

* Jardin Zoológico

SANTA FILOMENA

Plaza
Coupolican

RIO DE
LORETO
PATRONATO

BOMBERO
NUNEZ
PURISMA

SIGLO
XX

PIO
IX

ANDRES BELLO

Canal del Carmen

DARDIGNAC

CONSTITUCION

MALLINKRODT

BELLAVISTA

BELLAVISTA

AVENIDA SANTA MARIA

FORESTAL

JOSE MARIA CARO

* Museo de
Bellas Artes

AV. ANDRES BELLO

ISMAEL

VALDES VERGARA

Parque GRAN BRETAÑA

AV.
MACKENNA

AV.

PROVIDENCIA

MOSQUETO

MERCED

Foresta

USA

GRAL. SUSTAMANTE

ROSAL

JOSÉ V. LASTARRIA

A. BURHLE

CARNICER

SUBERCASEAUX

Vera
Cruz

Museo Arte
Popular

A.SIMPSON

*

SANTA LUCIA

O'HIGGINS

PORTUGAL

MARCOLETA

Parque Metropolitano

Cerro
Santa Lucia

Parque Metropolitano

Av Presidente Kennedy

BERNARDO

LIRA

Clinico
Universidad
Católica

Virgen del San Cristobal

* San Cristobal

Club de Golf

Avenida Apoquindo

CARMEN

Museo de Arte
Contemporaneo

* Museo de Ciencias
Naturales

Av. Providencia

Av. Francisco Bilbao

Ossa

P. of Wales
Country Club

SAN
ISIDRO

Quinta
Normal

Universidad
Técnica del Estado

*

Club Hipico

Parque
Cousiño

San Diego

Av. Santa Rosa

Av. Vicuña

Av. Yrrarraval

ESTADIO
NACIONAL

Av. Yrarrazaval

MACKENNA

ITEMS OF INTEREST
beyond the
Town Center

0km   1   2   3   4

This fighting spirit of the Araucanian Indians most probably accounts for the fact that the majority of Chileans are of Spanish descent; in the early days few of the Chilean Indians intermarried with the Spanish, unlike the softer-natured Indians of Peru. Even today, although a quite notable Indian strain runs through some sectors of the working classes, mixed Spanish and Indian blood is rare in the middle and upper classes.

This is not the case with other races, however. In the battles for independence, the Chileans' leader was named O'Higgins, their navy was formed by Cochrane, and in recent years the biggest private bank was the Banco A. Edwards & Co. The last three presidents were Alessandri (Italian origin) and Frei (Swiss) and Allende's mother was named Gossens. Of the four members of today's military junta, one is named Pinochet and one Leigh. Thinking casually of Santiago shops and factories, the names of Küpfer, Graham, Haddad, Bercovich, Luchetti and Mackenzie come easily to mind. They are all Chileans.

It could be that this vast mixture of European races has something to do with the beauty and poise so often found in Chilean women. But you'll hear all about that from the Chileans.

A Long History—and a Short One

In the north of Chile not far from the great Chuquicamata copper mine, complete, organized villages of some pre-Inca civilization have been unearthed. But no record of who these people were survives. The Incas came later, extending down as far as central Chile and bringing their civilization with them. The native Chilean Indians, the Chango coastal race, the Araucanians, the Onas (the last living Ona died early in 1975) and the Alacalufes and Yaghans of the south were all of inferior civilization. It was the cooking fires of the Alacalufes that caused sailors to name the southern tip of Chile "Tierra del Fuego" (Land of Fire).

The first European to see Tierra del Fuego was Hernando de Magallanes (Magellan in English) who sailed in 1520 through the straits which today bear his name.

Around 1535, an expedition under Don Diego de Almagro started down from Cuzco in Peru on the inevitable Spanish search for gold and silver. He reached Santiago—after tramping heedlessly over the copper deposits which are Chile's mainstay today—and returned empty handed. A further optimist, Don Pedro de Valdivia, a captain under Pizarro, also led an expedition. He reached the central zone and in 1641 founded the city known as Santiago del Nuevo Extremo at the foot of a small hill called Huelen (pain) by the Indians. Today this hill is a park in the center of modern Santiago and is called the Santa Lucia

Hill. There for all to read is a stone facsimile of Pedro de Valdivia's letter to his king, praising this new territory and urging the king to send settlers.

His second expedition, in 1549, was aimed principally at suppressing the Araucanian Indians; but he was captured and, under the orders of Caupolican, their chief, put to death. An avenging mission under Garcia Hurtado de Mendoza fought its way much further south and in turn captured and executed Caupolican. A story of the Spaniards' war against the Indians is told in a famous poem "La Araucana" by Alfonso de Ercilla y Zuñoga.

Life under the rule of the Viceroyalty in Lima progressed slowly, developing a farming colony whose coast was forever at the mercy of raiding English and French pirates. Restive under this regime, the criollos (Spaniards born in Chile) began to long for independence, and their first Junta de Gobierno was formed on September 18, 1810, a date still celebrated in Chile as Independence Day.

When in the following year they nominated Jose Miguel Carrera president, the Viceroy could endure no more of their insolence and sent an army to crush the upstart "Chileans." Fighting continued until 1818 when an army under the Argentine general San Martin and Bernardo O'Higgins, won the final victory.

O'Higgins became Director Supreme, but he got into difficulties as ruler and finished his life in voluntary exile. He was succeeded by Ramón Freire; still the country remained divided and chaotic until around 1830, when Diego Portales won the battle that ended what was virtually civil war. Portales was shot in a military uprising in 1837, but his victory left Chile tranquil until 1879, a quiet broken only by Chile's brief alliance with Peru against the Spaniards, which led to the bombardment of Valparaiso, after due warning, by the Spanish Navy.

The Pacific War

For some time there had been wrangling with Bolivia over the rich guano deposits and later over the nitrate fields in the Atacama desert. Chileans began to work these deposits under the most grievous conditions and the burden of a ruinous tax. Threatened by Bolivia with embargo of the factories, the Chilean government took a hand, and in February 1879 their army landed at Antofagasta and captured the town. The War of the Pacific was on. Peru allied herself with Bolivia, and the fighting continued for four angry years, until Chile finally emerged victorious in 1883. Chile acquired the Bolivian provinces of Antofagasta and Tarapaca and the Peruvian provinces of Tacna and Arica. Chile later (1929) returned Tacna to Peru, but retained

Arica. The 1883 treaty cost Bolivia her sea coast; an outlet corridor is now being negotiated by Chile, Bolivia and Peru.

The nitrates brought great wealth to Chile but not political stability. In 1891 there was another civil war, this time between pro-Congress and propresidential factions. The former won, and the president (Balmaceda) committed suicide.

From then on, although presidents were occasionally removed forcibly, there was no serious warlike action until 1973 when the late Salvador Allende was dismissed by the combined action of the three armed forces and the Carabineros. Allende was elected by a bare plurality (36%) and his attempts to enforce wholesale expropriations of farms, commerce, industry and the banks were a failure. Economic and disciplinary chaos reigned, widespread strikes and street rioting racked the country; and after Congress had ruled the government illegal, the armed forces moved and took over control.

The Junta has brought order and econimic recovery, and presently legislates through decree-laws which undergo prior study by a Council of State which includes, among other dignitaries, all ex-presidents of Chile. Four constitutional acts have so far been promulgated, leading to a new constitution. Meantime, it seems that the Junta proposes to remain in power until Chile is completely stabilized, politically and economically.

The Economy Today

With 6,000 million tons of proven copper reserves, and five major, unworked deposits still not fully blocked out, it seems that Chile's installed capacity for producing 1,200,000 tons of copper annually will remain for some time the backbone of the economy. Nevertheless, in 1976 non-traditional, non-mineral exports increased to US$600 millions; and in spite of relatively low copper prices, there was a US$476 millions surplus in the balance of payments, even after the service of foreign debts.

The foreign-owned copper mines had been expropriated by the Allende government, but the Junta has negotiated full payment terms with the former owners, Anaconda, Kennecott and Cerro, and the mines, now State-owned and operated, are proving profitable.

Chile is still the world's greatest producer of natural nitrates and their by-product, iodine. The nitrates are coming into their own once again as petroleum-based synthetic fertilizers experience heavy cost increases. In all, Chile heads the list of mineral producers in Latin America with two-thirds of the total, including coal, iron, gold, silver, oil, manganese and sulphur.

Industry suffered a set-back during the Allende period, when 500 factories were expropriated, but the end of 1977 will see 486 of these de-nationalized, and today there are nearly a million people working in industries that include: textiles, wine, leather, beet sugar, footwear, paper and pulp, cement, steel, petroleum products, appliances, freight and passenger cars, locomotives, small ships, tractors, glass, cigarettes and cigars, tires, fish and meat products, timber, synthetic fibres and many others. Non-mineral exports increased by 60% in 1976.

Much of Chile's development is due to the Development Corporation (Corporación de Fomento), always called CORFO, and its subsidiaries. Apart from assisting industrial development, its electrical subsidiary ENDESA generated 6,730 million KVA in 1976, mainly hydro-electric. Oil extraction and refining is the job of another CORFO organization, the National Petroleum Enterprise, and the partly state owned, partly private Pacific Steel Company's integrated steel plant at Huachipato began as a CORFO entity.

The pressure is on today to increase farm output. Between the half-completed Land Reform of the Frei government (1964–1970) and the subsequent Allende reform (1970–1973), Chile was importing $700 millions in foodstuffs by 1973, a burden quite unjustifiable in view of the farm capacity of the country. This figure is now down to something over US$200 millions, and the break-even point is being strenuously pursued.

Whether wine should be discussed as a consumer product or an export item is a matter of opinion. Certainly the Chileans consume plenty, but France is one of Chile's chief wine customers. It is a product worthy of the attention of the most critical and experienced wine fancier.

All this suggests that Chile definitely falls into the category of a "developing country." And as the country develops so does its middle class, already the largest and most powerful on the continent. It provides the governing class of the country, politicians, industrialists, artists, professional men and women, the engineers, the scientists and the doctors. Incidentally, there is no antifemale bias in Chile. Women rise to the highest posts in the Administration, education and business.

Arts and Artists

Thus, it comes as no surprise that one of the two most important poets was a woman: Nobel prize winner Gabriela Mistral, the pen name of a former provincial school teacher, Lucila Godoy. The other Chilean Nobel Prize was awarded to Pablo Neruda (whose real name was Neftali Reyes) who came home to die in 1973 from his ambassadorial post in Paris.

For Spanish-speaking students histories of Chile are numerous, but for the English-speaking there is the excellent "A History of

Chile" by Luis Galdames, an English translation of which was published in 1941 by the University of North Carolina Press.

Chilean artists have exhibited in several of the world's capitals: Juan Francisco Gonzalez, Alfredo Valenzuela, Camilo Mori, Roberto Matta, and sculptors Nicanor Plaza and Rebeca Matta. Among internationally known musicians are violinist Alfonso Montecinos and pianists Rosita Renard and Claudio Arrau, the latter recognized as one of the best living interpreters of Beethoven.

Wining and Dining

As Chile is a cosmopolitan country, this is strongly reflected in her food and drink. Santiago, for instance, is filled with French, Chinese, Italian, Spanish restaurants, and so on, all around the world. But the real charm of wining and dining in the capital—or in any of Chile's cities—lies in the great quantity of foods and beverages which are typically Chilean.

Chile's world-famous grapes are the base of its four most popular drinks. First, of course, is wine itself. Then comes *Pisco*, a powerful liquor distilled from grapes and most often seen in the *Pisco Sour Cocktail*. Grapes are also used to make *Chicha*, a medium-brown sweet beverage somewhat reminiscent of apple cider with added punch. The last, and most powerful, is *Aguardiente*, which translates literally into "fire water."

Chilean wines are world famous, and the fame is well deserved. As was already mentioned, countries like France, Canada and the United States import Chilean wines of the better qualities. A bottle of good quality costs only $2–$3.

The variety of types of Chilean wine is extremely wide. At the bottom of the scale are the common wines (which are of a remarkably good quality) which are normally consumed at home and in the bars.

At the other end of the scale are the excellent high quality table wines used on special occasions. Such well-known types as Cabernet, Borgoña (Burgundy), Rhin, and Pinot are a common sight on Chilean tables or in bars and restaurants. Due to the confusion that arises from having some 20 well-known brands of wine, each of these with its individual classifications, the tourist would perhaps be best advised to decide on *tinto* (red) *or blanco* (white) and let the waiter supply the details. Or, if one wants to go *a la chilena*, he can just ask for *vino de la casa* (house wine).

Chileans boast of their wines, and they drink them in quantity. You would do well not to try to drink glass for glass with a Chilean, for it's odds on that he has been drinking since childhood. From the time they are very small, kids are given a little wine and water with their meals; the water is gradually eliminated as they grow older. Thus by the time they reach maturity, they are not only connoisseurs but have also acquired a considerable immunity to the alcoholic content.

Pisco is made only in Chile and Peru. It is colorless and has a slightly sweet smell and a very distinctive taste. In all its forms it looks and tastes innocent—but beware, for it never is. Commonest probably is the cocktail Pisco Sour, made with pisco, lemon juice, and sugar shaken together in ice and then made frothy by the addition of beaten white of egg. A mixture of pisco and vermouth is called a Pichuncho. Also, dry ginger ale is used to make a long pisco drink.

Right after the grapes are in—around May—and during the September Independence Day celebrations, a favorite drink is chicha, a fermented grape-juice drink. Like pisco, this innocent looking, slightly sweet beverage has a kick like the proverbial mule.

Aguardiente is the most alcoholic of the four national drinks. Distilled from grapes and ordinarily clear in color, it also comes as a kind of brandy, *Armañac*. Aguardiente is the drink responsible for the fact that Chilean teatime goes under the name *las once*. Among the many legends told about the origin of this custom, this is one of the most interesting: In colonial days the men and women used to gather to have tea in the afternoon. The men would soon get bored with such a "lifeless" drink and slip off, one by one, to the kitchen pantry to uncork the bottle of Aguardiente. When someone noticed the absence and asked about it, the tolerant wife would explain, "Oh, he's having his once." "Once" in Spanish means eleven, and Aguardiente has eleven letters.

Aguardiente is also the base for one of the most popular drinks in the country, *Cola de Mono* (monkey's tail). Made with Aguardiente, coffee, milk, sugar, cinnamon and egg yolk, it is served in most Chilean homes during the Christmas season but can also be found in some downtown bars throughout the year.

Beer is one of the drinks consumed in largest quantities in the country, perhaps because of the large German element in the population. Very popular because of its low price, beer can be found in many types throughout the country. Generally considered superior are the Royal Guard, Escudo and Kayser brands in bottled beer and the draft beer (*schop*).

Also locally manufactured are a number of other liquors. The Chilean version of London Gin is quite good; locally made vodka is acceptable. Whisky sold under local trademarks is imported and bottled in Chile; its quality is usually better than many U.S. or Canadian whiskies. However, it should be noted that imported whiskies are very expensive, and a shot of Scotch in a good bar costs more than $3. In Chile it is possible to find most of the soft drinks well known throughout the world, such as Coca-Cola, Pepsi Cola, Orange Crush, Ginger Ale and Orange Fanta, plus a number of refreshers which are strictly Chilean: Bilz, fruit juices in bottles (*Nectar de Fruta*) and several brands of mineral and soda waters.

Typical National Dishes

Although the cuisine in Chile is mainly international, there are a number of typical dishes which generally go over well with visitors. The highly flavorful dishes are for the most part rather simple to prepare and can be repeated back home with few difficulties.

At the head of the list comes the *Empanada*. A very unsuitable translation would be meat pie, but at least that gives some sort of idea. Inside a flour pastry shaped like a small turnover goes a combination of meat and onions cut into small pieces, hard-boiled egg, raisins and olives. The "pie" is baked in a hot oven until the crust is somewhat hardened and generally served with red wine as the first course of a meal. It can also be made using chicken or fish as the staple ingredient.

Humitas are made from corn—the first of the season, since it must be tender. The corn is ground into a paste, seasoned, then wrapped in corn husks. These small bundles are then placed in a pot of boiling water for almost an hour. Separate the husks, and you have a Chilean dish, rather like the Mexican tamales but seldom so highly seasoned.

Pastel de Choclo (freely translated as "corn pie") is something of a cross between an Empanada and a Humita. The same *pino* (small pieces of meat, onions, raisins, and boiled egg) used in the Empanada are placed in an earthenware oven dish and topped with pieces of chicken and ground corn. The mixture is baked until the corn is brownish in color, then served hot.

The *Cazuela de Ave* is a kind of souped-up soup. It contains rice, corn, green beans, chicken, carrots, pumpkin, salt and a number of herbs. After the mixture is boiled, it is served piping hot, often as the second course of a Chilean luncheon after the Empanada. Known as a common man's dish, it is often served in the best households as well.

Bife a lo Pobre is the name for a steak served as the poor Chileans used to eat it, but these days it would be difficult for a really poor man to eat one. (Some have suggested the name be changed to *Bife a lo Rico*.) It is a big steak with fried potatoes and onions, and a pair of fried eggs is placed on the top of the steak when served.

The *Parrillada* contains a selection of meat grilled over hot coals. In most restaurants the Parrillada is served on its own small grill, so that the heat is conserved as the diner makes his selection. Ordinarily accompanied by fried potatoes and/or some kind of salad, the Parrillada is a very popular and tasty dish. But a word to the squeamish eater: if you are not prepared to eat parts of a cow you had no idea were edible, you had better pass up the Parrillada and stick to a conventional *Filet* or *Entrecot* (T-bone).

Curanto is not so much a dish as a complete dinner. In Santiago it is served in some restaurants, made in pots, but this is hardly authentic. In the southern region of Chile around Puerto Montt and especially on Tenglo Island which faces Puerto Montt, the Curanto is prepared in a very different way. A hole is dug in the ground and stones placed in the bottom. Fires are lit on top of the stones. When they are red hot, the wood and ashes are swept away and the food, in sacks, is placed on top of the stones. Wet sacks go atop the food sacks, and on the wet sacks go several layers of earth and grass to conserve the heat inside. After several hours the "oven" is opened and the feast begins. The food inside the sacks is a rather mad combination of peas, pork, seafood, potatoes, and any number of other ingredients. But the result is incredibly tasty—and unforgettable.

Also common, especially in the countryside, is *Pan de Horno*, a country bread baked in an earthen oven. *Sopaipillas* (fried pumpkin patties) are very popular, especially on rainy days. And *Pan de Pascua* (fruitcake) is in almost every household at Christmastime.

Chile's seacoast (the longest in the world) naturally offers an immense variety of seafoods. And the list would be much longer if the Chileans so wanted, as there are many kinds of fish which are simply ignored by the population.

Best known of the *mariscos* (shellfish) are the huge lobsters from Juan Fernández Islands, among the best in the world. But equally enjoyable are the *centollas* (marine crabs with spotted scales). These are found in the south and are especially famous around Punta Arenas.

EXPLORING CHILE

"Santiago," as Chileans are often heard to say a bit critically, "is Chile." And they are very right. Santiago is not only the capital politically, but economically, culturally, and otherwise-ly as well.

Not that there is no activity outside the big city. Such cities as Valparaíso (principal port on the Pacific coast), Viña del Mar (the Pacific coast's most fashionable vacation spot) and Concepción (home of a fine university and center of the steel and coal mining industry) cannot be bypassed so easily. Nor can Arica in the far north, Punta Arenas in the far south, and a series of other cities in between.

But Santiago is the center of it all. And this centralism is accentuated by the system of government, in which all decisions come from someone living and working in Santiago. All the government agencies and principal offices are in the capital; thus, headquarters of the biggest industries and companies are too. By sheer weight of the population, now over 3,500,000, Santiago is also the center of cultural life and boasts three of South America's top educational institutions: the University of Chile (state-run and the largest), the Catholic University (private) and the Technical State University, which specializes in training "technicians," as distinct from engineers, in many technical professions.

The tourist's interest in Santiago is centered around the many activities and the generous Nature which serves as hostess. The most striking feature of the city is Nature-endowed: the mountains so very near and the hills within the city itself. The downtown area is one of Latin America's busiest, its streets overflowing with people rushing about shopping or tending to their businesses. However, this city seems to suffer more than a normal amount of demolitions, street excavations and general untidiness, which prompted a well-known Chilean cartoonist to quip: "Santiago is going to be a nice town—if they ever finish it."

The main downtown street is called Avenida Bernardo O'Higgins, or, more simply, the *Alameda*. Once a branch of the Mapocho River, it was later dried up and converted into a modern, wide thoroughfare. Right downtown on this main street stands Santa Lucía Hill, an amazing example of what can be done with a useless place. The hill may be regarded as the birthplace and bulwark of Santiago, as it was here Don Pedro de Valdivia founded the city and from here Don Casimiro Marcó del Pont, the last Spanish governor, defended the city from attacks by Independence-seeking Chilenos. Mapuche Indians had earlier dedicated it to the God of Pain (Huelén) and Christians erected on its summit the very first hermitage and the first Cross of the Conquest.

National hero Bernardo O'Higgins first had the idea of using it as a cultural attraction when he tried to build an observatory and a parthenon atop it. But centuries were to pass before historian, politician, writer and great patriot Don Benjamín Vicuña Mackenna made the dreams of O'Higgins come true. From 1872 to 1874 he directed the work by convicts which transformed the hill from a garbage dump to the lovely unique park it is today.

The hill is a kind of living museum, since two fortresses constructed by Marcó del Pont still remain: one, the Castillo González, overlooks the "Alameda" and provides a wonderful view of the city from its main terrace; and the other, Castillo Hidalgo, now houses the Popular Arts Museum in what were once the dungeons.

Many claim Santa Lucía is one of the loveliest parks in the Americas, and it may well be. Vicuña Mackenna's additions of plants and trees (convicts carried the soil on their backs) and of monuments and ornaments transformed the junk heap into a public park of rare beauty. That it is romantic is obvious. A Sunday afternoon stroll through the parks will reveal plenty of *amor al aire libre* (love in the open air), as the Chileans call it.

San Cristobal Hill or Metropolitan Park

Santa Lucia, at 240 feet above street level, is just a midget compared to its big brother, San Cristóbal Hill. The first thing to impress many an air visitor about Santiago, this hill is 1,200 feet high and adorned with a statue of the Virgin Mary, France's gift to Chile. At night the big statue is flooded with lights and can be seen from almost any point of the city. San Cristóbal is within easy walking distance from downtown, four blocks across the Mapocho River. Its summit can be reached by car or by funicular, a train that goes straight up. At the top is a terrace with a small café and many gardens and walkways. A *Casino del Cerro* (no gambling) serves dinner with a wonderful view.

About the view: it is absolutely marvelous. Take off a couple of hours and get to the top just before sunset; then wait to watch the lights begin to twinkle on until the whole city stretched out before you becomes a giant birthday cake. Needless to say, this place is a favorite spot for lovers.

A third of the way up San Cristóbal is the city zoo, which can be reached by car, funicular or (for hiking enthusiasts) walking. The animals are kept in places very similar to their natural habitats, taking advantage of the hill's mountainlike appearance. Especially interesting is the zoo's collection of typically Chilean animals and birds.

There is also the very attractive Tupahue swimming pool surrounded by lawns and gardens.

In the same group of hills to which the San Cristóbal belongs is the Pirámide, so called because of a small monument there honoring Don Manuel de Salas, one of Chile's founding fathers. The monument was erected by British merchant John O'Brien, who sided with the South American colonies and joined General San Martín's forces to fight the Spanish. He became San Martín's principal collaborator and lived many years in Chile, his second country. Because he used to live in what is now Pirámide del Salto del Agua, he decided to dedicate a monument to the man who had been kind enough to give him the place. San Martín himself used to go there after fighting to rest his nerves and restore his energies.

The place is now one of the most beautiful in Santiago, with lush gardens and a delightful restaurant which has become one of the favorite spots for Santiaguinos.

But once you are off the hills and back downtown, a logical place to start seeing the center is La Moneda, the Presidential Palace. The Palace was designed by Joaquín Toesca and completed in 1805 and now houses the Ministry of Interior and the Foreign Affairs Ministry as well as the Presidential offices. On two sides of it are tall buildings housing governmental offices, the postal and telegraph building, and the *Hotel Carrera*. One plaza behind La Moneda (toward the Alameda) has a statue of former President Arturo Alessandri Palma, and another in front of it (on Moneda Street) doubles as official parking lot and site for the changing of the Palace Guards ceremony, when the Palace is in use as the Presidency.

At present the Presidential Palace is closed and under repair, but since the Moneda occupies a whole block, busy Santiaguinos used its two main entrances, which connect Moneda with Alameda, as a shortcut by walking through the connecting patio. It was perhaps the only Presidential Palace in the world that could be so freely entered and used by its citizens.

Five blocks from La Moneda, as you walk away from the Alameda, is the main square, the Plaza de Armas. On its fringes are the relic-filled Cathedral, the sprawling Central Post Office and the Municipality of Santiago. Plans call for the demolition of all these old buildings to build a big modern commercial center with ample parking space and wide streets. On two sides of the plaza—east and south—is a commercial and residential center with large apartment houses.

Behind the Cathedral, on Bandera Street, is the National Congress. Since political parties have been declared temporarily "in recess," it is presently used by one of the ministries. It was designed by French architect Ambroise Henault, who is also responsible for the University of Chile headquarters on the Alameda and the Municipal Theater at Augustinas and San Antonio. The Municipal Theater is the most important cultural center, and top national groups perform there throughout the year, as do international attractions like the Bolshoi Ballet and the Chinese Opera. There are also performances by the Ballet Nacional Chileno and the Ballet de Arte Moderno.

The Churches of Santiago

As a Catholic country, Chile's churches are among its most important monuments. Santiago has many, ranging in architectural style from modern to colonial. Santo Domingo, located on the street of the same name, was inaugurated in 1771 and was one of the most beautiful churches in Chile—"was," because a 1963 fire destroyed its interior and roof completely. Only the stone walls remain, but its style can still be appreciated from outside. Work has already begun to rebuild it, and it has been declared a national monument (which means that any future plans for Santiago must be made bearing in mind that the Church will remain there forever).

The Cathedral was built in 1558. Most of its relics and holy figures are of Jesuit origin, brought to the country or made here by that order. Notable are the wooden figure of Saint Francis Xavier and the 17th-century silver lamp weighing more than 50 pounds. In the sacristy, full of furniture several centuries old, is a magnificent painting of the Last Supper. The monstrance is the most striking piece in this collection of religious objects. More than 30 pounds of silver went into its making; it is adorned with emeralds and rubies.

The Church of San Francisco, begun in 1568 and finished in 1618, is of a style inspired by the Italian Renaissance. It was constructed with enormous stones, and practically no mortar was needed to unite them. Inside it, in the cloister, are paintings by Juan Zapata, a member of the Quito School of the 17th century. Separating the cloister from the sacristy is a three-leaved door with evident Renaissance inspiration, and in the main altar is an image of Our Lady of Mercy; carved of wood and standing 11 inches high, it was brought to Chile by Don Pedro de Valdivia. Other notable images are those of Saint Francis of Assisi, founder of the order that lives in the adjoining monastery; Saint Michael, dating from 1594; and the Christ of La Caña, brought from Lima in 1630.

Other churches worth a visit are San Agustín, Agustinas and Estado Streets; La Merced, at Compañía and McIver; Santa Ana, Cathedral and San Martín; Recoleta Dominica, seven blocks from Mapocho Train Station on Recoleta Street; and Recoleta Franciscana, at the beginning of Recoleta Street.

In this Recoleta area is Santiago's central market. An old building, its main attraction is the variety and incredible array of shops around it, ranging from ultramodern supermarkets to simple baskets on the street. Within the market itself are a great variety of foods and souvenir objects—ceramics from Pomaire and Quinchamali, baskets from Linares, saddles from Chillán and Rancagua, rugs from Temuco and Osorno, dolls from Santiago.

Santiago's Museum

Santiago has sixteen places called museums, although art galleries are also called "museos" which may confuse the tourist. Under this heading are the Popular Arts Museum, the Colonial Art Museum and the Fine Arts Museum (Museo Nacional de Bellas Artes) in Forestal Park. There are some fine paintings

here, and the Wittgenstein Collection is worth seeing. There is an
Historical Museum downtown at Miraflores 50 and a Natural
History Museum in the park called the Quinta Normal. Classical
painting and sculpture may be found in the Palacio de la
Alhambra at Compañia 340, but check first, as it has recently
been closed for repairs. The Cathedral has its own museum in the
Plaza de Armas, as does the San Francisco Church at Londres 4.
For the mechanically minded, there is an aviation museum and
a vintage car museum, the former in the Quinta Normal, the
latter in the street 10 de Julio.

The Vitacura and Las Condes areas in suburban Santiago are
filled with lovely homes and beautifully kept plazas and parks.
They are also located very near the mountains and offer beautiful
glimpses of superb scenery.

Excursions from Santiago

Chileans have another saying (they're full of them) about
Santiago: "The nicest thing about the city is that it's so easy to get
away from."

The latter part, at least, is quite true. Take Las Vertientes, for
instance. Only forty minutes away by car in the direction of San
José de Maipo through Puente Alto, it has a fine swimming pool
set among marvelous mountains at *Hosteria Las Vertientes,* and
the Maipo River which runs by offers an extra attraction.

Or go to El Arrayán, located on the banks of the Mapocho
River on the road to the Farellones ski resort. It is but 20 minutes
from downtown Santiago by car, and buses and *liebres* also make
the trip. *Hosteria El Arrayán* has a swimming pool for guests and
offers a magnificent view of the mountains and rivers together
with the crisp mountain air. On the road to El Arrayán are several
restaurants, some of them rather rustic. In the Las Condes area
is "La Rueda" which features Chilean music and singing, and
good food.

Continuing on the same road you will reach Farellones, 30 miles
from Santiago and some 7,400 feet above sea level. It has six ski
lifts, one of them a chair lift which rises all the way to the top of
Colorado Hill—10,664 feet above sea level. The fields of Farellones and Colorado have acquired a well-deserved international
fame, and many competitions are held there during the skiing
season—from the last of May through mid-October. Accommodations are good, if somewhat scarce. There are 75 *refugios,* 15
belonging to clubs and 60 in private hands. A store rents all the
necessary equipment, and there are several snack bars. Transportation is pretty good during the whole season, with a daily service of
buses, cars and trucks. It's a fine weekend or one-day trip.

Three miles further up on the road to Farellones are the La

Parva slopes, very popular with Santiaguinos. La Parva has three poma lifts, one over a mile long. There is a small restaurant for the public, but most visitors lodge at nearby Farellones, as mostly private homes are found at La Parva.

Lagunillas ski fields are further along the same road to Las Vertientes. There the fields are good and the accommodations good enough. Several clubs and private refugios take guests. There is a chair lift about a mile long, and Lagunillas offers several long ski trips, some of which must be taken with a guide. Transportation to Lagunillas is provided by cars and buses in a two-hour trip. It is also possible to take the mountain train up to San José de Maipo on the El Volcán Railway, and from there to Lagunillas by car or bus, a two and a half hour trip. Toward the end of the season the picturesque La Lola ski competition takes place.

Still further up the same road into the Andes is the mountain town of El Volcán, from which many mountain hikes can be taken, and further up Lo Valdes, practically the Andes themselves. Nearby are the Morales Thermal Baths, 6,000 feet above sea level (58 miles from Santiago, 8 from El Volcán). These are supposedly good for respiratory ailments, as is the climate.

Another well-known thermal bath near Santiago is Colina, 20 miles from the city at the altitude of 2,700 feet. Water temperatures vary from 65 to 90F., and the hotel (3rd class) is complete with thermal baths, swimming pool and restaurant. Buses leave from the side of Mapocho Station, and the trip takes about an hour.

The Central Valley has its own share of attractions. The town of Maipú, where the great Battle of Maipú took place, has a museum, a monolith commemorating the battle, and a temple to the Virgin of Carmen built after O'Higgins' promise. A Parthenon of the Heroes pays homage to the men who took part in the famous independence battle. Maipú also has a famous swimming pool with a good restaurant; the top rodeo of the year is held there with competitors from all over the country.

A scant 37 miles from Santiago, near Melipilla, is the town of Pomaire, famous for its pottery and ceramics. The craftsmanship has been handed down from father to son for countless generations, and collectors of original folkloric art will find many pieces worth taking home. The trip is best made by car. Pomaire pottery can also be found in Santiago's central market and at many art stores.

Santiago province is blessed with many beach resorts famous for their beauty, climate, and cool waters: San Antonio, busy seaport and seafood center; Cartagena, (overly) popular vacation spot; San Sebastián; Las Cruces; Isla Negra; El Tabo—all with beautiful beaches and agreeable climates. El Tabo has a white sand beach; from there to the north they are yellow-white, to the south grey-white. El Quisco is one of the best beaches of the region, and in summer it is heavily populated with Santiaguinos and tourists. Algarrobo, last of the series, has extremely peaceful waters because a big rocky island just off the coast breaks up the waves. The sea here is as peaceful as a pond, and for this reason it is a top spot for yachting, skin diving and water skiing. Transportation to and from all this area is excellent, especially during summer. A train services Catagena, and buses reach every other spot of the area.

Special mention is due to Rocas de Santo Domingo beach resort, located in the same area south of San Antonio. The road to the resort passes through Llo-Lleo, famous for its wonderful climate, and Tejas Verdes, and before arriving in Santo Domingo one must cross a bridge stretching more than a mile over the Maipo River. The town has marvelous gardens and houses, and order and care ever evident. It has a large sea-water swimming pool and a splendid golf course. Recent additions include an airport for private planes and a car racetrack. Several clubs and organizations have casinos and bars, and there are two hotels, the Imperador and the Club Hotel.

Other famous beach resorts are located in the nearby province of Aconcagua. Papudo, Zapallar, Maitencillo and Los Molles are all easily reached by bus or car; the trip to Papudo, the most distant, takes about three hours.

The world-famous ski resort of Portillo, site of the 1966 world Ski Championships, is also in Aconcagua province. Located at 9,300 feet above sea level, Portillo boasts ski slopes more than 2,000 feet long, plus ice skating rinks. Classes for novices in both ice-skating and skiing are given by champions from the U.S.A., France, Austria and Chile itself. The winter sports season begins in June and lasts through September. The natural beauty of Portillo is further enhanced by Laguna del Inca, 300 feet from the *Hotel Portillo*. During winter it becomes a skating rink, and during summer it is a sailing and fishing spot.

Portillo has first-class facilities. With several ski lifts and two chair lifts and a snazzy six-floor hotel, it is easily the best resort of its kind on the continent. Transportation is provided by the Transandino Railway leaving Mapocho Station and transferring in Llay-Llay, or by tourist bus or private car. Travel agencies will help make arrangements during the season.

Valparaiso and the Coast

The tourist arriving in Chile by boat may well think that his first view—the many hills surrounding the port with houses miraculously clinging to their sides—cannot be surpassed by anything else in the country. And the visitor who has arrived by air or by way of Los Andes will be equally surprised when he takes the trip to Valparaíso and its nearby sister, Viña del Mar.

Valparaíso is divided into two sections: the already mentioned hills and the "basin" section which serves as the commercial center. Each of the hills is like an individual city, and the twisting streets that go up and down them will enchant any tourist—especially if he has a color camera at hand. The view from these hills over the bay and on to Viña is one of the most striking in all of Chile.

The taste of the port is found in its twisted streets next to the Mercado, with its myriad bars, underground taverns and sailor hangouts. The cultural life of the port is as busy as its maritime one and centers around the Arturo Prat Naval School, Beaux Arts Museum, Severín Public Library, Catholic University of Valparaíso, branches of the University of Chile, and the Technical University Federico Santa María, one of Latin America's most outstanding. Valpo's poets and writers have enriched Chilean literature since the beginning of the republic.

Valpo's historical spots are many. Among the most important is the Miradero O'Higgins, located in Alto del Puerto. This spot offers the best view, and for this reason it was used by General O'Higgins when he saw the Chilean Navy off to aid Peru in its War of Independence with Spain. Another famous spot is Cerro Los Placeres, where Diego Portales was murdered.

Valparaíso's beaches must take a back seat to those of Viña. The principal, most central one is Las Torpederas, surrounded by plazas and gardens. From there a tour can be taken around the various fishing towns, and another to visit such places as the Paseo Rubén Darío, the park of Playa Ancha, and the football stadium of the same name. A bit more time is required to visit such spots as the Quebrada Verde Park. There is also the historical field of Placilla, where the Revolution of 1891 was decided and the fate of President Balmaceda sealed. After defeat, he took his life.

Viña del Mar, 10 minutes further up the coast from Valpo, is a true gem—"The Pearl of the Pacific," it is called. Its natural beauty is a year-round attraction, and in the summer a flurry of activity makes the place even more enjoyable. A series of beaches —some almost downtown—draw thousands of sunners daily in the summer.

El Recreo, the first after leaving Valparaíso, is wide and comfortable, with terraces full of vacationers and a sea-water swimming pool. It is followed by Caleta Abarca, with a splendid view of the port and surrounded by beautiful gardens and walkways. At one end of the beach is the *Hotel Miramar* with its nightclub and swimming pool, and the beach also has a comfortable restaurant for dining and dancing. Other beaches are spotted along the ten-mile coastal road connecting Viña with Concón, and whether the vacationer prefers crowded beaches with many activities or isolated spots inhabited only by the visitor and nature, he can find either extreme—and all the in-betweens—in the Viña area.

But Viña's charm takes in far more than its beaches. The city is set amidst a forest, and man's hand has been used to complement the marvelous work done by Nature. Beautiful modern buildings which form the city's skyline gracefully combine with the more traditional chalets and even castles. Here the President of Chile has his rustic Summer Palace on Cerro Castillo (Castle Hill). Wide, well-designed avenues decorate the city, such as the Avenida de la Marina, lined on one side by palm trees and apartment buildings and on the other by the *estero*, an inlet of the sea with multiple bridges and illuminated fountains.

The abundance of flowers have given Viña the name, "The Garden City." Apart from the thousands of private gardens, tourists may visit the Quinta Vergara, an old mansion converted into a park with huge beautifully kept gardens and walkways. Here during the summer many outdoor cultural events are held, such as the annual Song Festival. Other lovely parks include the Plaza Vergara in the heart of town and the Plaza Mexico with its lighted fountains.

Places to visit: the Municipal Theater, offering top dramatic and ballet presentations; the Benjamín Vicuña Mackenna Municipal Library; the Academy and Museum of Fine Arts in the Quinta Vergara; the Naval History Museum overhanging the sea; the Valparaíso Sporting Club, one of Chile's best racing tracks; Sausalito Stadium, set amid the forest on the banks of El Tranque lake; and the Granadilla Country Club with a magnificent golf course. Viña is small enough and friendly enough that the tourist will have no trouble finding his way from one spot to the next

But *the* place to visit in Viña is the Municipal Casino. Gamblers can while away their money (or make a pile) at roulette or baccarat (punto y banca) in elegant surroundings during the September 15–March 15 season. And for nongamblers, the Casino has a full-scale nightclub and boite with top national and international acts, excellent food and drink, and plenty of dancing space. Funds from the Casino have contributed much to making Viña the clean, attractive, progressive city it is.

In Viña take advantage of the *victorias*, horse-drawn carriages that are found everywhere. They are fun for drives along the shore road and through the quiet shaded streets, and they are less expensive than cabs. (In Viña, as in many other Chilean cities, these have no meters. Be careful not to get taken; ask *cuánto* before leaving.)

North of the Capital

Around Valparaíso and Viña del Mar are a number of towns in Chile's Central Valley. Quillota, according to Charles Darwin, is a bit of the tropics installed in Chile. Its main attraction is as a resting place, and its fruits are exported to the rest of Chile. Other resorts are Limache, Olmué, Quilpué ("City of the Sun"), and El Granizo. Algarrobo, a small town 50 miles south, has become a very popular middle-class vacation spot, boasting small sailing boats, good seafood restaurants and hotels. Villa Alemana is famous as a rest spot. An important railway center is La Calera.

To the north lies the great Atacama, the driest desert in the world. Endowed with a special beauty all its own (sunset on the Atacama is a wonder, with the sands taking on a thousand different tones), it would nonetheless be a bit bare without the many oases spotted all the way up to the northern border.

The first major city to the north—and one of the most charming —is La Serena, more than 300 miles from Santiago. The region is famous for its climate and fruits, and ex-President Gabriel González Videla, a native son, gave the city great impetus by rebuilding many of its public buildings in a picturesque Spanish style. Its plazas contain well-designed gardens, and flowers can be seen almost everywhere. Big trees along Francisco de Aguirre Avenue lend their shadows and their ancient beauty, and two hills, the Santa Lucía and the Cerro Grande, provide excellent views of the city and the sea. La Serena also has an archeological museum, located in the great mansion of Count Villaseñor, highlighted by a collection of art by the Diaguitas Indians.

Near La Serena is the La Silla Observatory. This observatory, second in the world in the size and sophistication of its equipment, is located here to take advantage of the region's extraordinary air conditions. It has more days of sunshine than anywhere else, there is no overcast of any kind day or night, and the air is totally smog free. Astronomers declare the site unequaled for atmospheric clarity.

La Serena's well-known beaches are El Faro, which takes on a festive look during holidays; Punta Teatinos; Las Cuatro Esquinas and Caleta del Arrayán. Four miles from the city by paved road is the famous Balneario de Peñuelas with its extraordinary view, cabins and restuarant service. A nearby racetrack and airfield complete the picture.

Coquimbo is La Serena's seaport, and near it is Guayacán with a hotel and caves where Sir Francis Drake is believed to have hidden a lot of treasure. Nearby Vicuña is the birthplace of Chile's Nobel Prize poetess Gabriela Mistral, and she is buried (according to her wishes) in Monte Grande. Andacollo, another of the region's attractions, has colorful religious celebrations that attract about 100,000 believers and tourists yearly. Tongoy, a famed beach resort, is as well known for its delicious seafoods. Also well known are the beach resort of Los Vilos and the beach of Pichidangui.

Copiapó, another 150 miles to the north, was one of Chile's most important cities during the fat years of the last century. Most of the cultural life of the country was centered in it, and Santiago,

compared to Copiapó, was practically a provincial city. The
Southern Hemisphere's first railroad and the country's first public
lighting service, technical education system and state school for
girls are credited to Copiapó. All the bills were paid by the mining
revenues, especially from the silver mines of Chañarcillo, which
were discovered by the famed Juan Godoy.

North of Copiapó are the two-mile-apart seaports of Chañaral
and Barquito, from which the copper production of nearby
Potrerillos and El Salvador is shipped. The latter copper center is
at an elevation of 7,800 feet and some 15,000 persons live there.
Vallenar, south of Copiapó, is near the iron ore field of El Algarrobo, one of the most important in the country. Huasco is Vallenar's port, 30 miles away, and is famous for its wines and its
Pisco, as well as for its seafood. Caldera is 52 miles northeast of
Copiapó; in 1851 the first railway in the hemisphere was built
between these two cities. The main activity of this port is the load-
ing of minerals.

Antofagasta's Days of the Sun

The province of Antofagasta, still further north, is renowned
because it has the highest solar intensity in the world for 360 days
of the year. Its geysers (of Tatio) attract many tourists, and like
the rest of the north it is chiefly desert and mountain ranges.
Famed archeological zones such as Pucará are in the region. The
capital city of the province is also named Antofagasta, center of
copper and nitrate mining activity. The city is also an important
railway center through which pass the international lines to La
Paz, Bolivia, and Salta, Argentina. Much of Bolivia's international
commerce passes through Antofagasta, according to the treaty
signed after the War of the Pacific.

Antofagasta is a progressive city. Its beautiful plazas and parks
are a tribute to man's conquest of the desert. The Plaza Colón has
a big Westminster Clock donated by the British residents, and the
Spanish and Yugoslavian communities have also contributed monuments and adornments for the city's beautification.

For sports enthusiasts, Antofagasta has a fine Sporting Club,
tennis courts, a golf course, and an Automobile Club complete
with magnificent building. Deepsea fishing is a favorite sport, and
the Hotel Turismo maintains boats to take the visitors out.

Best-known beaches are the Balneario Municipal, the Isla de la
Chimba (also known as Guamán) and La Portada, famous for
a rock arch located in the sea facing the beach. The action of
the waves over the centuries carved a hole in the rock leaving
the arch that looks like a doorway (*portada*) from which the
name is derived. On the city's highest hill is painted an enormous
anchor, which greeted the arrival of the *Peru* steamship in 1886,
one of the first to arrive in Antofagasta Bay.

Calama, 136 miles from Antofagasta, is a desert oasis located more than 6,000 feet above sea level. Its *Calemeño* wine has become quite famous, as have its melons and sweet corn. Its chinchilla farms provide luxury furs.

A few miles north of Calama is Chuquicamata, the largest open pit copper mine in the world, and the nitrate plants of Maria Elena and Pedro de Valdivia. Also near Calama is *Dupont* explosives factory, which supplies most of the explosives used in Chilean mines and exports some to Bolivia.

The province features the additional seaports of Tocopilla and Taltal. Through Tocopilla goes much of the nitrate from the pampas and the copper from the Chuquicamata mine. It has some very good beaches (Punta Blanca and Caleta Bay, the latter with seawater swimming pool) and is famous as a site for deepsea fishing. Swordfish and black marlin abound in its waters.

Throughout the area are many ancient towns lost among the salt and the desert sand, some truly prehistoric and others reminders of the golden days of nitrate. Sixty miles from Calama, in San Pedro de Atacama, Jesuit priest Alfred Le Paige of Belgium has worked for many years uncovering secrets of the Atacameño Indians who long ago inhabited the area. He is in charge of the local parish and has founded an archeological museum now internationally famous. Many scholars come to Chile with the sole purpose of visiting it, and the last of its distinguished guests was ex-King Leopold of Belgium. An old church adds to the touristic and historic value. Tourists are allowed to dig for their own relics in San Pedro, with the condition that anything of significant value must go to the museum. A comfortable inn helps in a pleasant stay.

Only 22 miles from San Pedro is Toconao, rich in archeological treasures such as the legendary *Camino del Inca*. It provides a superb view of the Láscar Volcano.

Chiu-Chiu is 23 miles from Calama. The baptismal basin in its parish dates from 1557, and documents found there to 1611. Also nearby is the town of Pukará de Lassana, which means desert fortress—and which it was. The geysers of Tatio in the same area shoot astounding hot water columns in the midst of the scorched plains.

A Battle Lost, a War Won

Patriotic Chileans have a special place in their hearts for Iquique. It is not because of the battle won, as in the case of Arica or Maipu, but because of the battle lost at sea by Arturo Prat during the 1879 War of the Pacific. The war was just beginning on May 21, 1879, when the great warship *Huáscar* of the Peruvian Navy arrived at Iquique accompanied by a smaller warship. Two small wooden ships under the command of Captain Arturo Prat were Chile's only defense. But Prat fought the giant enemy until his own craft was practically broken in half. When the ships collided, Prat, and a few of his followers who could hear his shouts, jumped aboard the enemy ship, only to die under the bullets of Peruvian guns. But his heroic gesture fired up the whole country, and this fervor continued until the war had ended in victory for Chile.

Iquique was a great nitrate seaport; now it is the center of the country's rapidly growing fishing industry, and oil drilling is also underway in the region. The city offers much local color to the tourist. Many plazas seem to defy the desert with their gardens, the best known being, naturally, Plaza Arturo Prat. Here is a famous clock tower and the Casino Español, an artistic imitation of the Alhambra Palace in Spain. Iquique also has an archeology and anthropology museum with a collection of mummies unearthed in the desert surrounding the city. The *mercado*, with all kinds of local and imported merchandise, is a favorite tourist spot and is surrounded by many popular restaurants with local, Peruvian and Asiatic dishes.

Iquique's beaches attract large crowds almost year round. Cavancha has a beautiful street running beside it and is very close to town. The Balneario Municipal is four miles away, Playa Blanca eight miles and Piedras Buenas twelve miles. It also offers fine opportunities for fishing, and several national and international records have been set here.

Iquique's Pica Valley, 85 miles from the city, is famous for its lemons, grapes, oranges, "guayabas" and "mangos." It was discovered in 1536 by Captain Ruy Díaz, and Don Pedro de Valdivia was also in the valley when he made his conquering expedition in 1540. The church and bell tower of Mattias, near Pica, were built about this time. North of Pica Valley is Mamiña, 72 miles from Iquique and famous for its thermal baths. The Pampa del Tamarugal, 186 miles long and 25 to 30 miles wide, is named after the "Tamarugo," a small but hardy spiked bush that grows on it. La Tirana, a fresh oasis with a famous religious celebration, is situated on the Pampa.

On the coast 60 miles north of Iquique is the small port of Pisagua, known as the land without winter. The bay, surrounded by high hills, has very quiet waters, the natural setting forms a kind of overcoat over the whole town.

The Highest International Railway

One of the world's highest railroads operates from Arica, the International Railway to La Paz, Bolivia, offering commercial and passenger service between the two countries.

Among the city's attractions are the Vicuña Mackenna Park, the Juan Noé Park (named after the doctor who fought malaria in the Azapa Valley) and the Church of San Marcos, designed by French architect Gustave Eiffel and declared a national monument.

Sports fans have the Estadio Carlos Dittborn, named after the late organizer of the World Football Championship in Chile in 1962, a race track, polo fields, a golf course and a swimming pool. The beaches are beautiful with wonderfully temperate waters, and you can swim at night at La Lisera, a mile from town, and at Chinchorro and Miramar on the northern side of the city.

There are also a gambling casino and several of the best hotels, bars, restaurants and boites in the country.

The valleys around Arica are true oases in the desert. Lluta Valley, a scant 10 miles from Arica, is a center of cotton, corn, wheat and tomatoes, and some agricultural produce comes out of the Chaca and Camarones valleys. Putre, on the Arica Altiplano, has 500 inhabitants living in 100-odd houses, all at over 10,000 feet. Parinacota looks like a ghost town, with its ancient church and closed houses. And the magnificent 18,000-foot Payachatas Volcano, with the Chungará and Cotacotani lagoons at its foot, makes an impressive sight.

Nearer Arica is the livelier Azapa Valley, famous for its olives and other tropical fruits. Sugar cane is also found in some of these valleys, which now and then break up the dry and almost tragic monotony of the forbidding northern desert.

In the valley there are still vestiges of ancient hamlets, petrographs and pre-Spanish cemeteries. About 30 minutes by car up the valley from Arica is an interesting museum with displays of well-preserved mummies, implements and household items, all recovered in this area.

Santiago to the South

The provinces south of Santiago are mostly agricultural and do not hold a great deal of tourist attraction until the lakes region is reached. Several thermal baths are spotted along the way, among them the Cauquenes (12 miles from Rancagua by car or bus), San Fernando (province of Colchagua, 56 miles from San Fernando, because of the altitude not recommended for weak hearts) and Mondaca (Talca province, off-limits for heart cases). Another 22 recommended thermal baths stretch from near Iquique in the north all the way to Aysén in the south and are said to have remarkable healing powers.

At Rapel, some 60 miles from Santiago, a new 40-mile long lake has been formed by the backup from a hydroelectric dam. This lake has become very popular for fishing, sailing, swimming and water skiing.

The first important city on the southern trek is Talca, 150 miles from Santiago. Situated on the River Claro, Talca is smack in the middle of grape, wine, wheat and cattle country, and its traditionally proud people claim that the great cities of the world are Talca, Paris and London—in that order. The town has a golf course, polo field, swimming pools, clubs and theaters.

The Laguna del Maule is 90 miles from Talca. It offers good rainbow trout fishing; however, the fish are small by Chilean-lake standards. Boating, sailing and other water sports may be enjoyed here, although because of the altitude temperatures tend to be rather low. Near the lake is the Altos de Vilches summer resort with a hotel open from October through to March. Several thermal baths are in the area, the best of them being Pani-mávida, 35 miles by road. Other impressive sights are La Mina, with an inn for visitors; the small Maule Lagoon just before the big one; Las Balustradas, overlooking a 900-foot cliff; the 180-foot Maule Falls and the Penitentes, an incredibly beautiful sight with mountains, lava formations and exuberant vegetation.

Constitucíon, a port some 60 miles from Talca, has fine bathing beaches and is known as a summer resort. It is surrounded by pinecovered hills, and the coast is noted for its unusual rock formations and peaceful waters that allow almost all water sports to be practiced. There is a yearly Carnaval Maulino in February with a masked ball and a Venetian promenade down the Maule River.

Next stop on the southern tour is Chillán. One section, Chillán Viejo, retains much of its colonial air; the house where Bernardo O'Higgins, liberator of Chile, was born still stands. The other section, known simply as Chillán, has modern buildings, wide avenues and all the comforts of the twentieth century. Among its attractions is the Mexico School decorated by world-famous Mexican muralist David Alfaro Siqueiros. The Cathedral is ultra-modern and the plazas and parks really beautiful. The "mercado" is also a tourist attraction with its many regional products, among them ceramics and pottery from Quinchamalí and other nearby towns which can be visited. The mountains surrounding Chillán are among the most striking of the thousands the tourist will see in Chile.

Leaving the city, near Recinto, one may visit the Cueva de Los Pincheira, huge caves in which the Pincheira brothers used to hide after their cattle stealing raids. A series of pottery-making towns—Quinchamalí, Colliguay, Huechupin, Cuca, Chonchoral and Confluencia—offer collectors original creations of the famous black pottery.

Some 58 miles from Chillán at the altitude of 5,400 feet are the Chillán ski slopes with two refuges accommodating 60 guests, and near the slopes are the mineral springs which make the area famous, with a complete hotel.

A University Run by a Lottery

Concepción, capital of that province, is a triply important city —industrially, culturally and touristically. As an industrial center it boasts the Huachipato steel plant, coal mines, and textile plants in Tomé and Chiguayante. Nine miles away is the sister city and port of Talcahuano, also the principal military port of the country. Its intellectual life is centered around the University of Concepción, financed by contributions and by a twice-a-month National Lottery. The tourist attractions are many: in the center, the historical Cerro Amarillo (Yellow Hill) offers a very good view of the town; the central plaza is lovely; the modern campus of the University is the only real university city in Chile; Cerro Caracol, 300 feet high, offers a grand view of the valleys and the great Bío-Bío River, the largest in Chile. Across the river is San Pedro, with beautiful forests and lagoons. In the largest of the lagoons boating and other water sports are practiced. The principal beaches are Las Escaleras, reached by stairs carved in rock; Ramuntcho, named after one of the novels by French writer Pierre Loti who visited the place in 1875; and La Desembocadura del Río, one of the most striking places for the visitor who goes there for the first time. Near this beach is the Pedro del Río Zañartu Museum, located on a farm and featuring local and Araucanian art objects.

La Planchada Fort is maintained by the city as a landmark. For two centuries this fort defended Concepción. It is near Penco, an industrial area well known for its sugar refinery and its crockery factory.

Only 19 miles from Concepción is the textile center of Tomé, famous for its products of exceptional quality. Tomé also has good beaches and other attractions.

Near the port of Talcahuano is the Quiriquina Island, where the Naval School has an establishment for its students, as well as the giant Huachipato steel plant. Seventeen miles from Concepción is Coronel, which with Lota shares the leadership in the country's coal production. The Lota mines extend for several miles under the sea. In Lota is the famous Parque de Lota, with 80 years of care behind it. In the Gulf of Arauco is the Island of Santa María, and in the same area is the beach resort of Laraquete, a seven-mile golden-sand beach about an hour by car from Concepción.

Los Angeles of the Lakes

The fabulous Chilean lake region begins in Los Angeles, some 320 miles south of Santiago, where the Laja Lake is located. The most famous sight in the Los Angeles region is the Laja

Falls, probably the most inspiring piece of scenery in the country. The Falls start at the Laja Lake, 4,500 feet high and covering 48 square miles. The Antuco Volcano is reflected in the lake, and every year fishing competitions are held there. Fifteen miles north of Los Angeles the Laja River, which flows from the lake, drops some 200 feet to form the Laja Falls, or Salto del Laja. This region is famous for its views, and there are four volcanoes in the area: the Antuco, the Copahue, the Tolhuaca and the Collapén.

Almost 200 miles further south, after the Araucanian center of Temuco, is one of Chile's loveliest and most famous lakes, the Villarrica. Its 66 square miles of waters change colors throughout the day. Viewed from the lake the nearby Villarrica Volcano is an awesome sight. On the banks of the Villarrica are the internationally known vacation spots of Pucón and Villarrica, with luxury hotels and ample opportunities for fishing and water sports. A legend says that if a small *morro* (hill) near the lake is visited by a recently married couple the lake becomes furious. So honeymooners had best watch out.

Fifty miles from Temuco, on the slopes of the Llaima Volcano, is the Llaima ski resort in the Los Paraguas National Park, so named because of the lovely snow-covered trees that resemble umbrellas. Two lodges can accommodate about 170 guests, and there is a mile-long ski lift. Here you can ski year round.

Near the Llaima are the thermal baths of Rio Blanco, and in the same province, 11 miles from Curacautín, are the Manzanar springs.

But back to the lakes: Next in line is Lake Panguipulli, whose name means "puma hill" in English. It is located in the province of Valdivia, and very beautiful; there is a small, new and very good privately-owned hotel ("hosteria"). Excursions can be made from the Hosteria Cancahuasi (ex-Rainbow Fly Club), a good fisherman's hotel in Chan Chan. Also in Valdivia are the Lakes Pirihueico, closer to the border with Argentina and with a hotel on its bank offering excursion services; Calafquén, offering excellent fishing but no hotel; Riñihue, connected with Panguipulli by the truly beautiful Enco River, down which a one-day fishing excursion can be made; Ranco, a lovely lake with 23 islands well known for its excellent (up to 18 pounds) fishing; and Riñinahue, considered by many the best fishing spot in the whole lake district, and offering the most beautiful scenery imaginable as well.

The province of Osorno holds forth even greater wonders. The first lake, Puyehue, contains some wonderful islands filled with native birds and has marvelous waterfalls and a big, good hotel for tourists. Near the lake are the Puyehue Thermal Baths, considered by many the finest hot springs establishment in all of South America. The fishing is, again, superb. Further south,

Lake Rupanco, a bit nearer Osorno itself, has top fishing and famous hot springs, but unfortunately tourist facilities are limited.

On to the south in the province of Llanquihue is the biggest of them all: Lake Llanquihue. Near Puerto Montt, and with marvelous Puerto Varas on its banks, Llanquihue measures 320 square miles and in some parts is 1,500 feet deep. Its waters are deep blue, and it is the scene for many water sports and some very good fishing. The lake is surrounded by some of the world's most beautiful volcanoes, especially the Osorno with its eternally snow-capped peak. The sight is absolutely breathtaking.

Osorno Volcano also lends its majestic presence to Lake Todos Los Santos, or Esmeralda—the first name because it was discovered on All Saints' Day, the second because of the emerald color of its waters. Theodore Roosevelt described this lake as the most beautiful he had ever seen, and most tourists must agree. It presents one of the most striking views in the world.

Steamboats operate on the principal lakes of this region—Esmeralda, Llanquihue and Ranco—and the trip is always fun and inspiring. Most of the hotels on the banks of these lakes have ways to organize excursions that the tourist will greatly enjoy.

South to the Chilean Bavaria

Of course this region offers more to the tourist than these spectacularly beautiful lakes. As cities go, the "big three" mentioned have an individual charm which makes each of them worth a good, slow visit.

Valdivia, with its Calle-Calle River full of boats, was founded by Don Pedro in 1552 and is an important and busy place. The climate is humid, and beautiful lakes, woods, beaches and rivers are all around the cities. Along the waterways are countless little islands, cool and green. One recommended side trip is to Llifén, on the banks of Lake Ranco, with a marvelous hotel complete with radio and airstrip.

Osorno is one of the many cities inhabited by great numbers of German descendants whose forefathers colonized the region. Here the German language is used almost as much as Spanish. Even road signs and menus are printed in German in some places, and its wonderfully organized streets look like a bit of old Europe. Among the many interesting excursions (besides those to the lakes) are the La Picada and Antillanca ski resorts. The first, 53 miles from Osorno, includes a view of Osorno Volcano with top quality slopes, and transportation is provided by car or bus to the 120-guest refuge run by the *Club Andino de Osorno*.

Antillanca, 62 miles away and 12 miles from Puyehue, is 4,200 feet above sea level. Here the Club Andino has a 50-bed refuge and provides buses that leave Osorno every Saturday at 2:30 p.m. and return Sunday evening.

Puerto Montt is famous for its seafoods and its seaport, from which the trip through the zone of canals begins. It also has Isla de Tenglo with its famous *curantos*. Nearby is Maullín, with its lovely river; Peulla or Ensenada, an inn in a beautiful setting and worth a visit, is across from Puerto Varas.

For those with a pioneer spirit, this trip is highly recommended. The region is not well developed to receive tourists, but the trip is unforgettable. The boat leaving Puerto Montt makes the run of the ports and touches scores of fishing villages. The trip takes about ten days and visits a great variety of picturesque towns. The tourist will pass dozens of small islands so covered in vegetation that they seem to be plants sprouting from the water. Sailors and those living in the area call them *maceteros* (flower pots). The fishermen who populate the area will be seen around the hundreds of canals—a hardy people in a beautiful but cruel nature.

On the big Island of Chiloé are two towns with tourist accommodations. The first, Ancud, the capital of the province, is four hours from Puerto Montt by boat. The bay of Ancud is famous for its beauty, and the many attractions include the Cerro Caracoles, from which the panorama of the city and its surroundings can be seen. Near Ancud is the fort of San Antonio, the last Spanish stronghold in the War of Independence, as well as *La Máquina* (the machine), so called because there the first mechanized timber mill in South America was installed in 1828. Other attractive places are the thermal baths in Llancahué across the bay of Ancud and such spots as Faro de Aquí, Faro de Punta Corona, Mar Brava and Chacao.

Castro, second city of the province, is located on the banks of the Castro Canal and surrounded by small islands and towns. As all ships going or coming in the southern region must stop there, its commercial and maritime life is very important. Of special attraction in the area are the towns of Huillinco, Queilén, Quellón and Chonchi, the latter with a wooden church 165 by 36 feet.

The famous zone of canals lies south of Puerto Montt and Chiloé, and a boat trip through the area provides views almost impossible to believe. Among them are the Cumbre de los Farellones, an incredible rock formation that rises almost straight up and makes the ship seem a tiny toy in comparison, and, further south, the San Rafael Lagoon at the foot of imposing glaciers. When the great masses of ice fall into the lagoon they break into irregular blocks of fantastic colors. The wonders continue until the boat reaches its destination of Punta Arenas, capital of the province of Magallanes. Here tourism is well developed, and the Hotel Cabo de Hornos has a well-deserved reputation for service and organization.

The province's main activity centers around industry and agriculture. Great herds of sheep are there, which later go frozen to London and other European cities. The production from oil fields there practically supplies Chile with one-third of the petroleum consumed in the country. Seals and whales in the area also provide a large source of revenue. An interesting 4-day, 3-night tour can be arranged from Punta Arenas to Tierra del Fuego, with visits to ranches, oil fields and a tour of Punta Arenas.

The city's attractions include Cerro La Cruz, from which the city and the Strait can be seen; racing tracks, golf course and tennis courts at the Club Hípico; an ice skating rink and indoor stadium for sports fans; a zoo at the Pudeto Artillery Regiment; and the María Behety Municipal Park for a day out. Its Salesiano Regional Museum is filled with information on the culture of the Yagane, Ona and Alacalufe Indians.

Four miles from Punta Arenas, atop the Patagonian Andes, are ski slopes that feature runs of more than a mile with a 1,200 feet difference in levels. Punta Arenas' *Club Andino* owns a refuge for 100 guests, and car or bus transportation is available. More information is available from Santiago's *Club Andino de Chile*. Also nearby are fox farms, Seco (Dry) River, Loreto Mine and the historic site of Fort Bulnes where the first settlers managed to survive. Boat trips can be made to the islands of Magdalena, Marta and Contramaestre.

The Rugged South

About 150 miles north of Punta Arenas is Puerto Natales, accessible by a very good road that goes through forests and beside marvelous lagoons. The whole region is incredibly beautiful, and two hotels have been built at the foot of the spectacular Paine Towers. Soon the region may become a tourist center, but now it is only for the rugged or very adventurous. It's the same with Cuevas de Milodón, Valle del Río Serrano and Ultima Esperanza, all in the same area.

But anyone who has made any of these trips agrees on one thing; they are unforgettable and well worth any inconvenience. From its northern desert to its icebergs and fjords in the far south, Chile is a land as blessed by nature as any in the world— and it's all there waiting for the visitor to this "long and friendly land" to enjoy.

PRACTICAL INFORMATION FOR CHILE

CAPSULE COMMENTS. *Physical Features.* A 2,625-mile-long country only 312 miles across at the widest point. A country of every climate and landscape, Chile stretches from a barren northern desert to fertile valleys near Santiago over hundreds of miles to the famed lake district of forests, mountain rivers and green fields and finally to a wild southern wasteland of glaciers, fjords and unexplored islands.

Climate. Because of Chile's unique geography, almost every climate classified by geographers lies within its boundaries. Santiago's pleasant climate is similar to Southern California's, except it has more rain.

Population. 14,590,000. Santiago has over 3,500,000.

Language. Spanish.

Archeological Attractions. Atacama region and Easter Island.

Principal Industries. Copper, wine, steel, paper, iodine, wheat, and food processing.

WHEN TO COME. Depends on whether you want to ski or to fish for trout and bathe. For the former, May to October; for the latter, October to April. Remember that Chile's seasons are reversed: it is summer here during the Northern Hemisphere's winter months and vice versa. Easy calculation: take the Northern month and subtract 6 and that gives you the Chilean weather. Thus February (2nd month) has the climate of the Northern August (8th month).

SPECIAL EVENTS. The Santiago, Valparaíso and Viña del Mar opera, theater and ballet season runs from April to November.

The International Song Festival (February) in Viña del Mar is truly international. Held in a magnificent natural amphitheater. Mainly for the young.

Flower shows are held around October and November. The two biggest take place in Santiago and Viña del Mar. You may see the Chilean grey rose, but all blooms are most attractive.

An industrial and agricultural exhibition held in Santiago in October also features some very fancy riding by Chilean "huasos" (cowboys) and the Carabineros "Green Team," a cossack-type exhibition riding group.

The two main horse races of the year are the Derby (Viña del Mar, January) and "El Ensayo," (Santiago, October).

The national golf championship is held in Viña del Mar in January, and international golf events continue through March.

There are more than twenty religious festivals, mostly with colorful processions. Near Santiago is "Cuasimodo" on the first Sunday after Easter, with what is called the "running of the Host" as the priests visit the sick to take them Communion, acompanied by crowds on horseback, in carts or on bicycles, all fantastically decorated.

In the fishing ports and villages, June 29th (the day of St. Peter and St. Paul) is celebrated by taking the effigy of the saint from the church through the streets and in a boat round the fishing grounds.

July brings the Feast of the Virgen del Carmen, patron saint of Chile's armed forces. After the decisive battle for Chile's independence, Barnardo O'Higgins ("the father of the country") promised to build a temple on the site in Maipú. It was completed only in 1975 and is an imposing building.

The same Virgen del Carmen is celebrated in La Tirana in the north near Iquique, and that of the Virgen del Rosario in Andacollo near La Serena in the middle north. Both these feasts have in common oriental-style costumes and dancing by teams which practice all the year round to oriental-sounding music played on strange traditional instruments. The origin of this touch of the East is unknown. These very picturesque ceremonies, which last a week, command audiences of over a hundred thousand visitors from all over the world who camp on the hillsides.

September 18th is Independence Day, and on September 19th the armed forces stage their big parade in the Parque Cousiño, attended by the President and ministers and the diplomatic corps. For the country in general, "El Dieciocho" (the 18th) is mainly a drinking holiday, with much red wine and Chicha (a fermented grape drink which tastes innocent but isn't) accompanied by "empanadas."

Ski championships are held in Portillo and Farellones in July and in a smaller way in Villarrica and Antillanca in August.

Association football season is from early spring right through summer. The twice yearly contests between the two major universities, called "Clasicos," have an elaborately produced show on the field before the games.

In January is the International Horsemanship Championship in Viña del Mar, where some first-class riding can be seen. Chileans usually carry off the honors, although the show is truly international.

Holidays. The following legal holidays are observed in Chile: January 1; Holy Week; May 1; May 21; August 15; September 18 and 19; October 12; November 1; December 8; December 25.

HOW TO GET THERE. By air. The major airlines of the Western world now reach Santiago through Pudahuel Airport. This new airport (not yet completed) takes all the international traffic.

From the United States, *Braniff* has four flights weekly from New York and Miami (two via Washington, D.C.); two flights from San Francisco and Los Angeles. *LAN-Chile* has seven weekly flights from New York and Miami; *AVIANCA* from New York and Los Angeles; *Aerolineas Argentinas* from Miami; *Varig* from New York and Miami, via Rio de Janeiro; *Air France* from Miami via Pointe-à-Pitre. *Lufthansa* from New York. *Canadian Pacific Airlines* flies to Santiago from Canada by way of Mexico. *Aeroperu* from Miami and Lima.

From Europe comes a steady flow of traffic, and nine major airlines now connect Santiago with the capitals of Europe: *Air France*, whose flight originates in Paris; *Alitalia*, from Rome and Milan; *British Caledonia Airways* from London, Lisbon and Madrid; *Iberia*, from Madrid; *KLM*, from Amsterdam; *Lufthansa*, from Frankfurt; *SAS*, from Copenhagen; *Swissair*, from Geneva and Zurich; and *Sabena*, from Brussels. *LAN-Chile* from Frankfurt, Paris and Madrid, Easter Island, Fiji and Tahiti.

By sea. Chile can be reached by boat through any of its major seaports. Principal point of arrival is Valparaíso, one of the busiest ports on the Pacific Coast. The steamship companies reaching Chile are many and their services varied, but some of the most important ones are *Compañia Argentina de Navegación Dodero* from Buenos Aires; *Compañia Sud Americana de Vapores* from New York and the main ports of Europe; *Prudential-Grace Lines,* from the United States via the Panama Canal; and *Royal Netherlands S.S. Co.* from Rotterdam and Le Havre.

By train. From La Paz, Bolivia, there are railways to Arica and Antofagasta. The "Transandino" connects to Buenos Aires, Argentina.

By road. The Pan American Highway enters Chile through Arica. The Chilean portion is entirely paved, but a few poor stretches remain. TEPSA buses come to Chile from as far north as Ecuador.

PASSPORTS, VISAS. Passports are required of all visitors except nationals of Argentina, Brazil, Uruguay and Paraguay, who need only their national identity cards. Visitors under 18 may be included on their parents' passports, but if traveling alone need both individual passports and authorization from their legal guardians. Visas are not required except for citizens of African countries, stateless persons and citizens of countries with which Chile has no diplomatic relations. Carriers will supply the obligatory Tourist Card, valid for 90 days and renewable up to 180 days. This must be handed in upon leaving the country. Onward or return passages should be confirmed as soon as possible after arrival.

A smallpox vaccination certificate is required of every person arriving in Chile.

CUSTOMS. Tourists may bring in personal belongings, 500 cigarettes, 500 grammes of tobacco, 100 cigars, 2 open bottles of perfume, two liters of alcoholic beverages and gifts. On leaving the country they may take souvenirs and handicrafts not exceeding 500 dollars.

CURRENCY AND BANKING. Banking hours are from 9 a.m. to 2 p.m., Monday through Friday. All banks have a foreign exchange section, but some work only in dollars. Local currency is the peso, which is devalued daily to a total of 3%-4% per month. At mid-March 1977 the peso stood at approx. 18 pesos to the U.S. dollar. Most hotels are permitted to change foreign currency but never accept offers from hotel staff (porters, etc.), since it is illegal and may land you in serious trouble. Don't offer to pay shops in foreign currency either.

CABLES, TELEPHONES, MAIL. Internal telephone service in Chile is automatic and fairly efficient. International service via satellite is excellent. Santiago is directly south of Boston, Massachusetts, so that the time of day in Chile is the same as in the Eastern zone of the U.S. The seasons, of course, are reversed in the Southern Hemisphere. Telex is available to all the usual countries. There are several international cable services; for English language messages, *West Coast Cables* (Bandera 156) is recommendable.

Mail services to all parts of the world are good, but incoming deliveries are often slow. Don't use sea mail since delays are enormous. Hotels will mail your letters. Postage to the United States is approximately 10 cents for a two-page (airmail paper) letter.

 TIPPING. Restaurants and bars add 10% to the bill, but waiters will expect 10% cash tip in addition. City taxi drivers do not expect a tip, but for long distance or hire for long periods in the city, a tip may be given according to the service received. Taxis in the city are metered, but with the high inflation conditions you may find the meters haven't been adjusted, in which case the driver will have a "conversion card."

 WHAT TO WEAR. The visitor must remember that Chile is south of the Equator, that the ski season is during the Northern Hemisphere summer, and that swimming and fishing season is when the Northern countries are freezing.

Unless the visitor visits the Antarctic, he can expect temperate weather. From Santiago to the south, however, waterproof clothing is needed for the year-round, unpredictable rains. Santiago and Viña del Mar have rainy spells in winter; the former has no rain at all in summer, although the coastal areas may have a little.

Briefly, city wear is much the same as for any temperate country. For the women, suits and dresses, slacks and pants suits; for the men, suits and ties.

In resort areas, sports clothes are acceptable during the day, and a suit is usual for men at night. Women shouldn't wear shorts in the cities, although they are common in resort areas. Evening dress should not normally be necessary, but pack a cocktail frock.

 HOW TO GET AROUND. Santiago's city and suburban bus services are not really recommended for the tourist. With the exception of very brief periods between rush hours, public transportation is drastically overcrowded; you may find yourself standing with eighty others under a sign reading "22 standing passengers only." Highly skilled pickpockets abound; so it's really cheaper and better to take a taxi. Most of the hotels have a group of taxis which serve that hotel alone. Their fares are the same as all others. In town there are both cruising taxis and cab ranks. All charge according to the meter or the "conversion card," which they must carry. There is a 50% surcharge after 10 p.m. Hotel taxis are painted sky blue; the others black with yellow roofs.

Hertz and Avis have car renting agencies in Santiago and Valparaíso. A Peugeot 404 costs (Avis) US $88 per week (in February 1977) plus 17 cents a mile, all subject to 20% tax. Buy your own fuel. Chilean renters ATAL autos and Iberia are also good. For brief stays in Chile, the visitor's home license is sufficient; for longer stays, bring an international license.

Intercity buses are good and comfortable, and some have bar and toilet facilities. Chileans travel mostly by bus, because they are cheaper and have more frequent service than the railroads.

The State Railways offer acceptable service to Valparaíso and the South in "automotor saloons" with bar service and music (which tends to get a bit loud).

For many out-of-town runs—Viña del Mar, for instance—there are collective taxis which make quick excursions at modest rates.

The State airline, 48-year-old LAN-Chile, has frequent service to all main towns throughout the country. Fares are reasonable and the line has an excellent record. LADECO also flies to some major cities. Air taxis can be obtained by calling the local aero club; or, in Santiago, TAXPA, New York 53, Room 102, and Helicop Services at Huerfanos 1178, Office No. 611. Airfields are usually far from the cities; thus for the normal tourist travel, road or rail is quicker in the end.

With its long coastline, obviously the best way to see Chile should be by boat, but unfortunately the coastal lines are not basically passenger ships and don't offer much in the way of amenities. A trip south through the canals is really worth the trouble, though. Contact Chilena de Navegación Interoceanica, Casilla (P.O. Box) 1410, Valparaíso.

Transportation between Santiago and the Valparaíso area, including Viña del Mar, is excellent. Trains, although not frequent, include automotors with bar, and there is a good road. Buses are frequent, and collective taxis are available all day. There is also frequent bus service to the coast villages and towns to the south and north of Valparaíso.

Looking northward, La Serena is a town likely to attract the visitor. It lies on the northern system of the State Railways, but the best connections are the frequent buses along the Pan American Highway. There are bus services—frequent in summer, less so in winter—to the local places of interest, and there is a delightful little railway up the valley to Rivadavia, via Vicuña, Gabriela Mistral's birthplace. If you think you may be late for the down service after your visit, tell the driver, and he'll probably wait for you.

Copiapo, the mining district and attractive town, has air service from Santiago and the usual buses.

Antofagasta, the largest town in the north, can be reached by road, air or sea.

For Tocopilla and Calama, use either LAN-Chile airline or LADECO (this is an abbreviation for "Linea Aerea del Cobre," or Copper Airline, which was formed primarily to serve the copper mines of the north).

To Iquique, travel by bus or plane.

Finally, sitting right on the Peruvian border is Arica, served by LAN-Chile and frequent buses (which provide a fascinating ride—although rather tiring after 1,500 miles—over the desert). The valleys behind Arica have very little transport, and almost the only way to see them is by rented car.

Going south from Santiago, Talca is on the main rail route and also on the Pan American Highway bus routes. It is also united with Argentina by way of a road through the Pehuenche Pass. The Lagoon is reached by paved roads, and there are bus and car services.

Bus service connects Constitución with the capital, and rail service links it with Talca. It is possible to arrive in private plane by landing at Quivolgo.

Chillán is connected to Santiago by bus, train and airplane service. Side trips to the ski slopes and thermal baths can be made by train part way and then by car, and the ski slopes can be reached on horseback.

Concepción can be reached by land, sea and air with well-established services in all three systems. The airport is Hualpencillo and is used by LAN-Chile. The State Railway has a Santiago-Concepción run, and the bus service is quite good. The road is paved all the way. Steamships on their way to Puerto Montt and Punta Arenas stop at Talcohuano.

The best transportation to and from nearby places is by bus. Some are serviced by trains on certain days (like Sundays and holidays, when a train makes the Concepción-Laraquete run). Regular train runs connect the industrial towns of the area with Concepción.

Los Angeles is connected with round-about train service from Concepción, but these spots are more easily reached by car or bus on the Pan American Highway, which runs right through Salto del Laja. An international road connects Los Angeles with Chos Malal, Argentina.

To get to Villarrica you can take a train from Santiago to Loncoche and connect with another train for the remaining 56 miles of the trip. In summer a sleeping car goes all the way from Santiago to Villarrica. You can arrive by road as well—by car down the Pan American Highway or by bus from Temuco, about 100 miles north, or from Loncoche in summer.

The State Railways Information Bureau on Avenida Arturo Prat in Temuco can give the current complete information on the many excursions possible from this city. As a general rule, the starting point for all of them is Temuco.

Many of the lakes are in the province of Valdivia, and most excursions start from there. A road connects Valdivia with San Martín de los Andes, Argentina, and the Pan American Highway links it with Santiago. Las Marías and Pichoy are the airports, and a branch of the Santiago-Puerto Montt railroad goes there. For the most part, it's a bit difficult to make such arrangements on your own. To get to Lake Ranco, for example, several train combinations are necessary. This, combined with the difficulty of getting reservations in season, makes it almost imperative for the tourist to let a travel agency help him to see the south. There is good bus service from Santiago but, again, only to the principal cities.

As is the case of Valdivia, there is excellent transportation to Osorno and to Puerto Montt by plane, train or bus. But to get from these centers to the lakes themselves is more complicated. Some taxis fare passengers where there are no local buses, but this information varies from city to city and lake to lake. For this reason, it is always best to

consult a travel agent before heading south. They know the ins and
outs to unravel what might otherwise become too complicated. Many
times private planes are used to simplify the trips.

Boat service to Easter Island and Robinson Crusoe Island is infre-
quent and unreliable. TAXPA private airline (Nueva York 53, Room
102) operates nonscheduled service to Robinson Crusoe. For Easter
Island, LAN-Chile makes twice-weekly stops outward bound to Fiji,
and the same on its return flights to Chile. Transportation is also available to tour the island.

Punta Arenas has boat and air contact with the rest of Chile. The
boats leave from Valparaíso or Puerto Montt, and planes fly from
Santiago to Chabunco airport, run by the Chilean Air Force. For
excursions within and outside the city, contact the efficient Touring
Club de Magallanes.

There are almost 150 tourist agencies in Chile, 78 of them in
Santiago. Many specialize in different parts of the country. Hotels will
put the visitor in touch with the appropriate agency and make
recommendations.

HOTELS. Scattered all up and down Chile are a
number of fine hotels which can do much to make
a visit more enjoyable. However nice the nicest
of these may be none can come up to the inter-
national "luxury" classification. But whatever they may lack in that line
is made up by the comfortable, homey atmosphere they offer. The
famous Chilean hospitality even extends to the hotels, especially in the
provinces where it is not uncommon to see the owner or manager sit
down to dinner with his guests.

The real problem with hotels is not in their quality but in their
quantity. Many places in Chile which are truly marvelous are almost
unknown because the facilities for people to visit them simply do not
exist. Progress has been slow in this sense, and the pace is still none
too fast. This is a great pity, for the wonders of Chile deserve a wider
attention than that now given them.

Chile's Tourist Department has bestowed its luxury classification on
a few hotels in the country. As these are scattered throughout the long
land, almost any region will have at least one. Some of them, as much
because of their natural setting as their architectural beauty, are
fabulous. The *Hotel Portillo*, for instance, is located at the famous ski
resort and between May and August offers some of the world's most
beautiful snowscapes plus a beautiful frozen-over lagoon.

The Tourist Department lists 34 hotels, of which 8 are classified
deluxe and 9 first class. Some of these hotels may claim to offer more
comfort and better service than the luxury group, and their prices are
on a lower scale. These classifications are made from the point of
view of facilities offered and not from the health standpoint. After
the Tourist Department has given a hotel a rating, it can be safely
asserted that the sheets are clean and the beds are bugless.

Between domestic inflation (8–10% per month in early 1977) and
the daily alterations of the exchange rate, it is quite impossible to say
what a given hotel will cost at any future date. The following must be
taken as indications only and not regarded as firm rates.

The last survey by the Tourist Department showed *deluxe* hotels charging $13–$30 single, $16–$50 double; *first class* $14–$15 single, $11–$19 double; *moderate* $7.50–$12 double; all EP and all with 30% tax over rates above. Many of them offer suites at widely varying prices. Out of the capital rates are usually lower, and the resort areas have a reduced tariff for the off season (mid-March to mid-November). At Portillo, for example, a single with bath runs about $36, double with bath about $48, including meals. Advance bookings in the resort areas are essential during the season.

SANTIAGO

Ask the National Tourist Board (Agustinas, opposite Hotel Carrera) for their *Practical Guide to Santiago*, in English.

Deluxe

SHERATON SAN CRISTOBAL. 350 rooms with bath, TV, air conditioning. In elegant residential district, 10 min. by taxi from downtown. Good international, local specialties in rooftop restaurant. Superb mountain views. Cocktail lounge. Pools, shops.

CARRERA SHERATON. Facing Plaza de la Constitución and La Moneda Palace, right downtown. 355 recently decorated rooms—singles, doubles, and suites—all with private bath and telephone. Excellent meals served in four different dining rooms. Rooftop dining beside swimming pool from December to March, with lovely view. Air conditioned. Excellent bar. Orchestra for dancing. Discotheque. Address: Teatinos 180.

TUPAHUE. New, modern building. Downtown. 209 double and twin rooms, all with private bath, completely carpeted, air conditioned. Music, telephone and TV. Dining rooms and self-service cafeteria, grill. Music bar, disco "Carroussel." Temperate swimming pool.

APARTHOTEL. Americo Vespucio 121. New. Excellent motel-type suites with bath, kitchenette, individual air conditioners, telephone and TV. Grill, bar and very good food in the restaurant. Also **Aparthotel II**, uptown Providencia in Luis Thayer Ojeda Street.

First Class

CRILLON. One of Santiago's most fashionable hotels, offering 145 rooms with private baths and telephones. Charming atmosphere. Excellent French, Chilean and international cuisine in its restaurant; separate bar, cocktail lounge, tea room, snack bar and outdoor patio. Meeting spot for local society. Room service, laundry, shoe shine. Agustinas 1025.

EL CONQUISTADOR. A new first-class hotel in the very heart of business, shopping and entertainment center. 133 single and twin-bedded rooms and suites, all with private bath and telephone. Good international cuisine, grill room, coffee shop, and American Bar. Miguel Cruchaga 920, and Estado.

PANAMERICANO. Two blocks from the Moneda Palace on Teatinos Street. 90 rooms with private baths, all looking toward the street facing the magnificent Andes. All rooms with telephone and radio. Room service. Bus service. Garage. Good bar. Huérfanos and Teatinos.

Moderate

SANTA LUCIA. 65 rooms with private baths and telephones occupying three floors of modern downtown building. One or two bedroom suites with living room and kitchenette. Monthly rates available. Terrace Restaurant and Winter Garden Restaurant serve good meals. Room service, laundry, shoe shine, beauty parlor, and parking facilities. Huérfanos 779.

GRAN PALACE. 72 rooms, some suites, in modern new building, all with private bath and telephone. Grill, American bar, roof terrace garden. Room service and valet service at all times. Transportation to and from railway stations, bus sta-tions, airport. Garage for parking. 1171 Huérfanos and Morandé.

RITZ. 54 rooms with bath. Near shopping, business area. Estado 248.

EMPERADOR. Good location, on the Alameda facing old San Francisco church. 115 rooms, each with phone, radio, bath. Restaurant, laundry and room service. In the same building: beauty parlor and Turkish baths for ladies. Bernardo O'Higgins Ave. 853.

FORESTA. Excellent location facing Santa Lucia Hill. 40 suites. Spanish dining room, bar, tea room, conference room.

CANCILLER. Uptown, 10 minutes from city center. Small, quiet, 44 rooms with bath. Eliodoro Yañez 876.

ANTOFAGASTA AND SURROUNDINGS

First Class

TURISMO ANTOFAGASTA. "Honsa." A five-story luxury hotel with all the necessary comforts. 108 double rooms with private baths and magnificent view of the Pacific. Large hall, bar (American bar facing sea), terrace with gardens, swimming pool (with outdoor restaurant), big dining room opening onto terrace, internal gardens, boite, beauty parlor, barber shop, shops inside the hotel. Good service. The hotel owns boats and private transportation.

Moderate

HOSTERIA TAL TAL. Paved road from Antofagasta to the south leads to Taltal. At seaside, with 10 double rooms, each with private bath. Terrace facing the sea, sitting room, dining room-restaurant, bar. Near Taltal is the Chiu-Chiu Lagoon, over 900 feet deep, where legend claims some of the Inca treasures were sunk. Chiu-Chiu is still a colonial town in its way of life and its architecture.

HOSTERIA SAN PEDRO DE ATACAMA. "Honsa." A modern, comfortable inn in the town where time seems to have stopped at the beginning of the colonial period. It has a single room, five doubles, and two triples, all with private bath, plus a sitting room, dining room and bar. San Pedro de Atacama is full of incredible archeological treasures, and a famous museum has been built for the mummies found there and for the ceramics and Indian art of the zone.. The project is directed by Jesuit Father Le Paige. The town is 60 miles from Calama.

HOSTERIA CALAMA. A modern building with 14 rooms opening onto terraces, sitting room, dining room-restaurant and bar. Calama is 140 miles from Antofagasta and very near Chuquicamata, the largest open pit copper mine in the world.

HOSTERIA TOCOPILLA. A modern building decorated with contemporary art, it has 14 rooms with private baths and faces the sea. Beautiful gardens flank the inn, which also has three very comfortable sitting rooms, a dining room-restaurant, and a bar. The inn is half a mile from Tocopilla by paved road. Tocopilla embarks nitrate from nearby deposits. Deepsea fishing is famous in Tocopilla; swordfish and tuna are sought by fishing fans from many parts of the world.

ARICA

Deluxe

MOTEL AZAPA. One of the country's best hotels. Suites with kitchenette, refrigerator, private baths, terraces and tropical park. Boite, bar, elegant swimming pool. Transportation for guests.

First Class

EL PASO. Modern in design, surrounded by tropical parks and gardens. Located a mile from the city of Arica by paved road. 40 double rooms with private baths. Sitting room, dining room, bar, large comfortable terraces.

HOSTERIA ARICA. Facing sea, Morro de Arica. 60 double rooms with private baths. Also offers motel-type cabins. Dining room, sitting room, bar. Terraces and covered gardens overlook the Pacific. Private transportation for tourists.

MOTEL SAUCACHE. Ten cabins each with own parking space. Two or three bedrooms, bath and complete kitchen. No restaurant or bar. Out in the country on the Azapa road four miles from the center of Arica. Pleasant gardens.

Moderate

EL MORRO. At the skirts of the famed "Morro de Arica," surrounded by tropical vegetation. All rooms with private baths, air conditioning. Features bar, restaurant and swimming pool.

COPIAPO AND SURROUNDINGS

First Class

COPIAPO. Facing the plaza of the important mining center of Copiapó. 30 double rooms with private baths, several sitting rooms, ample gardens, dining room-restaurant, bar, card room, tea room. Near Copiapó is the great Paipote smelting center.

Moderate

HOSTERIA VALLENAR. "Husa." Modern two-story building surrounded by terraces, gardens, ponds. 19 double rooms with private baths, big sitting room, bar, dining room, restaurant. Vallenar is an important mining city, and the great Algarrobo ore fields are 28 miles away.

HOSTERIA DE CALDERA. At seaside. 7 double rooms with private baths, dining room-restaurant, bar, sitting room in new building. Caldera is 53 miles from Copiapó by paved road running through the Pampa Salitrera (nitrates). Several great mining establishments can be seen on the way. A picturesque place, considered the beach resort of Copiapó.

HOSTERIA DE CHAÑARAL. "Honsa." Also at seaside, a modern building with 9 single and 10 double rooms, all with private bath and a view of the temperate Pacific. Terraces, dining room-restaurant, bar. Chañaral is an important embarking port for iron ore, nitrate and copper.

IQUIQUE AND SURROUNDINGS

First Class

PRAT. "Honsa." In downtown Iquique, at one corner of the Plaza de Armas, 25 singles and 26 doubles, each with private bath. Big sitting room, dining room, bar, and covered and open-air gardens where meals are served. Boats available for fishing and water skiing. Nearby are the Mamiña Thermal Baths, with a great medical reputation.

HOSTERIA CAVANCHA. Inn. 3 minutes south from Iquique City near Cavancha Airport. 32 double rooms with private bath. Beautiful gardens with terraces facing the Pacific. Private seashore. Modern. Excellent typical and international cuisine. Laundry and garage service station.

Moderate

HOSTERIA PICA. 8 double rooms with private baths, comfortable and decorated with a modern touch. Dining room-restaurant, sitting room, bar. Swimming pool and several individual cabins. Located more than 3,000 feet above sea level, Pica offers many natural attractions.

LA SERENA AND SURROUNDINGS

First Class

TURISMO FRANCISCO DE AGUIRRE. La Serena's largest hotel, a modern three-story building with 73 double rooms with private baths. Large sitting room, bar, restaurant and boite. Large terraces surrounded by gardens. Ample facilities.

BUCANERO. Located at Guayacán, near La Serena's seaport of Coquimbo. Seascapes in view from the private balconies. Excellent restaurant and bar. For a really smashing drink, try the "Bucanero Special," already famous in Chile.

CABINAS DE PENUELAS. American-style motel four miles from La Serena by paved road. The motel has several cabins located by the sea, each with sitting room, bedroom, bath and terraced garden. Each cabin accommodates six persons. The Casino (no gambling) provides excellent restaurant service. The view is magnificent, and water sports can be practiced in the temperate waters of the sea, especially water skiing and skin diving.

Moderate

TURISMO OVALLE. Located at one corner of the plaza in the city of Ovalle. Comfortable rooms—13 singles and 19 doubles—with dining room, bar, tea room, large sitting room. Thirty miles from the famous beach of Tongoy, well known for its seafoods and temperate waters.

HOSTERIA VICUÑA. "Honsa." 35 miles from La Serena by paved road. 14 double rooms with private baths, dining room, bar, sitting room, terrace, swimming pool. Vicuña is a quiet city with a wonderful climate and is near the "Termas de Toro" (Bull Thermal Baths).

VIÑA DEL MAR

First Class

O'HIGGINS. Elegant and comfortable hotel on Arlegui Street, facing Plaza Francisco Vergara, beside the sea inlet called the estero. Near Municipal Casino, beach. 300 rooms and apartments with baths and phones. Charming Winter Garden. Reception and convention facilities. Top quality restaurant specializing in international cuisine, grill room and boite with orchestra, American bar. Room and valet service, laundry at all times, beauty parlor, barber shop, swimming pool, terraces and gardens. Garage and service station.

SAN MARTIN. At San Martín and Siete Norte Streets. 120 rooms with private bath and telephone, some with view of the ocean. Large sitting room with huge windows overlooking Avenida Peru and the Pacific. Only three short streets from the Casino. American bar with highly skilled barman. Room service, laundry, shoe shine, messenger service. Restaurant and snackbar.

MIRAMAR. Located on the rocks of Caleta Abarca beach, literally overhanging the sea. Semimodern design; 100 rooms with telephone and private bath. Suites with two bedrooms and living room. American bar, restaurant overlooking the Pacific on large terrace enclosed by glass panels. Boite with orchestra and dancing every evening during summer. Outdoor terraces and sea water swimming pool. Fashion shows at the hotel several times during year, especially in summer. One of the best views of Viña.

Moderate

ALCAZAR. Comfortable old hotel with new ultramodern addition of separate cabins. 75 rooms with private bath and telephone, restaurant and bar. Room service and laundry. Garage and parking lot. Well located, only one block from train station and two blocks from downtown Viña. Alvárez Street 646.

CHALET SUISSE. Comfortable; partly old, partly new. A great favorite with the older generation of both Chilean and foreign residents. 16 rooms with private bath, off-street parking lot, restaurant with a steady reputation for good, plain food. Downtown, close to the railroad station.

SOUTH OF SANTIAGO

CHILLAN. *Gran.* Sitting rooms, smoking room, big dining room, private supper rooms, bars. Big comfortable bedrooms, with a sitting room on each of the three floors. 2 singles and 58 doubles with private baths. Gran offers thermal baths and nearby ski slopes, plus the interesting crater of the Chillán Volcano. Located in the center of Chillán. *First class.*

CONCEPCION. *City.* This very old building houses a comfortable hotel with sitting room, bar, dining room and boite. All double rooms with private baths. Concepción is a cultural center with a famous university and also boasts several tourist attractions such as San Pedro Lagoon, complete with sand, beach, boats, and casino. Near Concepción are the most important coal mines of the country—Coronel, Schwager and Lota. Seaside towns such as Penco, Tomé and Dichato have earned a well-deserved reputation as beach resorts. *First class.*

Araucano. Elegant and comfortable hotel in the heart of the city. 300 apts. with bath and phone. Furnished in Spanish-Araucanian style. Temperate swiming pool. Restaurants with excellent meals. Disco, shops. Room service, laundry, garage and service station. *Deluxe.*

CONSTITUCION. *Hosteria Constitucion.* Recently constructed, the inn is located on the banks of the Maule River and is surrounded by gardens. The bar has large windows and a terrace overlooking the river; the dining room has a cozy fireplace, terrace and small tables from which the view can be seen. The sitting room also has a fireplace, plus a glass roof to make it more attractive. 25 double rooms with private baths, all looking on the magnificent Maule. Constitución is famed for its large beaches, clean and peaceful waters, and rock formations. *First class.*

LAJA FALLS. *Mariscal Alcazar.* This modern building located in the center of the city features a sitting room with fireplace, dining room opening onto terrace, bar, 25 double rooms with private baths. Near the city are the famous Laja Falls (120 feet high), a beautiful natural attraction. *First class.*

Motel Salto del Laja. Veritably beside the Laja Falls, this modern, very comfortable inn is designed to provide its guests with a beautiful view without ever leaving the motel. A bar, dining room, and swimming pool added to the visitors' comfort. *First class.*

LAKE CALAFQUEN. *Hosteria Calafquen.* On the banks of the lake bearing the same name, this inn is of rustic design and offers almost every tourist comfort. Three floors and a bar, dining room, sitting room, terraces. 3 single rooms and 50 doubles, each with private bath. The region offers unlimited opportunities for good fishing, hunting and water sports. From the inn the tourist can reach San Martín de los Andes in Argentina. *First class.*

LAKE PUYEHUE. *Gran Hotel Termas de Puyehue.* Located on the banks of Lake Puyehue, the hotel has thermal baths as an added attraction. The building is modern with many extras: swimming pool with hot thermal water, tennis courts, riding stables, boats for fishing and water skiing. 100 single and double rooms. Near the hotel is the Salto del Pilmaiquén (Pilmaiquén Falls) and the Antillanca Volcano, with famous ski slopes. *First class.*

Refugio Antillanca. A short 12 miles from Puyehue, on the Antillanca Volcano ski slopes. The refuge has 40 comfortable rooms, and the natural beauty makes the visit worth while even out of the skiing season. *Moderate.*

LAKE VILLARRICA. *Pucon Gran.* Located on the banks of Lake Villarrica and offers an overwhelming view of some of the world's most beautiful scenery. Sitting room, bar, dining room, private supper room, game room, tennis courts, terraces overlooking the lake, large gardens, "pergolas" (summer houses), and docks on the lake. Offers water skiing, horseback riding, places for hikes, excellent fishing and hunting. Hotel has boats and transportation facilities for guests. 130 rooms, all with private bath. *First class.*

Antumalal. Near Pucón. One of Chile's most fabulous, on the banks of Lake Villarica. Famous for its views and its service, it has been visited by such personalities as Queen Elizabeth, Prince Philip and Senator Barry Goldwater. The hotel organizes fishing and hunting trips for its guests. 20 rooms with private baths. Located on a small hill surrounded by forests. *Deluxe.*

Motel Yachting Club Villarrica. On the banks of the lake, with broad gardens. Swimming pool, sauna. Boats for fishing and yachts. *First class.*

LINARES. *Linares.* The city's best hotel, right in the center of town. Dining room, sitting room, private supper rooms, bar. 28 double rooms with private baths. 25 miles from Linares is the Achibueno River with good trout fishing. Also nearby are the Panimávida Thermal Baths. *Moderate.*

OSORNO. *Gran.* 100 rooms with private baths, large dining room, bar, sitting room. Nice building. Osorno is famous for its nearby tourist attractions, among them Lake Rupanco and Puyehue, both of which are well worth the visit. *First class.*

PORTILLO. *Portillo.* One of South America's outstanding ski resorts. 420 comfortable rooms, chalets, pool, skating, sauna. *Deluxe.*

PUERTO MONTT. *Perez Rosales.* Of rustic design, its balconies were carved by Chilean artists to represent typical scenes of the "Chilote" people who live along the channels of the Reloncavi Gulf. 5 floors, large luxurious sitting room, big dining rooms beautifully decorated and with fireplaces, bar, private supper rooms, beauty parlor, barber shop, commercial shops. 52 double rooms with small sitting room, one three-bed room and one six-bed room. Pureto Montt is a must for the visiting tourist. A clean city on the sea, it has a great panoramic view of the Reloncaví Gulf, Tenglo Island and several volcanoes. Its seafood is famous all over the country, especially "centollas." *First class.*

Hosteria Ancud. A rustic, solid building with sitting room, bar, dining room, 12 singles and 12 doubles, each with private bath. The region is famous as a touristic attraction because of the many picturesque towns found on the Island of Chiloé. Its forests and mountains are much admired by visitors.

Hosteria Castro. A modern building with bar, sitting room, dining room, 12 singles and 12 doubles with private baths, plus an extra 12-bed room. In the same region as the Hosteria Ancud. *First class.*

PUERTA VARAS. *Gran.* On the banks of Lake Llanquihue in marvelous Puerto Varas, a city which seems to have been transplanted from Germany. The hotel is very large—three floors surrounded by gardens and terraces. Big dining room, new cassino, bar, private supper room, sitting rooms, terraces. 400 rooms with private baths. Puerto Varas is located is one of the most magnificent spots of the lake region. The imposing figure of the Osorno Volcano always provides a breathtaking view. Bariloche, on the Argentine side of the Andes, can be reached from Puerto Varas. *First class.*

PUNTA ARENAS. *Cabo de Hornos.* New seven-story building with 150 deluxe rooms, each with private bath and telephone. Large reception hall, restaurant, bar, Winter Garden, laundry and valet service, garage. Punta Arenas is an important seaport and cattle and industrial region. Oil is found in several nearby fields, and the area offers many attractions to the enterprising tourist. *First class.*

TALCA. *Plaza Gran.* Talca's finest, in a three-story building facing the Plaza de Armas. Large sitting room, dining room, private supper room, bar on the first and second floors. 70 rooms with bath. Near Talca is Constitución, a famous beach resort, and 90 miles away by paved road is the Laguna de Maule, located near the border with Argentina. *First class.*

TEMUCO. *La Frontera.* 60 rooms with private bath. Centrally located. Has the same private owner as the Chalet Suisse in Viña del Mar. Reputed for good food, drinks and company. *First class.*

VALDIVIA. *Pedro de Valdivia.* Modern building surrounded by gardens, with large sitting room, dining room, magnificent bar. The hotel is decorated with beautiful murals and has an elegant boite, 85 double rooms with private baths. The city is famous for its beauty, located on the banks of the Calle-Calle River. Several picturesque towns along the river can be reached by boats leaving Valdivia. The region is also famous for its forests.

 SANTIAGO RESTAURANTS. Traditionally, the Chilean is a homebody. When he entertains, he uses his home to do so, and when he is entertained, it is in someone else's abode. For this reason Santiago was, until a few years ago, a very difficult town to paint red. At the time of this writing (1977) the main difficulty is the curfew which, though variable, is usually in effect from 2:00 a.m. to 5:30 a.m. The normal hour to begin dinner, either at home or in a restaurant, still remains 9–9:30 p.m.

The arriving tourist can find plenty to enjoy himself, no matter how long his stay. Of course, most of this activity is centered in Santiago, but Viña del Mar and Valparaíso have their own fine offerings, especially in the busy summer season. In all three cities there is a noticeable lack of nightclubs; most places offer fine meals as well as opportunities to dance, and many have their own floorshows. Price range for a complete meal at a very expensive restaurant: U.S. $30; expensive $20; medium-priced: $6. Dining/dancing restaurants, boites and discotheques $4–$20. All restaurants add 10% service charge, but a tip is expected in addition.

DINING ONLY

ENOTECA. In San Cristobal. Hilltop. A super view of Santiago, city of glass walls. Excellent music and fine food. A special place downstairs for learning about vineyards and to taste the finest wines, piscos of the North and South zone.

LA PORTADA COLONIAL.
Calle Merced. Excellent cosmopolitan cuisine and rich old world colonial elegance in former home of Chilean aristocrat. *Very expensive* but highly recommended. Fine wines and good seafood.

EL PARRON.
Sumptuous steaks served on individual grills—enough to whet lazy appetites. "Parrillada" is a specialty. Grape arbors cover the dining rooms. Fine wines, separate bar. Providencia 1184.

JACARANDA.
Delightful outdoor dining in summer, fine service, consistently excellent international menu. One of Santiago's best restaurants—a bit more *expensive* than the usual but worth it. Huérfanos 640.

BRIC Á BRAC.
French cuisine, elegant setting. Abadía 25.

RESTAURANT EMILIO.
For gourmets. From the kitchens of this simple building come what many agree is the best cuisine in town. Merced 477.

MUNCHEN.
Large outdoor and indoor restaurant specializing in German food. Excellent beer. Where many of the German colony gather nightly and on Sundays. Providencia, corner of Thayer Ojeda. 15 minutes from downtown.

BELLEVUE.
Good, fairly *inexpensive* food with top service. Added attraction: beautiful view of Santiago, from 12th floor of a modern building. Huérfanos 878.

LA CASCADE.
Excellent French food. Fairly *expensive*, but worth it. Ave. Francisco Bilbao 1947. Also **Cascade II**, Avenida Manuel Montt 260, Providencia.

MAISTRAL.
French, Chilean, international cuisine. Exclusive and *expensive*. Air conditioning. Spanish, English, French, German, Italian spoken. Mosqueto 485.

INNSBRUCK.
In suburbs. Excellent international cuisine.

RENDEZVOUS DES GOURMETS.
In outskirts of Santiago, Vitacura. International. Closed Sundays.

EL ESCORIAL.
French and Spanish; entertainment. Central, in Plaza Bulnes.

EL CASERIO.
Basque. Manuel Montt 126.

RESTAURANTE CANTON.
Merced 572, and next door,

EL DANUBIO AZUL,
Merced 564. Both good Chinese restaurants, serving very good meals and taking advantage of the existence of many Chilean foods—especially seafoods—which blend perfectly into the Chinese pattern for some dishes that surpass the authentic oriental plates. Also Lung Fung, at Agustinos 562.

DINING AND DANCING

ALERO DE LOS DE RAMON. In a typical Chilean colonial house in outskirts of city. Traditional Chilean dishes and Latin American music; sing-a-long led by Ramón family. Av. Las Condes 9389.

CANTA GALLO. 150-year-old beautiful building with the "Comilona a la Chilena" (eat all you want at a *reasonable* price) every Mon. and Fri. Show with most typical Chilean music. Characteristic ancient carriage identifies it. Av. Las Condes 12345.

EL POLLO DORADO. Serving the diner's choice of half a "golden chicken" (the translation of the name) or a huge steak. Dancing to "Pollo's" band. Floorshow features typical Chilean groups dancing the national dance, "The Cueca." At Agustinas and Estado, basement.

LA PIRAMIDE. Perched on a hilltop, this chic restaurant has glass walls for a super view. Flaming dishes are a specialty here and there is a Swiss chef to see that they really flame. In the evenings there is an orchestra for dancing. Really fine food service. Out Americo Vespuccio Norte to the end, then halfway up San Cristobal Hill on a gentle knoll. Expensive.

SAN CRISTOBAL RESTAURANT-BOITE. Situated atop Chile's famous San Cristobal Hill, the restaurant offers dining and dancing with a breathtaking view of the city by night.

LO CURRO. Charming, thatched-roof restaurant set in a forest of towering eucalyptus trees some 30 minutes by car from town. Delicious food, well prepared drinks and good service. Open for tea, cocktails, dinner and dancing all year. Soft music from a live orchestra. Filled with younger set until 10 p.m., when their seniors take over. Out Vitacura to Luis Pasteur, then over Mapocho bridge to Lo Curro Road.

WALDORF. Upstairs-and-downstairs restaurant, but downstairs there is also a boite with an adequate international floorshow. In both places, very good international food, and drinks downstairs are quite good as well. Downtown at Ahumada 131.

NURIA. Good attention and a good orchestra in the downstairs restaurant, specializing in international dishes. With separate bar, quite good. Agustinas 705-715.

INTERNATIONAL RESTAURANT (Hotel Carrera). Good food, with a menu that changes each day to offer three international specialties. Music by orchestra and by the Carrera's "Fantasia de Cuerdas" (Strings Fantasy) adds the proper touch to the elegance. Also in the Carrera is the Copper Room and, in summer, the rooftop restaurant beside the pool.

LAS BRUJAS, P. de Gales, far into the suburbs where it is possible to eat. But most go there to dance in the almost complete darkness and sip the excellent drinks offered.

Discotheques are unstable, but a few which seem to be achieving a certain permanence are: *Eve,* Vitacura 5480; *Hipopótamo,* Costanera 2873; *Le Moustache,* Nueva Costanera 2905; *Play Train,* Camino Las Condes; *Las Brujas,* Parcela 158; *Principe de Gales,* La Reina.

RESTAURANTS IN VIÑA DEL MAR

CHEZ GERALD. Good French cooking; dancing; two outdoor terraces; good bar; Ave. Peru, corner of 6 Norte.

CHEZ JACQUES. Excellent food in main dining room, outdoor grill. Discotheque with good music. Next door to Municipal Casino.

ARMANDITO. Sumptuous Argentine-style steaks on individual grills. 1 block from Hotel San Martin.

SAN MARCOS. Good Italian food, next door to Armandito, above.

NIGHTLIFE. The curfew, variable but currently (early 1977) 2 a.m. to 5:30 a.m. has decimated Santiago's "night clubs," which used to come to life about 1 a.m. and remain open until dawn. Among the survivors shows are mediocre and drinks expensive. The best late-evening entertainment is found in the "boites" of the good hotels, where the food is good and the gin isn't made in the kitchen. The *Bim Bam Bum* is a burlesque theater at Huérfanos 837, with variety acts and girls that show off but do not strip.

Humoresque, Picaresque and *La Sirena* are strip joints where there is no limit to the strip, but the audiences are far from distinguished

CASINOS. *Municipal Casino.* The biggest of the casinos, in Viña del Mar, is open daily September 15 to March 15, and weekends the rest of the year. Large gambling salons, full-size cabaret and boite with Chile's best dance bands. Saturday evening there is also a show in the main dining room. The new casino in the Gran Hotel in Puerto Varas also operates Sept. 15–March 15. Another new one, at Peñuelas (La Serena) was to be operating for the 1977 tourist season.

Arica has a casino open throughout the year which offers baccarat, roulette and vingt-et-un. There are also a good restaurant and a late-night cabaret.

SHOPPING. There are today almost no import restrictions in Chile, and the shops are well-stocked with imported goods of all kinds, fairly expensive because of customs duties. Most brands of American cigarettes are available everywhere, and a few English, at an average price of a dollar per pack of 20 cigarettes.

Among Chilean goods, the excellent textiles are worth mentioning. For "typical" items, colorful hand-woven ponchos are a good buy, and also vicuña rugs, and—although perhaps a little heavy for air travel—there is excellent artisan copper work.

Chilean stones have achieved much popularity abroad, and there are many "rock shops" in the city and suburbs selling quality work in lapis lazuli, Chilean jade, amethyst, agate, onyx and others. For beautiful work in pigskin, go to the *Talabateria Inglesa* in the Hotel Carrera and in Bandera Street.

There are enormous price differences from shop to shop, so it is as well to look around before buying. In some of the smaller shops it is still possible to bargain for a lower price, but not in the big department stores. Take a slow wander through the many arcades (*pasajes*) in the city center and in Providencia, which has become a big shopping area.

CASA LOBEN. Represents Bell & Howell. Well-stocked photo store with wide selection of color slides. 24-hour photo service, camera repair and a projection room for clients. Agustinas 1070.

REIFSCHNEIDER. The largest photo dealer in Chile, complete photographic supplies for the camera fan. Quick photo processing, plus a wonderful selection of color and black-and-white slides for sale. Agustinas 1151.

CHILEAN ART. A complete collection of Chilean souvenirs—ceramics, copper work, ponchos, vicuña. Agustinas 1010.

CASA BARROS. Old, reliable jewelry firm. Estado 310.

JOSE SANCHEZ Y CIA. Fine quality woolens and worsteds manufactured in Chile. Agustinas 931. No tailoring.

LEO SCHANZ. Custom-made pants for ladies, men, children in 8 hours, whatever type or color. Merced 535.

GALERIA CENTRAL DE ARTE. New modern, and perfectly lighted, close by hotels. Permanent exhibition of paintings, sculpture, ceramics and engravings and big enough to hold simultaneous exhibitions. Moneda 920, corner of Estado.

CEMA-CHILE. Permanent exhibition of typical handicraft of Chiloe, Toconao, Chillan and others. Nataniel 441.

CHILE TIPICO. Full of typical souvenirs, with artistic copperware and articles made of horsehair, silverware, blankets, ponchos, rugs and ceramics. Agustinas 1022, locals 149 and 153 (Windsor Theater Arcade).

GEO ROCK SHOP and **VENEZ VITE.** Located in the same arcade at Huérfanos 1160, both shops specialize in Chilean stones such as jade, lapis lazuli, amethyst, agate, onyx and the attractive pink "Rosa del Inca," or rhodocrosita, which is also found in Argentina.

JUVEN'S. Wide selection of clothing—mostly sport-type—for men. Two locations: Unión Central 1038 and Huérfanos 1024. Also Providencia.

FLAÑO. Elegant fashions for both men and women. The world's most famous brands are found among Flaño merchandise, as well as many local creations worth taking home with you. Huérfanos 964, and Providencia.

FATH. On the corner of Ahumada and Huérfanos. Very high-class silversmith and jeweler. Maintains a repair service with a qualified watchmaker.

 **SPORTS.** Chile participates in almost every sport common to countries in the Western Hemisphere. Without spectacular success, but with plenty of enthusiasm, Chile has been represented at the Olympic Games (summer and winter), the World Championship of Football (soccer), riding championships, international athletic meets, and a host of other competitive events.

As a Latin American country, Chile is well within the football (soccer) area of the world. And at this game Chileans have happily seen their teams grow from adolescence to maturity in a short time.

While Football is King, there are other sports in which Chile has an outstanding record. Recently its participants won the South American Riding Championship, and Captain Larraguibel still holds the world record in high jumping with the horse appropriately named "Huaso." A finalist in the 1976 Davis Cup championships.

With the abundance of mountain ranges come an abundance of places to ski (June to Sept.), mountain climb and camp, such as the ski resorts of Farellones, Lagunillas and Portillo and the new Ski Center with a ski lift in the south of the slopes of the Villarrica Volcano. Portillo, located five hours by train from Santiago is the country's ski capital and boasts fine accommodations, several chair-lifts and tows, and a six-mile run. Other smaller runs are located as close as 32 miles from Santiago. Swiss and Austrian ski pros operate Chile's ski schools.

Beaches and lakes all through the country give ample opportunities for every water sport from skin diving to water skiing. Boating is another favorite pastime with Chileans and visitors, and there are facilities for deepsea fishing in the north, at Tocopilla and Antofagasta (Mar./Sept.) Skin diving is good along the whole coast.

Chile is a fisherman's paradise. A license is required, which may be obtained from the "Club de Pesca y Caza" in any city (Rod and Gun Club).

In the north there's deepsea fishing all year round for tuna, bonito, swordfish, black marlin, striped marlin and shark. In the central valley are found brown trout and pejerrey. The really good rainbow trout fishing is in the south, where a 10-pound fish is a little fellow.

There is no agency organized to set up fishing tours down south, but the Rod and Gun Club secretary can be helpful if you're interested. The same club will arrange for licenses to hunt quail, partridge, snipe, doves, rabbits, ducks, and others.

A number of country clubs and stadiums allow visitors to participate in or watch such sports as basketball, tennis, volleyball, golf, horseback riding, track events, hockey, polo, rugby, and bowling. Many of the resident foreigners belong to country clubs where all sports are practiced.

In sports spectacles, football again occupies the No. 1 spot. The Football Association organizes many international games in which the most famous teams of the world have come to play, though they have never found it easy to beat the Chilenos. These matches, as well as most other sporting events, are held in the state-owned National Stadium, with a seating capacity of 80,000. The World Basketball Championship took place there, as did part of the World Football

Championship of 1962. Much of the national competition in football takes place in the stadium each year, and important swimming, tennis and track events are usually held there.

The National Stadium was built in 1935 when the late President Arturo Alessandri (father of President Jorge Alessandri, 1958-64) was in office. At that time it was considered a white elephant, ostentatious and useless, but it soon proved too small for the needs of a city as large as Santiago. Before the 1962 World Championship it was necessary to enlarge it to accommodate the large number of visitors expected, and in spite of those efforts it was still too small. Now, when a particularly hot game takes place between national teams or when an important international event is scheduled, there are always large numbers of fans unable to get seats. Fortunately, two of the football clubs are building stadiums with seating capacities of more than 100,000.

Horse racing fans have plenty of opportunities to enjoy the sport. In Santiago there are two race tracks, the *Hipódromo Chile* open mornings on Sundays and holidays and the *Club Hípico* open afternoons on the same days. Occasionally races take place during the week, especially on Wednesdays. In Viña del Mar races are held at the Sporting Club, open all day on holidays.

 GETTING THE RIGHT PICTURE. With such scenic wonders and such a variety of climate and geography, the camera bug will have wonderful opportunities for great pictures in Chile—if he keeps a few pointers in mind. Expensive cameras and/or accessories must be declared in customs when entering the country, as well as the types and number of rolls of film. At any rate film can be found almost everywhere in the country, at least such common types as 620 or 120 and 127. 35 m. film is very common, especially in Santiago, Valparaíso, and other larger cities.

Every major brand of film can be found in the country. Kodak is the big name, and its yellow sign is seen in some of the most remote places. Other brands, such as Agfa and Ilford, are well known to the national camera bugs. If more film is needed for that added trip to the provinces, it is best to be on the safe side and buy it from any of the camera stores scattered around downtown Santiago or Valparaíso.

It is advisable to bring along a set of filters—especially a haze filter —for black and white film, as skys and clouds will look better. Use your light meter to be sure of the correct exposure for desert and snow shots and for photos taken in the exceptionally clear sunshine of the middle north.

No special precautions need to be taken with the camera before coming to Chile. The temperature and humidity of the country are such that the camera will require no special oils. Neither is there any special problem with the film.

If the visitor plans a rather long stay, it is advisable that he have color film developed, either within the country or by sending it abroad (delay, about 4 weeks). Kodachrome II, for instance, must be sent out, but all other kinds such as Agfacolor, Ektachrome can be developed. And if the need arises, efficient camera mechanics are available in Santiago through important camera stores.

**USEFUL ADDRESSES.** Embassy of United States, Agustinas 1343 (near Hotel Carrera); U.S. Consulate Merced 230; British Embassy and Consulate, Avenida Concepción 177; Canada, Ahumada 11, 10th floor; LAN-Chile Airlines, Agustinas 1109; Dirección de Turismo, Agustinas opposite Hotel Carrera. All in Santiago. Automobile Club, Pedro de Valdivia 195, Providencia.

AMERICAN EXPRESS AGENTS: Santiago, *Turismo Cocha*, Agustinas 1122.

ARGENTINA

Big Land - Big Hopes

BY

HERBERT M. CLARK and GEORGE HILLS

(Herbert Clark was a veteran foreign correspondent who reported on South America from 1937. He spent most of his time in Argentina where, we regret to report, he died before being able to complete this chapter. Upon the death of Mr. Clark, George Hills, a South American expert for the BBC, accepted the task of finishing this section, to which he made substantial contributions. William L. F. Horsey, for 17 years United Press International's general news manager for South America, brought this chapter up to date for the present edition.)

The traveler who comes to Argentina will be visiting at least two peoples and the equivalent of a score of countries.

The *porteño*—remember that word; it means "resident of the port," and Buenos Aires, the capital of Argentina, *is* the port of that country—is a rough-and-ready type. Sometimes he's described—and by himself—as a *vivo*, a "live one" who knows how to get along in life. One-third of all Argentines (all but a small percentage are pure white, a mixture generally of Spanish and Italian with Irish, English, German and Central European strains which have emigrated to southern South America over the centuries) lives in Greater Buenos Aires, the capital and its circling suburbs. This area covers only some 1,100 square miles (one one-thousandth of Argentina) but has 6,364 people per square mile in contrast to the 20 people who occupy each square mile of the country of 25,000,000 as a whole.

Outside the capital the *provinciano*—inhabitant of the farm-land, even if he comes from such another population center as Rosario or Córdoba—is a kind, gentle, courteous and helpful soul who will be delighted to walk blocks out of his way to make sure you find what you want and would be insulted by being offered any pay for his services.

Argentina, though not so big as the United States, is as large as the combined countries of Western Europe. It is the eighth largest country in the world. You'll never be disappointed in the scenery, whatever you seek. Argentina is a giant right-angled triangle which stretches from the 22nd parallel of south latitude down to the South Pole itself and from the snow-capped Andes mountains east to the Atlantic Ocean. It is some 980 miles, west to east, at its broadest, and stretches 2,150 miles south to north on mainland South America from Bolivia to Cape Horn. It is 4,600 miles long on the basis of Argentina's claim to the South Pole. It covers 1,100,000 square miles at the southern end of the continent; Chile, its western neighbor, runs as far south and files diplomatic counterclaims to the south polar area.

Argentina embraces an assortment of climates from the freezing pole up to the subtropic north along contiguous borders with Bolivia and Paraguay. Brazil and Uruguay lie to the northeast. And Argentina's regions range from rocky deserts in the Andes to the fertile green pampas, flat grassy plains along the Atlantic. You'll find everything you want from mountains (Aconcagua, at 22,834 feet, is a challenge to climbers and the hemisphere's highest peak) to the sea-level plains, from a set of waterfalls at Iguazú (stretching around a 9,000-foot semicircle and booming from a crest 230 feet high down to the bed of the Paraná River, a tributary of the River Plate system) to grazing lands. Far to the southwest you'll find a miniature Switzerland, where a string of icy lakes with the Andes mountains for a backdrop are filled with salmon trout weighing up to 25 pounds and ready to fight the hardiest of fishermen.

El Libertador

Whichever city, town or even large village you reach first in Argentina, you will come across a main square dominated by a fine equestrian statue: a noble figure of a general upon a horse worthy of its rider. Usually, but not invariably, the pedestal will bear the name of the man so prominently commemorated —General José de San Martín, El Libertador, the liberator; not always, because there is no more need for it in Argentina than for an effigy of George Washington to carry its identification in the U.S.A. San Martín's portrait has a hallowed place in every state school, and though new postage stamp issues are frequent,

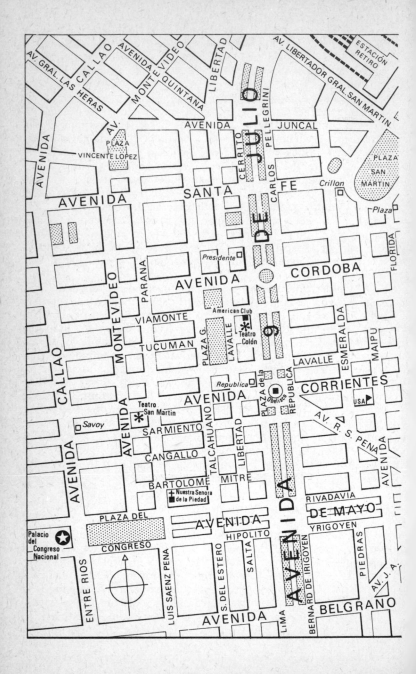

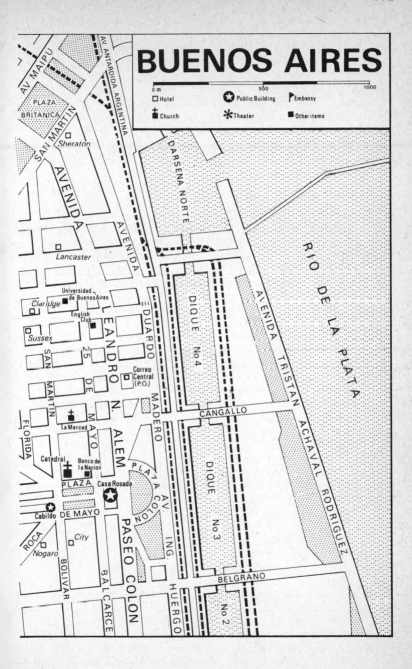

BUENOS AIRES

0 m   500   1000

☐ Hotel   ★ Public Building   ▶ Embassy

✝ Church   ✳ Theater   ■ Other items

AV MAIPU

AV ANTARDIDA ARGENTINA

PLAZA BRITANICA

SAN MARTIN

Sheraton

DARSENA NORTE

AVENIDA

AVENIDA

RIO DE LA PLATA

Lancaster

Claridge

Universidad de Buenos Aires

English Club

LEANDRO

EDUARDO

DIQUE No 4

AVENIDA TRISTAN ACHAVAL RODRIGUEZ

Sussex

SAN

25

DE

MADERO

Correo Central (P.O.)

MARTIN

N.

ALEM

La Merced

FLORIDA

Catedral

Banco de la Nacion

CANGALLO

DIQUE No 3

PLAZA

PLAZA A AV. COLON

Casa Rosada

Cabildo

DE MAYO

PASEO COLON

ROCA

City

ING.

Nogaro

BOLIVAR

BALCARCE

HUERGO

BELGRANO

No 2

there is always one series in circulation which portrays the General.

No man did more to make Argentina an independent nation than did General José de San Martín, and his memory is therefore given pride of place everywhere. One of the main railroad systems has been given his name. There are three important towns called after him—one close to Buenos Aires, a second a port up the Paraná River and the third a tourist center of particular charm in the Andes. The least that a village can do is to have its one street bear his name: the center of Buenos Aires has a square and a street, and its finest avenue of all is the Avenida del Libertador.

The European Influence

The history of Argentina figures in street names at every turn in Buenos Aires and as far northwest and south as you can go from the capital. *Reconquista*, 25 *de Mayo*, 9 *de Julio* recall three major steps in the independence of Argentina. *Rivadavia* was Argentina's first elected president. In other countries of Latin America the people among themselves still refer to squares and streets by their centuries-old names as often as by their modern official ones. Not so in Argentina. Nevertheless Argentina takes pride in her European origins. There is little vilification of her Spanish past, and the essential continuity of her history from the arrival of the earliest Spanish settlers four hundred and fifty years ago to the present day is generally recognized. The history taught to schoolchildren pays tribute to the fearlessness of the Spanish explorer and settler as well as to the French 18th-century philosophers who influenced the settlers' decision to secede from Spain, to the British who served with General San Martín and to those of many nationalities who helped the young free nation to develop economically.

Though Argentine nationalism may seem to the observer to take extreme forms at times (as when, to quote one example, an American journal with a world-wide circulation published a feature article in which General San Martín's character was judged not without faults, and Argentine schoolchildren were officially herded in procession solemnly to lay wreaths at the foot of his monument "in reparation"), the Argentine looks upon himself as European through and through in race and culture; and indeed he is. Even his very nationalism has had its parallels in France and Germany.

He will insist also that he is American, that is, an inhabitant of the American continent. The narrowed use of the word "American" as a synonym for "a citizen of, or pertaining to, the U.S.A." consequently arouses in the Argentine as much resentment and indignation as does among Europeans, including the insular British, the French politician's equation of Europe with France.

The Argentine himself, it is true, will refer to the people of the U.S.A. as "North Americans," but then the Argentine feels he has less in common with Mexico than with Spain, less with Canada than with Britain, and far more in common with the Russians, Poles and Yugoslavs, the Italians and the Germans of Europe than with those of such countries who emigrated due westward and are now in and of the United States. Yet there is a very real link between the U.S.A. of a hundred years ago and modern Argentina; the Argentine federal constitution, for all the changes it has undergone, still bears a distinct resemblance to that of the U.S.A. (for all its amendments). The Argentine constitution of 1853 was consciously modeled on Washington's original. The architectural similarity between the Congress Building in Buenos Aires and the Capitol in Washington is more than coincidental, and there may have been a tribute to the north when the Argentine Presidential Offices Building came to be called the "Casa Rosada" (the "Pink House"). The events of 1776 in North America had a direct influence on the events of 1810 in the southern half of the continent.

A Country Named by a Poet

This first one-third of the history of independent Argentina (the name by which a Spanish poet, Martin del Barco Centenera, had called the region in 1602 and which was officially adopted in 1860) can be summarized in terms of the ideals for which many died. Firstly there was war over the concept of kingship, between one group of its inhabitants loyal to the person of the hereditary King of Spain and the other to the office of kingship. Secondly war over the concept *patria*, one group, mostly but not entirely men of peninsular birth, who looked on the Spanish new world as an extension of the motherland, and the other group, born in the new world, who interpreted the term as the land of their birth. Mixed in with all this is the reaction against the absolutism introduced into Spain by the French Bourbon kings and which made acceptable among Spaniards and Spanish colonists the doctrines of the French philosophers who had reacted against it in France. Thirdly there was war between those who would fragment the concept of "motherland" still further and those who would not, and again between those who hoped to reproduce in Buenos Aires a replica of the absolutism once exercised in Paris and Madrid and those who believed them betrayers of the cause for which they had gone to war in the first place. There were in all these wars commercial interests and economic forces, but their importance must not be exaggerated: General San Martín would have been a wealthy man had he remained in the service of Spain. He did not fight for vainglory (he could have done this in Europe) or for gain, but for an ideal.

Many Argentines who have held the same rank have been motivated to military and political action by baser motives, but by no means all; and it is relevant to the present political condition of Argentina that when the armed services have intervened in government, some of their leaders have acted out of high motives and with General San Martín, the Liberator, as mentor. The fifty years of wars had a second effect relevant to today's situation. Under Spanish rule there was an old tradition that local birth should be no bar to executive or administrative posts, even the highest. Argentina, then, was not born without a body of able and experienced civil servants and civilian politicians, but the protraction of internal strife did leave the country without the means to bring the armed services under full civilian control in the country's formative years, as happened in the U.S.A. Thus, the Army to this day has the political power necessary to make or break a president.

It must not be thought, however, that strife was continuous or that it totally impeded the development of the country, far from it. Rivadavia, elected President of the United Provinces in 1826, founded banks, made satisfactory commercial treaties with foreign powers, encouraged the importation of fine cattle, and established schools, universities, and hospitals. By mid-century the white population totalled about one and a quarter million. It had agricultural produce adequate to its needs. Towards the end of the colonial period the colonists had begun to realize that the "silver mines" of the Jesuit *reducciones* had been none other than good soil and husbandry. The lands of the *reducciones* (the modern provinces of Misiones, Corrientes and Formosa along the rivers) had reverted to jungle, and their inhabitants scattered, but colonists and newly independent Argentines had found that the fringes of the Pampa were ideal for the cultivation of fine grasses and fodder. The cattle and horses which from the earliest time had multiplied without the need of much attention from the landowners or their *gauchos* were now to become a vital asset worth some conscious effort.

Agriculture and Industry

Internal peace in Argentina coincided with the population explosion (and famines) of mid-19th-century Europe. There was a demand for cheap food in Europe. Argentina had the land, and Europe the tools. Ploughs and harvesters, well-drilling machines and windmills to raise water to the surface and immigrants from Spain, Italy and elsewhere to make use of them came in the new steamships, to be followed rapidly by British and French engineers and Irish laborers to build railroads of which over the next seventy years 25,000 miles were to be laid.

Now in theory all land to the south of Buenos Aires and westward to the Andean chain was Argentina, but in fact south of a line of forts along the Rio Salado (Salty River) a hundred miles to the south of the capital few had ventured since the expulsion of the

Jesuit missionaries from there as from the northern regions. The Indian tribes had reverted to barbarism. From time to time they would raid the "civilized" zone on the Buenos Aires side of the forts for cattle. They were inhospitable to the would-be settlers among them. A young officer, Julio A. Roca, undertook the pacification of the south. He carried it out in the years 1878-83 using the same methods as were employed against the North American Indians (and against the Scottish Highlanders by the English in their pacification following 1745) and justifying them with the same excuses. The results were also similar. The Indians were virtually exterminated. The way was open for Argentina to become one of the world's major sources of agricultural produce.

Julio Roca's reward was the presidency. His officers received tracts of land no less than one hundred thousand acres apiece. The really vast estate had been the exception rather than the rule under the Spanish rule, but in the troubles following independence there had been many opportunities for the few to dispossess the many, for estates to be joined together and for as many as a million acres to come into the ownership of one man or family. The Army officers, it must be said in passing, were not the only recipients of virgin land. Many of the laborers laying the railroad tracks availed themselves of the opportunity of being paid in kind with land adjacent to the tracks, thus laying as well the foundations of considerable fortunes. For the land cleared of the Indians was pampa with never less than six feet of top soil on which Lucerne grass (alfalfa) would be grown to feed the beef cattle for which there was a huge market in industrial Britain. Hides, tallow and salt beef had been Argentina's exports during the whole of the Colonial period, but with the development of refrigeration chambers in ships it became possible to send frozen beef. But the toughness of the Argentine breeds then became apparent. Their upgrading became necessary, pedigreed bulls were imported from England, and today Argentine meat eaten in Argentina is second to none in quality and taste.

Herds to provide the meat for which there was a European market required man power; the tilling of the soil for the sowing of forage and its harvesting required it even more. Immigrants flocked by the tens of thousands, mostly from Italy and Spain; in half a century there were over one and a quarter million who came, and stayed. The landowners were interested not so much in the land or what was done with it as with the cattle which could be reared on it and on the alfalfa to feed them. They let the immigrants have plots of land on which to grow wheat for three years and keep the profits, provided that they planted alfalfa in the fourth year and moved on. The alfalfa in this rotation was cuttable twice a year for up to ten years. The land was then leased again.

Now the market for the wheat proved almost as profitable as that for beef cattle, and it began to be grown for its own sake, not merely to the south and west but to the north of Buenos Aires in the province of Entre Ríos (Between Rivers, and hence often referred to as Mesopotamia). While Buenos Aires grew into one of the world's great cities and ports with the cattle trade (and with the sheep trade for which the bulge south of it was discovered to be particularly suitable), Rosario, across the Paraná in the province of Santa Fe, became the world's greatest grain port.

The pattern of agriculture has changed in detail since those nineteenth-century days; but though the economy is more diversified today with the development of several other agricultural products and with industrialization, it still depends for the most part on wheat and meat.

The comings and goings of presidents and political parties in the period 1860 to June 1943 are of relatively slight importance. Radicals alternated in office with Conservatives. Socialists date their origins back to the 19th century but had little power before the 1930s. The Communist Party of Argentina is technically the oldest in South America, but even today it appeals only to young university men and frustrated skilled workers.

The Perón Era

In June 1943, the President, Ramon Castillo, a former judge and university professor, was deposed by these generals. The Army however was far from united. The first Army President, Rawson, lasted one day; the next, General Ramirez, nine months; the third, Farrell, two years. But the real power behind the scenes did not emerge till 1946. That was Colonel Juan Domingo Perón. He had a remarkable woman at his side, Eva Duarte.

Perón during the next nine years evolved a personal mixture of authoritarianism and national socialism which is called *justicialismo*. One of its aspects was its intense nationalism. At the end of the 1939-45 war Argentina had truly remarkable assets from the sale of her agricultural products to the allies. With them, and bearing in mind the oil and gas resources of Argentina, Perón could have developed his country into an industrial giant without impairing its agricultural capacity. Instead, for domestic reasons, he bought out the foreign-owned railways (which were in need of urgent repairs and modernization), harassed established foreign enterprises and undertook various large prestige schemes. On the other hand he gave a favorable hearing to industrial, transport and dock workers. In the face of ever-reducing national productivity, he raised their wages and raised them again.

With such a policy he came to be worshipped by a majority of the working classes; his wife, Eva, even more so, for apart from her considerable ability, she was seen by them as the poor girl from the wrong side of the tracks who had risen to be the president's wife, and who even (some hoped) might be the world's first woman president. Perón's, and even more Eva's, personality cult was more than those in the armed services could stand. As it happened, Eva died. Every night thereafter at the hour of her death there was a commemoration on all radio and television. Relations between the Church and the State, only momentarily good at the beginning of Perón's regime when he promised to permit religious instruction in the public schools, reached the breaking point. A band of soldiers led by Generals Leonardi and Aramburu rose against him, and over half of the ordinary men and women rallied to their support. This was, in fact, the first popular revolution (popular in the sense that civilians participated in it) since the 1810 rising against the Spaniards.

After Peron was forced to leave the country, Generals Leonardi and Aramuburu took over as joint presidents. In 1958 Dr. Arturo Frondizi, a member of a faction of the Radical Party, was victorious in a constitutional presidential election. His success was attributed mainly to the backing he received from the supporters of the exiled Peron. Peron was said to have made a secret agreement with Frondizi for that support, subject to certain conditions laid down by the former president.

Frondizi faced a lot of opposition and there were several attempts to force him out of office. However, his policy of encouraging foreign financial sources resulted in some sizable foreign investments in Argentina during that period, particularly in the oil industry which expanded to a point where there was almost national self-sufficiency. But before his term of office expired, he was ousted by a group of officers.

The year 1962 was a time of political drama—there was one day when Argentina witnessed three separate individuals being announced as president. But that day, following some strategic sleight of hand by the Radical Party, the president of the Senate, Dr. Jose Guido, moved into the top job.

Guido was replaced in October 1963 by Dr. Arturo Illia, a comparatively unknown family doctor from upcountry, who belonged to the Intransigente, or left-wing of the party. His first act in office was to cancel all contracts with foreign oil companies, a decision that set the country back for years, said his opponents. He was forced from office in June 1966 by General Juan Carlos Ongania, being physically ejected from the Casa Rosada Palace by federal policemen.

At first, Ongania appeared to have overwhelming popular support, but as time went by his regime gave many Argentinians the impression that he was modeling himself and his government on that of the Franco government in Spain, and that he had no intention of ever willingly giving up his power. The armed forces

LANGUAGE/30
For the Business or Vacationing International Traveler

Now in 20 languages! A basic language course on cassette tapes (up to 2 hours) complete with a pocket phrase dictionary and social guide...Only $14.95 EA.(plus shipping)

Now that you have this Fodor Guide please don't overlook another key to a more enjoyable and successful trip: the ability to speak basic words and phrases in the language of the country you are visiting.

To help you gain this invaluable knowledge FODOR is pleased to offer the new DUN-DONNELLEY LANGUAGE/30 CASSETTE SERIES in a choice of 20 of the world's languages at the low price of $14.95 per course. (Ten additional languages in preparation.)

Language/30 is now available commercially after its exclusive testing and use in preparing U.S. government personnel for overseas duty. Programmed for fast learning, each basic mini-course allows you to learn, simply and effectively, the useful words and phrases needed in your travels. Each course offers guided practice in greetings, introductions, asking questions and general conversation for the traveler at hotels, restaurants and places of business and entertainment— plus a special section on the social customs and etiquette of each country. The pocket dictionary can be used for on-the-spot reference.

Let Language/30 be your passport to successful international travel, and remember—by making an effort to speak their language you will be showing an interest in people which will open countless doors to the friendship, hospitality and business opportunities that await you the world over. Language courses currently available:

ARABIC	FRENCH	INDONESIAN	NORWEGIAN	SERBO-CROATIAN
CHINESE	GERMAN	ITALIAN	PERSIAN	SPANISH
DANISH	GREEK	JAPANESE	PORTUGUESE	SWAHILI
DUTCH	HEBREW	KOREAN	RUSSIAN	TURKISH

dismissed him in June 1970 and recalled General Roberto Livingston from Washington to take his place. But Livingston was soon accused of leaning too heavily toward a form of populism, and by March 1971 he, too, was superseded—by General Alejandro Lanusse, a man who for long had been regarded as "the power behind the throne."

The country had had almost seven years of military-dominated governments, but now Lanusse promised that there would be democratic national elections. Peron was constitutionally debarred from running as a candidate because he was living in Madrid. Lanusse went on record as saying that he thought Peron would be afraid to return to Argentina.

But the Peronists were by no means finished as a political force. Some of the Frejulia alliance chose Dr. Hector Campora, a country dentist and a former chairman of the House, as their presidential candidate along with another erstwhile conservative, Dr. Vicente Solano Lima, as vice presidential candidate. Fighting under the slogan "Campora to the Presidency and Peron to Power," Campora won by a massive majority.

Campora's mere 49 days in office were accompanied by much unrest. His opponents occupied factories, universities and hospitals, and attacked army bases. May 25, 1973 was a particularly bad day with the extremists trying to take over the government. The president had to flee from the Congress building by helicopter, and many foreign diplomats were prevented from entering the Casa Rosada Palace.

That night the jails were emptied of political prisoners, and in the confusion many hardened criminals also escaped.

Campora flew to Spain to invite Peron to return home. Peron was in poor health, but he returned with Campora on June 20. Even his return from exile was marred by disturbances. As his plane approached Ezeiza International Airport, 120,000 of his followers, gathered there to welcome him home, clashed with a large group of opponents. To help reduce tension, Peron's plane was diverted to the Moron Seventh Air Force Base, but the day ended with many casualties.

Campora resigned and was appointed ambassador to Mexico. New elections were held and Peron was once again swept into power with a big majority. But along with the problems of poor health, Peron found that the times had changed and that not everybody acclaimed him. At one huge rally in the Plaza de Mayo, 20,000 members of the Monteneros abused him and marched from the meeting to form an underground opposition.

Peron paid a state visit to Paraguay in June, 1974, against his doctor's advice. His physical condition worsened, and on June 29 his wife Isabel, who was visiting in Madrid, was recalled home. Peron handed over the presidential duties to her. He was nearing 79 and suffering from several respiratory and cardiac complications. On July 1 he went into a coma and three hours later he was dead.

Isabel attempted to continue governing with the support of the Peronist entourage and the trade union leaders of the C.G.T. But within a year it was apparent that the country was on the verge of bankruptcy.

On March 23, 1976, after 20 months of uncertain government, and racked with an annual inflation rate of more than 600 percent, Argentina once again experienced a political coup instigated by a military junta. This was commanded by General Rafael Vizela. The junta appointed a cabinet of military men, and this has since been battling with the problems of a rabid inflation and the country's general, financial disarray.

EXPLORING ARGENTINA

It would be an understatement to call Buenos Aires the heart of Argentina. With 3,000,000 people in the city proper and 10,000,000 in "Greater Buenos Aires," it accounts for nearly a third of the body of the country as well, even though it comprises only a thousandth of Argentina's area.

Buenos Aires

Biggest city in Latin America, and biggest of all Spanish-speaking cities, Buenos Aires is as cosmopolitan as any city in the world. Its theaters, shops, hotels, subways and public buildings are large, luxurious and modern. True, it does not show much of a past, for there is little left of the original 16th-century settlement here (Buenos Aires was first founded in 1536 by Pedro de Mendoza, but settlers had to move out in the face of fierce Indian attacks, and a permanent colony was established on the site by Juan de Garay only in 1580). But Buenos Aires lives for the present.

Pot-holes are a nasty hazard for drivers, but all sidewalks and streets were to be repaired by last year. *Porteños* themselves are wont to froth at such inconveniences, but they are only minor when stacked alongside the elegance and the power of this city with its mighty avenues (Ninth of July Avenue, with ten lanes of traffic, is the widest in the world) and imposing buildings.

It is a lush city in many respects, with an increasing number of skyscrapers spotted through a host of parks. Its port teems with ships of all types and flags. Elegant Calle Florida and pushing and booming Avenida Santa Fé afford superb shopping centers where you can buy anything from an automobile to a wallet —made in Argentina. Buenos Aires has a horde of museums and stresses its culture with myriad art exhibits. The Colón Opera House is acoustically one of the world's best; a handsome Grecian building from the outside, inside it displays comfortable red-plush seats and boxes (some used to be covered by carved grilles so that families in the so-common Latin mourning could see the performances without themselves being on public view) and a splendid stage. Buenos Aires offers 42 theaters, among them: the Teatro Municipal General San Martín—an ultramodern building housing separate auditoriums as well as the Museum of Modern Art—and the Teatro Nacional Cerventes.

The largest and prettiest of the Buenos Aires 150 parks, the Palermo Park, is located on Avenida Libertador General San Martín. Adjoining it are the Zoological and Botanical Gardens, a splendid polo complex (2 fine fields) and close by a handsome rococo race track called the Hipódromo Argentino. Another similar turf track, seating 45,000 people, is located at San Isidro, a suburb of Buenos Aires.

A quick tour of the capital might start with the Plaza de Mayo and the Casa Rosada (the pink—and it is!—Government House), the Cathedral where General San Martín lies entombed in state, and the Cabildo, Argentina's town meeting hall, where the first local Government was formed on May 25, 1810. Behind this plaza stands the War Ministry, one of the grandest buildings in Buenos Aires. Continue on to Avenida Libertador General San Martín and the Plaza Britania, with its big clock tower, donated by the English and Anglo-Argentines. Also on this avenue are located the Museum of Fine Arts as well as the new Buenos Aires Sheraton Hotel.

For straight sightseeing, try the Avenida de Mayo, commercial hub of the capital and adjacent Rivadavia Street, longest in the world stretching 115 blocks in Buenos Aires and another 20 miles west and north after it crosses the city limits and enters the provinces of Buenos Aires.

La Boca to Belgrano

For a more picturesque part of town, go to La Boca (preferably by night), graced by now-abandoned traveling-crane bridges put up a century ago to haul horse-drawn beef drays from one side of the river to the other. It was here that the tango was adopted. In summer don't miss a musical or comedy performance at the open-air Teatro Caminito, in the closed street La Vuelta de Rocha. It's a unique experience. It's a fascinating part of Buenos Aires on the southern outskirts, bounded on the south (the city limits of Buenos Aires) by the "Riachuelo," an arm of the River Plate which serves as a freight dock and as Buenos Aires' fishing port. Houses there were slums not so long ago. An artist named Benito Quinquela Martin has done wonders for the region, however. He himself is a superb painter of the port scene, and he loves the port so much that he has built a primary school and given it to the city, housing a museum of waterfront paintings in it. He has spurred a drive to paint homes in sharp primary colors, and some of these houses have become restaurants for gourmets as well as gourmands. At Pedro de Mendoza 1835 is La Boca Fine Arts Museum, open daily.

From the Boca to Belgrano, you will find the streets dotted with stalls, flower vendors to book dealers to kiosks selling newspapers, magazines and paperback books.

If you become interested in the Argentine economy, you might drop by the local Stock Exchange (at the intersection of 25 de Mayo and Sarmiento), or, if you're in Buenos Aires around July, go out Santa Fé to the 4,800 area at Plaza Italia with its fine statue of Garibaldi and to the fairgrounds of the Argentine Sociedad Rural and see the livestock show that organization sponsors annually. You will be impressed by the number of fine, pudgy cattle on display, not to mention the superb horses.

Florida, the world-famous shopping street, is no longer what it was in the days when the likes of Harrods and Cartier's were found there. It is now a ten-block shopping mall for pedestrians, adorned with ornamental flower pots, and, as happened on Fifth Avenue in New York, the banks are slowly moving in. Now for a deluxe shopping expedition take a saunter along Avenida Santa Fé, and venture into the numerous arcades and adjacent side streets, for purchases in exquisite taste. Avenida Corrientes is the "Broadway" movie center. Ninth of July Avenue features dry-goods establishments, streams of traffic and a mammoth underground parking plaza that is a model of its kind. The obelisk monument is also on this avenue.

Culture at All Levels

Buenos Aires' National Art Museum, Av. del Libertador 1473, (open daily except Wed.) has a sound permanent collection of world masters and also just about the best grouping extant of Argentine painters and sculptors. The Museum of Argentine Folk Art Jose Hernandez, Av. del Libertador 2373, has a marvelous collection of colonial Argentine, Indian and religious art, as well as articles related to the gaucho (closed Mon.) The Museum of Decorative Art, Av. del Libertador 1902, is noteworthy for its tapestries and antiques. The National Museum of Oriental Art is in the same building on the first floor. The Museum of Spanish-American Art Isaac Fernandez Blanco (Suipacha 1422), open Wednesday to Sunday, is a replica of a lovely old colonial home with an outstanding collection of antique silver from "mate" cups (gourds from which that herb tea is sipped through a "bombilla" like a soda straw) to spurs and the silver stirrups the gauchos used. There are a score of other art salons, from public museums to private galleries, and all work their hardest in the cool months.

The Colón Opera House (the season starts May 25 with a white-tie gala attended by the president of the republic) is the home of great opera, with a changing stream of imported talent to bolster the local which has provided La Scala Milan and Glyndebourne with exports. It is also headquarters for the National Ballet Theater and for the fine National Symphony Orchestra. In the summer the Ballet gives open-air performances in Palermo Park, where the Planetarium is located.

Many millions of dollars have been spent on a complete overhaul of the Colon Theater, including construction of an underground complex covering a whole city block. It is today perhaps one of the finest opera houses in the world. Its cavernous storage rooms have sets for every known opera, thousands of costumes, wigs and shoes.

To get in you will probably need a "fixer," as seating is limited and the demand enormous; but your concierge will probably have a page stand in line from dawn onwards to get you tickets. Dark suits for gentlemen and long dresses for ladies are the normal wear.

Some 42 theaters are open almost constantly, from those presenting Argentine dramatic works or translations of foreign plays to "revue" theaters with comics who strike out at local political mishaps (and always find material) and choruses notable for the brevity of their costumes.

A recent development in Buenos Aires is the steady growth of "café concerts." They usually take place in a small salon, often a cellar, and consist of a one-man or one-woman show, with tables and drinks. There must be a score of such places today, and they all seem to be doing well. And playgoing is cheap; a ticket can cost you 50 cents, less than a movie, and can't possibly run to more than $2.00. Be sure to look at the Teatro General San Martín at Corrientes 1532, a modernistic building with three separate stages and an art gallery.

Or if you're a movie fan, there are some 200 houses, obliged by law to show one Argentine film in every ten (and the local product can be excellent on occasion) but preferring American, British or European pictures, all with Spanish subtitles.

For the scholar, there is the National University of Buenos Aires, with colleges for everything from agriculture to medicine, law to chemistry scattered throughout Buenos Aires, and Buenos Aires Catholic University, Belgrano University and El Salvador University.

Buenos Aires had six fine colonial churches. On the night of 16 June 1955, five of them were set on fire by the Peronistas. San Ignacio, architecturally by far the finest, and San Francisco were completely gutted. La Merced and San Miguel were severely damaged. Santo Domingo, where the remnants of the British General Whitelock tried to reform before accepting defeat in 1806 suffered least, but the equally interesting *convento* (or Priory) adjoining it was badly damaged. So was the Archbishop's Palace, by the Cathedral, which contained an invaluable library and all the historical records of the River Plate since 1600. The Cathedral itself suffered little. Even the Peronistas did not dare to destroy the tomb of General San Martín: but the Cathedral is quite without architectural merit. The one old church left unharmed was the fashionable El Pilar (at Junin 1904). It is quite a little jewel of its kind.

Outskirts and Environs

Less than half an hour from the center of Buenos Aires you will cross Avenida General Paz, the belt highway which is a city limit. Northwest along the River Plate you will begin traversing a series of suburbs where lush homes with private swimming pools and handsome gardens are the residences of the "upper-crust," mainly foreigners; these are generally too expensive for the average Argentine. Nine of those suburbs stretch in an unbroken chain from Vicente Lopez-Florida through San Isidro and its racetrack to the Tigre, where the River Plate spreads into a score of delta channels, with hotels and restaurants sprinkled throughout the islands which dot the region. Center of a citrus fruit area, it is also used for truck farming, produce coming in to the mainland city of Tigre, a rustic Venice, where the markets are as colorful and as well-stocked as Les Halles of old in Paris.

Best way to see most of the Paraná Delta and its 1,200 channels and streams is by the new tourist service by giant catamarans, carrying 120 passengers in comfort in the big-windowed restaurant and another 40 on the sight-seeing deck above. Boats leave Tigre marina every hour on Saturdays, Sundays and holidays. Cruise takes about two hours and covers the rivers Luján, Sarmiento, Capitan, San Antonio and Urión.

Or you can go southeast just about as far, through another unbroken chain of suburbs, winding up at Quilmes (site of a brewery which turns out excellent beer) or Temperley, home of a large British settlement.

A 40-mile drive will take you to Luján, a place of popular pilgrimage. It has a good Colonial Museum. And two hours from downtown you can find a typical Argentine *estancia* (ranch); a travel agency can arrange for you to visit a 6,300-acre estate where, for $24.50 a head, you can have cocktails and lunch with the charming owners and tour their stud farm and cattle breeding establishment for a day. A shorter tour, equally typical of the traditional Argentine life, is a full day at an *estancia* nearby, only eighteen miles from town, where your genial host, courtesy of $20.50 a person to the travel agent, will greet you with overflowing hospitality, including a barbecue (itself a sight in Argentina, with sheep or lambs spread-eagled on a metal crucifix over a charcoal fire) and entertain with "gaucho" music and his sentimental, sensual dances.

In Palermo Park, quite near the U.S. Embassy, there is an Andalusian patio, the gift from the people of Granada to the "opulent city of Buenos Aires." There is everywhere a natural opulence of flora and fauna, of mountain and plain. To see it you must explore the provinces; but even if you have time only for the cities, you will find that though no other compares in size with Buenos Aires, each has its own marked individuality, even in this day of ferro-concrete. Many are far richer in ancient monuments: after all, there were a dozen cities in Argentina before there was a group of huts in New England or Virginia.

EXPLORING THE PROVINCES

Argentina has a well-developed network of internal airlines, but it is best to book as far in advance as possible, as some of them are rather overworked. She is proud, too, of her 27,284 miles of railroad. Food is good on the trains and sleeping accommodations reasonably comfortable. You can go up river by boat well beyond Asunción in Paraguay. There are in all 3,000 miles of navigable water. In addition, there are over 100,000 miles of roads. These vary from fast, well-surfaced macadam arteries on which high speeds are quite safe to tracks which will test the durability of any car. Some of these tracks are impassable in wet weather and others equally impossible after a drought. If you are going to tour the country by car, go first to the A.C.A. (Argentine Automobile Club). Its headquarters is an imposing building along the Avenida del Libertador. The club can provide detailed route maps and information on the state of the roads. It runs also a number of service stations where you can refuel, have repairs done efficiently or get advice as to where to have them done, eat a good meal and take a rest—and a rest can be welcome after a long fast stretch in the heat of a summer's day.

Today the average tourist can get to almost any place along paved highways, though some of the more remote places are still served by unpaved roads. Of course, if someone invites you to his ranch, you can expect a foot of dust in summer on the approach roads or a foot of mud in winter.

A.C.A. is a wonderful institution with nearly a million members, operating scores of motels throughout the country, camping sites, service stations, hundreds of break-down trucks and even a fleet of light planes and a country-wide communications network.

If you are going through the less-frequented and rougher highways you would be well advised to take two spare wheels, a tow rope (to help others squelching in a morass or to be helped out yourself) and a spade and some hessian or boards to dig yourself out of a sand or snow drift and to give your tires a firm grip out of it. You will not, of course, need any of these along the principal arteries.

The Pampas

Head out of Buenos Aires in any landward direction and you are in the Pampas. The administrative unit now called the Province of La Pampa is only a part of them. They extend like a fan from the capital for between 300 and 400 miles. On their produce and fertility the economic well-being of Argentina depends almost in its entirety. But for three groups of low hills, one towards the northwest, near Córdoba, one towards the southwest, near Bahia Blanca, and the third by the small town of Tandil almost due south, they are as beautiful, or monotonous, as a motionless ocean; where wheat is planted on them, when harvest time nears and a soft breeze blows, the resemblance is even greater. Barbed-wire fences delimit pasture and tillage, each "field" varying from between 100 and 5,000 acres; owls perch on the wire, and the posts of the very hard quebracho wood which grows in the north are beloved of the Hornero, or oven-bird—so-called because its nest is shaped just like the traditional earth-oven of Europe. There are next to no trees. Those there are are usually avenues of eucalyptus leading to the palatial *estancia* (ranch) house; but there are not many of these, for the holdings are large by European or even North American standards. Much more plentiful than houses are the pylons and vanes of the windmills which pump water to the surface, for there are few rivers and fewer streams. (That surface is several feet rich in topsoil except towards the southwest where it has eroded into sand.) The water is pumped into troughs for the cattle, sheep and horses which graze together.

On these pampas, cattle rearing is still the main industry and therefore alfalfa is a major crop, but rotation and commercial interest demand the cultivation of wheat, maize and linseed in quantities which would have surprised the earlier owners of these estates. Though there are among the owners some progressive men, the 19th-century tradition of absenteeism among the landlords and of a lordly house for the manager and hovels for the farm hands still has deep roots.

With its avenue of eucalyptus or other fine tall trees the estancias, as we have said, stand out of the flat plains. So do the towns of the pampas, of which there are dozens, prosperous little centers of supply for local needs and clearing houses for the cattle and grain. Invariably they follow the Spanish pattern of a main square, with a church on one side of it and the local authority on the other, one or more cinemas and cafes, and a railroad station; and a surprising number of them have an aircraft landing strip.

Mar del Plata

250 miles south of Buenos Aires, 35 minutes by air, seven hours by train or Pullman bus and, on a week-day, five hours by car—is the Mecca of Bonairensian holiday-makers of all classes. The resident population is 385,000, but between "spring-week" early in November and Easter it is flooded with well over a million people, who stay there on average 20 days. There are luxury hotels and flats for the wealthy, "family hotels" for the more modest, and cheap hotels, boarding houses and lodgings for the lower income groups. There are five miles of clean sandy beaches. In front of the large "Provincial Hotel" (an architect's nightmare) people are crowded, but further away you can have a large stretch of beach to yourself. Externally identical with the Provincial Hotel and next to it is the Casino.

From Mar del Plata you can make side-trips to the estancias at Chapadmalal (12 miles away) and Ojo de Agua (35 miles away). Tourist agencies can arrange package visits for tourists which may include horse taming and Argentine popular singing and dancing. (*Música folklórica* is not to be mistaken with *música autóctona*, this last being what European musicologists would call folk music. For that the traveler must go to the frontier areas between Argentina and Paraguay, Bolivia or Chile; but he may encounter the genuine ballad singer in the Pampas.)

During the summer season, December to March, the Roca Railroad runs a diesel streamliner express called "El Mar Platense" which makes the run to Mar del Plata in 5½ hours. It is air-conditioned, with piped music—mostly tangos—and an excellent dining car, with a table d'hôte menu.

There are less-crowded beaches strung along the stretch of coast termed "Atlantida". North of Mar del Plata the best are Villa Gesell (entirely the work of a single visionary German who shored up sand dunes by proper planting of pine trees) and Pinamar, literally "pines by the sea", which is becoming the fashionable place to go. South of Mar del Plata, the principal beach, Miramar, is now crowded with high-rise hotels, and there is also a casino.

Farther south is Necochea with a beach 15 miles long which is
developing rapidly. The new casino there is said to be the largest in
the world.

South from Buenos Aires

Mar del Plata is much publicized, and rightly so for the benefit
of the residents of Argentina, but for the foreign tourist it has
no more to offer than several other resorts in South America.

Some 200 miles west southwest from Necochea or 300 from
Mar del Plata stands Bahía Blanca, the most important city
south of Buenos Aires, most easily reached by going straight
there from the capital, just under 400 miles. It is the outlet
for the grain produce of the southern Pampas and the fruit
from the Río Negro valley in the extreme west; but again, it
has little to commend it above other towns. It is, however, on
the quickest road route from the capital to Neuquén and the
Argentine lake district, regions worth every foot of the long
journey to them. The car driver heading south will find Bahía
Blanca just right for a day's journey from Buenos Aires (the
400 miles can be done comfortably in 8 hours actual driving).
It has several good hotels (Austral, Gran Hotel del Sur, Belgrano and Central Muñiz). On the next day the motorist must
head for Neuquén, crossing the dust-bowl of the southern Pampas, and no greater contrast could meet his eyes after the rich
grain fields and pastures of the previous day than the bleak
panorama which will flank him for some 250 miles as he goes
westward. Sometime in the afternoon however, the scenery will
change as he enters the area irrigated by the Río Negro dam at
Neuquén. The development of this region out of desert into a
major fruit producing area was pioneered by the British owners
of the now nationalized railroad. The full extent of the zone is
therefore best seen by the rail traveler, but the road gives a
good next-best idea, all the same.

At Neuquén the traveler has a choice. He can continue westward to Zapala and head straight for the Andes, via the Copa-
hué National Reservation, a volcanic region with thermal baths,
and the Laguna Blanca National Park, famous for its animal
and bird life. There are clouds of flamingoes, and the black-
necked swan is a common sight. At Zapala he can turn south
and head for Bariloche, center of the Lake District, via Junín
de los Andes and San Martín de los Andes. Close to Junín there
is the very beautiful lake of Huechulafquen—and if you have
the time for a detour, take the 75-mile road to Pucon on Lake
Villarrica in Chile for really superb scenery. The best views of
the snow-capped Lanin Volcano are those from that road. From
Junín, which is famous for rainbow trout and salmon, head south
25 miles to San Martín de los Andes on the shores of Lake

Lacar, and a further 95 miles brings you finally to Bariloche by the very side of Lake Nahuel Huapí.

The alternative route from Neuquén to Bariloche follows the river Limay through the Valle Encantado (enchanted vale) where every turn of the road reveals ever more phantasmagoric rock formations. Even the least gifted imagination will be kindled by them. If your car breaks down here, you can always live on the trout from the crystal clear river.

So then, either through the enchanted valley or along the Andean foothills you can come by car to San Carlos de Bariloche on the shore of Nahuel Huapí ("Island of the Tiger"), tourist center of a region of mountain and lake. Of course jet aircraft will accomplish the journey in 2½ hours against the minimum of three days allowed for the road from the capital, 28–39 hours by train, or 26½–28 hours by bus. If time is limited, then choose the airline.

This region is often likened to Switzerland, but in all fairness it outdoes Switzerland in natural beauty. The snow-capped Andes are more rugged than the Alps, the lakes more glimmering and more vivid in coloring. There are in the series of national parks in this region three million acres of forest teeming with wild life, of lake and stream flashing with rainbow trout and salmon, and of mountains for "alpinismo" (mountaineering) and skiing. Needless to say, guides are available, and there are refuges on the more favorite mountains. Six ski lifts, a cable car, chair lift, a restaurant and a hotel have made the Cerro Catedral (Cathedral Peak) the most popular for skiing. The peak that dominates the scene is the 12,342-foot-high extinct volcano, the Tronador, or thunderer, its glacier now reachable by road. Near San Martin de los Andes a new ski complex has been developed at the summit of Cerro Chapelco. A "Short-Circuit" bus tour ($1) stops at the *Llao-Llao*, a most luxurious hotel with an 18-hole golf course and private dock. For the sportsman, the area offers fishing and shooting; for the tourist, horse-riding, or simply resting in deck-chairs on the lake steamers. There are many hotels and plenty of free camping ground. An all-day outing (about $5) on a modern cruiser takes you to Victoria Island.

Patagonia and the South

Bariloche, an Alpinelike village with a large shopping area, cooperative apartments for tourists, iceskating rink, indoor swimming pool, bars and soda fountains, is in Río Negro, but by the older nomenclature it is part of Patagonia—"the land of the people with long feet"—who no longer exist, if ever they did. Indeed the population density over the 450,000 square miles of Patagonia (the provinces of Neuquén, Río Negro, Chubut and Santa Cruz, and the territory of Tierra del Fuego), is one person per square mile and, incidentally, 40 sheep, with a high wool yield. It was to mind sheep that Welshmen sailed about 100 years ago (1865) and established, 300 miles south of Buenos Aires, the port and colony with the very Welsh-sounding name of Madryn. There, as in a second colony, Trelew, you can to this day hear perfect Welsh spoken as well as Spanish, but little English. Highly recommended is the excursion from Madryn to Peninsula Valdes, 117 miles, where 2,000 or more enormous elephant seals bask on the pebbled beaches. This is the only elephant seal colony in the world which is on continental land. *Lindblad* fans already know about this tour. The discovery of natural gas and oil in Comodoro Rivadavia, a further 200 miles south, and of coal in Tierra del Fuego may eventually alter the generally desolate character of the area. Ushuaia, on the extreme tip of the continent, is already attracting tourists with its rightful claim to be the world's southernmost town. It can be reached in five days by ship or a few hours by air.

South of Bariloche, nestling in the foothills of the Andes and millenary forests is the little town of Esquel, whose inhabitants are largely of Welsh descent. (A nearby village was originally called Trewellyn but the name has been corrupted to Trevelin.) Six modern hotels are being built at Esquel, and what should develop into the largest ski complex in Argentina is underway. The scenery here is fantastically beautiful, and the fishing superb. Esquel is reachable by bus from Bariloche over primitive roads or by narrow gauge railroad from Ingeniero Jacobacci, but the best bet is by air from Buenos Aires.

West of Buenos Aires

The largest town in the West of Argentina is Mendoza, on the foothills of the Andes 660 miles from Buenos Aires. It is best reached by air; the road to it is excellent but of no particular interest, though to approach it at evening through the vineyards is a singular experience. Mendoza is 2,480 feet above sea level. Behind it the Andes rise sharply to 13,000 feet and more.

Mendoza now is a rapidly expanding city with a population of some 230,000 persons. Though founded over four hundred years ago, there is in it no building of any size more than one hundred years old; for in the year of the third centenary of its foundation the city was razed to the ground by an earthquake. There was severe loss of life. To avoid a repetition it was rebuilt with streets abnormally wide. It was from Mendoza province that General San Martín organized his army of the Andes, first to liberate Chile from Spanish rule, then Peru. The event is commemorated by a vast monument on the Cerro de la Gloria (the Peak of Glory) in a huge public park. It rises a hundred feet to a statue of Liberty breaking her chains. On the plinth are various high reliefs, the best that of the women of Mendoza giving their jewels to the General to defray the expenses of the expedition. In front of the block the General sits astride his horse; above and behind it a bronze condor eagle hovers.

The provinces of Mendoza and its neighbor San Juan comprise the vine-growing district of Argentina. The wines of the region are good, and at their best very good. The city of San Juan has now been fully rebuilt after the major earthquake which practically destroyed it in 1944.

It is worthwhile taking the transandine railway, if not all the way to Chile, at least up to Puente del Inca. There is some fascinating wild territory beyond Uspallata (5,740 feet above sea level); at Río Blanco (7,000) there are raging torrents. Then the train passes a valley dominated by the cone of Tupungato, a giant volcano rising to 22,310 feet, and on the other side of the valley there is an awe-inspiring view of Aconcagua, the highest mountain in the Western Hemisphere (22,834 feet). Puente del Inca, 100 miles from Mendoza and 6,500 feet higher, is an ideal center for skiers and mountaineers; from there too there is an easy ride by car or on horseback to the La Cumbre pass on the frontier. There, upon a deep red hill amid the glaciers rises the statue of Christ the Redeemer, put there by the workers of Argentina to prevent further frontier fighting with Chile. The pedestal carries the legend: Sooner shall these mountains crumble than the peoples of Argentina and Chile break the peace they have sworn at the feet of Christ the Redeemer.

Northwest of Buenos Aires

The city of Córdoba is 432 miles northwest of Buenos Aires; an hour by air, an overnight journey by train, a long day's journey by car (via Rosario and Bell Ville for the better surface). It was for many years the capital of the Spanish province of El Tucumán. Further to the north and west lie the modern provinces and ancient cities of Jujuy, Salta, Santiago del Estero, Rioja, Catamarca and the modern province and city of Tucumán. Almost every one is worth a visit for their scenery and agriculture as well as their churches and other survivals from colonial times.

Even if time is limited, Córdoba is a "must." It is a rapidly expanding industrial city with a population of nearly a million, as well as the center of a vast agricultural area and of a region of *sierra*, or low mountain; cool in the summer and temperate in winter, it is therefore beloved of the holiday makers for whom all the usual amenities and sports are available. The *Córdobes* will delight in showing you the best views of and from his beloved sierra, but he is prouder still of his university, established in 1613 by the Jesuits under the protection of the Bishop Fernando de Trejo y Sanabria, and of his colonial buildings, the

Cathedral, half a dozen churches and Cabildo. There is a solidity about them which has a kinship with, say, the early Norman style of Britain, or of Herrera in the Escorial, and a simplicity of decoration (where later enthusiasts have not been at work with deplorable flamboyance) unusual in 17th- and 18th-century architecture. The best of them, the original university building, the College of Monserrat which adjoins it, the church of the Compañía (i.e., the Jesuits) and the greater part of the Cathedral were all built and embellished by Guaraní craftsmen under the direction of a group of Jesuit lay brother architects, sculptors and painters. The work of the group can be seen also in the ex-Jesuit *estancias*, or agricultural research stations and houses of study in the neighborhood of Córdoba (Santa Catalina and Alta Gracia are the best preserved) and throughout the north of Argentina. It could also be seen in Buenos Aires, for they were the architects of San Francisco, San Ignacio and La Merced to which the Peronistas set fire in 1955. The names of the group will astonish those accustomed to the thesis that foreigners were excluded from the Spanish Empire. The more famous, who span the period 1650–1767 include Primoli, Blanqui, Wolff, Lemer, Krauss, Harls and Klasner, Italian, Austrian, Flemish, Czech (Bohemian) and German; there was also a José Smid (Joseph Schmidt or Smith?) Primoli, incidentally, also designed the simple Cabildo of Buenos Aires where the independence of Argentina was first proclaimed.

The University was in its apogee when the Jesuits were expelled by order of Charles IV of Spain. It declined rapidly over the next fifty years and might have perished but for the interest taken by Dean Funes, very much a local hero. Today it is a State University of considerable size, and there is also a newer private Catholic University.

The Garden of Argentina

Tucumán, 325 miles to the north of Córdoba, is called the garden of Argentina, and its beauties are indeed great. The 2-hour daily flights from Buenos Aires includes a stop-over at Córdoba. The road to it from Córdoba crosses a huge salt flat, but thereafter the vegetation takes on the luxuriance to be expected from a subtropical climate. There are in the province over a million acres given over to sugar cane, land irrigated by the waters of the Sierra de Aconquija which lies to the north of the city; there are also substantial maize plantations. The city itself is on the plain, but at the very foot of the sierra so that the wealthier businessmen commute between the two.

The Spaniards descending the Andean plateau through the Quebrada de Humahuaca founded Tucumán city just over four hundred years ago, in 1565; not indeed on its present site, but somewhat to the south of it (on the spot today called Pueblo

Viejo). It was moved after a disastrous flood in 1580, but it did not begin noticeably to develop for another hundred and fifty years. Its colonial buildings therefore are principally of the 18th-century. The Cathedral houses the cross used in the foundation ceremony of the original city. It has a fine façade giving on to the main square where the Independence Monument commemorates the fact that it was in Tucumán that on 9 July 1816 the Congress of the United Provinces of the River Plate irrevocably proclaimed their independence from Spain. The plain little house where they met, (the Casa Histórica) is carefully preserved. It was at Tucumán also, and with the help of its citizens, that General Belgrano won one of the major battles of the War of Independence in 1812. There is now a "Sound and Sight" spectacle, held daily at 7 p.m.

The sugar cane area extends northward into the province of Salta, but there the land and climate is good also for tobacco and vine cultivation and for livestock ranching (other than sheep). There is good timber in the forests, and the mountains are rich in silver, lead, copper, gold and marble, but transportation difficulties have yet to be overcome to make their exploitation economic. Oil, however, is being pumped to the Paraná River.

Salta boasts an old cathedral with a balanced and well-proportioned façade. It has everywhere an air of elegance and distinction, and as the local authorities give financial inducements to builders who seek to tone the new with the old, it is likely to preserve its "colonial" charm. Its gold altar is famous.

Anyone with an eye for natural beauty or an interest in old churches should however make Salta a base for further operations rather than journey's end, even though it is one thousand miles from Buenos Aires. Salta is at the meeting point of two valleys, one the Quebrada del Toro, running over 350 miles westward into Chile and rising to 14,680 feet at the frontier, and the other the Quebrada de Humahuaca, northward through Jujuy for 220 miles into Bolivia at a height of 11,358 feet. There is a railway line in each, and scenery of breathtaking beauty can be seen from the trains, but the best way to travel along them is by mule or on foot to experience the desolation of the area and realize how freezing the wind can be even on a summer's day and even well within the Tropic of Capricorn. One of the more interesting groups of simple chapels and oratories built by Dominican and Franciscan friars from 1550 onward and by the Jesuits from 1585 is accessible to the really first-class car driver going up the Toro valley to the Puna de Atacama, and a second beyond Jujuy to the Humahuaca. But whether on foot or in a car, it is well to remember that the air is very thin. Very slight exertion will therefore prove trying to some people, while the air intake of the carburetor will need frequent adjustment; otherwise the mixture will be too rich and the engine will lose all its power. There is a point on the road to Bolivia which reaches a height of nearly 14,000 feet, higher than most mountains in Europe. In other places the river bed serves as the road.

About a third of the people in the Jujuy province are kindred to the Ayamará Indians of Bolivia. Their women, like their Bolivian cousins, wear bowler hats (and if you stand in the wind you will appreciate how wise they are). A fascinating sight is to watch them go into a church. They will remove their bowlers, put a shawl over their heads, and deposit their hats with all the loving care of a London man-about-the-city or Guards officer.

In the more sheltered spots there is a wide variety of wild cactus. On the high plateau there are droves of miniature donkeys and of llamas, alpacas and vicuñas who pick their way with the grace of ballet dancers on points.

The city of Jujuy lies between the Xibi-xibi and Grande rivers. Many Spanish-American paintings and images are preserved here. While its Spanish origin is clearly visible, the modern part is steadily growing. There are comfortable hotels, a casino and, just north of the city, the Reyes thermal spring baths.

The Chaco

Between the province of Salta and the River Paraná to the east, Argentine has within her frontiers a part of the Gran Chaco. It is a broad lowland of alluvial soil. The western area, which includes the city of Santiago del Estero, has little rain; the eastern half down to Resistencia on the river is better favored. There is swamp and impenetrable forest, but there are grasslands which will support "unimproved" cattle and goats, forests of Quebracho (a tough wood ideal for fencing posts and in its red variety rich in tannin), and the ground when cleared will yield cotton. There are two major pests: ticks and locusts. The highest temperatures ever recorded in South America were registered in the Argentine Chaco. With all this it is the naturalists' and ornithologists' paradise. The easiest approach to the western half is through Tucumán and Santiago (the oldest city in Argentina); and to the eastern, up river from Buenos Aires.

Northeastern Argentina

There are three attractions to the north and east of Buenos Aires: the rich pasture lands of Entre Ríos (Mesopotamia, between the Rivers Paraná and Uruguay) where the winters are mild; Misiones, wealthy in timber and mate tea; and in the ruins of the famous politico-sociological religious experiment of the Jesuit *reducciónes* and the falls of Iguazú.

In the last two years travel has been greatly eased by the large

Shrouded in legend as well as mist, Machu Picchu remains one of the world's greatest tourist targets.

Photo: E. Fodor

Typical of the continent's European heritage is this architecture at Viña del Mar, Chile.

Photo: E. Fodor

Market Day in the Andean Altiplano brings out that peacock urge.

Photo: E. Fodor

Argentine beef is as attractive as the photographic models, if not more so.
Photo: Pan American World Airways Inc.

suspension bridge over the Paraná River between Resistencia and Corrientes; the Hernandarias tunnel under the Paraná which links Santa Fé with Paraná, and shortly the vast rail and road complex between Zarate and Brazo Lago nearer Buenos Aires over the lower reaches of the Paraná. There are also two new bridges between Entre Ríos and Uruguay, and a third when the Salto Grande dam across the River Uruguay is finished. There are now daily bus services from Buenos Aires to most places in the northeast.

There are a number of modern highways and also direct railroad expresses, and frequent air services, but the ideal way to tour this whole area is by boat. On the way it will call first at Rosario, still Argentina's second largest city, though just barely so with the expansion of Córdoba; but it was once the world's major grain port. The second port of call will be Paraná, capital of Argentina for eleven years during the 19th century and chief city of Entre Ríos. From here onward, at the right time of the year, seemingly uncontrolled fires may be seen on the banks of the river. In this way the land is cleared of grasses which cattle find unsavory. Opposite Paraná is the city of Sante Fé, a university town but without major attractions. Three days after leaving Buenos Aires, the steamer reaches Corrientes, a city which long defied incorporation into either Paraguay or Argentina, and since it had such a commanding position over the river, it played havoc with communications between the two countries. At Corrientes the river road divides: west to Asunción in Paraguay and east to Iguazú.

There's a one-day river tour along the Paraná-Tigre Delta for about $10 per person, including lunch.

For a base from which to visit the ruins of the *reducciónes* open to the public, it is best to continue a further 217 miles up river (towards Iguazú) to Posadas. There are daily buses from Posadas to Iguazú. Only one of the 30 *reducciónes* is easily accessible, San Ignacio Mini. The journey takes about two hours by car or four by launch.

San Ignacio Mini up to 1767 had a town housing 2,000 Guaraní Indian families, people whom the sword of the conquistador was never able to conquer. Under the tutelage of a Jesuit priest aided by a lay brother, they formed a township among whom no Spanish merchant was permitted to stay. Each family had its own stone-built house; that they were of standards better than most Argentine city workers enjoyed until recently can be seen from the ruins. Each family had its own plot of land. However there was also land tilled, cultivated and harvested on a communal basis. The sale of the produce in Buenos Aires provided the money for the payment of taxes to the king and the purchase of all the needs of the community which it could not provide for itself. All children attended school and were taught to a level equivalent to that of an American high school or an English grammar school; music and the arts were in the curriculum as was Latin. There was a hospital and a home for widows, orphans and old folk, whose care and welfare was a charge on the community. Government was in the hands of the Indians themselves. They regularly elected an *alcalde* (a mayor, but with considerably greater powers in the administration of the law) and other officers. Suffrage was limited to the male adults; elections were decided by simple majority. The whole community voted on any major decision. The powers exercised by the priests in charge of those *reducciónes* has often been exaggerated by historians. In the early days at the beginning of the seventeenth century, when they were offering the Indians a refuge from slavery or near slavery under the Spanish colonist, the Indians were not only warlike but in as primitive a state as those of the wilder parts of Africa. The degree of civilization they reached can to some extent be judged from the ruins now kept clear of jungle growth by the Argentine authorities. From Corrientes to Iguazú the journey takes about two hours by air.

If you have seen Niagara Falls and thought them "great," wait till you have seen Iguazú (Guaraní for "The Great Water"). At Niagara the American Falls are 192 feet high and 1,100 feet wide; the Canadian 160 feet high and 2,500 wide. Argentina's Iguazú drops 200 feet and it is 8,100 feet wide. But it is not merely a question of height and width. Iguazú is in a more rugged setting; forests surround it. Iridescent butterflies and birds abound.

Argentina has finally become aware of the enormous international tourist value of the world-famous Iguazú Falls. Hitherto a local joke was that Argentina put on the show—for two thirds of the falls are in Argentine territory—while the Brazilians took in the tourist dollars.

Until recently, most travel agencies routed their tourists to Foz da Iguazu, a drab frontier town in Brazil, but which has 40 hotels and 8,000 beds, including the sprawling caravanserai of the Brazilian national parks administration above the falls themselves. The Salvatti Hotel in Foz da Iguazu, for example, is 17 stories high.

But now the Argentines are moving in in a big way with the construction of six new, large tourist hotels, a new airport with a long runway, more amenities in Puerto Iguazu, and something Brazil cannot hope to match: Ortega brothers and other travel agents will take you on a day trip which covers a visit to the Paraguayan hydro-electric complex at Acarai, the large new tourist Hotel Acaray, complete with casino and gaming machines, the Ponte da Amistad Bridge of Friendship over the mighty Paraná (longest concrete span in the world) and finally to the Brazilian side of the falls.

Where the river Iguazú flows into the Paraná, you may see on different headlands far above three monoliths painted in the national colors of Paraguay, Brazil and Argentina, for it is there that the three countries meet.

Having looked at the falls from the Argentine side, go round to the Brazilian. Needless to say there is every provision for tourists on either side: splendid fishing for trout, salmon, dorado and pacu. The piranha which delights in tearing human flesh to the bone down river is a rare visitor this far up. You can go hiking or riding to your heart's content in the huge national park area all round the falls—or you can just sit and watch them as you will.

PRACTICAL INFORMATION FOR ARGENTINA

CAPSULE COMMENTS. *Physical Features.* There is great variety in Argentina's geography, ranging from the torrid heat of the northern Chaco to the pleasant middle regions of the central pampas to the frozen Antarctic lands of Southern Patagonia.

Climate. Because of Argentina's vastness, her climate is as varied as her geography. Buenos Aires has mild conditions. The best months to visit are October to March. And the visitor should remember that the farther south he goes the colder it gets.

Population. 25,000,000. Buenos Aires 9,000,000.

Language. Spanish.

Archeological Attractions. Petrified forest in southern Patagonia, caves in Tierra del Fuego y Ongamira, Cordoba. In the valley of the Cachaquies (an extinct race), some parish churches, notably at San Carlos, have mummified remains. Finest archeological museum in Argentina is at La Plata, famous for its field expeditions and exhibits of prehistoric animal life and fossils.

COSTS. Argentina is no longer a cheap place to visit. Inflation roars merrily on. It is true the military regime has slowed the pace but it is still a fast one. Since January 1, 1977, the fiscal policy has been to devalue the peso by one peso per dollar every other day but in the opinion of exporters, especially in the all important meat trade, a substantial devaluation is called for.

Apart from exchange considerations, ever-increasing taxation, the end of the frozen rent law, and mandatory pay raises for all, have contributed to a terrific increase in the cost of living, which may not be comparable yet to Stateside prices but seem headed that way.

Tourists may now exchange their foreign currency at the official tourist rate at any of the numerous money changers. The rate is only a few pesos lower than the blackmarket where plainclothes police watch for the unwary. Arrest, fines and jail await those caught, so think it over.

Hotels. New hotel construction has fallen far behind in recent years, with the big chains' plans for expansion having to be postponed. Other problems are plaguing the hotel scene as well. Very large numbers of refugees from other South American countries are aggravating the housing shortage and filling hotels. About 25,000 visitors are expected for the World Rotary Convention in 1977, and probably four times that many for the World Football Cup in 1978. So be sure your travel agent has solid reservations for you, before you leave home. In general, hotels here can be found to meet anyone's needs or pocketbook. In the deluxe category, for freespending executives on an expense account, are such plush establishments as the *Buenos Aires Sheraton*, the

Plaza, Claridge Presidente and *Alvear Palace*. Here you may have to pay an average of $30 a night single and $45 double plus more for suites.

Large grants of credit have been made by the Government to hotel builders to house the horde of soccer fans expected in 1978 for the World Championships. Some 60 new hotels are now going up in Buenos Aires and the provincial sub-centers of the Championship.

The Plaza Hotel is adding a new wing and is generally refurbishing the two older wings. Nine new hotels are being built in Buenos Aires including a 250 room tower at Callao 250 and the five star 20 story tower *Hotel Libertador* at Cordoba and Maipu streets with 210 rooms.

Hotel Santa Catalina on the site of the old downtown air terminal will have 440 doubles in its 22 story edifice and ten suites. It will have a roof restaurant with a panoramic view of the River Plate and the metropolis which sprawls as far as eye can see.

The Continental Hotel has been completely refurbished and restored to its old deluxe category and so has the International Hotel at Ezeiza airport.

Then comes a group of large hotels like the 400-room *City*, or the *Nogaro, Republica, Lancaster, Lafayette, Crillon,* and *Buenos Aires,* where you can probably get a single for $12 and a double for $20.

Finally, perfectly satisfactory for foreigners are many smaller hotels like *Tres Argentos, Gran Hotel Dorá, Sussex, Gran Hotel Argentino, Eibar, Promenade, Shelltown, Embajador, Victory, Liberty, King's* and the like, from about $10 for a single to $15 for a double.

Except for the huge caravanserai, it is usually possible to get a low rate for an inside room.

Restaurants are now classified by the state into categories: "five forks" is the top rating, but you can safely eat in places with four and even three forks. You'll probably spend about $10 per person at a five-fork establishment down to as little as $3 in a three-fork. You can eat for a dollar or so in the rest. The larger hotels like the *Sheraton* and the *Plaza* now operate inexpensive coffee shops, and almost all have snack bars.

Taxis cost about 60 cents U.S. for a short ride; a longer one, say to the suburbs, is about $5. Unless someone meets you at Ezeiza airport, take the airline bus to town. A taxi is outrageously expensive since the distance is 30 miles.

Drinks. Excellent local whiskeys or gin tonics (there are local distilleries of such world-famous names as *Hiram Walker, Gordon's, Long John, Cinzano, Martini, Rossi, Bols,* etc.) are available at about 30 cents U.S. a shot, and a tippler of real Scotch will be about $2.

U.S. cigarettes like *Lucky Strike* and *Chesterfield* are usually smuggled in, liable to be stale, and certain to be costly. British and American firms make many famous brands here: *Marlboro, Parliament, Benson and Hedges, Kent,* and others. Argentina exports tobacco.

City sightseeing tours. Several companies operate sight-seeing tours in and around the Argentine capital, including Teletour with its double-decker deluxe buses. You can sign up for a variety of mini-tours at your hotel desk and the bus will call for you. For first-timers it is an excellent way of seeing something of Argentina with multi-lingual guides, and equally so for those whose time is limited to a day or so. Here are the principal mini-tours offered at the latest price equivalents in U.S. $. However, local costs are going up faster than the official dollar rate.

City Tour. About $4. You will see the Government House (Casa Rosada), the Congress building which is startlingly like the U.S. Capitol, the Palermo Parks, the main avenues but not Florida which is now a ten block shopping mall; a whirl around the famous Italian quarter of La Boca with its multi-colored houses and the northern riverside suburbs, including the picturesque ports of Olivos and San Isidro and so on.

Tigre. About $6. Bus to Tigre Marina thence a two hour trip through the islands of the delta of the Paraná River. There is also another service in the summer months (December through March) from the old flying boat station in Dock F in the New Port with day and night sailings with dinner, show and music, and week-end trips for children.

Boca. About $9. A brief tour of the Boca district and dinner with singing waiters in a pseudo-Italian trattoria or cantina where the menu will probably be: cold meats, spaghetti, chicken or a small beef-steak with salad. Fine for those who seek atmosphere but not for gourmets.

Night Life. About $12 to $18. A trip through the Boca, then a couple of cabarets with one drink on the house.

Fiesta Gaucha. About $9 to $12. Coach trip to countryside with open-air barbecue of an immense array of steak, sausages, kidneys, sweetbreads and so on, to a guitar accompaniment.

Estancia Show. About $18. Trip to a ranch out in the province where apart from the barbecue and flagons of red wine a troupe of artistes dressed as country folk perform typical dances such as the pericón, gato, malambó samba, carnavalito, and many others. Singers will give haunting refrains of local folklore, some like the cueca bright and breezy but most with a plaintive note.

La Plata. About $5. Day visit to the capital of the province of Buenos Aires with its famous Museum of Natural History, Zoo and race-track, with a stop at the Children's City, a predecessor of Disneyland!

Lujan. About $8. Majestic cathedral with towering spires and two national museums, one being the old city hall. The Spanish seaplane *Plus Ultra* which flew from Cadiz to Buenos Aires in 1926 is on show. There are ancient Vice-regal coaches too. By the Lujan riverside there are numerous open-air restaurants under shady trees. Look for the restaurant "Eaux Vives" run by French nuns.

Cutting Expenses in Buenos Aires. Food. All restaurants are now compelled to list a cut-price menu which offers two to three dishes at a low price. It is called the "Tourist Menu."

There are almost no bad restaurants, and even if you eat in a lowly "one-fork" place, the food will be substantial, and you'll get it for half the price charged in restaurants with more "fork" ratings.

A lunch for the frugal is served by *Club Comega* on the 19th floor of the Comega Building, where there are fabulous views of the River Plate and the city. The kitchen is small and so the food may be simple, but the bar is excellent.

Transportation: It is faster and cheaper to travel by one of the five subways, which charge a nominal 6-cent fare. Taxis are so often held up by traffic jams in the business quarter that it can be faster to walk.

Shopping: for cheaper prices, stay off Florida and Santa Fé. Try Avenida de Mayo, Avenida Callao, Maipu and Esmeralda. Calle Libertad is the center for gold jewelry, watches and objets d'art at realistic prices. Avenue Cabildo in the Belgrano suburb is packed with branches of the chain stores and is a large and reasonable shopping center in itself. Fashion-conscious ladies will do well to seek out the numerous boutiques, many operated by former society ladies, in the side streets off Avenida Santa Fé.

 WHEN TO COME. Argentina has two lovely seasons: spring and fall (and remember to reverse your calendar in deference to the Southern Hemisphere; spring south of the equator centers on October and November; fall on March and April). Summer temperatures can go as high as 104 degrees and the humidity as rough as 100 percent; winter can be cold, windy and frosty as far north as Buenos Aires; to the south it can become extremely cold, to the north, on the other hand, it remains mild, if rather damp. Skiing in the Bariloche region, and hotels there are properly heated for you. But if you're just on a fun-tourist visit, stick to spring or fall, when you'll be comfortable wherever you go. There is no appreciable change in hotel tariffs (rates go up in January-February at the seaside resort of Mar del Plata, even so it attracts over a million holiday makers).

 TRADITIONAL EVENTS CALENDAR. If you are seeking "culture," winter is your best bet, from art exhibits to opera: from 25 May onwards. Buenos Aires holds the National Cattle Show, really an international affair with judges from the U.S.A. and England. One of the finest in the world, it takes place around July 10 and lasts two weeks.

Teatro Colón Grand Opera Season includes opera, symphonic concerts, ballet. The Teatro Colón is said to be the largest opera house in the world. May–Sept.

Other scheduled Argentine features: Wine festival, Mendoza, Mar.; Olive festival, Córdoba, Apr.; Mar del Plata festivities, Dec.; Fishing contest, Nov.–Dec., at southwestern lakes strung west toward Chile from San Carlos de Bariloche (the winner may net 25 pounds of salmon or trout from the icy waters); International fishing tournament up the Paraná by the Iguazú falls, Nov.; Gran Premio Nacional, horse racing at Buenos Aires, Oct.

July is the month for international skiing and the Snow Festival in Bariloche and up the Andes beyond Mendoza. The skiing centre in Sept. is Neuquén.

The Festival of the Miracle is held in Salta in Sept.

Carnival, the Mardi Gras season before Lent, has been dropped from the official calendar, but it is still the focal point for balls and masquerades at the clubs in the capital. There is water and flour throwing in La Rioja. Authentic customs are still upheld in the province of Salta.

HOLIDAYS. Jan. 1, *New Year's Day;* Jan. 6, *Day of Kings. Maundy Thursday. Good Friday.* May 1, *Labor Day;* May 25, *Anniversary of* *the Cabildo Abierto of* 1810. *Corpus Christi:* June 20, *Flag Day.* July 9, *Independence Day.* Aug. 15, *Anniversary of San Martin's death* Aug. 17. Oct. 12, *Columbus Day.* Nov. 1, *All Saint's Day.* Dec. 8, *Immaculate Conception.* Dec. 25, *Christmas Day.*

MOTORING. A tourist is allowed to bring his own car in for a limited stay, but talk with your travel agent before you get into a muddle. Or you can rent a car in Buenos Aires (the number of agencies is constantly increasing). By all means use the "extra" or "especial" rather than regular gas in Argentina. Avis, National and Hertz rentals are available.

One drives to the right in Argentina and usually feels he is taking his life in his hands; speeds are in excess of what you'd regard as "safe," and the Argentine driver weaves back and forth between lanes in a "wild-man" fashion. Get the required International Driver's License from your local AAA.

TRAVEL DOCUMENTS. You will need a passport, but no visas are required if you are from the U.S., Canada, Great Britain, Holland, Ireland, Norway, Sweden, West Germany, Austria, Belgium, Spain, France, Lichtenstein, Luxembourg, Switzerland, Denmark, Finland, Japan and Italy. For others you can have a tourist visa lasting 90 days (renewable, but don't get a transit visa if you can help it). You will also need a smallpox vaccination certificate and round-trip ticket. Airport tax: neighboring countries, 75¢; all others, $1.50.

WHAT TO TAKE? Argentina's climate is technically mild, the seasons reversed because you're on the other side of the equator, the occasional summer day unbearably hot, the winter night very infrequently down to freezing. The farther north you go in Argentina, the hotter it gets; the farther south, the colder—provided you stay at the same height above sea level, for it can be very cold, for example, in the rarified atmosphere of the Humahuaca valley. Dress for the climate as you would in Europe or San Francisco—if you're a blue-jeans person, so be it, but it *is* a style-conscious place; dress, at least for the upper brackets, is very Savile Row for men and Faubourg St. Honoré for ladies. In Buenos Aires in winter you will need a fur or heavy coat, suits and heavy afternoon dresses. In summer ladies go in for silks and linens or cottons. Now in summer men wear jackets only at very traditional places. There is no rainy reason, the rain being spread out evenly; so take a raincoat. Tuxedos and tails are so rarely worn now that you can forget about them.

HOW TO GET THERE. By air: At the southern tip of South America and stretching from the tropics to the frigid polar regions, Argentina is at the end or beginning of a hundred travel routes which fan out to such places as Easter Island, Tahiti, South Africa, North America, Latin America, Europe and the Far East and Australia.

Argentina has the only ice-free air base in the Antarctic at Marambio, which is the center for trans-Antarctic flights to Australasia.

Ezeiza, Argentina's national airport 30 miles from the city center, handles 6,000 take-offs and landings a month, but downtown the Aeroparque takes care of 9,000 movements, mostly domestic flights, although there are many from neighboring countries. Some 28 airlines use these airports.

From New York: Pan American, Aerolineas Argentinas, Braniff, Varig and LAN-Chile.

From Miami: Aerolineas Argentinas, Avianca, Braniff, Aero-Peru, LAN-Chile, Pan Am and Varig.

From Los Angeles and San Francisco: Aerolineas Argentinas, Avianca, Pan Am, Varig, and Braniff.

From Toronto, Montreal and Vancouver: CP Air.

Aerolineas and Braniff have non-stop flights from New York covering the distance in 10 hours. Varig has a daily non-stop flight from New York to Rio, where you can change planes for Buenos Aires. Pan Am has four flights a week to Buenos Aires, three of them via Rio, one non-stop.

Air France now flies three Boeing 747 Jumbos a week from Paris and Aerolineas Argentinas one flight a week from Frankfurt and one from Rome with the 747. The new Concorde service from Paris to Rio includes a connecting plane for Sao Paulo, but travelers bound for Buenos Aires must wait around for a local plane.

Present fares from New York to Buenos Aires (subject to upward revision in line with currency changes and operating costs): one way First class $782, Economy class $509; round trip excursion fare $856, valid for 28 days tour. Note: At press time, these were about to be raised 6%.

Provided you purchase your ticket before leaving the U.S., you can buy a "Discover Argentina" pass for $180, which is valid for domestic flights for 30 days (from the day of your first Argentine domestic flight), with unlimited stop-overs within the country, although no city may be visited more than once. Baggage allowance on local flights is 15 kilos.

For those with time and money, Prudential Lines' luxury liners sail from Vancouver to Buenos Aires twice a month, via Tacoma, San Francisco, Los Angeles, Buenaventura, Guayaquil, Callao and Valparaiso, passing through the Straits of Magellan; about 120 passengers. For adventurers, Moore-McCormack freighters carry 12 passengers from New York, Baltimore, Philadelphia, Norfolk (and sometimes Boston and Charleston) twice a month.

From Great Britain: British Caledonian four times week, including one flight which continues to Chile. Aerolineas Argentinas, twice a week. Or you can fly from London to Rio de Janeiro by Varig and change there. Alitalia has three flights weekly to Buenos Aires via Rio from Rome. Ibera has two flights a week from Madrid to Rio and on to B.A. Lufthansa has three multi-stop flights each week from Frankfurt. The average London to Buenos Aires time is about 14 hours.

One way fare: First class $1,147, Economy class $753. Round trip: First class $2,144, Economy class $1,408. Excursion rate for 60 days round trip $1,100. Note these fares are about 25 percent higher in the "high season" from June to September.

Charter flights from Europe are much cheaper, but you must be a member in good standing of the group organizing the trip for at least six months. Time limits for the trip vary from 30 to 60 days but are usually short.

Visitors from Australia, the Far East and South Africa may use the new joint service of Aerolineas Argentinas and South African Airways, twice weekly via Cape Town and Rio de Janeiro. Aerolineas only flies from Cape Town, but SAA has connecting flights with all parts of the world.

 By Sea. *From North America.* If you can afford it, the most enjoyable (but most expensive) way is to sail in one of the fine liners of the Prudential-Grace Line from Vancouver, calling at Tacoma, San Francisco, Los Angeles, Buenaventura (Colombia), Guayaquil, Callao, Valparaíso and then a day-long trip through the fascinating Straits of Magellan to Buenos Aires. They carry 100 passengers and have all the amenities and American food. One way: $1,910.

Moore-McCormack Lines has express freighter services from New York to Buenos Aires about twice a month. It is an old established line of great tradition, but passenger-carrying may cease, so check ahead. About 12 passengers per ship pay $685 dollars one way. Norwegian Ivarian Lines has a monthly sailing from New York for 6–8 passengers. Fares: single $775, double $750 each. Service is said to be excellent and the passenger quarters comfortable.

ELMA, the Argentine state merchant fleet, operates large freighters on an irregular schedule from New York and other U.S. ports. They carry a few passengers, but a knowledge of Spanish would be desirable.

From Britain: Lamport and Holt freighters from Liverpool carry from 5 to 12 passengers for £228 one way. Time for voyage about 17–21 days depending on ports of call. Blue Star carries six passengers usually from London or Southampton for £600 round trip. Houlder Brothers' flagship "Hardwicke Grange" carries 12 people but has no regular schedule at present because of the meat crisis; it normally runs from London and/or Southampton for £320, one way.

For the more adventurous who have the money, the best bet is to use the Spanish Ibarra Lines or the Italmar or Costa Lines of Italy, which still run real ocean liners from Spanish and Italian ports, some of them of 30,000 tons. They make the River Plate in a couple of weeks amid luxury which is something out of the past.

From other countries of South America you can reach Argentina with the greatest of ease by air, landing in Buenos Aires or in one of seven other cities. From Paraguay, Bolivia, Brazil, Venezuela and Chile you can come by plane, or by bus and train if the lines are not blocked by snow; but of all railway journeys anywhere, none is more fascinating or rewarding than that in the narrow-gauge pinion-helped pullman which runs from Mendoza in Argentina to Los Andes in Chile, with connections to Buenos Aires one way and Santiago the other. There is a newer line between Antofagasta and Salta but it's not a quarter the fun.

Or you can *drive* over from Uruguay, Brazil, Paraguay or Chile. From Rio you would go by São Paulo, and down the Uruguayan coast, or over west to see one of Argentina's natural wonders the powerful Iguazú falls. From Bolivia you'll come down from nearly 14,000 feet through Salta to Buenos Aires at next to zero feet above sea level. All cross-country highways in Argentina and Paraguay are now paved and well equipped with signs. From Paraguay there are car ferries at Asunción and Encarnación, and the Friendship Bridge links Paraguay with Brazil and the Iguazú Falls where there is a car ferry into Argentina.

There are daily *bus* services by air-conditioned pullmans between Buenos Aires and Rio de Janeiro, to Asunción with a change at Mendoza for Chile.

From Chile you could take off due east from the capital at Santiago, climb the Andes and come down through Mendoza over a good highway. Or you could head south toward Puerto Montt, take an *Austral* or *LAN-Chile* jet to San Carlos de Barilloche, a 35-minute, spectacular flight over snow-capped peaks. A boat also operates between these two points through a chain of lakes in southwestern Argentina. You can also drive or fly from Bariloche to Buenos Aires. *Aerolineas Argentinas* has an extensive internal network of flights.

 TRAINS IN ARGENTINA. The State Railways have a network of 25,000 miles, one of the largest in the world. All name trains like *El Libertador* to Mendoza, *Los Arrayanes* to Bariloche, *Rayol del Sol* to Cordoba and the crack *Expreso Buenos Aires* are Diesel-drawn, with new deluxe dining cars and sleepers built by Fiat in Cordoba. Many carry uniformed hostesses and have wall-to-wall carpeting. Sleepers nicely decorated and most are air-conditioned. You can travel to Asunción by the Urquiza line; to La Paz by the Belgrano line or to Chile via Mendoza or Salta. Belgrano is meter gauge, but the rest are 5 ft. 6 in. broad gauge, which makes for smooth travel.

 CUSTOMS. If you come directly to Buenos Aires by air or ship, you will find customs officials generally most cooperative and helpful. If you are bringing special equipment (typewriter, radio, guns, fishing equipment, cameras, binoculars, tape recorders or such), it is wise to inform your travel agent or the airline or shipping company in advance; they can arrange proper clearance.

All personal clothing and effects are admitted free of duty provided they have been used; so also, personal jewelry and professional equipment, such as a typewriter. When you leave, you may take leather articles and fabrics up to a value of about $300 without an export permit.

Three quarts of spirits and 500 cigarettes or half a pound of tobacco will not be dutiable; whisky (all sorts) is expensive in Argentina, but there are good local gins and cigarettes to suit British, Continental European and North American palates.

 CURRENCY. The monetary unit is the new peso worth 100 of the old pesos, or "*moneda nacional.*" The rate of exchange fluctuates, but the peso was growing in strength during the first months of the new military regime, and in mid-1976 international banking sources expected it to strengthen further, as a measure of stability was seen.

In Buenos Aires you'll find branches of banks from every part of the world jostling next to each other all round the junction of the Calle San Martín and Bartolomé Mitre, as well as in the provinces.

CHANGING MONEY. You can save valuable time (and get your full rate for a dollar or a pound sterling) by going to certain *Cambios*, or exchange brokers, along Corrientes and Calle San Martín or the hotel desk.

 TIPPING. Gratuities have theoretically been outlawed in Argentina, but your hotel or restaurant adds a stiff 24 percent service and tax charge to your bill, and if you expect to come back for a meal or such you'd better add a little extra, a maximum of 10 percent of the cost, though 5 percent is enough if the bill runs high. The same service charge is added in a bar. One quarter of the listed service charge is a fair rule of thumb. If you give a taxi driver 1.00 to 1.50 new pesos you've made his week. 50 cents is fine for the usher who shows you your theater seat.

 TRAVEL AGENCIES. There are hundreds of travel agencies in Buenos Aires. They operate under strict control by the State Tourist Bureau. All are helpful in booking you for local tours, sightseeing, plane, train or bus tickets to beach resorts, the lake district, the Falls, the Cordoba hills or across the river to Uruguay. Top hotels usually have a branch office in their lobbies.

The *Sol-Jet* organization, a subsidiary of Austral airlines with its own network of fine new hotels, local excursion buses and launches on the lake, offers the most comprehensive tours and requires only a few days notice. Most are 8-day visits which take in two or three cities or points of interest. The price averages $300, which includes all excursions and most meals. Sol-Jet also owns and operates large ski complexes at Cerro Catedral in Bariloche and Cerro Chapelco near San Martín de los Andes, so ski packages are of course also available.

A trip you will always remember is to Argentina's oldest cities: Jujuy, Salta and Tucumán with a night in a mountain hostel in the Calchaquíes Valley in the Andes. Other interesting tours are: the sea elephant preserve in the Welsh colony in Patagonia; Iguazú Falls; Mar del Plata; La Cumbre in the Córdoba hills, a famed British-type resort with golf, casino and wonderful scenery. Or there are foreign package tours to Punta del Este, Uruguay and Itapema, the new Brazilian beach.

Exprinter and other travel agents offer numerous package tours: among them deluxe steamer travel to Asunción, Paraguay, or to Montevideo, Uruguay. A new ski complex is being built at Esquel in southern Patagonia. Or perhaps you'd like to visit the world's largest glaciers.

Other leading agencies are: *Wagon Lits-Cook*; *City Service Travel*, which also handles American Express; *Casa Piano*; *Houlder Brothers*, steamship and air passages; *Mitchell's*; *Furlong*; *Trade Travel Company*; *Delfino and Waldron*.

Outside the capital, rates vary considerably. In the offseason, Mar del Plata hotels will quote you reduced rates. In general, things run like this:

Expensive (not very many), $15–20 single, $20–30 double. *Moderate*, $12–15 single, $18–25 double. *Inexpensive*, $8–12 single, $12–18 double.

Buenos Aires hotels will not quote you for board and many have no dining rooms. Hotels in the far provinces will usually quote you for board.

NOTE: Hotel rates are going up all the time because of compulsory wage increases, and operating costs in general from inflation, higher social security contributions, and so on.

 GETTING AROUND IN BUENOS AIRES. Moving around is easy, by cab, hired car if you're feeling luxurious, bus or subway if you're in a saving mood—and Buenos Aires' public transport goes everywhere. The city has five subway lines, one crossing the city from west to east, the other four interconnecting to the north.

Taxis have yellow roofs. They are, like everything else in Argentina, reasonable but increasingly expensive. Or through your agency or at your hotel, there are private cars called "remises" to hire by the hour, the trip or the week, usualy with a translator as driver. A Fiat rents for $6.30 per day, plus 10¢ per mile; a Chevy, $12 per day, plus 12¢ per mile.

Buenos Aires still runs fiacres, though those horse-drawn carriages are here called *mateos*; you might like to ask your hotel doorman to get one of those to take you on a tour, especially through the Palermo Park area past the Zoo (at Libertador's intersection with Sarmiento Avenue) and past a host of Embassy residences.

 HOTELS. There are few modern hotels in the capital of Argentina (the *Hotel Presidente*, the *B.A. Sheraton* and the *Republica*, overlooking the wide Avda. 9 of July) but there are a handful of highly elegant hotels, comparable to the palace-type hostelries of Europe. These feature elegance, excellent service and usually, very good food. The standards of service in all Argentine hotels and restaurants, as a matter of fact, are much higher than those in the United States. The enthusiasm of the service may more than make up for any other deficiencies. All hotels add three percent Tourism Tax, and 23 percent service charge, but tipping is expected, especially for unusual courtesy or helpfulness. Room service takes quite a while in most hotels and it is wise to order well in advance of the time you actually need something. All hotels are European plan (room only) unless otherwise mentioned. Most hotels in the large cities are air conditioned.

The government grades all hotels by the following scale: Luxury, first class special, first class, first class A, first class B, Grand Tourism (mostly in the provinces), second class, second class A, second class B.

Our listings, based on government classifications and our own appraisals by editors and readers, are simpler, since they are based primarily (but not exclusively) on Buenos Aires prices to help you in planning ahead: *Deluxe* means $30–$34 for single, $35–$41 for double; *First Class*, $24 up for single, $27 up for double; *Moderate*, $12 up for single, $20 up for double; *Inexpensive*, below the above figures.

BUENOS AIRES

Deluxe

BUENOS AIRES SHERATON. San Martín 1225/1275. 800 rooms. The best hotel in Buenos Aires, the only one with heated swimming pool. Health club, tennis, sauna, rooftop bar, shopping arcade. Disco.

CLARIDGE. 535 Tucumán, has 180 rooms, all with private bath. American as well as European plan available. Excellent service and one of the best restaurants in town. Dignified atmosphere.

PLAZA, 1005 Florida. Elegant, but not quite luxurious, with fine service. 350 rooms, all with private bath.

REPUBLICA. Cerrito 354-78. New; 250 rooms. On Nueve de Julio Boulevard in city center.

CONTINENTAL. Diagonal Norte 725. Newly re-opened, completely refurbished. 200 rooms. Air conditioned throughout. Television and personal refrigerator in each room. Restaurant with fine food, tea-room and boite. Across from Pan-Am office on avenue lined with stately buildings.

ALVEAR PALACE. 1891 Ave. Alvear. A well-run, residential hotel, about 15 minutes from downtown. 350 rooms with bath. Food recommended.

First Class

PRESIDENTE. 9th of July Av. and Córdoba. 300 rooms, air conditioned. Good restaurant, excellent bar, underground parking. Convenient. American tone.

Moderate

CRILLON. 796 Santa Fé. 150 comfortable rooms with bath. Faces Plaza San Martín. Bar.

GRAN BUENOS AIRES. Marcelo T. Alvear 767. Central location. 100 small but pleasant rooms. Good service.

LANCASTER. 405 Córdoba, has 125 rooms, all with private bath. A very comfortable establishment with a good reputation.

REGIDOR. Tucumán 451. 100 rooms, excellent service, garage.

SUSSEX. Tucumán 572, corner of Florida, the main shopping street. 120 rooms with bath.

Inexpensive

CITY. 160 Bolivar, has 400 rooms, all with private bath, and boasts the same facilities as the Plaza and Alvear Palace. The atmosphere is more down-to-earth. Grill room features fine food. Good bar.

GRAN DORA. Maipu 963. Central location, 100 air-conditioned rooms.

GRAN HOTEL ARGENTINO. 37 C. Pellegrini, has 160 rooms, all with private bath. Choice of European or American plans. Central heating and air conditioning.

NOGARO. 562 Ave. J.A. Roca, has 100 rooms with private bath. Air conditioning in most rooms. Good restaurant and bar.

SAVOY. 181 Callao, has 250 rooms with private bath. Restaurant, grill, beauty parlor, barber. Also: *Salles.* Rather new hotel. 120 air-conditioned rooms. Excellent service. Cerrito St. (on 9 of July Av.); *Liberty,* 626 Corrientes Av.

Note: The formerly run-down *International Hotel* at Ezeiza airport has been renovated and refurbished, so if your delayed plane arrives at an ungodly hour, this is the place.

OUTSIDE THE CAPITAL

BAHIA BLANCA. A busy port city, mostly a stopover point for travelers going by car to the Lake District. Good hotels: *Austral*, 159 Av. Colon, 100 rooms with bath; *Belgrano*, Belgrano 44, 100 rooms with bath; *Gran Hotel del Sur*, Colon 24, 195 rooms with bath.

MAR DEL PLATA. In this bustling resort, dozens of hotels are adequate for the fun seeker. *Château de Frontenac*, Alvear 2010, 80 rooms with bath. First Class. Others: *Provincial*, next to the casino, 500 rooms with bath. Moderate. *Astor*, 1638 Entre Ríos, 106 rooms all with bath. Inexpensive. *Hermitage*, 2657 Blvd. Maritimo, 200 rooms, all but 10 with private bath. First Class. *Sasso*, 3545 Av. P. Ramos, 150 rooms, all but 10 with private bath. Deluxe. *Tourbillon*, 49 San Lorenzo, 100 rooms, 90 with private bath. Moderate. *Flamingo*, Moreno 2155, 150 rooms, near casino and beach. Inexpensive. *Piccadilly*, 50 rooms, casino close by. Inexpensive. *Dos Reyes*, Colon 2129, 132 rooms with bath. Moderate.

GRAN HOTEL DORÁ. A home from home for most middle class folk. Part of the chain of the same name. It faces the Casino and has 120 rooms, restaurant run by Japanese, and 24 hour room service.

MIRAMAR. This resort further down the coast is less expensive and almost as much fun as Mar del Plata. Favorite hotels here are the *Atlantico*, 60 rooms with bath; *Gran Rex*, 50 rooms, bath; *Normandie*, 66 rooms with bath; *Plaza*, 100 rooms with bath; *Platamar*, 18 rooms with bath; and *Hispania*, 61 rooms with bath. All are in the First Class or Moderate category.

NECOCHEA. A rapidly rising beach resort 70 miles further south than Miramar. The new casino (for 5,000 patrons) is one of the largest in the world and futuristic in style. Many new hotels have been recently built. Best hotels: *Trocadero*, 93 rooms, 80 baths; *Marino*, 80 rooms with bath; *Atlantico*, 50 rooms with bath; *San Martín*, 62 rooms with bath (Deluxe).

THE BARILOCHE LAKE COUNTRY

LLAO-LLAO is one of the best-known tourist "musts" in Argentina at the foot of Cerro Lopez, overlooking the incredible postcard scenery of Lakes Nahuel Huapi and Moreno. President Eisenhower stayed a night here on his way to Chile and found time to try his luck at trout fishing on the River Limay. 175 rooms with bath. Deluxe.

NOTE: Travelers are recommended to book their rooms with other hotels in Bariloche with some travel agent before leaving.

SOL-BARILOCHE, formerly Hotel Italia, Mitre 212. Best hotel in city itself. Right on main stem. 135 rooms with bath. First Class.

TUNQUELEN. Near Llao-Llao overlooking lake. 60 rooms with bath. An exclusive place; food included at higher rates. Deluxe.

CATEDRAL SKI HOTEL. At foot of the mountain whence cable cars go up to Cerro Catedral and chairlifts to the southern end of the massif. Used mostly by winter sports enthusiasts but much less spartan than it was. 80 rooms with bath. This hotel is for those who want to get away from it all but be quite near town. Moderate.

HOTEL CASINO BARILOCHE CENTER. This is a huge block of 200 apartments in the Civic Center, fully equipped with baths and kitchenettes. Reservations can be booked in Buenos Aires through Cantegril International, Florida 683. Moderate. There are lower rates in the spring (March to June) and fall (September to December) between the avalanches of summer tourists and those of winter sports enthusiasts.

On the slopes of the Cerro Otto Hill rising behind the main street are several fine hotels with magnificent lake and mountain views: *Bellavista*, 62 rooms with bath, splendid public rooms. Deluxe. *Roma*, 70 rooms with bath. First Class. *Edelweiss*, 80 rooms. Deluxe.

Hard to get into, but a gourmet's paradise, is *Hosteria El Jabali*, only 12 rooms (all with bath). The dining room is a tourist's must for wild boar and venison, and fish are flown over from the Pacific Ocean every day. Deluxe.

Lakeside hotels in the town are: *Tres Reyes*, a truly sybaritic home from home. 58 rooms. First class.

Along the shores of Lake Nahuel Huapi, Argentina's second largest lake, amid beautiful settings but still near to town are: *Amancay*, near Llao-llao. 57 rooms with bath. Open the year round with central heating in winter. Swimming pool. First class. *El Casco,* 22 rooms. Deluxe.

There are more than 50 hotels in Bariloche and more are going up every day. There are also hundreds of modestly priced "residenciales" and hostrelries, all excellent.

Tourists would be advised to get bookings from travel agents in Buenos Aires before they leave, for they buy up blocks of tickets in planes and trains and hotel space.

CORRENTOSO. A German-run hotel which is a veritable Shangri-La, with views across the lake of the millenary forests and the snow-capped Chilean volcanoes. The hotel has its own port and runs excursions into the forests on the other side, impressing tourists by blazing the trees to record the path taken. Not much fishing in the lake any more but plenty in the abundance of smaller lakes. You can climb a mountain from the hotel—if you take a guide—or visit Villa Angostura, the nearby village. All rooms with bath; price includes full board. Hotel has only 30 rooms and is much sought after. Deluxe.

SAN MARTIN. On Lake Lacar with day trips to Chile via Puerto Huahum. Top hotel with casino: *Sol Andes*, 99 rooms with bath, perched atop the little town with full view of the lake and surrounding mountains. Moderate.

Alternatively, try *Residencial Berna*, Swiss-run, 25 rooms with bath. No dining room. Very modern. Inexpensive. *Lacar*, old fashioned but comfortable. 43 rooms, 34 with bath. Inexpensive. *Los Andes*, 16 rooms, 11 with bath, and a good restaurant. Price includes board. Moderate.

LOS ALERCES NATIONAL PARK. *Futalafquen*, on the lake of the same name, is a reasonably priced resort hotel. Reached via Esquel, it has 37 rooms with private bath.

NEUQUEN. Top hotel is the *Sol Neuqúen* of the Sol-Jet chain. New 14-story building with 99 air-conditioned rooms, all with bath; swimming pool. Right place to see Latin America's largest hydro-electric complex at Chocon. Or the largest man-made lake in South America, Lake Ramos Mejia, with fishing and yachting facilities. Moderate.

The new *Hotel Royal* almost alongside the Automobile Club is said to be most comfortable in Neuquen. All rooms with private bath. Conference facilities. Room service. Attractive lounges.

Also: *Charbel*, 50 rooms with bath. *Ideal*, 41 rooms with bath. *Huemul*, 45 rooms with bath. All inexpensive.

MENDOZA. Top hotels: *Plaza*, operated by provincial government, with casino inside. 85 rooms with bath. Air conditioning. First Class. *Sussex*, new, 120 rooms with bath. Moderate. *Internacional*, 60 rooms with bath. Moderate. *Gran Ariosto*, 55 rooms with bath. Inexpensive. *Gran Hotel Mendoza*, 90 rooms with bath. 10-story hotel near Casino. Inexpensive. Local residents try hard to get into the *Balbi*, 108 rooms with bath. Moderate.

ROSARIO. Argentina's second city, with about 1 million people. Top hotel is the traditional *Grand Hotel Italia*, with 200 rooms (ask for the modern section). Excellent food. Also: *Riviera*, San Lorenzo 1460, 100 rooms. First class. *Plaza Hotel,* Baron de Maná 26; *Presidente,* Avenida Corrientes 919. Air-conditioned. Moderate.

SAN JUAN. Outstanding and top hotel: *Nogaro*, with 133 rooms, part of Nogaro chain. Center for visiting famous vineyards and fantastic Andean scenery. Moderate.

SAN LUIS. The *Nacional de Turismo* here is the city's best. 45 rooms, all with bath. Frequently booked up in season with vacationing government workers, as all Nacional de Turismo hotels are likely to be.

There are many new hotels such as: *Gran Palace*, 70 rooms with bath, high class. *Gran Hotel San Luis*, 60 air-conditioned rooms with bath. Rooftop swimming pool. *Regidor*, 40 rooms with bath. *Novel*, 40 rooms with bath. All inexpensive.

CORDOBA. Best hotel (and food) is still the *Crillon* at Rivadavia 85. Reservations absolutely necessary. 120 rooms with bath. Moderate. *Sussex*, 120 rooms with bath. Fine view of city from dining room on top floor. Moderate. *Córdoba Palace*, a new hotel, 132 rooms with bath. First Class. *Gran Hotel Dorá*, 120 rooms with bath. Excellent service. Moderate. *Grand Alexander*, 48 air-conditioned rooms with bath. Inexpensive. *Windsor*, 59 rooms with bath. Inexpensive.

LA RIOJA. Best bet here is the *Gran Hotel Casino Provincial*, Blvd. Sarmiento 1275. Inexpensive.

CATAMARCA. If you have to stay here, try the *Nacional de Turismo*, 52 rooms, 40 with bath; or the *Ancasti*, 100 rooms with bath.

TUCUMAN. Newest hotel is *Metropol*, air-conditioned, with swimming pool, art gallery, convention facilities. Most of its 100 rooms face the jungle-clad mountains. Moderate. *Gran Hotel Premier*. 110 rooms with bath. Air conditioning. Inexpensive. *Versailles*. 62 rooms with bath. Much favored by artists and operates with *Hotel Francia* next door under same owner. *Francia,* 40 rooms with bath. Inexpensive. *California.* 45 rooms with bath. Moderate. *Savoy.* Run by the provincial government. *Casino.* 100 rooms with bath. Inexpensive. *Canciller.* 45 rooms with bath. Moderate. *Claridge.* 70 rooms with bath. Air conditioning. Moderate.

Other inexpensive hotels worth a visit: *Astoria,* 50 rooms. *Bristol,* 37 rooms. *Congreso,* 48 rooms. *Coventry,* 70 rooms. *King,* 50 rooms. *Miami,* 30 rooms. All with private bath.

SALTA. Best is the *Salta,* largest and with full amenities. Seignorial on corner on main city square. Swimming pool with bar service. 87 rooms with bath. Moderate. *Victoria Plaza* makes much of ex-King Leopold's having stayed here. No dining room. 100 rooms with bath. Moderate.

Very good, but with only a snack bar and no dining room, is the new *Provincial,* 72 rooms with bath. Hotel is right on main street. Also recommended: *California,* 70 air-conditioned rooms with bath. *Flamingo Motel,* in a picturesque setting just outside city. Swimming pool and grill room. *Gran Hotel Premier* with 70 air-conditioned rooms. Restaurant. All Inexpensive.

JUJUY. If you can get in, the best bet is *Alto La Viña,* perched on an Andean hillside with fantastic views of the city and up Humahuaca Canyon, especially at night. 70 rooms with private bath. Swimming pool. Moderate.

In the city itself: *Internacional Jujuy,* multistory new hotel with 110 air-conditioned rooms with bath. First Class. *Augustus,* 42 rooms with bath. Moderate.

SANTIAGO DEL ESTERO. Best bet: the new and monumental *Grand,* 110 outside rooms with bath. Air conditioned. Moderate. Others: *Savoy,* 75 rooms with bath. Inexpensive. *Gran Hotel Coventry* has 31 rooms with bath. Inexpensive. *Florida.* Restaurant. Inexpensive.

Nearby are the famous thermal springs of Rio Hondo. Best among many hotels there are: *Grand.* 200 rooms with bath. Rates include one meal. Deluxe. *Gran Hotel Los Pinos,* 105 rooms with bath. Includes meals. Deluxe. *Independencia,* 90 rooms with bath. First Class. *Crillon,* 70 rooms with bath. With board. Deluxe.

CORRIENTES. Newest and best hotels: *Guarani,* 150 rooms with bath. *Corrientes,* 120 rooms with bath. *Buenos Aires,* 72 rooms with bath. *Orly,* 68 air-conditioned rooms with bath. *San Martin,* 44 rooms with bath. All Inexpensive.

CONDORIA. Entre Rios province. New *San Carlos Hotel,* atop a hill overlooking Salto Grande falls where work has started on one of the world's largest dams, with road and rail connections across the river to Uruguay. Locks will allow ocean-going ships to proceed farther up the Uruguay river. 62 rooms with private bath, most with private balconies. Pool and golf course. Good fishing. Near to newest National Park, the Palm Forest of Colón.

IGUAZU FALLS

There is a series of steel footbridges built on the rim of the falls—which number 287 in all—right to the Devil's Throat, which is the major fall. You can also get there from upstream in a sort of large canoe with an outboard motor, except after a heavy rain when the current and volume of water are excessive.

For the moment, the new *El Libertador*, deluxe, with 112 rooms with bath, is the best bet. The Sol-Jet tourist group, an affiliate of Austral Airlines, will fly you there for 5- to 8-day stays in an all-inclusive package which is a very good deal, not much more than the price of the flight.

The National Park's *Tourist Hotel* has 104 rooms with bath, but is usually block-booked by tourist agencies. With board. *Casino* operates here in winter months from July. First Class.

SANTA FE. The best bets: *Hostal Santa Fé de la Vera Cruz*. 80 rooms with bath. *Conquistador*, 72 rooms with bath. Both Inexpensive.

Others are *Corrientes*, 60 air-conditioned rooms with bath. *Castelar*, 100 rooms with bath. *Hernandarias*, 41 rooms with bath. *Gran Hotel España*, 50 rooms with bath. All Inexpensive.

The new *Hotel International Cataratas* of 181 rooms all looking outside and most of them over the falls themselves has four presidential suites for people with money to spend.

It has convention facilities for 600 delegates, pool, self-service coffee shop and a de luxe restaurant, shopping arcade and many other things, like a cabaret for example for those who love the flesh-pots rather than the wonders of Nature.

ROUGHING IT. Argentina has a network of camp sites and motels throughout the republic. The Automobile Club has pioneered the field and owns scores of motels, and private enterprise operates many more. Living in tents is today commonplace and one of the fast-growing local industries is the manufacture of "dormobiles," or traveling houses which you hitch to your car.

Resort cities welcome campers—there is even a campsite beside the Iguazú Falls!

RESTAURANTS. In Buenos Aires you may find the same food you get at home wherever you come from. That means typical dishes of the U.S.A., Britain, France, Spain, Italy, Greece, Germany, Russia, Hungary, China, Japan, Denmark, Sweden, Norway, Switzerland, Portugal and the Middle East. But rising costs are forcing many places to close up.

But you would be foolish not to sample the local dishes, largely an amalgam of Basque, Spanish and Italian food which might prove a gastronomic adventure. Many places catering to foreigners advertise their specialties daily in the Buenos Aires *Herald*.

BUENOS AIRES

Expensive

CLARIDGE HOTEL GRILL, without doubt the city's best public restaurant. Highly elegant in the Continental manner. Quite expensive. Tucumán 565.

PLAZA HOTEL GRILL is in the same class as the Claridge Hotel Grill, and features fine Continental dishes and the ubiquitous Argentine steak. The specialty: pepper steak. Good service, elegant atmosphere. 1005 Florida St.

AU BEC FIN, 1223 Arenales, claims to be the finest of the many French restaurants in town. Decor is simple but prices are steep. Favored by expense accounters.

LA CABANA. 436 Entre Ríos, is a must. Best steak house in Buenos Aires; rather expensive. Gracious service, tremendous servings—so come with a good appetite. Also specializes in local, or native, dishes.

EL LAGAR DEL VIRREY. Ayacucho 1669. International menu, superb decor.

LA PIGALLE, Roberto M. Ortiz 1839, said to be the most luxurious restaurant in town. Violinists. Closed Mondays.

LONDON GRILL AND OYSTER BAR. 455 Reconquista, is a refuge for the English-speaking community and specializes in businessmen's lunches. Good chops, lamb and beef, curries.

THE ALEXANDRA. San Martín 774. A break off from the London Grill and also has menus in English. Traditional British atmosphere from kippers to Christmas puddings and mince pies. Air conditioned.

EL ALJIBE. Sheraton Hotel Plaza Britannia. International cuisine, American and local dishes.

SWISSAIR. Santa Fé 846, 1st floor. A daily food festival for gourmets. Closed Sundays.

EL CALDERO. Gorriti 1972. Medieval restaurant with ancient music and songs. Help yourself to all you can eat and drink.

LA VEDA. Florida 1. Five-forks restaurant much in favor with executives. Features top quality steaks, by the allegedly finest grillmasters.

IRISH PUB. San Martín 979. Half a block from Plaza Hotel.

Specialties: roast beef, chicken pie and Irish stew. Air conditioned. Note: Their sign now says 'Matias Downtown' but it's still *the* Irish pub of B.A.

HOSTAL DEL LAGO. Palermo Park. Very plush restaurant on a lake in Palermo Park. Continental food.

THE JOCKEY CLUB. Downtown next to the French Embassy, is without doubt the very best place to eat in all Argentina. By invitation only.

LA CAUTIVA. Sucre 1546. An exotic place frequented by cattle ranchers and turfmen for its prime beef and native dishes, served in upper rooms above a livery stable and overlooking an equestrian jumping course.

EL CABALLITO BLANCO. 479 M.T. de Alvear, has an international menu, better-than-average service. Folkloric and tango shows.

BISTRO. Demaria 4700. French cuisine, lovely atmosphere.

Other fine restaurants are *Il Pozzo del Poeta*, Av. Libertador 6649, elegant, Italian, orchestra but no dancing; *Meson Espanol*, Caseros 1750, picturesque, Spanish, entertainment. Also recommended are the grill rooms in the *City Hotel, Alvear Palace, Continental* and *Nogaro Hotel*.

Reasonable

LA ZI TERESA DI NAPOLI. 2939 Las Heras, serves very good southern Italian specialties in pleasant surroundings.

CASA SUIZA. 254 Rodriquez Pena, features Viennese cooking, better than what you might expect, and Swiss dishes.

MUNICH is the short name of a chain of excellent restaurants which are plain in appearance but which serve good food for a very reasonable price. Spaghetti and meat dishes are the specialties. Among the best of the chain are *Munich Recoleta* on the street of the same name and the *Munich*, 965 Av. de Mayo.

LIGURE. At 855 Juncal, offers quite good northern Italian food in pleasant surroundings.

TORNA A SORRENTO, Lamadrid 701. Morsels of the sea cooked to perfection, including *cazuela de mariscos*.

ABC. Lavalle 545. German restaurant open from 10 a.m. to midnight. Trout and German dishes featured.

CHIQUIN. Cangallo 920. First air-conditioned place in Buenos Aires. Old-time atmosphere. Famed for roast beef, at lunch only.

CORRIENTES II. Corrientes 135, the ground floor of grain exchange. Famed businessmen's meeting place with a vast menu and large dining room. Excellent steaks.

NAPOLI. Bouchard 470. In front of Luna Park indoor stadium, the local Madison Square Garden. Italian atmosphere. Simple but superb food, especially the meat dishes.

LO PRETE. Luis Saenz Peña 749. An enormous hangar-type saloon with Italian decor and wide choice of dishes.

VUONO. Solis 659. Famed for Italian spaghetti dishes. Try *alle vongole*, spaghetti with shellfish. Air conditioned.

Inexpensive

PARILLA SAINT TROPEZ. Mouthwatering steaks at unbelievably low prices.

RIVERSIDE RESTAURANTS. There are some 50 restaurants known as *Carritos* along the river towards Palermo. Recommended are *Happening No. 55, Los Hermanos No. 51, Jacaranda No. 52.* Steaks, chicken.

ROMA. Lavalle St. Large pizza parlor.

LA ESTANCIA. Lavalle 941. Steak house.

Argentine Cuisine

EL CEIBAL. 2263 Las Heras, is very good, inexpensive. Try the *carbonada*. Several branches in city.

LA CARRETA. 6902 Av. Libertador, is famous for its good local food and its *mate*. Tables outdoors.

IL PICCOLO-NAVIO. Suarez y Necochea (Boca district), is a fun place, informal and colorful, with good food served with bags of wine. Speciality of the house is seafood.

EL PESCADITO. 1475 Pedro Mendoza (Boca district), features music with its seafood dishes. Old-fashioned harborfront atmosphere.

EL TIBURON means *The Shark*, but the restaurant at 1561 P. Mendoza (Boca) features Italian cuisine, snails.

SPADAVECCHIA. 1180 Necochea (Boca district), is another native place, with a devil-maycare atmosphere, music, dancing.

SPARAFUCILE. 1111 Necochea (Boca district) is similar to the Spadavecchia.

Chinese

Several Chinese restaurants in Buenos Aires serve Cantonese specialties. Among them are: *Cantina China,* 967 Maipu; *Canton,* 945 Córdoba (upstairs);

Pagoda China, 614 Av. R. Saenz Pens; and the luxurious *Wa Tu* at Rio Bamba, between Santa Fé Ave. and Charcas. Excellent food and service.

The Suburbs

PERIGORD is the best restaurant in San Isidro, unless you eat at any of the nightclubs, which can be risky but exciting if you have courage. Some typical nightclubs in the suburbs are *Sunset* *Club* and *Golden Pub*. Good restaurants: *La Palmera* and *El Hueso Perdido*, patronized by resident Americans.

We recommend taking a tour which includes a visit and meal at **EL MANGRULLO**. Almost like visiting an *estancia*. "Gaucho" waiters, songs, dances. Traditional food; or **PINAR AZUL**. A delightful operation 30 kms. from town, at José Paz. Swimming pool, riding. Excellent barbequed beef. About $10. Folklore show.

 NIGHTLIFE. Buenos Aires has numerous theaters and there are frequent visits by foreign ensembles like the Comedie Francaise, Bolshoi Ballet, Moscow Circus, occasional U.S. groups, sometimes a British company and of course many Spanish and Italian performers.

Hard times have come with the attempt to restore financial sanity the hard way after three decades of pie in the sky economics with ever-rising prices and ever heavier taxation.

So nightlife as such has dwindled somewhat except for tourists, but the old-time big cabarets like the Tabaris, world-famous in its time with clients like the late Duke of Windsor; the Chantecler where you chose between hostesses in bathing suits for the heated pool or in long dresses for the dance floor; the Casino, Casanova, Novelty, the famous Embassy and many others have all passed into history.

Today there is a large number of smaller intimate boites though many stage shows. Dance floors are usually tiny. Newest and for the moment most spectacular is *Cabaret*, corner of Florida and Marcel T. de Alvear, near the *Plaza Hotel* and facing the same main square. *Salon Blanco* for the more sedate features a musical variety show with drinks and *Salon Dorado* features a string of strippers in its "Sexy Revue."

Buenos Aires is a gay city, with a variety of night life entertainment from nightclubs, small boites, discotheques to B-girl level bars. Among the better places are: *Golden Horn*, at the top of Sheraton Hotel. Dancing "among the stars" in a most beautiful atmosphere; *Gong* (Córdoba 634).

L'Horizon, Junin 1460. For those who like things hot, you may get warmed up for a larger evening from the Lebanese fare mingled with Middle Eastern belly dancers—who incidentally expect a handsome tip.

El Almacen de Rivero is an old 1800 corner-house converted into a typical tango "cavern," in the old San Telmo section at Balcarce and Independencia Sts. *Malena al Sur* is another two-storied cabaret with turn-of-the-century decor and an excellent tango orchestra.

Karim (C. Pellegrini 1143), cabaret and striptease popular with visitors; *Karina* (Corrientes 636), Cope's Tango Show, cabaret and dancing; *Maison Doree* (Viamonte 548), "distinguished place for distinguished men," sophisticated and select with show.

Favorite bars with the international set are the *Queen Bess* (Santa Fé 868), *El Reloj* (between Lavalle and Maipu), a popular place serving drinks in 17 different flavors, and the *Claridge* (Tucumán 565). The place to watch your pocket is 25 de Mayo Street, where a whole line of B-girl bars awaits the unwary.

Those who want to hear the best tango, should go to *Caño* 14 (Talcahuano 975). Newest and very "in" is *Michelangelo* (Balcarce 433). No dancing but floorshow and drinks.

CASINOS. There are casinos in Mar del Plata, Bariloche, Mendoza, Córdoba, Necochea, Pinamar, Río Hondo, and north-western spots but none in Buenos Aires. There is a national lottery, but selling tickets for it is forbidden except to authorized, licensed spots and provincial lotteries.

THE PACE OF LIFE. An evening out in Buenos Aires will be timed for eight-thirty, if you're only an hour late you'll still be in time for a cocktail before the meal. It is most appropriate to send your hostess flowers, the same day if it's to be a dance or a large affair, otherwise next day. And that won't hurt your wallet; flowers are cheap and delightful in Buenos Aires. If you (or your travel agent) have contacts, that may be a fairly constant practice, since Argentines prefer to dine and entertain in their homes. Since street doors to apartment buildings are locked at 9 p.m., you'd best be within reach by then.

TEAROOMS AND SIDEWALK CAFES. An important factor in social life in Argentina is the *confiteria* or tearoom. And your Argentine, who has had a very light breakfast and lunched at about 2 p.m. and knows he is not going to dine until about 10 p.m., is a steadfast tearoom client, though he will probably take coffee or a soft drink rather than tea. This is one of the few places in Argentina where tipping has been really abolished; it is rare to see a customer leave as much as a single peso but 10 percent is now expected if his "pick up" runs to sandwiches (Argentina offers a "chip," a soft roll sliced and sandwiching a slice of ham or cheese or both—the latter a *mixto* or "mixed") and cakes and cookies delivered by as many as four waiters. Your Argentine acquaintances will be delighted if you invite them to tea in some such place.

Sidewalk cafes are only to be found in the wider Boulevards: Belgrano, Avenida de Mayo, Córdoba and the gigantic north-south artery, Nueva de Julio, the world's widest street. There are none on the local "Broadway," Calle Corrientes, because there is too much traffic.

Your bill will be slightly higher if you sit outside because the city council charges rent for using the sidewalks. But you may take your fill of the passing scene and the pretty girls.

A favorite tearoom is the *Richmond* in the Florida shopping mall —longest in Latin America at 10 blocks. Modern decor, deluxe, excellent bar. Florida 468.

The century-old *Tortoni* in Avenida de Mayo, among the many sidewalk cafes in this Avenue, is the traditional haunt of artists, painters, newsmen and intellectuals. The walls are covered with paintings and plaques. It has a barber shop and runs through the block.

El Molino, at Rivadavia and Callao, is full of society folk and was also a favorite spot, until recently, of politicians from the National Congress across the street, now indefinitely suspended by the regime. Faces one of the largest city squares.

The Ideal, at Suipacha 384, is a rococo room paneled in a dark walnut and crowded.

The *Wa Tu*, on Rio Bamba between Santa Fe and Charcas, is a new, interesting Chinese tearoom and restaurant.

 DRINKING WATER. Argentina's water supply is plentiful and pure, though you may have some stomach troubles because its bacteria are different from the ones you know at home. Milk is also pasteurized and safe.

 YOUR HEALTH. Argentina has some of the best doctors and surgeons in the world. Any embassy, hotel, or local travel agent can give you a list. Better hospitals: British (near town at Perdriel 74), or the Pequeña Companía de María (Little Company of Mary, an order of English-speaking Catholic sisters at San Martín de Tours 2944). Buenos Aires has some 91 other hospitals. And there are good hospitals and doctors in the provinces. Emergency, phone: 34-4001.

FARMACIAS (drugstores or chemists) sell pharmaceutical and medicinal supplies only. One of the largest in the world is the *Franco-Inglesa*, with multilingual clerical help, at the corner of Florida and Sarmiento in Buenos Aires. There are many others in every district, alternating at staying open all night. You can obtain anything you want, and most of them deliver. For beauty preparations, go to a *perfumería*, or dealer in perfumes and cosmetics.

 MUSEUMS. There are dozens of museums in Buenos Aires of every conceivable nature and also innumerable art galleries, most of them private, though visitors are welcome, especially to buy. Most interesting museums in the capital include;

The Cabildo, facing the Casa Rosada government house, has captured battle flags of the British Royal Marine Battalion and the 71st Highlanders, given up during the invasions of 1806, and many items of Argentina's struggle for independence. Open from Thursdays to Sundays from 5–9 p.m.

The National Historical Museum, at Defensa 1600, where you may sometimes see the Liberator General San Martín's famous curved sabre and many other items.

In Tigre there is the *Naval Museum* on the waterfront at Avenida Victoria 125 with ship models from triremes to battleships, old maps, naval guns, lighthouse equipment and relics of shipwrecks.

The Star Group is the two-block-long complex in the ancient Cabildo buildings in Lujan, 40 miles distant in a lush riverside setting. One houses Colonial history and the other transport, from the former Viceroy's ceremonial coach to the "Plus Ultra" Spanish seaplane which first linked Argentina by air with Europe in 1922.

Pueyrredon Museum, the former home of the general who governed Argentina while San Martín was fighting to free Chile, is located in suburb of San Isidro on bluffs overlooking the River Plate Estuary. You may see the peppertrees under which they planned the invasions of Chile and Peru which ended Spanish power. There is not much in the museum, but it does give an example of life as it was lived in those far off days, and the setting is one of the most beauti- ful spots in Buenos Aires. Usually open in afternoons.

A most famous museum is in nearby La Plata, with many exhibits of fossilized prehistoric animals found in Argentina and much archeological lore, all housed in a palatial building.

For sea lovers, the ancient sloop Sarmiento is open for visitors on Saturdays, Sundays and holidays from 2 to 5 p.m. This was one of Argentina's first warships and was until a few years ago the Navy's historic schoolship. Moored in north basin near most hotels.

 NATIONAL PARKS. Argentina has 16 national parks with another coming up in the little known Esteros de Ibera an area comparable to the Everglades of Florida.

The parks cover the Iguazu falls area, part of the Pilcomayo river area, a virtually virgin jungle zone in the far north; areas in the Chaco and Formosa in the tropical far north; the almost unknown jungle area between Salta and the Chaco, where big game and similar wildlife is still abundant.

Then comes a string of parks along the eastern foothills of the Andes mountains from Neuquen province to south of Bariloche. In the far south is the Glacier National park with some of the largest glaciers in the world both for length and size. There are others in Tierra del Fuego which is still largely in its virgin state, the petrified forest in Patagonia.

One of the latest is the Palm Forest in Entre Ríos. This area is the western terminal of a singular belt of palm forest which stretches across northern Uruguay right to the Atlantic coast.

The yatay palm has an average age of 200–300 years but some last up to 800 so they must have been there when the Conquistadores came. Fibre from the leaves has long been used to weave hats and more recently by the Alpargatas group for making shoe soles.

Tourist accommodation in the Glacier National Park has advanced from tents to small hostelries and regular tours are operated from Buenos Aires. If you want to tackle the continental ice-cap second only to Greenland's and at 9,000 feet about the same height but much narrower, you will have to contact the National Parks administration before you leave Buenos Aires.

 FLORA AND FAUNA. Argentina will delight you with its flora and fauna. The latter ranges from brilliant butterflies (especially in the north) to doves, duck and partridge among birds; puma, lynx, jaguar and deer among wild game. Vicuña, smaller than the llama, provides a soft wool for scarves, sweaters and ponchos, very warm. Fish include everything from trout and salmon to the *pejerrey*, a cross between a sunfish and a sole. The national bird, incidentally, is the *hornero*, or oven-bird, small and gray and making its home of mud and straw with a curving, tunneled entrance to protect it from rain. And in contrast the tremendous condor sails through the lofty Andes peaks. In the far south, the state annually auctions off sectors of the national parks for deer-shooting. Titled people come from Europe every year for this sport. One can also go boar-hunting; this is an exciting but dangerous sport since some boars are as big as small steers and very fierce. Specially-trained "dogo" hounds are used, and high-powered rifles. In the Patagonian wilderness you may see droves of guanacos, a relative of the vicuña and llama; flocks of the "nandu" or local ostrich and of a giant hare called "vizcacha".

Since Argentina lies in three climatic zones, its flora is as varied. Jungles and tropic forests lie to the north; the *quebracho* (a tree with wood hard as steel) is abundant. The national flower is the *ceibo*, a reddish and almost pulpy bud. Even more spectacular, and lining Buenos Aires' streets, are the *paraíso* (paradise) and jacaranda trees which paint the landscape with purple and yellow feathers of blossoms. Flowers are so abundant and inexpensive that stalls dot the street corners of any city.

 SPORTS. Sport is popular throughout Argentina, so that though Buenos Aires offers the widest variety, you can expect a pretty good choice anywhere. If you're a sportsman, active or spectator, Buenos Aires offers *tennis* at the Hurlingham Club or the Buenos Aires Lawn Tennis Club (see your agent for cards); *horse racing* (the Jockey Club, San Andres, Hurlingham, Olivos, etc., again with cards), the year round; *golf:* Jockey Club and Blue Course, Buenos Aires, Links Golf Club, Club Nautico San Isidro; high-goal *polo* in the fall in Palermo and the suburban San Isidro, Hurlingham and Tortugas; top-flight *football* (soccer) all year; Argentina has intermittent high-quality *auto racing* from road races to Grand Prix contests with international star drivers. The January "Gran Premio de Argentina" is the opening race of the annual Formula 1 championship. *Pato* or "duck" is an exciting blend of polo and basketball-on-horseback. Exhibition matches on Sun.

Buenos Aires' Palermo Park has public *tennis* courts and a public *golf* course, with equipment to rent. There is *boxing* and *wrestling* at downtown Luna Park.

There is *boating* (sculls and yachting) on the Tigre 45 minutes northwest of Buenos Aires with craft available if you get a card. *Horseback riding* is also good, with miles of handsome bridle paths in Buenos Aires' Palermo Park and stables from which you can rent mounts.

There is excellent *skiing* in the Bariloche region. You can go *mountaineering* and for real tough exploration of glaciers turn further south.

Shooting is a year-round sport, best in November when a good shot may bring down a hundred perdiz (almost but not quite a partridge) in a day, or knock over as many duck on the Paraná River just a day northwest of Buenos Aires. Dove shooting is great in Buenos Aires province.

International *boxing* bouts at Luna Park indoor stadium. *Waterskiing* on San Antonio River in the Tigre Delta region. Field hockey, up-and-coming rugby football every Sunday, basketball, baseball (largely by Japanese), yacht races in Plate River, billiards and chess tournaments, international lawn tennis, target shooting (including running deer and skeets), bicycle races and numerous track and field events.

FISHING. Every little resort on the Atlantic Coast has a lengthy fishing pier, but many people make good catches of large fish from the beaches. Chief species: rock salmon, conger eel, corvina, sharks, skate, mackerel, hake, brotola, kingfish and many others.

Some exciting fishing can be had in the upper reaches of the River Paraná. King of the river is the Dorado, a real fighter and a big fish. Best spot is at Paso de la Patria where the Paraguay meets the Paraná. Bungalows and launches for hire.

The surubi sometimes weighs 600 to 1000 pounds, and the Mumbucurá is even bigger and can get a man's head in its mouth.

There are many other varieties like sting ray, kingfish, bagré (a sort of dogfish), tarariras, bogas, pati and pacú.

All of Argentina's many artificial lakes are stocked, mostly with large kingfish, and some with trout.

For salmon and rainbow trout fishing the smaller lakes near Bariloche are best. The farther south you go the bigger and better the fish.

When President Eisenhower fished in the River Limay, once noted for trout and salmon, patriotic locals released 150 live trout and salmon round the bend up river. But Ike still did not catch any.

**SHOPPING.** Big stores are open from 9 a.m. straight through to 7 p.m., which is valuable to know if you have a shopping excursion planned. Some smaller stores close for from two to three hours for lunch, generally to include a siesta, or short afternoon nap.

Calle Florida houses some fine shops, from department stores, such as *Harrods* between Paraguay and Córdoba, to big-game couturiers (*Drecoll,* at Florida 764, is one) to branches of internationally famous jewelers (*H. Stern*, Hotel Plaza and Hotel Sheraton, for fine gems and jewelry; ask for free local "charm"). Men's suits, readymade and tailored—at places such as *James Smart, Rhoder's* or the very modern *Gonzalez.* Dress goods are generally top quality; your travel agent should be able to find you a seamstress. For benchmade shoes, try *Botticelli, Lopez Taibo* or *Guante.* Other stores like *Ostende* at Florida 371 will offer you handmade shoes off the rack and fit you well. For luggage and leather goods, *Pedro Mayorga, Pullman, Frenkel's, Etons, Lopez, Carlos Pisk* and *Antique.* Suede coats and accessories at *El Trebol.* Balenciaga perfume and cosmetics cost 50 percent less than in the U.S.

If you're out for souvenirs, preferably with some utility, try *bombachas*, the baggy, long-bloomered pants worn by the hard-riding *gaucho* cowboy, the *chiripa*, an overgrown diaper-scarf he strings through his legs, or the *rastra* of silver coins fastened to chains which is the buckle for his wide belt. Or that gaucho can give you other ideas from the scabbarded, usually in silver, knife he wears in his belt to his spurs or boots to the *mate* cup from which he sips his herb tea and the *bombilla*, the silver tube through which he drinks that tea.

But don't be tempted by aigrettes, birds of paradise or the plumes of the ostrich which roams southern and western Argentine; you'll just have customs troubles when you get home. You'll be far better off with leather gloves (fine in Argentina) or with antelope jackets, coats and purses, as good. Hand-embroidered blouses are excellent. Such fur coats as nutria are cheap if you feel like splurging. Antique shops (try *Regalos Paraná* at Tucumán 1721) can turn up fine bargains. On Sun. the flea and antiques market in San Telmo is a major attraction.

Shifting from purely mun* ane commodities, try *Iriberri* on Florida (or any of a hundred other music stores) for recordings of Argentine music—camp or gaucho songs similar to American "westerns" to the tango.

Then there is native art, especially wood carvings of the gauchos, done in keeping with the country paintings of the late Florencio Molina Campos. A great calendar artist, some of his lithographs are still available, mainly at a stationer's called *Gilardi* at Calle San Martín 56, and while they're expensive, they're worth the price. They can be framed with glass and passe-partout into handsome and exotic place mats, or will brighten your "South American Room."

Color photography processing is now no problem in Argentina, as several large companies have opened plants, so tourists will find pharmacies and camera stores prepared to develop and print their pictures.

CLUBS. Among useful organizations you will find the American Club (Viamonte 1133), the Stranger's Club (Bartolomé Mitre 430), the American Women's Club (Córdoba 630), the Argentine Automobile Club (Libertador 1850, and especially valuable if you plan any motoring), the Y.M.C.A. (Reconquista 439), the Y.W.C.A. (Tucumán 884). See your agent or air or shipping line for cards. Rotary International is at Florida 229. English Club, 25 de Mayo 586. The Jewish Club is *Hebraica*, at Sarmiento 2233.

NEWSPAPERS. The Buenos Aires Herald is one of the best English-language dailies published in a non-English-speaking country. Airmail editions are available of the principal American and British newspapers, but they arrive of course a day or two late. If you read Spanish you can have your pick from the voluminous and staid La Prensa, through La Nación to the tabloid Clarin. Magazines, too, such as *Time, Newsweek, Vogue* and *Harper's Bazaar* are available at news agents.

CHURCHES. Argentina is by its Constitution a Catholic nation, but there is complete religious freedom. You'll find a Catholic Church without difficulty and others as well. The American Church (Methodist-Episcopal) is at Corrientes 718, the Anglican St. John's Cathedral is at 25 de Mayo 282. The Presbyterian Church, Belgrano 579, holds English services on Sun. at 11 a.m. There is a Lutheran Church at 2000 Naon St. There is a Synagogue at Libertad 785. You'll find seven Christian Science churches.

MAIL AND TELEPHONE. Mails are slow within Argentina, but if you want to write home your letters go fast. For current rates ask at your hotel. Telegrams (cables) are expensive, and will cost the equivalent of half a dollar a word to New York, 20p a word to London.

International telephone service is excellent and will cost $20 for three minutes to New York, £10 to London. But local calls are very cheap.

 ELECTRIC CURRENT. Argentina runs on 220-volt current and uses the continental European plug, so you won't be ironing or shaving unless you've thought to buy equipment ahead. Converter plugs are readily available, however, as are transformers to make your 110-volt gear function. Current is 50-cycle, so that your U.S.A. tape recorder or record player will need special spindles to get the correct "drive"; but not the European models.

 USEFUL ADDRESSES. The United States Embassy and Consulate are at Sarmiento 663, with the Embassy residence out in Palermo at Libertador 3052, the British Embassy Chancery and Consulate at Luis Agote 2412 and the residence at Gelly y Obes 2301. The French Embassy and Consulate are at Cerrito 1373, with the Ambassador's residence in suburban Martinez at Montes Grandes 1301. Tourist Information Center, Avda. Santa Fé 883.

Police headquarters are at Moreno, 1550; the Foreign Office at Arenales 761; Ministry of Interior in the Casa de Gobierno (Government House) at Balcarce 49; Ministry of Tourism, Uruguay 291; National Tourism Bureau, Suipacha 1111; International Assoc. for Medical Assistance for Travelers (IAMAT), Paraguay 609, Buenos Aires.

AMERICAN EXPRESS AGENTS: *Buenos Aires*, City Service Travel Agency, Florida 890; *Bariloche*, Alun-Co Turismo, Bartolome Mitre 5.

URUGUAY

The Tight Little City-State

BY

HENRY LEE

While discussing Uruguay and its people, two foreigners took distinctly opposite viewpoints. One said that Uruguay was really a small geographical appendage of big Argentina where excessive freedom had degenerated into license, where city people spent too much time striking, talking and playing, and where religion and rural people were disregarded. He deplored the fact that in this welfare state almost all received public benefits from cradle to grave. "Did it ever occur to you," interrupted the other visitors "that it might be good for people to be free, secure, and have time for cultural activities, politics over coffee, and fun at the beaches?"

The interesting thing about Uruguay is that both these visitors were largely correct in their observations.

There is nothing quite like Uruguay, speaking geographically or historically, although it has often been described as the "Switzerland of South America" or "another Riviera." Actually, its government is like Switzerland, its beaches like the Riviera, its economy somewhat like Argentina, and its people like nothing else. Uruguay is really a city-state and could be compared to ancient Athens. Its main characteristic is its people—a product of the nation's unique institutions, in turn derived from Uruguay's geography, history and the resulting economy, politics, art, literature and other aspects of its culture.

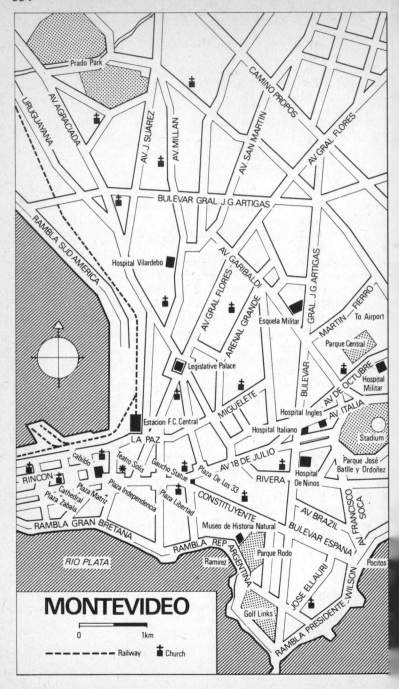

MONTEVIDEO

```
0                    1km
------------  Railway
✝  Church
```

A Little Geography

Uruguay doesn't have much geography. This second-smallest South American country (72,172 square miles) might be described as a big city with a large ranch that spreads over gently rolling hills (none above 2,000 feet) with very few trees native to the land. Most are newly planted in a remarkable reforestation program.

Uruguay's climate is temperate, subject to swift and uncomfortable variations and always windy and somewhat damp. In winter, June through August, the temperature sometimes dips as low as 23°F. but averages about 58°F. Summers, December through February, averages about 75°F, and are tempered by Atlantic breezes. Well-distributed rainfall is about 40 inches yearly at Montevideo and 10 more inches in the north. The soil is black and rich in potash, producing good grasses for the grazing of sheep and cattle. Only eight percent of the land is farmed, while 90 percent is used for grazing.

Montevideo, the most southern point of the nation, fans out from the center into the hinterland. All roads and railroads lead to or from Montevideo, depending on which you travel. It has the nation's largest university (the newly created University of the North will concentrate students from the northern and central areas), about half the secondary schools, half the newspapers with 90 percent of the circulation, half the radio stations, half the doctors and two-thirds of the hospital beds. Moreover, Montevideo has almost half the population; thus, it controls public opinion, the majority of votes and, therefore, the machinery of government.

This leaves about 100,000 working ranchers and farmers and their families who support Montevideo's 1,450,000 residents in a manner to which they have become accustomed. Those in the south and east grow fruits and vegetables for the big city appetites. Those of the west produce the grains and thus may be called the breadbasket. Those in an eastern area produce the rice. Cattle and sheep ranching are concentrated in the north central plateau, although these activities are found everywhere outside Montevideo. Livestock is the business that earns money abroad and enables Montevideo to live well. The big ranch owners generally live most of the time at one of their Montevideo properties.

Struggle for Existence

Uruguay's geography was the key to its history. While the Spanish conquistador, Juan Díaz de Solís, still thinking the Western Hemisphere a large land mass that was blocking the route to what was hoped would be the spice lands of the Far East, probed down the coast of South America in 1516, he entered the wide Plata River, perhaps thinking he was skirting the southern end of the continent. As the water became less salty and more muddy, he decided to land about 70 miles east of what is now Montevideo. The savage Charruas Indians killed all the landing party but the cabin boy. Solís' senior officer, Sebastian Gaboto, survived because he remained aboard the vessel anchored in the river.

Gaboto returned 11 years later and found the cabin boy, thus concluding that the Indians were not cannibals as thought—just savage. That, along with the absence of precious metals and stones, was enough to discourage much settlement for a long time. Gaboto did build a fort along the shore, where the town of Salvador existed for a while.

While sailing around South America to the Philippines, Ferdinand Magellan sailed some distance up the Plata River. Legend has it that a lookout muttered in Portuguese "I see a mountain" (Monte vide eu), a phrase finally twisted around to Montevideo. This name, actually, is probably derived from old manuscripts describing the region.

Little occurred in this land, called "Banda Oriental" (East Bank), until the dawn of independence. It remained a buffer area over which Spanish Buenos Aires and Portuguese Brazil fought a continuing struggle. It remained inhabited mostly by two species: the wild cattle turned loose by the Spanish and which multiplied on rolling, natural pastures; and the wild "gauchos," Uruguay's counterpart of the cowboy, whose food, clothing and mode of living were derived from the products of his neighbors, the cattle. Both these inhabitants were greatly to influence Uruguayan life.

Few Uruguayan institutions developed from the "God, Gold and Glory" of the Spanish conquest and colonial era. Few missions were developed by the priests, as the savage Indians finally became only four in number; they were captured and taken to Paris in 1832 for study and exhibition. Few inhabited the area that offered no mineral resources.

As the once great Spanish Empire's strength ebbed in the first decade of the 19th century, two other empires looked at possible expansions. France occupied Spain and Portugal, while Britain took Buenos Aires, then the seat of the Spanish vice-royalty that had nominal control over Bolivia and the Plata River countries. The British that occupied Montevideo for seven months in 1807 sowed the seed of revolt along the so-called Eastern Bank, but the essentially military post of Montevideo refused to go along with Buenos Aires in establishing an independent junta (governing committee) in 1810.

José Gervasio Artigas had other ideas. This captain of the Spanish forces in the interior of Uruguay mobilized the gauchos and other part-time bandits to fight with Buenos Aires for Latin American independence. He took Las Piedras and besieged Montevideo in the winter of 1811. After Portuguese troops moved into Uruguay, an agreement was reached between the conflicting forces for the siege of Montevideo to be lifted.

Artigas then organized an exodus of all wishing to join him to an area north of Salto on the west bank of the Uruguay River. About one-fourth of the nation's estimated 60,000 population joined him in what has been compared to the later Boer trek in South Africa. Paysandú was one of several communities almost completely abandoned by this force of about 13,000 civilians and 3,000 troops.

Influenced by the young United States federal republic and its new constitution, Artigas became the leader of a federal form of government in opposition to Buenos Aires and its desire to control the Plata River area under a centralist form of government. Artigas drove Buenos Aires forces from Uruguayan soil in 1815 and held together a federated area of what is now Uruguay and northern Argentina.

Driven out of Uruguay by a Portuguese army from Brazil in 1816, Artigas fell back to Northern Argentina, where he continued to fight Buenos Aires' central government. He was finally beaten and forced to flee to Paraguay in 1820. There, he lived in poverty and solitude for 30 more years. All nations must have one great hero; so many years after his death, Artigas was given his due immortality, and the Parks of Uruguay today feature his statues that provide vast parking areas for pigeons.

Thirty-three Uruguayan exiles from Buenos Aires slipped into Uruguay in 1825 and led a successful revolt against a strong Brazilian occupation force. Fructuoso Rivera, former Artigas lieutenant, joined the "thirty-three" under Juan Antonio Lavalleja and others to vote union with Argentina. This meant war between Argentina and Brazil, fought on Uruguayan soil and adding to the nation's potential for battle monuments. Britain, wanting peaceful commerce in the area, negotiated a peace in 1828 in which all concerned recognized Uruguay as an independent republic.

Wars of Red and White

The most colorful thing about Uruguay the rest of the century was recurrent hostility between two political forces that were to shape Uruguay's subsequent history: the "Colorados" (Reds) and "Blancos" (Whites). While fighting for government control, Rivera's forces began using the color red in 1836 and Lavalleja's forces turned to white to distinguish themselves in battle. Giuseppe Garibaldi, Italy's liberator, led a force of 3,000 French Basques under the Colorados for several years. Sporadic armed conflict continued between the two political forces the rest of the century.

Meanwhile, several factors were introduced that set the stage for Uruguay's political maturity. Streams of European immigrants had no inherited political passions. The dominant Colorados in 1872 began granting the Blancos, mostly ranchers, needed peace to ship their improved beef to a hungry Europe for higher prices. Political influence of the army, which had replaced the old gauchos, ebbed. The Colorados also pacified the Blancos with a few political posts and some of its funds. José Batlle y Ordoñez came on this stage in 1903 and made Uruguay mostly what it is today—essentially a mixed socialist-capitalist economy, an urban cradle-to-grave welfare state, and a great democracy. The son of a president, he served twice as president himself, 1903-1907 and 1911-1915, and dominated the nation's politics until his death in 1929. He had the combined physical features of a judge, professor and "Kentucky colonel"; he had a mental insight into political problems that were to label him one of the world's first and great reformers, although some feel he reformed too much for the urban proletariat and too little for the rural peasants. He knew what democracy was and how to obtain it—he emancipated the women and built an advanced system of free, public education.

In his climb to the presidency, he enlisted the erstwhile inarticulate and incohesive middle class that had been enlarged by European immigrants. Instead of starting his own reform party, he started his own newspaper and shaped the disordered Colorado Party into his own image. He cited both his Colorado and Blanco parties in demanding honest elections and civic responsibility. His first term of office was spent mostly in putting down another bloody civil war with the Blancos. But, meanwhile, he was promoting democracy by organizing "grass-roots," neighborhood political clubs that still characterize Uruguay's active political life.

Democratic Growth

During four years in Europe between terms, he was impressed with Switzerland's executive council, social legislation and state-operated industries as a cure for Uruguay's problems. From the editorial page of his "El Día" newspaper, he fashioned his ideas for a new Uruguay during his second term. For better government, he obtained a modified national council, a limited proportional representation in congress, direct presidential election and complete separation of church and state. For labor, he instituted an eight-hour work day, minimum wages, old-age pensions and other benefits. For small industrialists, he secured high tariffs to counter what he regarded "foreign economic imperialism." For rural workers who would provide the production to pay for these benefits, he offered little but rural schools. For women, he obtained a divorce (women don't have to say why) law and arranged for their education. For his enemies, he provided sufficient displeasures to be called an atheist, among other things.

"The modern state unhesitatingly accepts its status as an economic organization," he explained. "It will enter industry when competition is not practicable, when control by private interests vests in them authority inconsistent with the welfare of the state, when a fiscal monopoly may serve as a great source of income to meet urgent tax problems, when the continued export of national wealth is considered undesirable." And then he showed just what he meant. He brought the government into insurance, utilities, railroads, banking, meat processing, tourist hotels and even a "pawn shop."

Gabriel Terra, leader of the conservative faction in the Colorado Party, reversed Uruguay's democratic development in 1933 by installing himself as virtual dictator in collusion with the army. His regime, however, was unable to still the democratic forces that had become a national heritage.

A nine-man national Council replaced the president as executive head of the government on March 1, 1952. The Colorados had been consistently defeated at the polls; so they finally agreed to a system that would give them at least a minority voice in the government.

Pastoral, Socialist-Capitalist Economy

Uruguay basically has a pastoral economy that is highly dependent on whims of the world market. The country has traditionally exported wool, meat and hides for foreign exchange earnings to pay for manufactured imports. To liberate itself from the flexibility of world markets, it has tried in recent years to industrialize by importing raw materials and erecting protective tariff walls for developing its own industries. These efforts have contributed to recurring trade imbalances, balance of payments deficits and falling monetary reserves.

The small nation has no significant industrial raw materials, and water- and diesel-generated electricity are the only sources of power. Light industries have been developed for providing national consumption needs like textiles, food processing, electrical appliances and machinery. There has been an increase in exportations, and in official and private circles there is a continual search for new markets and new goods to export. Such nontraditional exports as clothing, glass, leather, shoes, honey and extracting industries (marble and granite) are now being shipped to those countries which have traditionally been good markets for Uruguayan products: Argentina, Brazil, Germany, Italy and Japan. New restrictive measures are helping to curb smuggling.

Broad social benefits have imposed high production costs on industries, both private and public. The form of the economy is a mixed socialist-capitalist one in which the government either monopolizes or competes with private enterprise in electric power, telephones, fuels, alcohol, cement, aviation, railroads, insurance, fishing, meat processing, hotels and port facilities.

Still, Uruguay has one of the highest living standards in Latin America (about $600 per capita income). Its problem could be compared to a family that spends more than it makes, requiring the use of savings and persistent trips to the bank as an alternative to austerity or harder work. Average per capita consumption of beef is about one pound daily.

Uruguay's membership in the Latin American Free Trade Association (LAFTA) may boost the economy and permit exports of certain manufactured goods to Argentina, Bolivia, Brazil, Chile, Colombia, Ecuador, Mexico, Paraguay, Peru and Venezuela. LAFTA was formed in 1960 to make members less dependent on selling raw materials at declining prices in world markets and on buying manufactured goods at rising prices. To create larger markets for national industries, the association expected to have a free trade area by 1972 through annual negotiation of tariff cuts. It would then become a customs union and common market. Basic differences in the economies of these countries have made this goal impossible to accomplish, and the deadline has been postponed to 1980.

Economic Crisis

Meanwhile, Uruguay has been going through an economic crisis, stirred by overconsumption and underproduction. For several years the number of government workers was steadily increasing while the number of those not on the public payroll was declining. The law provided retirement at 55 with full salary plus bonus during lifetime.

The result was that three productive workers were supporting one pensioner and four private sector workers supporting one civil servant. This meant that roughly 450,000 nonproductive workers were supported by 850,000 productive ones. "Is it possible," a 1963 report asked, "that the labor of three persons can generate enough income to support a pensioner, in addition to providing his own consumption and generating the economy, while his own individual production is falling?"

These and other factors lowered individual production and stunted economic growth. "From 1955 to 1961," the report continued, "the growth rate was 3.1 percent. Since 1961, it has been only 0.6. In terms of per capita growth rate, the figure is negative (−0.6)." This meant there was actually more individual consumption than production.

Falling production resulted in recurring inflation and overvalued currency, requiring periodic devaluations. The peso dropped from 250 (in 1963) to 2,330 to the U.S. $1 by late 1975. But latest indications are that this trend is being successfully reversed.

The new peso that replaced the old (see MONEY section) has strengthened. Month by month the number of public sector employees has been dropping; an example is the national airline, P.L.U.N.A., which not long ago had 1200 on its payroll; in early 1976 the figure was down to 450. The retirement age has been raised to 65. The unemployment rate has been dropping. A State Department report prepared in late 1975 says, "An improvement in Uruguay's position is hoped for after 1976, when marketing conditions for Uruguay's exports are expected to improve and the fruits of Uruguay's current economic reforms materialize." The position of the nation between Argentina and Brazil—two rapidly industrializing countries—was cited as a favoring factor, and "most important, Uruguay is a land-rich country and one of the areas of the world where food production can be increased with relatively low investment." The report summarized the situation optimistically: "While short-term prospects for the Uruguayan economy are mixed, there are good reasons to believe the country will eventually regain its position as one of the most prosperous of the continent."

Neighborhood Democracy

Uruguay needs a sound economy for the high costs of maintaining what is perhaps the highest form of democracy and an expensive welfare state. Per capita cost of government operations has been estimated at about $500 yearly, a figure almost as high as that of the U.S. and in a nation with a small defense budget.

Until 1966 Uruguay inaugurated a new president every year, who served as the nation's ceremonial head and presided at the nine-member National Council meetings.

Uruguay's unique elector system placed the government's executive power in the council, composed of six from the winning party and three from the loser. The first four runners took one-year turns at the council presidency during the council's four-year tenure. Now all this has changed again. As a result of national elections in November 1966, Uruguay returned to its former system of a single executive administration, the people having disposed of the former nine-man national council by vote.

But that doesn't explain the real nature of Uruguay's crazy-quilt politics, where anyone with 50 friends can have himself a real party. One can get a list of candidates on the election ballot with 50 signatures. The group functions as a standard party, but members also identify themselves with one of the two major parties: "Colorados" (Reds) or "Blancos" (Whites). Thus voters cast their ballots for individual party lists and also for a major party. The major party with the most votes now wins the presidency. But factions within that party function as an organized force, somewhat like Democrats in the United States Congress.

Colorados vs. Blancos

The Colorados, whose great leader, Don José Batlle y Ordoñez, shaped Uruguay into a super democracy, socialist economy and welfare state early this century, lost the last election by about 20,000 votes. Their 90-year grip on the government was broken by the Whites in 1958. Luis Alberto de Herrera had become to the Blancos what Batlle had been to the Colorados. He had admired Hitler, Mussolini, Franco and Perón almost as much as he disliked Great Britain and the United States. He wrote 40 books and will probably be recorded by history more as a writer than politician. Well-dressed and well-bred, he could deftly drive his old car among rural folk and inspire their confidence. He was a typical example of Latins following personalities rather than political programs.

In the 1966 election, however, the Colorados again returned to power, placing Oscar Gestido, a retired air force general, in the presidency. Their names are derived from the colors the two parties used in many civil wars for almost a century before ballots were better than bullets for deciding political questions.

The "parties" within these two major parties range from "leftist" to extreme conservative. And each of these parties has neighborhood political clubs around which each community's activities are centered.

Faction Parties

A major party can grant or refuse to grant the use of its name to another political faction or organized political force. The advantage thus obtained by the major party is that the votes of this faction are totaled up with what is considered the total party vote. The advantage to the faction is that its influence is determined by votes it can deliver to a major party. This procedure amounts to both a nominating primary and election at one stroke, which all who know both will agree is a rather bold stroke. While these political factions are usually highly organized, they are also generally identified by such slogans as "Long Live Batlle" or another phrase that demonstrates support for a person or idea.

Uruguay has found this machinery quite suitable for electing a stable and democratic government. Elections held every five years, according to the Constitution of 1967, will choose the president, 31 members of the national senate and 99 members of the chamber of representatives, as well as the governor and 31-member legislative council for each of the 19 departments. Since Uruguay has a centralized government, the departments have little power and thus cannot break the strong hold Montevideo has over the rest of the nation—the reverse of the strong rural blocs in the U.S.

The other branch of government, the judiciary, is headed by a

Supreme Court of Justice. Its five members are elected by the two houses of Congress for 10-year terms, and they cannot be reelected until after a lapse of five years.

The early welfare legislation of Batlle has been expanded by subsequent regimes. The nation has about 80 statutes relating to such labor or social benefits as limited work periods, rest, vacations, domestic labor, minimum wages, severance pay, unemployment compensation, sick and accident benefits, female and child protection and old-age pensions. Medical care is provided for the poor and many of the big middle class get this and other benefits from more than one hundred mutual aid societies. Most of the urban population is covered by some pension or retirement plan.

It is important to consider that these benefits came to a society that can count freedom as its greatest benefit. All these benefits developed within the framework of democratic procedures and advanced political machinery. In this process, Uruguayans have fashioned themselves into an essentially middle-class society in which there are few very rich and few very poor.

President Gestido, who assumed power in 1967, embarked on an austerity program, which cut back on welfare and government spending. Gestido died in December 1967; Vice-President Pacheco Areco, although belonging to the same party, has not strictly followed in his predecessor's footsteps. The current president, Don Juan María Bordaberry, has concrete goals for public work projects and popular support for the elimination of the slums.

Invested Freedom

Such fortune, of course, costs money. In this advanced democracy, long and intensive campaigns sap energies and consume resources; and complex election machinery is expensive. "We have the costliest electoral system per capita on the continent," said President Baldomir during World War II, "but it is cheaper than revolution."

But Uruguay has a democracy and a life that perhaps cannot be priced or discussed in terms of monetary values. The nation's democracy is aptly symbolized by the obscure building, home of the executive branch which looks like a run-down county courthouse, and the ornate legislative building, which houses the Congress and is considered one of the continent's outstanding structures. The humility of the police, the pride of the people, the pace of daily life, the intellectual bent of many scholars—all these things that might be visions in other lands are realities in Uruguay. The people know what they have, and they want to keep it that way.

A Unique People

Social scientists say that particular institutions of a nation fashion what they describe as a national culture or national personality. This thesis is well supported in Uruguay. It is obvious even to the casual observer that Uruguayans, although from the same predominately Italian and Spanish stock as the Argentines across the Plata River, are different. They are not impulsive like so many other Latins; they would rather consider emotional issues over a cup of coffee. Although more emotionally involved with football (soccer) than any other activity, they do not resort to riots and excessive fisticuffs that have characterized the game among neighbors. They would agree that an intolerant person should be educated not punished.

Some have observed that Uruguay has reached the far side of freedom, holding that individualism at times degenerates into license. What would be regarded as irresponsible conduct elsewhere is apt to be regarded here as individual expression. They might admire discipline elsewhere, but they feel no compulsion to practice it. They might respect Anglo-Saxon efficiency, but they want no part of it. It is the better part of valor to express individualism in a school strike, a political demonstration or as participant or spectator at a sports event. This extreme individualism often appears selfish and might antagonize a foreigner.

"Uruguayans admire the discipline and efficiency of the Anglo-Saxon," the *London Times* reported ("The Land of Beautiful Disorder," August 21, 1956), "but their admiration is tinged with pity. 'What do they get out of life?' they ask, 'Only patient, placid queues waiting for the bus, where is the adventure, where the initiative? Even if you don't get away with queue-jumping, you have the fun of a fine argument. Traffic lights add to the spice of driving. There is a thrill in being able to squeeze past a red light, or in crossing traffic screaming invective, which is really admiration.' They feel contempt for the man who tamely obeys the regulations, allowing himself to become a slave to coercion."

This national personality is reflected in attitudes toward the military and police. Soldiers or sailors are not seen swaggering down the street as in so many other Latin communities. While unsuccessful or unemployed peasants in other Latin countries often go to the capital and get a job driving a taxi, in Uruguay they often join the Montevideo police force. Sometimes seasonal workers take a job on the police force. Yet, Uruguay does not seem to need more money for a stronger army or better police force.

Uruguay's political advancement and cultural development have, fortunately, extended beyond its borders. Its greatest contribution has been in international affairs, especially in making the Inter-American community of nations what it is today. The influence of the nation's literature, art and medical science have also captured widespread attention.

Few realize to what extent Uruguay has shaped the present order of international affairs, especially the Western Alliance. This role began on June 18, 1917, when Uruguay decreed that "no American country, which in defense of its own rights should find itself in a state of war with nations of other continents, will be treated as a belligerent." This was the beginning of the Inter-American political system formally organized later as the Organization of American States.

The U.S. agreed to the concept of equality of nations at the 1936 Inter-American conference at Montevideo and also accepted the principle of nonintervention. Then Uruguay's idea of a collective stand in World War I was expressed at the 1938 Inter-American conference at Lima this way: an aggression against one American state should be considered an aggression against all.

Uruguay figured in two World War II incidents. The eyes and ears of the world were turned on Montevideo when in December 1939 the German battleship *Graf Spee* escaped into the harbor from three nearby British cruisers. In accordance with international law, Uruguay required the vessel to depart after three days in which the injured were attended. Instead of confronting superior British firepower waiting down river, the German commander scuttled the battleship dramatically before an audience lining the river bank and others pinned to radios throughout the world.

Seed of the Western Alliance

The 1942 Inter-American foreign ministers conference at Rio named a hemispheric Advisory Committee for Political Defense of the continent during the war. Alberto Guani, Uruguay's foreign minister, proposed to this committee, whose seat was in Montevideo, a collective recognition device for sorting out desirable and undesirable neighbors. This idea remains an issue today in the Inter-American Community.

The war left many deep scars in its wake. One was the reluctance of the U.S. to accept Argentina into the postwar America of nations after the latter helped the Nazis when it looked like they might win the war and went against them only when it was certain the Allies would win. This issue developed at the 1946

Inter-American conference at Mexico City. Eduardo Rodriguez Larreta, another Uruguayan foreign minister, salved this scar by proposing what he called "collective action" of the American states against a common enemy. This made Argentina's re-entry into the community more palatable to the U.S. This idea became known as collective intervention, which became the famous Article Six of the 1946 Inter-American Treaty at Rio. And this article became the basis for the North American Treaty Organization, the Inter-American Alliance and the Southeast Asia Treaty Organization.

A national decline started in the '50s in the wake of the slump in world prices of raw materials which are the basis of the Uruguayan economy. Political instability followed recession. Tupamaros, the Castro-inspired intellectual revolutionaries, created bad publicity for tourism after a number of successful political assassinations. At present, the country is led by a conservative government, dominated by the military, that ended up with the Tupamaros organization that damaged Uruguay so much socially and economically. Now a new order is found among the working and studying classes and thus Uruguay is recovering its erstwhile image as "the Switzerland of South America."

But there is also something in Uruguay's national culture that removes it from the usual catalogue of nations. With several exceptions, no Uruguayan has made any great impact on world culture. Things of literature, art and related subjects are organized on the intramural level for the joy of all and great prestige of none in particular. It is the enduring stress on the individual and his equality in the national society that characterizes the Uruguayan.

This affinity for the individual and democracy perhaps began with José Pedro Varela, the father of Uruguay's extensive public education system. While visiting the U.S., he came under the constructive influence of Horace Mann, noted U.S. educator, and Domingo Faustino Sarmiento, Argentine statesman-educator. Varela and Sarmiento returned to South America together in 1868—Sarmiento to become president of Argentina and Varela to inspire the formation of the Society of the Friends of Popular Education in his native land. Uruguay's middle-class society, responsible citizenship and advanced democracy stand today as living monuments to the Uruguayan who did so much for education in 11 years before death stilled his boundless energies at the age of 34.

One big exception to Uruguay's intramural type culture is José Enrique Rodó (1872–1917). One of Latin America's several great writers, Rodó exerted considerable political influence with his magic pen. In his "Ariel," he aroused the fear and perhaps hate of many Latins against the U.S., then extending the "big stick" policy of Teddy Roosevelt about the Caribbean. He found such virtues as freedom, education and dignity in the U.S., but he thought these too mixed with materialism. He wanted a united Latin America that could stand together against the feared U.S.

A group of novelists covered the taming of the gaucho from wild primitive to reluctant cowboy. Others captured the gaucho's folk songs and music. The latter resulted in Uruguay's national dance, the "pericon," a triple-time round dance resembling the French minuet.

Musical concerts are held often and are well attended. But Uruguay's top composer, Eduardo Fabini (1883–1951), is little known beyond the land. The national symphony orchestra has been compared well with large symphonies in the U.S., and it has broadcast programs across the Plata River to sophisticated Buenos Aires.

The first native Uruguayan painter of note was Juan Manuel Blanes (1830–1901), who recorded on canvas much of his nation's rich history. Pedro Blanes Viale (1879–1926) was an impressionist who has two well-known historical scenes now hanging in the Legislative Palace and National Museum of Fine Arts. Pedro Figari (1861–1938) became perhaps the nation's best artist with his colorful works of Montevideo's 19th-century life.

José Luis Zorilla de San Martin and José Belloni have erected notable pieces of sculpture: the first, the famous gaucho on horseback; and the second, the famous covered wagon. The monuments range among the finest of Latin America's artistic landscape.

EXPLORING URUGUAY

Uruguay has no medieval history or regal colonial past such as Peru and Mexico, therefore it has no ancient ruins or colonial monuments of great splendor. If the traveler has plenty of time, it is a pleasant place to relax and get to know the country, especially in the good weather from December to March. If the tourist is doing South America, he should not pass up this unique nation, which can be impressive during as little as two or three days.

Montevideo is well laid out for the tourist.

The first day one might start at the port and customs area and cover the Old City that has not changed much since the last century. Since about three-fourths of Uruguay's extensive foreign trade is funneled through Montevideo, much of this area involves businesses related to shipping, banking and commerce. Almost all the nation's 73 banks are in this area—an industry probably resulting from the nation's political stability and inefficient banking practices. Boats of major shipping lines stop at the port and thus give the area an atmosphere often associated with major shipping points: honkey-tonks with loud music and inviting hostesses, street vendors and small stores openly selling smuggled goods, and ex-seamen who have their own good reasons for living quietly on this "beach." In conformity with the nation's style, one can invade such areas without the risks involved with similar places in other lands.

About five blocks in any of three directions from the waterfront, one finds the first of many combination parks and monuments. This is Plaza Zabala, with a monument to Bruno Mauricio de Zabala, the Buenos Aires governor who brought seven families here and founded Montevideo in 1726. The spot is marked by an outstanding piece of architecture, the Palacio Taranco, built by a wealthy merchant in French style and filled with its original imported furniture, marble floors, statuary, draperies, clocks, and paintings by prominent European artists of the period. At present the Ministry of Education and Culture is responsible for its preservation and runs it as a center for cultural activities. One of the reception rooms has been transformed into a small auditorium that can hold up to 140 people where the best of opera, chamber and recital concerts, plays and ballet are offered from March to December. All performances are free of charge.

The colonial atmosphere of the city is found four blocks up Rincon at Plaza Matriz, or as it is sometimes called, Plaza Constitucion. This is the heart of the Old City. Fronting the plaza is the old "cabildo" (municipal building), which has been renovated but still looks colonial. Here is also the old cathedral.

From this plaza, the Río Plata can be viewed to the right and one can there see the walls and gun emplacements that once protected the city from foreign foes. The British stormed this bastion in 1806 and held Montevideo for several months. Their breakthrough occurred near the site of the present Anglican Church, another symbol of British influence in Uruguay's early economic development.

From Plaza Matriz, two blocks eastward stands the big gate that was once part of the wall. This wall empties onto Plaza Independencia. This blends the old with the new and marks the colonial era from the republican one. In contrast to the trim and modern Victoria Plaza Hotel is the old Salvo Building, undoubtedly the continent's ugliest structure.

The story goes that the owner was an eccentric man who liked odd things. When he explained to the architect the kind of building, the architect was quoted as saying: "All right, I'll arrange your building, but I refuse to have my name on it." It is the city's only major edifice without the architect's name.

The Old and the New

Artigas, the national hero, is mounted on his equestrian statue as if he were riding his horse out of the colonial into the republican era. The "Casa de Gobierno" (Government House) sits across the plaza from the Victoria Plaza Hotel and symbolizes the nation's democratic heritage. This old building looks like a second-class courthouse inside and outside, despite erect guards with brilliant-hued, colonial-style uniforms.

The Teatro Solís is located a half block off the plaza. This is the center of the community's regularly scheduled musical concerts and cultural activities. It also includes a museum of natural history.

Continuing eastward down Avenida 18 de Julio, one passes through the main shopping and theater area. After three blocks through this street, one might well choose to top off a day of sight-seeing by turning slightly left or northeastward down another broad avenue, Agraciada, to visit the imposing Legislative Palace. This building, commanding the view down the avenue, was built of granite and marble for $17 million at a time when this was considered a large sum. The ornate furnishings inside reflect Uruguay's devotion to democracy. Stained-glass windows reach back to ancient Athens to demonstrate present enthusiasm for democracy and education. Busy legislators, who remain in session about nine months yearly, rush about opulent woodwork, lush carpets and beautiful paintings in this democratic stronghold. Several female legislators can be seen here, symbolizing the nation's complete emancipation of women.

Beyond the Legislative Palace is a bay that leads north and northwest to an old area of Montevideo that is noted for many old but still splendid homes. Another mile northward is the so-called Prado. In mid-19th century this area had many country estates that were a warm-weather retreat from the heat and flies of Montevideo. The Prado has now been enfolded in Montevideo's continuing growth.

The most famous 19th-century resident of this area was José Buschental, a financier who built a 175-acre estate here and married the niece of Don Pedro II, the Brazilian emperor. He brought fish from the Orient to stock the streams that were created by dredging the nearby Miguelete River. He brought flower plants from throughout the world to beautify his extensive gardens. And the animals, both domestic and foreign, added to the exotic scenery. This area now has a statue of Buschental, 800 varieties of roses, and is known as Prado Park, Montevideo's oldest.

The visitor thus far would have a sense of early Uruguayan history, an acquaintance with its government and an enduring memory of dingy streets studded with picturesque plazas and a beautiful park. One could do this by foot and taxi in a single day, but he would have to hurry.

Picking up at the broad intersection of 18 de Julio and Agraciada, one travels only two blocks eastward to confront another plaza symbolic of Uruguayan life. This is, of course, Plaza Libertad, also known as Cagancha. There is a column to liberty in this plaza, and the space is often occupied by discordant groups exercizing their liberty and expressing their displeasures. Across the intersection and to the left on 18 de Julio is the Ministry of Foreign Relations, an unpretentious building from which men and ideas have influenced world affairs.

The Famous Gaucho

Continuing down the avenue for three more blocks, one arrives at an apex that steers 18 de Julio slightly to the left. Here is the famous gaucho on his horse, one of the two best examples of Uruguayan sculpture. Zorrilla de San Martin was at his best in freezing into bronze the true character of the gaucho; his dashing courage, threatening smile and enduring freedom.

Another plaza four blocks down 18 de Julio marks another of Uruguay's historical mileposts. This one is named for the 33 brave ones who returned to their native land and expelled the Brazilians, thus progressively casting in stone and metal the second chapter of Uruguay's independence movement. The city's central fire station is located on this plaza, housing firemen who do not have much work because of widespread fireproof construction in Montevideo. Little children must be satisfied with an occasional and relatively quiet fire truck.

There has been plenty of noise down a few blocks at the main University of the Republic campus (but student demonstrations have now apparently become a thing of the past). These buildings house the schools of law and economic sciences and also the national library. Schools of medicine, engineering and architecture occupy more modern buildings in scattered parts of the city. Despite a passion for politics, university students are a serious group, and the professions they later practice are a tribute to their intellectual energies. Many also hold fulltime jobs and thus spend as much as 18 hours daily between work and study. The university is renowned for its education in medicine and architecture.

This wide avenue finally ends at Parque José Batlle y Ordoñez, a park that introduces the visitor to the man who created the contemporary phase of Uruguayan history. The importance of the sites in this big park depends on one's tastes. If you like football (Latin brand), then this is the most important place in town, for here is the 75,000-capacity Centenary Stadium that was built in 1930 to mark the nation's 100th anniversary. The British introduced the game here late last century, then the Uruguayans took it from there and made it a national institution. Uruguay has won four world championships; and in the process, the young have found the game enjoyable wherever space and a ball were available, and adults have found pleasure whenever the stadium gates opened. But if one's taste leads to sightseeing, in this park there is Belloni's famous bronze statue of the covered wagon, which reminds one of the covered wagon days on the western frontier of the U.S. or the Boer trek in South Africa. This life-size statue depicts six oxen hauling the covered wagon and a gaucho directing the oxen.

The third interesting travel route in Montevideo is the riverfront drive, called Rambla. This drive begins in the port area and runs along the beach area to Punta del Este and will some day continue to the Brazilian border. The first beach along this route is Ramirez, popular in warm weather because of its proximity to the downtown area. Behind the beach is the spacious Rodó Park, named for one of Latin America's greatest literary figures. This park, widely known for its artificial lake with many gondolas and small boats, is surrounded by beautiful eucalyptus, paradise, palm and ombú trees. And the park, of course, has a statue of Rodó. The cluster of amusement facilities and refreshment stands give the park a Coney Island atmosphere. The beach and park are designed to form eventually a large waterfront recreation area.

In conformity with this plan, an excellent municipal golf course adjoins the park as one continues along the drive. Uruguay's democracy shines even on the golf course, where waiters or bartenders might be found playing in a tournament with socially prominent persons. On Sunday afternoon, golfers must abandon the links so that young lovers may hike along the fairways and old people rest among green, shaded lawns.

Continuing along the Rambla eight more blocks, one passes the small beach of La Estacada. Then about four more blocks rises the ornate skyline of Pocitos Beach, one of the great playgrounds of the country. This is still part of the residential area of Montevideo, but in warm weather it becomes something else —Argentines come across the river and occupy most available apartments in the modern buildings, and residents of Montevideo line the beaches. Government employees, for example, work in the mornings instead of the afternoons, as in the rest of the year, thus giving the beach the attention they feel it deserves. Many of these modern apartment buildings, forming a beautiful high crescent along the beach, were built from the proceeds of wool and meat exports that brought good prices during the Korean War.

Rich, Cool Breezes

As one travels east along the beaches, he finds the air more snobbish and the breezes cooler. The last so-called metropolitan beach is at Carrasco, a fashionable suburb of Montevideo whose streets are shaded by big trees and whose houses reflect a con-

centration of the few actually rich persons Uruguay has. The
beautiful beach is lined with small sand dunes banked by incessant winds. In contrast to so many modern brick houses is the
old cavernous casino that remains a popular place for Uruguayan society when the gaming tables are opened in season.
Montevideo's international airport lies just beyond Carrasco,
nine miles from downtown Montevideo.

After Carrasco, the highway turns somewhat inland, with
branches leading to several of the major beaches. Atlantida, 35
miles from Montevideo, is surrounded by beautiful forests of
pine and eucalyptus. This beach also has a casino, golf course,
movies, tea rooms and fine fishing to enjoy. The next major
beach resort is Piriapolis, with its horseshoe-shaped bay and well-
planned streets stretching inland toward the high hills that ring
the community. The popular sport here is hill climbing, especially atop San Antonio, where a small church dedicated to St.
Anthony attracts pilgrims during June. Punta Fria, a suburb of
Piriapolis, is noted for its rock gardens.

Punta del Este has, of course, become world famous as a
popular site for international conferences and movie festivals.
This peninsula-type beach, 85 miles from Montevideo, draws
wealthy vacationists from many foreign countries, especially
Argentina. They occupy modern apartment buildings, hotels or
privately owned residences set among tall pine trees and facing
two beaches of white sand and ocean of blue. They have a
December-March average temperature of 69 degrees while enjoying golf (18-hole course hosting international matches), fishing
(mostly from rented motor boats), yachting (centered around
Yacht Club), water skiing (in smooth waters) and horse racing.
Social events are centered at the suburban Cantegril Country
Club, built by a development firm that concentrated such entertainment features as a huge theater, swimming pool, residential
bungalows, motel-type apartment buildings, tennis courts, restaurants and other recreational facilities.

Although a relatively new development for the international
set, Punta del Este is already being associated with famous
Acapulco of Mexico and Copacabana of Brazil. Some find it a
handy name to drop at cocktail parties. Some foreign governments have found it useful to have consulates here. All visitors
find it proper to wear sports clothes to most social events in
this "live as you please" resort. During the summer Season (December to March) of 1976-77, Punta del Este received about
500,000 visitors.

A nearby island, Seal Island, is inhabited by an estimated
half-million seals, whose furs make beautiful coats.

The small town of Maldonado, capital of the department of
the same name, is three miles inland from Punta del Este and
has some colonial ruins. Otherwise it is only important as a point

for continuing on the Rocha, northeastward and 115 miles from Montevideo. This community, several miles from the Atlantic Ocean, can be reached by rail or road. Palm groves stretching from sand dunes provide Rocha with an unusual beauty. At the nearby coast is La Paloma, protected by two small islands and endowed with a lake for fishing and attractive scenery for viewing.

Battle Monuments

Beyond Rocha, on the highway to Porto Alegre, Brazil, is the reconstructed fortress of Santa Teresa that has been converted into a museum. This fortress, built by the Portuguese when they held this area in the 1750s, is part of a national park lined with palm trees and featuring a bird sanctuary along with freshwater pools for swimming. Two miles away on the coast is La Coronilla, where people can fish in the ocean for sharks and among the rocks for black corvina and skates (the latter weighing up to 100 pounds).

Another old fortress at San Miguel, near the Brazilian border town of Chuy, has also been adapted to a national park. The park has many plants and animals, both foreign and domestic. There is a museum at the fortress and good surf-bathing at nearby Barra del Chuy.

If not as fancy, Uruguay's interior unfolds unique scenery and sites for visitors. Much of this area was opened by the Pan American Highway that stretches from the Brazilian border town of Acegua southwestward across Uruguay to Montevideo, then westward to Colonia, across the Plata River from Buenos Aires. This highway opens several trips that can be made in a day's drive or extended to several days.

One might choose a trip to Colonia, which would bring into view some of the nation's richest farming area, rolling hills, neat towns and varied scenery. Santiago Vazquez is reached after 14 miles on the banks of the Santa Lucia River. This town is famous for what is known elsewhere as fish-fries, the fish weighing up to 75 pounds and being landed from the river. The concentration of pleasure craft reflects the popularity of boating in this area. Two hours out of Montevideo and a small distance from the Pan American Highway is "Colonia Suiza," settled by immigrants from Switzerland more than a century ago. This little tourist resort features Swiss-style entertainment: clean and comfortable hotels, fine cheeses and quiet rest in beautiful surroundings. Nearby are "Colonia Valdense" and "Nueva Helvecia," noted for fine fruits, vegetables, cheese and quaint, locally manufactured music boxes. Colonia Valdense, founded by evangelical followers of Peter Waldo (12th-century French religious leader), retains much of the customs and puritanical practices of its ancestors.

Colonia, about two and a half car-hours from Montevideo, is a hub of traffic toward Buenos Aires and up the Uruguay River. A hydrofoil connects with Buenos Aires three times daily. This 17th-century Portuguese settlement retains more of its colonial atmosphere than other Uruguayan communities: old houses with barred windows line narrow cobblestone streets. Sights to see: historic parochial church, municipal museum, viceroy's mansion and the lighthouse. San Carlos, a warm-weather resort, is four miles from Colonia. The community's bull ring (Plaza de Toros) stands in ruins as a memory of bullfights that attracted many Argentines from across the river before the sport was outlawed a half-century ago.

Fifty miles north of Colonia is the picturesque river port of Carmelo, a popular yachting center and resort area. The sheltered waters of a stream flowing into the Uruguay River, Arroyo de las Vacas, form sort of a naturally endowed yacht club catering to craft from rowboat to luxury dimensions. Historically, Carmelo features the ruins of a Jesuit orphanage, where José Artigas was elected leader of the revolutionary movement in 1811.

River Country

Continuing 18 more miles up the Uruguay River is Nueva Palmira, a port of call for river steamers. Another 12 miles is La Agraciada, where the famous 33 patriots landed from Argentina and organized a Uruguayan force that expelled Portuguese occupation troops. A statue to General Lavelleja, group leader, is on the beach. The livestock and resort center of Mercedes lies 30 miles up from where the Río Negro empties into the Uruguay River. This can be reached by continuing on the road from Colonia or by rail from Montevideo, 186 miles away. Yachting and fishing is popular here in warm weather. Paysandu, on the Uruguay River 299 miles from Montevideo, is a popular fishing area for the dorado game fish.

Little of tourist interest is found in the other river ports on the Uruguay River until Salto, about 365 miles from Montevideo. Tourists can travel here by road or car. On the high banks of the Uruguay river above this community are many rapids that shut off river travel except for small boats. People make excursions by launch to the waterfall of Salto Grande and the rapids of Salto Chico. Fishing facilities are available at the former for rolling and surf-casting for the famous game fish, dorado. Motor launches also ferry travelers across river to Concordia, Argentina. There is a statue in Salto to the famous Italian patriot Giuseppe Garibaldi, who commanded a contingent of Italian and French-Basque immigrants in two victorious battles against Spanish royalists during the independence struggle. Uruguay's plans for a big dam and hydroelectric power projects near Salto have become a reality this year.

For beautiful scenery and interesting sites, one might travel north from Montevideo through Florida, Durazno and the surrounding valley of the Yi River, and Tacuarembo to the Brazilian border town of Rivera, where one can continue on to São Paulo, Brazil. Although not heavily populated this trip through almost the country's dead center can be made by bus, car or train. And one could choose as little or as much of it as he pleases.

From Montevideo, the traveler soon picks up a variety of interesting scenery that includes the vineyards providing the good wines consumed with even better steaks, dairy and poultry farms, and fields of alfalfa, corn and tobacco. At Florida, 78 miles from Montevideo, one enters the city through a historically important display of smooth stone. Here, the Uruguayan patriots declared their independence and freedom from foreign domination August 25, 1825. There is good fishing on the Santa Lucia River that flows by the city. Nearing Durazno on the banks of the Yi River, the so-called "purple land" of Uruguay comes into view. This scenery was made famous by William Henry Hudson in what is perhaps the best travel literature yet done on Uruguay, "The Purple Land." This book, first released in 1885, was one of Theodore Roosevelt's favorites and perhaps induced him to travel to South America. At Paso de los Toros (Pass of the Bulls) in the heart of the country, is a railroad junction linking Montevideo with other parts of the nation. The nearby hydroelectric plant of Rincon del Bonete produces power from South America's largest artificial lake, stocked with many varieties of fish for the attention of increasing tourists. Plenty of game and fowl are found at Tacuarembó, 279 miles from Montevideo. Visitors here enjoy the caves about 10 miles distant in this hill country. Rivera lies 73 miles beyond on the Brazilian border, spread over two hills that feature a park, Plaza Internacional, the Cuanpiru Dam, and the pleasant aspects of good relations with Brazilians living in the adjoining community of Santa Ana do Livramento. The international boundary line is like a main street in other communities, and both nationalities walk back and forth freely. Two bridges, both bi-national projects, joining Uruguay to Quarai, Brazil (at Bella Union, in Artigas, northernmost state) and to Colón, Argentina (at Paysandú) have brought noticeable economic benefits to the two regions.

The Pan American Highway, running northeast from Montevideo to the Brazilian border, offers several interesting places to visit. As elsewhere in Uruguay, rail lines generally parallel this highly traveled highway. Minas, about 75 miles from Montevideo, is found by some tourists to be a useful change from the beach resorts. Capital of the Department of Lavalleja, named for the leader of the famous 33 patriots, Minas features mineral deposits, beautiful marble ranging from pure white to black, mineral springs used for baths and excellent drinking water, nearby caves and the equestrian statue of Lavalleja. The mineral water of Minas is also used in the excellent beer that Uruguay produces.

Instead of continuing northward to Melo and the border town of Acegua, most prefer to turn off at Treinta y Tres and travel northeastward to the border town of Rio Branco. Treinta y Tres, 200 miles from Montevideo, can also be reached by rail. Travelers along this route see what was Uruguay's last frontier that has now been recorded in its folklore. It was here that cattle roamed unattended until the gauchos would come along with their baggy trousers, lasso, guitar and mate to camp along a stream. Here they would slaughter and skin the cattle, then move on. Here developed one of the most important words in the Uruguayan vocabulary: "estancia" (to be located), known as a ranch. When the ranges were finally fenced in, the adventurous gaucho began to disappear. But, like his counterpart in Argentina and Brazil, he is remembered in the nation's songs and dances. Some modern gauchos still ply their trade somewhat and retain the customs of their forebears, but they are bucking the 20th century.

At Rio Branco, a large international bridge spans the Yaguaron River. Some of the funds for this bridge were part of a loan Brazil refused to accept from Uruguay. The latter then with similar grace appropriated the money for the bridge and other public works designed to benefit both nations.

PRACTICAL INFORMATION FOR URUGUAY

CAPSULE COMMENTS. *Physical Features.* The smallest country in South America. Uruguay means "The Purple Land" and the name is well chosen for the country's vast prairies are often covered with purple flowers and a dark soil rich in potash that grows the world's most superior grasses for cattle and sheep. There are a few rolling hills and no mountains. Uruguay's spectacular beauty comes from her 200-mile coast line of famed beaches—the site of many outstanding resorts.

Climate. Exceptionally fine climate. Both summers and winters are mild. The Uruguayan summer (December-March) is the best time to visit the country, although the other seasons offer bright, invigorating days and cool nights. Never any snow.

Population. 3,036,000. Montevideo 1,450,000.

Language. Spanish.

Principal Industries. Wool, meat packing, hides, textiles, wine.

WHAT WILL IT COST? Even if the country is not known for accurate statistics, Uruguay's cost of living is still the lowest in the continent. A government-controlled price freeze on the basic necessities plus an efficient campaign to stop the so-called "economic crimes" have practically put a stop to black market dealings.

However, the Uruguayan economy based primarily on the land and virtually dependent on oil importation was hit severely by the oil crisis; this led to a general rise in prices. The actual cost of gasoline is U.S. $2 per gallon. In addition, a heavy importation tax on cars makes automobiles cost three times as much as in the U.S. As a result, beautifully kept 1928 (or older) Chevrolets or Fords run around the city, to the envy of the American tourist who wants to take one home. Excellent mechanics manufacture parts for them, and they look and run like new. But rarely are they for sale; automobiles are such valuable items in this country that they almost become part of the family, and nobody wants to part with theirs. Even if they were for sale however, complicated and expensive paperwork makes it really costly to take one of these cars back to the U.S.

The large middle class, which for a long time had been the base of Uruguay's population, is now weakening. Some 25 years ago, any middle-class family was able to afford two homes, one in town and one in a resort, because long-term mortgage loans with very low payments were readily available. This was the time when most of the beach resorts were built. Fully paid pensions, retirement beginning as early as

LOCAL PRICES COMPARISON TABLE

Food expense for an average family (generally 2 children to a family) is comparatively reasonable.

Some food costs:

1 kilo (2.2 pounds) filet steak	US $1.25
1 kilo T-bone steak or prime ribs	1.00
1 kilo ground beef	.80
1 kilo potatoes	.20
1 pound butter	.50
1 dozen eggs	.50
1 large beer bottle	.35
1 pound sugar	1.00
1 snack-size ice cream	.30
1 kilo oranges (about six)	.20
1 head lettuce	.10
1 can SMA baby formula	1.70
1 tube tooth paste	.40
1 liter of local wine (good)	1.40
1 haircut (lady's)	3.00
Shampoo and set	3.00 to 6.00
1 cinema ticket	.70
One opera, ballet, or symphonic concert, orchestra seat ticket	2.00
Local telephone calls	.05
Coca-Cola	.20
Color film, 20 exposures	3.50
Toilet tissue	.10
Picture postcards, each	.20
Airmail postage to U.S.	.15

40 years of age and a prosperous economy made life pure enjoyment in this lovely city.

Those days are gone now, perhaps forever, and it is very hard for a young couple to get started here. With an average income of US $250 a month, both members of the family have to work, sometimes at more than one job. Rentals run from $100 and up, depending on the area of the city.

Education in Uruguay is free at all levels, from the compulsory six years of elementary school and four years of high school to a doctoral degree in a profession. Vocational training, mechanical and industrial schools, handicrafts, home economics, liberal arts, painting, music and business administration are among the many professional careers for which education is provided.

As a result, Uruguay has the lowest illiteracy rate in South America. On the other hand, there is a surplus of professional people; these often have to take a second job to better their standard of living, or they leave the country for the greater opportunities available abroad. The government is trying to offer more attractive jobs to these educated youth, especially in the rural regions up country, to put a stop to this "brain drain."

RESTAURANT SAVINGS

Besides those places known as excellent restaurants, a healthy, good-tasting, economical lunch or dinner can be had anywhere along the main street or in the downtown area.

Although lunch for the average Uruguayan means a three-course meal at home during the two-and-one-half hour noontime break, any of the sidewalk cafes, called "bars," will serve you an excellent steak sandwich ("chivito"), grilled ham and cheese ("sandwich caliente"), or tuna fish, turkey or club sandwich ("Olímpicos") for two or three dollars including a beer or coke.

As an attractive alternative, you might order a drink ("copetin"), and with it you'll get at least half a dozen hors d'oeuvres included in the price. Keep in mind that imported whisky is expensive, and it is more economical to settle for a local one at half the price. A "copetin" with local whisky costs about US $1.

Dinner is generally late; no restaurant will serve it before 8 p.m., and local people usually wait until 9:30 or 10 o'clock. However, around 5 or 6 p.m., local tea rooms get crowded with ladies who stop shopping to have "tea," a must at this time of day. Tea means having toast, marmelade, grilled sandwiches, cakes and pastries, which, together with hot tea or coffee, you get for US $1.50 at any downtown elegant tea room. Ask for a "te completo."

RESTAURANT COSTS

The following list suggests prices for a meal, with wine, in different categories of restaurants in Uruguay.

Category	Montevideo	Major Interior City	Beach Resort (in season)
Luxury	US $6	US $4	US $7.50
First Class	4	3	5
Moderate	3	2.50	3
Inexpensive	2	2	2.50

A MODERATE-RANGE DAILY BUDGET

Here is a breakdown of a typical day's basic expenditure to help you work out your own budget.

First-class hotel, breakfast, tax and service charges included, per person, in a double room	US $ 6
Lunch in a middle-priced restaurant	3
Dinner in a middle-priced restaurant	3.50
Bus, city transportation, basic fare	.10
Taxi transportation, basic fare for 2 kilometers, no tipping	1
Theater ticket, middle range	.80
One pack of cigarettes, local brand	.45
One coffee, at a popular coffee shop	.20
One beer, in a popular bar	.35
10% for contingencies	1.54

TOTAL: US $16.94
(or £7.58)

 WHEN TO COME? Because of Uruguay's beaches and climate, most tourists come here in the relatively warm weather from December to April. When Uruguay's exchange rate is not out of line with Argentina, some of the more popular beach hotels might be filled during these months. The chilling winds of July and August make Montevideo uncomfortable and the beaches actually undesirable. But the nation's interior resorts, scenic sites and interesting places might be found attractive all year. Of course, all Uruguay is more conducive to travel in the better weather months of December to April. Light clothing and sports wear is better for this season, but warmer clothing is necessary from June to September, especially in Montevideo and along the coastal area.

 WHAT TO TAKE: Winter in Uruguay is from mid-May to early September and requires quite heavy clothing, with overcoats, scarves and gloves advisable. Men, in general, wear suits and ties, though there are irregular exceptions now (e.g. the Casino). Women's dress is fashion-minded and follows European patterns—fur coats, woolen suits and sweaters, cocktail dresses, and at least one long dress for many evening occasions. Pant-suits and slacks are less favored than skirts or dresses. For summer (December through March) in town, summer dresses or skirts with tops are right, although among younger people blue jeans and various combination outfits are common. For evening wear, have a long skirt and blouse, and a sweater or shawl too, as it may suddenly turn cool.

For resorts, like Punta del Este, one of the smartest and most popular in South America, men wear sport jackets, trousers or Bermuda shorts, and no ties even for formal occasions. Women wear caftans by day, long dresses at night, and enjoy a wide range of freedom and imagination. Both sun hats and rain wear are good to have along for both men and women; heads need not be covered in church anymore.

SPECIAL EVENTS. Carnival Week is the gayest occasion of the year in Uruguay. Although this "fiesta" is official only for the Monday and Tuesday preceding Ash Wednesday, irreverent and anti-clerical Uruguay closes down most of its shops and business for the entire week and plays carnival. People masquerade, sing, dance, and parade the streets of Montevideo. Fun makers, including many foreign visitors, crowd hotels, clubs and casinos, dancing the tango and samba. Houses and streets are appropriately decorated and humorous shows are staged at open-air theaters. Because of the complete separation between church and state since 1918, Uruguay has changed the name of Holy Week to Tourist Week, when most businesses close down—not for spiritual reasons, but for such recreational activities as camping in the woods and playing on the beaches. National Cattle Exhibit is in August and in December the Festival of Nations, prepared with the various embassies under the auspices of the country's First Lady, features exhibits of products of many countries and various events and festivities. La Semana Criolla comes in late March or early April and is a festival-type week involving horse breaking and stunt riding by cowboys, along with singing and dancing. International horse races with champions from most South American countries are held Jan. 6, at Maronas. An International Piano Contest is held in Montevideo in November. Theater, ballet and symphonic concerts are staged in Montevideo from March to January.

 HOW TO REACH URUGUAY. This country is well connected with others by air, boat and bus. *Pan American* and *Varig* airlines have several flights weekly from the U.S. direct to Montevideo. An alternative route is down South America's west coast by *Braniff International Airways* to Buenos Aires. *LAN-Chile Airlines* has flights between Miami and Montevideo. *Cruzeiro do Sul* flies from Brazil. *Lineas Aereas Paraguayas* from Asunción and Lima.

Since Buenos Aires is just across the Plata River, the passenger from Europe might consider *Iberia, Air France, KLM, SAS, Varig, Lufthansa, Alitalia, Sabena* and *Aerolineas Argentinas*, which all have flights to both Buenos Aires and Montevideo. There is a 1000 peso departure tax for passengers leaving Uruguay.

For internal travel, *PLUNA*, Uruguayan government-owned airline, *Austral* and *Aerolineas Argentinas* have convenient, four daily half-hour flights from downtown Buenos Aires to Montevideo. One can also travel from Buenos Aires by the Alimar's hydrofoil boat to Colonia (4 round trips daily), then to Montevideo by bus, a trip lasting about 3½ hours. Or one might wish to take one of the Argentine river passenger boats, which is both a pleasant way to travel from one country to the other and to spend the night.

A few shipping lines from Europe and the U.S. stop at Montevideo, amongst them *Lamport & Holt Line*. This port is also served intermittently by a few passenger-cargo boats. The *Argentine State Line—ELMA*—offers sailings between Montevideo and New York. These cargo boats have facilities for about 12 passengers, and these individual shipping lines are the best or perhaps only sources of information about their intermittent schedules. Boat travel is a pleasant way to reach

Montevideo from Asunción, Paraguay. An Argentine line, *Cia. de Navegacion Fluvia l Argentina*, provides comfortable weekly travel down the Paraguay River to Buenos Aires. *Moore-McCormack Lines* offer one-way or roundtrip freighter cruises. *Sunline Agencies* cruises from Buenos Aires call here.

Overland travel is becoming popular with travelers between Brazil and Uruguay. ONDA and T.T.L. bus lines operate comfortable buses between the two neighboring countries. The distance between Montevideo and Porto Alegre, Brazil, is 14 hours and Rio de Janeiro is 59. Many budget-minded Brazilians find a pleasant vacation in traveling to Montevideo by bus, then returning from either Montevideo or Buenos Aires by boat. The recently established bus line *COIT* has two departures weekly for Asunción and Iguazú Falls, plus excursions, on new Mercedes-Benz buses. Hostess and bar service.

DOCUMENTS AND CUSTOMS. British, U.S., German and many other nationals may enter Uruguay with a passport and without a visa for a period of three months. This stay can be extended easily. A smallpox vaccination certificate must accompany the passport. It is wise for travelers to carry their passports with them for identification purposes. One carton of cigarettes, or 50 cigars, and one opened bottle of liquor are allowed duty free. No other restrictions on personal effects in limited quantities.

MONEY. The new peso (N$) is the monetary unit in Uruguay and amounts to 1,000 of the old variety. Notes of 1, 5, 10, 50 and 100 have been issued, but the old notes and coins will still be in circulation for some time as well. Present exchange rate: N$4.10 = $1 U.S. Exchange is allowed only at official or private banks.

TIPPING. Hotels and restaurants bill guests with extra charges ranging from about 10 percent, which are supposed to be tips but are actually what they consider wages for their service employees. These people expect another 10 percent on top of the bill. These extra charges are usually distributed among all workers but elevator operators on a point system. Figure $N.60 ($600 in old pesos) for two pieces of luggage at the airport and other points of arrival and departure, 10 percent for taxis and N$.30 for theater ushers.

TOURIST AGENCIES. For a tourist center and a nation that counts tourism as an important industry in its depressed economy, Montevideo has few good tourist facilities. The Ministry of Communications, Tourism and Transportation, Agraciada 1409, and its information center across the street in the square, is a refuge for political retainers.

Bueme's Travel Service, main offices at Colonia 997, branch offices in the Santos Dumont Building at Punta del Este, has a highly developed tourism service department. Well known for its personalized services, it features a two-night Ranch Package Tour, giving a completely different approach to the country than regular tourists get. They also have in addition to their usual private car services, regular seat-in-a-car basis daily tours to a nearby Estancia or to some private stock-yard; city tours at 10 a.m., 3 p.m.; summer Montevideo by Night Tour, at 9 p.m.; all-day tour to Punta del Este, at 9 a.m. A visit to a meat-packing plant can be arranged at any moment.

Beware of chauffeur-guides obtained by hotel clerks, who get a 30 percent kickback. And also beware of businesses that sometimes try to combine tours with real estate, etc., on a commission basis.

Besides Bueme's there are: *Exprinter*, Sarandi 700; *American Express*, Bartolomé Mitre 1318; and *Wagons-Lits/Cooks*, Río Negro 1356.

 WHAT TO SEE. For the visitor who has two or three days in Uruguay, there are several musts. A city tour with a guide would be desirable, but if this is not propitious, then one should do the central area of the Old City and part of the New City by foot. The ornate Legislative Palace is a must, along with at least one of the major parks. And it would be equally essential to take a taxi ride, a half-hour or an hour trip, along the Rambla drive and metropolitan beach area, always remembering to take a taxi with a meter that is functioning and avoid the sharp operators who make a profession of swindling non-Spanish-speaking foreign tourists. The Information Center of the Ministry of Communication, Tourism and Transportation has done little to protect such tourists from these hustlers and con men, who usually hang out in front of major tourist hotels. Outside Montevideo, the traveler must consider that a trip to Uruguay is not complete without a trip to Punta del Este, especially in season. And a ride to a good cattle ranch, not further than 80 miles from Montevideo, could be arranged.

 HOTELS. In Montevideo, at the country's best, singles are from $21, doubles from $28. At other good hotels, singles from $9–$13, doubles $13–$17. Most resort hotels in sophisticated Punta del Este are expensive by South American standards. Deluxe accommodations are from $23 single. Many of the country's fine, small resort hotels are available for less than $10 per night and fully-furnished apartments for $30 a day, accommodating up to three persons.

HOTELS IN URUGUAY

MONTEVIDEO

Superior

VICTORIA PLAZA. Air-conditioned; gourmet restaurant, cocktails and dancing.

First Class

AMERICA. Good location; 80 rooms with cocktail lounge.

CASINO CARRASCO. An old luxury hotel renewed, on the beachfront, 20 minutes from downtown; 120 rooms. Casino, restaurant, cocktail lounge and night club.

COLUMBIA PALACE. On the riverfront; 150 comfortable rooms. International restaurant, cocktail lounge and dancing.

CRILLON. 80 rooms. Cocktail lounge. A few steps off the main street of town.

LANCASTER. 80 rooms. Cocktail lounge.

LONDON PALACE. In downtown area. 100 rooms, cocktail lounge. Garage.

PRESIDENTE. On the main street. 75 rooms, congenial service, large shopping arcade.

There are several lower-priced hotels for those adventurous tourists not expecting first-class service or bi-lingual staff.

PUNTA DEL ESTE

(Advance reservations advisable from December to March.)

De Luxe

SAN RAFAEL. On beach, 150 rooms with casino, restaurant, cocktail lounge, and night-club. A major resort.

First Class

SAN MARCOS. Among pine trees, on the beach, 80 rooms, restaurant, cocktail lounge, card rooms, swimming pool.

Other first class hotels are:

Marbella, Shelton, Iberia, Península, Playa, Palace, Riviera.

COLONIA DEL SACRAMENTO. *Hotel Mirador.* First class hotel with excellent restaurant, bar, swimming pool.

COLONIA SUIZA. *Hotel Nirvana.* First class countryside hotel with 120 rooms. Tennis court, swimming pool, restaurant, bar.

FRAY BENTOS. *Fray Bentos Hotel* and *Plaza Hotel.*

LA CORONILLA. *Costas Del Mar* and *La Coronilla Hotel,* both on the beach.

LA PALOMA. *Casino Hotel* on the beach, with casino.

MERCEDES. *Hotel Brisas Del Hum.*

PAYSANDU: *Grand Hotel* and *Nuevo Hotel Paysandu.*

PIRIAPOLIS. *Argentino Hotel,* 500 rooms on the beach, with casino, swimming pools, restaurant. Moderate.

SALTO. *Gran Hotel* and *Los Cedros.*

SAN MIGUEL PARK. *San Miguel Inn* near the historic San Miguel Fortress.

 RESTAURANTS. Uruguayan national dishes are built around beef, and to a lesser degree mixed salads and wine, which is the way it should be in consideration of availability. Good food is a national pastime here, and most of the population can afford a good appetite.

MONTEVIDEO. An old French castle, once belonging to a French Marquis, has been converted into an excellent restaurant, cocktail lounge and discotheque called *Lancelot* (formerly Le Chateau), at Friburgo 5817. The exterior stone walls were hand-worked by Italian stonecutters, the slate roof was imported from France. A meal with wine at an expensive restaurant costs about $5–$6; at a moderate one: $3.

In the Carrasco residential district, 10 minutes by taxi from downtown Montevideo, is a new restaurant, *Matias*, offering first class French cuisine in an elegant atmosphere.

For U.S. or European dishes, the *Victoria Plaza* has excellent food at reasonable prices. The *Aguila*, across the plaza and adjoining the Teatro Solís' aged architecture, provides the Uruguayan elite and foreign visitors good food at higher prices. For the budget traveler, there is good food at reasonable prices at *Sorrento's* on Plaza Independencia and *Morini's* a half block off the plaza on Reconquista 714. But wherever in Montevideo one sees a spit turning in what is called *parrilladas*, he can go in and eat good beef with a good salad at incredibly low prices.

Along the beach route, there is the very expensive *El Galeon*, a French-type restaurant at Leyenda Patria 3096 in Pocitos, best for European and local food. The *Bungalow Suisse* in Carrasco, caters to the Uruguayan elite. A new Bungalow Suisse has been opened downtown. It offers the same famous and tasty variety for both lunch and dinner. For good Italian food, *Catari*, Colonia 971. *Portofino*, Belastiquí 1325, for Italian food, with floor show and dancing. *La Azotea*, at Pocitos, for the best parrilladas. Also try: *El Malecon* at Juan Benito Blanco 1269, good steaks, chicken; *Panamericano*, Larranaga 1042, generally good; *Mi Tio*, Av. Rivera, and Soca, for barbecued beef, chicken.

In Carrasco, *Cottage Hotel* and a Swiss restaurant near the airport are good.

Punta del Este Restaurants. *Marisconea* for seafood, *Bungalow, Swisse, Floreal* and the expensive and small *Karakatoa* offer the best food and service. For Italian food visit *Catari* or *Stromboli*. *Club de Pesca, Daiquiri, La Brochete, Los Caracoles, El Chalet* and *El Sargo* are very good restaurants with reasonable prices.

At the hotels, the best restaurants are at *San Rafael, San Marcos* and *Palace*. Punta del Este's best restaurant is at the very exclusive *Yacht Club*, which is, however, open only to members and invited guests.

But the English-speaking traveler should always remember that only in the more pretentious restaurants and hotels is English understood. Tourists not speaking Spanish should learn a few restaurant words before going to the more popular and locally patronized restaurants.

NIGHTLIFE. This is not one of Uruguay's tourist attractions or an attraction for Uruguayans, for that matter. But there are several places where the visitor may relax, without expecting too much. There are popular and attractive discotheques in the Carrasco area, some with good floor shows, among them; *Lancelot, El Mar de la Tranquilidad, Zum Zum* and *Tom Tom Metek*. There are several dinner-dance places in Montevideo but these come and go without much tenure. The best discotheque is *Zum Zum* near the Panamerican Bldg. The casino hotels at Carrasco, Atlantida, Piriapolis and Punta del Este usually provide dinner dancing along with the gambling. Several first-class nightclubs and bars are springing up in booming and relatively expensive Punta del Este.

The Montevideo hotels mentioned above have good bars, and the

Victoria Plaza provides music for listening and sometimes for dancing. But remember that when there is music for dancing, prices on the drinks are hiked inordinately. Stay away from the "intimate" bars in Montevideo, where "hostesses" ply innocent visitors with bad drinks and confront them with a big bill.

Near Punta del Este there is a unique discotheque, *Las Grutas*. In Punta del Este, good discotheques and nightclubs are *Afrika*, *"05"*, *Gong, Carousel, La Fusa* and *Barrabas*.

 MUSEUMS. The Museo Histórico Nacional (National Historical Museum) is located at Rincón 437 with an annex at Zabala 1469. These, residences of General Fructuoso Rivera and General Juan Antonio de Lavalleja in their times, contain 20 rooms displaying distinct steps in the nation's history. The Museo de Historia Natural (Natural History Museum), at Buenos Aires 652, displays in ten sections Uruguayan fauna and flora, also archeological objects and fossils. Other museums are the Museo Nacional de Bellas Artes (National Fine Arts Museum) in Rodó Park; and the Museo Oceanografico y de Pesca (Oceanography and Fish Museum) at Rambla República de Chile 4215, which is located on the beach at Puerto Buceo. The *Planetarium*, at the Zoo, Av. de Rivera, has 4 weekly showings. The *Military Museum*, on top of Montevideo Hill, has a collection of colonial Spanish uniforms and guns; *Museo Romantico*, 25 de Mayo 428, paintings and antique Spanish furniture; *Museo Joaquin Torres Garcia*, Constituyente 1467, paintings, contemporary sculpture; *Museo Precolombino*, Mateo Vidal 3249, excellent Indian art, fossils. Pre-Columbian and Colonial Museum, in the City Hall building, has a good collection of Indian art from various primitive cultures of the continent.

 MAIL. Don't mail letters through local postal service, for it often takes as much as four days for a letter to pass through the hands of Uruguay's extensive bureaucracy that includes its post offices. Mail can be posted in the downtown offices of Pan American and Varig Airlines the afternoon before or just several hours before departure of these planes. Mail can be posted at an airport post office branch up to about an hour before plane departures. Airmail costs from 300 pesos and takes three to four days for delivery in the U.S. Hotels generally will determine how much postage you need and sell you the necessary stamps. There is no parcel post.

TELEGRAMS AND CABLES. Charges for telegrams inside Uruguay and to Argentina and Chile are nominal. Cables can be sent world wide through Italcable Company, British firm of Western Telegraph Co., Ltd., and U.S.-operated All America Cables and Radio, Inc. The *Victoria Plaza Hotel* has an All America branch office.

 TELEPHONES. Local telephone service is reasonably adequate and is operated by the Uruguayan Government. Long-distance calls within Uruguay might require a considerable wait, depending on the traffic (numbers are 213 and 210) but the principal touristic areas are now connected to Montevideo with a dialing system. The country is now connected by satellite to systems throughout the world, and long-distance calls to elsewhere (dial 218) no longer present difficulties. The time in Uruguay is one hour later than that in the Eastern zone of the U.S.

SWIMMING. Since Uruguay is so small (North Dakota size) and is almost surrounded by water, there are plenty of places to swim when the weather permits. The so-called metropolitan beaches (from Ramirez and including Pocitos) are not recommended, because the water is not particularly clean. Many of the resort areas in the interior have swimming pools, and those beaches along the Atlantic Coast are considered especially desirable for swimming. The mineral baths at Minas should not be forgotten, if one considers that swimming.

FISHING. This is excellent in Uruguay. Three happy fishing grounds are pointed out in an English-language pamphlet on the subject, produced by and available at the National Tourist Commission. The zone along the Plata River from Colonia to Piriapolis is used a lot for surf-casting. From Piriapolis to Punta del Este is labeled the best fishing area in the world by the International Fish Bureau. The third zone is along the Atlantic Coast to the Brazilian border. Dorado will give fishermen a good fight around Salto and Paysandú. Boats and tackle can be rented in fishing clubs in: Salto, Paysandú, Fray Bentos, Punta del Este, Montevideo and Mercedes.

GOLF. The golf club, on the outskirts of Montevideo and by the Rambla drive, is municipally operated, considered a first-class course and has a good restaurant, open to the public. Victoria Plaza guests can obtain guest cards for this course without charge. And there is the course of the Punta del Este Country Club, where international matches are held. Although golf is played year round, there are some days in July and August when most golfers would find it more comfortable inside. There are days when heavy winds hinder golfing.

HUNTING. The hunting season runs from December 1 until March 31, and Uruguay's abundant hunting potential is generally limited to this period. There are wild boar, armadillo, partridge, duck, hare and pigeons. The snipe, a bird whose survival is enhanced by speedily changing his altitude, is popular with hunters. And there is the "martineta," a big partridge-type bird with beautiful feathers. Many Uruguayans mix their camping with their hunting, but camping facilities are not readily available for visitors.

BOATING. Boating is a favorite pastime among Uruguayans on the nation's many and varied streams. Santiago Vazquez on the St. Lucia River, for example, is one of several popular boating centers. *Bueme's Travel Service* can arrange for rental of motor or sailboats in Montevideo and elsewhere. At Salto one could combine boating with a visit to the nearby spa, where the Uruguayan Government is building a hotel for lease to a private company to facilitate such activity.

HORSE RACING. There are two main tracks: *Hipodromo de Maronas,* (Sat., Sun. afternoon); *Las Piedras* (Thurs., Sat., Sun.). Entrance fee 30¢, minimum betting 40¢.

CASINOS. Casinos, operated and controlled by the government, are found at the *Parque Hotel* in Montevideo, the *Hotel Carrasco* in Carrasco, *Hotel Atlantida* in Atlantida, and the *Hotel Argentino* at Piriapolis. There is a casino at Punta del Este, *Hotel San Rafael,* and at Rivera.

WHAT TO BUY. There are several items that should be in the luggage of every departing visitor. The best buy is a suede or antelope jacket for either man or woman. Some claim the amethyst jewels here, along with those of Siberia, are the best in the world, and they are moderately priced. (For all fine gems and jewelry, try *H. Stern,* Victoria Plaza Hotel; ask for free local "charm.")

The same claim is made for Uruguayan nutria furs, with additional claims that the hair is longer, thicker, softer and better colored than others. In any event the price is much less than elsewhere. And seal furs, from the estimated half-million seals on an island off from Punta del Este, are also popular with tourists. Alligator bags, shoes and purses are other good buys. A Uruguayan specialty is a variety of gift items made from the hide of unborn calves (*nonato*). Antiques and paintings can also be very good buys.

TRAVEL WITHIN THE COUNTRY. Every place the visitor might wish to see in Uruguay may be reached by either plane, train, bus, boat or car. All buses are air conditioned. Cars rent for about U.S. $15 a day. Government owned and operated rails are poorly maintained. Four main trunk lines and their branches connect Montevideo with all major cities and with Brazilian railways at four different points on the border.

There are no scheduled boat lines along the principal rivers, but the Uruguayan River is navigable from Colonia to Salto, and the Río Negro, flowing across the country from northeast to northwest, is navigable to the port of Mercedes, an important rail hub.

PLUNA (Primeras Lineas Uruguayas de Navegación Aerea) is an Uruguayan airline with daily flights to all major points within the country.

Three bus lines—CITA, COT, and ONDA, provide comfortable travel throughout Uruguay, enable the traveler to see more of the beautiful landscape, and also connect at Brazilian border points. Cars are available for rent from *Sudamcar,* Mercedes 908 (Volkswagens, $18 daily plus 10¢ per klm).

USEFUL ADDRESSES: *American Consulate and Embassy*, Calle Lauro Müller 1776 (tel. 40-90-50). *British Consulate*, Rincón 454. *International Association for Medical Assistance for Travelers* (*IAMAT*), Avenida Italia 2484, tel. 404364—409011. *All America Cables*, Victoria Plaza Hotel, Plaza Independencia. *Western Telegraph* corner of Cerito and Misiones. *Correo Central* (Central Post Office), corner of Misiones and Buenos Aires. *Express Leather Factory*, the best antelope, suede and leather goods, the only groundfloor shop on Plaza Independencia. *Revillon Furs* for nutria, seal, ocelot, pony, calfskin, at 18 de Julio 853. *August Wild*, for amethysts, 25 de Mayo.

AMERICAN EXPRESS AGENTS: Montevideo, *Turisport Ltda.*, Bartolomé Mitre 1318 (only for credit cards).

PARAGUAY

A Paramilitary Paradise

BY

HENRY LEE

Although Paraguay has not lived up to its original billing as a paradise, it is perhaps one of the few remaining undiscovered tourist attractions in South America. Legends of primitive wanderers once described this California-sized, landlocked nation of about 2,700,000 inhabitants as a Garden of Eden with lush prairies, rich cedar forests, and great rivers with healing qualities. One can understand in a casual trip down the Paraguay River just how people in another era and even some today could impute such character to the country.

Whatever Paraguay was supposed to be then, it is now a striking contrast to any other South American country. Fashioned by a military tradition and authoritarian philosophy, traces of Ancient Sparta are found among this integrated population whose warm friendship, handsome stature and disciplined behavior often hide hunger, illness, or ignorance. Even the clean-uniformed street cleaners go about their work with their chins high and their brooms stretched across their shoulders in a paramilitary manner.

Paraguay's geography has shaped much of the nation's history, economics, politics, and culture. The Paraguay River splits the country vertically into two distinct areas. On the westward side is the Chaco area, a sparsely populated region of mostly scrub forest, comprising roughly two-thirds of the nation. The grassy plains along the river support a few river-town settlements, then further inland the land becomes dry and the scenery bleak. This part of the Chaco, with the classic title of "Green Hell," is not too severe for three Mennonite colonies who produce cheeses and other foodstuffs for sale.

Most of the other residents are 40 thousand pure-bred Indians. Paraguay's part of the Pan American Highway runs through this area from Asunción, from Villa Hayes, through Filadelfia (with 3,000 residents, 254 miles from Asunción), then to Gen. Eugenio A. Garay, 10 miles from the Bolivian border. This road is expected to link with the scheduled highway that will connect the continent's major river systems in Bolivia, Peru, Ecuador, and Colombia. The Parana Plateau, between the Paraguay and Parana rivers, includes about one-third of the nation's land and the vast majority of its people. This area involves a low, flat plain that rises from the high cliff hanging over the Parana River and occasionally features rolling, wooded hills that stretch to Concepcion on the Paraguay River. Another plain stretches to Asunción and southward, providing hill lands above the Paraguay River where much of the nation's population is concentrated. Along the wet savannah of the upper plain are found sugar, rice, cotton, and grains. Elsewhere is found the famous "yerba" *mate* that provides the national drink.

While Paraguay has no seacoast, few countries are more influenced by water. The Parana River slices southwestward out of Brazil, forming the eastern and southern boundaries of the country. This river forms the Guaira Falls at the northern boundary with Brazil. Iguazu Falls are on the Iguazu River between Brazil and Argentina, about 20 miles from where the Iguazu flows into the mighty Parana. (Name of falls often spelled Yguassa or Iguassu.)

The major port city on the Parana is Encarnacion with about 47,500 inhabitants. Exports of *mate*, timber, hides, cotton, and tobacco are shipped from here through the Plata River estuary to world markets. Encarnacion is across from Posadas, Argentina, and Paraguayan trains for Buenos Aires are ferried from Encarnacion across the river to Posadas. A bridge joining the two cities is in the planning stages.

The highway from Asunción to Encarnacion was completed in 1969, making the old Jesuit settlements more accessible for tourists, providing an alternative route to Iguazu Falls and making the famous Dorado fishing spot more accessible.

The Paraguay River, however, is considered the nation's major transport funnel, with the capital of Asunción as the central point of departure, with about one-fourth the population and all that goes with the political and economic center of a nation. Almost every attraction in the country, water-wise and otherwise, leads out of the capital city.

The opening of a new highway bridge across the Parana River between Paraguay and Brazil in 1965, however, indicates a

ASUNCION

0 miles ¼
0 kms ½

Aduana y Puerto

Bahia de Asuncion
(Rio Paraguay)

DON BOSCO
HERNANDARIA
GRAL. DIAZ
AV. COLON
E. V. HAEDO
MONTEVIDEO
OLIVIA
ESTRELLA
PALMA
PTE. FRANCO
B. CONSTANT
EL PARAGUAYO INDEPENDIENTE

RIO APA
RIO JE JUY

J. OLEARY
15 DE AGOSTO
14 DE MAYO
J. B. ALBERDI
CHILE

Plaza Constit.

RIO VERDE

Plaza de Los Heroes

INDEP. NACIONAL

YEGROS
ITURBE
TTE. FARINA

FR. MORENA
M. DOMINGUEZ
A. DE HERRERA
AZARA
CERRO CORA
25 DE MAYO
McAL ESTIGARR.
E. AYALA

Plaza Uruguay

MEXICO
PARAGUAY
ANTEQUERA
TACUARI

RIO ACARA
Station

McAL
LOPEZ

AVE. ESPANA

AVE. ESTADOS UNIDOS

lessening of the importance of the river route through Argentina, as overland transport from Asunción to the Atlantic Ocean is now possible. A good highway running eastward from the capital city across the new bridge and ending at the Brazilian port of Paranagua has already begun to see fleets of trucks racing back and forth on the 600-mile run, some 250 miles shorter than the river route.

The highway from Clorinda, Argentina, to Buenos Aires is now completely paved, linking the two cities by land in 18 hours driving time. Clorinda is reached from Asunción by ferry. A bridge between the Chaco and the Eastern Region is also under study, and will make access to Clorinda easier and quicker.

Subtropical but Capricious

Although Paraguay's climate is described as sub-tropical, fast switches in the weather can send one in a sport shirt looking for a heavy sweater, or vice versa. The hot weather season, between December 21 and March 21 ranges between 77 and 110 degrees, and can be uncomfortable. Fall lasts through June, and while the days are mild the nights are often cold. From then until September's end, the temperature may fall as low as 32 degrees, sometimes rapidly from warm weather. The weather starts warming up again after September. While there is some rainfall year-round, most falls in December and March. Asunción, as an indicator, has about 79 rainy days yearly, 72 cloudy ones, and 214 clear ones.

This geography and its climate seem to have done something to the people of Paraguay—they are different, and among the friendliest in South America toward the foreign tourist.

History has shaped the people of Paraguay into a brave and hospitable people, inured to hardship and intensely proud of their country. They are well-disciplined, bilingual, have the harp for their national musical instrument, and bathe often twice daily. Although Spanish is the official language, most people outside Asunción speak the ancient language of Guarani of their ancestors by preference. Books, periodicals, and plays are produced in the Guarani language. And, interestingly enough, the language has sort of a status symbol, in contrast to the Indian languages of the Andean countries that are sometimes considered embarrassing. Public officials are expected to speak Guarani.

Paraguay's unique history explains this. Some have quipped that Paraguay spent 60 years getting into trouble and has been trying to get out of it ever since. And it has been said that domestic tyrants and foreign foes have shaped the nation's history. But this history is too interesting to dismiss so lightly.

The Spaniards discovering Paraguay in 1537 married the

Indians instead of killing them, thus developing the first "mestizo" (Indians-whites) nation in Latin America with a national conscience. Among the 200,000 Indians subdued by the Spanish captains, Juan de Salazar and Pedro de Mendoza, were the Tupi-Guarani linguistic group. Although primitive and primarily hunters and fishermen, these handsome, sturdy, and friendly people were to influence to a large degree the development of what is today Paraguay's national character. They were then disposed to gather numerous wives, and were addicted to bathing. Today nine-tenths of the population is descended from this Spanish Guarani mixture.

The capital of Asunción some 20 years later had about 1,500 inhabitants, a cathedral, textile mill, and the beginning of a stock industry. For the next two centuries, this city remained the major Spanish seat of power in the southern tier of South America. This was the staging area for the Spanish colonization of what is today Eastern Bolivia and the Plata River area. But Paraguay had no minerals, so Spain gave little help to the area, except for the Jesuit missionaries who reached Asunción in 1588. Before their expulsion in 1776, these priests gathered about 100,000 Indians into resettlement projects, protected them from Spanish exploitation, and taught them farming and other skills. These militant missionaries fashioned the Indians into an effective army that in 1640 helped fight off the Portuguese invading from Brazil, who, like other neighbors, in succeeding years wanted to conquer or divide up Paraguay but could not decide just how to do it. These Jesuit missions or "reduccíones," as they were called, have been described as socialist communities where the Indians were forged into a highly disciplined and economically productive group.

Losing its grip as a center for colonization, Asunción began falling into the orbit of the expanding community of Buenos Aires. When Paraguay obtained its independence from Spain painlessly in May, 1811, Buenos Aires tried to draw all the old Vice-royalty of La Plata under its power. A hastily improvised Paraguayan Army prevented this political move, but Argentina was able thereafter to convert the inland nation into a virtual economic satellite, which it remained for nearly 150 years, until recently.

Hermit Republic

Early dictators shaped the subsequent history of Paraguay. José Gaspar Rodríguez de Francia grabbed control shortly after independence and sealed the nation off from the outside world for 30 years. Paraguay was thus called by some writers an 18th century Japan and an "American China." Bloodthirsty, but honest, Francia improved farming methods, tortured his enemies, and made the hermit republic self-sufficient in a primitive way. Carlos Antonio Lopez opened the country to immigrants and trade, started public works, freed the few black slaves. His son, Francisco Solano Lopez took over in 1862 and involved Paraguay in a savage war (1864–1870) with Argentina, Brazil, and Uruguay. Impulsive and egoistic, but also brave and intelligent, this Lopez billed himself as a South American Napoleon while studying in France as a young man. There, he also picked up his famous mistress, Elisa Lynch, who was to share her lover's hardships and pleasures until he was killed in battle near her side.

When the War of the Triple Alliance ended, the quiet that hovered over Paraguay was the stillness of a graveyard. Outnumbered ten to one, Paraguay's population was reduced from about 525,000 in 1864 to about 221,000 in 1871. Only 28,746 males survived the carnage—mostly old men and young boys. Elisa Lynch retreated to Paris with her fortune and jewels. And Paraguay entered 68 years of political instability climaxed by another bloody war.

Paraguay developed politically in a sense during its early years. Its population was about the only cohesive society in Latin America, and perhaps it was the first Latin nation with a national conscience. But the nature of this highly disciplined and submissive society did not appear very conducive to democracy as universally understood. General Bernardino Caballero, war hero, formed the Colorado (Red) Party among planters and army officers in 1874, about the same sort of alliance that now rules the country. Caballero and another general made and unmade presidents until a Liberal Party, a reflection of growing commercial interests, gained control of the government by revolution in 1904. Various dictators ruled under the banner of this fractured party, which did however move the nation a couple of stumbling steps toward what could be called 19th century liberal democracy, despite military influence actually functioning as a thinly veneered oligarchy.

A border dispute with Bolivia over the Chaco area developed into a furious war in 1932. Paraguay was in possession of some 20,000 square miles of the disputed area when truce was signed in 1935. Paraguay paid the lives of two soldiers for each square mile won, while Bolivia paid three for each one lost. Poisonous snakes, malaria, dysentery, and lack of water claimed as many victims as enemy fire.

The belief that this dry and infested scrub forest contained oil was said to have promoted the war. Foot soldiers soon found that the area did not even contain adequate water, let alone oil. No oil has yet been found on the disputed land, but Exxon and Texaco have recently resumed intensive exploration.

Meanwhile, the Chaco provided prosperity for the Mennonite colonists, who also help the 40,000 still-primitive Indians here, and ample space for the cattle that graze on the land. An international loan was granted for the construction of a 300-mile paved highway on the Transchaco road, which should change Chaco's present isolation. Construction has begun.

Heroes of the Chaco War have since played musical chairs with the presidency. Several apparently tried to lead Paraguay out of political disorder and economic disaster, and several reflected a new political philosophy that had developed in the wake of the nation's most recent war and its militant history. This philosophy referred to the "New Paraguay," which rejected 19th century liberal democracy for an authoritarian state perhaps somewhat inspired by Nazi Germany's then existing concept of national socialism. Paraguay's military tradition should be recalled at this point and it should be noted that the nation's only major writers had recently outlined an authoritarian society to fill its needs.

This philosophy was first shaped by Dr. Juan Stefanich, later foreign minister, who envisioned a new world of justice that might be raised from the wreckage of turmoil, tragedy, death, and sorrow; he called for a new democracy extending beyond 19th century liberalism and in harmony with what he viewed as a new "world rhythm." Followers of this thinking moved Colonel Rafael Franco into the presidency in February, 1936, and the authoritarian "Febrerista" Party was thus born. The movement was joined by a majority of army officers and Chaco War veterans. Franco completed the Pantheon begun by Francisco Solano Lopez, where remains of all the nation's major military heroes have been placed.

The major architect of the Chaco victory, General Jose Felix Estigarribia, took over in 1939 and incorporated this new authoritarian philosophy into the 1940 constitution. This constitution still exists; thus Paraguay may ironically be described as a "constitutional dictatorship."

General Alfredo Stroessner has held the presidential reins since 1954. He maintains a firm grip on the post and appears to be bringing order out of chaos. Curiously, Stroessner has a broad political base in the Colorado party, widely supported by the *compesinos* (peasants).

Primitive but Sound Economy

Paraguay has a very primitive yet sound economy. It is based on the export of meat, forest and agricultural products to world markets that can bear high transport costs, and import of machinery, foodstuffs, and fuel. Although it has vast lands that are rich but uncultivated. Paraguay imports about one-fourth of its food, mostly wheat, although new varieties of wheat are now being successfully grown and could make the country self-sufficient in the near future. "There are vast areas of potentially rich and virtually unutilized land," a recent economic study disclosed. "The climate is favorable, with adequate rainfall usually well distributed." Still, the country has a good balance of trade, its exports amounting to US $200 million yearly and its imports at about the same figure. This enables it to maintain a fairly orderly balance of payments, and the money is relatively sound. The Guarani runs at about 135 to the U.S. dollar in the fluctuating market, and is exchanged freely at that rate in the "Casas de Cambio" (exchange brokers). The official rate is still 126 to the dollar, unchanged for 20 years, and is used for commercial transactions. The Eximbank has recently issued a laudatory report on the country's economic situation and handling of its finances.

Meat products, sugar, and wood account for about half the exports. Paraguay's long staple cotton runs second to Egypt in prestige and accounts for another $1.6 million. Hides provide about $2 million in exports, as do such edible oils as those derived from Coco palm, cottonseed, and peanuts. Enough tobacco is produced for local consumption and about $1.5 million for export.

Paraguay has little mineral wealth, although the Chaco region holds possibilities for oil and natural gas, with surveys now under way. There are rich deposits of iron ore in the north, but they are not exploited. Limestone is quarried for making cement, in which the country is now self-sufficient and even has a surplus for export. Salt is obtained from the Lambare area. The apparent paucity of minerals, however, remains unimportant so long as the nation's vast agricultural resources remain unexploited.

Paraguay has little industry and, apparently not much immediate potential, although its Acaray hydro-electrical project has made it self-sufficient, now bringing electricity to remote towns and villages. Surplus energy is already sold to the Northern Province of Misiones, Argentina, and will be shortly to a part of the state of Parana, Brazil, in what will eventually be the world's biggest hydro-electrical project. The joint Brazil-Paraguay "Itaupú" dam is being started and is expected to completely modify the country's economic structure. It has already changed the small town of Pto. Presidente Stroessner across the Paraná River from Foz Iguazú, into a booming frontier town, where housing projects for the workers and other developments have made land prices soar dramatically. The nation is exporting wood products to an expanding area. Meanwhile, local industries are geared mainly to local consumption. These involve textiles from locally-produced cotton, sugar, meat products, soft drinks, mineral waters, beer and ice, cigars, and tobacco. The only industrial items for export involve meat canneries, sugar mills, saw mills, quebracho-extracting plants, essences, and vegetable oils.

Paraguay's politics are more difficult to assess than its economy, in the face of current thinking that traditional and highly illiterate societies must suddenly burst forth with democratic forms inspired by foreign aid and technical assistance. This nation has a president who was elected in a free election in which there was an opposition candidate who openly criticized the current government while he was campaigning for the job of president. There is an opposition Liberal Party bloc in Congress that got its seats merely by running a slate of candidates against the ruling regime, an alliance between the Colorado Party and the yet unchallenged military.

Yet, this is what most describe as a "tamed" opposition—an opposition party that can criticize the government on minor issues but knows where to draw the line on substantive ones that might rock the boat, a minority leader explained. "But this situation is better than no Congress. We expose smuggling, graft, and the excessive military budget (estimated from 26 to 65 per cent of the national budget)."

EXPLORING PARAGUAY

The nature of Paraguay's geography and limited economic development determines greatly how one travels about the country. The Paraguay River, bisecting the nation vertically almost through the middle, and the Parana River, forming the southeastern boundary with Argentina and Brazil, are major tourist attractions. While public railroads cover only 309 miles, private industrial companies have another 455 miles of rail lines of narrow gauge running into forest areas. In general roads are primitive, but they are being steadily improved and extended.

Unless the traveler enters Paraguay by bus or by car from Argentina or Brazil, he is likely to fly into Asunción and begin his travels. This capital city of almost a half million inhabitants is a good pad from which to fan out in all directions by road or air.

But first there are some considerable sites in Asunción, and several nearby attractions that can be viewed in day long or overnight motor trips. Like many old river-port communities of this type, the city's life is centered around the customs house and its surrounding streets lined with the nation's past history and present activity. Traveling along Calle El Paraguayo Independiente and the river front towards the center of modern Asunción, the most impressive site is the Government Palace, where many of the executive branch's offices are located, including the president's office, the equally ornate foreign minister's office, and space for ceremonial activities. This building may be classified along with some of the continent's most interesting buildings. It was built by Francisco Solano Lopez before the War of the Triple Alliance, but he did not get much time to enjoy it. Like his mistress, he imported the voluminous marble and much of the building's beautiful interiors and furnishings from Paris. Both the president's office and those of the foreign minister have been attractively designed with large and splendid mahogany pieces of furniture, set off with well-blending red-colored leather. Only the splendor of the age in which it was made enables one to recognize the various attractions of this building through its amazing preservation and maintenance. Another 100 yards or so along El Paraguayo Independiente is a square in which the Congressional Palace and cathedral, recently remodeled, are located.

Turning away from the river at this point and toward the downtown center, one comes upon the Plaza de los Heroes. Here is the Pantheon of Heroes, begun during the War of the Triple Alliance and only completed in 1937. Here are the hallowed tombs of Carlos and Solano Lopez, Marshall Estigarribia, and two unknown Paraguayan soldiers who were killed in battle. And here one can actually feel the nation's deeply engrained military tradition. Fashioned after the Invalides of Paris, it is often visited as a national shrine.

To the side of the Pantheon is Calle Palma, the city's main business street, along which are located the major stores. Then across the small plaza stands the Guarani Hotel, one of Asunción's most striking buildings.

Paraguay has something preserved from the past that is interesting for youth and reminiscent for elders: old trolleys that have defied the ages with good operation and maintenance. President Stroessner is said to have turned down their retirement because of their attraction for tourists and his affinity for the past. They offer a pleasant ride from downtown Asunción, Avenida España, Padre Cardozo Street to the turnaround point at Las Mercedes church.

The Gran Hotel del Paraguay is also a tourist attraction in itself on the outskirts of the city. This old but still comfortable hotel was once the country estate of the Lopez family. The spacious dining room was once the private theater for Madame Lynch, the mistress of Francisco Lopez. Air conditioning has invaded the nostalgic features of the place, but some of the old environment is still there, including several murals.

Asunción has several good parks and many pleasant plazas. Parque Carlos Antonio Lopez commands an excellent view of the city and stretches over several square blocks that form an apex at the intersection of Antonio Lopez and Rios Gallegos. Parque Caballero stretches along a riverside area at the foot of Estados Unidos, featuring the old country home of the war hero for whom the park is named, small lakes, waterfalls, and gardens. The Botanical and Zoological Garden is located four miles from downtown in the community of Trinidad. This area contains examples of the varied flora of the country and what is known as the Museum of Natural Science, housed in another former Lopez residence.

Several hundred pure blooded Maca tribe Indians may be found at an island in the Paraguay River that is only row-boat distance from downtown Asunción. A tour for good sized groups can be organized combining a short train ride to the Jardín Botánico station, a visit to the Maca Indians and return to Asunción by bus. Daily boat tours are now available. These interesting people, who were brought from the Chaco area, are familiar sights downtown in their tribal garb while peddling their handicrafts. Their distinct and attractive features are not likely to persist in their new world, but meanwhile they are considered a tourist attraction. Another nearby attraction is the large suburb of Luque, which became the nation's capital during the War of the Triple Alliance.

The Lake that Inspires

The nearby lake community of San Bernardino is a must for any tourist spending as much as two or three days in the country. It is located 35 miles away on inspiring Lake Ypacarai, whose shores are lined with tropical trees and growth. This lake, measuring 3 by 15 miles, may be reached by road. Many of the more prosperous Paraguayan families have vacation homes here and many others find their way here between November and March. This lake has inspired some of Paraguay's famous music.

Most road travel and almost all rail travel out of Asunción is concentrated in the southeastern part of the country. A new highway runs through the area where the ruins of the Jesuit missions are concentrated to the transportation hub of Encarnacion on the Parana River. There is also the nation's only major rail line, slicing across the same area. And there is a road from Asunción running horizontally across to Brazil and the famous Iguazú Falls.

Before arriving in the mission area on the improved road, one arrives at Yaguaron after about 30 miles. This small-grain producing center features a typical early 18th century Paraguayan church, with magnificent hand-carved altars, choir lofts, etc., tinted with dyes made by Indians from plants.

Carapegua, another 23 miles, is the northern entrance to the mission ruins, but the first site of interest is not found until reaching San Ignacio, another 89 miles. This first Jesuit settlement is still outlined by its ruins that have stood through the ages, reflecting the advanced development of this area in a time when much of the New World had not even been discovered or settled. These ruins include a church, school building, and work shops. These are preserved as a museum. Ten miles off this road to the northeast is Santa Maria, which has a new church with about 65 sculptures in its chapel.

Continuing on the trip along the road to Encarnacion about 10 more miles, the traveler arrives at the most famous Jesuit ruins of Santa Rosa. A fire swept these ruins in 1883 and little remains but a reconstructed painting of Our Lady of Loreto and a sun clock. The area of the ruins terminate at Coronel Bogado, another 12 miles. Encarnacion is the next point of interest, 230 miles from Asunción, center of boat traffic on the Parana River and where rail passengers from Asunción are ferried across the river to Posadas and then Buenos Aires. The road, however, extends another 17 miles to Trinidad, where the remains of a great Jesuit church are overgrown with orange trees. A small museum near the church ruins has two large carved wooden images of Christ. The backs of these images were carved so thin that priests standing behind them could impress the Indians by simulating the Creator.

Encarnacion, a city of 47,350 people is not otherwise interesting except for exporting the timber, mate, tobacco, cotton, and hides of the region.

Paraguay's other major stretch of highway across plains and hills provides the traveler more variety and different scenery. Traveling eastward, the Mariscal Estigarribia Highway unfurls interesting markets where the women smoke big cigars and sell local merchandise. It takes little time to find that the dominant language of the rural areas in this bi-lingual nation is Guarani.

The most interesting place on this road is Itagua, about 19 miles from Asunción, where the famous spiderweb lace, or "nanduti," is woven by hand into table cloths, handkerchiefs and other items that characterize the artistic talent of Paraguayans. These attractive handicrafts are an exclusive art of the women and they sometimes spend five years with an item before they are satisfied with its quality. Aho-pof embroidery, used for shirts and dresses, is also available in this town.

Another 15 miles is Caacupe, a popular resort and religious center. Pilgrims come here from throughout the nation on December 8 to celebrate the feast day of the Blue Virgin of the Miracles at the city's beautiful church of the same name. Swimming pools in nearby streams are popular with both tourists and the community's 21,500 inhabitants.

Arriving at Coronel Oviedo, 83 miles from Asunción, one can branch off southward for 24 miles to Villarrica, where the railroad passes from Asunción to Encarnacion. Since this community of 54,000 people offers nothing more special than a scenic hill-top view of surrounding orange groves, the traveler might choose for various reasons to continue on the Mariscal Estigarribia Highway. This highway continues another 121 miles through bush forest and across the Caaguazu forest to the Parana River. This river is spanned by a 550-yard international bridge at the town of Presidente Stroessner on the other side. One can stop at a 50-room hotel-casino here or continue on the road to Brazil to Iguazú Falls, or even to Paraguay's free port facilities at Paranagua on the Atlantic Coast.

The railroad trip between Asunción and Encarnacion could only be justified by the desire of the hearty traveler wishing to see more by traveling between the Paraguayan capital and Buenos Aires by rail and returning by boat. The distance of 928 miles between Asunción and Buenos Aires takes five days. Travelers describe the train trip as dusty and difficult.

Travel by river boats in Paraguay is something else. This is natural since transportation experts say man-made travel routes should complement what nature has already done, and nature has already done a lot of rivers here and endowed them with attractive scenery. Because so much of Paraguay is well threaded with two major rivers and laced with smaller streams, much of the nation's economic and social life is centered in communities along the rivers.

For Hunters, Adventurers

It is obvious by this time that highway travel in Paraguay is limited, but it is increasing in potential with completion of the Paraguayan section of the Pan American Highway from Asunción to the Bolivian border. This highway opens up the vast and now forbidding Chaco area to the traveler who wants to see something different, to the hunter who wishes to test his skills in an area that is still relatively wild, or to the scholar who wants to study Indian tribes almost unbrushed by civilization. The first community encountered on this road is Villa Hayes, just north of Asunción, which is a department of the same name. Both are named for the American President, Rutherford B. Hayes, who successfully mediated a border settlement between Paraguay and Argentina after the War of the Triple Alliance. There is also another bit of Americana about the Chaco. The late United States Senator, Huey Long, of Louisiana, argued on behalf of Paraguay in its Chaco War with Bolivia and had a Chaco community named Long for his efforts. Besides Hayes, no other community of any consequence exists in the Chaco but Filadelfia, 245 miles from Asunción. This is where the Mennonite colonies are located. The only other village along this road is Mariscal Estigarribia.

The traveler along this road will not be rewarded with variety. He will find that about 54 percent of the Chaco area is forest land, 40 percent is pastoral land with some cattle and plenty more potential, only 4 percent suitable for farming, and only 1 percent cultivated. The population density is less than two to a square mile.

And these isolated inhabitants include a few nomadic Indians, the Mennonite colonists, a few river-bank settlements, and Texans who are raising cattle deep in the interior. But, like the upper Paraguay River, this area is slated for more development.

PRACTICAL INFORMATION FOR PARAGUAY

CAPSULE COMMENTS. *Physical Features.* The country is roughly divided into two major areas—the *Chaco* and *Paraguay Proper*. The *Chaco* is a vast, thinly populated wilderness of scrub forests and large cattle ranches. *Paraguay Proper* is a smaller, richer area where population is concentrated and is composed of flat plains, some gentle hills, and a small area of high cliffs. The division between the two areas is the Paraguay River.

Climate. Best time to visit Paraguay is from April to November when the weather is pleasantly mild. Other months are often very hot. The rainy season is from December to March.

Population. 2,703,000. Asunción 464,000.

Language. Spanish, Guarani.

Principal Industries. Cattle, agriculture, mate (tea), timber.

WHEN TO COME? The best time to visit Paraguay is from fall through spring, April to November; the heat is not oppressive and the cold not severe.

Although the climate is sub-tropical, there can be swift changes from hot to somewhat cold weather during most of the year. Summer, December 21-March 21, temperatures range between 77 and 110 degrees and make tropical clothing like sports shirts and slacks comfortable. Fall, March 21-June 21, temperatures are usually mild but sweaters or coats are sometimes needed at night. Winter, June 21-September 21, temperature is mild with a few cold days when warmer clothing is needed. The other three months of spring can bring some cool days in the beginning and very hot days in the ending. While it rains year-round, rainfall is heavier from December to March. Dress tends to be informal and sportswear is popular in warm weather.

FESTIVALS AND SPECIAL EVENTS. *Celebration of San Blas*, Patron Saint of Paraguay. Feb. 3. *Independence Days*, May 14, 15. *Eve of St. John's Day*, religious and pagan rites, dancing around huge bonfires, June 23-24. *Founding of Asunción*, Aug. 15. Sept. 12. Fleet formation in Paraguay River. *Virgin of the Miracles of Caacupe*, Dec. 8. Thousands of pilgrims, carrying heavy stones on their heads, congregate and worship in villages.

HOW TO GET THERE. Asunción may be reached by air, road and rail. The last means is not recommended, unless the traveler is prepared for discomfort. A ferry between Posadas, Argentina, and Encarnación offers an alternate route to Buenos Aires, about 200 miles longer, by way of the Argentine provinces of Misiones and Corrientes, and then across the new bridge over the Paraná River to Resistencia, Capital of the Chaco Province. Those who prefer to continue along the left bank of the Paraná river, travel instead to the City of Paraná, Provincial Capital of Entre Rios, crossing under the mighty Paraná in the new tunnel between the cities of Paraná and Santa Fé. Two boats, built in Spain with German power plants, operate for Flota Mercante del Estado to Concepcion to the north, and Corrientes, Argentina to the south. Cabins, with private baths, are air-conditioned and nicely furnished; food aboard is good. *Braniff International Airlines* has flights from the U.S. east and west coasts, Panamá, Lima, Guayaquil, La Paz and Buenos Aires. Several other airlines also have regularly scheduled flights: *LAN-Chile* (from New York and Miami via Santiago); *Varig* (from New York, Miami, and Europe via Rio, Sao Paulo, Iguassu Falls); *Aerolineas Argentinas* (from Buenos Aires, Corrientes or Resistencia); *LAP* (Paraguayan) from Montevideo, Buenos Aires, Lima, Santa Cruz, Rio, Sao Paulo; *Iberia* (from Madrid and Buenos Aires); *Lufthansa* (from Frankfurt); *Pluna* from Montevideo.

There is daily bus service from/to Yguassú, São Paulo and Rio, Brazil and Resistencia, Santa Fé, Rosario, Cordoba, Buenos Aires and Argentina.

WHAT TO WEAR. Remember the best season is from April to September.

Dress tends to be informal and sportwear is popular. For more formal occasions, or business, women wear suits or dresses, slacks and pant suits, for men light weight suits are the most comfortable, sweaters or coats are sometimes needed for a very short spell in June or July.

PASSPORTS. U.S. citizens need a valid passport, a tourist card and a smallpox vaccination certificate. Most other nationalities, with the exception of iron-curtain countries, may enter with these requirements. Airport tax: $4 if you go on to Argentina, Brazil, Bolivia or Uruguay; $5.40 otherwise.

CUSTOMS. 200 cigarettes, or 50 cigars, or 1 lb. tobacco, and 1 bottle of liquor allowed duty free.

CURRENCY. The Paraguayan unit of currency is the Guarani, exchanged at the rate of about 135 for the $1 and about 235 for the pound sterling. Paper notes range from 1 to 10,000 Guaranies (plural). New stainless steel coins are circulating in the 1, 5, 10 and 50 denominations.

WHAT TO BUY. No visitor should leave Paraguay without a record of Paraguayan music, because this treasured music is not easy to buy elsewhere. The same can be said for the "nanduti" lace, made by the women of Itagua, also "aho poi" sport shirts made from very handsome material in a variety of colors and designs. Other appealing items include leather goods (not as good as those in Argentina or Uruguay), wood handicrafts, silver mate cups and native jewelry.

HOTELS. Our categories in Paraguay are as follows: First class, $25-35 for singles; $30-40 doubles; moderate, $18-28 singles, $25-33 doubles. **Asunción:** The new resort *Hotel Casino Itá Enramada* is located on the Paraguay river, out of town, with 150 rooms. The hotel runs a shuttle bus into Asunción. Fully air-conditioned, it offers a magnificent view of the river and the Paraguayan Chaco. Besides the elegant casino, it has a large pool, offers tennis, water skiing and fishing, and has become the principal tourist attraction of the area. *Hotel Guarani*, 13 floors, air-conditioned, with an imposing view of Asunción from most rooms. It has recently been remodeled. Designed for looks as well as comfort. Playground area, swimming pool. Try H. Stern shop here for gems and jewelry. Opened 1975: the small and very nice *Chaco Hotel*. Also first class: *Armele*, 115 air-conditioned rooms near port. *Grand Hotel Paraná*, centrally located, air-conditioned, and *Premier*, air-conditioned, a bit out of town, on a hill with a beautiful view.

The pleasantly situated *Gran Hotel del Paraguay* belongs to another century but has some air-conditioned rooms and much environment the tourist is not likely to forget. The pleasing contrast of this hotel might make it desirable for the lingering tourist to spend a little time here. Moderate.

Plaza. Fair-priced hotel adjacent to old RR station. Air-conditioned; recently updated. *Presidente* (24 rooms) across from the Hotel Guarani has air-conditioning, also *International* is good and is located downtown. Prices for both: inexpensive. *Asunción Palace* is an inexpensive downtown hotel.

San Bernardino, most popular Paraguayan resort: the *Hotel del Lago* is the best place to stay. *La Cordobesa* offers a good restaurant and serves a nice afternoon tea. Distance from Asunción is 30 miles. *Acuario* a new hotel on the lake; $12 for single and $20 for double. One hour tour by boat including one drink $5.25 per person. Lunch/dinner $4.50. Afternoon tea $1.80.

Puerto Stroessner: The air-conditioned *Gran Hotel Casino Acaray* is a first class base from which to enjoy the spectacle of Iguazú Falls, five hours by highway from Asunción. It also has a casino. There also are new smaller, comfortable hotels such as the *Catedral* and *Itaipú*.

 RESTAURANTS. Restaurants in the *Hotel Chaco* and *Ita Enramada* are good, with reasonable prices. The *Gran Hotel del Paraguay* has a good reputation for its food. The Wed. evening Indian curry is excellent. Relaxed atmosphere. Good Paraguayan music.

But no trip to Paraguay is complete without eating at one of the *parrilladas* located in the suburbs of Asunción. These eating places feature an open-air atmosphere, good Paraguayan beef, and unforgettable Paraguayan music played by a trio of one harp and two guitars. *The Hermitage* at 15 de Agosto and 2a; *Yguazú*, on Choferes del Chaco for good entertainment, dinner and dancing.

There are several other restaurants downtown in Asunción with good food, cleanly prepared, reasonably priced: *La Preferida*, at Estados Unidos 443/451; *La Pergola* at Estrella and Alberdi. *Hosteria El Caballito Blanco* at Alberdi, Haedo & Gral. Diaz. The *Amstel*, in Villamorra, has Dutch atmosphere, candlelight and soft music. The

Gondola is in front of Plaza Italia. Nice atmosphere and good Italian food. *Talleyrand* at Mcal. Estigarribia 932, nicely decorated, muzak, excellent air conditioning. *Uchiyamada*—modestly installed but good Japanese food, at Constitución 763 & Pettirossi. *Tao-Tao* (Chinese food) at Cnel. Bogado 847 almost Tacuari. *Dragón de Oro* (Chinese food) at Independencia Nacional 646.

There are some adequate restaurants outside Asunción, but the tourist making short journeys out of Asunción are advised to carry along prepared sandwiches and snacks.

Typical Dishes. Paraguay has an excellent "dish," actually a variety of soft corn bread, for some reason called *sopa Paraguaya.* It is made of mashed corn, cheese, milk, eggs and onion. There is a soup called *Soo-yosopy*, which has a base of cornmeal and ground beef. As in other beef countries like Argentina and Uruguay, the *asados* are good, meaning meat roasted on a spit. *La chipa* is an excellent type of cornbread, made of cheese, corn flour, and yucca starch. The national drink is called *caña*, distilled from sugar cane or from honey.

 SPORTS. Hunting and fishing are special attractions in Paraguay. The sparsely populated Chaco area offers the best in hunting but this sport can be enjoyed in all parts of the country. The jaguar is a popular subject of the sport and is particularly wild and dangerous. There are also a couple of species of wild cats, bear, and wild pig. It is said that thousands of species of birds exist in Paraguay. A 14-day safari, including transportation from Asunción, accommodations, meals, and hunting, costs $4695; additional day $305.

Fishing is, of course, limited mostly to the rivers, but there are plenty of fish there. The dorado, found in the Paraguay, Paraná and Tebicuary rivers, ranges in size up to 65 pounds, enough weight and fight to give fishermen a hard time. International fish contests in the landing of the dorado are held near Asunción occasionally. And there are many other smaller and less aggressive fish that are peculiar to the rivers of this sub-tropical, land-locked country: the *surubi, el pati, el pacu, manguruyus, armados, moncholos, bagres*, and others. There are also small lakes with trout and local varieties of fish. Fishing parties leaving Asunción via colorful riverboats cost about $920 for a 5-day, all inclusive trip. The Asunción Golf Club has 18-hole course and a pro. *Soccer* is Paraguay's national sport. Tennis is also available.

 NIGHTLIFE. Unless the enchanting parrilladas are considered as such, Asunción has very little nightlife. There is dinner dancing and entertainment at the *Yguazú*. The new casino at the Hotel Ita Enramada is impressive; admittance $1.60, tie and jacket required. There's also a casino at the border town named Presidente Stroessner, overlooking the Paraná river, where the "Friendship-Bridge" connects Paraguay with Brazil. The *Caracol*, a nice discotheque, is the present place for swingers. *Safari* in San Martin and España, also has a nice discotheque. And the sidewalk *confiterias* might be considered a sort of nightlife; people gather at outdoor tables and talk into the late evening. If there is not enough room on the sidewalk, then some tables are placed along the street, giving this institution its proper importance.

HOW TO GET ABOUT. Cars can be hired through local tourist agencies. Daily rental rates: $26–40 including 100 kms. and insurance. A scenic 225-mile highway now links Asunción with Iguazú Falls, a 5–8 hour ride by bus or car. Air-taxi service is popular with international sportsmen discovering the trackless Gran Chaco. Travel agencies offer daily city tours, Maka Indian tours, San Bernardino and Yaguaron tours. A new tour by boat is being offered daily by Paraguay River Safari to the Maka Indian Village. It leaves from the downtown port of Asunción at 3:00 p.m., returns 6:00 p.m. Refreshments and snacks are available. Cost US $10.00 per person. The boat seats 40 people on the upper deck, 25 lower deck. They also charter vehicles for round-trip visits to Iguazú Falls. Domestic air service by *TAM, LAP, Aeronorte* and *Aerosur*. Most popular visitor's flights are *Varig's* daily Asunción-Iguassú Falls service. One slow rail line runs 274 miles from Asunción to Encarnacion. Best bet for surface transportation in Paraguay is overland bus.

MUSEUMS. They may be rated in this order of preference: Ethnological Museum, on Calle España at the corner of Monpox; the National Museum of Fine Arts, at Mcal. Estigarribia, Iturbe and Caballero, which has some art from the Jesuit missions; the Museum of Natural Science, in the Jardin Botanico, and Museum of Modern Art, Independencia Nacional and Victor Haedo. Historic Military Museum in the Ministry of Defense at Mcal. Lopez & Vice Pte. Sanchez has interesting collections from the war of the Triple Alliance (1865–70) and the war with Bolivia (1932–35).

TIPPING AND SOCIAL CUSTOMS. It is customary to give a 10 per cent tip on top of the charges that are placed on hotel, bar, and restaurant checks. Entertainment is usually informal and sports wear is usually acceptable, especially in the hot season. Paraguay has retained the Spanish custom of the siesta, lasting from noon to about 3 p.m. People rise early and many offices and shops are open by 7:30 a.m. They close for the siesta and again at 6:30 p.m. Banking hours are from 7:30 to 11:00 a.m. in summer and in winter. Government offices are open from 7 a.m. to noon except in summer when they are open from 6:30 to 11:30 a.m.

USEFUL ADDRESSES: *U.S. Embassy and Consulate*, Avenida Mariscal Lopez and Kubitcheck; *British Embassy* and Consulate, 25 de Mayo 39; *Braniff International Airways*, Independencia Nacional 557; *Aerolineas Argentinas*, Independencia Nacional 365; *Varig*, Estrella and Alberdi; *Lufthansa*, Estrella and Chile. *Iberia*, 25 de Mayo and Yegros. *LAP* (Lineas Aereas Paraguayas), Oliva 467. *LAN-Chile*, Oliva 399. A number of shops and services are located in the building of the *Hotel Guarani*. *Adventist Hospital*, on Pettirossi 372/380; *Nicolás Breuer, Physician*, on Eligio Ayala 993; *Dr. Victor Boettner*, Dentist, on Eligio Ayala 1050. *Discos Folklóricos* (records of Paraguayan music), Mcal. Estigarribia 323, also in Independencia Nacional & 25 de Mayo, and on Estrella and Alberdi.

AMERICAN EXPRESS AGENTS: Asuncion, *Inter-Express S.R.L.*, Ntra. Sra. Asuncion 588.

TOURIST VOCABULARIES

English-Portuguese and English-Spanish

TEN-MINUTE SPANISH

Glossary of often used terms and phrases

ENGLISH	SPANISH	PHONETIC PRONUNCIATION
Good morning (afternoon) (evening).	Buenos días (buenas tardes), (buenas noches).	Boo-*eh*-nohs *dee*-ahs (boo-*eh*-nahs *tahr*-dehs), (boo-*eh*-nahs *no*-chehs).
I don't speak Spanish.	No hablo español.	Noh *ah*-bloh ehs-pahn-*yohl*.
I don't understand.	No comprendo.	No kohm-*prehn*-doh.
How are you?	¿Cómo está usted?	*Koh*-moh ehs-*tah* oohs-*teh*?
Very well, thank you.	Muy bien, gracias.	Mooee bee-*ehn*, *grah*-see-ahs.
Where are you going?	¿A dónde va usted?	Ah-*dohn*-deh *vah* oos-*teh*?
When are you returning?	¿Cuando volverá usted?	Koo-*ahn*-doh vohl-veh-*rah* oos-teh?
Many thanks.	Muchas gracias.	*Moo*chahs *grah*-see-ahs.
Please.	Por favor.	pohr fah-*vohr*.
No, (yes).	No, (sí).	Noh, (see).
Don't mention it.	De nada.	Deh *nah*-dah.
To the right.	A la derecha.	Ah la deh-*reh*-chah.
To the left.	A la izquierda.	Ah lah ees-key-*ehr*-dah,
Do you have a match?	¿Tiene usted un fósforo?	Tee-eh-*neh* oos-*teh* oon *fohs*-foh-roh?
Can you tell me?	¿Puede usted decirme?	Poo-*eh*-deh oos-*teh* deh-*seer*-meh?
I think so.	Creo que sí.	*Kreh*-oh keh see.
I don't think so.	Creo que no.	*Kreh*-oh-keh noh.
More slowly, please.	Más despacio, por favor.	Mahs dehs-*pah*-see-oh, pohr fah-*vohr*.
Repeat, please.	Repita, por favor.	Reh-*pee*-tah, pohr fah-*vohr*.
Pardon me.	Perdóneme.	Pehr-*doh*-neh-meh.
I don't know.	No sé.	Noh *seh*.
Do you know?	¿Sabe usted?	*Sah*-beh oos-*teh*?
Goodbye.	Adiós.	Ah-dee-*ohs*.

ENGLISH	SPANISH	PHONETIC PRONUNCIATION
Come here, please.	Sírvase venir acá.	*Seer*-vah-seh veh-*neer* ah*kah*.
It doesn't matter.	No importa.	Noh eem-*pohr*-tah.
Next week.	La semana próxima.	Lah seh-*mah*-nah *prok*-see-mah.
Yesterday.	Ayer.	Ah-*yehr*.
Don't forget.	No se olvide.	Noh seh ohl-*vee*-deh.
Call me ('phone me).	Llámeme (por teléfono).	*Yah*-meh-meh (pohr teh-*leh*-foh-noh).
What do you wish?	¿Qué desea usted?	Keh deh-*seh*-ah oos-*teh?*
The gentleman.	El señor.	Ehl sehn-*yohr*.
The lady.	La señora.	Lah sehn-*yor*-ah.
The young lady.	La señorita.	Lah sehn-yohr-*eetah*.
Monday.	lunes.	*loo*-nehs.
Tuesday.	martes.	*mahr*-tehs
Wednesday.	miércoles.	mee-*ehr*-koh-lehs.
Thursday.	jueves.	who-*eh*-vehs.
Friday.	viernes.	vee-*ehr*-nehs.
Saturday.	sábado.	*sah*-bah-doh.
Sunday.	domingo.	doh-*meen*-goh.
Black.	Negro (masc.)	*Neh*-groh.
	Negra (fem.)	*Neh*-grah.
Red.	Rojo (masc.)	*Roh*-hoh.
	Roja (fem.)	*Roh*-hah.
Blue.	Azul.	Ah-*zool*.
White.	Blanco (masc.)	*Blahn*-koh.
	Blanca (fem.)	*Blahn*-kah.
Green.	Verde.	*Vehr*-deh.
Yellow.	Amarillo (masc.)	Ah-mah-*ree*-yoh.
	Amarilla (fem.)	Ah-mah-*ree*-yah.
Zero.	Zero.	*Seh*-roh.
One.	Uno.	*Oo*-noh.
Two.	Dos.	Dohs.
Three.	Tres.	Trehs.
Four.	Cuatro.	Koo-*ah*-troh.
Five.	Cinco.	*Seen*-koh.
Six.	Seis.	*Seh*-ees.
Seven.	Siete.	See-*eh*-teh.
Eight.	Ocho.	*Oh*-choh.
Nine.	Nueve.	Noo-*eh*-veh.
Ten.	Diez.	Dee-*ehs*.
Eleven.	Once.	*Ohn*-seh.
Twelve.	Doce.	*Doh*-seh.

TEN-MINUTE PORTUGUESE

The following words are absolutely indispensable if you want to enjoy yourself in Brazil:

eu	I	eu vou	I go
você	you	você vai	you go
êle, ela	he, she	estou com fome	I'm hungry
nós	we	onde está	where is
êles	they	quanto é	how much is
um	one	vinte	twenty
dois	two	trinta	thirty
três	three	quarenta	forty
quatro	four	cinquenta	fifty
cinco	five	cem	hundred
seis (or meia duzia, or meia)	six	mil	thousand
sete	seven	meia duzia	six (or half dozen)
oito	eight	conto	1,000 old cruzeiros
nove	nine	kilo	2.2 pounds

dez	ten	kilometer	1,100 yards
Domingo	Sunday	hoje	today
Segunda-feira	Monday	amanhã	tomorrow
Terça-feira	Tuesday	dia	day
Quarta-feira	Wednesday	noite	night
Quinta-feira	Thursday	horas	hours
Sexta-feira	Friday	ano	year
Sábado	Saturday	semana	week

ENGLISH	PORTUGUESE	PHONETIC PRONUNCIATION
Good morning (afternoon) (evening), (or good night).	Bom dia (boa tarde), (boa noite).	bone dee'-uh (bo'-uh tar'-dee), (boh'-a noy'-te).
I don't speak Portuguese.	Nao falo portugues.	now faw'-loo Por'-too-gays
I don't understand.	Nao compreendo.	now comb-pree-en'-doo
How are you?	Como está?	comb-oo ess-taw'
Very well, thank you.	Man's answer: Muito bem, obrigado.	Mwee'-too bain, oh-bree-gaw'-doo
	Lady's answer: Muito bem, obrigada.	Moo'-ee-too baying, oh-bree-gah' da.
Where are you going?	Onde vai?	On'-djee vie'?
When are you returning?	Quando volta?	Kwahn'-doo vohl'-ta?
Many thanks.	Muito obrigado. (Lady-Muito obrigada).	Moo'-ee-too oh-bree-gah'-doo. (Lady-Moo'-ee-too oh-bree-gah'-da).
More slowly.	Mais devagar.	My'-ees de-va-gahr'
Pardon me.	Desculpe-me.	Dis-kool'pe me.
I don't know.	Nao sei.	Nah'-oong say.
Do you know?	O senhor (a senhora), (a senhorita), (voce) sabe?	Oo se-nyohr (a se-nyor'-a), (a se-nyoh-ree'-ta) (Voh-say') sah'-be?
Today.	Hoje.	Oh'-jee
Tomorrow.	Amanha.	Ah-mahn-yah'.
Yesterday.	Ontem.	On'-tain.
This week.	Esta semana.	Es'-ta se-mah'-na.
Next week.	A próxima semana.	A pro'-see-ma se-mah'-na.
Don't forget.	Nao se esqueca.	Nah'-oong se is-kay'-sa.
All right.	Muito bem.	Moo'-ee-too bayng.
See you later.	Até logo.	A-tay' loh'-goo.
Goodbye.	Adeus.	A-day'-oos.
Come here, please.	Venha ca, por favor.	Vayng'-ya kah, poor fah-vohr'.
It doesn't matter.	Nao tem importancia.	Nah'-oong tayng eem-poor-tahn see-a.
Let's go.	Vamos.	Vah'-moos.
Very good. (bad).	Muito bem (mal).	Moo'-ee-too bayng (mah'-l).
Where can I change my money?	Onde posso trocar meu dinheiro?	Ohn-de po'-ssoo troo-kahr' may'-oo dee-nyay'-roo?
Monday.	Segunda-feira.	Se-goon'-da fay'-ra.
Tuesday.	Terca-feira.	Tayr'-sa fay'-ra.
Wednesday.	Quarta-feira.	Kwahr'-ta fay'-ra.
Thursday.	Quinta-feira.	Keen'-ta fay'-ra.
Friday.	Sexta-feira.	Ses'-ta fay'-ra.
Saturday.	Sábado.	Sah'ba-doo.
Sunday.	Domingo.	Doh-meeng'-goo.
Black.	Preto, negro.	Pre'-too, nay'-groo.
White.	Branco.	Brahng'-koo.
Red.	Vermelho.	V-mel'-yoo.
Green.	Verde.	Vayr'-de.
Blue.	Azul.	A-zool'.

ENGLISH	PORTUGUESE	PHONETIC PRONUNCIATION
Yellow.	Amarelo.	A-ma-re'-loo.
One.	Um (uma).	Oong (oom-a)
Two.	Dois (Duas).	Doys (Doo'-as)
Three.	Tres.	Trays.
Four.	Quatro.	Kwah'-troo.
Five.	Cinco.	Seeng'-koo.
Six.	Seis.	Say'-ees.
Seven.	Sete.	Se'-te.
Eight.	Oito.	Oy'-too.
Nine.	Nove.	Noh'-ve.
Ten.	Dez.	Dayz.
Eleven.	Onze.	Ohn'-zay.
Twelve.	Doze.	Doh'-zay.

INDEX

(The letters H and R indicate hotel and restaurant listings)